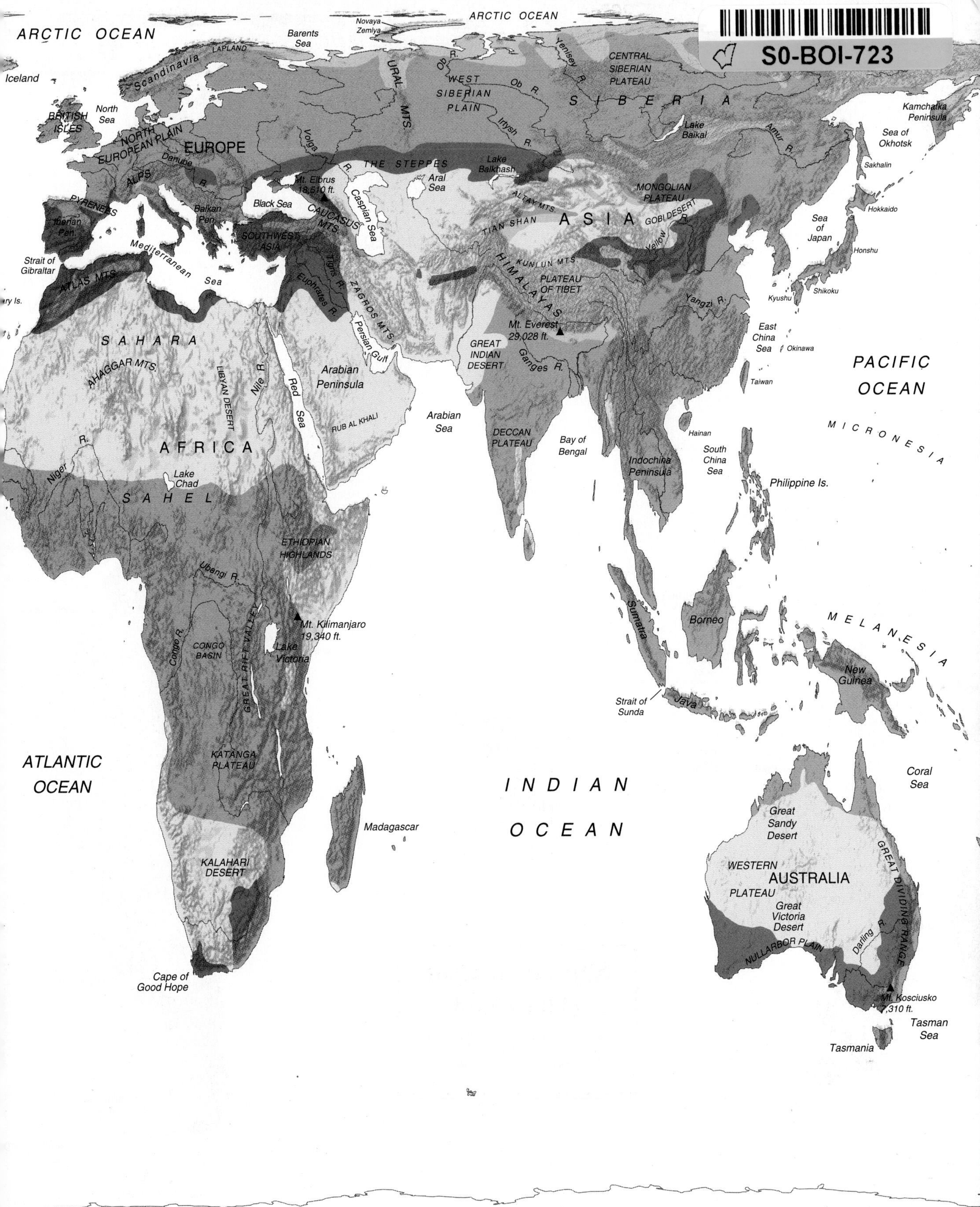
ARCTIC OCEAN
ARCTIC OCEAN
Novaya Zemlya
Barents Sea
Iceland
LAPLAND
Scandinavia
BRITISH ISLES
North Sea
NORTH EUROPEAN PLAIN
EUROPE
Danube R.
ALPS
PYRENEES
Iberian Pen.
Balkan Pen.
Strait of Gibraltar
ATLAS MTS.
Mediterranean Sea
Black Sea
Mt. Elbrus 18,510 ft.
CAUCASUS MTS.
SOUTHWEST ASIA
Volga R.
URAL MTS.
Ob R.
WEST SIBERIAN PLAIN
Irtysh R.
Yenisey R.
CENTRAL SIBERIAN PLATEAU
S I B E R I A
Lake Baikal
Amur R.
Kamchatka Peninsula
Sea of Okhotsk
Sakhalin
Hokkaido
Sea of Japan
Honshu
Kyushu
Shikoku
THE STEPPES
Aral Sea
Caspian Sea
Lake Balkhash
ALTAY MTS.
MONGOLIAN PLATEAU
GOBI DESERT
TIAN SHAN
A S I A
Yellow R.
KUNLUN MTS.
PLATEAU OF TIBET
HIMALAYAS
Mt. Everest 29,028 ft.
Yangzi R.
Tigris R.
Euphrates R.
ZAGROS MTS.
Persian Gulf
GREAT INDIAN DESERT
Ganges R.
East China Sea
Okinawa
Taiwan
PACIFIC OCEAN
S A H A R A
AHAGGAR MTS.
LIBYAN DESERT
Nile R.
Red Sea
Arabian Peninsula
RUB AL KHALI
Arabian Sea
DECCAN PLATEAU
Bay of Bengal
Indochina Peninsula
Hainan
South China Sea
Philippine Is.
MICRONESIA
A F R I C A
Niger R.
Lake Chad
S A H E L
ETHIOPIAN HIGHLANDS
Ubangi R.
Mt. Kilimanjaro 19,340 ft.
Congo R.
CONGO BASIN
GREAT RIFT VALLEY
Lake Victoria
Sumatra
Borneo
MELANESIA
New Guinea
Strait of Sunda
Java
ATLANTIC OCEAN
KATANGA PLATEAU
I N D I A N
O C E A N
Madagascar
Coral Sea
KALAHARI DESERT
Great Sandy Desert
WESTERN PLATEAU
AUSTRALIA
Great Victoria Desert
GREAT DIVIDING RANGE
NULLARBOR PLAIN
Darling R.
Mt. Kosciusko 7,310 ft.
Tasman Sea
Tasmania
Cape of Good Hope
ANTARCTICA

Political Divisions of the World

ARCTIC OCEAN
ICELAND
NORWAY
SWEDEN
FINLAND
RUSSIA
U.K.
IRE.
DEN.
NETH.
BELG.
ESTONIA
LATVIA
LITHUANIA
RUSSIA
BELARUS
POL.
GER.
UKRAINE
CZ. REP.
LUXEM.
SLOVAK.
MOLDOVA
FRANCE
AUSTR.
HUNG.
SWITZ.
LIECH.
SLOV.
CRO.
YUGO.
BOS.
ROMANIA
BULG.
ITALY
GEORGIA
Aral Sea
Caspian Sea
KAZAKHSTAN
MONGOLIA
UZBEKISTAN
KYRGYZSTAN
NORTH KOREA
SOUTH KOREA
JAPAN
SPAIN
PORTUGAL
ALB.
GREECE
ARMENIA
TURKEY
TURKMENISTAN
TAJIKISTAN
AZERBAIJAN
SYR.
CYPRUS
LEBANON
ISRAEL
IRAQ
IRAN
AFGHANISTAN
CHINA
TUNISIA
MOROCCO
ALGERIA
LIBYA
EGYPT
JORDAN
KUWAIT
BAHRAIN
QATAR
PAKISTAN
NEPAL
BHUTAN
East China Sea
Sahara (Mor.)
UNITED ARAB EMIRATES
SAUDI ARABIA
Red Sea
INDIA
MYANMAR (BURMA)
LAOS
TAIWAN
PACIFIC OCEAN
MALI
NIGER
OMAN
Arabian Sea
BANGLADESH
Bay of Bengal
South China Sea
PHILIPPINES
CHAD
ERITREA
YEMEN
THAILAND
CAMBODIA
BURKINA FASO
GUINEA
BENIN
SUDAN
DJIBOUTI
VIETNAM
NIGERIA
ETHIOPIA
CENTRAL AFR. REP.
MALDIVES
SRI LANKA
PALAU
CÔTE D'IVOIRE
GHANA
TOGO
CAMEROON
UGANDA
SOMALIA
MALAYSIA
BRUNEI
EQUATORIAL GUINEA
GABON
KENYA
SINGAPORE
INDONESIA
SAO TOME & PRINCIPE
RWANDA
BURUNDI
REP. CONGO
DEM. REP. CONGO
PAPUA NEW GUINEA
Cabinda (Ang.)
TANZANIA
SEYCHELLES
MALAWI
COMOROS
ANGOLA
SOLOMON ISLANDS
ZAMBIA
ATLANTIC OCEAN
ZIMBABWE
MADAGASCAR
NAMIBIA
MAURITIUS
INDIAN OCEAN
BOTSWANA
AUSTRALIA
MOZAMBIQUE
SWAZILAND
SOUTH AFRICA
LESOTHO
Key to Abbreviations:
Alb. Albania
Ang. Angola
Austr. Austria
Belg. Belgium
Bos. Bosnia & Herzegovina
Bulg. Bulgaria
Central Afr. Rep. Central African Republic
Cro. Croatia
Cz. Rep. Czech Republic
Dem. Rep. Congo Democratic Republic of Congo
Den. Denmark
Ecua. Ecuador
Fr. France
Ger. Germany
Hung. Hungary
Ire. Ireland
Liech. Liechtenstein
Luxem. Luxembourg
Mor. Morocco
Neth. Netherlands
N.Z. New Zealand
Pol. Poland
Rep. Congo. Republic of Congo
Slovak. Slovakia
Slov. Slovenia
Switz. Switzerland
Syr. Syria
U.K. United Kingdom
Yugo. Yugoslavia
ANTARCTICA

THE GLOBAL PAST

VOLUME TWO, 1500 TO THE PRESENT

Lanny B. Fields
California State University–San Bernardino

Russell J. Barber
California State University–San Bernardino

Cheryl A. Riggs
California State University–San Bernardino

BEDFORD BOOKS Boston

For Bedford Books
President and Publisher: Charles H. Christensen
General Manager and Associate Publisher: Joan E. Feinberg
History Editor: Katherine E. Kurzman
Developmental Editor: Jane Betz
Editorial Assistants: Thomas Pierce and Maura Shea
Managing Editor: Elizabeth M. Schaaf
Production Editor: Lori Chong Roncka
Production Assistants: Ellen C. Thibault and Ara Salibian
Copyeditor: Eric Newman
Proofreader: Paula Woolley
Text Design: Wanda Kossak
Photo Researcher: Carole Frohlich, The Visual Connection
Cartography: GeoSystems Global Corporation
Page Layout: DeNee Reiton Skipper
Indexer: Steve Csipke
Cover Design: Hannus Design Associates
Cover Art: "Head of Victory," 1907 or after, by Augustus Saint-Gaudens (detail). Helen and Alice Colburn Fund. Courtesy of the Museum of Fine Arts, Boston. Dance shield, early twentieth century (detail of back view). Kikuyu, Kenya. Photo by Heini Schneebeli. Courtesy of Marc L. Ginzberg.
Composition: Ruttle, Shaw & Wetherill, Inc.
Printing and Binding: Quebecor Printing Kingsport

Library of Congress Catalog Card Number: 97–72370

Manufactured in the United States of America.

2 1 0 9
f e d c b

For information, write: Bedford Books, 75 Arlington Street, Boston, MA 02116 (617–426–7440)

ISBN: 0–312–10332–8 (hardcover comprehensive vol.)
ISBN: 0–312–10330–1 (paperback Vol. 1)
ISBN: 0–312–10331–X (paperback Vol. 2)

On the Title Page: *Landscape painting in China began as early as the fourth century* B.C. *Generally, human figures did not dominate the landscapes; they fit into them naturally and were represented in proportion to the size of mountains. This serene village along the Yangzi River in the late–seventeenth century reflects the era's exceptional prosperity and political stability.*
Wan-go Weng.

Acknowledgments and copyrights appear at the back of the book on pp. 1119–1120, which constitute an extension of the copyright page.

THE GLOBAL PAST

VOLUME TWO,
1500 TO THE PRESENT

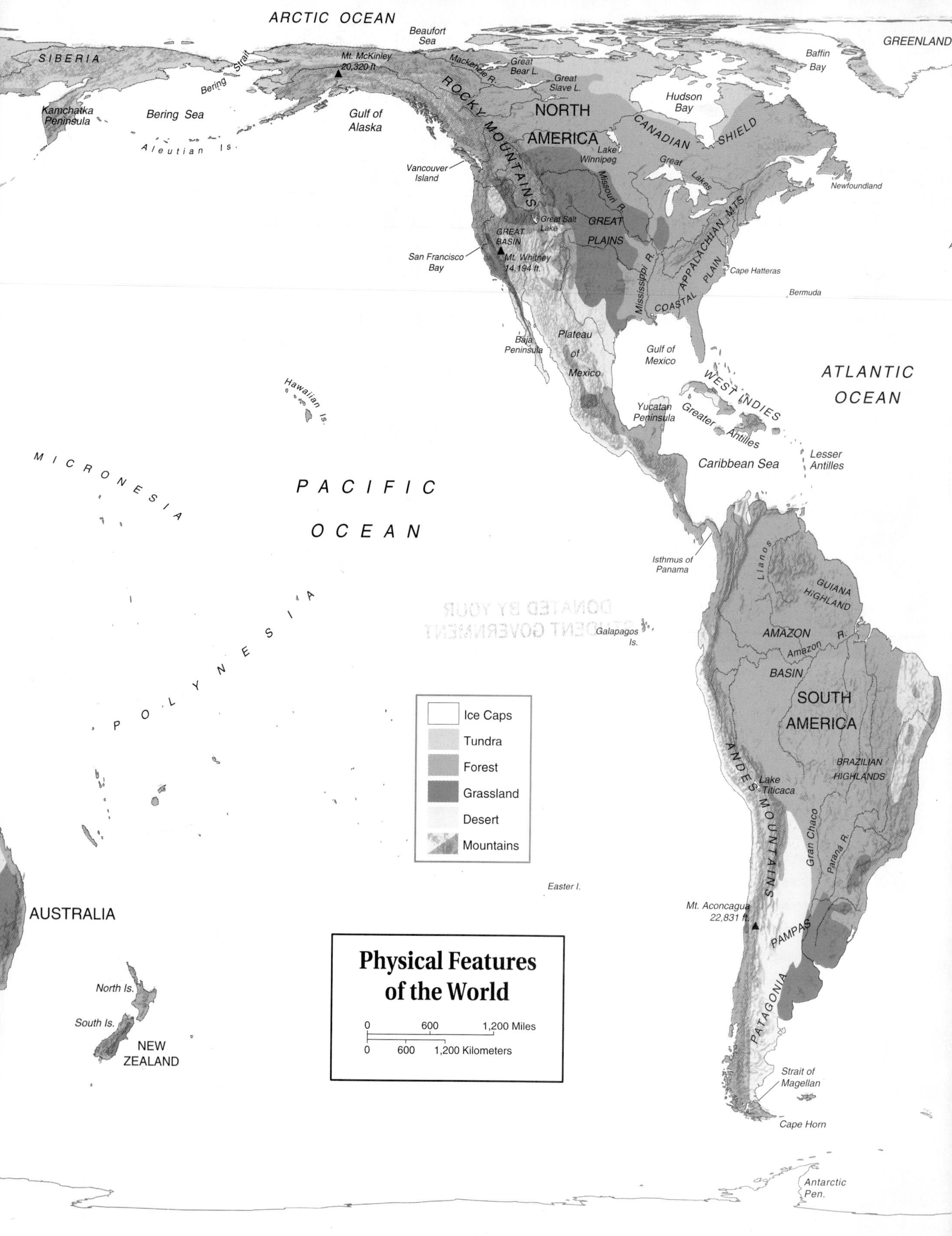

ARCTIC OCEAN
Beaufort Sea
GREENLAND
SIBERIA
Mt. McKinley 20,320 ft
Mackenzie R.
Great Bear L.
Baffin Bay
Bering Strait
Great Slave L.
Hudson Bay
Kamchatka Peninsula
Bering Sea
Gulf of Alaska
ROCKY MOUNTAINS
NORTH AMERICA
CANADIAN SHIELD
Aleutian Is.
Lake Winnipeg
Great Lakes
Vancouver Island
Missouri R.
Newfoundland
Great Salt Lake
GREAT PLAINS
APPALACHIAN MTS.
GREAT BASIN
San Francisco Bay
Mt. Whitney 14,194 ft.
Mississippi R.
COASTAL PLAIN
Cape Hatteras
Bermuda
Baja Peninsula
Plateau of Mexico
Gulf of Mexico
ATLANTIC OCEAN
WEST INDIES
Hawaiian Is.
Yucatan Peninsula
Greater Antilles
MICRONESIA
Caribbean Sea
Lesser Antilles
PACIFIC OCEAN
Isthmus of Panama
Llanos
GUIANA HIGHLAND
POLYNESIA
Galapagos Is.
AMAZON R.
Amazon
BASIN
SOUTH AMERICA
Ice Caps
Tundra
Forest
Grassland
Desert
Mountains
ANDES MOUNTAINS
BRAZILIAN HIGHLANDS
Lake Titicaca
Gran Chaco
Parana R.
Easter I.
AUSTRALIA
Mt. Aconcagua 22,831 ft.
PAMPAS
Physical Features of the World
0 600 1,200 Miles
0 600 1,200 Kilometers
North Is.
South Is.
NEW ZEALAND
PATAGONIA
Strait of Magellan
Cape Horn
Antarctic Pen.
ANTARCTICA

Contents

PART EIGHT
GLOBAL WAR AND REVOLUTION 886

Preface for Instructors

In 1991, Lanny Fields, who had been teaching world history for more than ten years, wrote an article criticizing the books then available for this course, urging both publishers and professors to be bolder in their goals and methods for teaching a global history. This brief piece was published in *Perspectives,* the newsletter of the American Historical Association, where it came to the attention of an editor who had also been searching for a way to approach a course that was clearly growing. The conversations thus started branched out to include two more professors at California State University–San Bernardino; Cheryl Riggs, also in the Department of History, joined Lanny Fields to add her own experiences in the classroom and to strengthen a commitment to social and religious history. Russell Barber, an anthropologist-archaeologist, was recruited when it became clear that to write something "truly global" meant to move beyond what history alone could encompass; his research and understanding of other social science models has proved invaluable to the project. After the efforts of many years, we are pleased to present a book that is global in scope, practically structured, and designed with our students in mind.

As instructors in world history courses, we have found that the most difficult part of teaching these courses is finding a way to cover such a huge topic: deciding what to leave out, how to integrate diverse strands, and how to give the course shape. We have written *The Global Past* with this essential problem in mind and used a variety of approaches to make the text comprehensive and coherent and to help make the introductory world history course a valuable learning experience for students.

Truly Global Approach

From the beginning, *The Global Past* has been designed to provide truly global coverage of world history. Many world history textbooks were born as Western civilization texts and expanded to incorporate sections on other parts of the world; these sections, however, are often poorly integrated into the textbook and overly brief. In contrast, these topics are given more extensive treatment in *The Global Past*—as their global significance demands—and are integrated into broader discussions throughout the book. Unique chapters on the Global Industrial Revolution (Ch. 32) and the effects of the Great Depression worldwide (Ch. 38) expand discussions traditionally reserved to coverage of the West.

This broad geographical coverage gives students a better picture of the range of unique world events and encourages them to make comparisons that lead to insights about recurring patterns in world history. Indeed, comparison of events and processes in disparate places and times is an important theme of the book, a theme that is reinforced in the "Issue" chapters and in the special features.

Multidisciplinary Perspectives

Many disciplines have made significant contributions to the study of the human past, and *The Global Past* draws freely on anthropology, geography, and other social sciences to complement the insights of historians. Models and other intellectual tools of the social sciences help to frame discussions, making recurrent patterns more evident and understandable. Models are a widely misunderstood tool of the social sciences. A discussion in Volume One explains to students that models are ideal constructs created by scholars and that real-world deviations from the expectations derived from models are revealing and frequently lead to new insights.

The presence of an anthropologist-archaeologist among the authors signals a commitment to examining human history before the existence of written records and in places where documents can be complemented with material evidence. The interests of modern archaeologists range from reconstructing past environments to exploring technological capabilities to explaining social change. *The Global Past* incorporates their findings throughout. Archaeological contributions are most obvious in chapters that discuss ancient times, but they also enrich our understanding of more recent times and events, such as plantation slavery in the Americas, the Industrial Revolution, and West African urbanization.

Balanced Coverage

In recognition that history is more than kings and battles, *The Global Past* explores political, economic, cultural, and social developments, attempting to provide balanced and integrated coverage. We have devoted entire chapters, for example, to such topics as "The American Exchange" (following the European voyages of discovery to the Americas) and "The Arts as Mirrors of the Modern World." A unique chapter on Populations in Change (Ch. 42) examines the issue of societies in flux after 1945 and sets the stage for the final chapters, which look forward into the future. Shorter treatments are integrated into chapters, linking political-economic events and cultural-social events. This recognition of connections between people, places, and different arenas of activity has been praised by reviewers.

A Variety of Special Features

A number of short sidebar essays are interspersed throughout the text to give students a sense of how people lived in the past, what their concerns were, and how historians interpret the past. These special features, which help to flesh out the coverage and provide a welcome change of pace, are of five types:

- "In Their Own Words," excerpts from primary sources, appear in every chapter. "*Haiku* Poetry and Commentary," for example, places *haiku* in the broader context of Japanese culture.
- "Paths to the Past," historiographic and methodological discussions, help students understand how historians know what they know. For example, "Lorenzo Valla and Textual Criticism" describes the fifteenth-century origins of a method now widely used by modern scholars.
- "Encounters," narrative accounts of contacts between peoples, examine the places where cultures and ideas met. "The Lay Reaction to Darwin," for example, discusses the attitudes of conflict and acceptance with which people encounter a new idea—in this case, the theory of evolution.
- "Parallels and Divergences," comparisons of particular topics across time and space, examine similarities and differences between cultures. "China's Taiping Uprising," for example, compares this abortive revolution to the successful revolutions to which the chapter is devoted.
- "Under the Lens" boxes examine individual events, people, or objects in depth. "Paderewski and Polish Nationalism," for example, focuses on the work of one notable individual in a chapter that touches on nationalistic movements around the world.

Topical-Chronological Organization

As longtime teachers of the world history survey, we are well aware of the dilemma instructors face in such courses. On the one hand, students need to see the chronological pattern of history in order to organize all the information covered in a text of this size; on the other hand, students need to make connections *across* time in order to make the information meaningful. A textbook organized strictly according to chronology can, of course, become encyclopedic and mired in the minutiae of specific cases. One organized strictly according to topics, on the other hand, can obscure the basic and important temporal relationships that are central to understanding causality. *The Global Past* steers a middle course, maintaining a largely chronological structure in this five-part volume while emphasizing important themes within each part in order to give the material coherence and meaning.

One of the great values of a topical treatment is its economy. Writing a truly global text means including sections often omitted in other books; providing balanced treatment of economic, cultural, and social history also adds length. The topical approach allows space for these essential elements while keeping the length of the book manageable; it is a way to emphasize important links without going into endless detail. It also encourages comparison, an important goal of this text. To make space for these new goals, we have scaled back on the traditional European coverage characteristic of the previous generation of world history texts. We hope instructors will agree that this tradeoff is more than compensated for in the truly global coverage that results.

The treatment of revolutions in Europe, Asia, and the Americas in a single chapter provides a good example. Grouping these varied events together draws students' attention to both their similarities and their differences. Further, the discussion of other revolutions can be shortened, since students will easily be able to see how they conform to the general pattern already established.

To give them coherence and thematic unity, each of the main parts of *The Global Past* closes with a brief chapter devoted to an issue—such as trade, empire, religion, or technology—that has shaped the events discussed in that part. These "Issue" chapters encourage students to step back and consider how events occurring in distant cultures connect to one another, and how they connect to events that occurred earlier and later in time.

Features to Assist the Student

The Global Past includes a variety of features to help students make sense of what they read, organize their thoughts, and study.

- An equal-area map at the beginning of each chapter, often with detail inserts, shows what geographical areas will be discussed in that chapter.
- 58 maps within the chapters are accompanied by detailed captions to encourage critical thinking.
- Full-color maps at the back of the book dedicate a two-page spread to each major geographical area and summarize the changes in each area over the period covered in the text.
- An outline at the beginning of each chapter helps students see how the topics covered relate to one another.
- Pronunciation guides, at the bottoms of text pages, give easy-to-read phonetic respellings for non-English words.
- Abundant, good-sized figures and charts are always accompanied by substantial captions to encourage critical thinking.
- Part and Chapter timelines place significant events and processes in time, helping students recognize the chronological relationships within and between geographical areas.
- End-of-chapter summaries are ideal for study and review.
- Suggested readings at the end of each chapter offer carefully selected, annotated lists of classic, recent, and specialized studies for students to explore.

In addition to the full-color map appendix, *The Global Past* includes two other reference tools:

- glossary of significant terms (which appear in boldface in the text), including pronunciation glosses where appropriate; and
- a full index, including cross-references, brief identifications, dates, and pronunciation glosses where appropriate.

Useful Ancillaries

Bedford Books has made available to the student three major ancillaries: a reader, a map workbook, and a study guide. The two-volume reader, *Reading* THE GLOBAL PAST (edited by Russell J. Barber, Lanny B. Fields, and Cheryl A. Riggs), is geared specifically to *The Global Past* and organized into similar parts. Each part offers an integrated set of readings organized around a critical theme of that part, such as the rise of civilization or the role of economics in empires. Most of the readings are primary sources such as travelers' accounts or political documents, but a few important secondary readings are included as examples of current historical thinking. Each part also contains a visual portfolio.

The two-volume map workbook, *Mapping* THE GLOBAL PAST*: Historical Geography Workbook* (written by Mark Newman at the University of Illinois–Chicago), gives students additional practice working with maps and analyzing the significance of geography in historical events.

The two-volume study guide, *Making the Most of* THE GLOBAL PAST*: A Study Guide* (written by Jay Boggis), gives students valuable practice in working with art, maps, timelines, outlines, summaries, essays, and test questions of all kinds.

Ancillaries for instructors help manage the formidable task of teaching an introductory world history course. An instructor's resource manual, *Teaching* THE GLOBAL PAST (written by Cheryl A. Riggs), offers summaries; sample syllabi; lecture suggestions; suggestions for student projects and paper topics; a general bibliography on teaching world history; a variety of references to books, films, and other teaching materials; tips for incorporating the other ancillaries; and more. A testbank (available in print, Macintosh, and Windows formats) offers multiple choice, true/false, fill in the blanks, short answer, reading art, and essay questions of graduated difficulty for all chapters. Color transparencies for maps and selected illustrations in the text allow instructors to focus on particular images in class. A unique *Audio Pronunciation Guide* lets instructors hear how unusual non-English words and phrases are pronounced, so they can speak confidently in class.

History has developed an increased awareness of how critical it is to study the totality of the human past: all arenas of human endeavor at all times and places. *The Global Past* will initiate students into that awareness as soon as they take their first survey course in world history.

Acknowledgments

It is trite but true to state that every book is a group effort; a textbook raises that statement to new heights. We have imposed on our colleagues at California State University–San Bernardino and elsewhere, regularly requesting information and comments. The School of Social and Behavioral Sciences at CSUSB and Deans Aubrey Bonnett and Ellen Gruenbaum assisted us by providing funds to facilitate the project.

At Bedford Books, Publisher Charles Christensen and General Manager Joan Feinberg have been both supportive and demanding, and their dedication to producing a quality book has been exemplary; Jane Betz has guided the text through its evolution; and Lori Chong Roncka has been responsible for its production. Carole Frohlich of The Visual Connection applied her skills and taste in researching the illustrations.

Louise Waller, formerly of St. Martin's Press, holds a special place in our gratitude. Her initial interest in and guidance of this project were very influential in shaping it, and we consider her an honorary author.

Finally, we extend our thanks to the various reviewers who read parts or all of the manuscript and shared their expertise and judgment with us. Not every comment was always welcome at the time, but it would be difficult to find one that did not ultimately help improve the text. We extend our thanks to that legion of reviewers: Roger Adelson, Arizona State University; Ruth Aurelius, Des Moines Area Community College; Norman Bennett, Boston University; Gail Bossenga, University of Kansas; Fritz Blockwell, Washington State University; Thomas W. Burkman, State University of New York–Buffalo; Captain Robert Carriedo, United States Air Force Academy; Ronald Coons, University of Connecticut; Captain Robert Cummings, United States Air Force Academy; R. Hunt Davis, University of Florida; Michael Fisher, Oberlin College; Vernard Foley, Purdue University; Robert D. Friedel, University of Maryland; Robert Garfield, DePaul University; Suzanne Gay, Oberlin College; Frank Garosi, California State University–Sacramento; Laura Gellot, University of Wisconsin–Parkside; Marc Gellot, University of Wisconsin–La Crosse; Marc Gilbert, North Georgia College; Christopher Gutherie, Tarleton State University; John S. Innes, Eastern Washington University; Doug Klepper, Santa Fe Community College; Gregory Kozlowski, DePaul University; James Krippner-Martinez, Haverford College; David Lelyveld, Columbia University; John Mandaville, Portland State University; C. Nicole Martin, Germanna Community College; David McComb, Colorado State University; Rebecca McCoy, University of Idaho; John Mears, Southern Methodist University; Gail Minault, University of Texas–Austin; David T. Morgan, University of Montevallo; Les Muray, Lansing Community College; Vera Reber, Shippensburg University; Donald Roper, State University of New York–New Paltz; Paul Scherer, Indiana State University–South Bend; James Shenton, Columbia University; Amos E. Simpson, University of Southwestern Louisiana; Leonard Smith, Oberlin College; Robert Tignor, Princeton University; Joseph Warren, Lansing Community College; Samuel Wells, Pearl River Community College; Allan Winkler, Miami University of Ohio; John Williams, Indiana State University; Marcia Wright, Columbia University. We would especially like to thank Marian Nelson of the University of Nebraska–Omaha and Robert Berry for their extensive help.

Lanny B. Fields
Russell J. Barber
Cheryl A. Riggs
San Bernardino, California
June 1997

THE GLOBAL PAST

VOLUME TWO,
1500 TO THE PRESENT

BEFORE 1400, MOST PEOPLES WERE LARGELY ISOLATED from one another. Certainly there were trade and diplomatic contacts, and pilgrimages and wars brought some individuals into contact with foreign lands. Nonetheless, deserts, oceans, and the sheer vastness of the space between many peoples were significant barriers, given the transportation technology available at the time. Most of Africa was cut off from Europe and Asia by the Sahara Desert, and contrary currents in the Atlantic Ocean made northward voyages along the African coast difficult or impossible. Africans, Europeans, and Asians had no idea that the Americas even existed.

While there was sporadic contact in earlier periods, the contact that began with the fifteenth-century European voyages of discovery was qualitatively different. The intensity of contact produced far-reaching changes that stretched across the next three centuries. Diseases and foodstuffs were transported from continent to continent with important demographic consequences; entire populations were subjugated; and some countries grew rich by exploiting newly found lands. Improved transportation technology was partly responsible for these changes, but other factors played important roles as well.

Part Six explores the contacts following the European voyages of exploration, the changes they brought about, and the reasons that underlay increasing European domination of the world in this period. These factors are aspects of the massive and rapid change that culminates in what we call "modernity." The development of modernity is the major theme of this volume of *The Global Past.*

Throughout this volume, we use two terms that require special consideration. The **Old World** refers to Asia, Africa, and Europe, while the **New World** consists of

	INDIA	RUSSIA	PERSIA
1300			
1400			
1500	Mughal Empire	Russian Empire	Safavid Empire
1600			
1700			
1800			

PART SIX

THE COLLISION OF WORLDS

the Americas and the Pacific islands. Some scholars object to these terms, feeling that they are based on a European perspective that is inappropriate for a global treatment of the past. We have adopted them, with some reservations, because we feel that they emphasize a fundamental distinction. The peoples of the New World and peoples of the Old World were unaware of each other's existence before the European voyages of exploration, and each had developed independently.

All of the chapters in Part Six explore the theme of developing global interaction. Chapter 22 discusses the factors that characterize modernity and its significance to the changing world order. Chapter 23 discusses some of the most important voyages of exploration (originating in both Europe and Asia), and Chapter 24 explores the colonization that developed from the European discoveries. The exchange of ideas, items, and species between the Old and New worlds is chronicled in Chapter 25, and Chapter 26 treats the new basis of slavery and the slave trade that developed in this period, bringing Africa into global prominence and contact. Empires of western Asia, southern Asia, and eastern Europe also were in contact with new peoples in this period, and they are discussed in Chapter 27; Chapter 28 treats contemporary East Asian states and their contacts with other peoples. Finally, Issue 6 places slavery in a broader context by examining its forms around the world and over time.

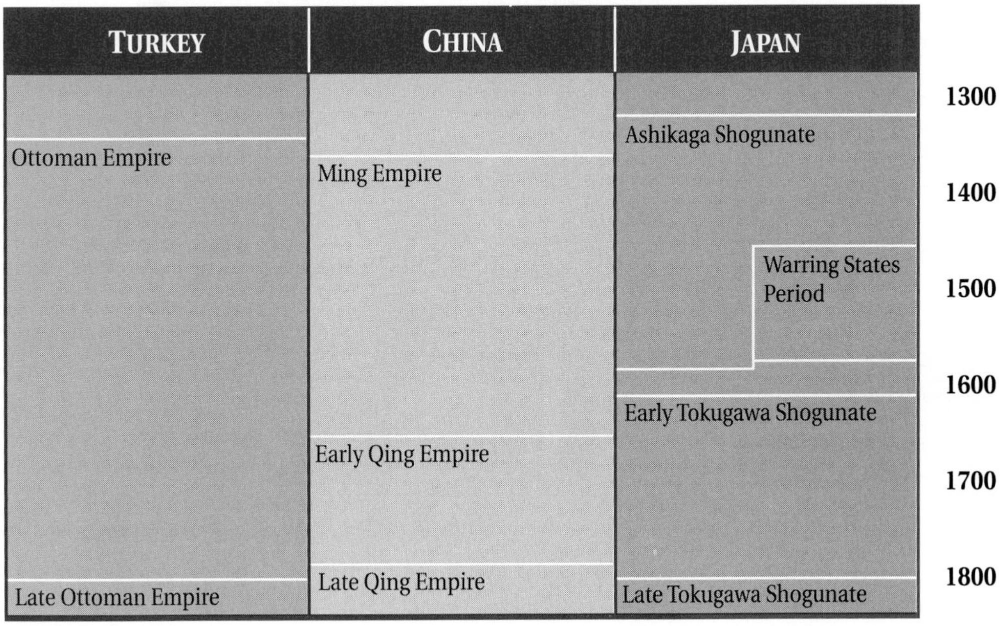

TURKEY	CHINA	JAPAN	
			1300
Ottoman Empire	Ming Empire	Ashikaga Shogunate	
			1400
		Warring States Period	1500
		Early Tokugawa Shogunate	1600
	Early Qing Empire		1700
Late Ottoman Empire	Late Qing Empire	Late Tokugawa Shogunate	1800

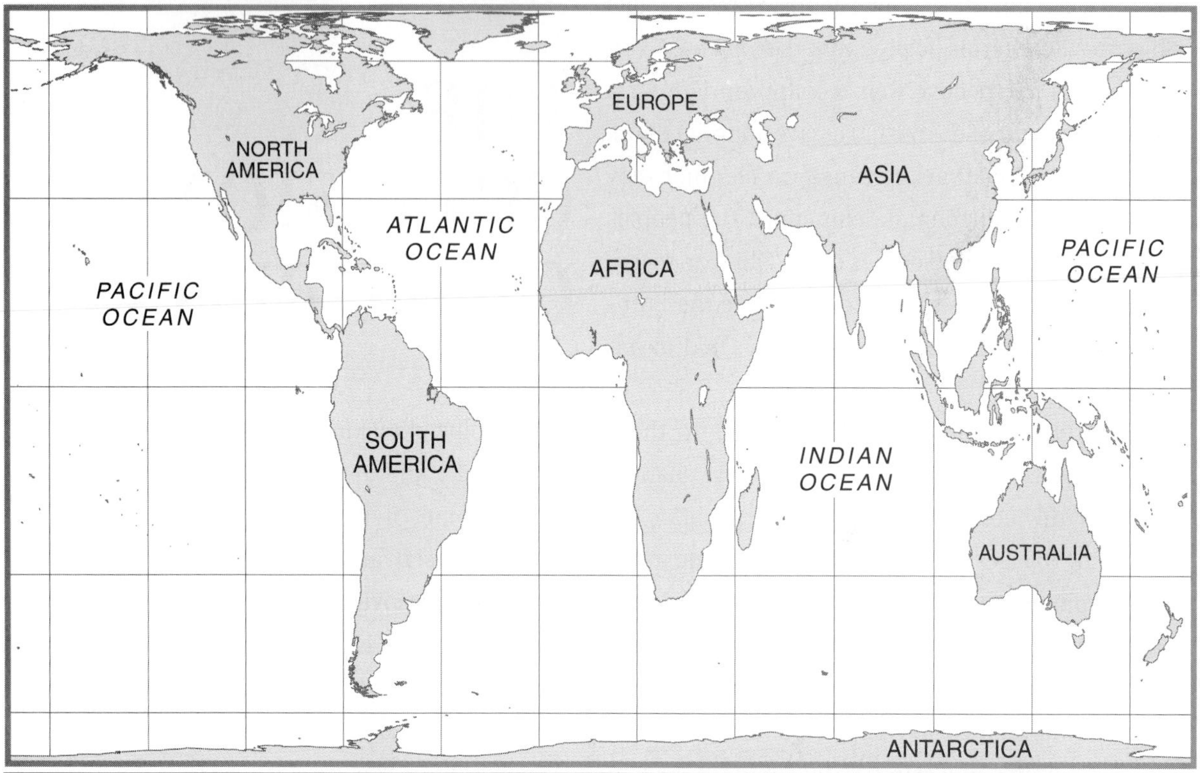

NORTH AMERICA
EUROPE
ASIA
ATLANTIC OCEAN
PACIFIC OCEAN
AFRICA
PACIFIC OCEAN
SOUTH AMERICA
INDIAN OCEAN
AUSTRALIA
ANTARCTICA

On the Edge. *Harold Lloyd, like many of his contemporaries in the 1920s and 1930s, felt caught up in the dangers of modernity. Lloyd, of course, was an actor who made a career out of generating thrills and fear among moviegoers. In this scene, he teeters on the edge of disaster, trying to cope with the hazards of a skyscraper under construction.*
Corbis-Bettmann.

CHAPTER 22

Exploring Modernity

If human existence were an apple, then civilization would be no thicker than its skin and the modern era would be no thicker than the insecticide on it. Human beings evolved from distant ancestors who lived more than a million years ago, and change came slowly until the invention of agriculture. Sedentary people lived in villages, towns, and eventually cities that soon became centers of civilization with characteristics such as social-class distinctions and long-distance trade.

Change accelerated, producing kingdoms and **empires**, groups of peoples and territories ruled by a single power. Over the centuries, empires rose, dominated, and collapsed, while long periods of rule by local and regional leaders alternated with domination by larger kingdoms and empires. Science and technology brought forth many important inventions and discoveries, such as metallurgy, paper, and gunpowder. In addition, religions met certain needs, and some faiths spread far beyond the places where they originated.

In this volume, we will explore the forces of change that led to modernity and the peoples who brought increasing global contact and often conflict. Modernity has accumulated some unfortunate associations, and it too often is assumed that modern societies are somehow superior to premodern societies, a judgment we will avoid. In this textbook, we will discuss modernity in terms of its characteristics. Not all of these features need be in place, but at least most of them must be present in order for a society to be considered modern.

What is **modernity**? Let us examine its features:

- —a cultural outlook that focuses on progress;
- —a perspective that seeks to accelerate the systematic application of science and technology to improve economic production;
- —a view that shifts from a predominantly religious to a predominantly secular understanding of the world and the universe;
- —governments, often nation-states, that usually seek wider participation of a broader spectrum of people in all aspects of life, especially politics;
- —an increase in the determination of social status according to merit rather than birth, and the breaking of social barriers to the advancement of talented people; and
- —the accelerating integration of regional economies into a global economic network that is increasingly dominated by capitalism or socialism.

Modernity slowly emerged in the western part of Europe and in Japan and by the nineteenth century across much of the world.

Progress is a crucial component of modernity. Beginning in the late eighteenth century, intellectuals developed and espoused **progressivism**, the idea that things are getting better and better. Thus, change is for the good and the result of change is always superior to the beginning. Optimism flowed from this perspective and characterized the thinking of a wide array of the ruling elite in the nineteenth century.

Part of this positive outlook developed from the systematic application of science and technology to the improvement of production. Although science and technology previously had been used to improve production, the applications had been unsystematic. In the mid–eighteenth century, Enlightenment thinkers like Denis Diderot implemented their vision of prosperity by writing the *Encyclopédie*. This reference work, illustrated with many drawings, offered information about many manufacturing techniques. Successful Japanese farmers printed and sold agricultural manuals to help increase agricultural yields throughout Japan. By the nineteenth century, German chemists developed fertilizers to help farmers, especially in Germany. One result of the great success in applying science to production was the belief that science can solve all problems.

Secularism, the practice of applying nonreligious ideas to the service of humanity, developed in the late eighteenth century and became an element of modernity. As scientists understood and explained a universe that ran according to natural laws, some people began to ignore religion as necessary to the society's functioning and well-being. A few Enlightenment thinkers espoused atheism, the belief in a godless universe, and some others gradually shrugged off spiritual concerns as irrelevant to progress. By the nineteenth century, scientists developed theories about nondivine origins of the earth and human beings. To some people, religion was outmoded and riddled with superstition. Science, they felt, had replaced religion in the modern era.

Wider participation in the nation-state became the characteristic policy in the modern age. Politicians realized that securing a broad participation of citizens in the governing process strengthened the modern state. Leaders of the American Revolution developed this concept when writing and implementing the U.S. Constitution. A significant development in that view came in the French Revolution, which created the modern military state. While other countries had elected representatives to national or local office, the franchise had been limited to the privileged and wealthy few. The French government purposely opened voting to nearly all men, and voting became a regular practice in modern France. Soon, other countries followed the French example, and people who participated in governing became enthusiastic citizens who supported their governments.

A related feature of the modern age was the opening of governmental service to people of talent. For a long time, state offices had been restricted to aristocrats and people of substantial means. Enlightenment thinkers sharply criticized this practice, arguing that many officials were incompetent. During the French Revolution, buying offices was abolished, and government service was opened to a broader spectrum of social groups. By the nineteenth century, civil service examinations were regularly used to select people for office holding. At the same time, evaluation of officials became commonplace so that ineffective

UNDER THE LENS

Japan's Path to Modernity

The Japanese played a significant role in international trade during part of the Early Modern Era, but they gradually turned inward and shut off nearly all contact with western Europeans. In that period of relative isolation (1640–1854), however, the Japanese created an integrated national market, a technologically advanced agricultural system, a prosperous middle class, a large intellectual class, and a stable polity. Most of these conditions facilitated Japan's transformation into an industrial country by the early twentieth century.

The period from 1540 to 1640 saw Japan enter international affairs in a major way. Westerners arrived in Japan in the 1540s and helped spark Japanese curiosity about Western ideas and technologies. Christianity became widely practiced, especially in the port cities frequented by Western merchants and missionaries. After the mid–sixteenth century, Japan used gunpowder technology to revolutionize warfare and began the effort to reunify a fragmented country. By 1592, Japan's rulers were looking toward Korea and China as places Japan could conquer and rule. New techniques of prospecting and retrieving silver from ores also opened significant sources of that metal for trade purposes. In fact, Japan was the second-largest producer of silver after the Americas. International trade received a significant boost from the introduction of Japanese silver in the first half of the seventeenth century.

Political and social stability concerned Japan's ruling class and triggered the closed-country policy. A small but significant number of provincial leaders and their subjects were Christians and therefore were seen as vulnerable to manipulation by Roman Catholic priests, who were usually foreign. An uprising by Japanese Christians in the mid-1630s fed the government's fears. In addition, foreigners could bring in the latest weapons and threaten political stability.

Instead of weakening Japan for future competition, Japan's isolation actually laid the foundations for modernization in the nineteenth century. Japan experienced rapid growth in its population, cities, and agricultural output. This brought urban prosperity as merchants turned to domestic trade. Roads improved and enhanced trade among cities, while peasants began producing specialized crops for urban markets. Schools multiplied in cities, towns, and villages, with the result that a significant percentage of men and women were literate by the mid–nineteenth century. Resources were carefully managed; waste products from fishing and soybean processing were used as fertilizers. Coal became a major fuel by the early nineteenth century. In all, the Japanese created the infrastructure necessary for industrialization and modernity.

people could be released, and effective officials could be retained or promoted. The development of universal education policies helped provide aspiring individuals with the means to take and pass civil service examinations.

Modernity brought forth increasingly integrated regional, national, and international economies. Transoceanic voyaging by Europeans expanded opportunities for trade and the prosperity that flowed from such commerce. They also benefited from the establishment of colonies as exploitative bases. Soon, Japanese and American silver circulated in China, India, and France. The Atlantic slave trade also increased the traffic in human beings by the tens of millions in exchange for goods, like rum from the Caribbean region.

The Industrial Revolution significantly increased the number of manufactured goods and the need to develop markets for their sale. Textiles were the major goods produced in the early phase of the Industrial Revolution, and they circulated in England, on the European mainland, and in other parts of the world. The need for regular and inexpensive supplies of raw materials and markets for finished products drove imperialism, the intensive subjugation of lands and peoples by industrialized powers. In the late nineteenth century, imperialist countries like Great Britain, the United States, and Japan had carved out their empires.

A by-product of this economic and political expansion was an increasingly integrated global market system. Gradually, regional economic blocks were joined in larger economic units as imperialist nations needed to trade with other countries as well as with their own colonies. By World War I's outbreak in 1914, the globe was loosely tied together in an integrated economic system. One manifestation of this was that economic problems in one country might ripple across its national borders, affecting other coun-

FIGURE 22.1 ***Thomas More's Utopia.*** *Information about the places explored by Europeans stimulated thinkers to imagine places of ideal or farcical conditions. One model was developed by the English official Sir Thomas More early in the sixteenth century. The fictional Utopia, which means "no place," was discovered by Hythlodaeus, "the dispenser of nonsense." Thus, satirical elements were evident in More's fanciful island, which was compared with England.* Warder Collection/ET Archive.

tries. Global economic downturns became increasingly widespread in the nineteenth and twentieth centuries.

Two groups are intimately associated with modernity: the **middle class**, the class of business and professional people, and the **intellectuals**, a group whose members live by the exchange of ideas. Most civilizations have these two groups, but in the modern age they have been viewed as leaders of change. Members of these two classes increasingly believed that all barriers to what they saw as advancement had to be eliminated, and they worked hard to accomplish that goal. They increasingly advocated universal education as a primary means of advancement.

MODERNITY'S FIRST PHASE: THE EARLY MODERN ERA, AROUND 1500–AROUND 1750

Transoceanic voyaging had a profound impact on Europeans. Knowledge and wealth, for example, greatly enriched many in Europe. Trade and the systematic exploitation of peoples and resources, especially in the Americas and Africa, yielded vast riches.

European ships reached the New World in the late fifteenth century, and they first sailed in the Indian Ocean in the same century. The Americas were progressively explored, and South, Southeast, and East Asia came within the sphere of European discovery. (Australia remained out of European reach until the seventeenth century.) The global age had arrived when the crew of Ferdinand Magellan's ship successfully circumnavigated the globe between 1519 and 1522. Parts of Africa were explored by Europeans, especially beginning in the fifteenth century.

The European printing press, developed in the fifteenth century, helped the new information about the non-European world reach a wider audience because books and pamphlets could now be made more quickly, more inexpensively, and more numerously. Early in the era, Protestant Reformation leaders like Martin Luther founded breakaway religious movements, successful in part because of the large number of tracts printed in support of their ideas.

FIGURE 22.2 ***Reading at Home.*** *This sixteenth-century painting captures the sense of seriousness and wonder associated with reading. Here a woman reads aloud to an old man. Although both European men and women could read, a far greater percentage of men were literate. In some Protestant territories, reading from the Bible was an expected daily occurrence that helped to spur literacy.* Louvre © R. M. N.

Parallel developments occurred with the expansion of an intellectual class and the improvement of literacy in the cities and towns of Europe. Intellectuals using scientific methodology helped spread knowledge in areas such as astronomy, medicine, and mathematics. Through a rudimentary postal system that permitted limited correspondence, these thinkers kept abreast of recent discoveries. In the same era, popularization of various discoveries informed the wider reading public.

Measures of literacy are imprecise, but there seems to be a consensus among historians that growing numbers of urban dwellers in Europe could read during the Early Modern Era. Silent reading in the privacy of one's home became popular around the sixteenth century and led to increased reflection about ideas. At the same time, the growth of private libraries mirrored the ease of attaining books, and it was not long before library rooms were being used as meeting places. By the mid–eighteenth century, intellectuals and members of other classes met to discuss all kinds of ideas, like the perspective that social status should be based on merit.

During the Early Modern period, Europeans played an active role in the accelerating integration of regional economies into a modern global economic network. The Portuguese established strategic bases around the Indian Ocean. The English and Dutch eventually followed the Portuguese, and they enjoyed a more stable financial backing in the form of the Dutch East Indies Company and the English East India Company. All of these efforts rapidly integrated regional Asian and African markets with markets in Europe.

Towns and cities benefited from the prosperity stemming from the growth of trade and the exploitation of resources in colonies. Merchants in Antwerp, Lisbon, and London often prospered, as did the artisans who produced the necessary goods to trade abroad. Much early modern economic growth and prosperity rested on technological developments from the thirteenth to the fifteenth centuries.

A combination of inventions and improvements to existing manufacturing techniques accelerated change, especially in Italy during the Early Modern period. Wind power was harnessed by windmills, bringing a significant source of power to manufacturers. New types of spinning wheels and looms appeared and facilitated the production of textiles.

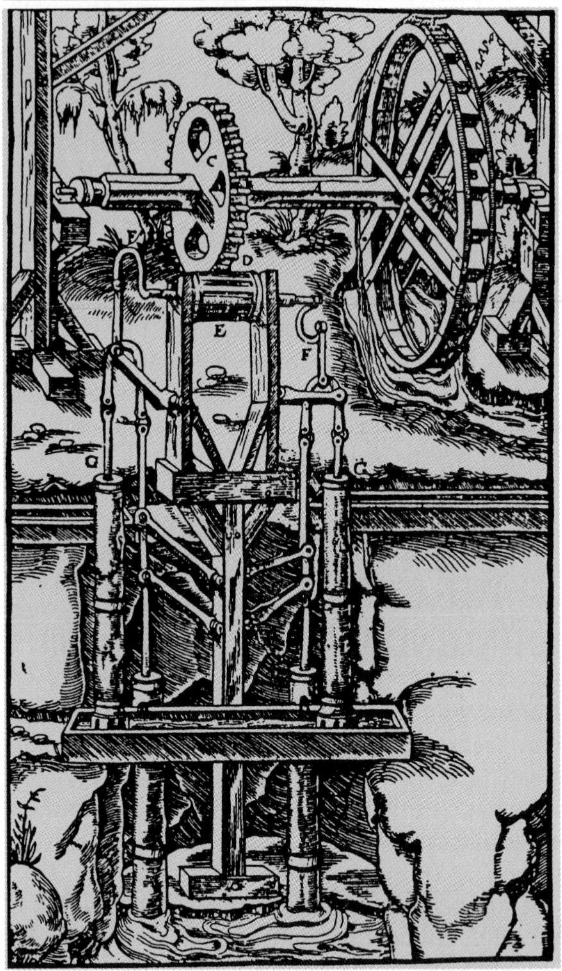

FIGURE 22.3 ***Mining Machinery.*** *This illustration from a book by Georgius Agricola, who popularized metallurgical technology in sixteenth-century Europe, shows a water-powered mining pump. Mining benefited from the application of such important inventions to the extraction process and from the need to secure metal for casting cannons and muskets.* From Georgius Agricola, *De re metallica*, 1556.

MODERNITY'S SECOND PHASE: INDUSTRIALIZATION AND WESTERNIZATION, AROUND 1750–1905

Beginning in the latter half of the eighteenth century, an industrial revolution centered in England, the Netherlands, and Flanders spread over much of the rest of west and central Europe by the mid–nineteenth century. Over the next several decades, the effects of this transformation swept across the globe, creating among many the need to Westernize.

Population growth increased markedly from 1750 to 1905. Cities of hundreds of thousands of people became commonplace in Europe. They often reeked of industrial pollution and poor sanitary conditions, but city life seemed better than rural life to many. This urbanization was the basis for industrialization.

Many other elements helped bring about the Industrial Revolution. One vital component was the application of knowledge to production techniques through Denis Diderot's encyclopedia. Underlying assumptions of this encyclopedia were that technical knowledge could be easily learned and that the skills of one industrial process might be transferred to another branch. Another assumption was that workers might be taught these things and should have some form of formal education. Monarchs influenced by thinkers of this era began calling for universal education.

In England, a companion development was the shift in the nature of patents granted by the government to reward inventors by guaranteeing them a fixed income or royalties from their discovery. This stimulated inventiveness and the application of knowledge to the improvement of manufacturing techniques.

The two most prominent social developments from 1750 to 1905 were the growth and dominance of the middle class and the emergence of an industrial workforce. These two economic classes often were hostile to each other. Union building and strikes were but two activities of the workers, while lockouts and strikebreaking were owners' responses. The guild system had been largely destroyed by industrialization, but in some places guilds gave way to unions.

The Industrial Revolution's need for resources was behind the growing power of many European countries, the United States, and Japan. They all used their industrial might to extend their control to less developed countries, fostering an imperialism that dominated global politics from 1850 to 1950. Other nonindustrialized or partially industrialized empires, such as those of China, Russia, and Austria-Hungary, could not compete and either disintegrated or fell under external control.

The ideas of democracy and liberty that flared up in the American and French revolutions were transmitted throughout the world in the nineteenth and twentieth centuries. Freedom excited many intellectuals in other parts of the world, especially those under domination by European powers. When Chinese intellectuals, for example, wished to transform their own culture, they promoted Westernization, especially democracy.

FIGURE 22.4 ***The Manufacture of Soda.*** *The glass industry boomed in the eighteenth and nineteenth centuries. Critical to the making of glass was the production of soda. This illustration shows the process, including the furnace where the reaction occurred (top), the vats where the soda was dissolved (center), and, finally, the method used to prepare soda for its use in the manufacture of glass. Huge factories were needed for the large-scale operations in the modern period.* After C. Tomlinson, *The Useful Arts and Manufactures of Great Britain,* Part II, Section: "The Manufacture of Soda," pp. 26, 33. London, 1848. E. Norman. D. E. Woodall.

IN THEIR OWN WORDS

A Critique of Eurocentrism in the 1990s

Late in the twentieth century, Partha Chatterjee, an Indian intellectual, wrote *The Nation and Its Fragments,* in which he examined the influence of British rule in India and Indian reactions to the British. At the same time, he subjected ideas and institutions of the West to a painstaking scrutiny and concluded that using European categories as the universal measure for various societies (Eurocentrism) severely limits intellectual discourse and understanding.

> One can see how a conception of the state-society relation, born within the parochial history of Western Europe but made universal by the global sway of capital, dogs the contemporary history of the world. I do not think that the invocation of the state/civil society opposition in the struggle against socialist-bureaucratic regimes in Eastern Europe in the former Soviet republics or, for that matter, in China will produce anything other than strategies seeking to replicate the history of Western Europe. The result has been demonstrated a hundred times. The provincialism of the European experience will be taken as the universal history of progress; by comparison, the history of the rest of the world will appear as the history of lack, of inadequacy—an inferior history. Appeals will be made all over again to philosophies produced in Britain, France, and Germany. The fact that these doctrines were produced in complete ignorance of the histories of other parts of the world will not matter: they will be found useful and enlightening.

FIGURE 22.5 ***Modern Art.*** *Pablo Picasso loved to startle art lovers with new images. Part of a wide movement beginning in the early twentieth century, this painting of three musicians clearly reveals a different way of seeing. Some artists of the period experimented with new forms and visions, while others protested the traumas of war.* The Museum of Modern Art, New York. Mrs. Simon Guggenheim Fund.

MODERNITY'S THIRD PHASE: UPHEAVAL AND REBUILDING, 1905–PRESENT

The smug optimism implied by the idea of progress during the early years of the twentieth century was shattered by the two world wars and several revolutions that brought a ghastly loss of human life. A general questioning of modernity's costs characterized the writings of intellectuals who saw many of their friends slaughtered in World War I. Antiheroes began to appear in fiction, and intellectuals began to question the value of progress and modernity itself.

War was a major feature of the period beginning in 1905. The Russo-Japanese War ended in 1905, two world wars succeeded it, and lesser conflicts also occurred; World War II dwarfed all previous wars in the loss of human life. In addition, civil wars in Russia and China either brought to power or kept in power communist governments that slaughtered additional millions of people.

Human catastrophe and the effects of industrialization and technological development compelled many intellectuals to question seriously whether the costs of progress and modernity itself were simply too steep. Can we, many asked, speak of progress, if tens of millions of people perish in building a new political and social order? Can we still speak of modernity when the ability to take life far outstrips our ability to preserve it? Can human beings live in a world of declining resources and heavily polluted skies and waters?

The global economy became even more closely interrelated than in earlier times. By 1914, it would be an integrated global economic system. The economic collapse from 1929 to 1941 deeply affected most nations and empires. After 1945, the global economy saw general growth of competition between the capitalist and Soviet socialist systems. The Soviet system developed until the 1980s, when serious problems helped bring about a general economic collapse there from 1989 to 1991.

Another impact of the twentieth century has been environmental degradation. The capitalist and socialist economic systems have severely damaged many environments on the planet. The disposal of nuclear wastes is especially disturbing because the effects may last for generations rather than for years, and some environmentalists have questioned the benefits of the Industrial Revolution and the atomic age. Indeed, many are questioning progressivism and whether things are always getting better.

The increasing advancement of women and ethnic minorities is one significant twentieth-century development. It relates directly to wider social participation of more people in modern life and to the breaking of social barriers to advancement that had begun in the sixteenth century.

Figure 22.6 ***Injustices Faced by Women.*** *This political cartoon, designed by Mary Lowndes, builds on the Western world's traditional female personification of Justice. Lowndes characterized British politicians as acting unjustly by excluding women from a reform bill. By 1912, people in England and elsewhere were seriously examining the implications of keeping women from power.* Fawcett Collection.

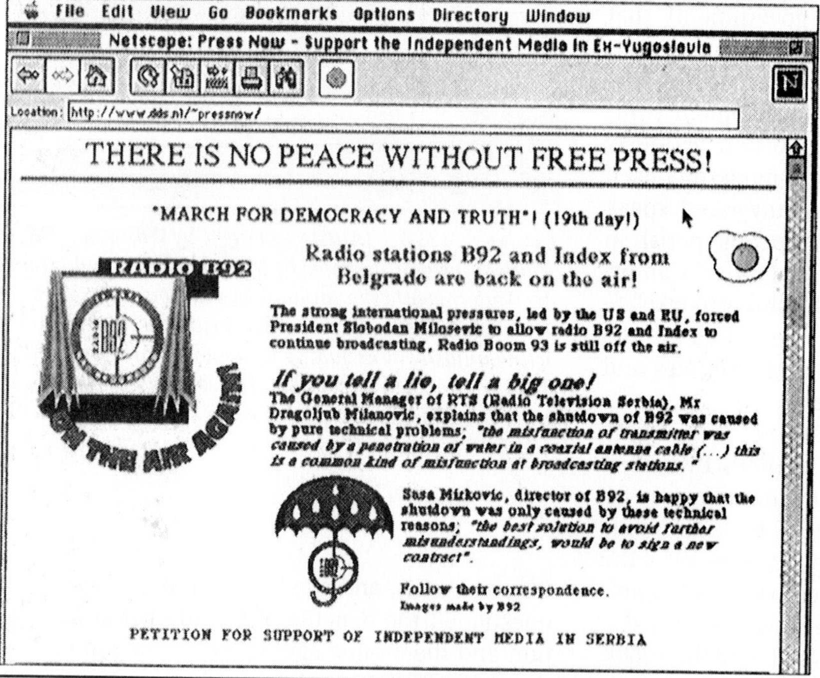

FIGURE 22.7 ***Modern Technology and Freedom.*** *This picture shows the use of computers in conveying information about political demonstrations. In late 1996, Serbs protested against their government, which had annulled elections won by opposition groups. To circulate information about these protest activities, teachers and others used the Internet. Authoritarian regimes found it difficult if not impossible to curb the flow of information because of the large numbers of computers, fax machines, telephones, and pocket radios. The communist government of Rumania once registered all typewriters held there; today such an effort would be almost impossible.* Photo by Alan Chin. Both images: New York Times Picture Sales.

In phase three of modernity, changes in travel, communication, and the economy have increased global integration. At the same time, disruptive elements like military conflicts, economic depressions, and environmental catastrophes have given governments much to consider. One theme is the questioning of progress, and another is the criticism of European ideas and values being used as universal categories. This latter debate has focused on Eurocentrism, the view that sees Europe as the measure by which everything else is judged (see "In Their Own Words," p. 552).

SUMMARY

1. Modernity, one way to characterize the era from 1500 to the present, has many important elements:

- —a cultural outlook that focuses on progress;
- —a perspective that seeks to accelerate the systematic application of new science and technology to improve economic production;
- —a view that shifts from a predominantly religious to a predominantly secular understanding of the world and universe;
- —governments, often nation-states, that usually seek wider participation of a broader spectrum of people in all aspects of life, especially politics;
- —an increase in the determination of social status according to merit rather than birth, and the breaking of social barriers to the advancement of talented people; and
- —the accelerating integration of regional economies into a global economic network that is increasingly dominated by capitalism or socialism.

2. The Early Modern Era was modernity's first phase, lasting from around 1500 to around 1750. Modernity's second phase of industrialization and Westernization lasted from around 1750 to 1905. Upheaval and rebuilding have characterized modernity's third phase, from 1905 to the present.

3. A transformation of Europe and Japan came in the eighteenth and nineteenth centuries and was associated with the Industrial Revolution. This shift gave many European states and Japan the power to carve out empires, some of which lasted for decades.

4. As human ingenuity perfected ways of killing, the losses from war and revolution reached tens of millions and caused many to feel disillusioned with change.

SUGGESTED READINGS

Blum, Jerome. *In the Beginning: The Advent of the Modern Age.* New York: Charles Scribner's Sons, 1994. An examination of elements of modernity that commenced in the 1840s, largely in Europe.

Chatterjee, Partha. *The Nation and Its Fragments.* Princeton, N.J.: Princeton University Press, 1993. A critique of prevailing interpretations of the history of India with wider implications for the study of global history.

Hodgson, Marshall. *Rethinking World History.* Cambridge, Eng.: Cambridge University Press, 1993. A collection of essays about Islam, Europe, and the study of global history.

McNeill, William. "The Age of Gunpowder Empires, 1450–1800," in Michael Adas, *Islamic and European Expansion.* Philadelphia: Temple University Press, 1993, 103–40. An essay about the role of gunpowder in Europe's rise in global affairs.

Mokyr, Joel. *The Lever of Riches.* Oxford, Eng.: Oxford University Press, 1990. A work examining the relationship between technological development and economic growth.

Totman, Conrad. *Early Modern Japan.* Berkeley: University of California Press, 1993. An examination of Japanese history in the Tokugawa period, including ecological and financial matters.

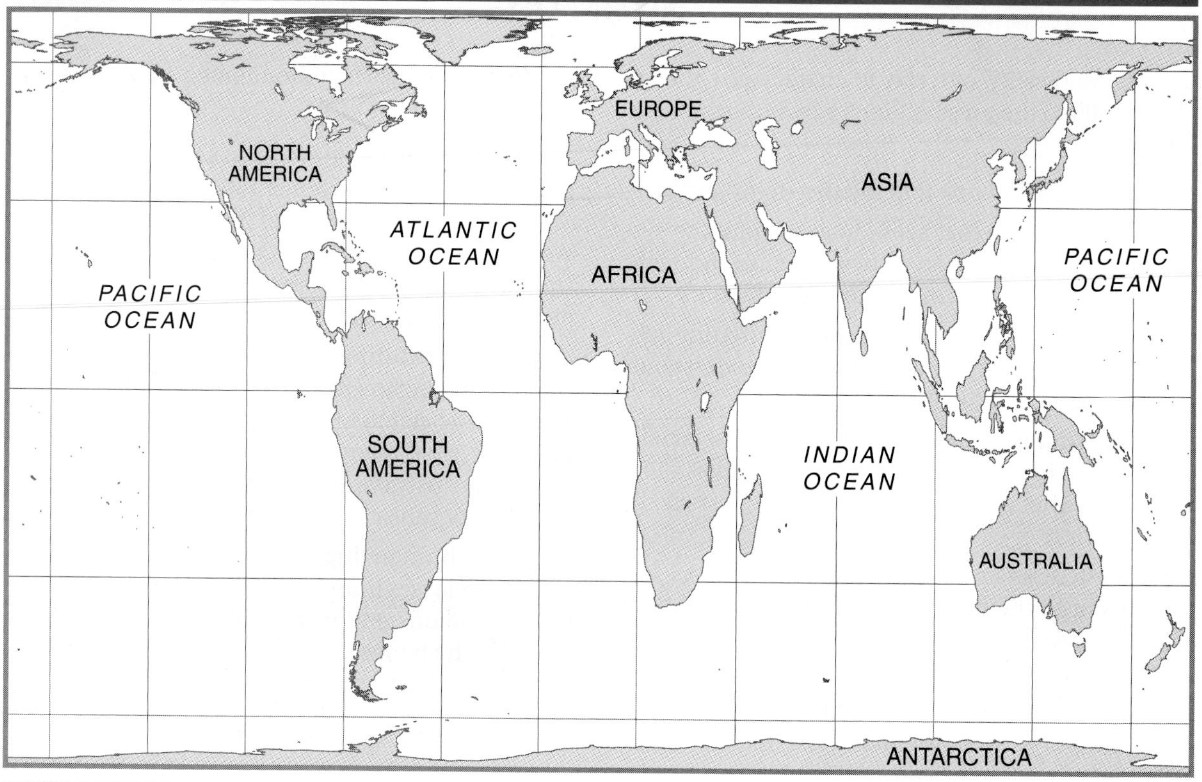

EUROPE
NORTH AMERICA
ASIA
ATLANTIC OCEAN
PACIFIC OCEAN
AFRICA
PACIFIC OCEAN
SOUTH AMERICA
INDIAN OCEAN
AUSTRALIA
ANTARCTICA

EUROPE
ASIA
NORTH AMERICA
AFRICA
ATLANTIC OCEAN
PACIFIC OCEAN
INDIAN OCEAN
SOUTH AMERICA
AUSTRALIA
ANTARCTICA

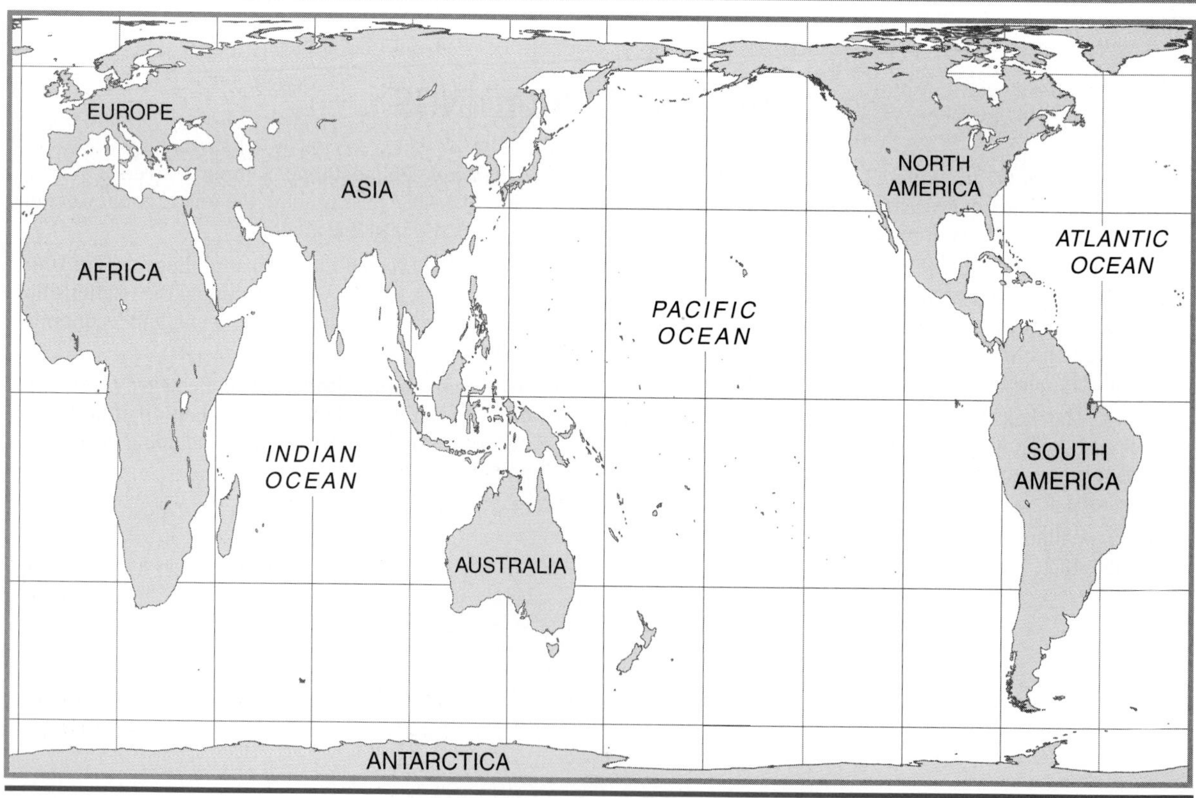

CHAPTER 23

Oceanic Explorations and Contacts

1405–1780

We have traversed . . . immense waterspaces and have beheld . . . huge waves like mountains. . . . We have set eyes on barbarian regions far away hidden in a blue transparency of light vapors, while our sails, loftily unfurled like clouds day and night, continued their course [as rapidly] as a star, traversing those savage waves as if we were treading a public thoroughfare. . . .

–ZHENG HE

These words carved in stone in China celebrate the achievements of Zheng He,[1] commander of China's seven oceanic expeditions in the fifteenth century. Chinese ships, some of enormous construction, sailed and then abandoned the South China Sea and the Indian Ocean a few decades before the Europeans arrived. The Europeans, however, came to stay and reaped substantial and lasting benefits from their efforts.

Sailing across the Atlantic and Pacific oceans on a regular basis began in the fifteenth and sixteenth centuries. Before that time, the hazards of sailing for long periods kept ship captains close to shore and rarely out of the sight of land. Without a compass, for example, ships could easily get lost, and ships had to carry their own supplies. During early long-distance ocean travel, fresh water turned bad, and the absence of fruit and vegetables in the sailors' diets brought on scurvy, a dreaded disease caused by the lack of vitamin C. Fierce storms terrified crews, and ocean currents

[1] **Zheng He:** JEHNG HUH

often snagged unwary ships and took them far off their intended paths. Frequently, many ships of an expedition would be lost in stormy seas, or others would turn back home after their crews were exasperated by extended voyages away from land and a varied and healthful diet. Illness and anger fueled many mutinies, and only the most self-assured or desperate sailors continued on the lonely, unexplored routes. The Polynesians, Micronesians, and Melanesians all sailed to different island groups in the Pacific Ocean. Most of these peoples stayed south of the equator, but some Polynesians established permanent settlements in the North Pacific. The Vikings sailed the waters around Europe, venturing into the North Atlantic as far as Iceland, Greenland, and Canada. The Chinese briefly dominated transoceanic voyaging in the early fifteenth century, expending large amounts of money and even reaching Africa, but they halted and withdrew from ocean travel to concentrate on domestic issues. Many Europeans increased their interest in seagoing exploration and, by the early sixteenth century, sailed the major oceans. They also circumnavigated the earth and inaugurated a global era in history.

OCEANIC VOYAGING BEFORE 1400

Water covers much of the earth and has served as a barrier between the New and Old worlds. Polynesians and Vikings, among others, often sailed the Atlantic and Pacific in earlier times before European sailors dominated the oceans for exploration, trade, conquest, and colonization in the Old and New worlds.

MAP 23.1 ***Oceanic Voyaging before 1400.*** *Polynesian, Viking, and Chinese sailors explored the waters far from their homelands, gaining knowledge of other cultures, trading, and settling in new lands. Their ships carried from a dozen to a few hundred people each, and their expeditions numbered from one hundred to nearly thirty thousand people.*

Polynesian Exploration

Beginning perhaps around 50,000 years ago, peoples from mainland Asia began exploring and colonizing islands along a path ending at the continent of Australia. Other groups, such as the Melanesians around 1500 B.C., went east to Pacific islands, like New Guinea, New Caledonia, and Fiji. Micronesians settled the more eastern and northern islands, like Palau and Guam. After 1000 B.C., Polynesians reached more remote islands, including New Zealand, Samoa, Easter Island, and Hawaii.

Polynesians achieved great navigational feats without the aid of the compass or the sextant used by other maritime peoples. Their boats were usually single- or double-hulled and often had an outrigger (a buoyant pole parallel to the hull and affixed to it by wood pieces) to stabilize the craft. The largest ships, catamarans, could carry as many as 200 people and their necessary supplies. The vessels could be propelled either by oars, in which case they needed a steering paddle or rudder, or by winds blowing into the triangular sail. With these devices, the Polynesians ventured over most of the Pacific Ocean.

To guide them, the Polynesians relied on the sun, moon, and stars as well as the flight patterns of migratory birds. On cloudy days and nights in open water, the sense of being lost must have given pause to many on board the ships. Familiar waters were mapped out and the particular places where sailors could get their bearings were noted, but new waters had no known markers to guide the explorers. Only a sense of adventure and the urge to locate new lands for colonization drove the sailors on.

Earliest human settlement in the Marquesas, Samoa, and Hawaii dates to the era from the second century B.C. to the second century A.D. The settlers fished, hunted wild animals and birds, gathered fruit, and tended gardens of taro and other tubers. The bark of trees was pounded into materials to make cloth and other products.

Polynesians also caused ecological degradation on many islands where they settled. By A.D. 500, Polynesians in Hawaii killed off nearly all flightless birds for food. Widespread deforestation of the Easter Islands brought serious erosion of agricultural fields. Saltwater marshes were used as

FIGURE 23.1 ***Palm-Frond Map from the Marshall Islands.*** *Various peoples of the Pacific have made nautical maps of string, twigs, or the central ribs of palm fronds. These maps show distances between islands measured in time traveled, not in actual miles, since currents and prevailing winds could cause two trips of equal distance to have very different sailing times. In its original form, this map from the Marshall Islands most likely had bits of coral and shell marking island positions. Maps similar to this probably were used by early Polynesian navigators.* Bishop Museum.

PARALLELS AND DIVERGENCES

Elements of Early Modern Sailing Technology

The Chinese and Europeans mastered the essential techniques of shipbuilding, rigging, and sailing in the fifteenth century, skills that opened the oceans to global voyaging. Over time, accurate sea charts were drawn indicating passages through straits, underwater reefs, and shoals, as well as unusual currents.

Ship construction and rigging improved significantly in the fourteenth and fifteenth centuries. Chinese ships were constructed as separate but interlocked watertight compartments, making them nearly unsinkable. Chinese sails were of square design and were made of cloth, permitting effective use of wind power. At the same time, European shipbuilders began using techniques that made lighter and larger vessels capable of carrying larger loads. They included square and triangular sails in their riggings in combinations designed to permit more effective use of wind power.

In the fifteenth century, the previously distinct northern and southern traditions of European ship design merged, producing the **full-rigged ship**, a ship of multiple sails in various positions, allowing it to take advantage of diverse wind conditions. Such ships, one type of which is the famous galleon, were superior to their predecessors in seaworthiness, size, and ability to control the direction in which they sailed. In addition, the development of the vertical stern permitted the use of a rudder that steered more precisely than the earlier steering oar, allowing the ship to avoid rocks and other obstacles. Finally, the extra space in the ship and the mounting of cannons in openings in the ship's sides made the full-rigged ship a floating arsenal that was a formidable military force used especially in India to reduce local resistance.

Both Chinese and Europeans used the compass and other navigational devices to permit sailing under all conditions. The compass was employed in sailing by the Chinese centuries before the Europeans developed it. To measure latitude, the Europeans adopted the astrolabe from the Greeks via the Muslims and adapted it, calculating the altitude of the North Star and indicating the observer's latitude.

The revival of previous cartographic knowledge also permitted the mapping of the global surface. Greek geographical works were translated into Latin by the early fifteenth century and provided models for Europeans to divide maps into grids of latitude and longitude. This made for more useful map projections and safer sailing for ships' crews.

sources of water for taro fields, leading to the salting of lands and rendering them unusable. Many birds on the Easter Islands were hunted to extinction for their colorful feathers.

Viking Exploration

The Norse Vikings, medieval inhabitants of the Norwegian coast, sailed the waters of the Baltic and North seas and often raided coastal settlements of continental Europe and the isles of Britain beginning as early as the eighth century. Major invasions commenced in the ninth and tenth centuries and even reached the Iberian Peninsula and places on the Mediterranean coast. The largest of the raiding vessels measured more than 100 feet long and carried as many as sixty-five fully armed Vikings; some of the fleets included as many as 300 ships. The Vikings had shallow-draft vessels for rivers as well as deep-draft ones for the oceans. The deltas of many European rivers attracted Viking settlement, and soon Viking colonies dotted much of the coastline of Europe. In England most early Viking homesteads were established along eastern shores. In addition, Vikings sailed down inland waterways in eastern Europe and Russia.

Eventually the Vikings crossed the short stretches (200 to 250 miles) of the North Atlantic to Iceland and Greenland, settling in Iceland during the first quarter of the ninth century. The only people preceding the Vikings to Iceland were Irish monks who used it for a place of retreat from worldly distractions. Greenland, about 200 miles from Iceland, attracted the attention of the Vikings in the tenth century, although European colonization did not begin there until the last two decades of the century. The Inuit had long inhabited small communities in Greenland.

The Vikings reached North America around A.D. 1000. They explored some of the coast of present-day eastern Canada and established a short-lived settlement in present-day Newfoundland. Archaeologists in the early 1960s found the remains of a Viking settlement in Newfoundland.

Norse Vikings could not sustain viable settlements in Greenland and North America. Contentious chiefs who frequently quarreled with one another ruled the Vikings, and leaders who had run afoul of more powerful chiefs ran the Viking settlements in Greenland and North America. In addition, overpopulation in some Viking lands drove some to seek lands suitable for settlement. Lands to the west were quite inhospitable to the Viking way of life, at least in the northern reaches accessible to them. Vikings were grain agriculturalists, yet no crops could be grown in the frigid lands of Greenland and adjacent North America; their houses and many of their tools were largely made of wood, but these places supported only sparse and scraggly trees. The Viking settlement in Newfoundland lasted only three years, and the Greenland settlement survived for scarcely more than a century.

FIGURE 23.2 ***Viking Ship.*** *This thirteenth-century seal of Bergen, Norway, depicts a Viking ship sailing the seas. While the typical Viking ship had but one dragon head on its bow, dragon heads were placed at both ends of this ship by the seal's designer, for aesthetic purposes. Bergen was a key port of trade with Viking settlements in Greenland.* Per Christoffersen, EGM-Foto. Courtesy of Rijksarkivet, Oslo.

Although the distances that the Vikings sailed did not compare with those of the Polynesians in the Pacific, these Europeans had sailed from the eastern to the western hemisphere, and they briefly established a small settlement in the new land. These facts attest to the sailing skills of the Vikings.

CHINESE VOYAGING IN THE INDIAN OCEAN, 1405–1433

Although the Chinese developed various navies in their history, they also maintained a strategic orientation to Inner Asia and land warfare, and centuries of conflict with various nomadic tribes from north of China helped solidify that inland orientation. In the fifth and fourth centuries B.C., northern Chinese states began building walls to protect themselves from nomad incursions, and the Qin Empire linked these walls to form the edifice now known as the Great Wall. This defensive posture against northern tribes symbolizes China's land orientation. Nevertheless, Chinese voyaging in the Indian Ocean suggests a naval tradition of consequence.

China's Emerging Naval Tradition

By the sixth century A.D., a necessity to defend their coastline and patrol their inland waterways caused the Chinese to develop a naval force. In the seventh century, a Chinese fleet defeated Japanese vessels off the Korean coast. A few centuries later, a Chinese flotilla (including paddle-wheel boats) patrolled the Yangzi River, keeping the Mongols from invading South China. When the Chinese fleet defected to the Mongols, swift conquest of the south followed.

The Mongols soon used the naval fleet to assert their political influence. Twice they attempted to invade Japan with an armada (generally of Korean ships and sailors as well as Mongol soldiers). The second attempted invasion of Japan in 1281 included a significant Chinese naval force. In the 1290s, the Mongols sailed the South China Sea, reaching the island of Java (in present-day Indonesia). Although the Mongols soon turned their focus away from maritime activities, Chinese ships continued to sail the waters of Southeast Asia.

IN THEIR OWN WORDS

Chinese Prayers for Safe Voyages

Sailors seem to be given to superstition when facing long-distance oceanic voyaging, and the Chinese are no exception to this. Even Zheng He, a devout Muslim, actively participated in prayers and rituals honoring the Celestial Consort and the patron goddess of sailors. Originally a historical figure who lived in the tenth century, the Celestial Consort was credited with saving sailors, and worship of her spread along China's southeastern coast. The Yongle Emperor built a splendid temple to her in the early fifteenth century.

Before each voyage, Zheng He and members of the crew sacrificed goats, pigs, and cattle, and they burned incense and gave prayers for guidance and a safe return. One prayer had the words:

> As the divine swirling smoke rises, with hearts pure and true, we bow down and beseech the messengers of merit to convey by means of the incense in this burner that in this year, in this month, on this day, at this hour, we respectfully entreat the patriarchs of the imperially created compass throughout the ages: Yellow Emperor, Duke of Zhou, immortal masters of former ages divinely knowledgeable . . . Dark Raven, immortal White Crane master. . . .
>
> [And] patriarchs of the ages who have traversed the sea; who know the mountains, the sandbanks, the shallows, the depths, the isles, the shoals; who are conversant with the sea lanes, the mountains, the mooring waters, the constellations and guiding stars; those from past times to the present day, those who first transmitted it and those who later taught it.
>
> [And] the great guardian spirit generals of the 24 directions; the great spirit generals of the 24 azimuth points of the patriarch of books, the compass classic; the page boy who sets the compass directions, the spirit of the water basin, the lord of the water changing, the strongman who sets down the compass needle, the guardian spirits of the direction of the needle, the master of the lookout, and all the other immortal masters and spirit soldiers and divine emissaries—all the efficacious spirits of the incense burner.
>
> [And] the protectress of our ships, the Celestial Consort, brilliant, divine, marvelous, responsive, mysterious force, protector of the people, guardian of the country.
>
> [And] the all-seeing and all-hearing spirit soldiers of winds and seasons, the wave quellers and swell drinkers, the airborne immortals, the god of the year, and all the local tutelary deities of every place.
>
> Come down one and all to this incense feast, partake of this sagely vessel.
>
> Come rising on auspicious clouds from the ends of the earth, come down and grace our incense table . . . to protect our ships and valuables.

Certain Chinese inventions facilitated travel in waters beyond sight of land. China employed the compass in maritime activities by the twelfth century. Naval engineers had developed watertight compartments for ocean-going vessels, and at the same time, the Chinese improved anchors to be useful during storms. Indeed, with these various technological successes, Chinese merchant ships garnered the reputation of being exceptionally seaworthy, and merchants from other countries preferred to ride aboard Chinese ships, believing that the vessels would best guarantee a safe arrival at a destination.

Motivations for the Chinese Voyages

In 1403, the Yongle[2] Emperor seized power in China (see Chapter 28) and became a dynamic Ming monarch who wished to do grandiose things. One was outfitting the Ming navy to follow existing trade routes in the South China Sea and on into the Indian Ocean. The Yongle Emperor's effort, monumental in scope and scale, reflected imperial ambition and a desire to project Chinese influence

[2]**Yongle:** YOHNG leh

abroad. The program did not seek exploration, promote trade, or push colonization. It was largely symbolic, and in that way it differed from the later European voyages. Perhaps it is best understood as the idiosyncratic policy of a powerful monarch.

Another factor in China's naval voyages was the eunuchs, one of whom was Zheng He, who commanded each of the seven expeditions. Ming emperors used eunuchs for many tasks, especially ones that might incur criticism and resistance by bureaucrats who believed these tasks to be costly. The monarchs often preferred working with eunuchs, who obeyed rather than questioned imperial policies. The Yongle Emperor, for example, heavily relied on trusted eunuchs and selected Zheng He to oversee the outfitting of the armada.

The Seven Voyages

The emperor ordered the fleet to be ready to sail in 1405. Many of the empire's shipyards, including a large one near Nanjing, built the required ships. Of the fleet, the largest ships had as many as nine masts and several decks and measured nearly 200 feet across and around 450 feet in length. These ships displaced between 2,500 and 3,000 tons and could carry between 450 and 500 people. They far outsized the largest Polynesian, Viking, or European ships up to that time or into the seventeenth century. In fact, they compare in size with the largest vessels of the eighteenth century.

The fleet of the first expedition numbered over 300 ships, including more than 50 large vessels.

FIGURE 23.3 ***Chinese Ship.*** *This fifteenth-century multimasted sailing vessel was of the type used in the Ming expeditions led by Zheng He. Around five times as big as the ships of Columbus or Vasco da Gama, the Chinese ships carried large numbers of sailors and huge amounts of cargo. They were generally seaworthy, surviving the great cyclonic storms of the Indian Ocean.* Ontario Science Center, Toronto.

The total human cargo of the two-year voyage numbered nearly 28,000 people, in contrast to the few hundred sailors of the Polynesians and Columbus or Magellan. Although the flotilla carried a small army, they did not fight much, because its major purpose was diplomatic rather than military. Special water tankers were constructed and could supply as much as a month's drinking water. There was also one physician for every 150 sailors and many linguists to translate for the diplomats.

Zheng He's first three expeditions sailed across the Indian Ocean to India, and each time the flotilla carried many diplomatic envoys back to China to feed the ego of the Yongle Emperor. Because the fleet followed trade routes previously used by merchant ships, some commerce was conducted. Yet one must remember the low position of merchants in Confucian Chinese society. In that kind of social climate, business ventures did not receive much imperial endorsement. China's diplomatic system, in fact, demanded that the emperor return gifts of greater value than those received in a diplomatic exchange. After all, China viewed itself as superior, and that superiority carried an obligation of generosity over into the exchange of goods.

The last voyages reached the east coast of Africa and made port at Mogadishu in Somalia and Malindi farther south. One result of the voyages was the collection of animals exotic to the Chinese. The tall giraffes particularly excited the Chinese, who saw them as a kind of unicorn, a mythical beast associated with good omens for a monarch.

FIGURE 23.4 ***Giraffe in China.*** *The Ming sailing expeditions of the early fifteenth century brought back many exotic creatures from the regions of the Indian Ocean. This picture shows a giraffe that was transported from Africa. Chinese rulers had collected strange animals for centuries, and giraffes were considered to be among the most peculiar.* Shen Tu (1357–1434), Tribute Giraffe with Attendant, 1403–1424. Philadelphia Museum of Art. Given by John T. Dorrence.

Termination of the Voyages

Of the possible reasons for the dearth of sea voyages between 1420 and 1433, the crucial factor was the death of the Yongle Emperor in 1424. Because he had been intimately connected with the voyages, his death ended that tie and permitted critics to assert themselves with less fear of imperial retribution. In addition, factional politics played a part in the termination of the expeditions. Eunuchs, who generally supported Zheng He, frequently opposed the scholar-officials, who derided the eunuchs' lack of education and their not earning government positions through the examination system. Most scholars adhered to Confucianism, which espoused Chinese self-sufficiency; it was unseemly, they argued, for Chinese to go abroad. Rather, the thinking went, barbarians must come to China. Scholars also opposed any hint of trade connected with the expeditions, because Confucians despised merchants. These views became more persuasive after the deaths of the emperor protecting the fleet and the influential eunuchs supporting it.

Strategic and financial considerations also played a role in halting the naval expeditions. China's Inner Asian orientation reasserted itself over time, especially after the Mongols became active in the north. (In fact, a Mongol army captured one emperor in 1449.) Ming laborers rebuilt the Great Wall in the fifteenth and sixteenth centuries. China simply could not afford a naval presence and a strong military campaign in the north. To build the great fleet, the Yongle Emperor had commandeered timber and other resources from many provinces, and the financial and material needs of the voyages severely taxed the empire's resources for defense.

Overall, China turned inward after having accomplished some remarkable naval feats decades before the Europeans arrived in the Indian Ocean. China's deliberate isolationist bent negated any influential role in global politics or relations. Coupled with the ban on overseas trade until 1567, China retired from the world naval stage at the height of its prowess. Pirates who had been swept from the seas reappeared along the China coast, and European ships arrived in China in the sixteenth century. Some Europeans became pirates or joined forces with East Asian pirates. The Chinese retreat from maritime activities was so thorough that in the late 1470s officials destroyed some records of their voyages kept in the War Ministry.

EUROPEAN EXPLORATION AND TRADE, 1434–1780

In the fifteenth century, Europeans embarked on a remarkable variety and number of exploratory voyages. Within a few decades before and after 1500, they mapped out the west coast of Africa,

PATHS TO THE PAST

The Myth of the Flat Earth

Contrary to popular belief, people in the European Middle Ages did not believe that the earth was flat. Christopher Columbus's voyage is often touted as the triumph of science over the ignorant view of medieval Christianity that the world was flat and any voyage into the unknown waters of the Atlantic Ocean would result in ships' falling off the edge into oblivion. This perception, however, was held by only a few medieval church leaders and some educated people in Europe prior to the transoceanic voyages of the fifteenth century.

How did such an error originate? The history of this little tale falls at the feet of two nineteenth-century men: Washington Irving (1783–1859), who wrote a semifictitious biography of Christopher Columbus, and Antoine-Jean Letronne (1787–1848), who wrote several works, including the four-volume geographical *Histoire de géographie moderne* (Paris, 1806). Unfortunately for later history, the sources these men used to weave their interpretations of medieval and Christian thinkers were not carefully checked by other scholars until recently, and, therefore, their imaginative embellishments were accepted as fact.

Washington Irving's biography included a completely fabricated story of a meeting with Columbus at a university. The clerics who attended supposedly declared heretical Columbus's idea that the earth was spherical. Irving's account created the encounter in order to make the biography interesting. His tale unwittingly created the basis for historical misinterpretation of medieval science. Irving's writings echoed a prejudice against medieval Christianity that had been common for centuries. In Irving's mind, Columbus represented the new science of the modern era in contrast to medieval science, and his literary scene depicted Columbus arguing the truth of a spherical earth against his oppressive persecutors. Irving wrote at the end of a scene, "Such are the specimens of the errors and prejudices, the mingled ignorance and erudition, and the pedantic bigotry, with which Columbus had to contend." Scholars believe that no such council met and no such conflict existed. The only arguments Columbus ever had concerned the accuracy of his calculations on distance.

Geography was a popular subject in the nineteenth century, and Letronne's influence as a scholar was significant. French scientific investigation often took a particularly antagonistic anticlerical stand on all issues. Letronne argued that medieval astronomers were forced to believe in a flat earth because of clerical pressure that had threatened persecution, prison, or burning at the stake. In reality this never occurred. Unfortunately, because of Letronne's influence on later geographical scholarship, the misinformation was picked up and perpetuated by scholars in other fields.

sailed throughout the Caribbean Sea, and thoroughly explored the eastern coasts of the two American continents. Diverse Europeans, including Spanish, Portuguese, English, Dutch, Scandinavians, French, and Basques, came to the New World.

What propelled these adventurers to brave the perils of oceanic crossing? Economic incentives drove many sailors into dangerous oceanic waters. Certainly many hoped to discover a new passage to India and Indonesia, whose spices were in great demand in Europe and fetched good prices. Precious metals also lured people and nations to undertake risky endeavors. The opening of new places for colonization and commerce drove many west and south from Europe. Soon, national and dynastic rivalries fed the competitive efforts to outdo the other European states.

Certainly new maritime inventions and techniques gave sailors more hope that transoceanic voyages offered a greater probability of success in returning home. The maritime compass permitted sailors to fix directions without recognizable land features on which to get a reckoning. Improved technology permitted sails that caught breezes and permitted easy maneuvering in case the wind changed direction, resulting in less chance of being becalmed. Portuguese sailors from 1434 mapped out the west coast of Africa, garnering much experience in sailing. This knowledge passed to others in the sailing community because crews of mixed nationality were common throughout this era. For example, Italians sailed with the Spanish, Scandinavians sailed with the English, and English sailed with the Dutch.

The Age of Columbus

Christopher Columbus certainly was not the first human to set foot in the Americas—he was preceded by the American Indians by many thousands of years. But his voyages made Europe aware of the Americas and initiated global integration.

Christopher Columbus sought a new way to the Indies, land of spices and immense profits. He sailed west rather than south and embarked on a risky venture that had been underwritten by the Spaniards. He outfitted three ships and a few hundred sailors, yet the consequences of his expeditions far outstripped those of the Chinese in global terms. The Europeans vied with one another to find additional lands and peoples.

FIGURE 23.5 ***Entrance to a Portuguese Mansion.*** *The Portuguese began to settle in India in the sixteenth century. This gate, built by the Portuguese, still stands in western India and features rampant lions and a coat of arms with triple-crossed lances. Portugal controlled the colony of Goa in India until the 1960s.* From K. N. Chaudhuri, *Asia Before Europe* (New York: Cambridge University Press), Plate 72, 349. Reproduced with permission. Photo courtesy of Library of Congress.

As noted earlier, Columbus actually was but one of many captains sailing from the Iberian Peninsula in the fifteenth century. The Portuguese probed along the west coast of Africa, eventually rounding the southern tip of that continent and sailing into the Indian Ocean, reaching East Africa and India in the late 1490s.

Portugal and Spain competed for new lands and wealth in the years after Columbus's first expedition. In 1493, Pope Alexander VI attempted mediation between the two countries and offered a line of demarcation between Portuguese and Spanish dominion. Envoys of the two monarchs negotiated a modification of the papal effort that was somewhat more favorable to the Portuguese. This led the following year to the Treaty of Tordesillas,[3] which divvied up the new-found lands. (The Protestant European countries ignored the division of the globe.) Brazil, claimed in 1500 by a Portuguese captain, was the only territory in the New

[3] **Tordesillas:** tor deh SEE yahs

World open to the Portuguese. The Spanish proceeded to explore the New World, while the Portuguese probed the Indian Ocean and sailed farther toward the islands off the Southeast Asian mainland and eventually to East Asia.

Most Spanish attention focused on Mesoamerica and South America, with the exception of Portuguese-dominated Brazil. The Spaniards undertook limited trading but concentrated primarily on exploration and conquest. One Spanish leader, Vasco de Balboa, saw a large body of water (the Pacific Ocean) from a peak in Panama. This excited him and others, because the ocean promised to be the waterway to the Indies. Some followed this speculation by sailing south and west.

The English and Dutch also undertook some tentative steps in exploration, beginning in the late fifteenth century. Some of their ships sailed along the upper coast of North America, but nothing of consequence followed in terms of exploration until the late sixteenth and early seventeenth centuries, when Henry Hudson, who sailed for both the English and the Dutch, made important explorations, including that of Hudson Bay in Canada. The French also conducted some far-ranging explorations in the Americas, but little trade or colonization occurred until the seventeenth century.

Both the Americas and Europe were strongly influenced by contact following Columbus's voyages. Millions of Native Americans perished from disease, and many others died fighting the European conquerors. Europeans grew wealthier because of the silver and gold from the New World. New foodstuffs transformed the diets of Europeans and promoted population growth.

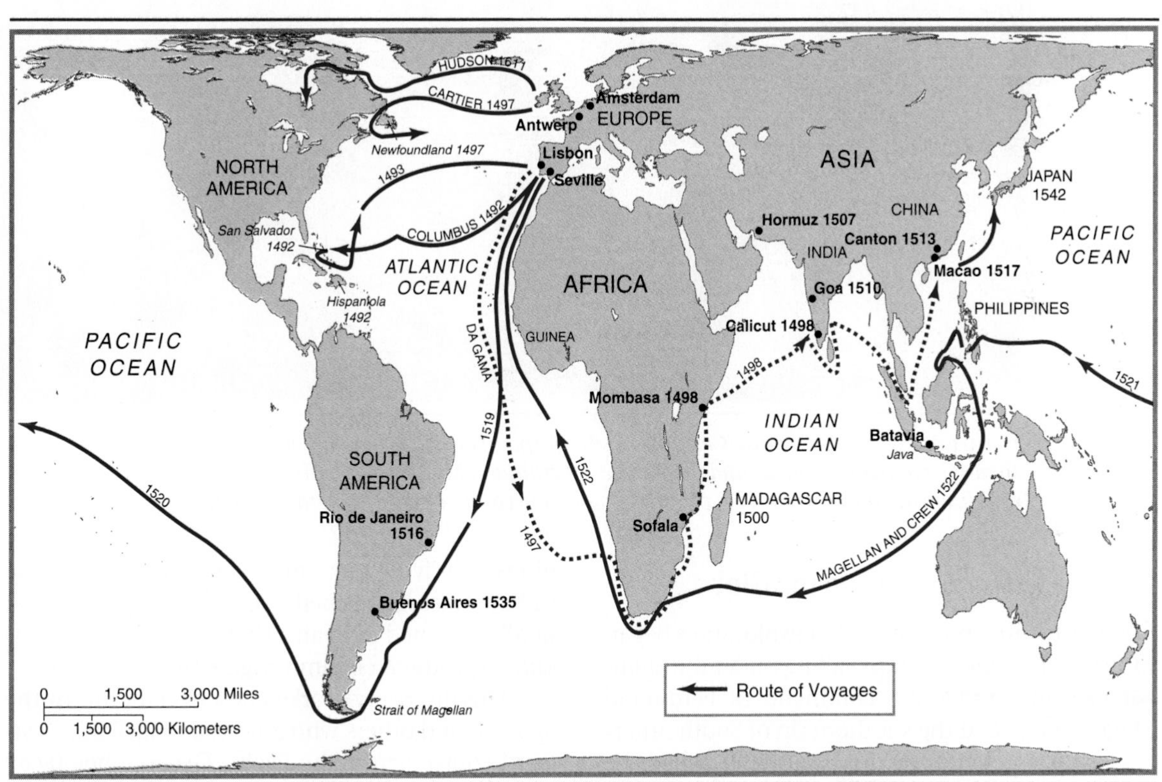

Map 23.2 ***European Voyages and Trading Posts in the Indian Ocean, 1492–1522.*** *The Portuguese explored the western coast of Africa through the fifteenth century, rounding the Cape of Good Hope in 1497. Vasco da Gama, who led that expedition, sailed on to India. His feat inaugurated a Portuguese presence in the Indian Ocean that dominated trade for most of the sixteenth century via strategically placed ports. Christopher Columbus and Ferdinand Magellan sailed west and south from Europe to reach the Americas. Magellan continued on across the Pacific Ocean to the Philippines, where he was killed; his crew returned to Spain in 1522.*

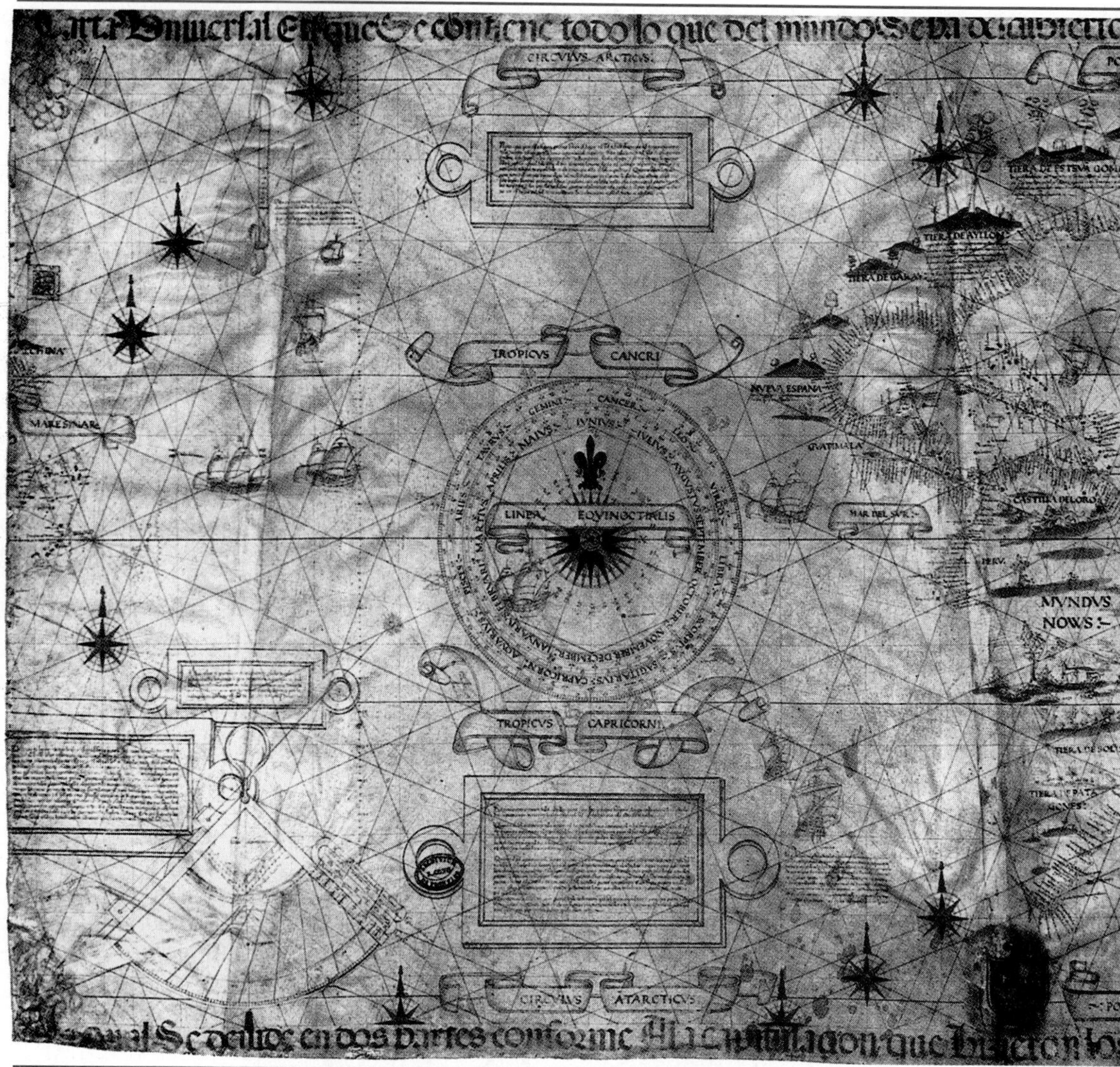

FIGURE 23.6 ***Sixteenth-Century World Map.*** *This 1529 map by Diego Ribero shows the major continents and the voyage of Ferdinand Magellan and his crew. Africa and India are rather accurately portrayed along the coasts, and the eastern coasts of*

Circumnavigating the Globe

A major turning point in global exploration began in 1519, when several ships sailing under the Spanish flag and under the command of Ferdinand Magellan reached the southern tip of South America and passed through the strait (later called the Strait of Magellan) into the Pacific Ocean. This voyage of exploration crossed the Pacific and reached various island groups, including those later known as the Philippines. By that landfall, many crew members had died and only a couple of ships remained. Captain Magellan became embroiled in a native conflict and also lost his life in the Philippines. Surviving crew members sailed across the Indian Ocean, reached the Atlantic Ocean, and finally returned to Spain. They were history's first-known group to circumnavigate the earth.

This discovery sparked new expeditions by the Spanish and others who followed Magellan's westward course across the Pacific Ocean. They faced many hazards, ranging from diseases resulting from poor diet and bad water to the great storm systems of the Pacific. Survivors also had to brave contact with local peoples, some of whom were hostile.

Westward routes across the Pacific eventually became the highways between Spanish posses-

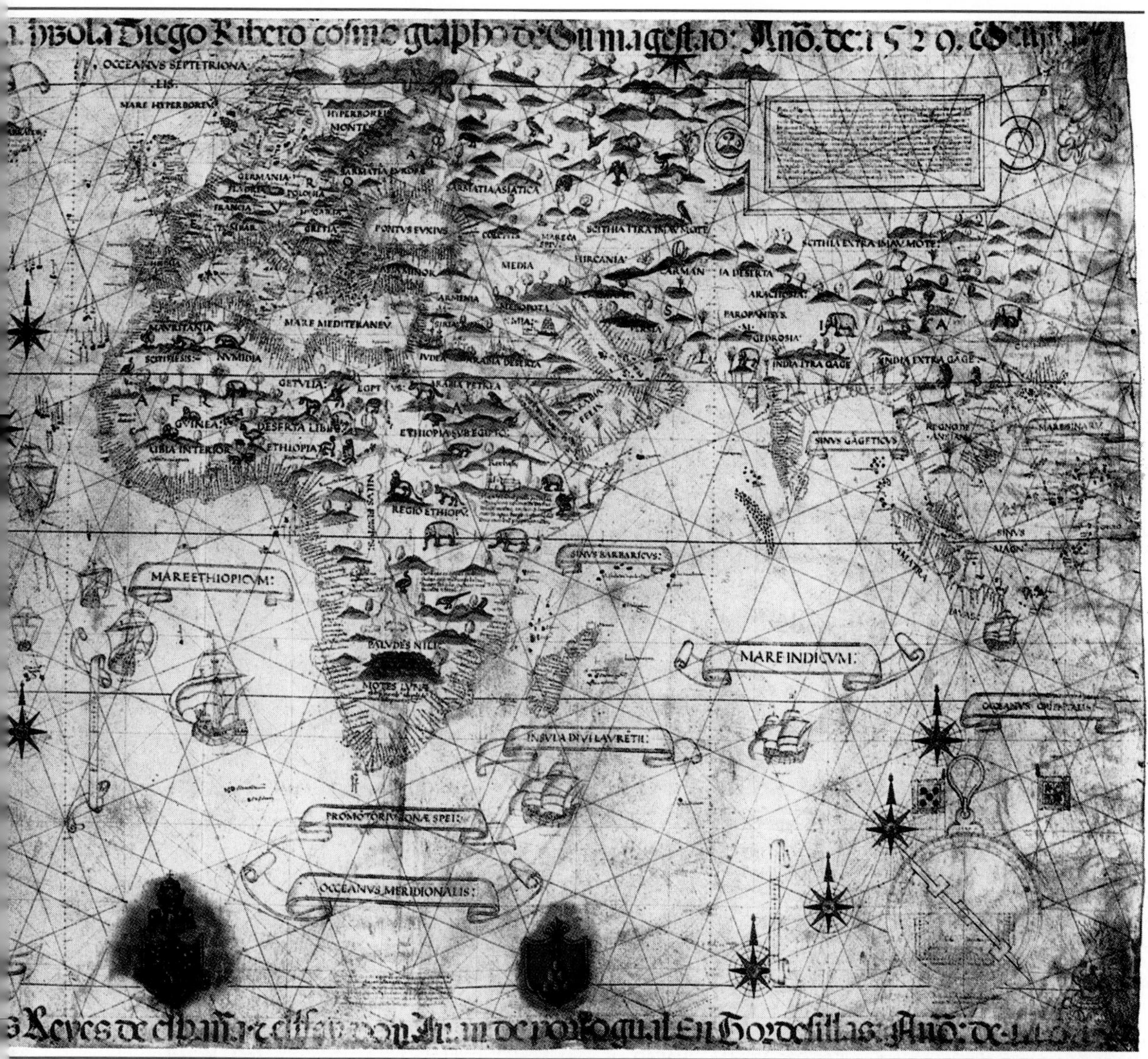

the Americas are clearly defined, unlike those in the west—a reflection of the state of mapping and European voyaging in the early sixteenth century.
Biblioteca Apostolica Vaticana.

sions in the New World and the Philippines. Soon Spanish precious metals and coins circulated across the Eurasian landmass, causing a variety of economic effects from inflation to growth of trade.

By the end of the sixteenth century, the Dutch also began to sail in foreign waters far from home. They explored the Americas, including Canada, the United States, and the Caribbean. Intrepid Dutch captains sailed to the Spice Islands (later called the Dutch East Indies and eventually Indonesia). One voyage even explored the waters off Australia in the mid–seventeenth century. The Dutch organized their explorations and trading missions in the East by chartering the Dutch East India Company, which played a major role in the seizure of the Spice Islands for Dutch colonization and economic development.

An English ship under the command of Francis Drake, who had been authorized by Queen Elizabeth to prey on Spanish ships, also circumnavigated the globe in the latter part of the 1580s. Drake reached the Pacific from the Atlantic and successfully raided the treasure-laden Spanish ships. Rather than return to the Atlantic and face possible capture by Spanish warships, Drake headed across the Pacific. He traded in the East Indies, sailed through the Indian Ocean, and reached the Atlantic, arriving back in England to a

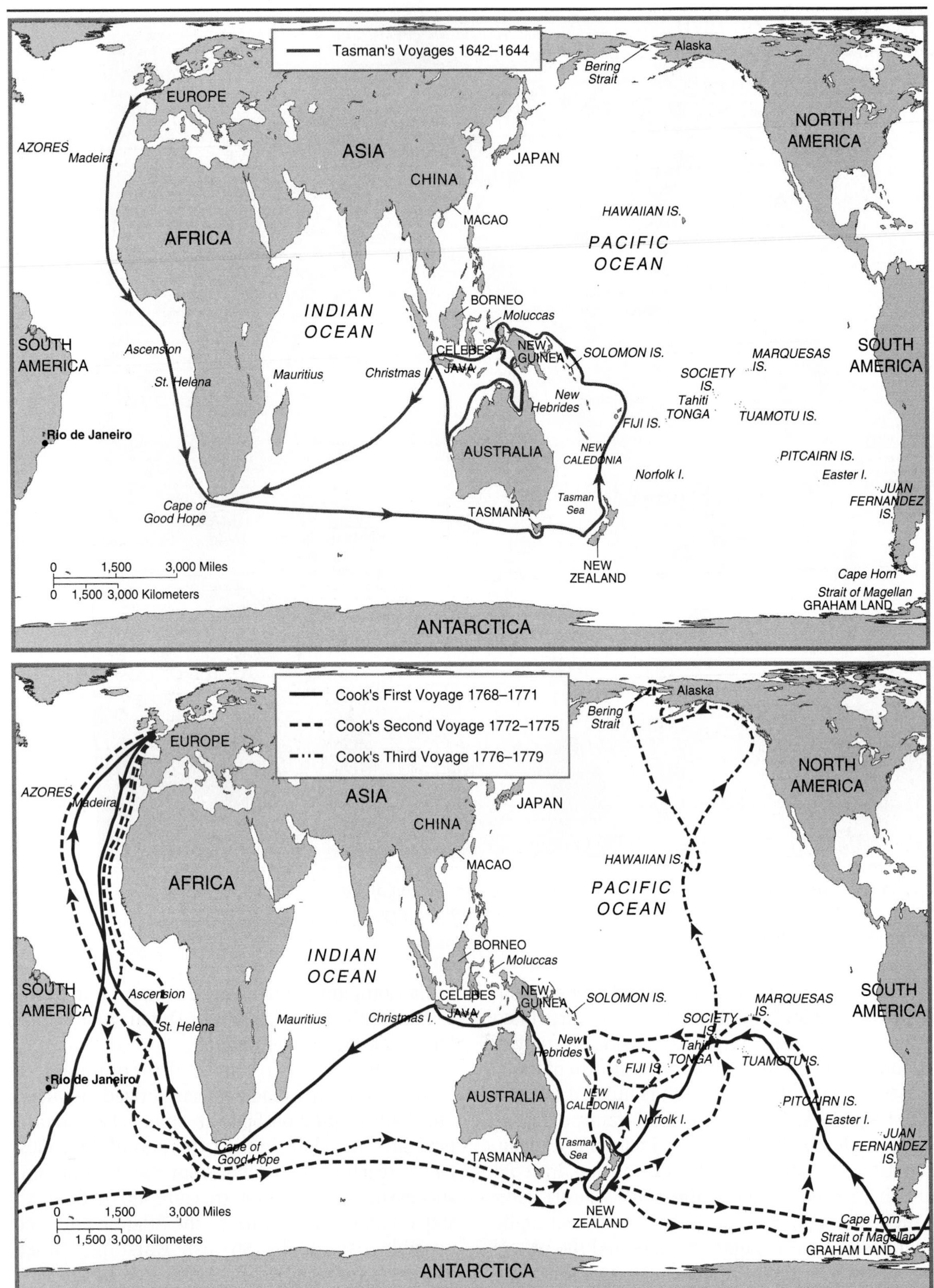

Tasman's Voyages 1642–1644
EUROPE
AZORES
Madeira
ASIA
CHINA
JAPAN
MACAO
AFRICA
Alaska
Bering Strait
NORTH AMERICA
HAWAIIAN IS.
PACIFIC OCEAN
INDIAN OCEAN
BORNEO
Moluccas
CELEBES
JAVA
NEW GUINEA
SOLOMON IS.
SOUTH AMERICA
Ascension
St. Helena
Mauritius
Christmas I.
New Hebrides
SOCIETY IS.
Tahiti
TONGA
MARQUESAS IS.
TUAMOTU IS.
FIJI IS.
Rio de Janeiro
AUSTRALIA
NEW CALEDONIA
Norfolk I.
PITCAIRN IS.
Easter I.
JUAN FERNANDEZ IS.
Cape of Good Hope
TASMANIA
Tasman Sea
NEW ZEALAND
0 1,500 3,000 Miles
0 1,500 3,000 Kilometers
Cape Horn
Strait of Magellan
GRAHAM LAND
ANTARCTICA
Cook's First Voyage 1768–1771
Cook's Second Voyage 1772–1775
Cook's Third Voyage 1776–1779

◀ MAP 23.3 ***Dutch (Tasman) and English (Cook) in Australian and Pacific Waters, 1642–1780.*** *In the seventeenth century, Abel Tasman sailed from the Netherlands, reaching Tasmania and New Zealand. He helped establish a Dutch presence in Asian and Pacific waters, especially in Indonesia (Dutch East Indies). James Cook arrived in those waters more than a century later and undertook much mapping and specimen collecting throughout the region. Both Tasman and Cook were nautical pioneers, advancing European knowledge and science.*

hero's welcome. This voyage excited other English captains and prompted them to emulate Drake. Moreover, the possibilities of great wealth inspired the chartering of the English East India Company, a private investment organization that funded many expeditions.

Another English explorer who circumnavigated the globe was Captain James Cook (1728–1779), and he headed three English expeditions to the Pacific that were charged by the British Royal Society to undertake scientific observations and explorations. He fully mapped the coasts of New Zealand and Australia, and his accurate maps have long been admired.

Cook's crew also included scientists who recorded various plants, animals, islands, and people. Cook landed on many islands, including Hawaii, and reached the continent of Australia. A conflict in Hawaii led to Cook's death, and reportedly King George III wept at the loss of the English scientist, cartographer, and sailor.

The Global Significance of the European Voyages

Oceanic voyaging greatly increased the contact between Europeans and others. From this activity came the beginnings of knowledge of peoples and customs in distant lands, including fanciful and dehumanizing portraits that had no factual basis.

FIGURE 23.7 ***A European Perspective on the New World.*** *Europeans developed fanciful images of the inhabitants of the Americas. This German colored woodcut of 1505 depicts cannibalism, a common impression that Westerners had of indigenous peoples. One can see various severed body parts, some of which are being eaten. The cannibal fantasy pervaded European literature.* The New York Public Library. Spencer Collection, Astor, Lenox and Tilden Foundations.

EUROPE	ASIA		
	Chinese voyaging, 1405–1433	1400	Zhu Di becomes Ming emperor, 1403
European voyaging, 1434–1780			Portuguese begin exploring African waters, 1434
			Columbus reaches the Americas, 1492
		1500	Portuguese arrive in Indian Ocean, 1497
			Magellan begins global voyaging, 1519
			Cartier explores Canadian rivers, 1534–1535
			Drake returns to England, 1580
		1600	Henry Hudson explores Canadian waters, 1610–1611
			Dutch land in Australia, 1644
		1700	
			James Cook killed in Hawaii, 1779
		1800	

Soon new perspectives based on comparative analyses drove Europeans to reform their own societies by using non-European models.

The new information, however, also facilitated the conquest and reduction of many societies through exploitation and widespread killings. The massive Atlantic slave trade played a major role in developing American plantations and economies, and European diseases ravaged large Indian populations in all of the Americas. These developments will be covered in some detail in subsequent chapters.

Europe greatly benefited from the global exchange of foodstuffs, precious metals, and other raw materials that enriched some European monarchies and many members of the middle classes, like merchants and artisans. Indeed, a powerful economic base developed from the sixteenth century and supported European domination of much of the world in succeeding centuries.

SUMMARY

1. The Polynesians and the Vikings mastered the complex skills and technology necessary to sail in open ocean waters. Both settled distant lands, and the Vikings briefly stayed in North America. The global impact of this voyaging was limited.

2. Chinese fleets plied the Indian Ocean in the early fifteenth century. Some ships reached and explored the East African coast. Because their purpose was associated with a single emperor and was therefore idiosyncratic, they stopped soon after his death and never resumed.

3. Christopher Columbus landed in the New World while looking for a passage to India. He and his successors slowly explored the Americas, while the Portuguese sailed into the Indian and Pacific oceans.

4. Colonies were established in the New World as Europeans systematically exploited the Americas' natural resources and people.

5. Ferdinand Magellan and his crew circumnavigated the earth between 1519 and 1522. This action inaugurated a global age and was followed by voyages by Iberians, as well as by those of Dutch, English, and others.

6. Conflict sometimes characterized European relations with non-Europeans between 1500 and 1800. Some countries expelled the Europeans or kept them at bay. Other peoples in the Americas, Asia, Australia, and parts of Africa succumbed to European power.

SUGGESTED READINGS

Hugill, Peter. *World Trade since 1431.* Baltimore: Johns Hopkins University Press, 1993. A broad interpretative perspective on the interrelationship among geographical, technological, and capitalist factors in global exploration and trade.

Landstrom, Bjorn. *Columbus: The Story of Don Cristóbal Colón. . . .* Trans. by Michael Phillips and Hugh W. Stubbs. New York: Macmillan, 1966. A critical account of Columbus, depicting him as a pious but essentially greedy man.

Levathes, Louise. *When China Ruled the Seas.* New York: Simon and Schuster, 1994. A detailed account of the seven Chinese voyages in the context of China's history of maritime activity.

Morrison, Samuel. *Admiral of the Ocean.* Boston: Little, Brown, 1942. A classic and favorable account of Columbus, stressing his tireless determination, practical virtue, and nautical talents.

Mote, Frederick, and Denis Twitchett, eds. *The Cambridge History of China.* Vol. VII: *The Ming Dynasty.* Cambridge, Eng.: Cambridge University Press, 1988. This collection of essays contains an excellent section about the Ming voyages of exploration.

Smith, Roger. *Vanguard of Empire.* Oxford, Eng.: Oxford University Press, 1993. A recent examination of the technology and organization behind the European ships that sailed in the fifteenth and sixteenth centuries.

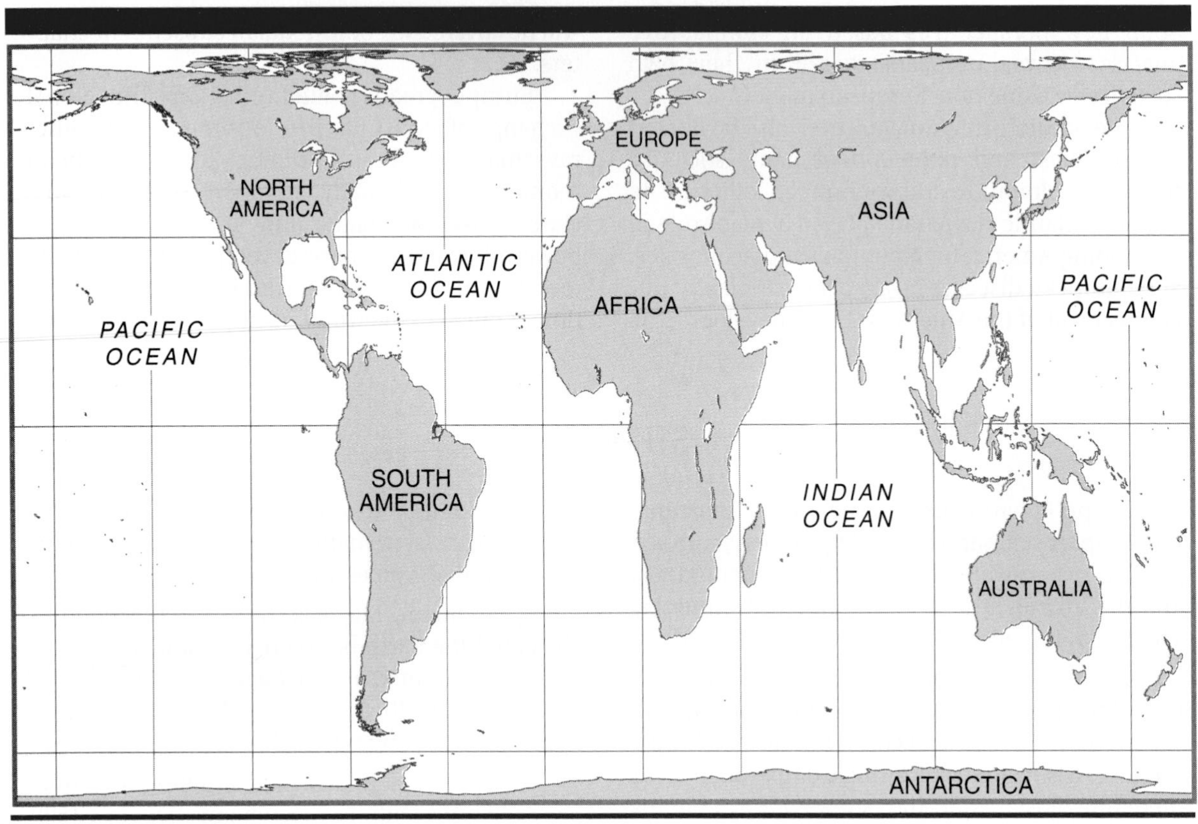

EUROPE
NORTH AMERICA
ASIA
ATLANTIC OCEAN
PACIFIC OCEAN
AFRICA
PACIFIC OCEAN
SOUTH AMERICA
INDIAN OCEAN
AUSTRALIA
ANTARCTICA

CHAPTER 24

Early European Colonialism

around 1500–around 1750

Infuriated by the exploitation of India by the Portuguese who had established a toehold there in the early 1500s, Saint Francis Xavier[1] wrote acidly that colonialism consisted of "conjugating the verb 'to rob' in all its moods and tenses." One-sided and narrow as this statement may be, it emphasizes the exploitation that was created by—indeed, that was the primary reason for the existence of—early colonialism. This chapter will explore some of the motives, processes, and outcomes of the European colonial effort in the sixteenth, seventeenth, and first half of the eighteenth centuries.

The European voyages of exploration were primarily economic investments. Certainly there were scholars and a few sovereigns who held academic interests in new lands and were eager to increase their store of knowledge. Such curiosity, however, was minor in comparison to the financial advantages that the explorers and their patrons hoped to gain. Initially, the primary motive of these voyages was to find a route to India and nearby parts of Asia, thereby making direct contact with spice and silk merchants. By circumventing the Arab agents who carried the trade in the fifteenth century, Europeans reasoned that they could increase the supply of these commodities, lower prices, and make a greater profit. As it became obvious that previously unknown lands existed, European explorers and adventurers became interested in finding new sources of

[1] **Xavier:** ZAY vee ur *or* HAH vee air

jewels, precious metals, wood, furs, and other valuable commodities.

The spirit of economic gain that pervaded the voyages of exploration was equally prominent in the centuries that followed. Once found, it was reasoned, a new land was of little use unless wealth could be wrested from it, and this meant establishing settlements in far-flung places. To be fair, there was a diversity of motives behind the settling of foreign lands, but the one that was most common, most compelling, and most significant in the creation of policy was the economic motive. The process of establishing colonies, administering them, and extracting wealth for the home country is known as **colonialism**. While there had been colonies in earlier times, such as in ancient Greece, this was the first appearance of a distinctive hierarchic relationship between colony and home country that was to endure in some parts of the world for several centuries.

THE EUROPEAN REACTION TO NEW PEOPLES AND NEW LANDS

When explorers first brought back stories of previously unknown peoples living in the newly discovered lands, Europeans scarcely knew what to make of them. Initially, European scholars argued among themselves about whether these were truly human beings and worthy of treatment as such. This initial confusion was serious, because explorers, conquerors, and colonists were interacting with these peoples and needed guidelines for appropriate actions.

Initial Confusion

According to the book of Genesis in the Bible, Noah had three sons: Shem, Japeth, and Ham. After the Great Flood, when everyone except Noah's family had been killed, it was from these three that all the people of the world descended. According to Christian tradition, Shem was the ancestor of all Asians, Japeth of all Europeans, and Ham of all Africans. The biblical tradition left no place for other races, and the European discovery of American Indians, Polynesians, and Australians left these peoples without a biblical basis. Were they really human beings created by God? Were they simply clever beasts, sent by the Devil to confuse soldiers of God?

Further complicating matters were the unreliable reports that quickly began coming back to Europe with exploring expeditions. An enduring story was that of the sciopods[2] ("umbrella-footed people"), wild men with only a single leg, who were reported to hop along at great speed, then sit down and raise a broad foot over the head for shade. Sir John Mandeville and other travelers reported these creatures from various continents but most especially Africa. Other tales recounted winged people, headless people whose eyes and mouths were in their chests, and people with multiple arms. While most contemporary scholars discounted the least anatomically likely of these stories, the combined weight of these various accounts led scholars and others alike to believe that humanlike creatures with curious structures were to be found in the new lands. Certainly they could not be considered human, or could they?

More tales returned to Europe of fantastic beings, particularly in Africa and South America. One of these beings from Africa was huge and hairy, with a forward-projecting face and huge fangs. It walked hunched forward and beat its chest when angered. Clearly a gorilla, this creature also was imputed to have a language, to take sexual license with people who crossed its path, and occasionally to build houses or wear clothes, characteristics decidedly unlike those of the apes. These stories seemed no more unbelievable than those of winged or umbrella-footed people, and they added to the confusion of learned opinion in Europe.

What with cultured apes and monstrous people and the absence of biblical guidance, the scholars of Europe entered a prolonged debate over whether Indians (as they called all peoples from unknown lands) were truly people. The kindling of vested interest fueled this fire, because some colonial powers would have found it most convenient if the Indians had been determined to be merely clever beasts who could be exterminated or otherwise treated without human regard. The conclusion of this debate came only in 1537.

[2] **sciopods:** SY oh pohdz

The Eventual Solution

In 1493, Pope Alexander VI ruled that Indians were truly people. His reasoning lay in the facts, reported to him, that the Indians were peaceful in nature, went naked (an important criterion for the innocence of wild people), and ate no human flesh.

Unfortunately, Pope Alexander had been misinformed, and, in the years that followed 1493, it became clear that some Indians were warlike, well clothed, and cannibalistic. In fact, reports of cannibalism were typical in descriptions of new peoples, even with societies that clearly carried out no such practices, leading some modern scholars to believe that a purposeful campaign of disinformation was being undertaken. In any case, this information demanded that the pope's decree be reconsidered. After a lengthy debate in papal court, Pope Paul III confirmed Alexander's decree in 1537. As an act of faith, European Roman Catholics—the vast majority of the population in the colonizing countries at this date—now had to accept that Indians were human.

FIGURE 24.1 ***Monstrous Humans from European Travel Accounts.*** *European travelers in the fifteenth and sixteenth centuries described a variety of bizarre human beings, such as those shown here. On the left is a chest-headed being, in the center is a sciopod (umbrella-footed person) shading himself from the tropical sun with an oversized foot, and at the right is an armed and noseless cyclops. Stories of these mythic creatures gained credibility in part by being attached to legitimate accounts; this illustration comes from an edition of the travels of Marco Polo, who never mentioned any such creatures.* Bibliothèque nationale, Paris.

DIFFERING COLONIAL AGENDAS

Each country that entered the colonial arena had a different set of goals and plans of how to achieve them: colonial agendas. As circumstances changed over time, so did these agendas, producing a variety of differing colonial experiences overseas. In addition, the individuals who carried out colonial projects had their own interests and agendas, some of which were quite independent of or even in conflict with those of their home countries.

Official Agendas

Portugal and Spain were the first to become active in colonialism, dominating the sixteenth century. They were followed near the end of the sixteenth century by the French and Dutch, and the English trailed along in the seventeenth century. Each country established policies that encouraged certain types of use of the new colonies.

THE SIXTEENTH CENTURY. The Portuguese and Spanish, by virtue of their early start, were able to focus initially on the most desirable commodity: precious metals. One of the questions Columbus asked the natives of Guanahani (San Salvador) when he first set foot in the Americas was whether they had any gold. Similarly, early explorers everywhere asked the locals whether they had any gold or knew where any was to be found. The immense wealth in gold in Central America was attractive to the Spanish, who named Costa Rica ("Rich Coast") in commemoration of the gold found there as well as in Panama and Colombia. In Peru and Mexico, the Inca and Aztec Indians had hoards of gold and silver that the Spanish appropriated for their coffers.

FIGURE 24.2 ***Peruvian Implement of Gold.*** *This artifact is a* tumi, *a sacrificial knife, used by the Chimú of coastal northern Peru in the early sixteenth century. It depicts a cultural hero named Ñaymlap, who has small wings projecting from his shoulders and wears an elaborate headdress and ear ornaments, all with inlaid turquoise. Objects like this were valued by Spanish conquerors primarily for their gold content, not for their artistic or cultural value. Tons of such treasures were melted down to make bars, which were easier to transport to Spain.* Boltin Picture Library.

This focus led the Spanish and Portuguese to establish themselves in such a way that they could effectively extract gold and silver for shipment home. This meant setting up settlements near or at native cities and towns, knowing that the masses of wealth would be focused there. When these treasure troves were exhausted, the towns and cities provided labor for the mines to produce more. Because the mines often were at some distance from major settlements, work parties were sent off to mine and refine the metals, which then would be sent back to the cities for shipment to the home country. This led to a settlement pattern of large, isolated concentrations of colonists surrounded by hinterlands that were composed almost entirely of native people.

This pattern typified the Americas, where conquest permitted the Spanish and Portuguese to do pretty much as they pleased. In Africa and Asia,

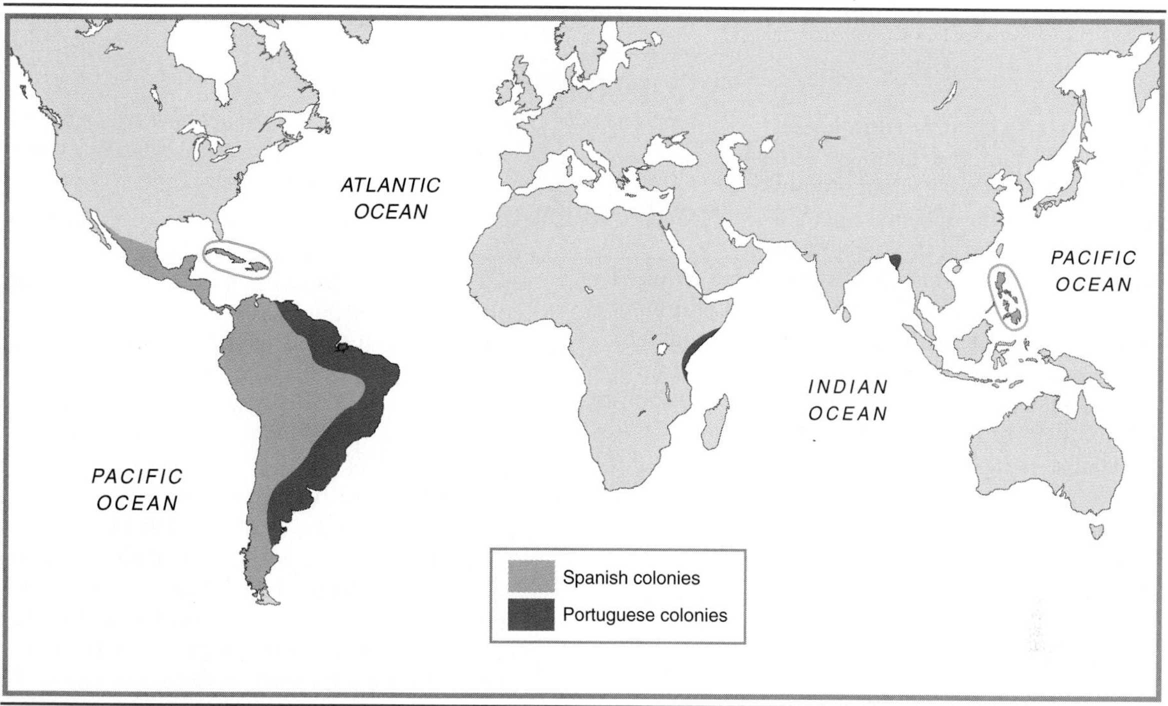

Map 24.1 ***Major Colonial Holdings in 1550.*** *The European colonial system was relatively small in 1550, restricted largely to coastal areas.*

however, colonists were foreigners in lands still controlled by their native populations. As a result, in these places the colonists were restricted to small settlements or precincts within coastal cities, from which points they carried on a commerce with local businesses. The Portuguese desperately wanted access to the gold of East Africa and the silver of Iran to facilitate the Asiatic trade, but they had to trade with local producers or wholesalers, rather than merely seize it, as in the Americas. The result, however, was similar, with the majority of the colonial population restricted to a few urban settings.

An additional aspect of Spain and Portugal's colonial agenda was the desire to convert the natives to Catholic Christianity. This desire grew out of pious convictions that their faith was true and correct and that passing it on to others was the greatest favor that one could perform, even if the local people failed to recognize it. Consequently, the Spanish and Portuguese established missions, scattered throughout conquered territory, "to convert the heathen." These missions were the exceptions to the urban concentrations that otherwise typified these colonies, and they often formed the nuclei of settlements for the expanded settlement that was to follow in the seventeenth century.

While other countries were not particularly active in colonizing during the sixteenth century, there are noteworthy exceptions. France, Holland, and England, frozen out of the major extraction of precious metals, founded colonies in the Caribbean to serve as bases for the **buccaneers**, pirates who raided Spanish treasure ships carrying gold and silver back to Spain. Some buccaneers were commissioned by European governments as privateers, and others merely took advantage of the situation to enrich themselves on their own initiative. State-sanctioned piracy was initiated by the French in 1555 when they attacked Havana in Cuba, but the English soon eclipsed the French in this regard, establishing a colony in Jamaica and raiding widely throughout the Caribbean. The Dutch, though never so thoroughly involved, distinguished themselves in 1628 by capturing the Spanish treasure fleet with tons of gold and silver.

IN THEIR OWN WORDS

The Requerimiento

The Spanish colonial effort linked religion and the military, and nowhere is this more evident than in the *Requerimiento*[a] ("Requirement"). The *Requerimiento* was a document that *conquistadores* from 1513 forward were required to read to the Indians whom they encountered. Amazingly, this document informed Indians that they would have to renounce their own religions in favor of Christianity; if they refused, they were held responsible for their own deaths. In 1573, the *Requerimiento* was abolished by the Spanish king, part of a broader program to reduce forcible actions against the Indians.

On the part of the King, don Fernando, and of doña Juana, his daughter, Queen of Castile and Léon, subduers of the barbarous nations, we their servants notify and make known to you, as best we can, that the Lord our God, Living and Eternal, created the Heaven and the Earth, and one man and one woman, of whom you and I, and all the men of the world, were and are descendants, and all those who come after us. But, on account of the multitude which has sprung from this man and woman in the five thousand years since the world was created, it was necessary that some men should go one way and some another, and that they should be divided into many kingdoms and provinces, for in one alone they could not be sustained.

Of all the nations God our Lord gave charge to one man, called St. Peter, that he should be Lord and Superior of all the men in the world, that all should obey him, and that he should be head of the whole human race . . . and he commanded him to place his seat in Rome . . . this man was called Pope. . . . One of these Pontiffs, who succeeded that St. Peter as Lord of the world, in the dignity and seat which I have before mentioned, made donation of these isles and *terra firme* [mainland] to the aforesaid King and Queen and to their successors, our lords, with all that there are in these territories, as is contained in certain writings which passed upon the subject as aforesaid, which you can see if you wish.

So their Highnesses are kings and lords of these islands and land of *terra firme* by virtue of this donation; and some islands, and indeed almost all those to whom this has been notified, have received and served their Highnesses, as lords and kings, in the way that subjects ought to do, with good will, without any resistance, immediately, without delay, when they were informed of the aforesaid facts. And also they received and obeyed the priests whom their Highnesses sent to preach to them and to teach our Holy Faith; and all these, of their own free will, without any reward or condition, have become Christians. . . . We ask and require . . . that you consent and give place [provide land for a church] that these religious fathers should declare and preach to you the aforesaid.

If you do so, you will do well . . . and we . . . shall receive you in all love and charity, and shall leave you your wives, and your children, and your lands, free without servitude. . . . But if you do not do this, and wickedly and intentionally delay to do so, I certify to you that, with the help of God, we shall forcibly enter into your country and make war against you in all ways and manners that we can, and shall subject you to the yoke and obedience of the Church and their Highnesses; we shall take you and your wives and your children, and shall make slaves of them, and as such shall sell and dispose of them as their Highnesses may command; and we shall take away your goods, and shall do all the harm and damage that we can, as to vassals who do not obey, and refuse to receive their lord, and resist and contradict him; and we protest that the deaths and losses which shall accrue from this are your fault, and not that of their Highnesses, or ours, nor of these gentlemen who come with us. And that we have said this to you and made this Requirement, we request the notary here present to give us his testimony in writing, and we ask the rest who are present that they should be witnesses of this Requirement.

[a] ***Requerimiento:*** ray kay ree mee EHN toh

FIGURE 24.3 ***Women Pirates of the Caribbean.*** *Piracy, sometimes state-sanctioned, flourished in the sixteenth and seventeenth centuries but was waning by the early eighteenth century. This woodcut shows Anne Bonny and Mary Read, women who sailed aboard* The Island of Providence, *an outlaw pirate vessel commanded by Captain Jack Rackam. Little is known of how these women became pirates, but they plied their trade with the same recklessness as their more numerous male colleagues, until they were captured and imprisoned in 1720.* The New York Public Library, Rare Books Division.

This raiding continued well into the seventeenth century, enriching buccaneers and serving the ends of their sponsoring countries.

While England, France, and Holland had limited interests in colonies during the sixteenth century, they still were active in exploiting the Americas as visitors, focusing on the most easily exploitable commodities: wood, fish, and furs. Their sailors arrived at the coast in ships, stayed briefly to collect the desired items, and returned home without establishing any settlements.

Northern Europe, especially Holland and England, had been running out of wood for years. The Tudor style of architecture current in this period featured thin veneers of wood that were set into stucco exteriors in lines paralleling the roof and walls of a house. In this manner, a minimum amount of wood could be used to its greatest advantage. In particularly short supply were the tall, straight trees required to make masts and spars for the fully rigged ships that had become common. The new-growth trees that dominated England were simply too small, but the forests of New England and Maritime Canada had such trees aplenty.

Similarly, the fishing banks of Europe had become depleted from decades of overfishing. The fishing banks of Newfoundland and New England, in contrast, yielded huge hauls of large fish with little effort, attracting fishermen from all over western Europe. The fish mostly were salted and packed in barrels to preserve them for the long voyage home.

Finally, Europe had made extinct or severely diminished its populations of fur-bearing animals in its zeal for furs to clothe the expanding middle class. The demand for fur remained, however, and only high-priced Russian furs could be consistently obtained. The North American continent became a competing source. Crews on fishing boats along the North American coast frequently traded copper kettles and iron axes to local Indians in return for furs, a transaction each perceived as an incredible bargain. It was common for a fishing boat in this period to increase its profits by carrying back a few trees for mast wood and several loads of furs, in addition to its cod and flounder.

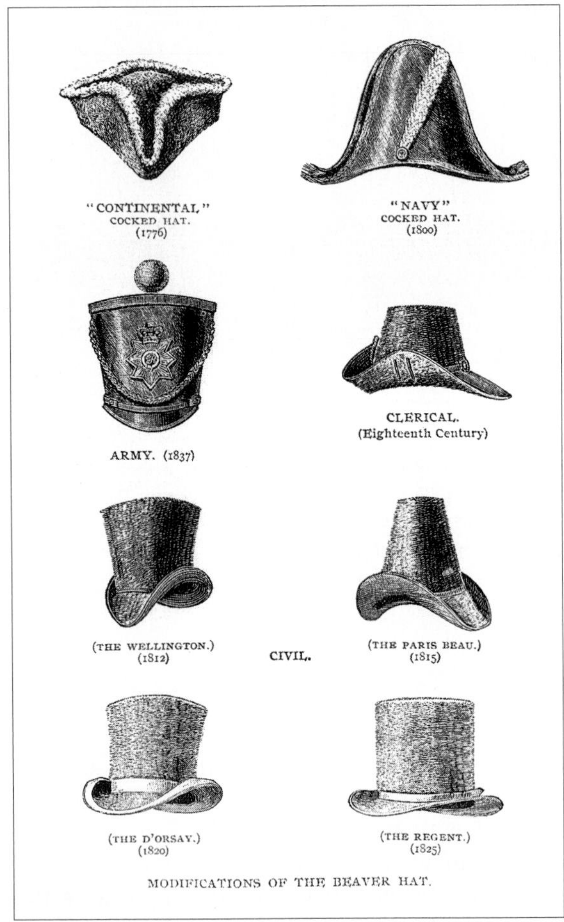

FIGURE 24.4 ***Beaver Hats.*** *The beaver produced one of the furs most valued by Europeans, especially for hats. After trapping had destroyed the European beaver, the discovery of vast populations of beavers in North America revived the industry. This nineteenth-century engraving shows just a few of the many styles of hats that required beaver fur and fueled the North American fur trade.* Public Archives of Canada, Ottawa/ Documentary Art and Photography Division (#C-17338).

THE SEVENTEENTH CENTURY. By the seventeenth century, much of the more readily available wealth had been drained off by the Spanish and Portuguese, and they were forced to turn increasingly to less lucrative, more labor-intensive enterprises. These included mining, ranching, and growing crops.

With the richest and most accessible deposits depleted, the Spanish were forced to expend more labor in extracting mineral wealth. This meant establishing permanent settlements near major mines to serve as provisioning and entertainment centers. These mining settlements began the process of spreading the Spanish population around the colonies, away from the urban centers.

In addition, ranchers began large operations for the raising of beef and the tanning of hides. Because such ranches required vast quantities of land and could use less desirable, semiarid areas, they tended to be located at some distance from the cities that had so dominated Spanish America in the previous century. Their isolation made the ranches centers for all that the ranchers would need to survive and thrive. Ranches often had facilities for such activities as curing olives, fermenting wine, making soap, and weaving cloth.

Finally, in wetter areas, particularly along the coast, planters developed vast plantations for the growing of various cash crops, especially sugar and tobacco. While plantations provided food for local consumption, they focused primarily on crops that could be shipped to the home country and sold for great profits. Sugar was the first of these, because Europe had acquired an immense sweet tooth, increasing its per capita consumption a hundredfold between 1500 and 1650. Tobacco was a bit slower to develop as an industry, because Europeans adopted the practice of smoking only after contact with American Indians in the 1500s. Nonetheless, it was a growth industry by the early part of the 1600s, especially in Brazil.

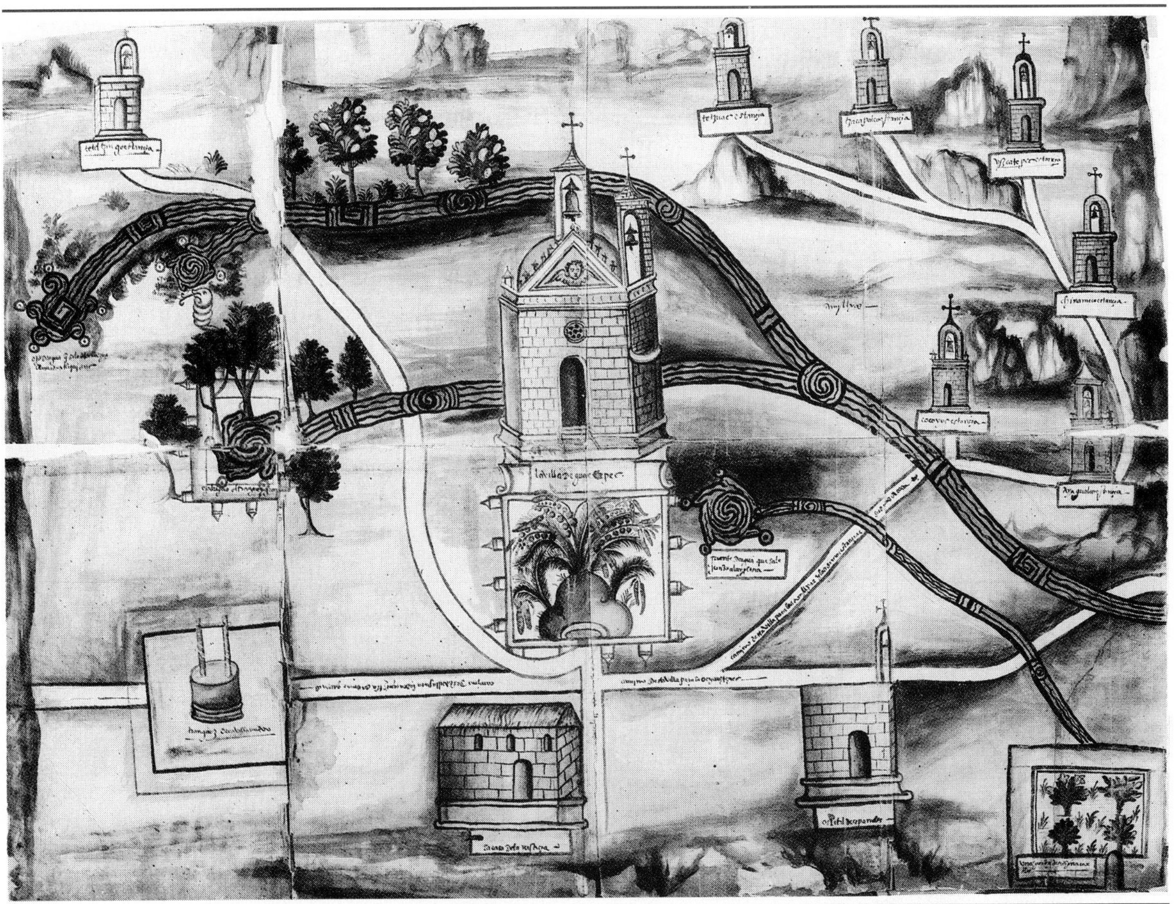

FIGURE 24.5 ***The Mexican Countryside under Spanish Rule.*** *This painting from around 1580 shows the fertile region to the south of the Valley of Mexico as it appeared to an unknown artist. The countryside is dotted with Christian churches and rich with village orchards that grew local and European fruits as well as Mexican corn and European wheat. The painting blends both native Mexican and Spanish styles, but the content focuses on the Spanish reshaping of the landscape.* University of Texas, Austin. Benson Latin American Collection.

The total effect of these shifts in activities was to transform the settlement pattern of Spanish and Portuguese America. The highly concentrated pockets of colonists that had dominated the sixteenth century gave way to a broader dispersal of colonists. They remained in pockets—ranches, plantations, and missions, as well as the cities—but the pockets were far more numerous and scattered much more widely in the seventeenth century. By 1750, relatively few places in Spanish America were more than a few days' ride from a colonial settlement.

To the Dutch and English colonies, where little mineral wealth was known, the first major wave of colonists came in the 1600s. The colonies of temperate North America were seen as similar to England and Holland, though plagued with severe winters, bellicose natives, and poor soils. Nevertheless, most colonists expected to build a version of the home country there.

Tracts publicized the official colonial agenda, and one of these, written by Richard Eburne in 1624, cited the reasons why a young English man should become a North American colonist. Building the colonies would augment the power of the king of England; it would ease the population pressures felt in England at the time; it would make for lower prices on commodities in England; it would "enrich the poorer sorts hence removed"; it would improve trade; and it would "root out idleness out of this land," a great danger to the way of thinking of English Calvinists (members of a Protestant denomination).

With this in mind, colonists set about reproducing England or Holland in their colonies. The Dutch were not very successful with their North American colonies, largely because they had difficulty convincing residents of Holland that they should leave the richest and most tolerant country in northern Europe. As a result, they lost New Netherlands to the English in 1664, and it became the colony of New York. The English colonists planted their stamp on the land, founding towns and cities with names and layouts borrowed from the home country. In large measure, the English colonies in North America—by their nature as reproductions of the home country—became economic competitors with England itself.

In the Caribbean, the English successes in buccaneering paid for the expansion of the colonies there, and the English established plantations as a way to reap the economic benefits of tropical colonial holdings. Sugar was the primary plantation crop, but dyes, cocoa, ginger, tobacco, and cotton also were important. The English toehold in Jamaica expanded to include the rest of that island, as well as St. Kitts, Barbados, and various other islands, mostly those abandoned by the fading Spanish presence. The English colonies in the Caribbean were so productive that, by 1700, they accounted for approximately 12 percent of England's imports.

The English and Dutch in Asia were limited largely to trading cities comparable to those of the Spanish and Portuguese in the previous century. The English were most interested in India and the

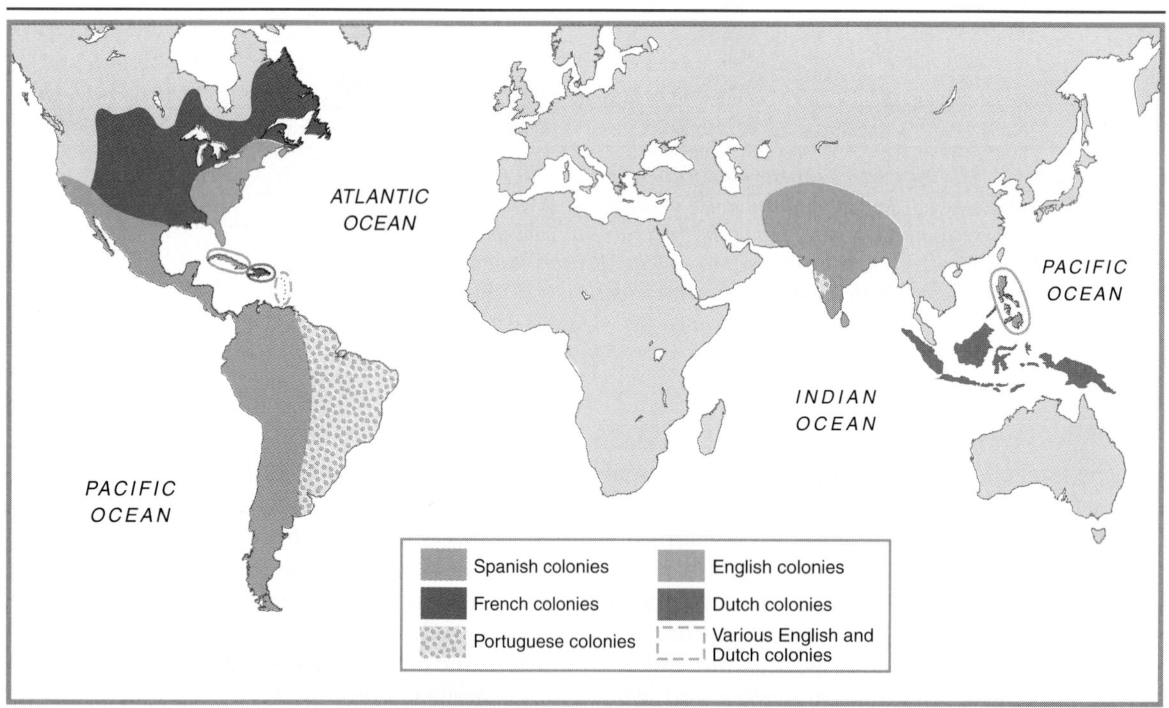

MAP 24.2 ***Major Colonial Holdings in 1700.*** *By 1700, Europe's colonial system had expanded so that most of the Americas and various areas of Africa and Asia were within its control. Compare the size and geographical spread of colonies at this date with those at 1550 (Map 24.1).*

Dutch in Indonesia, but neither conquered the local governments in this period. Rather, they carried on trade, which was especially lucrative for the Dutch.

France was not particularly successful as a colonial power but had its greatest successes in eastern Canada and the Caribbean. In eastern Canada, its attempts were driven by two-pronged efforts. First, the French were interested in establishing a trade in furs, the northern equivalent of precious metals. Second, they wished to establish a self-sufficient colony that reproduced France in North America, particularly along the St. Lawrence River. In the Caribbean, their interests were similar to those of the English and Dutch: to establish bases for buccaneers and sugar plantations.

Personal Agendas

Each country in the colonial competition had its own agenda, but the individuals who populated the colonies for them were not always moved by these state interests. Instead, most had personal agendas.

Above all else, colonists were moved by the possibility that opportunities in the new lands would bring them economic betterment. Accordingly, it is not surprising that colonists predominantly were drawn from the ranks of the poor. The first wave of Spanish colonists came primarily from Extremadura,[3] the central province of Spain that had suffered from centuries of environmental degradation. Wood supplies were devastated, soils were depleted and eroding, and travel to a new land was attractive. English colonists usually were the urban poor, lost on the streets of London with few domestic prospects and an urge to leave for the colonies. Prominent among the first wave of French colonists were impoverished petty nobles, able to claim a title but no land or wealth; they saw the colonies as opportunities to reclaim their rightful status in life.

Most of these colonists hoped to make a fortune quickly and return in triumph to their home countries. Many men left wives at home, expecting that their absence would be only for a few years. The exception was the English, who mostly realized that they were embarking on a path that might lead to economic betterment but was unlikely to result in real wealth. Eburne, in the 1624 tract cited earlier, provides a series of arguments—many based on biblical heroines—that a man could use on his wife to convince her of the wisdom of emigrating to the colonies. Most English colonists realized that moving to the colonies, at least those in North America, meant a permanent relocation.

Another important motive for becoming a colonist was the search for a place where one could practice one's chosen religion freely. By the 1600s, the Protestant Reformation was in full swing (see Chapter 29), and some colonists sought a more tolerant place. This was an important issue in the English colonies of North America, because Calvinists were persecuted in England during the early part of this period. Once in America, the persecuted sometimes became the persecutors, and the Calvinists of the Massachusetts Bay Colony actively attacked Quakers, forcing many to move to Rhode Island. Large numbers of Dutch and Portuguese Jews moved to Brazil, hoping to escape persecution in Europe but finding conditions equally difficult in South America; most moved on to Barbados and eventually to New York.

Still another religious motive was the urge to spread Christianity. This was especially prominent among French, Spanish, and Portuguese colonists, virtually all of whom were Roman Catholic, because Catholicism traditionally has been active in seeking converts. Most colonists with this motivation were clergy, usually priests or monks, and they often showed great zeal in their ministrations. French Jesuit missionaries, such as Isaac Jogues, were eloquent in their desires to be martyred in the cause of Christ. The Catholic Church saw to it that their eloquence was publicized widely in the form of the *Relations*, printed accounts of their trials and successes in North America and elsewhere; the *Relations* served as excellent recruiting materials for the next generation of missionaries.

There was, however, another class of colonists whose emigration was not motivated by such public-spirited concerns. A certain percentage of the colonists were convicts, either sentenced to banishment in the colonies or given the choice of prison at home or freedom in the colonies. Portugal led the way, banishing prisoners to its African territories and Goa (a colony in India) in

[3] **Extremadura:** eks TREH mah DOO ruh

the early 1500s and later to Brazil. By the late 1500s France began sending convicts to the St. Lawrence Valley, and England followed in the 1600s with convicts bound for Jamaica; in the 1700s, more convicts were shipped to English colonies in Georgia and Australia. The overall number of convicts among the colonists is currently unassessed, but it probably was only a small fraction.

The reasons prompting colonists to leave their homelands were diverse and idiosyncratic. A few were escaping unhappy marriages, fleeing in the face of debt, or running from the law; some were patriots who ardently believed that massive emigration was the only solution to their countries' demographic ills; still others were religious adherents bent on finding a place to practice their religion freely or to convince natives of the truth of that religion. The vast majority, however, were calculating opportunists, confident that their chances for economic improvement were better in the colonies than at home.

THE COLONIZING PROCESS

The details differed, but the general pattern of colonizing was much the same in most of the European colonies established before 1750. The earliest toeholds grew into thriving, more balanced entities that began to compete with the home country.

The Earliest Attempts

Like exploration before it, initial colonizing usually was financed by private capital. Governments saw these endeavors as long shots, gambles with low probabilities of success, and they rarely made state money available for them. Instead, private companies typically raised the financial backing to begin a colony.

The English East India Company (established in 1600), the Dutch East India Company (in 1602), and the English West India Company (in 1621)

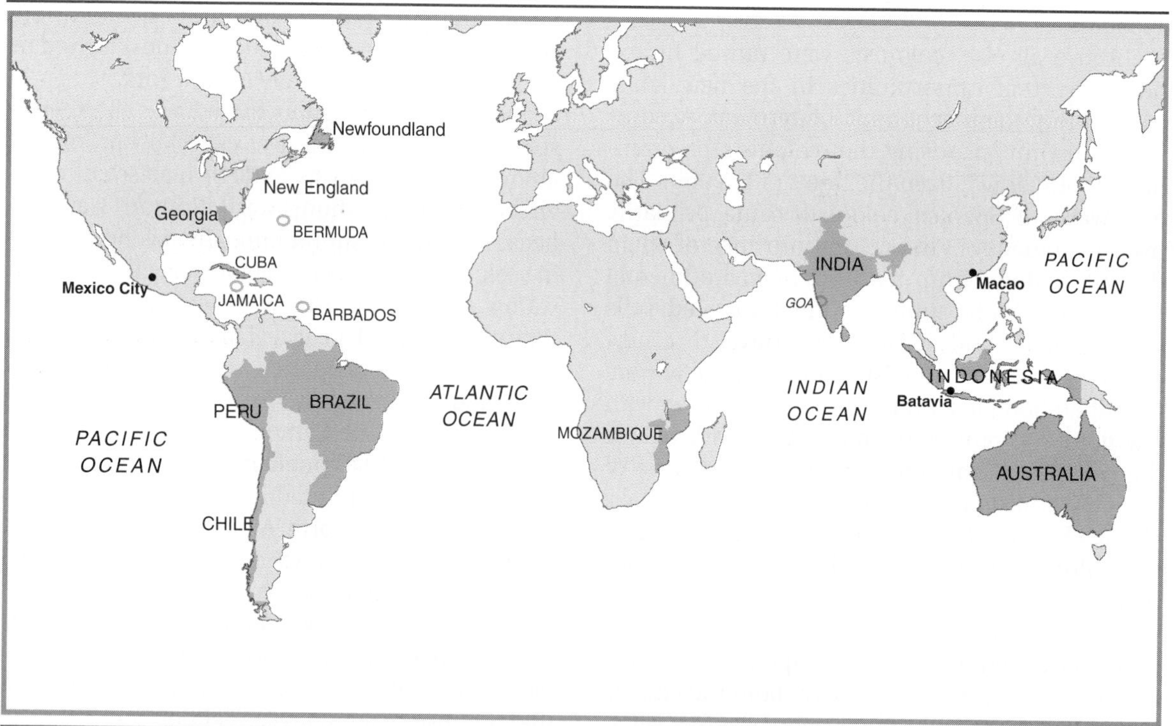

MAP 24.3 ***Colonies and Colonial Towns.*** *Most early European colonies and colonial towns were located on the coasts; in the Americas, some inland areas such as Mexico were conquered and colonized relatively quickly. As European expansion progressed, colonies in the interior of continents became more common.*

UNDER THE LENS

The Many Tactics of the Dutch East India Company

The Dutch East India Company, though a private corporation, appropriated for itself many of the rights of a sovereign country. It maintained a military force, conducted diplomatic missions, and presented decrees that it expected to be obeyed. In a sense, this was not surprising, because the directors of the company were the same urban merchants that wielded great influence in Dutch government. The company and the government were but organs of the same interest group.

The military branch was the strong right arm of the Dutch East India Company, particularly in terms of naval power. When it was desirable to blockade Manila and intercept the silver shipment coming to the Philippines from Mexico, it was this branch that did the job. Similarly, when it was necessary to conquer Malacca to open the spice trade of the Malay Peninsula, the military branch undertook and accomplished the task. When the Chinese needed to be taught that they could not infringe on Dutch trading prerogatives, it was the military that sank eighty of their vessels in retribution. The inhabitants of one island famed for its nutmeg plantations were starved out by the Dutch East India Company military, effectively removing a competitor.

The diplomatic skills of the Dutch East India Company were evident in its dealings with local rulers. Through the combination of threatened force and promised reward, company operatives managed to negotiate secure agreements with local Indonesian and Malay rulers for the supply of various spices. Importantly, these agreements usually were exclusive, forbidding any trade with Europeans other than the Dutch. At the same time that they secured a plum for themselves, the Dutch precluded success on the parts of their competitors.

The decrees of the Dutch East India Company supported their trading position and were backed by the naval authority behind the company. After the effective conquest of Ceylon (present-day Sri Lanka), the company set out strict guidelines for the trade of cinnamon, including prices, monopoly (held by the company, of course), and sanctions for disobeying the decree. The rigor with which this and other decrees were enforced is testament to the military and economic might of the company.

Despite its power and successes, the Dutch East India Company was faltering by the early 1700s. Its successes had earned it a sizeable tract of land that it controlled, and this taxed even its resources. Further, errors in judgment, such as abandoning the tea trade to England as inconsequential, weakened the company's position. Finally, the Dutch government took over the duties that formerly had been granted to the Dutch East India Company, ending its period of prominence and power.

---

were classic examples. (An even earlier English Russia Company was founded in 1583 to handle the fur trade with Russia, but it was eclipsed by these more successful companies.) Each was a private corporation operating under crown charter. To state it differently, the state was able to determine general policy for the companies through the charters, yet the funds hazarded were private, raised by the sale of stock. The first two companies directed trade and colonizing in India and Indonesia for the English and Dutch, while the latter served the same purpose for the English in the Caribbean. All three were wildly successful, posting huge profits and establishing thriving colonial communities.

Their success, however, was their undoing. As the countries under whose charters they operated realized the magnitude of the profits to be made, they decided that the charters should be suspended, permitting the state to control directly the colonizing process. By the early years of the eighteenth century, all three companies had lost their preeminent roles in trade, which by this time was controlled directly by governments.

There were other approaches to colonization. The Spanish, for example, placed the colonizing

FIGURE 24.6 ***The Portuguese Colony at Macao.*** *The Portuguese secured a favorable trading arrangement with the Chinese and established a permanent colony at Macao, called "Amacao" in this engraving from around 1600. This image shows the mixture of cultural practices common to such colonies. A public cross in the center proclaims the Christianity of the Europeans, while retainers, parasols, and sedan chairs exemplify the status symbols of the local Chinese. Although it is not documented in this view, the Portuguese traders also had a distinct district that was given over for their use.* From Theodor de Bry's *Indiae orientalis* (Frankfurt, 1607). Courtesy of the John Carter Brown Library at Brown University.

process under the control of the crown, letting trade be handled by the Seville Merchants' Guild, operating under royal monopoly; the Portuguese followed a similar practice in Brazil. English colonizing in North America was through various small private companies, usually one per colony and often without royal charter.

The early colonies were largely ***entrepôts***,[4] commercial centers that served simultaneously as collection centers for goods to be shipped to the home country and as distribution centers for goods coming from the home country. In places with strong native governments, such as Asia and Africa, colonies remained isolated *entrepôts* well into the eighteenth century or longer; Goa in India, Moçambique in East Africa, Batavia in Indonesia, and Macao in China were isolated European communities surrounded by native settlement.

In conquered places, however, the European *entrepôts* grew to become cities surrounded by

[4] ***entrepôts:*** ahn treh POHZ

other European settlements. As discussed earlier, the lure of riches drew colonists farther away from the *entrepôts*, leading to the beginnings of the next phase of colonial development.

Settling In

In conquered lands, colonists were not restricted to a limited range of commercial enterprises, and they became involved in a wide range of activities, mostly designed to make money. This economic and settlement expansion brought with it demographic and political consequences.

The earliest European colonies anywhere reflected in their demography the common belief that the colonists would be there only a short while: They were predominantly male. In Mexico City in the 1560s, Spanish men outnumbered Spanish women by a ratio of 10 to 1, and the ratios were higher in less urban places; in Batavia in 1620, there were no more than than five Dutch women; and Barbados had such a shortage of English women in 1653 that there were plans for mass importations of brides from "the lower classes" of London.

The imbalanced sex ratios in most colonies encouraged marriages and liaisons between European men and native women. In most places, such marriages were frowned upon by European colonial society, because natives were considered racially and culturally inferior; as a result, sexual liaisons or clandestine "temporary marriages" (with husbands abandoning their native wives when European women became available) were more common. These liaisons led to a new class of children of racially mixed parentage, called variously *métis*[5] (French), *mestizos*[6] (Spanish), or *mestiços*[7] (Portuguese). These mixed children usually were considered a distinct class, intermediate in status between Europeans and natives.

Different colonies took different approaches to redressing the imbalances in the numbers of European men and women. In Spanish and Portuguese America, a child with mixed parentage could be absorbed into colonial society, providing its appearance was not entirely at odds with this classification. Consequently, some children of colonists and native women were considered European by community consent, thereby increasing the numbers of women. Elsewhere, there were programs to ship European women to colonies, as to the French Antilles in the mid-1600s. Servant girls were in great demand in the colonies, and many began arriving as the living conditions became less severe. In a few cases, such as that of the Puritan colonies of North America, the ratio of men to women was more or less equal from the start, because married couples were the preferred colonists.

FIGURE 24.7 *Three Canadian* Métis. *One of the consequences of the mixing of peoples in the colonial era was the creation of new racial categories. In Canada, a child of mixed Native American and European ancestry was called a* méti. *The word comes from the Old French word for "mongrel" and was originally a term of contempt, though it became an acceptable term of self-identification by the 1700s. This tintype photograph from the 1870s shows three young* méti *men whose facial features and clothing reflect their mixed ancestry.* Provincial Archives of Manitoba.

[5] ***métis:*** may TEE
[6] ***mestizos:*** meh STEE sohs
[7] ***mestiços:*** meh STEE sohs

On the political front, colonists were beginning to identify with the emerging colonies. In some cases, such as that of Spanish America, it was clear by 1650 that the colonies held more economic power and perhaps more political power than the home country. While Spain's economy and military might were eroding, despite being buoyed up by massive infusions of wealth from its colonies, the Spanish colonies in the Americas were growing wealthier and stronger. In other cases, the remoteness of the home country made for weaker ties; it took an average of ninety-one days for a ship from Spain to reach Mexico, and nearly two years for the trip to Chile. Individuals whose grandparents were the last of the family to have seen the home country easily could begin viewing the colony as the entity with which they identified most strongly.

Economic realities were encouraging this identification with the colony. While colonial theory held that the colony should import its manufactured goods from the home country, this often was impractical. Many items were in short supply, and residents in the home country were loath to see goods shipped overseas when their needs had not yet been met. Colonists, therefore, often were left to fend for themselves, and local industries sprang up to serve local needs.

As the colonies grew, they developed local governments. Spain imposed the viceroy system in Peru and Mexico, appointing an individual to head the civil and military governments in the place of the king. Many viceroys were inept, and all were hampered by a cumbersome governmental system imported from Spain. The English colonies were ruled by governors appointed by the crown, but they developed various forms of local assemblies to deal with internal issues. As time went by, some of these local assemblies chafed under royal restraints, building tensions between the English monarch and the colonies. These tensions eventually erupted as the American Revolution.

COLONIAL CONFLICT

Many colonies were founded in the wake of military campaigns that destroyed the native governments, and others had ongoing military conflicts between colonial and native forces. The Europeans usually claimed the right to conquer these native societies because of their "sinful ways," reducing conquest to the saving of souls. In addition, the colonies were fields where the rivalries of European powers were played out, sometimes as military actions.

Hostilities between Colonial and Native Powers

Most of the Americas came under European control either directly by conquest or indirectly by the manipulation of societies weakened by disease. The success of European military operations was founded primarily on technology and organization, coupled with the population catastrophe resulting from diseases brought by the conquerors.

MILITARY TECHNOLOGY AND ORGANIZATION. The peoples of the Americas were equipped with military weapons that were inferior to those of the Europeans they opposed. The Aztecs of Mexico, for example, wielded razor-sharp swords made of volcanic glass blades set into the edges of wooden handles; they shot arrows from bows and hurled stones from slings; they wore padded cotton armor. These weapons were pitted against Spanish cannons, muskets, and steel armor. The greater efficacy of the Spanish equipment was in part responsible for the rapid Spanish victory.

The Spanish also introduced a factor previously unknown in American warfare: war animals. The *conquistadores* rode horses, an animal unknown to the Aztec; the popular notion that the Aztecs were amazed and believed the horse and rider to be one is fantasy, but an armored horse bearing down on an Aztec warrior was still a formidable weapon. In addition, the Spanish used mastiffs, large dogs bred and trained to attack the enemy. Protected by leather armor on its sides, a mastiff would be released ahead of foot soldiers, breaking the ranks of the enemy before they could attack. The mastiffs were far more feared than horses, because they could follow a fleeing soldier almost anywhere he could go, running him down and mauling him. Many Aztecs died from wounds inflicted by mastiffs.

Military organization was another advantage of the Europeans in most places where they encountered American Indian military forces. Aztec warfare, for example, was highly regimented and ordered, but its goal was the capture of enemy

Figure 24.8 ***Araucanian Warrior.*** *The Araucanians of Chile, known today as the Mapuche tribe, were among the fiercest resisters of European colonial intrusion into the Americas. Like the Plains Indians of North America, they adopted European weapons and the horse and took advantage of their mobility to conduct hit-and-run raids on sedentary Spanish settlements.* From Felix Best, Historia de las Guerras Argentinas (Buenos Aires: Ediciones Peuser), 1960. Reproduced with permission.

soldiers to use as human sacrifices. As a result, it had evolved in such a way that it favored capturing to killing the enemy. This was effective when battling other Mexicans whose goals were the same, but it put the Aztecs at a great disadvantage against the Spanish. In other parts of the Americas, warfare was small scale and undisciplined by European standards, and Europeans had a tactical advantage there, too.

Finally, Europeans were quick to form alliances with disaffected allies and with enemies of a people they wanted to conquer. The conquest of the Aztecs, for example, was made possible in part by tens of thousands of native troops who were fighting to remove the yoke of Aztec domination from their shoulders. They did not realize, of course, that it would be replaced by a Spanish yoke. Alliance politics was played by both native and European diplomat-soldiers, but the natives often were unaware of the scope of the European forces that eventually would come to their shores.

THE SUCCESS OF NATIVE RESISTANCE. The conquest of the Americas was neither complete nor immediate, however. While the Aztecs, possessing arguably the most powerful and well organized military in the Americas, were defeated in just two years, the Incas of Peru continued guerrilla warfare for several decades after the Spanish conquered their urban centers. In North America, the Iroquois of New York and Ontario resisted conquest for more than a century, succumbing only in the process of the American Revolution in 1781.

Successful resistance to European military conquest was most likely for nomadic or seminomadic peoples who could use their mobility as a weapon. The Apache of the American Southwest and the Chichimeca of northern Mexico are classic examples, but the Araucanians[8] of southern Chile stand out for their successful resistance. The Araucanians rapidly captured Spanish weapons, particularly the horse, pike, and musket, and learned how to use them effectively. They burned Spanish pastures, destroyed Spanish settlements, and employed Spanish tactics against the colonists. In 1586, Araucanian forces were fighting pitched battles using ranks of pikemen with bowmen among them, precisely in the Spanish manner. While the Araucanians exhausted the Spanish resources, their mobility and lack of permanent camps made it impossible for the Spanish to turn the tables on them. The Araucanians never were conquered, but in the twentieth century they voluntarily merged into modern Chilean society.

Hostilities among Colonial Powers

At the same time that colonial powers were battling native forces, they also were engaging one another in warfare. The rivalries and alliances that were in force in Europe were carried into the colonial holdings. The French and English, at war sporadically during the seventeenth and eighteenth centuries, carried their animosity into the colonies.

For the most part, these conflicts were expressed by arming natives hostile to the enemy power. In northeastern North America, for example, the French and English vied for power from the earliest colonies until 1763, when the French were defeated and forfeited most of their colonial holdings. The English armed the Iroquois, while the French armed the Huron and Algonquians; the Europeans could simply wait for their native allies to use those weapons against their traditional enemies.

Occasionally, however, active warfare broke out. The French and Indian Wars, for example, pitted French and English against one another off and on from 1689 until the eventual defeat of the French in 1763. These wars consisted mostly of frontier attacks on isolated settlements, but occasionally they erupted into full-scale battles. Though they have been given distinct names, such wars really were aspects of broader conflicts that involved Europe and all the colonial theaters.

[8] **Araucanians:** ahr oh KAYN ee uhns

ECONOMICS AND THE COLONIES

As extensions of the home countries, colonies had to solve economic problems if they were to be successful. Central to these problems was the relationship between colony and home country, one that often turned contentious. Labor and regulation of indigenous trade also were important areas of concern.

The Mercantile System

At the heart of the relationship between a colony and its home country was an ideal conception: the **mercantile system**. Defined as a relationship in which the colony provides raw materials for the home country while the home country provides manufactured goods for the colony, the ideal of the mercantile system was shared by all the colonial powers of Europe. To a greater or lesser extent, it was implemented in their actions.

In theory, the mercantile system should keep the home country strong and the colonies dependent. By providing manufactured goods to the colonies, the home country ensures that its own population is well employed, and the profits of manufacturing remain at home. The colonies, in contrast, are valuable primarily because they supply the home country with materials and an expanded market.

An example of how the mercantile system operated is provided by the **triangular trade** that the English set up. Ships left English ports laden with a variety of manufactured goods and arrived at West African ports. There they traded horses, guns, fabrics, and other items for slaves, sold by local slave traders. These slaves were carried to the Caribbean, where they were sold and the profits were used to purchase tropical products, especially sugar, molasses, rum, and indigo dye; the ship also sold iron tools, fabrics, and a wide variety of manufactured goods to the Caribbean colonists. The next stop was New England, where some of the Caribbean products and various manufactured goods from England were sold. The ship purchased furs, wood, salt cod, and other goods from New England, then returned to its English port. Each step of the way, manufactured goods flowed from home country to colony and raw materials flowed in the opposite direction.

Precious metals held a special place in the mercantile system. Because gold and silver were the foundation for all European money of this period, it was important that colonies provide these substances in whatever quantities were possible. In a very real sense, this represented an increase in wealth, resulting particularly in greater buying power in Asia.

The mercantile system was plagued by a major set of problems. To begin with, the home country was not always able to provide finished goods in the quantities needed in the colonies. This was especially true for Spain, whose sagging economic structure was taxed severely just to meet its internal needs, but it was true to a greater or lesser extent everywhere. Accordingly, it became necessary for the colonies to begin manufacturing on their own. Santo Domingo in the Caribbean began a glass industry by 1586; Bermuda began building ships by the 1630s; and Mexico instituted a major textile manufactory by the early 1600s. All of these industries were born of the need to provide for the local populace. Once these industries were begun, however, their owners chafed at the restrictions on entering the wider market, an entry that was opposed by the home country under the mercantile system. This led to resentment by colonists and many inventive ways of selling goods on the black market.

The mercantile system came to be a major point of contention between colonies and their home countries. By the middle and latter parts of the eighteenth century, economic theorists like Adam Smith (1723–1790) were criticizing the mercantile system. Smith argued that greater equality between colony and home country would stimulate the economies of both, increasing production and developing larger markets for both. He argued that this was the true benefit of foreign trade and that mercantilists had confused raw profit with overall benefit to the economic system. Such theories only fueled colonists' resentment of the mercantile system and its restrictions.

Labor

Many of the activities that colonies specialized in were very labor-intensive, demanding a great deal of labor to produce a product. Sugar manufacture, for example, required the field labor of planting, growing, and harvesting sugarcane, followed by the long process of pressing the cane and refining the fluid removed. Tobacco growing, cotton manufacture, mining, and many other colonial activities were equally labor-intensive. Colonial planters and others, accordingly, sought ways to obtain cheap labor to carry on these activities.

One way to obtain cheap labor was through slavery and related forms of servitude. Despite the initial cost of purchasing slaves, there were few ongoing expenses, and a great deal of labor could be extracted from each slave. In lowland parts of Central and South America, in the southeastern portion of North America, and in the Caribbean, slaves were the backbone of the labor force, particularly on plantations. The institution of slavery is discussed in Chapter 26 and Issue 6.

An alternative way to get cheap labor is with a labor requirement for conquered peoples. This alternative was used most extensively in Spanish America. Initially in the Caribbean and later in Mexico, Central America, and Peru, colonists implemented the ***encomienda,***[9] the institution whereby Indians were required to provide labor for the Spanish for free. An individual Spaniard would be granted an *encomienda* for service to the crown, and it would state the particulars of the arrangement. It might require, for example, all the adult males of a particular native village to devote one month of labor at the direction of the holder. In essence, it was tribute rendered by the conquered to the conqueror.

Encomiendas obviously were highly desirable for Spanish colonists, because this was labor at absolutely no cost. The *encomienda* replaced slaves in some parts of Spanish America as the labor source of choice, and the *encomienda* was dominant from the early 1500s to around 1650. By the mid-1600s, various conditions developed that made the *encomienda* no longer viable. Many conscripted laborers chose to flee rather than provide the required labor, and some villages threatened revolt. The ongoing increase in the number of colonists and the dwindling number of Indians surviving introduced diseases meant that there simply were not enough Indians alive to serve the needs of the Spanish colonists in some locales.

A third source of labor, wage laborers, replaced the *encomienda* in highland Spanish America and was always dominant in the northern parts of North America—places where there were few plantations. This source of labor, however, was not

[9] ***encomienda:*** ehn koh mee EHN duh

FIGURE 24.9 **Encomienda *Mining Practices in Bolivia.*** *The mountain of Potosí, shown in the background of this painting, was found by the Spanish in 1545 to contain vast quantities of rich silver-bearing rock. In the foreground is a refinery where the ore was crushed and mercury was used to extract the silver.* The encomienda, *a means of imposing a labor requirement on conquered people, was used to coerce the vast amounts of labor required to mine and refine the ore—such work was both grueling and hazardous.* Hispanic Society of America.

always cheap, because wages depended on local conditions of labor supply and demand. Consequently, it was the least favored alternative for labor-intensive activities, but it increasingly was the necessary resort in the years following 1650.

Adjusting Local Commerce to European Ends

In Asia and Africa, Europeans were resisted more effectively than generally was the case in the Americas, and a different approach had to be taken by colonists there. Because riches and labor could not simply be seized in Asia and Africa, European colonists tried to fit themselves into existing commercial networks, in the hope of gaining an advantageous position.

Portugal, for example, set its sights on the lucrative spice trade of India in the early 1500s. After a period of experimentation, the Portuguese declared in 1505 that the spice trade henceforth would be a royal monopoly conducted solely by the India House, a specially created royal office. The Ottoman Turks controlled the overland routes, so the Portuguese were forced to develop an oceanic alternative. Using silver obtained from

Brazil, Portugal purchased spices in ports along the Indian Ocean, then transported them by ship around Africa. Other sellers were largely excluded by decree, although a smuggling trade predictably emerged. Nonetheless, this and other monopolies proved a powerful tool for European colonial commerce.

The enormous infusion of American gold and silver pumped into Europe, especially Spain and Portugal, played a critical role in this redirection of trade. (Silver from Japan also played a significant, though less major, role.) Precious metals were more than mere wealth; they were the preferred medium of exchange in trade with Asia, and many Asian traders refused any other mode of payment. Prior to 1500, most of the trade between Asia and Europe had been in the hands of Arabs. They had been able to purchase spices with Iranian silver, sell the spices in Europe for various commodities, then sell those commodities in Iran and elsewhere in order to obtain more silver. After the infusion of precious metals from the Americas, Europeans were in a position for the first time to deal directly with Asian traders. Thus, they redirected major trade flows through their own hands, increasing their profits.

MISSIONS AND MISSIONARIES

Religion was mentioned earlier as a spur to colonization, encouraging some colonists to seek tolerant surroundings and others to try to convert the natives. The latter group, collectively known as missionaries, had a profound impact on some colonies.

In general, Protestants were not very active in attempting to convert natives in their colonies. A few Protestant churches, such as Quakers and Moravians, devoted significant efforts to missionary work, however. In the mid-1600s in New England, for example, Calvinists set up four **praying towns**, communities to which local Indians could come to learn the Calvinist religion, as well as other European skills and ways. The praying towns were very successful at teaching Indians the English language, technical skills (like repairing guns), and some superficial English manners, but the praying towns apparently had limited impact on Indians' religious beliefs.

Catholic approaches to conversion, in contrast, tended to be more energetic. Particularly among the Spanish and Portuguese, it was typical for several priests to set up a **mission**, a complex minimally consisting of a church, dormitories, and farm or ranch facilities. The ideal mission was self-sufficient, using converted Indians for its labor force and selling its surplus for the good of the church. Many missions approached this ideal.

Because Indians were accepted into the church as neophytes (provisional converts), they were considered committed to the mission. They were required to live there indefinitely and to perform their assigned duties. In return, they received religious and secular training, as well as various items of European technology. Leaving the mission, however, was not always permitted, and there are some cases of military-style capture and return of runaways. Alienated from their own society and often attracted to the material advantages of European technology, many neophytes and converts chose to remain at the mission; others seem to have genuinely been attracted to the religious message of the missions.

The successes of the missions in converting huge numbers of Indians in the first decades of colonization were heralded by the church. Thousands upon thousands of baptisms were conducted, and the membership of local parishes swelled. But doubts about the genuineness and persistence of conversion soon arose. In Peru in the 1560s, an end-of-the-world cult appeared among converted Indians, preaching that the diseases and catastrophes endured by the Indians were the revenge of offended ancient Peruvian gods. In eastern Mexico, priests realized that their success in conversion was due largely to the native practice of incorporating new deities into the ancient pantheon: Jesus was considered another god joining the company of older deities, such as Kukulcán[10] and Chac. To this day, Latin American Catholicism retains fragments of native religions within it.

In general, Catholic missions were most successful where they had the support of secular institutions. An isolated mission, many miles from the nearest colonial settlement, was unlikely to have sufficient material incentives to attract neophytes in the first place, and its workload might be so

[10] **Kukulcán:** koo kuhl KAHN

PARALLELS AND DIVERGENCES

Conversion by the Cross, the Sword, or the Copper Kettle?

Scholars continue to debate why so many native peoples in European colonies converted to Christianity. Some believe that the message of Christianity, stressing the dignity and potential salvation of the common person, was so appealing that it ensured success. Others argue that the military force that accompanied missionaries was a more compelling force. Still others contend that the material items that were associated with Christianity were the lure that attracted so many.

Certainly there is evidence that some missionaries were willing to use force or fraud to win souls. In the Yucatán Peninsula of eastern Mexico, 4,000 Indians are known to have been tortured into conversion by the military escort of Catholic priests operating there in the mid-1500s. In Portuguese colonies of Asia, orphans regularly were rounded up for mass baptism and subsequently were raised as Christians, despite complaints by local Buddhists. In Goa during the seventeenth century, beef was forcibly smeared on the lips of Hindus; contact with the forbidden meat meant that they were defiled and no longer acceptable to their faith, leaving them to turn to Christianity as the only available alternative. Anecdotes attesting to the willingness of some missionaries to call on force or fraud to coerce conversion are abundant.

But examples that seem to bear witness to the power of Christianity's message also abound. In the mid–sixteenth century, Saint Francis Xavier preached the doctrine of Christianity in the fish market of Cochin[a] in modern India, and children (coming from the despised fishing castes and having much to gain from espousing a religion that offered salvation to all) are said to have converted spontaneously. The Jesuit fathers in New France praised seventeenth-century Iroquois converts who withstood torture by enemies and refused to recant their faith. An Aztec man named Juan Diego[b] received in 1531 a vision of the Virgin María at Tepayacac[c] (present-day Guadalupe); such a vision was viewed by the priests as a sign of great faith.

Finally, many examples document the allure of technology as a major factor in conversion. Neophytes and converts were often given various material items as rewards for their faith, including copper kettles, metal knives, clothing, and guns. Among the most valued, however, were rosaries, sets of glass beads strung together in a loop with a cross attached at one end; these symbolized the sufferings of Christ, served as a memory aid in reciting prayer cycles, and were worn as personal decorations. When an Aztec, Iroquois, or Inca received a rosary, it underscored the authority of the Catholic Church, because only a powerful institution would give such a treasure to a common convert. Many converts clearly were impressed.

Which of these factors was responsible for the success of the Catholic Church in converting, to some degree, most of the Indians in the Americas and small but ardent communities in Asia? The answer probably is all three.

[a] **Cochin:** KOH chihn

[b] **Juan Diego:** WAHN dee AY goh

[c] **Tepayacac:** teh PY uh KAHK

heavy that they were scared off—and with no effective military support, neophytes could abandon the mission at will. Respect and sympathy for the natives seems to have enhanced success, and knowledge of their languages and customs also assisted. In recognition of this, several sixteenth-century Spanish and Portuguese universities established departments of American languages to train missionaries in local languages before they left for the colonies.

THE PERSISTENCE OF NATIVE SOCIETIES

There can be no doubt that the entry of Europeans as colonial powers had massive effects on native societies. Nonetheless, it would be an error to imagine that the European invasion simply wiped out local ways of life. As a simple generalization, the local elite culture was eradicated, while life among the common people sometimes went on little changed. In particular, rural people were more likely to retain their native culture than were their city cousins. Mexico provides a representative example of the changes wrought by European colonialism in the period before 1750.

For the nobility and royalty of the Aztecs, the conquest by the Spanish ended their way of life. Their sumptuous existence with palaces and servants was gone, and the nobles who survived found themselves sharing the lot of the common people. This meant earning a living through labor, losing special privileges, and submitting to the will and power of the new Spanish government. Many elite skills were lost or forgotten; native systems of court music, writing, painting, featherwork (for elaborate royal headdresses), and poetry were replaced with Spanish models. The elite simply merged with the mass of Aztec society.

For common people, however, everyday life often remained remarkably similar to what it had been before the conquest, especially in the countryside, far from Spanish influences. A farmer in a village remote from the capital carried on much as before. The same crops were planted as before, they were shared among family members as before, and a share was passed on as taxes rendered to the government as before. Christianity produced some changes, but many of the ancient native practices continued for decades, even centuries; sometimes a veneer of Christian symbolism was added to make the practices more acceptable to Spanish priests and officials.

For example, weavers continued to produce the folk costume for women and girls, consisting of some form of wraparound skirt and triangular over-the-head blouse (called a *quechquemetl*[11]). Either woven into the blouse or embroidered onto it were a series of animal figures in traditional forms. These figures represented ***nahualli,***[12] spirits of animals that would help protect the wearers from evils, whether disease or accident or spiritual mishap. The *nahualli*, while rejected and opposed by the Spanish clergy, nonetheless remained a potent part of religious belief for rural Mexicans, as they do in many parts of Mexico today.

FIGURE 24.10 *Modern Mexican* **Quechquemetl.** *Handwoven in the village of San Francisco in Mexico's state of Hidalgo, this garment was designed to be slipped over the head and worn about the shoulders. Based on an ancient pattern and executed in threads colored with bright European dyes, the delicate embroidery depicts various birds and animals representing protective spirits.* Anawalt/Berdan Collection, Museum of Cultural History, University of California, Los Angeles. Collected in 1985.

No native peoples could escape the disruption of disease and conquest entirely, but it is remarkable how many ancient practices have persisted. These are particularly strong in terms of religion, local government, cuisine, and folk culture. In truth, the ancient native cultures live on in the countryside.

SUMMARY

1. Colonialism developed as a means for Europeans to economically exploit newly discovered lands.

2. Initially, Europeans were confused about the status of peoples in the Americas, Polynesia, and Australia. In 1493 and again in 1537, popes declared them human.

3. Sixteenth-century colonies in the Americas were devoted mostly to procuring precious metals;

[11] ***quechquemetl:*** kehch KAY meht
[12] ***nahualli:*** nah HWAHL lee

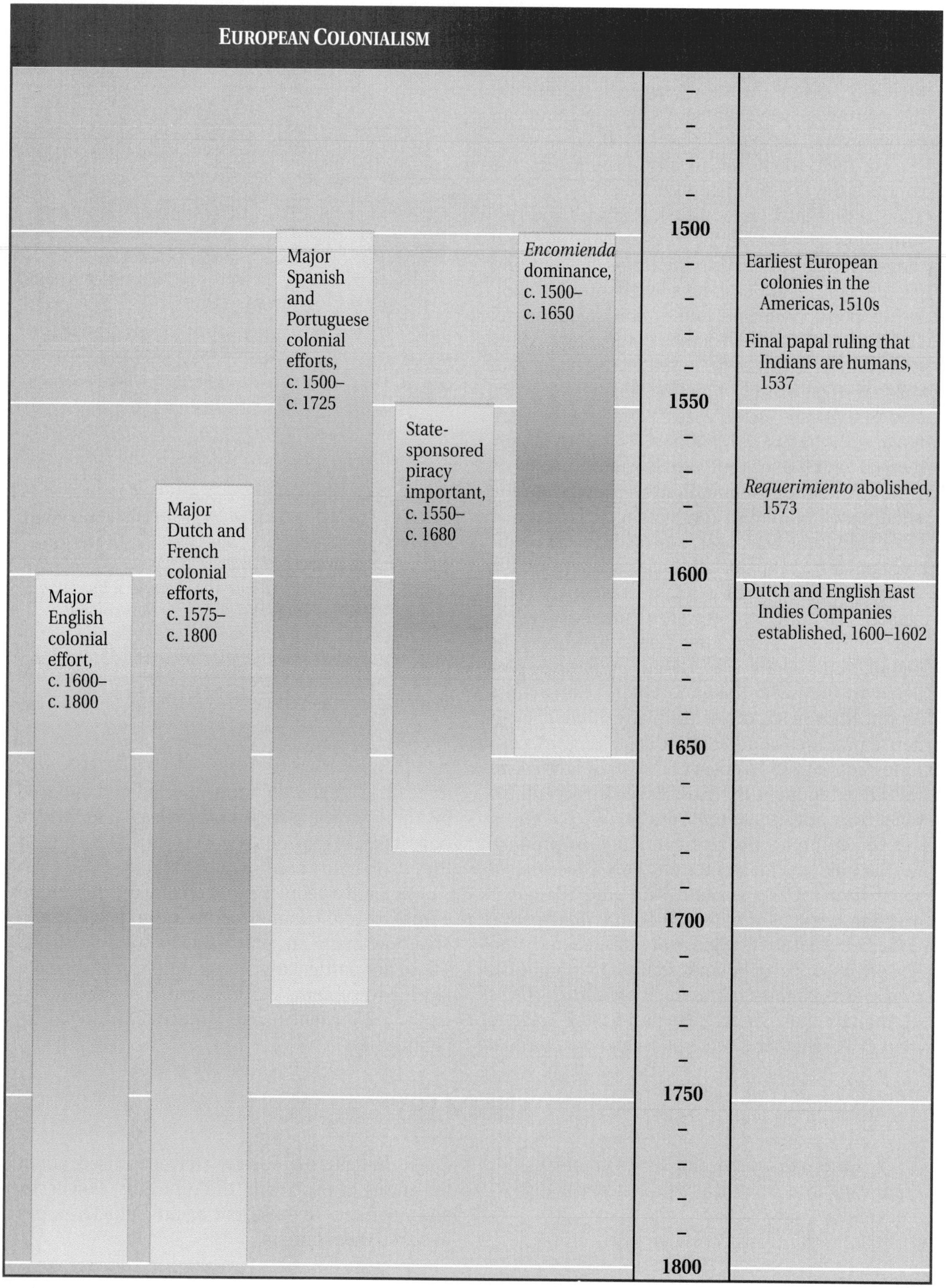

EUROPEAN COLONIALISM

Major English colonial effort, c. 1600–c. 1800

Major Dutch and French colonial efforts, c. 1575–c. 1800

Major Spanish and Portuguese colonial efforts, c. 1500–c. 1725

State-sponsored piracy important, c. 1550–c. 1680

Encomienda dominance, c. 1500–c. 1650

1500	Earliest European colonies in the Americas, 1510s
	Final papal ruling that Indians are humans, 1537
1550	*Requerimiento* abolished, 1573
1600	Dutch and English East Indies Companies established, 1600–1602
1650	
1700	
1750	
1800	

exploitation of resources (especially wood, fish, and furs) without settlement also occurred. By the seventeenth century, colonies were more attuned to mining, ranching, and planting as means to wealth.

4. In Asia and Africa, where native peoples were not conquered in this period, European colonies were restricted to *entrepôts*.

5. The English, Dutch, and French were especially interested in reproducing the lifestyles of their home countries in colonies.

6. Individual colonists had varying motives for joining a colony, including personal economic betterment, religious freedom, the opportunity to convert natives to Christianity, and patriotic urges to aid the home country.

7. Initial colonizing usually was funded privately, often by organized companies. When profits were clearly established, control often reverted to the state.

8. Most early colonies had few women, but by 1700 they became more common.

9. By the seventeenth century, many colonists were identifying with their colony more than with the home country.

10. Both native and colonial forces used alliances to further their military ends. The superior military technology and organization of the European powers permitted them to conquer most of the Americas. European rivalries were played out in the colonies.

11. The mercantile system retained colonies in a subordinate position, providing raw materials for the home country, which in turn processed them into manufactured goods to sell in the colonies. This led to colonial resentments.

12. Labor in colonies was primarily provided through slavery, the *encomienda*, and wage labor.

13. In Asia and Africa, European colonies tried to gain wealth by adjusting native commercial arrangements to their benefits. This was made possible, in part, by the massive infusions of precious metals coming from the Americas and lesser amounts from Japan.

14. Roman Catholics were more active and effective in converting natives in their colonies, especially through missions, than were Protestants. The missions aimed for self-sufficiency and used a variety of methods to attract converts.

15. Native culture persisted following European conquests. While elite culture often was eradicated, the folk culture of common people often persisted.

SUGGESTED READINGS

Eburne, Richard. *A Plain Pathway to Plantations*. Ed. Louis B. Wright. Ithaca, N.Y.: Cornell University Press, 1962. A reprint of the original English tract of 1624, promoting colonizing overseas. Also includes insightful modern commentary.

Ethnohistory. Society for American Ethnohistory. This quarterly journal includes many seminal articles dealing with aspects of early colonialism.

Koehn, Nancy F. *The Power of Commerce: Economy and Governance in the First British Empire*. Ithaca, N.Y.: Cornell University Press, 1994. A good recent treatment of the British colonial expansion.

McClintock, Anne. *Imperial Leather: Race, Gender, and Sexuality in the Colonial Conquest*. New York: Routledge, 1995. A feminist interpretation of colonial sexual politics and its impacts.

Pagden, Anthony. *Lords of All the World: Ideologies of Empire in Spain, Britain and France, c. 1500–c. 1800*. New Haven, Conn.: Yale University Press, 1995. A recent comparison of colonialist goals, attitudes, and strategies.

Parry, J. H. *Trade and Dominion: The European Overseas Empires in the Eighteenth Century*. New York: Praeger Publishers, 1961. The classic treatment of early colonialism, reflecting the ideas of the mid–twentieth century but still largely current. Its coverage extends later than that of this chapter.

Scammell, G. V. *The First Imperial Ages: European Overseas Expansion, c. 1400–1715*. London: Unwin Hyman, 1989. An excellent overall treatment of early colonialism, emphasizing the economic basis.

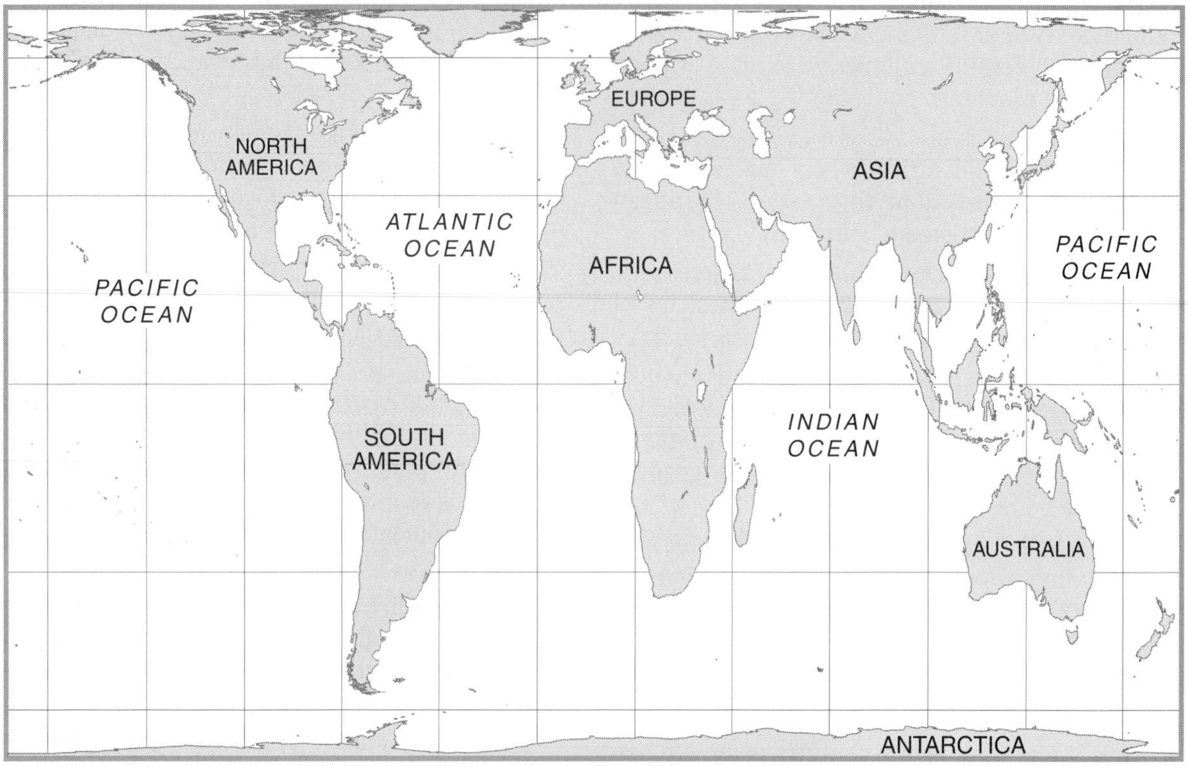

EUROPE
NORTH AMERICA
ASIA
ATLANTIC OCEAN
PACIFIC OCEAN
AFRICA
PACIFIC OCEAN
SOUTH AMERICA
INDIAN OCEAN
AUSTRALIA
ANTARCTICA

Columbus Exhibits West Indians. *Columbus captured several inhabitants of the Caribbean Islands on his first voyage to the New World and brought them back to Spain to show his patrons, the royal house of Spain.*
Mary Evans Picture Library.

CHAPTER 25

The American Exchange

1492–around 1750

When members of an African family in Ghana settle down to a meal of *fetri detsi*, a sauced chicken and vegetable dish, they may know that the okra in the sauce was domesticated in Africa and that the onions have been in use there since antiquity. But they are less likely to realize that the tomatoes and chilis in the dish came from America in just the past few centuries. Similarly, when tribal Yanamamö Indians of South America's Amazon rain forest have a periodic feast focusing on banana soup, they probably are unaware that bananas came to the Americas from the Old World. The European voyages of discovery opened a door between two worlds, and a variety of things previously isolated in one hemisphere passed between the Americas and the Old World in both directions. This process is known as the **American exchange**.

There had been many other exchanges in human history. Hellenistic Greece and the Roman Empire facilitated the movement of ideas and items in the Mediterranean basin and beyond. The Mongol conquests of Central Asia and adjacent Europe opened a corridor between East Asia and Europe, fostering the Mongol exchange. The establishment of a more or less uniform Islamic culture over a vast area led to trade and travel that carried items and ideas via the Islamic exchange. These and other exchanges, however, were different in the sense that they intensified interaction that already was occurring. In contrast, the American exchange initiated contact and exchange where none had existed before.

THE BREAKING OF AMERICAN ISOLATION

Viewed in broad perspective, most of the world's land lies in two masses: Africa-Europe-Asia and the Americas. Except in the inhospitable climate of the Arctic, these masses are segregated by the great expanses of open ocean. Prior to the voyages of exploration discussed in the previous chapter, contact between these great land masses was, at best, very limited.

History, legend, and folklore are full of heroes who departed on voyages over the sea, never to return. Prince Madoc of Wales, Rata-Wai[1] of Libya, Leif Ericson of the Vikings, anonymous Phoenicians, and many others have had their champions as early seafarers who accidentally discovered the Americas. Some of these figures probably never existed outside legend, and most of the others almost certainly were lost at sea, but it remains possible that several of them may have survived to wash up on American shores. But, with a single exception, there is no compelling evidence for American landings before Columbus's.

The Vikings (Norse) of Scandinavia, however, had vessels capable of oceanic voyages by the eighth century, and their settlements in Iceland and Greenland have been studied extensively by archaeologists. The *Greenland Saga* and *Erik's Saga* were composed around 1000 and were maintained as oral accounts until they finally were written down two or three centuries later. Scholars generally accept that they were maintained carefully, because the penalty for misremembering, at least nominally, was death. The sagas describe an expedition led by Leif Ericson to what must have been America. According to the sagas, Ericson and a small group of colonists set out from Norse settlements in Greenland, sailing westward. They ultimately came to a place they called "Vinland," where they settled for three years before returning to Greenland. The dates for their expedition usually are calculated as 1002 to 1004.

The Vinland tale long has fascinated scholars, and many sites for Vinland have been suggested, chiefly in New England. Misinterpreting *vin-* as meaning grape or wine encouraged this error, because grapes do not grow north of New England on the Atlantic coast of North America. In medieval Norse, however, *vin-* meant either berry, in general, or meadow. Using this translation, placing Vinland farther north makes sense.

In 1960, a team of Norwegian archaeologists and historians systematically explored the coast of eastern Canada, searching for a place that fit the description of Vinland. To fit the description, the place needed to have a good (though small) harbor, plenty of grassy meadows overlooking it, remains of several longhouses of the sort built by the Norse in that period, and evidence of a furnace for smelting and working iron, mined as ore from an adjacent bog. At a village in Newfoundland called L'Anse aux Meadows[2] they found just such a place, and eight summers of archaeological excavation revealed abundant evidence of an ancient Norse village.

The site produced remains of at least nine houses, a furnace for iron working, Norse-style boat sheds, domestic pigs, and abundant Norse artifacts, including iron rivets, spindle whorls (for spinning wool thread), and bronze ring-headed pins (for clasping cloaks). These items are indisputably Norse from around 1000; architectural styles and radiocarbon dating support that date. The site appears to have been occupied only for a short period, probably a few years, and all evidence suggests that this either was Vinland or another, unrecorded settlement much like it.

Why was Vinland abandoned? While it offered abundant fuel (peat from the bogs) and pasturage, it was very short on wood and other essentials of the Norse way of life. Further, the Norse had established terrible relations with the local people, whom they called ***skraelings***,[3] meaning "the impoverished ones," because they had no iron tools, woven cloth, or other items of technology considered essential by the Norse. Modern scholars have identified the *skraelings* as the Inuit[4] (Eskimo). After murdering curious *skraeling* visitors, the Norse Vinlanders were harassed constantly by the *skraelings*, who would use spears to pick off Vikings whenever possible. Far from home, short on essentials, and beleaguered by

[1] **Rata-Wai:** RAH tuh WY

[2] **L'Anse aux Meadows:** LAHNS ee MEH dohz

[3] ***skraelings:*** SKRAY lihngz

[4] **Inuit:** IHN oo iht

FIGURE 25.1 ***Norse Settlement in North America.*** *The archaeological site of L'Anse aux Meadows in Newfoundland is probably the remains of Leif Ericson's Vinland. The grassy hummocks of this picture are what have survived of the longhouses occupied by Norse Vikings around A.D. 1000. Abundant artifacts of Norse technology and style demonstrate that this was a Viking settlement, though the long-term effects on local Native American culture were minimal.* Parks Canada/Department of Canadian Heritage.

the natives, the Vikings found it best to return to Greenland.

The identification of L'Anse aux Meadows with Vinland is important for two reasons. First, it documents that the Norse did found a colony on the North American mainland. Second, it shows that it had almost no impact on the local people. The only cultural change brought about by Norse settlement among the Inuit of Greenland and Vinland seems to be that Inuit children began playing with toy tops that probably derived from the Norse spindle whorls. Otherwise, Inuit history and culture simply ignored the temporary intruders. To have profound effects, a colony must last longer and have greater interaction between peoples than at Vinland.

The colonies and explorations that followed the voyages of Columbus and others provided longer, more intensive contact between the intruders and the indigenous peoples, setting the backdrop for the American exchange.

THE CIRCUMSTANCES OF THE AMERICAN EXCHANGE

From the moment Columbus set foot in the Americas, the American exchange was underway. Some of the exchanges were accidental, but many were purposeful, and the circumstances of exchange had strong effects on its outcome.

First, the intensity of interaction between Europeans and Americans was an important factor in determining the degree of exchange between these peoples. Few Europeans entered some parts of the Americas, notably deserts, rain forests, and arctic regions. These areas were perceived as having few attractions, and the environments were sufficiently unhealthy or dangerous to incline Europeans to avoid them. In addition, native populations in these areas usually were dispersed and thin, making it unlikely that any Europeans there would encounter large numbers of inhabitants.

In contrast, an area endowed with rich resources and dense populations was attractive to Europeans. Wealth could be acquired in such a place, and the inhabitants there could be called upon as a labor force, as a source of information, or as an emergency support force if one needed food, shelter, or medical treatment. Central Mexico, the site of the Aztec capital, for example, was particularly attractive to the Spanish and received their early and intense attention; it also became a major theater for the American exchange.

A second factor is the purposes that spurred the European intrusion into an area. Missionaries, by definition, were agents of the American exchange, because their avowed purpose was to replace Native American religion with Christianity. In addition, many missionaries worked under the principle that Christianity could flourish only if Indians adopted "civilized" lifestyles, which to them meant European lifestyles. To greater or lesser extents, ranches, plantations, mining camps, and other European facilities also encouraged American Indians to adopt European ways. Sometimes the managers actively tried to persuade Indians to adopt European habits to facilitate the activities being carried out, as when learning the Europeans' language made communication more effective. Other times, seductive technology or styles that were perceived as sophisticated and prestigious were sufficient to entice Indians to adopt these elements of European culture.

Some Europeans actively discouraged Indians from adopting a European lifestyle. Notable here were the French fur traders in Canada, whose livelihood was anchored in a relatively intact native culture. For them to be successful, they required Indian trappers who traveled widely in their trapping expeditions and were willing to sell their furs for inexpensive European items. As many Indians began settling down near French forts, settlements, and missions in the seventeenth and eighteenth centuries, they stopped trapping, leading the traders to bemoan their own bad fortune.

The discussion thus far has focused on European traits that passed to the Americas, but the purposes of Europeans affected the flow in the opposite direction, too. Exploring expeditions, for example, often were sent out with a broad mandate to bring back information about a wide range of topics in the lands they would traverse. An explorer usually was alert to find new crops, medicines, mineral sources, and curiosities. Information on these might be presented to the public in a book recounting the expedition's adventures, and examples of items often were collected to be sent back to a sponsor in Europe. Such exploring parties were instrumental in transmitting ideas and items from the Americas to the home countries.

Third and finally, the degree of subjugation to Europeans had a profound impact on the degree of activity in the American exchange. The defeat of the Aztecs led to their status as a conquered people under the Spanish, so the only route to wealth, prestige, or power open to a Mexican native would have been through a Spanish lifestyle. Clothing, speech, housing, religion, and other aspects of culture had to meet Spanish standards if an individual were to partake of opportunities for personal advancement. Further, the thoroughness of the conquest ensured that large numbers of Spanish were living side by side with the descendants of the Aztecs, producing a fertile environment for the transmission of ideas and items in both directions.

The differing circumstances of contact were critical factors in the shape of the American exchange, affecting the items that were exchanged, the degree to which they were accepted, and the speed with which exchange took place. Among the most significant items to be transmitted from one hemisphere to the other were germs, plants and animals, technology, and ideas.

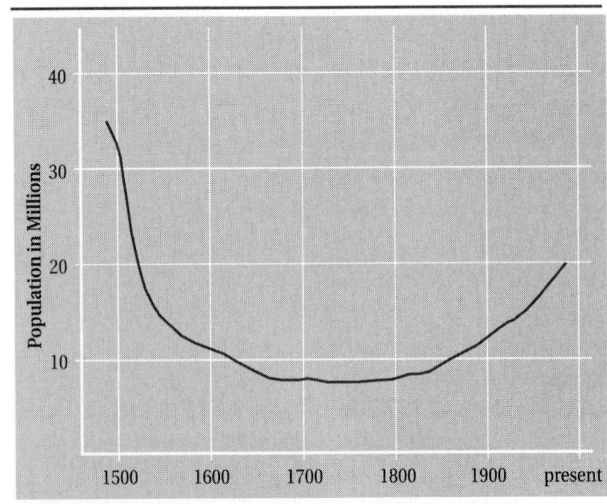

FIGURE 25.2 ***Estimated Native American Population in the Americas.*** *While such estimates are fraught with difficulties, an overall pattern of massive decline followed by slow rebound is evident.*

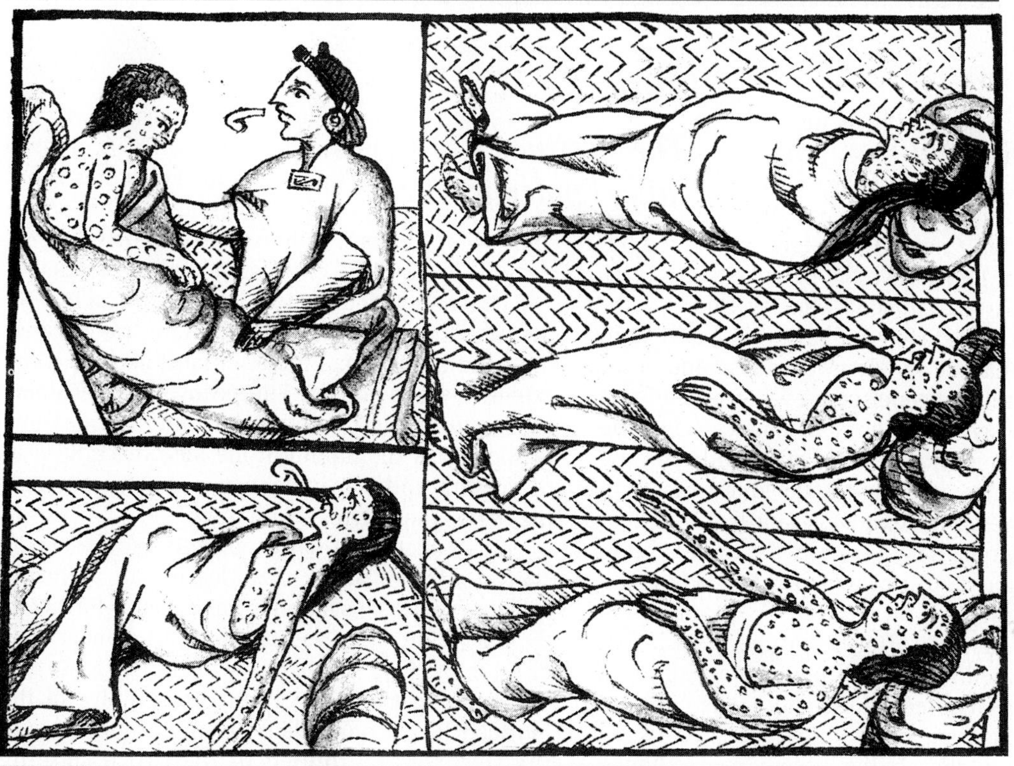

FIGURE 25.3 ***Aztecs and Smallpox.*** *Like other Native American peoples, the Aztecs had little natural immunity to the smallpox that Europeans unwittingly brought with them to the Americas. These illustrations by Aztec artists show victims' bodies covered in pustules and, ultimately, debilitated by the disease; the right central figure is probably deceased. The curved figures that extend from the mouths of the individuals at the left are speech scrolls, indicating that the person is speaking or (as in the bottom left image) groaning.*
Biblioteca Medicea Laurenziana.

DISEASES

Although few people realized it at the time, the first and most significant exchange between the Old World and the New World was disease. Because of an unlucky genetic history, Native Americans were particularly susceptible to Old World diseases.

People in these two hemispheres had lived in virtual isolation from each other for tens of thousands of years, and during that time they had developed slightly different genetic makeups. Some genes determine how many antibodies will be produced by the body to resist particular diseases. The Old World had been plagued by various epidemic diseases, probably since around 4000 B.C., including such killers as smallpox and influenza. In the earliest years of exposure, Old World peoples must have suffered devastating losses as those individuals lacking genes for disease resistance died. Over time, however, the mortality from diseases fell off, because an ever-increasing percentage of the survivors had genes for the production of antibodies to combat the diseases; the most susceptible to diseases had been weeded out before they were old enough to pass on their genes to their children. By the sixteenth century, the Europeans and others crossing to the Americas mostly had some level of resistance to the major deadly diseases of their era; many Europeans could be exposed to a major disease without contracting it, and still others who contracted the disease could survive it.

In contrast, Native Americans in the sixteenth century were at the same genetic point as their cousins in the Old World had been nearly six millennia before. Some had genes for combatting

UNDER THE LENS

The Merrimack Valley Epidemic, 1616–1617

The Merrimack River originates in the mountains of New Hampshire and runs through northeastern Massachusetts to the Atlantic coast. It is the third-largest river in New England, and many Indians lived along its banks in the early seventeenth century. During a few short months in the winter of 1616–1617, they were ravaged by a massive and destructive epidemic.

The Indians of the Merrimack Valley were of several tribes, loosely united into an alliance called the Pennacook Confederacy. Historical records cite the Pennacook as having around 3,000 adult males, and adult males averaged around one-fourth of New England Indian populations, leading to the standard estimate of around 12,000 persons for the Pennacook population in 1600.

In the winter of 1616–1617, three years before the establishment of the first permanent European colony in Massachusetts, a dreadful epidemic overtook the Pennacook. Descriptions recorded fifteen years later say that Indians were overwhelmed rapidly, sometimes as they walked between houses in their villages. Dizziness, high fever, and chills were the primary symptoms, and death often followed within a day or two. The first to be affected usually were the young men, but shortly after one person was afflicted, the entire village would succumb. Often the few who were well were insufficient to care for the many who were ill.

Writers of the era usually called the epidemic "the plague," but that term referred generally to any epidemic. Diagnosis nearly four centuries later on the basis of incomplete descriptions of the symptoms is not very satisfactory, but modern scholars mostly have concluded that the disease was some form of influenza. The infection of young men first was typical for epidemics in northeastern North America, because these individuals were the ones most likely to travel extensively and contact Europeans, thus becoming exposed to germs. Coastal traders from Europe came to shore near the mouth of the Merrimack River at this period, and the young men probably were trading goods—and germs—with them.

As a direct result of the epidemic, about 80 percent of the Pennacook died, leaving an estimated 2,500 survivors. This number was depleted further by the food shortages resulting from this demographic disaster that took such a heavy toll on the most productive segment of the Pennacook. Twelve of the fourteen Pennacook villages were abandoned, and the survivors regrouped in the two remaining villages.

While the most devastating, the epidemic of 1616–1617 was only one of three major epidemics that shook coastal New England before a European ever built a house there. Before a single act of hostility occurred, the Pennacook population was reduced to one-fifth its pre-Columbian level. The combined effects of disease, warfare, and cultural dislocation reduced the Pennacook to about 250 persons by 1675, and they ceased to exist by 1725.

smallpox and other diseases they had never encountered, but the vast majority had little or no resistance to these new diseases. As a result, Native Americans were genetically vulnerable to most Old World diseases when they were introduced to the Americas by the American exchange. Consequently, death tolls were appallingly high.

Europeans and Africans brought a remarkable array of deadly diseases with them to the Americas. Smallpox, influenza, cholera, yellow fever, bubonic plague, pneumonic plague, diphtheria, typhoid fever, measles, whooping cough, malaria, and many more Old World diseases all found their way across the Atlantic in the earliest crossings, and they found human populations biologically unprepared for them. All of these were serious diseases for Europeans, Africans, and Asians, given the state of medical knowledge of the day, but they were far more serious in American Indian communities, where 50 to 100 percent death rates were common upon first exposure to these killers. On the coasts, these diseases often came to be associated with the Europeans, but the diseases spread inland faster than the European invasion. Many of the people who died of disease in the first few decades of contact never saw a European.

Columbus's landfall on Guanahani (called San Salvador by the Spanish) provides a classic example of the insidious manner in which these diseases operated. Columbus noted no medical problems among the inhabitants of the island during his initial stay, but the next time Guanahani was contacted, it was devoid of people. Presumably all died of some disease that no one suspected was being transmitted, although a few may have survived and moved to other islands as refugees. A reasonable estimate of total population of the Americas in 1492 is 35 million, and probably 20 million people died of disease in the first half century of contact with the Old World.

The Americas had some diseases before Columbus. Aztec codices recorded epidemics, and Moche[5] art in Peru depicted individuals with erosive damage to their faces, probably the result of an insect-borne fungal disease. Analysis of skeletons and mummies shows that tuberculosis, pneumonia, hookworm, and amoebic dysentery plagued pre-Columbian Americans, just as they did Europeans, Asians, and Africans. But while the pre-Columbian Americas hardly were the disease-free paradise once envisioned by historians, they clearly had far fewer serious diseases than the Old World.

The reason pre-Columbian Americans were so fortunate lies in the nature of **disease reservoirs**, populations of animals that can contract human diseases, harboring the germs that cause them. Except in cities, human population concentrations were insufficient to harbor enough germs to keep most diseases from dying out; instead, the germs were harbored in animals in the Old World. Names of some diseases reflect this host relationship: swine flu, Asian duck flu, and cowpox (the milder form of smallpox). Other diseases also are well known for their animal carriers, as with anthrax and sheep. While the Old World had many of these disease reservoirs, few American animals were susceptible to human diseases, and epidemic diseases (if ever present) simply died out before they could become established. Even in cases where a New World animal could host a germ that attacked human beings, the scarcity of domesticated animals meant that that germ was unlikely to be in daily, intimate contact with human beings.

There is a possible exception to the generalization that few dangerous diseases afflicted pre-Columbian Americans. Venereal syphilis is widely considered an American disease, though the evidence is not conclusive. Clearly, there were no major outbreaks of diseases that unquestionably were syphilis in Europe prior to 1500, and no skeletons with unequivocal syphilitic lesions have been recognized in Europe prior to that date. In contrast, many pre-Columbian American skeletons bear lesions that appear to be the result of syphilis. Further, the rapid spread of syphilis in Europe around 1500 and the very high mortality rates associated with it are suggestive of a new disease for which Europeans had little biological immunity.

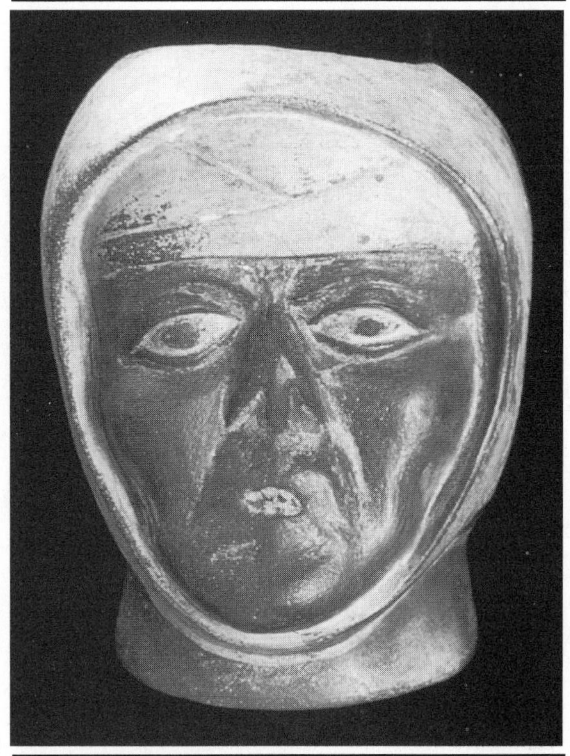

FIGURE 25.4 ***Pre-Columbian Pottery Depicting Leishmaniasis.*** *While the Americas before 1492 had relatively few deadly diseases, they were not completely free of destructive illnesses. This pot from the Moche Valley of Peru dates to around* A.D. *550 and shows an individual with a curiously depressed face. This person probably suffered from leishmaniasis, an insect-borne American disease that produces decomposition of the nose, palate, and lips.* Countway Library, Harvard. Courtesy of John W. Verano, Tulane University.

[5] **Moche:** MOH chay

The American exchange was unequal in terms of the transmission of diseases and their impact. The Old World acquired only a single major disease, one that could be contracted only through sexual contact; Europeans recognized the venereal character of syphilis by 1498, so it was avoidable. In contrast, the Americas received a host of virulent, highly infectious, fatal diseases that could be transmitted through the air. Although there are very few known cases of intentional infection of American Indians with diseases, rampant epidemics were a powerful ally in the European conquest of the Americas. As P. M. Ashburn so eloquently wrote:

> Smallpox was the captain of the men of death in that war, typhus fever the first lieutenant, and measles the second lieutenant. More terrible than the conquistadores on horseback, more deadly than sword and gunpowder, they made the conquest.

PLANTS AND ANIMALS

While many plants and animals were common to both hemispheres, many also were unique to either the Old World or the New World. This is understandable, given that the Afro-Euro-Asian and American land masses had been separated for about 35 million years, after continental drift tore them apart and propelled them away from each other, opening up a depression between them into which water flowed to form an ocean. During the eons intervening between this geological event and the American exchange, there was plenty of opportunity for evolution to produce unique species on each side of the ocean.

In addition, people in each hemisphere had been domesticating plants and animals for thousands of years. The domestication process involves selective breeding, resulting ultimately in a new form with a different genetic composition from

FIGURE 25.5 ***Making Indigo Dye.*** *Native to India, the indigo plant was transported to and grown in European colonies in tropical America to cut the cost of the dye, which was used extensively for coloring cloth. In this eighteenth-century image, slaves tote bales of indigo leaves to a processing station for the extraction of blue dye.* Courtesy of the Charleston Library Society.

FIGURE 25.6 *Potatoes Being Fed to the Poor of Seville.* *In some parts of Europe, the virtues of potatoes were largely unrecognized for centuries after they were introduced from South America. This 1645 painting by Murillo shows poor Spanish children being fed potatoes. In Spain, potatoes were often considered a coarse food that was acceptable for the lower class, but one that would upset the more refined nature of the upper class.* Accademia de San Fernando/MAS Barcelona.

that of its wild ancestors. Domesticated species are very important in the American exchange, because these were plants and animals that already had proven their usefulness to people and had been modified to better serve human needs.

Foodstuffs

Some of the most important plants and animals that passed between the hemispheres were new foods. For most farmers in Indonesia, Poland, or Ghana, discoveries of new lands in the Americas or seizures of gold for Spanish coffers were abstract and distant, but a new food to plant was an exciting and immediate prospect. Unfortunately for scholars, most of the incorporation of American foods into Old World agriculture was done by poor, often illiterate farmers, and records of dates or circumstances of adoption often are scanty.

STARCHY STAPLES FROM THE AMERICAS TO THE OLD WORLD. Starchy crops typically form the bulk of any diet based on agriculture, and two important starchy crops came to the Old World in the American exchange: potatoes and corn. In order to entice a farmer to adopt it, a new crop had to provide significant advantages over its competitors, especially competitors that already were part of the agricultural routine. Many of the new American crops offered just such advantages.

Potatoes were developed in Peru but rapidly spread to the Old World, particularly Europe. As early as 1536, Spanish ships leaving Peru stocked potatoes as a cheap food for sailors, and some of these potatoes made their way to Spain. The earliest Europeans to grow potatoes appear to have been the Basques of north coastal Spain, around 1590; by 1650 potatoes had reached Ireland; by the early 1700s they were in Germany; by 1760 they were in Poland; and by 1790 they had reached Russia.

The attractions of potatoes were three. First, they could produce more food per acre than competing crops. In the northern European plain, where rye grain was the only starchy crop that could be counted upon to mature in the short growing seasons, potatoes yielded almost four times the amount of food per acre as did rye. Further, potatoes could grow on rye fields being left uncultivated to rejuvenate the soil, producing a crop where none was possible before, yet not depleting the soil. In the highlands of western China and Tibet, potatoes also became important in small-scale plots where other crops were ill suited.

Second, unlike any Old World starchy crop, potatoes offered such balanced nutrition that they could be eaten to the exclusion of all other foods with only minimal deterioration of health. They also were reputed to increase one's sexual potency, a not inconsequential incentive.

Finally, grain had to be harvested when ripe and kept in a barn, where it was a convenient target for plundering soldiers during the many European wars of the eighteenth century. In contrast, potatoes could be left in the ground all winter and dug as needed—no plundering soldier was going to take the time or effort to dig potatoes. In effect, potatoes were plunder-proof, protecting a farmer's harvest. This last reason almost certainly was the most important in initially encouraging the growing of potatoes in northern Europe.

These advantages spurred the widespread adoption of potatoes, and in much of northern Europe they were sometimes cultivated to the exclusion of other crops that previously had been dominant. Unfortunately, potatoes have a serious drawback that was to devastate Ireland during the potato famine that began in 1846 and ended in 1851. Unlike dependence on grains, successful dependence on potatoes requires that there never be a year so disastrous that there is no crop to harvest; potatoes can be stored only a single year, lest they sprout and rot. Consequently, long-term storage to cope with such an emergency is precluded. When a fungus arrived from America and caused the notorious blight and subsequent famine in Ireland, there were insufficient stockpiles of food to fend off starvation.

Corn was the other major American staple crop to transform parts of the Old World. Like potatoes, it could produce more food per acre than its competitors, but it had two important drawbacks. First, it lacked certain amino acids and vitamins critical for health, and an exclusive diet of corn would lead to **pellagra**, a deficiency disease resulting from a lack of niacin, a B vitamin. This meant that corn never was used to the exclusion of other starchy staple crops, avoiding the danger of a disaster like the Irish potato blight. Second, corn requires more water than wheat, so it was adopted as an alternative to wheat primarily in areas where there was abundant rainfall, areas like northern Italy and West Africa.

The spread of corn in the Old World is documented less well than that of potatoes, but it appears that corn appeared first in Spain, to which it was carried by Columbus. By 1650, it had made its way to Venice and the western parts of the Ottoman Empire. Corn made great inroads in the mountain valleys of the Balkans, and it was the fuel that sustained late-nineteenth-century Greek and Serbian independence movements centered on mountain strongholds.

Potatoes and corn benefited all those areas that adopted them, but particularly Europe and China, because their environments were most favorable for their cultivation. Populations increased with the introduction of these crops, sometimes quite markedly, as in Ireland. These burgeoning populations provided the colonists who would consolidate the European colonial conquests, particularly in the Americas. Ironically, corn and other American crops in West Africa led to increased populations, allowing the slave trade to continue longer than otherwise would have been possible, further fueling the development of the American colonies.

OTHER FOODSTUFFS. Many other foodstuffs from the Americas were transported and adopted around the world. Indeed, it is hard to imagine many of the world's cuisines without ingredients from the Americas. Thai food without its searing chilis, southern Italian food without tomatoes and zucchini, West African dishes without peanuts, village Chinese cuisine without sweet potatoes—these are practically unthinkable.

Most of these foodstuffs were important for their taste contributions rather than for their caloric value. Some, like tomatoes, made important contributions of vitamins and minerals to peasant diets otherwise short on these nutrients. Others, like chilis, became important in terms of folk medicine.

In the Americas, too, various foods from across the ocean became standard parts of the cuisine. Wheat flour tortillas in northern Mexico, olives in eastern Mexico, chickpeas in Cuba, palm oil in

Brazil, beef in Argentina, and apples in Costa Rica—all these are Old World foods that have become part of New World cuisines.

OLD WORLD FOODSTUFFS COMING TO THE AMERICAS AS THE BASIS OF LABOR. Because many of the colonial powers in the Americas saw themselves as extensions of the home country, it is not amazing that important foodstuffs were transferred from there to the colonies. By 1650, well-to-do colonists in cities throughout the American colonies could duplicate most dishes to be had in their home countries. By that date, for example, cooks in Boston could obtain apples, pears, plums, cherries, quinces, spinach, garlic, chives, cucumbers, leeks, watercress, lettuce, endive, peas, carrots, turnips, beets, onions, cabbages, and various garden herbs, all European transplants to local gardens and orchards. Still more ingredients were available as imports from England or the Caribbean.

Some foodstuffs, however, were transferred from the Old World to the Americas for reasons other than the satisfaction of European palates far from home. Wheat, bananas, cattle, and especially sugarcane (whose value was spurred by the growing appetite for sugar in Europe) all were to be the basis of plantations and ranches, many of which ran on African and Native American slave labor. Sugarcane and bananas, both tropical crops that require abundant heat and moisture, became the staples of plantations in the Caribbean, Central America, and eastern South America. Wheat and cattle could tolerate less moisture and cooler climates, so ranches and farms at higher elevations and in more temperate climates focused primarily on them. The vast lands of the Americas, once sufficient labor was found to develop them, were the grounds for the making of fortunes.

DRUGS AND STIMULANTS. Although drugs usually are not conceived of as foodstuffs, the line between the two categories is blurry. Many important foods and beverages have some effect on the mind or body, and this could cause them to be classed as drugs. Drugs and related substances were used in both the Old and New worlds before Columbus and became objects of the American exchange.

Tobacco is a plant native to America, and there were several types at the time of Columbus's voyage. Domesticated forms were grown in northern South America (where it probably was first domesticated), Central America, Mexico, and southern parts of North America; wild forms grew almost everywhere. The wild forms usually produced a more marked psychoactive effect.

Tobacco was almost always used ceremonially among Native Americans. It most commonly was

FIGURE 25.7 ***English Tobacco Smoking.*** *This illustration from a 1641 London broadside shows two young dandies engaging in that new practice from the Americas, smoking tobacco. The broadside author considered this behavior socially and morally degrading, calling smokers "children of spirituall fornication." Nonetheless, the habit spread throughout England and other European countries during the seventeenth and later centuries.* The New York Public Library, Arents Tobacco Collection.

smoked, either as cigars (Caribbean and adjacent areas) or in pipes (everywhere else), particularly during religious rituals and at the sealing of intertribal agreements; sometimes it was smoked at a greeting ritual for visitors. In South America, it also was used as snuff and as a component of enemas, both of which were part of religious rituals.

Europeans, particularly the English, encountered tobacco through greeting rituals, which were prominent among the tribes of eastern North America. The tobaccos were strong, much stronger than those in use today, and the English seemed attracted to the euphoria and other psychological effects produced. By the late sixteenth century, pipe smoking was becoming popular among the English elite, and the elite of other European countries followed shortly. The technology of tobacco use by Europeans was adopted from Americans, but its purpose was radically different: The ritual use in America was replaced with recreational use in Europe.

Alcoholic beverages were known in the Americas, though they were rare. The Iroquois of northeastern North America made a light mead from maple sap; the O'odham[6] of the American Southwest fermented a wine from the juice of cactus fruit; the Aztecs made a wine from a cactus relative; and various peoples in South America made beers from corn and other starchy plants. With the exceptions of a few places in South America and Mexico, however, alcohol consumption was highly seasonal; wherever alcohol was drunk in the pre-Columbian Americas, its use was limited and highly regulated by ritual.

Europeans, in contrast, were very heavy consumers of alcohol. By the thirteenth century, they had mastered the technique of distillation, transforming wine or beer with low alcohol content into liquor with high alcohol content. They brought liquors with them to the Americas.

The introduction of liquors through the American exchange was disastrous for American Indians. Most had little or no experience with alcohol, and the few that had any experience had never encountered the potency of liquors. Without any traditional cultural rules to regulate the recreational use of liquor, American Indians usually learned its use from traders, who provided it free in order to secure more favorable terms in their transactions; needless to say, the traders encouraged overindulgence. Liquor became the scourge of many Indian communities, often leading to violence or mishap, a problem that remains widespread even today.

Coca is a leafy shrub that grows high in the Andes Mountains of South America. When its leaves are mixed with powdered lime, it releases an alkaloid that induces increased stamina, a feeling of well-being, and a distorted sense of time; it also is highly addictive. The exploitative potential of this combination was recognized by the Incas, the last Andean society before the Spanish conquest, and they used it to keep miners working for long hours of arduous labor. Because miners usually could not acquire coca through any other source, they were compelled to continue working in the government-operated mines. The conquering Spanish immediately recognized the power of this substance to control miners and continued supplying it.

Coca in its raw form never became popular among Europeans. Once it was refined and concentrated into a powerful narcotic, cocaine, in the 1870s, however, it became a popular drug in Europe and North America in the latter part of the nineteenth century. For several years it was believed to have only beneficial effects, particularly for the eyes. (This is why Sir Arthur Conan Doyle described Sherlock Holmes as a cocaine user and why, for a brief while, it was a component of Coca-Cola.) By the early years of the twentieth century, however, its role in heart attacks, strokes, schizophrenia, and brain damage was becoming recognized, and it no longer was considered benign.

The health dangers of tobacco, alcohol, and coca generally were not recognized in the early years of their adoption through the American exchange. Their perceived virtues, however, were readily appreciated by receiving peoples, and these substances have been incorporated into their cultures in varying degrees.

The Horse

The horse was imported to the Americas as the animal of choice for transportation, and herds of horses were brought to the Americas as early as the 1520s, particularly by the Spanish. Invariably, horses strayed, finding conditions to their liking

[6] **O'odham:** OH oh dahm

IN THEIR OWN WORDS

A Canadian Trading Frolic

In 1791, John Long published an account of his lengthy service as a fur trader in eastern Canada. Between 1768 and 1786, he had traded among various Indian tribes, but he had run short of funds and had needed to borrow money in order to return to England. His book probably was designed to help him pay off that debt. Long presents himself as an enlightened trader who was more concerned with the welfare of the Indians with whom he traded than were most of his fellows.

The excerpt presented here exemplifies several aspects of the American exchange, including technology and alcohol. Long describes this as a typical incident of trading in 1777, when a group of Ojibway Indians came to his camp to trade furs. The excerpt begins with a speech by Keskoneek, the Ojibway leader:

> "It is true, Father, I and my young men are happy to see you:—as the great Master of Life has sent a trader to take pity on us Savages,[a] we shall use our best endeavors to hunt and bring you wherewithal to satisfy you in furs, skins, and animal food."
>
> This speech was in fact intended to induce me to make them further presents; I indulged them in their expectation, by giving them two kegs of rum of eight gallons each, lowered with a small proportion of water, according to the usual custom adopted by all traders,[b] five carrots of tobacco,[c] fifty scalping knives,[d] gun-flints, powder, shot, ball, &c.[e] To the women I gave beads, trinkets, &c. and to eight chiefs who were in the band, each a Northwest gun, a calico shirt, a scalping knife of the best sort, and an additional quantity of ammunition. These were received with a full yo-hah, or demonstration of joy.
>
> The women, who are on all occasions slaves to their husbands, were ordered to make up bark huts, which they completed in about an hour, and everything was got in order for merriment. The rum being taken from my house, was carried to their wigwam, and they began to drink. The frolic lasted four days and nights; and notwithstanding all our precaution (securing their guns, knives, and tomahawks) two boys were killed, and six men wounded by three Indian women; one of the chiefs also was murdered, which reduced me to the necessity of giving several articles to bury with him, to complete the usual ceremony of their interment. These frolics are very prejudicial to all parties, and put the trader to a considerable expense, which nevertheless he cannot with safety refuse.

[a]Long also gives the speech in the Ojibway language, and in that version this phrase is rendered as *Nishinnorbay*: Ojibways.

[b]Diluting rum was for economic, not humanitarian, reasons.

[c]This region is too far north to grow tobacco, so it was obtained by trade.

[d]This term referred to any all-purpose knife.

[e]Et cetera.

particularly on the grassy plains of central North America and Patagonia in South America. By the latter part of the seventeenth century in North America and the middle part of the eighteenth century in South America, Native Americans had begun capturing and making use of horses. Particularly on the Great Plains of North America, the coming of the horse led to a revolution in the way of life.

Prior to this time, North American Plains tribes like the Arikara[7] and Pawnee were living a settled existence as farmers. Their sedentary villages had semisubterranean houses with sod roofs, and fields were carved out of the thick-sodded grasslands. These fields were owned by women, who organized their tending and the production of corn, squash, and beans. Bison were hunted seasonally, but this was laborious and only marginally successful on foot. There was little competition for land and only limited warfare.

With the advent of the horse, all this changed. Bison hunting from horseback was so successful that it became a year-round occupation. This, in turn, necessitated shifts in settlement, because the

[7]**Arikara:** uh RIH kah ruh

FIGURE 25.8 ***Plains Indians Hunting Buffalo on Horseback.*** *This detail from a painting by John Innes presents a romantic but also a fundamentally accurate picture of the use of the horse by Plains Indians in the central portions of North America. Introduced by the Spanish, horses permitted hunters to ride abreast of a buffalo herd rather than having to lie in ambush with only a single chance at success. The horse raised the status of men in Plains Indian society, placing more emphasis on the hunt and warfare.* "The Buffalo Hunt," John Innes, Glenbow Collection, Calgary, Canada.

bison shifted their haunts with the seasons, sometimes daily. Permanent sod houses were replaced with portable tepees, conical tents that could be collapsed, rolled up, and packed on a horse in a matter of minutes. Agriculture was abandoned, and the importance of women's economic roles diminished in direct proportion to the increased status of the male hunters. The horse turned these farmers into hunters, raiders, and warriors, as their increased mobility made them able to prey on people as well as on bison.

The popular image of the American Indian wearing a huge feather headdress, mounted on a horse, and chasing bison or fighting the cavalry has been immortalized in frontier art, in Hollywood movies, and even on U.S. coinage. Like most popular images, this image is oversimplified and stereotyped, but it is a reflection of one place and time in American Indian life. The irony is that this image existed only fleetingly and as a result of the introduction of the horse by Europeans.

Phylloxera, Grapes, and the American Exchange

The glory days of the American exchange of plants and animals were before 1700, and probably 90 percent of the important species that were to pass from one hemisphere to the other did so by that date. Nonetheless, the American exchange has continued into modern times. An example is **phylloxera**,[8] an aphid from the Mississippi Valley of North America that subsists by sucking plant juices from roots. It is particularly fond of grapevines, and, when it accidentally was introduced into France in 1863, the results were devastating. Phylloxera spread through the vineyards, killing great numbers of vines. The wine grapes of France (and eventually much of Europe and beyond) were nearly wiped out. Wine production in most of the affected areas dropped by 50 percent or more, raising havoc with the economy of France and, to a lesser extent, those of Italy and Spain.

Non-Europeans may have difficulty imagining the magnitude of the problem. In many regions of France, wine making was the major industry, employing more workers and producing more income than any other. This economic disaster, coupled with huge indemnities incurred by a failed war with Prussia, helped hurl France into a serious economic crisis.

The cure for the pestilence came from America. Because there were grapes native to the same area as phylloxera, agronomists reasoned that they must be genetically resistant to the aphid. They were correct, and when the European grapevines were grafted onto American root stocks, the scourge of phylloxera was controlled. The American exchange contributed the affliction of phylloxera, but it also contributed the cure through North American root stocks.

TECHNOLOGY

Of all the arenas where the American exchange operated, the results are perhaps easiest to see in technology. New tools, materials, and methods of manufacture passed from one hemisphere to the other for a variety of reasons.

Some pieces of European technology were such improvements over traditional American technology that they were adopted readily. Almost everywhere, but especially in North America, for example, American Indians saw the advantages of guns and tried to procure them. Many colonial powers tried to curb the gun trade to Indians, often with limited success, because the traders of a rival colonial power often were happy to trade guns for furs or other commodities. In New England, Indians in praying towns learned how to repair guns and manufacture many parts for them, attaining a measure of self-sufficiency.

In other cases, items were accepted but modified to improve their fit with perceived needs. For example, metalworking technology in native North American traditions before Columbus was limited, and no brass or iron was used; metals were much desired in the centuries that followed. Early trade between the English and Indians in New England included iron knives, iron hatchets, and brass kettles. While some of the kettles made their way into domestic usage as cooking vessels, many were used as fancy grave offerings; even more were cut into triangles and used as arrowheads.

Sometimes Indians adopted items not for their improvement over traditional technology but rather for the prestige associated with them. In colonial Mexico and Peru, European-style clothing bestowed a certain measure of status on the wearer; and the wearing of miscellaneous available scraps of metal armor conferred prestige but little practical advantage to seventeenth- and eighteenth-century Indians of the Great Lakes region of North America.

The process of adopting European technology was selective, and some items that might appear at first to have been advantageous were rejected. Wheeled vehicles in the Peruvian Andes, for example, were of little use, because the slopes were too steep to permit their safe or efficient use. European-style looms made little headway in Mexican home weaving, because a longstanding tradition of using backstrap looms was deeply engrained in the value system. And European grinding mills took centuries to supplant the grinding stones of Mexican households, because the cornmeal made in the mills was perceived as not tasting as good as that made by hand with a grinding stone.

Adoptions of indigenous technology by Europeans were fewer and even more selective. By and large, European technology was better suited for most colonial activities, because the colonists and most of their activities were transplants from Europe. The extensive and straight-rowed wheat fields of the Europeans were most efficiently tilled with an ox-drawn plow, not with the Indian-style

[8] **phylloxera:** fih LOK seh ruh

FIGURE 25.9 *Chief Tuko-See Mathla. Though this portrait of a leader of Florida's Seminole tribe was painted in the first half of the nineteenth century, it shows how thoroughly European technology and style had penetrated into Native American life by the eighteenth century. Tuko-See carries a rifle and wears a cast-metal medallion and gorget (a piece of armor) around his neck; his clothing is made mostly of woven European fabrics; his boots are even fastened with European laces and grommets.* National Museum of American Art, Smithsonian Institution.

FIGURE 25.10 *Louis, a Rocky Mountain Trapper. This painting depicts a French trapper of the early nineteenth century. Just as Native Americans had adopted European styles and technologies by the eighteenth century, Europeans on the American frontier had made similar adoptions from Native Americans. This trapper, for example, wears leather clothing, moccasins, and a native-style necklace. On the basis of material culture, it would be difficult to differentiate between this European and the Native American.* Buffalo Bill Historical Center, Cody, Wyoming. Gift of the Coe Foundation.

hoe, which was more effective with smaller, irregularly planted fields. As the conquerors, Europeans typically disdained the Indians; as discussed in Chapter 24, they felt themselves inherently superior. Consequently, Europeans and European Americans saw themselves as gaining no prestige (or other advantage) from adopting items perceived as native symbols. Indeed, wearing Indian-style hair or tattoos on the eighteenth-century American frontier usually was condemned as rustic and unsophisticated.

The primary area of adopting native technology was in frontier survival equipment. Snowshoes, fish traps, buckskin clothing, snow goggles—these items were the sort that Europeans adopted most frequently from Native Americans. This makes sense, of course, because people on the frontier, regardless of race or ethnicity, were living similar lives and meeting similar challenges. Many elements of the technology developed by American Indians over the centuries to meet those challenges were very effective and easily procured or produced by European colonists on the frontier. Any loss in prestige in the eyes of urbanites far from the frontier was a small price to pay for the increased ability to survive.

IDEOLOGIES

Diseases, plants and animals, and technology are relatively easy to recognize in the American exchange, because they have physical dimensions that can be seen, measured, and compared. Ideologies, in contrast, are difficult to trace. The same idea could have been developed independently in different places, and its presence in both Europe and the Americas does not necessarily mean that it passed from one place to the other. Further, ideas often are modified as they are transmitted from one people to another, making them difficult to recognize as coming from the same source. No doubt there are hundreds of cases of ideological exchange that remain unrecognized, but we shall focus on two examples where exchange is well documented.

Christianity

The preeminent European ideology passing to the Americas was Christianity. All of the countries with American colonies were Christian, and all imposed their creeds onto their American Indian subjects to greater or lesser extents. Missionaries are the most obvious agent of transmitting Christianity, but lay colonists also often felt an obligation to impress upon Indians the value of Christianity. The Indians, in turn, often felt that becoming Christian was a good course of action. Many Aztecs, for example, believed that the Spanish conquest occurred only because the Spanish god was stronger than the Aztec gods; consequently, it was only sensible to shift one's allegiance to the new, more powerful deity. In New England, Pequot[9] Indians sometimes converted to Christianity to gain access to the technological training available in the praying towns. In many places, becoming a Christian conferred legal rights or prestige that made conversion desirable. The potency of these factors working together is evidenced by the predominance of Christianity among Native Americans today, especially in Latin America.

But the type of Christianity adopted in the New World was often unlike that practiced in Europe. Maya Indians of eastern Mexico, for example, went to church on Sunday and worshiped the Christian god, but they continued making offerings and conducting rituals to their traditional gods and goddesses. The cross was interpreted as both the Christian symbol of Jesus' crucifixion and the Mayan symbol of the tree of life. Among the O'odham of Arizona, Catholic churches incorporated personal altars, where corn, pollen, and other traditionally sacred objects were placed in a hybrid religion that sprang from both Christian and traditional worship. Many American Indian groups modified the version of Christianity they adopted, adapting it to accommodate existing beliefs.

Sometimes, particularly in institutions operating with slave labor, African religions also blended with Native American religions and Christianity. These non-Christian influences were guarded against by most Europeans, but they persisted in folk religion, especially in the Caribbean, parts of the American South, and Brazil. The voodoo worship of Haiti, for example, intertwines African elements (like ecstatic trance and snake ritual) with Christian elements (like cross symbolism and the role of saints) and Caribbean Indian elements (like symbolic cannibalism and the use of triangular stones).

The Idea of Confederation

In general, we would expect the conquerors to adopt few ideas from the conquered, certainly fewer than passed in the opposite direction. Nonetheless, there is a good argument that the idea of confederation and a form of governmental structure were adopted by European Americans

[9] **Pequot:** PEE kwoht

from the Iroquois Indians of New York through the agency of Benjamin Franklin.

Benjamin Franklin, the colonial writer, politician, and scientist from Pennsylvania, was one of the earliest advocates of autonomy for the English colonies in North America. In 1754, the Albany Congress, a gathering of representatives from the colonies of British North America, met with an agenda of two items: approving a treaty with the Six Nations of the Iroquois and considering Franklin's plan for a central government over seven of the colonies. Franklin was present at the Albany Congress and used his considerable powers of personal persuasion to see his plan tentatively approved by it.

The Albany Plan of Union, as it came to be known, proposed joint government by a president-general, to be appointed for the colonies by the crown, and a Grand Council. The Grand Council was to be composed of representatives of each colony, to be elected by their respective assemblies. The central government was to have been charged with the basic duties of governing, including taxing, raising armies, waging war, and making peace. If it had been implemented, it would have been the first intercolonial government. The plan required approval by the assembly for each colony involved, and these bodies rejected it unanimously.

While Franklin never stated so, many historians suspect that the Albany Plan of Union was based on the League of the Iroquois. The League of the Iroquois was a confederacy-type government of six Indian tribes and had successfully bound them together since around 1300. Clearly, Franklin was familiar with the League, because this was the government with whom the treaty under consideration at the Albany Congress had been negotiated.

At the heart of both the League of the Iroquois and the Albany Plan of Union was the concept of **confederation**—a permanent union of equal states, cooperating for their common welfare—a concept alien to European political thought of the era. Many details of Franklin's proposed confederation were remarkably similar to the details of the League of the Iroquois.

The Albany Plan of Union, for example, stipulated that voting in the Grand Council was to be accomplished by first polling the members of a delegation, deciding the vote for that delegation, then having a single vote for each colony, a system absolutely parallel to that of the League. The selection of delegates was to be accomplished in a manner parallel to that of the League, and the duties of the Grand Council were to have been the same as those for their counterpart in the League. Even the name of the ruling body was the same as that of the League.

Franklin never revealed his inspiration for the Albany Plan of Union. He did, however, in 1751 exhort his colleagues to accept some form of union by noting that the English colonies should be able to achieve this if "Six Nations of ignorant savages should be capable of forming a scheme for such a union and be able to execute it in such a manner, as it has subsisted for ages and appears insoluble." Franklin's reference to "ignorant savages" attests to the tenor of the day and gives a potent indication as to why he might have chosen not to reveal any Iroquois inspiration for his plan.

While the Albany Plan of Union never went into effect, it had a profound effect on the course of government in America, and indirectly the world. It was the first proposal for a confederation of English colonies, and many of its principles survived to become part of the Articles of Confederation, the basis of the first government of the independent United States; many of these ideas, in turn, were incorporated into the U.S. Constitution, which still structures the government of the United States. There can be little doubt that the spirit of the League of the Iroquois has extended beyond the Six Nations to help shape the American political system and from there to have major impact around the world.

WHO BENEFITED FROM THE AMERICAN EXCHANGE?

But for the debilitating effects of diseases, it is conceivable that both hemispheres might have profited from the American exchange. On the face of it, the exchange of desirable foodstuffs could only increase the food supply, the exchange of technology would facilitate labor and production, and the exchange of ideas necessarily enriched both hemispheres.

AMERICAS

Period	Year	Event
	1000	Leif Ericson's colony of Vinland, 1002–1004
	1100	
	1200	
	1300	
	1400	Columbus opens the American exchange, 1492
Greatest virulence of introduced diseases, c. 1500–c. 1650; Greatest exchange of foodstuffs, c. 1500–c. 1700; Horses introduced into the Americas, c. 1520–c. 1710	1500	Potatoes carried to Spain, 1536
		Tobacco use established in England, c. 1580
	1600	Merrimack Valley epidemic, 1616–1617
	1700	

The devastation of the Americas by epidemics, however, outweighed any advantage that otherwise would have accrued to Native Americans through the American exchange. While there can be no way to know for sure, many scholars believe that the European conquest of the Americas never would have occurred if disease had not reduced populations and severely dislocated cultures there, paving the way. At the very least, Native American societies would have been better able to resist European incursions, resulting in very different events and consequences.

As events transpired, however, the primary benefits of the American exchange to Native Americans were new forms of technology and new foods. Demographic catastrophe, cultural calamity, and conquest far outweighed these benefits from the point of view of Native Americans. The Old World, on the other hand, particularly Europe, received tremendous benefits from the exchange, placing it in a position to embark on political and economic domination of the world.

SUMMARY

1. The American exchange was the transmission of diseases, plants and animals, technology, and ideology between the Old World and the Americas in the period after the European voyages of discovery.

2. While other pre-Columbian contacts between the Old World and the Americas may have occurred, only the existence of the Norse colony of Vinland is well documented. Even at Vinland the colonists had little effect on local Native American culture.

3. The type of contact between Europeans and American Indians had profound effects on the nature of the American exchange. Factors that most encouraged exchange were intense contact, European intent to modify the local cultures, and subjugation of the local population.

4. Old World diseases devastated American Indians, who had little biological immunity to them, paving the way for the European conquest of the Americas. For biological reasons, there were few American diseases that could afflict Old World peoples.

5. Potatoes and corn were the most important crops transferred from the Americas to the Old World. Particularly in Europe, they were the basis for great population growth that supplied the Americas with colonists. Other American crops like chilis became important for the tastes they imparted to cuisines around the world.

6. Most of the Old World crops transferred to the Americas were either to satisfy the tastes of European colonists or to support ranches and plantations for profit.

7. Tobacco was used in the Americas as a ritual drug, but Europeans adopted it for recreational use. Alcoholic beverages from Europe were widely sought by Native Americans, though alcohol abuse brought many problems. The Spanish continued the Inca practice of using coca to stimulate and pacify Andean miners; eventually a cocaine traffic with Europe and North America developed in South America.

8. The horse transformed the lifeways of the Indians of North America's plains. Formerly sedentary agriculturalists with a female focus to their societies, they adopted a male focus, becoming mobile bison hunters and raiders.

9. American Indians adopted various types of Old World technology for a variety of reasons, including practical advantage and acquiring prestige. European adoption of American technology was focused primarily on frontier survival tools.

10. The primary ideology to be transferred from the Old World to the Americas was Christianity. The primary transfer in the opposite direction probably was the notion of confederacy, which passed from Native Americans to European colonists in North America.

SUGGESTED READINGS

Crosby, Alfred W., Jr. *The Columbian Exchange: Biological and Cultural Consequences of 1492*. Westport, Conn.: Greenwood Press, 1972. The pioneering and classic discussion of the American exchange, still largely up to date.

———. *Ecological Imperialism: The Biological Expansion of Europe, 900–1900*. Cambridge, Eng.: Cambridge University Press, 1986. Discussion of the movements of plants and animals between Europe and colonial areas.

Ingstad, Anne Stine. *The Discovery of a Norse Settlement in America*. Oslo, Norway: Universitetsforlaget, 1977. The report of archaeological excavation and analysis at L'Anse aux Meadows, containing a wealth of detailed information and informative photographs.

Tooker, Elisabeth. "The United States Constitution and the Iroquois League." *Ethnohistory* 35 (1988): 304–36. The original and basic argument that the U.S. Constitution was inspired by the League of the Iroquois.

Viola, Herman J., and Carolyn Margolis, eds. *Seeds of Change*. Washington, D.C.: Smithsonian Institution Press, 1991. A collection of diverse essays on crops and associated economic systems transmitted through the American exchange.

Wissler, Clark. "The Influence of the Horse in the Development of the Plains Culture." *American Anthropologist* 16 (1914): 1–25. Though nearing its centennial, this remains the classic statement. Updates, primarily archaeological, are presented in an article in Viola and Margolis, cited above.

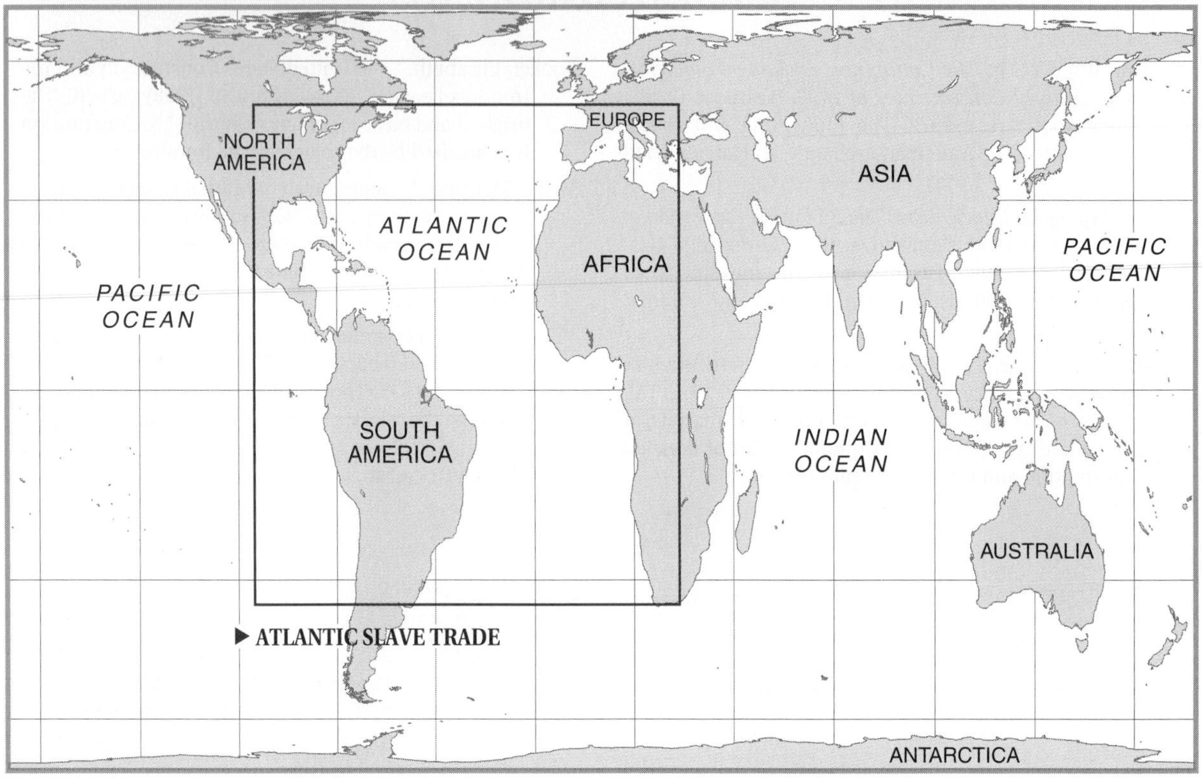

▶ **ATLANTIC SLAVE TRADE**

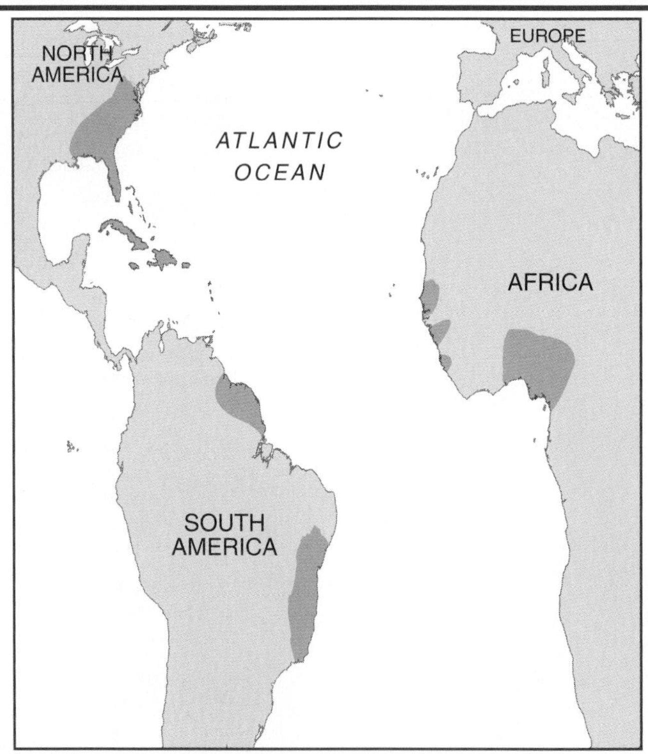

▶ **ATLANTIC SLAVE TRADE**

CHAPTER 26

The African Slave Trade

1441–1815

By a conservative estimate, nearly 30 million Africans were captured, enslaved, and forcibly removed to foreign lands over the course of the several centuries during which the African slave trade was active. Large numbers are notoriously difficult to grasp, so a comparison may bring this figure into focus. This number is approximately the combined population of the modern cities of New York, Los Angeles, Boston, Philadelphia, Toronto, Montréal, Detroit, Miami, Washington, Chicago, Dallas, Denver, San Francisco, and Seattle. Standing shoulder to shoulder, 30 million people would span a bit over 11,000 miles, approximately the distance from Los Angeles to New York, across the Atlantic Ocean to London, and across Eurasia into central Siberia.

Slavery is defined simply as the ownership and control of other people, and it has been a common institution around the world. Indeed, by 1400 it was practiced on all the inhabited continents of the world except Australia, and its various forms are discussed in the "Issue" section for this part. The slave trade in Africa, however, was far more extensive than that anywhere else, and its significance reached around the globe.

Sub-Saharan Africa (the part of the continent south of the Sahara) was a source for slaves at least as early as 1500 B.C., though the numbers of slaves at that date were few. By A.D. 700, two corridors of slave trading had become significant. The **trans-Sahara slave trade** was that which brought slaves from sub-Saharan Africa to the Arab Berbers of

North Africa. From North Africa some were distributed throughout the Mediterranean and to the Byzantine Empire. This trade was plied with caravans, usually carrying about 500 slaves, crossing from oasis to oasis over the Sahara. Most of the slaves were women, described as "well educated"; most scholars interpret this phrase to mean that they were trained and skilled in traditional women's tasks, such as cooking, conversation, and companionship. The total number of slaves carried across the Sahara has recently been estimated at about 8 million people.

The other major locale for the early African slave trade was coastal East Africa. The **Indian Ocean slave trade** was that which passed through the coastal cities and northward, particularly to the sugar plantations of Southwest Asia. The first leg of the Indian Ocean slave trade was carried out primarily by Swahili traders, local Africans who procured slaves from the inland tribes and brought them to East African coastal cities, where they were sold to Arab and other maritime traders. The scale of this facet of the slave trade is not fully known. Slaves in this trade were carried to various Asian ports, but the sugar plantations of Southwest Asia were their most common destination, especially in the years 500 to 900.

The slave trade across the Sahara and the Indian Ocean was dwarfed by the development of a third corridor in the years following 1441. The **Atlantic slave trade** was that which carried slaves from Africa to Europe and the Americas via vessels sailing the Atlantic Ocean. It centered on the West African coast and was operated primarily by Europeans and their descendants in the Americas. It soon marked itself as a departure from all other forms of the slave trade in its magnitude, the degree of its brutality, and the significance of its consequences. This aspect of the African slave trade is the primary focus of this chapter.

THE NATURE OF SLAVERY BEFORE THE ATLANTIC SLAVE TRADE

Both Africans and Europeans held slaves before 1441, the onset of the Atlantic slave trade, although the numbers enslaved were far smaller than after that date. In this earlier period, there were remarkable similarities in the ways slaves were perceived, treated, and procured in both Africa and Europe.

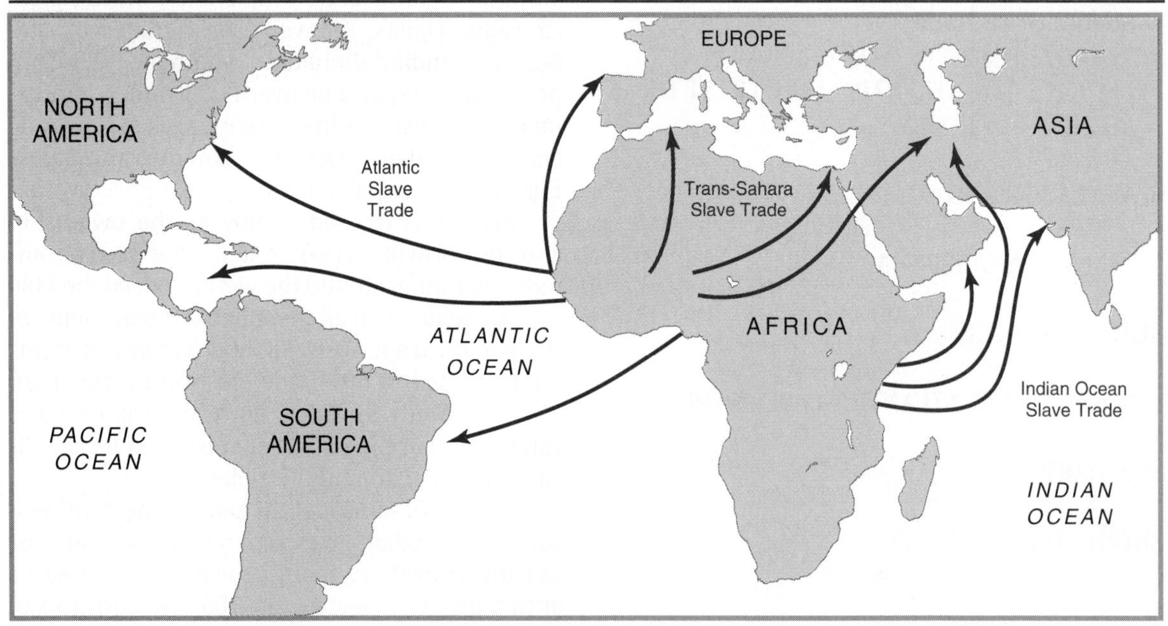

MAP 26.1 ***Corridors of the African Slave Trade.*** *The trans-Sahara and Indian Ocean slave trades shipped millions of Africans into foreign slavery, but both were dwarfed in magnitude by the Atlantic slave trade.*

In both places, slaves were viewed as persons whose labor was owed to their owner, but not as inanimate objects. In a fit of rage, the owner of a table could smash the table with an axe; in contrast, the enraged owner of a slave had no right to attack that slave with an axe. In either Africa or Europe, of course, a slave owner was permitted to punish slaves for wrongdoing, but the punishment was expected to be in keeping with the transgression. (The right to punish, by the way, also was accorded male heads of households over wives, children, and hired servants.) This conception of slaves as human beings with personal rights was in keeping with general conceptions of society in late medieval Europe and contemporary Africa. Both followed a hierarchic model, under which each person held obligations to social superiors, and slavery fit into this scheme well, as simply an additional tier at the bottom.

As persons, slaves could expect that their individual skills, talents, and hard work could improve their lot in life. By applying their talents, slaves could achieve greater status, better housing, more wealth, and even fame. Both in Europe and Africa, many successful slaves accumulated considerable power, sometimes owning slaves themselves. In many cases, slaves were encouraged to marry into their owners' families; a successful slave sometimes was adopted into the family, assuming the same rights as a son or daughter of the owner. **Manumission** (the freeing of a slave) was fairly common, and slaves could gain freedom through a variety of mechanisms, including a grant from the owner and purchase of their freedom with accumulated wealth.

In theory, slaves in both Africa and Europe before 1441 were to come from the ranks of those outside the mainstream of one's own society. Slaves in Africa were supposed to come from kingdoms other than one's own, and Muslims were forbidden by the laws of Islam to enslave other Muslims; in practice, these rules, though usually followed, sometimes were ignored in times of slave shortages. In Europe, slaves were supposed to come from the ranks of Jews, Muslims, or other non-Christians; in practice, however, many eastern European Christians served as slaves in western Europe, contributing their generic ethnic designation ("Slav") as the root for the modern word "slave." Several thirteenth-century papal directives decried the enslavement of white, Christian Europeans, although the practice seems to have been on the wane by the time those decrees were made.

THE BEGINNINGS OF THE ATLANTIC SLAVE TRADE

In 1434, a small technical advance in sailing technology changed the world. In that year, the Portuguese adopted the **lateen sail**, a sail on a slanted mast, which was already in use in the eastern Mediterranean. They modified it for ocean travel,

FIGURE 26.1 ***Lateen Sails in Seville Harbor.*** *The lateen sail revolutionized sailing between Europe and sub-Saharan Africa. In this sixteenth-century painting of the harbor in Seville, Spain, the lateen sails are furled. The yard for a lateen sail, visible on the boat in the center of the harbor channel, crosses the mast diagonally.*
Museo de America, Madrid/MAS Barcelona.

and for the first time European seafarers could sail almost against the wind. Prior to this time, Europeans had no desire to sail down the west coast of Africa, knowing that incessant winds blowing toward the south made a return trip impossible. The lateen sail opened coastal West Africa to European visitors.

Antam Gonçalvez,[1] the young commander of a vessel sailing for Prince Henry of Portugal, set out for West Africa in 1441, charged with collecting a cargo of the oil and skins of sea lions. After discharging his duty, Gonçalvez wanted to curry further favor with his patron, so he decided to capture some natives of the place to bring back to Portugal. He managed to capture a man and a woman, and he later threw in with another Portuguese captain to capture ten more Africans. These twelve people became the first spoils of the Atlantic slave trade.

Many of his advisors had doubted the wisdom of Prince Henry's sailing adventures. When the first consignment of African slaves arrived, however, most changed their minds; the second cargo of 29 slaves in 1443 won over the few doubters. One contemporary raved over a commerce where so many slaves could be "captured in so short a time and at so little trouble," and Portugal threw itself into the slave trade.

At first, Portuguese slavers were raiders, mounting military expeditions to capture Africans. By the early 1450s, however, this strategy was giving way to trading with local Africans. At least one earlier expedition had turned into a small war with a profit of only 165 slaves, and it became apparent that a more economical way of procuring slaves was needed. In the decades that followed, local Africans became the suppliers for the Portuguese slave trade.

From these modest beginnings, the Atlantic slave trade swelled rapidly. The first decade of Portuguese slave raiding and trading probably saw no more than a few hundred slaves sent to Portugal, and only about 35,000 slaves are estimated to have been brought to Portugal in the entire period before 1500. This number, great as it is in human terms, is merely a trickle compared with the millions of slaves who were exported from Africa in the centuries to follow.

[1]**Antam Gonçalvez:** AHN tahm gohn SAHL behs

EUROPE TRANSFORMS THE SLAVE TRADE

Within less than a century of its inception, the Atlantic slave trade evolved into something never before seen. As its scope escalated massively, attitudes toward slaves were transformed, and treatment degenerated. Fueled by economic greed, the slave trade became a lucrative business in which human suffering was little considered as a factor in the monetary equation. As might be expected, such a financially rewarding trade fostered competition among the European powers.

The Changing Nature of the Slave Trade

Shortly after 1500, the slave trade picked up in volume and was transformed. Current historical scholarship can document that at least 14 million slaves were exported from Africa by the Atlantic slave trade in the three centuries following that date. This estimate is based on numbers calculated from ship inventories, receipts, and similar documents, so it serves merely as a minimum estimate. The task of locating and examining these documents is huge and will require many more years to complete, and even then there will be gaps where records have been lost or destroyed. Consequently, the most conservative scholars believe that future research will push the number to at least 20 million; less conservative estimates range upward to

TABLE 26.1

Documented Destinations of Slaves in the Atlantic Slave Trade, All Periods

Receiving Slaves	*Number of Slaves*
Europe	250,000
North America	750,000
South and Central America	6,000,000
Caribbean Islands	7,000,000
Total	14,000,000

Note that these figures underestimate the volume of the trade as a whole, because they are based on arrivals at their destinations, and significant numbers of slaves died in transit. In addition, not all documents have survived or been located by historians.

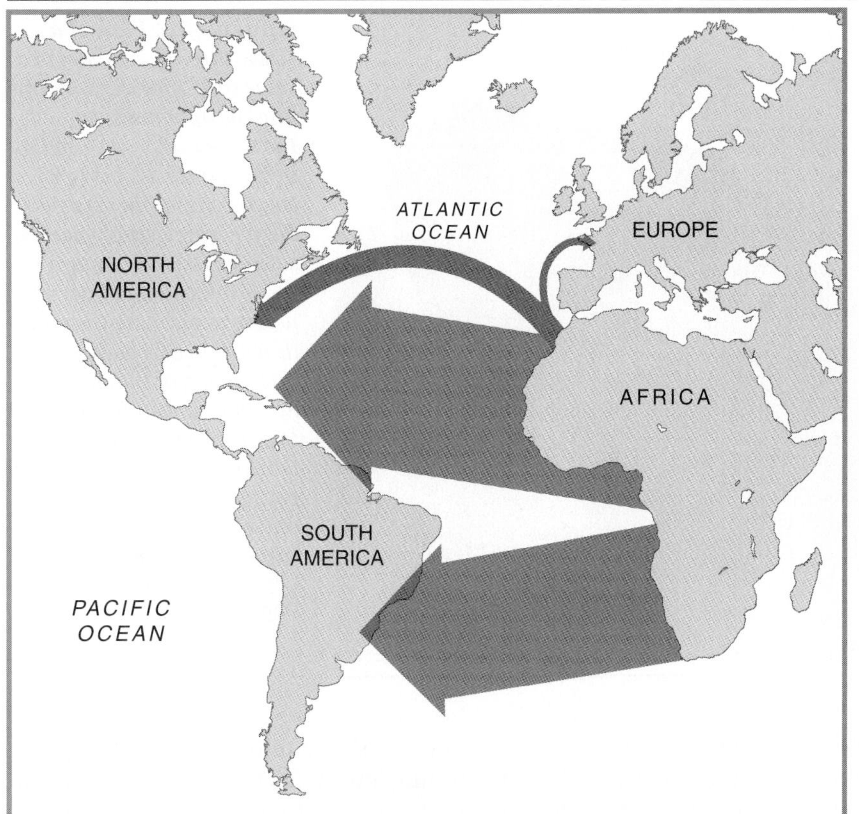

MAP 26.2 ***Slave Destinations in the Atlantic Slave Trade.*** *The widths of the various arrows indicate the relative volume of the trade. Tropical America was by far the greatest consumer, partly because of the short life expectancy of slaves there.*

40 million slaves or even more. No matter which figure is accurate, the number of slaves traded is staggering, amounting to an average of somewhere between six and twelve persons per hour, day and night, every day of every year.

A look at the destinations of these slaves helps explain this meteoric intensification of the slave trade. Historians disagree about details of the numbers of slaves traded, but we do have reasonable estimates of slave imports to various parts of the world (see Table 26.1). Clearly, slaves were being sent predominantly to the Americas. Less than 1.8 percent of all African slaves went to Europe (principally Portugal), and the vast majority went to South America, Central America, and the Caribbean; smaller but still significant numbers of slaves were sent to the southern parts of North America. Colonies in these places focused on agricultural plantations and were dependent on large numbers of slaves for labor; poor health conditions often resulted in early deaths for these slaves; their places had to be taken by more slaves brought in through the slave trade. These colonies created the demand that transformed the African slave trade into the massive and brutal commerce it became.

But the European slavers had accomplices among the Africans. Coastal West African kingdoms had traded in slaves with other Africans for some time, and they were happy to exchange captives for coveted European goods. Most of the coastal states that had access to Europeans actively engaged in the slave trade; Benin and Ife were especially active. Usually Africans from these kingdoms would conduct raids on their neighbors, particularly in the savannas, to procure slaves for trade, but sometimes Africans and Europeans conducted joint ventures. In 1765, for example, an English slaver named Isaac Parker cooperated with slavers from Efik[2] (a city of the Benin kingdom) in

[2]**Efik:** AYF eek

FIGURE 26.2 ***Plan of a Slave Ship.*** *This model of a slave ship, produced in England by opponents of the slave trade, was used to demonstrate the horrific conditions on these vessels. People were densely packed side by side; the amount of space allocated per person was scarcely more than the dimension of a body at rest. The tossing of the ship, foul air, and unfamiliar food led to seasickness and diarrhea, which made the two-month voyage to the Americas an ordeal that many failed to survive.* Kingston-upon-Hull City Council, Leisure Services Department.

an expedition inland. They hid in bushes near roads and paths near villages and captured "every one they could see." The African traders grew wealthy as the result of this trade, gaining large quantities of otherwise unobtainable European goods. In fact, the rise of Benin and Ife as prominent states can be traced in part to the wealth they gained from trading slaves to the Portuguese.

After the trauma of capture, the next trial for a slave was the **Middle Passage**, the sea voyage between Africa and the Americas. (The term, which derives from the triangular trade of the English, discussed in Chapter 24, is applied because this was the middle leg of the three-part loop that began and ended in England.) Typically, slaves were packed below the decks of the ships, often so closely that it was impossible to shift position during the voyage of several weeks. While women and children usually were spared, men typically were shackled to one another at the wrists or ankles. During this passage, many slaves died of disease, unsanitary conditions, dehydration, and cruel treatment, all of which were compounded by depression, called "melancholy" by the slavers.

In some cases, slave-ship captains committed atrocities with little likelihood of punishment. One of the most infamous of these cases took place in 1781, when Luke Collingwood, a British captain, was carrying 400 slaves to Jamaica. Realizing that he was running low on fresh water and might suffer a high rate of loss of his cargo, he schemed to transfer the loss to his insurance company. If the slaves died of thirst, the loss would be to the slavers, but if they died as a result of "the perils of the seas," the loss would be covered by insurance. Accordingly, he bound the hands of 132 of the sickest and weakest slaves behind their backs and threw them into the ocean, where they drowned. The insurance company initially refused to pay a settlement, but they were forced to do so when the British courts upheld the slave traders' claim.

Historians currently are debating the degree to which such atrocities occurred, and some historians feel that past conceptions of the Middle Passage have been influenced unduly by the political broadsides of abolitionists, whose interests were best served by publicizing the most extreme and horrific conditions. All historians agree, however, that death tolls were high and conditions were bad during the Middle Passage—the only question is how bad. Estimates for slave mortality during the Middle Passage vary from around 5 to 15 percent; for a ship carrying 400 slaves, between 20 and 60 would be likely to die during the passage. Clearly, slave traders in this period viewed their victims like fruit: merely a perishable commodity whose shipment inevitably produced losses.

It was in the early years of the 1500s that the conception of slaves changed among Europeans. Perhaps 1510 should be considered the watershed year, because this was the first time slaves were shipped to the Americas *for general sale.* Prior to this date, slaves were shipped to a particular destination and a particular owner who had ordered them for an expressed purpose, such as mining or performing domestic duties or cutting sugarcane. From this date forward, however, slaves usually were shipped to auctioneers, who resold them to the highest bidder, as they would horses or bricks. This change signaled the shift to **chattel slavery**, the system whereby a slave was considered to have no more value than any other object and a slave's humanity and personal rights were denied.

Of course, there was great variation in how slave owners treated their slaves. Both documentary and archaeological evidence indicates that some slave owners were compassionate and others

IN THEIR OWN WORDS

In the Hold of a Slave Ship

Olaudah Equiano[a] was born in 1745, the son of a chief in the remote Ibo[b] region of the Benin kingdom, in what now is Nigeria. He had little knowledge of the wider world in 1755, when he was captured by Benin slavers who sold him to English slave traders on the coast. After years of servitude in Barbados, he purchased his freedom and devoted himself to the abolitionist cause. He published *The Interesting Narrative of the Life of Olaudah Equiano*, an account of his travels, in 1789, and it became a bestseller. These selections from that work describe the start of Equiano's terrifying passage to the Caribbean.

> Quite overpowered with horror and anguish, I fell motionless on the deck and fainted. When I recovered a little I found some black people about me. . . . They talked to me in order to cheer me, but all in vain. I asked them if we were not to be eaten by those white men with horrible looks, red faces, and loose hair. They told me I was not. . . . I was soon put under the decks, and there I received such a salutation in my nostrils as I had never experienced in my life; so that with the loathsomeness of the stench and crying together, I became so sick and low that I was not able to eat, nor had I the least desire to taste anything. I now wished for the last friend, death, to relieve me; but soon, to my grief, two of the white men offered me eatables, and on my refusing to eat, one of them held me fast by the hands and laid me across I think the windlass, and tied my feet while the other flogged me severely. I had never experienced anything of this kind before. . . . I would have jumped over the side, but I could not; and besides, the crew used to watch us very closely who were not chained down to the decks, lest we should leap into the water; and I have seen some of these poor African prisoners most severely cut for attempting to do so, and hourly whipped for not eating. . . . I had never seen among my people such instances of brutal cruelty, and this not only shown towards us blacks but also to some of the whites themselves. . . . The stench of the hold while we were on the coast was so intolerably loathsome that it was dangerous to remain there for any time, and some of us had been permitted to stay on the deck for the fresh air; but now that the whole ship's cargo were confined together, it became absolutely pestilential. The closeness of the place and the heat of the climate, added to the number in the ship, which was so crowded that each had scarcely room to turn himself, almost suffocated us. This produced copious perspirations, so that the air soon became unfit for respiration from a variety of loathsome smells, and brought on a sickness among the slaves, of which many died, thus falling victim to the improvident avarice, as I may call it, of their purchasers. This wretched situation was again aggravated by the galling of the chains, now become unsupportable, and the filth of the necessary tubs [toilet tubs], into which children often fell and were almost suffocated. The shrieks of the women and the groans of the dying rendered the whole scene of horror almost inconceivable.

[a]**Olaudah Equiano:** oh lah OO day ehk wee AH noh
[b]**Ibo:** EE boh

were ruthless. The high death toll of slaves in much of the Americas, however, suggests that the greater number of slaveowners found that harsh methods served their ends best. In the South American colony of Surinam, for example, between 1676 and 1814 the standing population of slaves remained around 30,000, but this was maintained only by importing 1,500 new slaves each year; to keep the slave population constant, the entire population had to be replaced every twenty years. Clearly, life expectancy working the plantations there was very low. As elsewhere, life spans increased after the eventual abolition of slavery.

The European Scramble for Control of the Atlantic Slave Trade

The providing of slaves to the Americas was a lucrative trade, and many European powers wanted to capitalize on it. In early times, before 1600, the Portuguese had sole control of the trade. Their nautical innovations had made them the first Europeans in West Africa and had given them opportunities to develop the slave trade there, and they were eager to exploit those opportunities. Setting up trading colonies along the West African coast (and, to a lesser extent, the East African coast), Portuguese traders developed strong ties with the local suppliers of slaves. Coupled with Portuguese sailing capabilities, these ties gave Portugal initial control of the Atlantic slave trade.

By the early to mid-1600s, however, the English and Dutch were starting to eclipse the Portuguese. Portuguese sailing technology by this time had spread throughout Europe, and both England and the Netherlands constructed vast commercial networks, simply outcompeting Portugal in the slave trade. By the end of the 1600s, England was the leading slave-trading nation, and the Netherlands was second. France belatedly entered the scramble in 1713 and by the middle 1700s had displaced the Netherlands as the second-largest slave trader. England, however, remained by far the leading slave-trading nation until its abolition of the trade in 1808.

It at first seems surprising that Spain had no great stake in the slave trade, given its huge colonial holdings in the Americas. In truth, though, Spain's colonies imported a bit over one and one-half million slaves, a huge number, but only a fraction of the millions of slaves traded. In part, this resulted from the fact that the economies of the Spanish colonies were attuned more toward ranches than plantations and thus were not particularly well suited to slave labor. Another factor hampering any major active involvement in the slave trade by Spain was its very limited colonial holdings in Africa, from which a slave-trading operation could be based. The Treaty of Tordesillas had defined most of Africa as too far south for Spanish colonization, and Spain's withering military strength was insufficient to permit it to ignore the treaty and seize African territory of its own for such a base.

Because of these factors, Spain purchased its slaves from slave traders of other countries. While the slave trade in Spanish holdings officially was controlled by the Spanish monarch, the actual trade was assigned to foreign traders, usually through a kind of subcontract known as the ***asiento***.[3] The *asiento* permitted a foreign trader to sell slaves in Spanish lands at fixed prices, usually

TO BE SOLD on board the Ship *Bance Iſland*, on tueſday the 6th of *May* next, at *Aſhley-Ferry*; a choice cargo of about 250 fine healthy

NEGROES,

juſt arrived from the Windward & Rice Coaſt. —The utmoſt care has already been taken, and ſhall be continued, to keep them free from the leaſt danger of being infected with the SMALL-POX, no boat having been on board, and all other communication with people from *Charles-Town* prevented.

Auſtin, Laurens, & Appleby.

N. B. Full one Half of the above Negroes have had the SMALL-POX in their own Country.

FIGURE 26.3 ***Slave Auction Advertisement.*** *Bills such as this were posted widely to advertise the auctioning of slaves arriving from Africa. This bill was posted in South Carolina in the late eighteenth century*
British Library.

[3]***asiento:*** ah see EHN toh

Figure 26.4 ***Planting Cane on a Sugar Plantation.*** *Field slaves were worked hard by most plantation owners, and mortality rates were high. In this scene from nineteenth-century Antigua, slaves plant sugarcane that will later be transported to the mill in the background.*
From William Clark, *Ten Views in the Island of Antigua,* 1823, by permission of the British Library.

quite favorable to the trader. The *asiento* became important around 1600, and for the next century and a half slave traders competed hotly for these economic plums. By the middle of the 1700s, Spanish sentiments were coming to favor free trade over the *asiento,* and the *asiento* was officially discontinued in 1789.

EFFECTS OF THE ATLANTIC SLAVE TRADE ON AFRICAN SOCIETIES

In general, coastal African states gained in the short term from the Atlantic slave trade, while interior states lost. Viewed in a broader perspective, however, the African slave trade was a disaster for most of sub-Saharan Africa. West Africa, the primary source of African slaves, was most adversely affected.

The coastal West African states, called "the Guinea states" by the slavers, made great economic profits from the slave trade. The slaves themselves, of course, were an important commodity that brought wealth, but so were the food stores that were sold to slave ships to support slaves and crews during the Middle Passage. The profits from this trade, however, were concentrated among the elite royal and warrior classes, thereby increasing the degree of class stratification. In addition, the enhanced resources of the warriors led to an increased reliance on warfare as a means of dispute settlement.

At the same time, the interior African states of the savanna were devastated. These had been supported by economies geared to commerce in a broad range of goods, carried on both within West Africa and across the Sahara. The commerce that had brought them prosperity was disrupted beyond repair, dynasties were toppled, and political systems broke down, usually to be replaced by governments closely tied to slaving. Droughts are a regular feature of the savanna environment, and the traditional mutual-help networks that moderated their effects were destroyed by the political unrest and economic ruin. The upshot of these changes was that regional dominance shifted from the savanna states to the coastal states.

Another major effect of the Atlantic slave trade was its impact on African demography. No region can have tens of thousands of persons plucked from it annually for centuries and not suffer. To make matters worse, those taken by slavers typically were children or young adults, the members of society who had the greatest productivity ahead of them. Recent studies have concluded that 35 percent of those taken for the Atlantic slave trade were young women, and, because women are the demographic basis for the next generation, the impact of their loss on overall population levels was significant. During the years of the slave trade, sub-Saharan African populations as a whole either declined or remained steady, despite productive new crops introduced through the American exchange, crops that spurred major population growth everywhere else.

As the Atlantic slave trade increased and African governments oriented more to it, the nature of African slavery changed. By the 1700s, slaves in many African states were treated as commodities; as in the European colonies, chattel slavery had developed. At the same time, the proportion of slaves increased dramatically. By the early 1800s, one-half to two-thirds of the people in some African states were slaves.

Islam had entered West Africa by 800, and it had become important in the precolonial trading states of West Africa, particularly among rulers and traders. Its importance continued in the sixteenth and following centuries, however, as a response to the rising tide of slavery, largely for two reasons. First, because Islam forbade the enslavement of Muslims, Africans who embraced Islam could enjoy a certain level of protection from being taken as slaves, at least by fellow Muslims. For this reason alone, many Africans converted to Islam. Second, Islam provided an orientation for governments to turn away from focusing on the slave trade. Islam encouraged civilian governments and mandated moral codes that challenged the leadership of the warrior-elites that were linked so intimately to the slave trade.

It is ironic that the Islamic states of West Africa, despite their discouragement of concentration on the slave trade, included some of the largest slaveholding communities in Africa. While religious leaders urged moderation in slave trading, favoring a balance of trade that included a broad diversity of products, individuals realized that their greatest personal profit often was to be made through slaves.

The immediate and short-term harm to Africa by the Atlantic slave trade is clear. The long-term effects have been equally damaging. Before the Atlantic slave trade, West Africa had a healthy economy based on a combination of resource extraction, manufacturing, and commerce. Political disruptions attending the slave trade destroyed most of the commerce, and local manufacturing was replaced by dependence on European goods traded into Africa. Horses and firearms were particularly sought after, the former as a symbol of warrior status and the latter as a tool for the slave trade. In the end, West Africa reduced its economy to the export of slaves and little else, placing it at an international disadvantage that many scholars see extending into the present.

SLAVE LABOR AND COLONIAL ECONOMIES

Most of the Europeans who conquered the tropical Americas had no expectations that the African slave trade would be so important to the economies of the new colonies. Initially, some envisioned using Europeans for the workforce, either as slaves (Jews and Muslims) or wage laborers. Europeans, however, soon gained a reputation as unable to survive the conditions of labor in the American tropics, and this idea was largely abandoned. Others expected to use the local American Indians as slaves. Indeed, American Indians were enslaved in various places throughout the Americas, and in Brazil the capturing of Indians for slaves was so widespread that an occupational category, *paulistas*,[4] was designated for the individuals engaged in this activity. American Indians, however, usually proved to be unsatisfactory as a labor force, because the Old World diseases that

[4]***paulistas:*** poh LEES tahs

were part of the American exchange (discussed in Chapter 25) destroyed so many of them. European overlords had to look elsewhere for labor.

In a sense, Africa was the logical place for Europeans to look for labor. The African slave trade had been in existence for centuries, and its Atlantic branch was well established half a century before the establishment of the first colony in the Americas. In addition, European attitudes labeled Africans as inferior and therefore well suited to lives of servitude. Finally, experience with African slaves showed greater survival rates in the tropical environments of the Americas than for any other laboring group.

Nonetheless, the mortality rates for African slaves were appalling. A planter on the Caribbean island of Saint Christopher calculated in 1798 that 25 percent of the African slaves brought to his plantation died within the first few weeks of work. The greatest threats to slaves were oppressive work conditions. Mortality rates among slaves were always greatest in hot, damp lowlands, where disease and heat prostration were most dangerous. Next most lethal were the mines, followed by agricultural plantations in more healthy climates. Slaves with indoor jobs as servants fared best of all, with mortality rates approximately comparable to those of Europeans. The nature of the tasks assigned most slaves meant that many would die prematurely, and their ranks would be replenished through the slave trade.

Viewed from the perspective of the colonial powers, the slave trade was part of a broader pattern of commerce. European colonial powers, as discussed in Chapter 24, operated under the mercantile system, so one of their goals was to maximize the flow of raw materials into the home country while keeping their colonies dependent on the home country for finished goods. Another goal was to have a net surplus of money flowing into the home country. The only way to ensure the flow of imported raw materials was to provide a labor source for the colonies. The traders purchased slaves for that labor with finished goods and sold them in the colonies for either money or raw materials, which came back with them to the home country. From the mercantile view, the system was ideal.

A special place in the trade between Europe and the Americas was reserved for sugar. In 1400, most Europeans had never tasted sugar refined from cane, and the few who had done so typically used it as a medicine or a spice. (Honey and fruit juice were the only sweeteners available to them before the introduction of cane sugar into Spain by the Moors.) By the middle 1600s, however, Europeans had developed a great sweet tooth, and the demand for sugar had skyrocketed. Nowhere in Europe could sugarcane grow well, so sugar had to be imported. All the major colonial European powers had holdings in the Caribbean, and all produced sugar there. Refined and shipped in bulbous cones, sugar was used as a sweetener for various concoctions, including cocoa, newly introduced from Mexico. Reduced from the squeezings of the cane to a thick syrup, it became molasses, used primarily in the production of rum. By 1650, sugar had become a major import into Europe.

The volume and importance of sugar in European commerce directly affected the need for slaves. More than most crops, sugar required a great deal of labor. Aside from the work needed to grow the crop, its bamboo-like canes had to be cut by hand at harvesting and hauled to a mill, where they were pressed to squeeze out their juice. The juice was boiled until thick, then cooled and hardened in molds. To produce the needed quantities of sugar, huge amounts of labor were required, and that labor came from slaves.

Another crop that stimulated the use of slaves was cotton, particularly in the southeastern United States. Both picking cotton and separating the fiber from the seeds were very laborious tasks when performed by hand. The invention in 1793 of an efficient cotton gin automated and sped up the process of separating the seeds and fiber, meaning that the time spent picking cotton was the only barrier to greatly increased cotton production, which would result in greatly increased profits for plantation owners. Effective mechanical cotton pickers were not devised until the late nineteenth century, so the only solution open to the cotton planters of the early nineteenth century was to increase the number of cotton pickers. Because most cotton pickers were slaves, this meant increasing the number of slaves. It is ironic that in this case mechanization, which usually reduced the demand for labor and slaves, was a spur to increase the number of slaves on cotton plantations.

In recent years, scholars have debated whether or not slavery was an efficient system. On

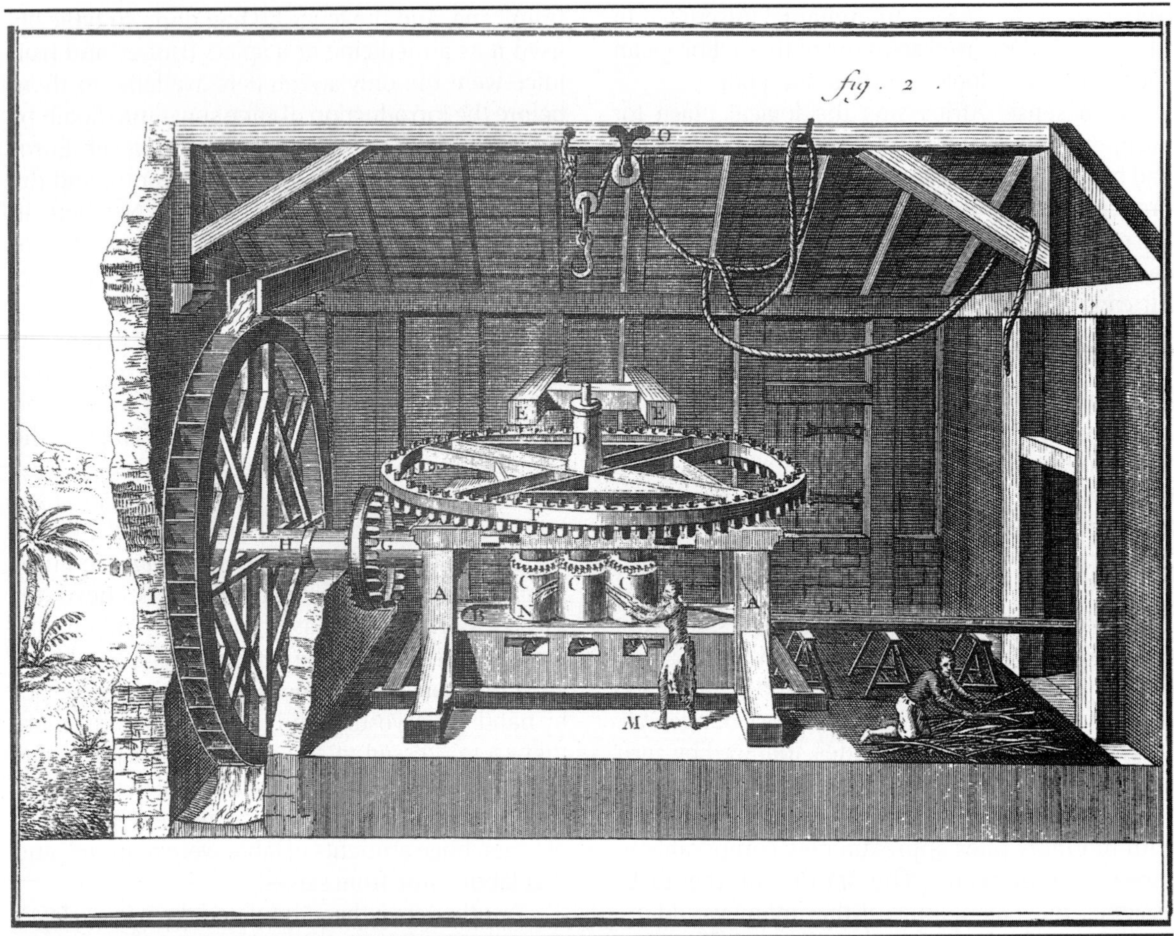

FIGURE 26.5 ***Sugarcane Press.*** *This eighteenth-century engraving documents the details of a sugar mill for extracting sugary sap from the cane. Flowing water turned the wheel (I) at the left, which then rotated the horizontal wheel (D) in the center; the central wheel turned the rollers (C) that pressed the cane itself. Sap collected in the basin (B). This sanitized image does not illustrate such factors as the oppressive heat of the operation, the physical exertion required, and the risk of maiming accidents.* Courtesy of Dover Publications.

the one hand, it was inefficient, because one hour of slave labor usually produced less than one hour of wage-earner labor did. Further, slaves were not trusted to perform certain tasks, particularly ones that used expensive machinery, because slaves often made "mistakes" that wrecked the machinery. (One may suspect sabotage, because slaves had little reason to respect owners' property and every reason to carry on some form of resistance against the owner who enslaved them.) On the other hand, seen in terms of work produced per slave, the system was very efficient: A slave produced more in a week than did a wage earner. The reason for this apparent paradox is simply that slaves worked longer hours with fewer breaks than did wage earners. They made the system efficient by the hard labor they were forced to perform and the long hours they were forced to work. Even considering the initial investment of purchasing slaves and the ongoing costs of feeding and housing them, the system was a bargain for the slave owner. The profits were extracted from the slaves' welfare. As one planter wrote, "We grew rich because whole races died for us. For us, continents were depopulated."

UNDER THE LENS
African Food in America

No movement of people, no matter how brutal or dislocating, occurs without the movement of culinary traditions. Even the African slave trade brought with it a part of West African cuisine.

By the early 1700s, it was typical for African slave ships to carry huge cargoes of African foods, and their occupants usually were fed at least one African meal a day. This cultural accommodation was no act of kindness, merely a self-serving recognition that fewer slaves died if familiar foods were fed them. Manuals of the day written for slave traders explained which foods would be best for slaves from the most common areas.

Yams were especially popular, because they were cheap, stored well, were easy to prepare, and were a common food in traditional West Africa. In 1732, John Barbot recommended that slavers carry 200 yams per slave; with as many as 500 slaves in the hold of a vessel, this meant a staggering 100,000 yams. Several African foods of somewhat lesser importance also made the voyage: black-eyed peas, sesame, okra, eggplant, *ackee*[a] (a starchy fruit widely used today in the Caribbean), and watermelon (originally grown for its seeds, not its pulp). Significantly, all are foods that carried their seeds (or other plantable parts) within the edible portion and could later be propagated in the Americas.

Once in America, slaves found that some African foodstuffs were unavailable and turned to local equivalents. Common substitutions included sweet potatoes (Americas) for yams, collard greens (Europe) and wild lamb's quarters (North America) for *sokoyokoto*,[b] *craincrain*,[c] and bitterleaf greens; Asian rice for African rice; and corn or potatoes for cassava.

[a]**ackee:** ah KEE
[b]**sokoyokoto:** soh koh yoh KOH toh
[c]**craincrain:** krayn krayn

In addition to ingredients, culinary techniques and recipes crossed the Atlantic in the memories of slave women. Corn mush, a thick corn porridge, was one of the most common of slave dishes in the Americas, and it is simply African *foo foo* (cassava porridge) with corn meal substituted for cassava flour. Gumbo, an American soupy stew thickened with okra (an African vegetable), is a direct transfer from Africa, where one name for okra is "gombo." Hotpot, a Caribbean stew, is a direct transplant from West Africa.

Two African-inspired dishes in America warrant special attention: fritters and long-cooked greens. The idea of taking a soft, starchy paste (often heavily spiced) and frying it in oil is a basic and longstanding West African technique, though it was not in use in Europe until the past couple of centuries. This technique produces fritters, such as the spiced corn balls called "hush puppies." The black-eyed pea fritter Brazilians call *acarajé*[d] is identical to the Nigerian *akara*.[e] Even quintessential southern fried chicken is dredged in a spicy batter before frying, an African technique alien to the Western food tradition.

In Africa, greens are most often prepared by long cooking them with a little piece of fatty meat, then eating the greens and drinking the vitamin-rich liquid left at the end of the process. This practice was carried to the Americas, and the traditional greens and salt pork is a direct reflection of it. In folk African American society, it also was traditional to drink the "pot likker" (juices) that remained after cooking.

Over the centuries, African contributions to American cooking have made their way into culinary traditions of all ethnic groups in the Americas. What could be more American than fried chicken, more Jamaican than hotpot, more Brazilian than *acarajé*?

[d]**acarajé:** ah kah rah HAY
[e]**akara:** AH kah rah

FIGURE 26.6 ***Marketplace in St. Johns.*** *This 1902 photograph shows the market on the island of St. Johns in the Caribbean. Such markets began at the same time as the establishment of slavery and the plantation system, and were critical as means for slaves to exchange goods. The markets' economic importance was supplemented by their social importance, since they provided a venue for meeting people, holding conversations, and making friends. For just these reasons, markets were often deemed potentially subversive and were shut down when plantation owners feared slave uprisings.* Library of Congress.

THE AFRICAN DIASPORA

The enforced dispersal of Africans during the slave trade— the **African diaspora**[5]—was the largest dispersal of its kind in history. There may never have been another migration of comparable scope, and all other massive migrations have allowed the migrants to bring with them at least some of the items, ideas, and usages that characterized their cultures. In contrast, Africans rarely could bring any physical items, and their activities as slaves were restricted in ways designed to obliterate their past. In many slave communities, for example, slave owners forbade the speaking of African languages, the use of African names, the performance of African music or the use of African instruments, and the practice of African religions. Despite these attempts at cultural eradication, an African stamp has persisted in many aspects of life among the descendants of African slaves in the Americas.

As far as we know, no musical instruments came on the Middle Passage. Nonetheless, African music came with African slaves, and in few places is African heritage more clear than in traditional African American music. For example, the **call-and-response pattern**, wherein a leader calls a line and a chorus responds with the same or a similar line, is distinctive to West Africa and the Americas. The complex rhythmic patterns of African American music from Brazil to the American South also can be traced directly to West Africa.

The conditions of slavery encouraged the development of a special class of African American

[5]**diaspora:** dy AS poh ruh

music: the work song. Work songs have strong and regular rhythms, allowing a group of workers to perform their tasks in unison. For some tasks, such as picking cotton, working at a single pace was not really necessary, but for others, such as propelling the multiple handles of a rotary mill, coordination was critical. Typically following the call-and-response pattern, work songs were sung during most group labor—fixing the work pace, coordinating movement, and buoying spirits. Variations and innovations of words and melodies were encouraged, but the rhythm was kept invariable. Slaveowners encouraged the use of work songs by slaves, one of the few cases in which an African practice was actively supported by owners.

On Caribbean plantations, Sunday traditionally was reserved as a rest day for slaves and others. By the early 1600s, slaves had established Sunday market days, when individuals (mostly women) would meet to exchange produce, handicrafts, and other items. This was a recreation of the traditional West African market, held on a regular day of the week. In the Caribbean as in Africa, women dominated this arena of commerce, using this traditional exchange mechanism to distribute homemade or home-grown items throughout the community. In addition, the market served important functions in spreading news and socializing.

While some of the African slaves brought to the Americas had practiced Islam in Africa, most had practiced native African religions or a combination of Islam and native religions. It is small wonder, therefore, that aspects of African religion were brought through the Middle Passage and thrived in the Americas. The design symbolizing the cosmos in the Kongo kingdom of Angola, for example, was (and is) placed on bowls and other vessels for preparing ***nkisi***,[6] magical preparations used in religious ceremonies. It consists of a right-angle cross in the middle of a circle or oval, and the design was believed to carry great spiritual power. The same symbols have been found on ceramic pots excavated by archaeologists from slave quarters in early-nineteenth-century South Carolina; the symbol also is used on iron pots used in preparing magical medicines in modern Cuba, where it is called ***la zarabanda***.[7]

[6]**nkisi:** NKEE see
[7]***la zarabanda:*** lah sah rah BAHN dah

Figure 26.7 ***African Religious Symbol in America.*** *This design is incised into the base of a food bowl from eighteenth-century South Carolina. Such designs are found over a wide area of exclusively slave settings. The design always appears on food bowls, never on cooking pots. The similarity of this design to a Kongo religious symbol suggests that it came to North America with slaves.* Courtesy of Dr. Leland Ferguson.

The gods of precolonial Africa survived in the spirits of **voodoo**, also known as *santería*.[8] (The word "voodoo" itself comes from West Africa, probably from the Dahomey word "vodu," meaning spirit.) Despite its reputation—gained mainly from paperback novels and "B" movies—voodoo is a religion given over primarily to healing. While its practice was forbidden under slavery, it continued underground and served as a potent link with an African past. It continues today in the Caribbean and in many areas with large populations of immigrants from there.

[8]**santería:** sahn tah REE ah

Even the notion of complex handshakes, important at various periods in African American history, is a direct transplant from West Africa. Traditionally, West African men had personal handshakes, consisting of from three to ten grips and movements in a fixed sequence. When such men met friends, these handshakes were exchanged as a greeting, much as complex handshakes may be today from Jamaica to Toronto.

The wearing of large or extravagant hats by women, another West African custom, has carried over into the Americas as well, particularly in the Caribbean and the American South. Related is the custom of wearing several hats at one time, still common in the Caribbean, although rare in the United States now.

SLAVE UPRISINGS

During most of the period of the Atlantic slave trade, few slaveowners and others of European extraction had much concern about violence at the hands of slaves. Slaves usually were forbidden to have weapons, but even more influential was the widespread belief among European Americans that African Americans were, by their nature, compliant and happy with their lot, no matter how dreadful it was. In the sixteenth, seventeenth, and eighteenth centuries, a few violent encounters on a small scale had occurred in such places as Antigua and Jamaica, and there had been individual cases of violence wherever there had been slaves. These, however, typically were dismissed as aberrations rather than as indications of a persistent or serious threat of uprising. At the end of the eighteenth century, however, this situation changed radically.

Two factors led to the most influential of all slave uprisings, the Haitian Revolution. The first was the chasm between the living conditions for slaves and those for the owner class in Haiti. Like much of the rest of the Caribbean in the eighteenth century, Haiti was overwhelmingly devoted to the raising of sugarcane and the refining of sugar. These labor-intensive tasks were performed by African slaves, who constituted more than three-quarters of the population. Conditions for slaves in Haiti were even worse than in most places, because the ruggedness of the terrain, the poverty and exhaustion of some of the soils, and the prevalence of disease made their lot especially burdensome. In contrast, the French elite who owned and operated the sugar plantations and other businesses prided themselves on being able to maintain an opulent lifestyle far from Paris.

The second factor was the French Revolution, which began in 1789. It will be discussed in more detail in Chapter 31, but its importance in terms of Haiti is that it championed the idea that the common people could resort to violence to rid themselves of rulers who cared little for the people's desires or needs. To a Haitian slave, this could be seen as a mandate to overthrow the French owners. The oppressive and unequal conditions in Haiti were the tinder, and the French Revolution was the spark.

Fanning the flame were Haitian patriots who instigated and led violent action against the French. The first of these was Vincent Ogé[9] (around 1750–1791). A slave from birth, Ogé initiated and led an uprising in 1790; in 1791, he was captured by the French and was tortured to death after a summary trial. His martyrdom established him as a rallying symbol for his cause.

François Dominique Toussaint L'Ouverture[10] (1744–1803) then took up the responsibility of leading the uprising, which rapidly grew into a full-scale revolution for independence. Toussaint L'Ouverture had been a slave until he was given his freedom in 1789, and, although his formal education was scant, his organizational and diplomatic abilities were spectacular. Through a series of alliances and military actions, he successfully defeated most of the French forces, and the revolution was nearly won by 1801. Through treachery, the French military captured Toussaint L'Ouverture in 1802 and sent him to France, where he died in a prison cell the following year.

The final leader of the revolution, Jean Jacques Dessalines[11] (1758–1806), was a ruthless commander whose armies committed well-publicized atrocities against the French and their Haitian allies. His methods were successful, however, and

[9]**Vincent Ogé:** vehn sehn OH zhay
[10]**François Dominique Toussaint L'Ouverture:** frahn SWAH doh mih NEEK too SAHN loo vehr TOOR
[11]**Jean Jacques Dessalines:** zhahn zhahk day sah LEEN

Figure 26.8 ***Vincent Ogé Returning to Haiti.*** *The first phase of the Haitian Revolution was spearheaded by Vincent Ogé, who returned from France in 1791 after his unsuccessful plea for increased civil rights and freedoms for Haitians. Thwarted in his attempts to bring about peaceful change, he led an abortive uprising that inspired Toussaint L'Ouverture and others to launch the successful Haitian Revolution in the early nineteenth century.* Bibliothèque nationale, Paris.

Haiti achieved independence in 1804. Dessalines expelled all persons of European extraction and proclaimed himself emperor. Haiti thus became the first African American state in the Americas and only the second independent nation in that hemisphere since the European conquest. The political implications of the Haitian Revolution will be explored further in Chapter 31.

The Haitian Revolution was a chilling episode to slaveowners around the Americas. It provided evidence that African American slaves were neither docile nor contented, and it proved that they were capable of effective, well-planned, and ruthless warfare, as well as postindependence retribution against slaveowners. Slaveowners and others of European extraction feared that the Haitian Revolution would serve as an inspiration for slaves elsewhere to rise up against their owners. While no other uprisings comparable to that in Haiti developed, the events in Haiti were a potent reminder that violence was possible anywhere there were slaves. Ultimately, it was one of several factors that led to the abolition of slavery throughout the Americas.

THE END OF THE ATLANTIC SLAVE TRADE

There always had been critics of slavery and the slave trade, but the intensity of their condemnation increased sharply in the second half of the 1700s. Led by Quakers and other humanitarians, criticism focused first on the slave trade.

Statements decrying the slave trade usually were couched in idealistic terms. Quakers condemned it because it debased and harmed people, running counter to their precept of brotherly love; Enlightenment philosophers (discussed in Chapter 31) condemned it because it violated the natural rights of slaves; and humanitarian philosophers condemned it for the suffering it imposed on its victims. These religious and philosophical movements were on the rise near the end of the eighteenth century, and condemnation of the slave trade followed naturally from them.

While idealist reformers were very important in the abolition of the slave trade, they were joined by allies with less lofty motives. In the United States and various other parts of the Americas, fear of slave insurrections like that in Haiti led some to support abolition of both the slave trade and of slavery. Some slaveowners who bred slaves for sale also favored abolishing the slave trade, reasoning that limiting the supply would drive up their value on the market. The Atlantic slave trade had not been particularly lucrative in some places, such as Denmark, and relinquishing it was little concession there.

Condemnation of the slave trade initially rose to prominence in the United States, but soon the focus shifted to England. There, various commissions inquired into the horrors of the Middle Passage, and hundreds of tracts were published advocating the end of the trade. In the meantime, voices denouncing the slave trade were being heard throughout Europe and its colonies and former colonies around the world.

The first country to abolish the slave trade was Denmark, a minor player, in 1792. It was followed by the United States in 1807, England in 1808, the Netherlands in 1814, and France in 1815. U.S. ships continued to carry small numbers of slaves into Cuba until this practice was outlawed in 1862. In a brief span of nine years, however, the vast majority of slave importation was made illegal.

FIGURE 26.9 ***A Slave's Gravestone.*** *This eighteenth-century gravestone in Jamaica memorializes Scipio Africanus, an African slave who became a Christian. While some Christian groups actively tried to convert slaves to Christianity, others feared this would lead to egalitarian aspirations, making slaves more difficult to control.*
Ikon/National Trust, Trevelyan Collection.

How could the slave trade, the product of four centuries of lucrative commerce, have been eradicated in such a brief time? Certainly this was a period when humanitarian concerns were affecting public policy more than ever before. And certainly the rising literacy rate in the Western world meant that the impassioned arguments of humanitarian reformers were reaching a broader audience than they would have in earlier periods.

AFRICAN SLAVE TRADE

			1400	
		Portuguese dominance of Atlantic slave trade, 1441–c. 1700		Adaptation of lateen sail for ocean use, 1434 Gonçalvez captures slaves in Benin and delivers them to Portugal, 1441
			1500	
Asiento in force in Spain, c. 1600–1789			1600	
	Dominance of chattel slavery in West Africa, c. 1700–1862	English dominance of Atlantic slave trade, c. 1700–1808	1700	
			1800	Haiti becomes independent following revolution, 1804 Slave trade abolished in primary trading countries, 1807–1815 Slavery abolished in most countries, 1840–1870
			1900	

Humanitarian sentiment probably was the most important factor underlying the end of the Atlantic slave trade.

An additional factor, however, was the changing economic nature of European and European American society. The old elites, based on royal lineage and agrarian landholding, had dominated politics for centuries. But following the onset of the Industrial Revolution (discussed in Chapter 32), power was shifting, and the new power base was rooted in industry and had little economic need for slaves. While it would still be about half a century before slavery itself was abolished in the same countries, the abolition of the slave trade was—in part—a symptom of the emerging dominance of the industrial middle class over the agrarian elite.

SUMMARY

1. Slavery existed in precolonial Africa in a form wherein slaves retained their personal rights. The early years of Portuguese slave trading (1441–around 1500) followed this general pattern.

2. The trans-Sahara slave trade and Indian Ocean slave trade carried substantial numbers of slaves from Africa to the Mediterranean and Asia. Following 1441, the Atlantic slave trade was centered in West Africa and conducted primarily by Europeans.

3. After around 1500, the nature of the African slave trade changed: Its volume and brutality increased, and slaves increasingly were viewed as devoid of personal rights.

4. Portugal controlled the Atlantic slave trade until around 1600, when it was displaced by England, which dominated from then on, while the Netherlands and later France became important traders. Other countries had small roles in the trade.

5. In Africa, coastal states participated in the Atlantic slave trade, providing slaves for the European traders. As a result, the traders and their states became rich and politically powerful.

6. In contrast, interior African states suffered from the effects of the Atlantic slave trade. Their governments were weakened or toppled, and their populations were robbed of their most productive members.

7. Chattel slavery (slavery in which a slave's value is considered in monetary terms only) developed in West Africa after the onset of the slave trade with Europeans. Increasingly, many Africans embraced Islam in an attempt to gain the protection it offered against being enslaved by other Muslims.

8. Both interior and coastal West African states suffered in the long run from dependence on European goods and underdeveloped economies.

9. In the Americas, where most slaves were sold, high mortality rates and labor-intensive occupations created a great demand for slaves. Sugar played an especially important role.

10. The triangular trade with slave trading as its middle leg supported the goals of the mercantile system.

11. The African diaspora was the dispersal of Africans by the slave trade. Despite the massive cultural dislocation, slaves were able to retain African cultural traits, many of which survive in the cultures of their descendants today.

12. The Haitian Revolution grew out of a slave uprising and resulted in the establishment of an African American state by 1804. It shocked slaveowners and other European Americans, who feared that similar uprisings could engulf them.

13. The slave trade in the major trading countries was abolished between 1807 and 1815. Humanitarian interests probably were the most critical factor in bringing about the abolition of the slave trade, but the rise of industrialization at the expense of the interests of the agrarian elite also shifted power away from those who gained the most advantage in the use of slaves.

SUGGESTED READINGS

Allison, Robert J., ed. *The Interesting Narrative of the Life of Olaudah Equiano.* Boston: Bedford Books–St. Martin's Press, 1995. The only known account of capture as a slave, the Middle Passage, and subsequent purchase of freedom by an African. Originally published in 1789. Includes an introduction and other interpretive aids.

Curtin, Philip. *The Atlantic Slave Trade: A Census.* Madison: University of Wisconsin Press, 1969. The seminal quantitative estimates from which all modern treatments begin.

———. *Economic Change in Precolonial Africa: Senegambia in the Era of the Slave Trade.* Two vols. Madison: University of Wisconsin Press, 1975. A classic treatment of the slave trade, focusing on economics alone.

Davidson, Basil. *The African Slave Trade.* Revised and expanded edition. Boston: Little, Brown, 1980. General treatment of the African slave trade, focusing on the effects in Africa.

Ferguson, Leland. *Uncommon Ground: Archaeology and Early African America, 1650–1800.* Washington, D.C.: Smithsonian Institution, 1992. An informative synthesis on the findings of archaeology regarding slave life in the southeastern United States.

Fogel, Robert. *Without Consent or Contract.* New York: Norton, 1989. The classic account by the economist on the efficiency of the American slave system. This work caps the research that won him a 1993 Nobel Prize.

Inikori, Joseph E., and Stanley L. Engerman, eds. *The Atlantic Slave Trade: Effects on Economies, Societies, and Peoples in Africa, the Americas, and Europe.* Durham, N.C.: Duke University Press, 1992. Excellent collection of papers discussing the "winners and losers" of the slave trade.

Rawley, James A. *The Transatlantic Slave Trade: A History.* New York: Norton, 1981. A general treatment with emphasis on the quantitative reconstruction of the trade.

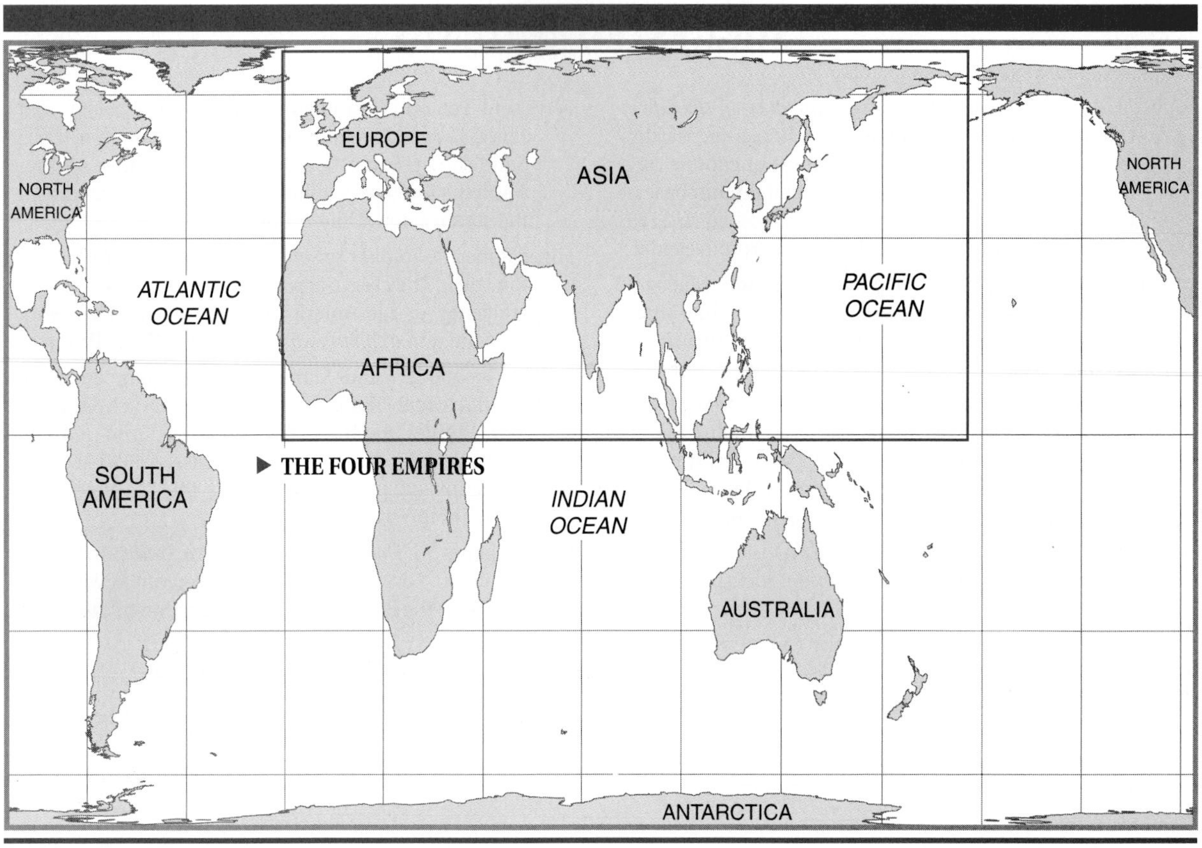

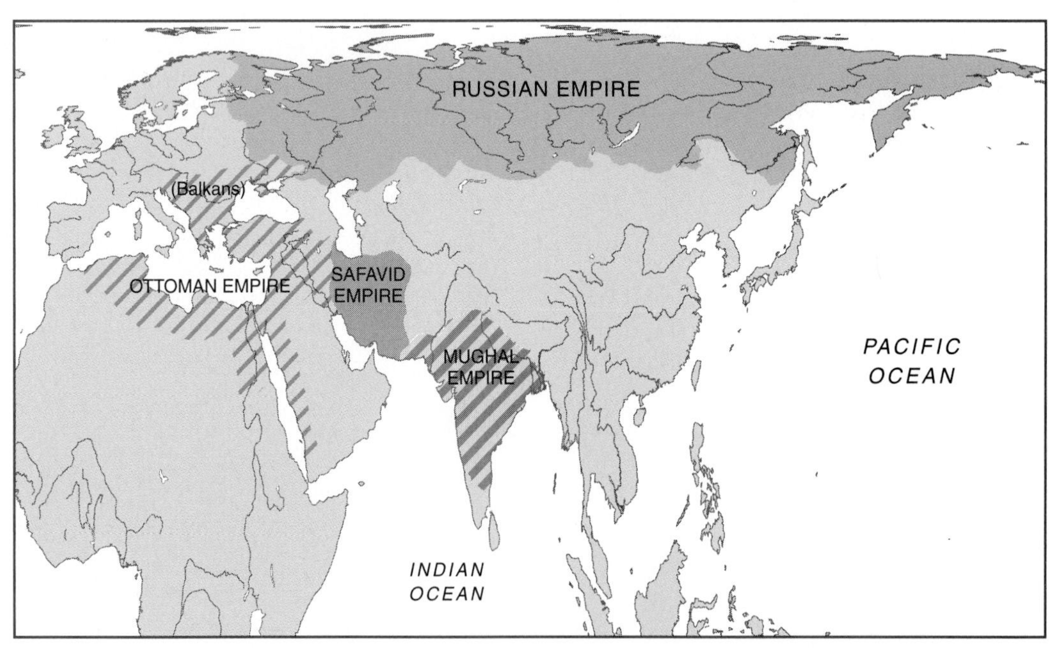

▶ **THE FOUR EMPIRES**

CHAPTER 27

Empires in Central Eurasia, South Asia, and North Africa

around 1350–around 1700

Several European travelers observed that they felt more comfortable in the Islamic Ottoman Empire than in the Christian Russian Empire. Perhaps those feelings reflected their familiarity with Ottoman cities, like Constantinople (modern-day Istanbul), that welcomed Europeans. Russian cities, on the other hand, had few non-Russians, who often were regarded with suspicion. Although western Europeans traveled to the Ottoman, Russian, Safavid, and Mughal[1] empires, they came as traders or advisors rather than as conquerors.

Trade and religion became dynamic elements of the Eurasian empires discussed in this chapter. The Ottoman Empire lay astride key trade routes between Europe, Asia, and Africa. The Safavid Empire controlled commercial roads between Southwest, Central, and South Asia, while the Mughal Empire dominated trade arteries in South Asia. Ottoman, Safavid, and Mughal monarchs also derived profits from maritime trade. Russian rulers had to content themselves with land trade routes within Europe but eventually conquered additional roadways between Europe and Central Asia. Islam was the dominant religion of the Ottoman, Safavid, and Mughal empires, helping their rulers to found and maintain long-lasting states. Russian rulers embraced Russian Orthodoxy, a branch of Christianity, and Russian Orthodox leaders rallied Russians to fight against invaders, like the Roman Catholic Poles in the seventeenth century.

[1] **Mughal:** MOO ghahl

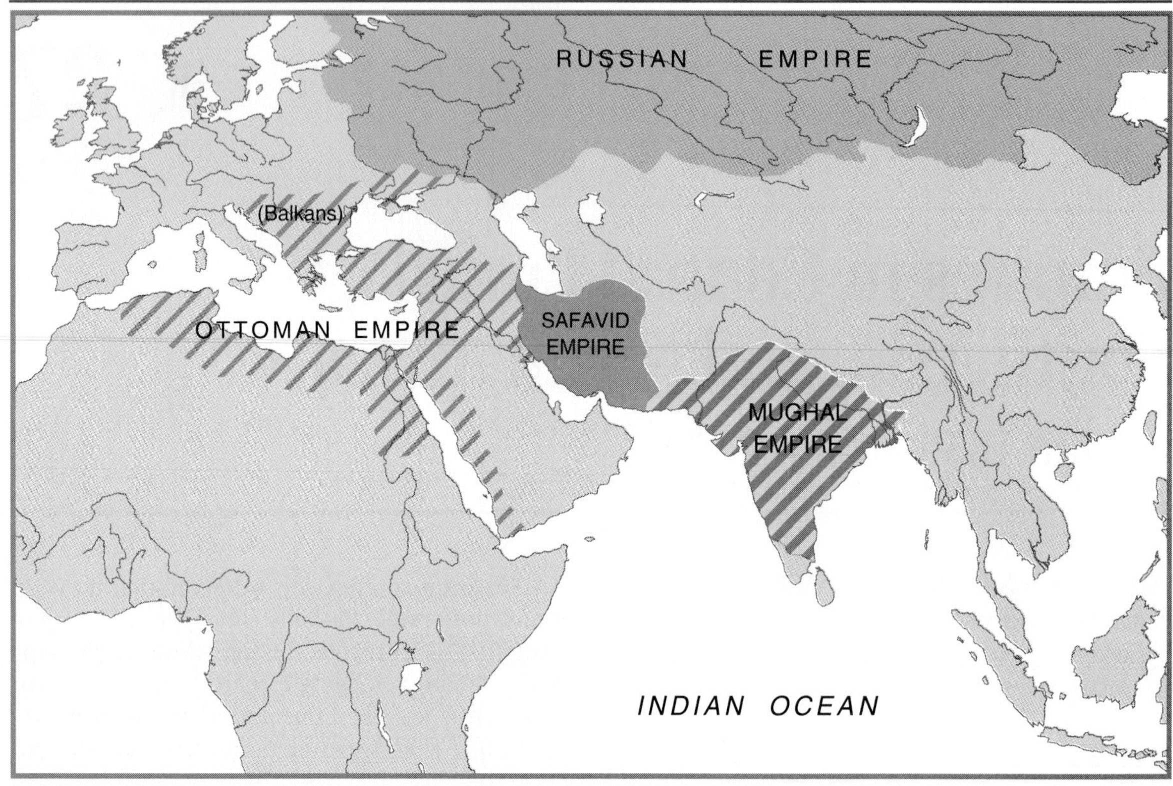

MAP 27.1 ***The Four Empires, around 1700.*** *The dynamic expansion of the Ottoman, Russian, Safavid, and Mughal empires brought some of them into direct contact with one another. The Ottoman Empire surrounded much of the Mediterranean Sea and covered parts of three continents. The Russian Empire controlled a vast territory, including the relatively uninhabited Siberia to its north. The Safavid Empire controlled much of present-day Iran, while the Mughal Empire united most of the Indian subcontinent.*

THE EARLY OTTOMAN EMPIRE, 1352–AROUND 1700

The Ottoman Empire began in the fourteenth century. It lasted until the twentieth century and is one of the longest-lived empires in history. One reason for this longevity was the tolerance by the Ottoman rulers of ethnic and religious differences. Religious tolerance, for example, was practiced by the Ottoman rulers, who welcomed Christians and Jews into their realm. Many served in the Ottoman government and played important social and economic roles. The Ottoman realm spanned parts of three continents, and its population reached nearly 30 million people in the seventeenth century. Although its leaders were Turks, the language of religion was Arabic and the main language of literature was Persian.

Expansion into Southwest Asia and Eastern Europe

The Mongol conquest of the Baghdad Caliphate in 1258 forced nomadic Turkic tribes, one of which was the Ottoman Turks, into the Anatolian Peninsula. Successive leaders of these Ottomans proclaimed a holy war against the Byzantine Empire in the fourteenth century; Ottoman successes brought other Muslims into the fight. A major development came in 1352 when Ottoman forces, allied with a claimant to the Byzantine throne, landed in Europe. Soon Ottoman armies began conquering the Balkan Peninsula, which lay open to expansion because of a paucity of able leaders and stable kingdoms. Imperial conquest was facilitated by the respectful treatment of Greek Orthodox Christians and by modest taxes on peasants. By 1400, the Ottoman Empire ruled parts of Islamic Asia and Christian Europe.

One significant consequence of the Balkan conquest was the formation of the **Janissaries**, warriors of European extraction who composed the elite Ottoman military force. Recruiters went into Balkan villages and selected teenage males for training as soldiers and administrators. These young men became slaves of the Ottoman **sultan**, the leader of the Ottoman Empire, and they were converted to Islam and trained as warriors or officials. Coming from Christian backgrounds and being the sultan's elite group set the Janissaries apart from other military groups. They were feared as fierce fighters.

Another feature of the Ottoman expansion into the Balkans was the forced relocation of peoples. Turkish groups were forced to resettle along and guard strategic highways that moved armies and their equipment to battle sites. Some Balkan peoples were transferred to the Anatolian Peninsula.

Capture of one sultan in 1402 caused a group of rivals to fight for control of the empire. This pattern of conflict, which often erupted early in the imperial era, led Sultan Mehmed II (reign dates 1444–1446 and 1451–1481) to promulgate the Law of Fratricide. This law made it legal for a monarch to kill his immediate male relatives who might pose a dynastic threat.

Figure 27.1 ***Janissaries.*** *The Janissaries faithfully served leaders of the Ottoman Empire for centuries. They adopted colorful ceremonial garb and were often at the forefront of heavy fighting involving the Ottoman armies. They played a crucial role in the conquest of Constantinople in 1453. In later centuries the Janissaries, like the imperial system they served, grew complaisant.* Österreichische Nationalbibliothek.

Ottoman Splendor: Mehmed, Selim, and Suleyman

In 1453, Constantinople fell to the Ottoman army under the command of Mehmed II; looting was kept to a minimum by the Ottoman sultan, who wished to keep his new capital unharmed. Known as Istanbul, the capital grew into a metropolis of around 400,000 people by 1550 and perhaps 800,000 by 1600. Mehmed was interested in Istanbul's architecture and cultural life. He oversaw the construction of the Topkapi Palace, with its immense gardens tended by perhaps 1,000 gardeners. Mehmed was a passionate gardener who planted exotic plants and trees. A major building complex of mosques, ***medreses***[2] (colleges), libraries, and hostels was erected in Istanbul under Mehmed's direction. Funding for this center came from a large nearby market endowed by the sultan. This income ensured a permanent income for those who lived and worked in the complex; at the same time, the complex was administratively autonomous. Three hospitals were also built,

[2] ***medreses:*** MEH dreh sehs

FIGURE 27.2 ***Diplomatic Embassy to the Ottoman Court.*** *Italian painters sometimes worked for the Ottoman monarchs. Gentile Bellini, for example, was sent by the Venetian government to paint Mehmed II in 1480. Bias crept into the scene depicted here. Ambassadors abased themselves before the Ottoman rulers, but Bellini's painting shows a meeting of equals (center) rather than the normal submissive kneeling depicted in more accurate paintings. Note the tame deer and camels in the foreground.* Alinari/Art Resource, N. Y.

including one for women and another for non-Muslims, and each had a pharmacy.

Although *medreses* had long been in Muslim cities, they became a significant part of the Ottoman educational system. The first Ottoman *medrese* was founded in 1331 (later, Istanbul alone had 95 *medreses*), and the *medreses* of Mehmed and Suleyman I were the elite educational institutions. Famous scholars were invited to head a *medrese*; they and all students received room, board, books, and a monthly income. At the same time, top officials donated land and income for *medreses* and hostels, and men and women gave funds and lands to *medreses* and other charitable institutions.

The Ottoman sultans resumed their conquest of the Balkans and invaded lands bordering the Black Sea, where by 1500 Ottoman ships sailed unchallenged. Major trade routes in Russia and Central Asia passed into Ottoman control, and the Crimean Khanate became an Ottoman tributary state, supplying slaves for the Ottoman Empire.

Although Selim[3] I (reign dates 1512–1520) ruled only briefly, he had a significant impact on the Ottoman Empire. In 1514, his army decisively defeated the Safavid army. A few years later, Selim conquered Egypt. He also won the title of Guardian of the Two Cities (Mecca and Medina), which had been held by the ruler of Egypt. Thus, Selim became head of the Sunni sect of Islam. In addition, he was obliged to organize the annual pilgrimages (*hajj*) to Mecca, highly prestigious and profitable enterprises. Syria also fell to Selim, with Egypt and Syria soon supplying more than one-third of the imperial budget. Thus, Ottoman rulers gained access to the Red Sea, and trade routes

[3] **Selim:** SEH lihm

IN THEIR OWN WORDS

A Diplomatic Exchange between Suleyman I and De L'Isle Adam

Ottoman expansion brought complex diplomatic relationships and often clashes with many European rulers. Thus, sultans had to cultivate diplomatic subtlety and military threat in their letters. In 1521, Suleyman I, newly ascended to the Ottoman throne, desired to conquer the island of Rhodes, a key threat to Ottoman maritime trade and an obstacle to Ottoman control of the eastern Mediterranean. In September 1521, the sultan sent an intimidating letter to the new Grand Master of the Knights of Rhodes, De L'Isle Adam.

> Suleyman the Sultan, by the grace of God, King of Kings, sovereign of sovereigns, most high Emperor of Byzantium and Trebizond, all powerful King of Persia, Arabia, Syria, and Egypt, Supreme Lord of Europe and Asia, Prince of Mecca and Aleppo, Master of Jerusalem and Ruler of the Universal Sea to Philip Villiers De L'Isle Adam, Grand Master of Rhodes, greeting and health: I congratulate you on your new dignity and upon your safe arrival in your estate. I hope that you will rule there in prosperity and even more gloriously than your predecessors. It rests with you to share in our favor; accept therefore our friendship, and as a friend congratulate me that emulating my father who conquered Persia, Jerusalem, Arabia, and Egypt, I have made myself master of that most important city, Belgrade. . . . I took many other strongholds and beautiful cities, destroying their inhabitants by the sword or fire, and selling the rest into slavery. Now after sending my large and victorious army home for the winter, I myself am able to return in triumph to my court in Constantinople. Farewell.

The Grand Master shrugged off the intimidation and replied in the plain language of a soldier.

> Brother Philip Villiers De L'Isle Adam, Grand Master of Rhodes, to Suleyman, Sultan of the Turks, I have well understood the purport of your letter, which has been delivered by your ambassador. Your proposals of peace between us are as agreeable to me as they will be unwelcome to Cortoglu [a Turkish privateer]. That pirate omitted no efforts to surprise me on my passage from France; but having failed to stop me, as I sailed past him by night . . . he tried to carry off two merchantmen, but the galleys of my fleet drove him off and forced him to flee. Farewell.

Suleyman launched the invasion during the next summer, and after a long siege the island capitulated. Suleyman gallantly permitted the knights to depart with their weapons and possessions; he also vowed to treat the people of Rhodes well. Although a few historians question the validity of Suleyman's letter, most accept it as genuine.

to sub-Saharan Africa and India came under Ottoman influence.

Perhaps the height of Ottoman power came during the reign of Suleyman I, Suleyman the Magnificent (reign dates 1520–1566). He conquered Belgrade and briefly besieged Vienna in 1529. Like his predecessors, Suleyman supported the various opponents of his main European foe, the Hapsburgs, who ruled Spain, Austria, and much of Germany. Thus, Suleyman allied the Ottoman Empire with France, which vigorously opposed Hapsburg expansion policies. Suleyman gave the French special trading privileges, and soon income from this trade became a major revenue source.

Suleyman built architectural masterpieces, including the Suleymaniye, a mosque complex that still dominates Istanbul. The mosque itself had four slender minarets and a vast dome, impressing subjects and travelers alike. Its architect, Sinan[4] (around 1490–1588), has been regarded as the greatest Ottoman designer, and he grew up in the Palace School, learning his architectural trade there. Sinan built many other splendid works, like the Imperial Mosque, which was commissioned by Mihrimah,[5] one of Suleyman's daughters.

[4] **Sinan:** see NAHN
[5] **Mihrimah:** MEE ree mah

FIGURE 27.3 ***Ottoman Canteen.*** *Artisans were favored with financial support by the Ottoman political and social elite. This piece dates from the era of Suleyman the Magnificent in the second half of the sixteenth century. The complex gold-leaf pattern studded with jewels is meant to dazzle the viewer.* Courtesy of Topkapi Saray Museum.

Suleyman was also nicknamed the "Lawgiver." This epithet reflected the fact that the sultan issued many decrees that supplemented the traditional law of Islam. In fact, Suleyman was regarded as the model of virtue, one who was stern but just, warlike but cultured. Legal decisions were often reached by consensus after debate, and the Ottoman justice system became famed among imperial subjects for its fairness.

Class and Gender

The Ottoman leaders maintained a social system with clear distinctions. The basic one was between the rulers and the ruled. Top government officials, both in the capital and in outlying provinces, came from the Palace School. Merchants and artisans enjoyed a favorable standing in Ottoman society because of the importance given to production and trade in Islamic societies. Artisan associations, or **guilds**, not only regulated production of goods along craft lines, but they also provided important social services, like emergency loans, for their members. Some guilds even had close associations with Sufi orders and therefore assumed a religious character. Slaves from Europe and Africa also served their Ottoman masters, although Islamic law forbade the enslavement of Muslims.

Although Ottoman society was dominated by men, individual women sometimes played important roles. Muslim women generally remained confined to the **harem**, a place of forbidden entrance to adult males, except the household head. Islamic law permitted four wives to one husband, but usually only wealthy men maintained many wives and children. When a sultan was a minor or indifferent to politics, his mother allied with palace eunuchs and wielded influence, especially in the seventeenth century. Wealthy and socially prominent women had an impact through charitable activities, because Islam required all to be generous in giving to needy people. Women donated money, property, and their time to worthy causes, including educational institutions.

Arts and Literature

Although elite arts flourished, a tension developed between those who pursued or developed new ideas and those who believed in the strict adherence to Islamic law and its practices. Molla Lutfi[6] (died 1494), for example, was a famous scholar and freethinker. Because he mocked what he considered to be outmoded Islamic beliefs, Molla Lutfi made enemies among the religious leaders, who found him guilty of impiety and executed him. Ibn Kemal[7] (1468–1534), one of Lutfi's students, wrote more than 100 religious treatises and a ten-volume history of the Ottoman Empire. Other scholars wrote encyclopedias concerning political or religious matters.

From earliest Ottoman times, Muslim scholars vigorously pursued studies of mathematics and astronomy, maintaining a long tradition of expertise. In 1577, the sultan's astronomer commissioned the building of a state-of-the-art observatory that used a clock system employing European

[6] **Molla Lutfi:** MOO lah LOOT fee
[7] **Ibn Kemal:** EE bahn keh MAHL

FIGURE 27.4 ***Turkish Bridal Procession.*** *This seventeenth-century painting shows a bride proceeding to her wedding. Several pages, each festively attired, lead the heavily veiled bride and her companions. In most Muslim areas, women were veiled in public.*
After Tueschnor, F., *Alt-Stambuler Hof und Volksleben*, Hanover, 1925.

clock technology. Religious authorities soon objected to the observatory because it supported research that challenged some tenets of Islam and had it razed; this kind of activity drove underground research that might conflict with Islamic law. In fact, such rulings effectively ended Islamic science as religious leaders gained control.

Turkish literature and arts developed in Ottoman times and were strongly influenced by Persian literature. For example, Turkish poets were inspired by Rumi (1207–1273), one of the greatest Persian poets and mystics. Rumi founded the Mevlavi Sufi mystics, and they influenced other Turkish arts, like music and dancing.

THE SAFAVID EMPIRE OF PERSIA, 1501–1736

The Safavid Empire (named after Shaykh Safi,[8] 1252–1336) came to power and helped Persia (modern Iran) become a major player in Southwest Asia. Ismail[9] (reign dates 1501–1524), the founder of the dynasty, proclaimed Shi'ism, an Islamic sect, as the ideology of the Safavid state. Conflicts between the Safavids and Ottomans soon assumed the character of a religious war, as the Ottomans were Sunni believers. Thus, the spread of Safavid rule was also the spread of Shi'ism, and strong animosities between the Sunnis and Shi'ites may be seen today.

One development connected with the collapse of the Abbasid Caliphate in the thirteenth century was the growth of folk Islam. **Folk Islam**, the religious practices of ordinary Muslims, lay beneath the surface of religious life as long as the great Islamic centers of Baghdad and Damascus flourished. With the subsequent loss of the Abbasid state in 1258, adherents of folk Islam began openly to practice their religion. Sufis attracted followings of common folk, and tombs of Sufis became sites for the faithful to visit.

Founding and Early Expansion

In 1501, Ismail (a descendant of Shaykh Safi) proclaimed the Safavid Dynasty, and early victories rallied Turkish tribes that had supported Ismail's ancestors. Having Turkish and Persian ancestry aided Ismail in building an army composed of

[8] **Shaykh Safi:** SHAYKH SAH fee
[9] **Ismail:** EESH mayh uhl

Turkish warriors and a government dominated by Persian officials. Ismail's success was in uniting them into a formidable whole.

Ismail used religion to weld his supporters tightly to himself. Because folk Islam permitted claiming divine status, Ismail proclaimed himself a god-emperor; he commanded absolute obedience, and his soldiers garnered a reputation for extreme ferocity. A string of victories fueled a sense of godlike invincibility and helped Ismail to forge an expansionist state.

Rather than confront the powerful Ottoman Empire and prematurely risk a defeat and total disaster, Ismail turned to other areas, which he easily subdued. The Ottoman sultan, however, knew that the Safavids presented a serious challenge to his empire; after settling internal disputes, Selim marched against Ismail, and Ottoman cannons and rifles shattered the Safavid force. Ismail escaped and ceased hostilities; having lost his ardor, he became passive after the battle against the Ottomans. Successor Safavid monarchs fought Ottoman forces, surviving several campaigns that brought loss of much territory. To stay in power, rulers permitted the growth of Turkish influence in the government and in the army. Turks under the Safavid leaders formed an elite bodyguard unit that eventually meddled in court affairs.

The Rule of Shah Abbas

Shah Abbas (reign dates 1587–1629) came to the throne at the age of sixteen years. He restructured the Safavid government and economy, recapturing land lost to the Ottomans. The first task for this **shah**, the Persian equivalent of sultan, was the

ENCOUNTERS

The Armenian Trade Connection

Among the great variety of traders in the seventeenth century, the Armenians played a significant role in the transportation and distribution of goods across wide parts of Eurasia. The cornerstone of Armenian commercial activity was the family or clan. In that sense, the Armenians are similar to the Jews of Cairo in the twelfth century or to the Overseas Chinese of Jakarta (Indonesia) in the twentieth century; each group built and sold commercial relationships on family ties.

The Armenians played crucial roles in many kinds of trade and could be found in China, the Philippines, Tibet, Russia, India, and Persia, among other places. One trademark commercial item was textiles, and one East India Company official admitted that Persian markets, under Armenian control, sold a wider variety of English broadcloth than famous stores in London. Armenians also specialized in the trade of indigo, raw silk, and wine. The prominent Armenian trade role in the Philippines came when the Spanish forbade Protestants from trading in the Philippines. This opened a place for the Armenians. Armenians traced their Christian lineage to long before the Protestant Reformation.

Because Armenians had no independent state in the seventeenth century, many had been forcibly relocated to Isfahan by Shah Abbas. From this center, the Armenians spread along caravan and maritime trade routes. One English merchant noted that

> the Armenians being skilled in all the intricacies of trade at home, and traveling with these into the remotest kingdoms, become by their own industry, and by being factors of their own kindred's honesty, the wealthiest men. . . . They are a kind of privateers in trade, no purchase, no pay; they enter the theater of commerce by means of some benefactor, whose money they adventure upon, and on return, a quarter part of their gain is their own: From such beginnings do they raise sometimes great fortunes for themselves and their masters.

The families developed a training and apprentice system to bring younger members into the family businesses. Young men were trained in handwriting, foreign languages, and accounting practices. Upon reaching adulthood, they were given a sum of money to manage and were promoted according to their financial and business success. The merit-based system seemed to work for several generations as the Armenians became major players in the commercial development of the Indian Ocean region.

elimination of the Turkish guards and the conquest of their tribes. Abbas created units composed of prisoners of war from the Caucasus area; these men had settled in Persia, and most had converted to Islam. The new force became an elite element in the reorganized Safavid army; with intensive training, these soldiers became the backbone of the forces that maintained Safavid rule.

Attacks against the Uzbeks resumed in the seventeenth century, and Abbas regained the vital silk-producing regions of northeast Persia. He also asserted control over important trade routes. By 1603, Abbas felt strong enough to confront the Ottoman Turks, and he slowly won back the lands lost early in his reign. In 1622, Shah Abbas also ousted the Portuguese from Hormuz, an island fortress in the Persian Gulf. This action gave the Persians access to Indian Ocean trade, especially with the Mughals of India.

Abbas not only fought wars and reformed his government, but he also embarked on a complex series of economic reforms. Realizing that political strength rested on economic prosperity, Abbas captured vital trade routes. He built roads and refurbished old highways. ***Caravanserais***, or inns where merchants could recover from arduous journeys, were founded at strategic intervals along trade routes.

The Persian capital was relocated to Isfahan, far from Ottoman areas and at the nexus of key trade routes. To promote trade, Abbas forcibly uprooted 3,000 Armenian families to settle in his new capital. These Armenians applied themselves to commerce and played a key role in the growth of trade in Persia. At the same time, the mass industrial production of ceramic wares, textiles, and carpets fueled prosperity. Silk production became a government monopoly, as did other vital industries. The royal artisans played a major role in the production of export goods. Abbas invested in trading ventures and encouraged Persian large landowners to do likewise. For diplomatic and economic purposes, Abbas maintained relations with the Mughals of India, the Crimean Tatars, and various European powers.

FIGURE 27.5 ***Armenian Church in Persia.*** *Armenian merchants played an important economic role for the Safavid rulers. In return, they were accorded special privileges, including the construction of their own churches in Isfahan, the Safavid capital. This domed church is dedicated to Saint Astavtzatzin, the Holy Mother of God.* Courtesy of Nice Vecchione.

Arts and Literature

The relocation of the capital stimulated Isfahan's growth from a sleepy town to a world metropolis. Abbas hired architects to create monumental buildings, such as the Isfahan Mosque, the Gatehouse, and the Royal Square. One mosque had a double dome and was built on an unprecedented scale, taking twenty years to complete. Master calligraphers decorated the building with graceful calligraphy. Chahar Bagh was an avenue nearly three miles long with fountains, cascades, trellised walls, and shaded walks with streams, flowers, and trees. People rode, walked, and conversed on this urban thoroughfare, which proclaimed Isfahan as one of the world's spectacular cities. Abbas built a Christian church for the Armenians and permitted Jews to build a synagogue.

Painters received royal patronage and much stimulation from Shah Tahmasp[10] I (reign dates

[10]**Tahmasp:** TAH uhm ehsp

1524–1576), who painted miniatures. Persians had a flair for miniature painting; long before the Safavids, outstanding Persian miniatures had been painted, some showing the influence of Chinese paintings brought to Persia by the Mongols. One famous miniaturist worked on a manuscript that contained more than 250 miniatures and consumed ten years of his life.

FIGURE 27.6 ***Persian Tile Mosaic.*** *Persian artists of Isfahan often painted on tiles. This tile painting depicts a woman at leisure, holding a vase and being offered fruit by a servant. Gardens were often favorite sites for domestic scenes; note how the floral pattern of the woman's gown complements the flowers in the garden.* Victoria & Albert Museum.

Shaykh-i Bahai (1546–1631) was perhaps the most admired scholar of the Safavid period. He was born in Lebanon and went to Persia. Shaykh-i Bahai mastered Persian and composed many poems in that language. He wrote more than ninety works on theology, rhetoric, Arabic grammar, mathematics, astronomy, law, and mysticism.

MUGHAL RULE IN INDIA, 1526–1707

The Central Asian ruler Babur[11] (reign dates 1526–1530) founded the Mughal Empire in India. At its height, the Mughal domain covered nearly all of the Indian subcontinent, and the Mughal emperors ruled a population of nearly 150 million people. Persian became the state language, and Persian artists, architects, and officials imparted a Persian character to an emerging Indian cultural synthesis. Although the Mughal leaders claimed Mongol and Turkish ancestry, most viewed themselves as Indians and professed Islam as their faith.

Akbar's Conquests and Administration

Akbar (reign dates 1556–1605), one of India's greatest rulers, brought Mughal rule to the western coast of India, controlled vital maritime trade routes, and expanded south to the Deccan Plateau. To overawe and protect his subjects, Akbar built four huge forts, which guarded the central area of the Mughal realm. He also massacred the population of an enemy city in 1567 to show that resistance to him could bring utter destruction.

Although Akbar came to the throne as a teenager, he and able advisors soon devised and implemented long-range solutions that brought peace and prosperity. By the age of twenty, Akbar assumed full command of his government, and one of his first actions was to marry a Hindu princess. Later he married additional wives: another Hindu, a Christian, and a Muslim. This showed Akbar's religious tolerance, according to some scholars. Akbar followed a policy of building a stable government by appointing different peoples to the administration. A Hindu commanded Akbar's army, and other Hindus served in the

[11] **Babur:** bah BUHR

Figure 27.7 ***Mughal Monumental Architecture.*** *Akbar built a capital, Fatehpur Sikri, which was briefly occupied and later abandoned for lack of adequate water sources. This scene conveys the overwhelming majesty of the capital's main building, meant to convey the might of Akbar's rule. Among these buildings is the mosque at the tomb of Shaykh Salim Chisti, the Sufi saint who was revered by Akbar.* Roland and Sabrina Michaud/Woodfin Camp and Associates.

financial administration. They were given charge of the state's tax collection because Akbar believed that Hindu tax agents would not gouge their fellow Hindus.

Todar Mal,[12] Akbar's Hindu finance minister, devised a revenue-raising system that transformed state finances and society. Finance officials developed a survey form that took into account agricultural land size, soil fertility, and average yields of various crops (over ten-year cycles). Each crop was expressed in monetary terms, reflecting average prices in local or regional markets. Because tax receipts were to be paid in cash, peasants or their agents sold their crops in order to get tax funds. Local leaders who had dominated areas of 20 to 100 villages were forced to become state revenue collectors in exchange for 10 percent of the tax revenues. This policy and others gave the Mughals a reputation for promoting stability and prosperity, thereby helping to prolong Mughal rule of India.

The mixture of diverse influences at Akbar's court may be seen in the patronage of various courtiers. Akbar welcomed writers in Hindi and Urdu, two languages that evolved from the admixture of Persian with local Indian dialects or languages. He also encouraged Hindu painters who specialized in drawings of India's flora and fauna. Persian poets, artists, and scientists who immigrated from Persia enjoyed imperial favor and support in and after Akbar's era.

Architectural development received great impetus during Akbar's reign. He worked on two capitals, Delhi and Agra, and planned a third. The last had to be abandoned for lack of sufficient

[12] **Todar Mal:** toh DAHR mahl

water to support an urban population. Akbar commanded architects and builders to construct forts, palaces, and mosques in his cities.

Akbar was illiterate, but he had books read to him, and his European contemporaries remarked on his vast knowledge and retentive memory. Avidly curious, Akbar welcomed adherents of various beliefs, including Hinduism, Christianity, and Zoroastrianism. Akbar would discuss religion with them, but, until his later years, he retained the essence of his Islamic beliefs. His realm was noted for its religious tolerance, which was especially shrewd, given that the majority of Indians believed in Hinduism.

Some of Akbar's actions and policies angered Muslims. Perhaps in deference to his Hindu subjects, he also abstained from eating beef and finally became a vegetarian. Many Muslim leaders opposed these departures from orthodox Muslim practices. Akbar's assumption of power over judging Islamic law, especially in capital offenses, caused additional grumbling by Islamic religious leaders. Part of Akbar's motivation stemmed from a case in 1578 in which a *brahman* (Hindu priest) was tried and executed for the crime of insulting the name of Muhammad. Akbar also investigated the entitlement of Muslim officials to claim state funds and found many cases of corruption.

UNDER THE LENS

Sikhism under the Mughals

Sikhism, a monotheistic religion founded in North India, began as an attempt to bridge the religious differences between Islam and Hinduism and was transformed into a religion of resistance to Mughal oppression. In the process, it appealed to commoners in northern India. By the eighteenth century, a major Sikh uprising erupted and helped bring about the decline of the Mughals, especially in the north.

The founding of Sikhism (Sikh[a] means disciple) originated with Guru (spiritual teacher) Nanak (1469–1539). Guru Nanak grew up in northern India and learned Arabic, Persian, and Sanskrit, languages associated with Islam and Hinduism. A man of great personal charisma, Guru Nanak loved to travel and walked across North India; later he went to Mecca and other cities in South and Southwest Asia. He taught that because there is one god, the creator, there is no Hindu, no Muslim. Guru Nanak welcomed all people irrespective of belief, gender, or social station. All people ate together, contrary to caste principles of strict segregation and separateness. Men and women, as well as people of different castes, shared dining facilities. Early Sikhs were exhorted to call on God's name, share earnings, and work hard.

Sikhism spread slowly through the sixteenth century, but its modest success led to persecution. Trouble for the Sikhs grew out of the succession dispute associated with Akbar's sons. Jehangir eventually succeeded his father and executed the reigning guru, who had favored one of his brothers. This was the first of several martyrdoms that sparked the growth of Sikhism.

Aurangzeb attempted to quell Sikhism but ended up making it even stronger. Fearing the successful spread of Sikhism, especially with the conversion of Muslims, Aurangzeb arrested, tried, and executed a charismatic leader. This and other attempts at repression drove Guru Govind and the Sikhs into open resistance. Govind transformed Sikhism by turning the Sikhs into an Army of the Pure. He and his followers took the family name Singh (lion), distinguished themselves by refusing to cut their hair, by wearing a steel bracelet, and by wearing a knife or sword.

After Guru Govind's assassination, a major uprising of Sikhs engulfed much of India north of Delhi, a major Mughal city. The Sikhs were inspired by Banda, an ascetic follower of Guru Govind. Banda traveled across the northern plains preaching and welcoming all groups, including many lower socioeconomic groups. Religious fervor and hatred of elite groups drove the Sikhs to success against cavalry and cannonballs hurled against them. Cities fell to the rebels, and inhabitants who refused to convert were killed; temples were desecrated and homes were looted. Only a major effort by the Mughals in 1715 quelled the uprising, with much bloodshed and reprisal. Sikhism continued to enjoy mass support in the north.

[a]**Sikh:** SEEKH

FIGURE 27.8 ***Lively Discussion.*** *This Persian miniature of the late seventeenth century depicts an unveiled woman engaged in a lively discussion with a religious teacher. Some Sufi organizations accepted women as equal members of their orders.* Museen des Kunsthandwerke, Leipzig.

At one point, Akbar created his own religion (Akbarism), which espoused one deity, the Sun God, without the need of a priesthood. He planned to unite his subjects spiritually as his government united them politically. Because of this tolerant approach to the old faiths, Akbar did not try to compel people to believe in his new one. As a consequence, the religion died with him.

Prominent families also played key roles in the Mughal government. The favorite wife of Jehangir[13] (reign dates 1605–1627) was Nur Jahan[14] (1577–1645), who initiated many Mughal policies. Jehangir was seriously ailing for his last decade of rule, partly because of his addiction to alcohol and other drugs. Nur Jahan, in alliance with her father and brother, dominated the government, and she is regarded as one of several influential Muslim and Hindu women in the Mughal era.

Shah Jahan (1627–1658) is another Mughal ruler who merits mention. He maintained a luxurious lifestyle in which dancing, singing, and gambling entertained the court. Shah Jahan indulged himself in his harem of hundreds of wives, yet he favored one, Mumtaz Mahal, who gave birth to fourteen children. She died in childbirth, and he mourned her death by erecting a mausoleum, the Taj Mahal. One of the world's architectural masterpieces, the Taj Mahal shows a strong Persian character but also combines Hindu features and echoes the stylistic synthesis of Akbar's era.

The Reign of Aurangzeb

Aurangzeb[15] (reign dates 1658–1707), one of Shah Jahan's sons, rebelled against his father and imprisoned him until he died. Aurangzeb reacted against many previous trends in the Mughal era. He abolished the court entertainments and used religious texts to support his actions. He imposed previously revoked taxes on nonbelievers, including an assessment on Hindu pilgrims. He also revived the policy of razing Hindu temples; hundreds of architectural masterpieces fell to the destructive policies of Aurangzeb and his ardent followers.

Aurangzeb resumed the conquest of India, planning to subjugate the entire subcontinent. Because the military effort took decades, it bankrupted the treasury. Even though tax revenues had doubled from 1589 to 1689, taxes were increased to fight the wars. The contracting out of tax revenues to Muslims who purchased the right to collect the expected sums and then pocketed the excess monies brought a rapacious exploitation of Hindus, who rebelled. By his death, Aurangzeb's administration was beyond repair and eventually collapsed.

[13] **Jehangir:** jeh HAHN gee hyr
[14] **Nur Jahan:** NUHR jah HAHN
[15] **Aurangzeb:** AH rahng zehb

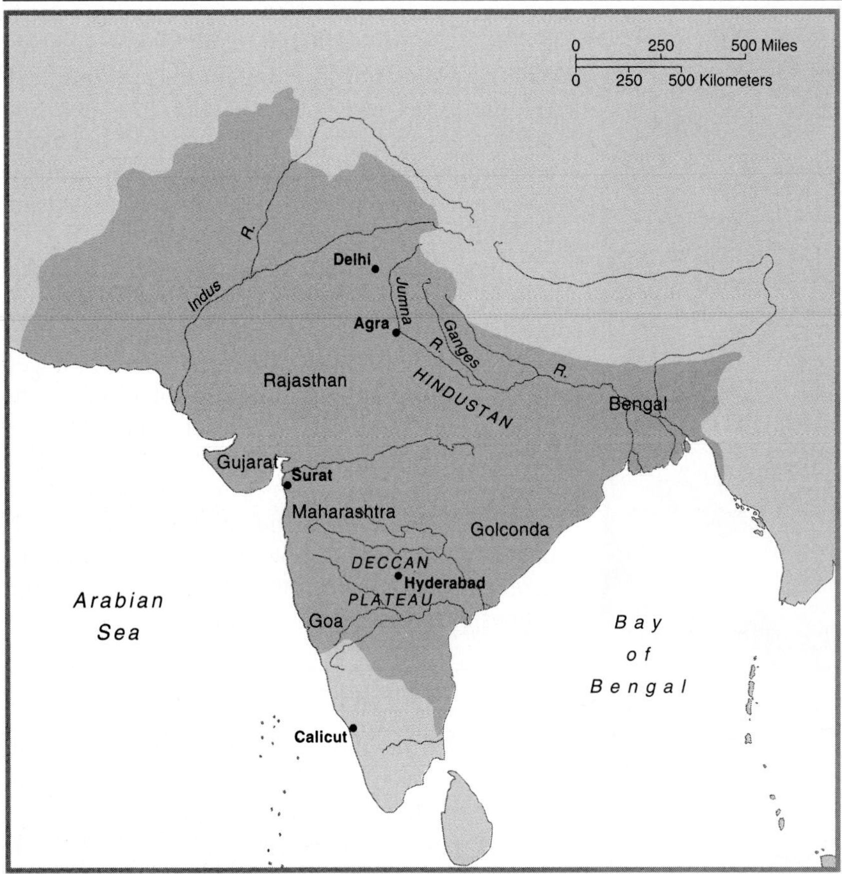

MAP 27.2 ***The Mughal Empire, around 1710.*** *Akbar and Aurangzeb conquered much of present-day India, Pakistan, and Bangladesh. Though pockets of resistance held out against the Mughals, especially in the west, they ruled a vast area by 1710—one that gradually succumbed to the British.*

Class and Caste

Mughal rulers presided over a traditional Islamic social structure with courtiers occupying the top of the social system, Muslim officials enjoying moderate prominence, and Muslim merchants having some prestige.

But the Mughals ruled over a majority population of Hindu subjects who were socially governed by a caste system that had endured for centuries. Although a loose, religiously defined social structure existed (the four Varna castes of *brahman* priests, warriors, commoners, and peasants), most Hindus were grouped by occupational castes (*jati*). Thus, there were scribal *jati* (lower officials), merchant *jati*, artisan *jati*, and peasant *jati*; most *jati* had regional or local identities and were largely self-regulating. The *jati* interacted economically and politically but seldom socially; members of a *jati* did not marry outside of their *jati*. One was born, married, and died within the *jati*. Thus, the Mughals ruled over two distinct social systems, which meshed at the court.

THE EMERGENCE OF THE RUSSIAN EMPIRE, 1462–1682

The Russian Empire emerged in the fifteenth century and eventually straddled Europe and Asia. Russian leaders directed a centralized state with an economy heavily dependent on the labor of serfs, peasants bound permanently to the land. Rulers of Moscow gradually became the tsars (emperors) of the Russian Empire.

Why did Moscow prevail over the other contending political entities? It was ruled by a series of leaders who usually managed peaceful successions to the throne. These far-sighted monarchs expanded their domains by all available means, including purchase and warfare, yet they understood that expansion depended on patient planning. A major success was the agreement that the Russian Orthodox Church would accept Moscow as its capital. Moscow also occupied a strategic position in northern Russia, lying between rivers along which trade goods easily moved.

The Accomplishments of Ivan the Great

The monarch Ivan the Great (reign dates 1462–1505) embarked on a series of policies to strengthen Moscow's dominance in the north. His foreign policy embodied the reconquest of western lands lost to the Lithuanians and the defeat of the khanates in the east. Ivan allied with the Crimean Khanate to defeat a Mongol-Lithuanian alliance. Victory came in 1480 and freed Moscow from two centuries of Mongol domination. Ivan fought the Lithuanian monarchy, which oppressed Russian princes under its control. Through a series of wars, many princes defected to Ivan, who claimed to rule all Russian peoples. Ivan also brought the Kazan[16] Khanate of the middle Volga River under his protection.

Aside from these diplomatic gains, Ivan conquered Novgorod and other city-states in northern Russia. Each campaign followed a carefully scripted scenario wherein Moscow's troops intervened in an internal dispute and gradually took control. Ivan understood that to conquer and rule, he must reform his government. He gained control over his officials by establishing the **service gentry**, landlords who joined his army and served in his administration. They owed their positions to Ivan and adhered to his demand for complete obedience, serving the same purpose that the Janissaries did for the Ottomans. To secure the support of the service gentry, who served away from their estates for long periods, Ivan permitted serfdom, binding peasants to the land.

Ivan established long-lasting institutions and practices. He oversaw the codification of law, which created a legal foundation for the state in 1497. In addition, a judicial system was established to dispense the monarch's justice, while other decrees directed government officials to be honest, loyal, and hardworking. Special investigating officials designated by Ivan served as a check on his subordinates.

After great personal trials, Ivan curbed the influence of his immediate family members and in-laws. He finally decided the succession in favor of his son, Basil. More than four decades of cautious rule and steady growth of Moscow's power warranted most historians to name Ivan III "the Great."

[16] **Kazan:** KAH zahn

The Reign of Ivan the Terrible

Ivan IV (reign dates 1533–1584) earned the appellation "Terrible" because he left Russians traumatized by his policies. A regency of Ivan's mother and aristocrats brought grief for Ivan, whose mother died in his eighth year. It is likely that she was poisoned; at least he suspected foul play. Aristocrat princes accorded Ivan public honor but scorned him in private. Ivan took power for himself in 1548, crowning himself tsar. In 1553, Ivan suffered a serious illness and wished to name his son heir, but he was thwarted by the princes. Finally, a suspicious Ivan turned against his top officials and aristocrats in the 1560s, launching a one-sided civil war that killed many. In the 1570s, thousands more were tortured to death, and the succession itself was affected when Ivan killed his adult son during a rage.

Ivan IV ruled effectively for many years. He reformed the government to improve its administration; a law code was published in 1550. The military was restructured and better trained in order to make it more efficient. The church was brought under governmental supervision, and church priests obeyed state law. Ivan followed his grandfather's (Ivan III) policy of expanding Russian control to the Baltic Sea, yet these early military successes united Russia's traditional enemies, Lithuania and Poland.

Ivan IV's greatest victories came in the east and southeast. The Kazan Khanate tamed by Ivan III became restive in the early 1550s, and Ivan IV launched a campaign that brought its annexation. Soon after, a second expedition conquered the Astrakhan Khanate, bringing the Volga River Valley under Russian control. A major reorientation had taken place, because now Russia, a European power, lay astride strategic Asian trade and transportation routes.

Russia's eastward expansion took a different route when the Stroganov merchant family supported the crossing of the Ural Mountains by a military force. With relative ease, Russians conquered the Siberian Khanate in the 1580s. When a group of Siberians tried to retake the khanate's capital, Ivan IV sent military support, defeating the Siberians. This opened the massive area of Siberia to Russian exploration, colonization, and exploitation. Furs, precious metals, and other materials could be easily gathered and traded. Part of the ease of Russian

FIGURE 27.9 ***Ivan the Terrible's Reign of Terror.*** *This woodcut shows the Russian tsar leading a group of subjects who are bound, awaiting punishment. Ivan is carrying the severed head of one victim, while another subject, perhaps a child, is impaled, framed by the horse's legs. In the background others are being beheaded and hanged. Thousands of people met similar deaths that were overseen by the tsar during his reign of terror.* The New York Public Library, Slavonic Division.

expansion is attributable to the many deaths caused by epidemics among Siberians, who could not withstand the diseases that the Europeans carried.

To conduct his foreign policy and expand central control of the land, Ivan IV relied heavily on the service gentry. He honored their growing appetite for permanent peasant labor by expanding serfdom. Peasants resented being bound to the land, and many fled to frontier areas in the south. The state tried to support its officials by outlawing the practice of flight and by returning apprehended serfs to their lords.

The Crimean Khanate, which had been allied with Ivan III, turned against Ivan IV, launching raids against Moscow and capturing many citizens. Perhaps 100,000 people were taken from their homes to slavery in the south. The loss of taxpayers caused a fiscal crisis, prompting authorities to raise taxes. A general depopulation resulted as many fled the ever-increasing taxes.

Ivan IV died, and, because his successor was ineffective, power devolved to capable officials who instituted reforms, reversing Ivan IV's harsh policies. Yet beneath the surface calm, the larger demographic issue of the depopulation of central Russia and the decline of tax revenues meant that any state crisis might lead to collapse. When this successor died, the line of Ivan IV ended. Rule passed to Tsar Boris Godunov (reign dates 1598–1605), an in-law of the dynastic house, but within a short time Russia found itself immersed in civil war, beset by foreign invasion, and faced with revolt by commoners.

Crisis and Revival

The Time of Troubles (1598–1613) saw Russia in collapse and chaos. The tsarist system failed to cope with its massive problems, and major social uprisings and foreign invasions imperiled Russia. Sweden took territory in the north, and Poland invaded, captured Moscow, and left a Polish ruler in charge. By 1610, it seemed that the threat of extinction haunted the Russian state. Members of the religious elite rallied the Russian people, and finally a group of landlords and merchants raised an army that defeated the foreigners. A social crisis in which the have-nots challenged the haves sputtered through various conflicts. By 1613, the people of Russia agreed that a new dynasty should rule, and they sent representatives to an assembly that elected a member of the Romanov family as the new tsar.

The first three Romanovs ruled from 1613 to 1682 and wielded power in a moderate fashion. Taxes lightly burdened the people, and foreign policies concentrated on regaining lost lands. A new law code was published in 1649, codifying the procedures and practices of serfdom for the succeeding two centuries.

Religious leaders in the 1650s and 1660s attempted to reform the Russian Orthodox ritual. Many Russians (Old Believers) viewed the changes in ritual as blasphemous and refused to accept them. This controversy in Russian Orthodoxy became political as well as religious because the state persecuted the Old Believers.

UNIFYING FEATURES OF THE FOUR EMPIRES

The Ottoman, Safavid, Mughal, and Russian empires had certain things in common, including the use of gunpowder technology, the significance of religion in defining each empire's cultural tradition, and the relative insignificance of European culture in imperial life.

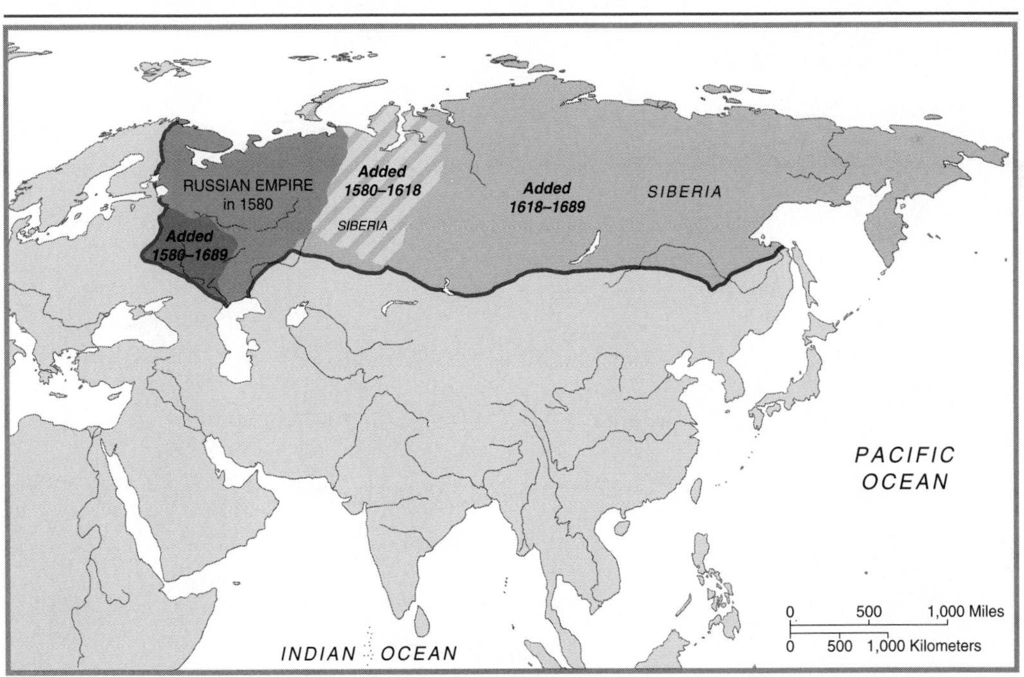

Map 27.3 ***Expansion of the Russian Empire, to 1689.*** *Although Ivan the Terrible briefly added territory reaching to the Baltic Sea in the northwest, these lands could not be held until the eighteenth century. Ivan's more enduring imperial legacy was the expansion southeast to the Caspian Sea and east into Siberia, which claimed vast lands for the sprawling Russian Empire.*

The Role of Gunpowder Technology

Gunpowder technology strongly influenced the expansion of each empire. Ottoman leaders were among the first to employ cannons. They unsuccessfully battered the formidable walls of Constantinople in 1422, but more accurate and devastating cannon fire helped shatter its defenses in 1453. In 1514, Ottoman cannonballs and musket shot smashed a Safavid army poorly trained in gunpowder warfare, but Safavid commanders soon employed cannons to deadly effect against their enemies in the east. Mughal cannons devastated city walls during sieges, and Russian monarchs formed regiments of musketeers. Each empire added units of musketeers who became elite guards.

Religious Influence

Religion strongly influenced politics, social life, and the arts of the four empires. The Ottoman Turks ardently believed in Islam and often declared ***jihad***, a holy struggle against their enemies, either Christian or Muslim. In the early 1500s, Egypt and Palestine were conquered, and Jerusalem, Mecca, and Medina, the three holiest cities of Islam, came under Ottoman jurisdiction. From that time, the Ottoman rulers undertook the responsibility for defending Islam, especially the Sunni sect. The major Ottoman rivals, Safavid Persians, embraced Shi'ism. This brought religious oppression in both empires because Sunnis repressed Shi'ites and vice versa. Political rivalries caused Muslim rulers to be more intolerant of other Muslims than of Christians or Jews.

Religion played a significant role in Mughal India and in Russia. Hinduism was the religion of the majority of Indians, and Islam had been in India since the eighth century. Early Mughal rulers (Muslims) practiced religious toleration, but later rulers attempted to compel all to embrace Islam. Resentment against growing intolerance by the state undermined Mughal rule in the late seventeenth century.

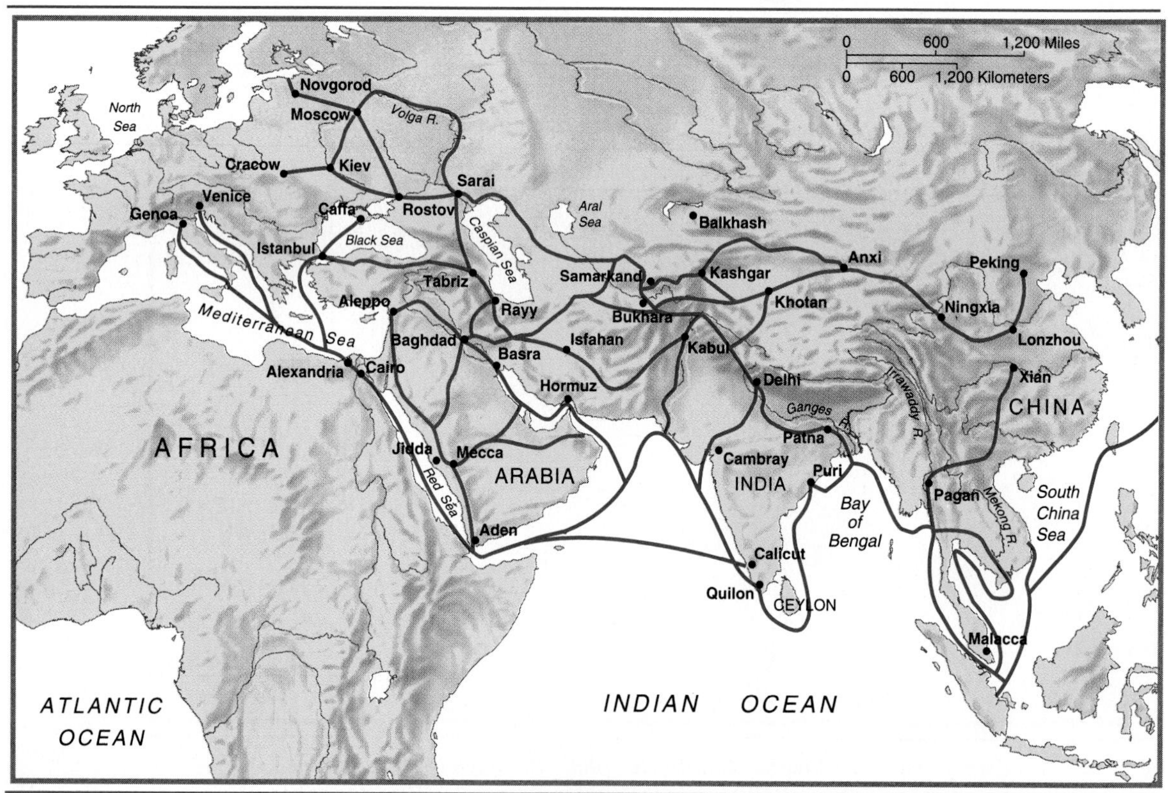

MAP 27.4 *Trade Routes of the Four Empires. The Mughal, Ottoman, Russian, and Safavid empires straddled vital trade routes passing from Europe and Africa through Asia. As European maritime power expanded, the land routes among the four empires became more important for intra-empire trade.*

CENTRAL EURASIA	SOUTHWEST ASIA	Date	Events
	Folk Islam in Southwest Asia, c.1200–c.1450	1300	
	Early Ottoman Empire, 1352–c. 1800		Ottoman army lands in Europe, 1352
		1400	
Early Russian Empire, 1462–1682			Ottoman Turks take Constantinople, 1453
			Ivan the Great stops a Mongol invasion, 1480
	Safavid Empire, 1501–1736	1500	Ottoman army defeats the Persian army, 1514
Mughal Empire, 1526–1707			Akbar assumes power in India, 1556
			Ivan the Terrible dies, 1584
		1600	Portuguese ousted by Persians in Hormuz, 1622
			Shah Jahan builds the Taj Mahal, c. 1640
		1700	Aurangzeb dies, 1707
		1800	

Moscow princes used the Eastern Orthodox Church to help solidify their rule by claiming to support all Eastern Orthodox adherents. During the early seventeenth century, invasion and rule over Russia by Catholic princes (Poles) brought a general rising of the Russian people led by Eastern Orthodox priests. The successful uprising had patriotic and religious overtones.

European Influence

Perhaps the most significant impact of the Europeans on the Ottoman, Safavid, Mughal, and Russian empires related to trade. Long-established trade routes brought goods to the peoples of the empires, and European merchants became important participants in trade. The Ottoman, Safavid, and Mughal monarchs played off merchants against one another, favoring those of their European allies or Europeans with whom they wished to do business. Russian rulers traded with merchants from states around the Baltic Sea but increasingly sought trade ties with the Ottomans and Safavids. Russian furs were prized by rich people of the Islamic lands and other parts of Europe, while Persian silks were worn in Russia, India, and Egypt.

Although Muslim rulers appreciated European technological and scientific advances and adopted them, their impact on Ottoman, Safavid, or Mughal statecraft was slight. Gunpowder weapons arrived in South and Southwest Asia about the same time as in Europe. Occasionally, European artisans were hired by Muslim monarchs (and Russians), but these artisans' influence was limited. Turks and Persians had traditions of excellence in astronomy and mathematics, remaining abreast of European knowledge until the late sixteenth century. After that, European scientific leadership went unheeded as most Islamic scholars confined themselves to religious and legal matters.

SUMMARY

1. The Ottoman Turks built an empire that ruled parts of Europe, Asia, and Africa. The Ottoman leaders prospered as long as they controlled most key trade routes between Asia and Europe. Rulers like Mehmed II and Suleyman I significantly expanded the Ottoman domain, and Selim I added Syria and Egypt, two vital regions.

2. Ottoman architects like Sinan designed impressive mosques and *medreses*. Important scholarly works, including encyclopedias, were written during the Ottoman era. Turkish literature showed some influence of Persian literature.

3. Ottoman society had distinct social classes, including the ruling elite, merchants, artisans, and slaves.

4. The Safavids rose in Southwest Asia, then expanded their rule over Turks and Persians. The Safavid Empire promoted the Shi'a belief system, especially in Persia.

5. Like the Ottomans, the Safavids developed trade and seized Eurasian trade routes. Shah Abbas I laid the foundations of Safavid power by building a strong economy, conquering important territory, and developing a splendid capital, Isfahan.

6. The Mughals conquered India from their base in Central Asia. A strong Persian component characterized the emerging Indian culture, which also had Turkish Islamic elements.

7. Akbar ruled effectively and created expectations of fairness that thwarted his intolerant great-grandson, Aurangzeb. Muslim classes and a caste system regulating Hindus made up Mughal society.

8. Moscow rulers created an autocratic system that relied on service gentry who needed serf support. Tsars expanded from Moscow in all directions and were most successful in the east. They fought against Polish Catholics and Russian Old Believers.

9. The Ottoman, Safavid, Mughal, and Russian empires were similar in being gunpowder-based states, in being strongly influenced by religion, and in being little influenced by European culture.

SUGGESTED READINGS

Chaudhuri, K. N. *Trade and Civilisation in the Indian Ocean.* Cambridge, Eng.: Cambridge University Press, 1985. A work that analyzes trade's impact on civilizations from 600 to 1750, using the model of Fernand Braudel.

Dukes, Paul. *The Making of Russian Absolutism.* London: Longman's Press, 1990. A standard survey of the seventeenth and eighteenth centuries.

Inalcik, Halil. *The Ottoman Empire.* New York: Orpheus Publishing, 1989 (reprint of the 1973 edition). A classic study of the first three Ottoman centuries.

Jackson, Peter. *The Cambridge History of Iran.* Volume VI. Cambridge, Eng.: Cambridge University Press, 1986. A major treatment of the Safavid era.

Riasanovsky, Nicholas. *A History of Russia.* New York: Oxford University Press, 1993. Perhaps the best Russian history survey.

Richards, John. *The New Cambridge History of India: The Mughal Empire.* New York: Cambridge University Press, 1993. An excellent examination of the Mughal Empire, including social and economic history.

Walther, Wiebke. *Women in Islam.* Trans. C. S. V. Salt. Princeton, N.J.: Markus Wiener Publishing, 1993. An examination of Muslim women, with special attention to their social position and with excellent pictures.

Wheatcroft, Andrew. *The Ottomans.* London: Viking Press, 1993. A well-illustrated survey of Ottoman politics.

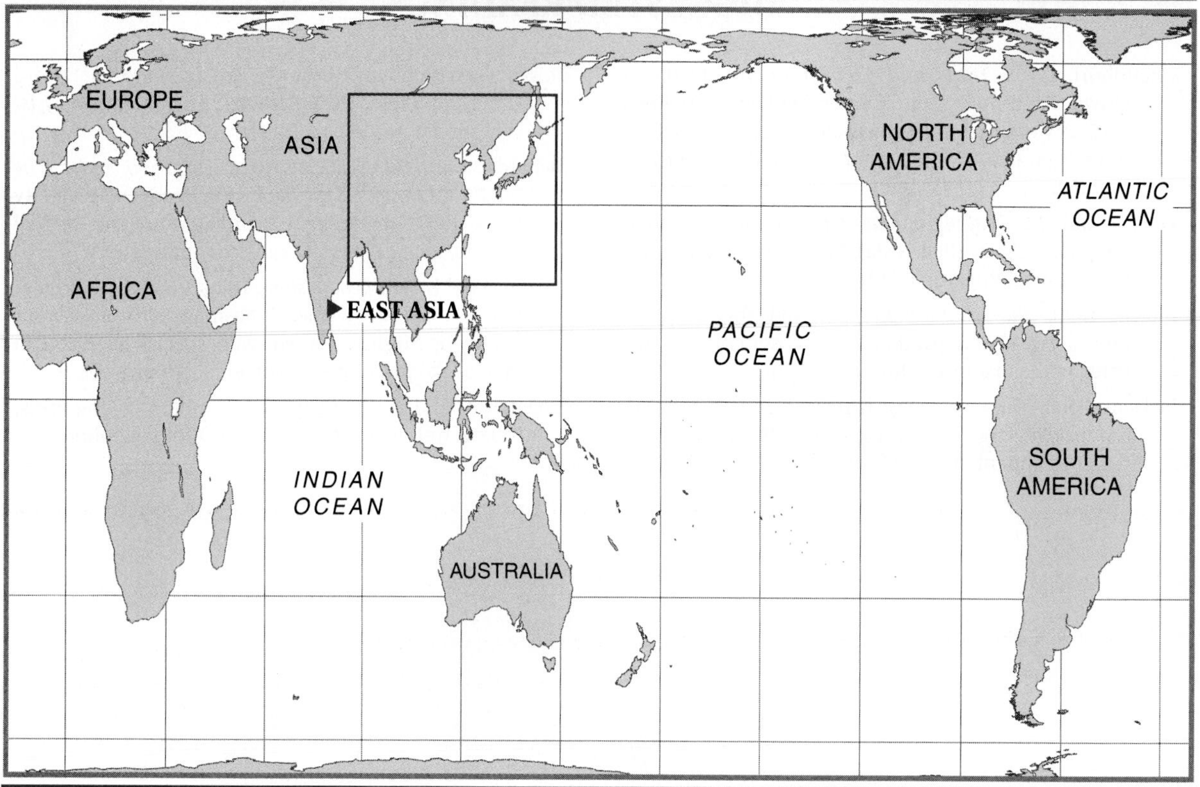

EUROPE
ASIA
NORTH AMERICA
ATLANTIC OCEAN
AFRICA
PACIFIC OCEAN
INDIAN OCEAN
AUSTRALIA
SOUTH AMERICA

▶ EAST ASIA

Sea of Japan
KOREA
JAPAN
Yellow R.
CHINA
Yangzi R.
East China Sea
PACIFIC OCEAN
South China Sea
Philippine Sea

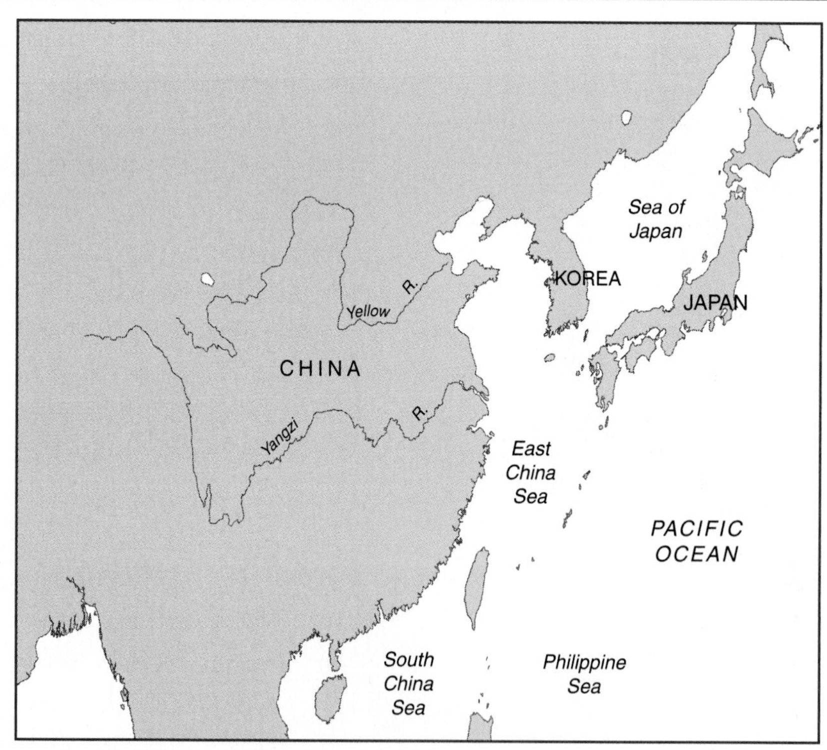

▶ **EAST ASIA**

CHAPTER 28

Colliding States in East Asia
around 1350–around 1800

In 1592, a Roman Catholic priest pored over intelligence dispatches from his contacts in Japan. They told of a large number of **samurai** *warriors gathering for an invasion of Korea and China. Tens of thousands of them were Christian Japanese soldiers, many of whom were musketeers. The massive army and naval force dwarfed the Spanish Armada, which had made a similar attempt to invade England in 1588. The Japanese military action, like that of the Spanish, failed.*

East Asian powers were in collision as states fought one another. Japan attacked Korea and China, while the Chinese invaded Vietnam or fought off the Mongols and Manchus. Europeans had only a modest impact on East Asian peoples before 1750. European traders brought guns and Christianity to the Japanese and Chinese, but soon Christianity had largely disappeared in East Asia, and the Japanese had abandoned guns.

MING EMPERORS CREATE A SINOCENTRIC WORLD ORDER, 1368–1644

A major Chinese uprising in the mid-1300s toppled the ruling Mongol Empire (1279–1368) and established the Ming Empire, which ruled for nearly three centuries (1368–1644). Early Ming rulers fashioned a stable government and created an inward-looking system of international rela-

FIGURE 28.1 ***The Hongwu Emperor.*** *This realistic portrait of the Ming Empire's founder, a former commoner, shows evidence of his having survived smallpox. The pockmarked face also helps convey the ferocity of a ruler who tyrannized his subjects and officials alike. Imperial absolutism grew as the Hongwu emperor gathered power into his own hands.* National Palace Museum, Taiwan, Republic of China.

tions. They believed that foreigners came to China to recognize the superiority of Chinese ways because China was the center of the world.

The Politics of the Hongwu and Yongle Emperors, 1368–1424

The Ming Empire, which succeeded the Mongol Empire, was founded by a commoner and orphan, Zhu Yuanzhang.[1] In order to survive, Zhu became a Buddhist monk and begged for a living, but his fortunes improved after he joined a rebel army. Within a short time, Zhu married the leader's daughter and assumed control of the force after the leader's death. Finally, Zhu Yuanzhang formed a government that administered some of China's most prosperous areas, and he gathered a core of advisors who had excellent skills in statecraft and military affairs. His Ming armies defeated all rivals, including the Mongols, and Zhu Yuanzhang was crowned and given the title of the Hongwu[2] Emperor in 1368.

The Ming government strongly reflected the founder's personality traits: suspicion about people's motives, scorn for the seemingly pretentious manners of the scholar officials, and a yearning for a return to the ways of earlier empires. The Hongwu Emperor created an inward-looking regime that shunned contact with the outside world except through a tributary system wherein emissaries bearing tribute came to China and pretended to acknowledge the superiority of its ways. Because the Chinese considered themselves superior, the emperor's return gifts had to be more valuable than those received. The Ming state formally outlawed international trade in 1372.

Administrative efficiency was severely hampered by a major purge and governmental reorganization. The Hongwu Emperor killed his prime minister and his commander of the armies. Executions and purges against suspected enemies caused perhaps 100,000 deaths; many who had connections with the prime minister and army commander suffered. These actions and the subsequent restructuring hampered the state as the emperor abolished the prime ministership, meaning that the emperor would thereafter decide all matters previously handled by the prime minister

[1] **Zhu Yuanzhang:** JOO yoo wahn jahng
[2] **Hongwu:** HOHNG woo

Figure 28.2 ***Dragon Robe.*** *Only the monarch or royal appointees could wear clothes with dragons on them. Dragons were the most powerful creatures in Chinese folklore, and the emperor was the most powerful of humans. People caught wearing unauthorized dragon-adorned clothing were treated as rebels and punished accordingly. This was especially true in the Early Ming era, when dragon robes came into fashion.* From Nagogawa Chusei, *Shinzoku Kibur*, 1798.

and his staff. Even the most dynamic monarch wilted under the hundreds of items demanding daily decisions. Another result of the abolition of the office of prime minister was the growing use of eunuchs to assist with various state tasks.

The Hongwu Emperor outlived his heir apparent and named his grandson to that position. When the emperor died in 1398, his grandson ascended to the throne and reigned, with several adult uncles governing parts of the empire. Within a few years many uncles had been deposed. In North China, one uncle, Zhu Di,[3] rebelled and ousted his nephew. A key ploy in Zhu Di's actions was feigning illness so that his sons, who were imperial hostages, would be released to visit their father. Soon after their freeing, Zhu Di revolted and eventually took power in a bloody civil war, reigning as the Yongle Emperor (1403–1424).

Of the Ming monarchs, only the Yongle Emperor was eager to explore the known world. He championed several Chinese naval expeditions (1405–1433) that sailed the Indian Ocean, reaching the east coast of Africa. (See Chapter 23 for more information.) Yet these maritime explorations went against China's fundamental strategic outlook, which was centered on Inner Asia (Mongolia, Manchuria, and Chinese Turkestan). In fact, the Yongle Emperor's shift of the capital from the Lower Yangzi River Valley to Beijing in the north heightened China's insecurity. While Beijing was the Yongle Emperor's power base, it lay so close to the homeland of the Mongols that later Ming rulers, fearing a Mongol revival and conquest of North China, terminated the naval expeditions and rebuilt the Great Wall.

Isolation and Trade

The Ming Empire's inward orientation resumed after the Yongle Emperor's death. Ming rulers turned their backs on earlier financial policies like the use of paper money and large amounts of coinage, as well as the Yongle Emperor's promotion of external trade. Once again, Ming rulers ordered merchants to desist from trading abroad and consistently refused to trade with the Mongols. When Japanese and Chinese pirates preyed on the China coast, the monarchy forcibly moved the coastal population inland, denying the predators any resources. Despite these actions and the hobbling effect of poor monetary instruments, Chinese merchants fared well in internal trade and held their own against foreign competition. By the late sixteenth century, the massive infusion of Mexican and Japanese silver into the world economy assisted the growth of China's economy. At the same time, cities along the coast and others inland prospered because of the increasing trade. Even the government ignored its own trading ban and made profits from maritime trade.

Expanding Intellectual Horizons

The Ming era saw the development of a growing intellectual class, especially in the cities. Education was the ladder of success in providing not

[3] **Zhu Di:** JOO dee

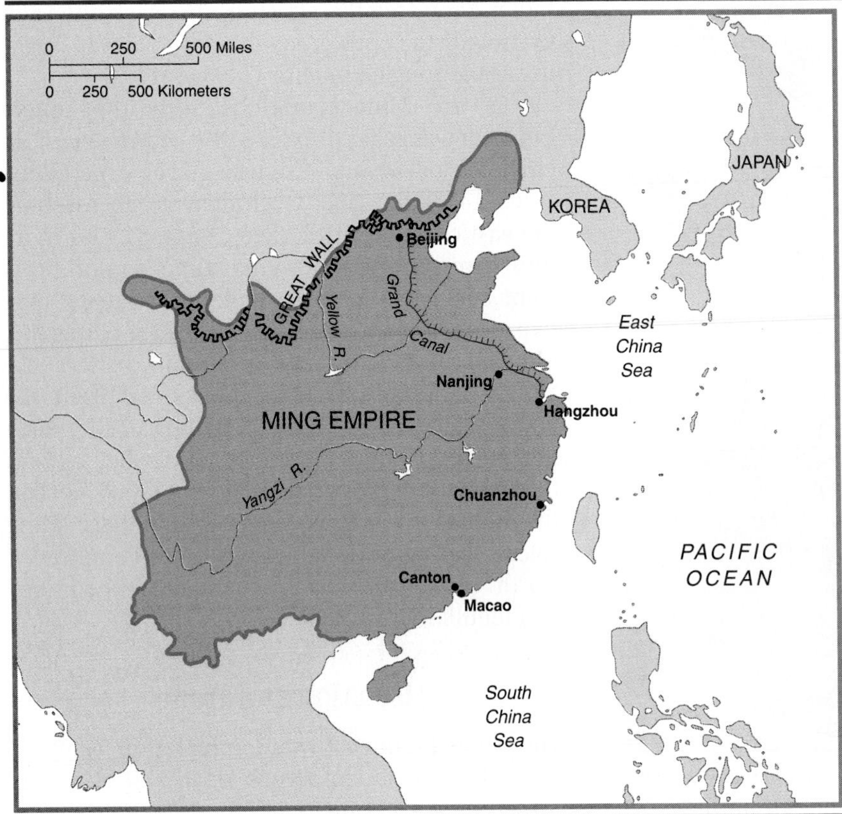

MAP 28.1 ***The Ming Empire around 1600.*** *Although the early Ming emperors were vigorous conquerors, the territory that they and their successors ruled included only Manchuria and small lands in the west. For most of its existence, the empire was inward-looking and defensive. The Grand Canal, which had been expanded and improved by the Mongols in the fourteenth century, linked the prosperous Yangzi delta region with the capital, Beijing. Grain barges regularly plied the artificial waterway, bringing rice and other foodstuffs.*

only the way to governmental service but also a way a person could enter the social elite. Thus, many went to school or learned from hired tutors.

All Ming rulers presided over an imperial examination system through which civil servants were recommended for government service. Memory was the most important element in passing the extremely difficult examinations, which required knowing by heart the Confucian classics and relevant commentaries. The Confucian ideological system became a unified political culture. The majority of officials served efficiently and provided political stability even in times of imperial incompetence. Only between 1590 and 1620, when one monarch deliberately ignored the bureaucracy, did the imperial system seriously deteriorate.

One significant intellectual and social development tied to the implementation of the imperial examination system was the expansion of social mobility. Schools sprang up in cities and towns to educate a growing number of people, some of whom read popular literary works. People, especially city folk, delightedly read short stories and novels, which were often shunned by academicians as "low-brow" writings. Short-story collections became very popular. The great achievement of the Ming era, however, was the novel. Chinese novels originated from prompt books kept by storytellers who traveled within cities and told story cycles over a period of several days. Writers wove these cycles into long narratives, including historical novels like the *Romance of the Three Kingdoms*, fantasy novels like *Journey to the West*, and erotic novels like *Golden Lotus. Golden Lotus* mirrored society, especially in depicting Chinese women as sex objects and playthings of men.

Arts and literature were produced and supported by the intellectual class. Chinese philosophy, for example, was enriched by Wang Yangming[4] (1472–1528), who stressed that reality was as the mind perceived it. His Confucian ideas maintained a practical bent—he was a highly successful official—as seen in his adage that "knowledge is the beginning of action, and action is the completion of knowledge." Thus, book learning was the first step to knowledge.

[4] **Wang Yangming:** WONG yahng mihng

Historical studies became popular as scholars took a critical interest in their past. Chinese historiography remained a special intellectual pursuit, and Ming rulers maintained a bureau of history, where scholars prepared an official history of the Mongols, and a special office kept a record of each reign's special events for future histories. Some scholars also collected artifacts from earlier eras, and a whole field of antiquarian research opened.

FIGURE 28.3 ***Scholar and Attendant.*** *A renewed interest in Confucian ideas developed in the Ming era, and scholars became honored once again. These porcelain pieces capture the tranquil aura ascribed to persons of literary accomplishment. Ming potters excelled at making porcelain pieces that were prized in other lands, such as Persia.* Avery Brundage Collection/Laurie Platt Winfrey, Inc.

Porcelain reached a high level of development and was appreciated by collectors across the world. The famed Ming vases appeared under imperial patronage, and artisans at the imperial kilns perfected the techniques for making vases and plates. Persian potters occasionally used Chinese porcelains as models for their own pottery, which they passed off as Chinese ware.

Population Growth and Social Unrest

For much of the Ming era, a steady population increase took place, but after 1600, weak leaders and climatic changes created conditions for serious uprisings that gravely weakened the Ming government. Early population growth was based on stable political and social conditions; cities increased in size, and some urbanites enjoyed a prosperous existence.

Overcrowding became a problem by the early 1600s, especially when the weather got colder and affected food harvests. Some people migrated overseas, beginning a Chinese diaspora to the Philippines and other parts of Southeast Asia, but the numbers were too small to bring much relief. Bad weather reduced grain harvests and led to a famine and a series of devastating epidemics that killed tens of thousands of people. In addition, conditions forced some commoners to become wanderers or bandits, and widespread areas of North and Central China erupted in large-scale peasant uprisings. One revolt in north-central China saw the rapid advance of a force to the capital, and when the city gates were opened, the last Ming emperor committed suicide. The rebel, Li Zicheng,[5] failed to establish a viable government and fell in 1644 to the Manchus, a non-Chinese people who lived in the northeast.

THE EARLY QING EMPIRE, 1644–1796

The Manchus quickly overran China and established the Qing[6] Empire (1644–1912), a time of peace and prosperity. Manchu leaders adopted the traditional Chinese political system, welcoming obedient scholars who advised on how to effect a

[5] **Li Zicheng:** LEE see chehng
[6] **Qing:** CHEENG

FIGURE 28.4 ***Flower Painting.*** *Ming and Qing artists devoted considerable time to painting flowers. Magnolias and peonies were especially favored for still-life subjects. Wang Hui painted many flowers and landscapes in the styles of famous masters who lived centuries earlier. The inscription notes the artists who influenced Wang Hui, and explains his motivation for creating such a visual perspective.* National Palace Museum, Taiwan, Republic of China.

Chinese-style state. The real power lay in the northeast, where the Manchus allied with the Chinese commander of an army near the Great Wall. This combined force swept to the capital and soon established a new dynasty.

Stability and Expansion

Between 1600 and 1800, the Manchus were blessed with able rulers. Two of them, the Kangxi[7] Emperor (1661–1723) and the Qianlong[8] Emperor (1736–1796), were outstanding leaders because they created effective administrations and significantly expanded China's territory.

The Kangxi Emperor firmly consolidated Manchu rule over China, adding new lands to the empire. He fought a civil war to extend central control over South China and defeated pirates who terrorized the local seas. Beginning in 1690, the Manchus conquered Mongolia and Tibet, increasing Chinese territory by hundreds of thousands of square miles.

Under the Qianlong Emperor, Manchu armies invaded Chinese Turkestan and crossed the Himalayas into Nepal, fighting the Gurkhas, who had been raiding Tibet. The Manchus were unsuccessful in expanding control over Burma and Vietnam, states they invaded but could not conquer. Nevertheless, the extent of Manchu influence rivaled that of all previous regimes.

Inner Asian trade routes saw increasing traffic, including growing commerce with the Russian Empire. Seaborne commerce prospered, and by the eighteenth century, Chinese wares were in great demand in Europe. Internal trade grew in the Qing era, but merchants remained handicapped by discriminatory government policies.

[7] **Kangxi:** KAHNG shee
[8] **Qianlong:** CHEE yahn lohng

Collecting and Censoring Literary Works

Maintaining the imperial examination system continued to promote education and to slowly expand the number of literate people. One group that benefited from education was women, and, while accurate numbers are difficult to determine, various evidence suggests that a modest percentage of urban women were literate by 1800. The Kangxi and Qianlong emperors presided over the gathering and organizing of vast amounts of written materials. They also destroyed works that portrayed Manchus in disparaging terms.

The Kangxi Emperor actively employed his scholars in writing major works that would highlight imperial prestige and Manchu patronage. Soon after he began ruling, the emperor enticed several prominent scholars to work on the history of the Ming Dynasty. In addition, he sponsored another group of intellectuals who collected and published extant poems written during the Tang Dynasty, a time considered China's golden poetic age. Nearly 50,000 poems by around 2,200 poets

FIGURE 28.5 ***Imperial Birthday Celebration.*** *The Kangxi Emperor ruled longer than any previous monarch of China, and his birthdays were celebrated with great festiveness. Elephants and other live animals were sent to the emperor as tributary gifts from southern countries such as Vietnam and Thailand. Chinese officials and servants are distinguished from Manchus by the braids of hair that hang down their backs. A crowd gathers around the royal dais as shopkeepers look on. The foreground of this woodcut provides a glimpse into several inner courtyards.* Cabinet des Estampes, Bibliothèque nationale, Paris/Laurie Platt Winfrey, Inc.

graced the monumental collection. Among other tomes appearing in the emperor's reign was the *Kangxi Dictionary*, a vast work that recorded and defined the words used in Chinese history. These works have ably benefited scholarship ever since.

The Qianlong Emperor also promoted the gathering and categorization of massive amounts of written material. In addition, he presided over a long-lasting and widespread literary inquisition. More than his predecessors, the Qianlong Emperor was concerned about works with passages derogatory to the Manchus. He used the collection of works for a vast project, *The Complete Collection of Materials in the Four Categories* (it contained around 36,000 volumes), to peruse and censor suspicious works. More than 2,000 volumes were destroyed, and scholars who had written them were severely punished for seeming to disparage the Manchus.

Population Growth and Economic Prosperity

Perhaps the most dramatic occurrence in the Qing period was unprecedented demographic growth. The population of China in 1700 probably reached about 150 million people; by 1800, it exceeded 350 million people. Why did such a phenomenon occur, and what were its consequences? Internal peace, more widespread use of foodstuffs from the Americas, and the absence of withering epidemics all contributed to the growth. In the eighteenth

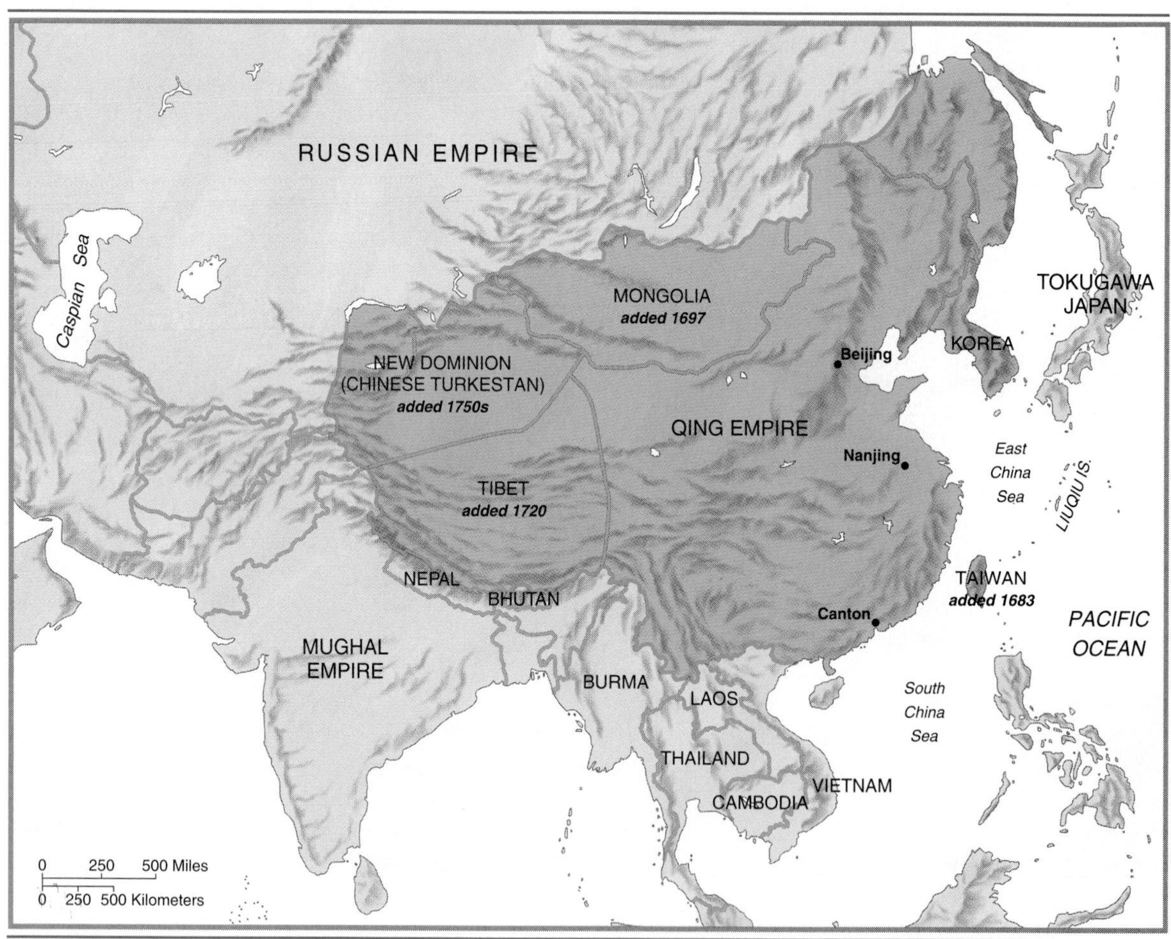

MAP 28.2 *The Qing Empire around 1770. The Manchu rulers of the Qing Empire significantly extended China's borders. Tibet, Mongolia, and Chinese Turkestan were added to the empire in the seventeenth and eighteenth centuries. At that time, China approximated its present borders with a territory of more than three million square miles.*

PARALLELS AND DIVERGENCES

Asian Encyclopedias before 1750

Eurasians displayed a propensity for organizing and presenting information in encyclopedic form, an attempt to bring together known information on various subjects. European examples will be explored in a later chapter; here we will examine Asian encyclopedias, including those of Chinese, Mughal, and Ottoman scholars. Asian encyclopedists generally prepared their information for officials who had to have accurate information in order to do their jobs effectively. Even encyclopedias about the Islamic sciences were primarily intended for judges and lawyers.

Ming and Qing intellectuals produced nearly 150 encyclopedias of all kinds, and they followed an encyclopedic tradition that had existed for several centuries. A major type of Chinese work dealt with political affairs; these often were written in the latter part of a dynasty, when political problems became more acute. The editors usually selected experts to write on specific problems or used the writings of former or current officials about matters of statecraft. Economic matters like administration of the salt monopoly or supervision of the silk trade also were often covered.

A seventeenth-century writer, Wang Qi,[a] wrote an important political encyclopedia and is noted for writing an illustrated encyclopedia of wide scope. The latter covered topics such as astronomy, cosmology, geography, biographies, painting, literary history, human physiology, and botany. This shows not only the author's varied intellectual interests but also those of his readers. The illustrations, of course, convey additional information, sometimes of a technical nature.

Abu'l Fazl,[b] a Mughal official, compiled an administrative encyclopedia that was widely used in the sixteenth and seventeenth centuries. He wrote in great detail on subjects such as architecture and the care and feeding of rare breeds of horses. Much of the encyclopedia's economic information came from the detailed land surveys that recorded the huge range of crops grown, their prices in different markets, data about land rights, and the availability of water resources. Modern scholars have begun to mine this and other information sources to paint a detailed picture of Mughal agriculture.

Ottoman officials made detailed land surveys and compiled encyclopedias for their officials; Ottoman scholars also contributed their own encyclopedias. Because Egyptians, Turks, and Indians also produced encyclopedias, an Islamic encyclopedist tradition existed, especially in the Early Modern Era. One group of scholars compiled an encyclopedia of Islamic sciences in order to meet the needs of religious officials who handled matters of Islamic law. Some of these sciences included practical ethics, etiquette, and other subjects tied to Muslim life and worship.

[a] **Wang Qi:** WONG chee

[b] **Abu'l Fazl:** AH buhl FAH zehl

century, foreign wars took place, but internal challenges to the government subsided, especially in heavily populated areas. Corn from the New World suited Chinese palates and could be grown on marginal lands; its cultivation over a larger area added significantly to the Chinese diet. The most important crops, however, were the varieties of potatoes and sweet potatoes. By the Qing period, the sweet potato had become a major component of Chinese cuisine, especially among the poor.

What effect did these changes have on politics and society? Long-term trends suggest that the amount of land available to each farming family shrank. Although new lands came under cultivation, the amount did not keep pace with the rapid demographic growth. Crowding on the land kept most peasants at the poverty level. In difficult times, people either starved or revolted. The elite also grew in number while government positions stayed relatively constant; the number of scholars taking the examinations mushroomed. When they failed to pass or enter government, discontent arose among these educated people who possessed the skills to mount political challenges.

THE ASHIKAGA SHOGUNATE, 1338–1573

The Mongols failed to conquer Japan in 1274 and 1281, but their two invasions weakened the ruling Japanese warrior government. It collapsed in the 1330s, and a dominant military leader, Ashikaga Takauji,[9] was proclaimed ***shogun***, military dictator. Although Ashikaga Takauji's descendants held the title of *shogun* for more than two centuries, they ceased to wield power after the mid–fifteenth century.

The Ashikaga Shogunate (1338–1573) governed from the city of Kyoto. For the first century, *shoguns* exercised effective control, and burgeoning trade with Korea and China helped generate prosperity. Using this wealth, the Ashikaga *shoguns* supported cultural leaders.

The most powerful *shogun*, Ashikaga Yoshimitsu (reign dates 1380–1408), dominated the capital and the country. He loved fine art, subsidizing artists and architects. Perhaps the most famous surviving structure of his era was the Golden Pavilion, a private retreat of this *shogun*; its sloping roof conveys a sense of uplift and lightness. A successor built the Silver Pavilion, in many ways a counterpoint to the Golden Pavilion. The latter showed best in the sunlight, while the Silver Pavilion, located in shady areas, exuded a more subdued effect.

Drama in the Ashikaga era is reflected in the appearance of the **Noh**, a dramatic form. Noh actors wear masks to hide normal facial expressions, forcing reliance on gestures and voice intonation to convey emotion. Financially supported by various *shoguns* and ***daimyo***[10] (territorial lords), Noh dramatists wrote plays for the political and social elite of Japan.

The Ashikaga state was overwhelmed by a civil war that erupted in 1467. The following decade of war devastated Kyoto and sparked a chaotic epoch known as the Warring States Period (1467–1568). The formation of provincial government centered on castle towns created by *daimyo*, who resettled their *samurai* warriors from the land to the castle towns. In exchange for the move, the *daimyo* guaranteed a fixed income for the *samurai*. In addition, village peasants farmed land, living self-sufficiently. They paid taxes to their village head, who remitted them to the *daimyo*.

[9] **Ashikaga Takauji:** AH shee kah gah TAH kah oo jee
[10] ***daimyo:*** DY mee yoh

JAPAN'S REUNIFICATION AND EXPANSION, AROUND 1560–AROUND 1600

A series of determined warriors envisioned and carried out the reunitification of Japan by military conquest. In addition, they promoted social, economic, and cultural policies imbued with ideas of loyalty and obedience to one's superiors. One major consequence of Japan's militarization was its attempt to conquer Korea and China, an action that ended in disaster for all parties.

The Unification Drive

Three outstanding warriors, Oda Nobunaga (1534–1582), Toyotomi Hideyoshi[11] (1536–1598), and Tokugawa Ieyasu[12] (1542–1616), forged a united Japan. Oda Nobunaga began the effort around 1560 by unifying his clan and then allying with other warlords. Oda Nobunaga defeated several opponents and occupied Kyoto in 1568, ending the Warring States Period; he formally ended Ashikaga rule in 1573. Nobunaga's assassination stopped his effort in 1582 but created the conditions that elevated Toyotomi Hideyoshi to the leadership of the national unification effort.

Toyotomi Hideyoshi was a remarkable figure, partly because of his success and partly because of his commoner origins. Only in the Warring States Period could a Japanese commoner rise to the top by ability and good fortune. In that sense he is similar to Zhu Yuanzhang, the founder of the Ming Dynasty. Toyotomi Hideyoshi's march toward unification climaxed with the defeat of the northern *daimyo*, one of whom ruled the Kanto,[13] Japan's largest plain, and Tokugawa Ieyasu was given dominion over the Kanto. In these later campaigns, 100,000 to 300,000 *samurai* were mobilized.

[11] **Toyotomi Hideyoshi:** TOH yoh toh mee HEE deh yoh shee
[12] **Tokugawa Ieyasu:** TOH kuh gah wah EE ay yah suh
[13] **Kanto:** KAHN toh

Toyotomi Hideyoshi conducted a land-survey program. This policy led to the measurement and registration of all arable land and told a ruler how much each *daimyo* controlled and thereby his wealth. It also focused attention on the village as the basic economic unit for the province and standardized information about potential agricultural production.

In addition, Toyotomi Hideyoshi imposed measures to foster stability in war-torn Japan. A sword hunt confiscated weapons from non-*samurai* so that ambitious people could not resort to the sword. The state prohibited people from changing their jobs, and by the Japanese modification of the Chinese four-class system (*samurai*, peasant, artisan, merchant), movement among the classes was forbidden. This policy differed from China's; there, education could provide mobility.

Japanese Expansion into Korea, 1592–1598

The final political effort of Toyotomi Hideyoshi was an invasion of Korea with the ultimate goal of conquering China and perhaps India. In 1592, more than 100,000 battle-tested *samurai* and their supporting logistical personnel landed in Korea and quickly overwhelmed Korean resistance. Chinese leaders soon realized the seriousness of the Japanese threat and mobilized armies in Manchuria, sending them to fight the invaders. A combination of Korean guerrilla warfare and a joint Chinese-Korean operation forced the Japanese south; negotiations took up several years. In addition, the Korean navy inflicted major defeats on the Japanese navy, threatening supply lines. A significant factor was the use of Korean "turtle boats," iron-clad wooden ships.

In 1598, the death of Toyotomi Hideyoshi terminated Japan's foreign adventure, leaving Korea in ruins, China in debt, and Japan relatively unscathed. Manchuria became a power vacuum where the Manchus eventually built their rival government. The Japanese treated the Koreans harshly, and carried many of them off to Japan as slaves; some Japanese brought home containers of pickled Korean ears and noses as war trophies. Korean potters and printers were compelled to move to Japan, where they helped revitalize Japanese pottery making and contributed to the printing of more books.

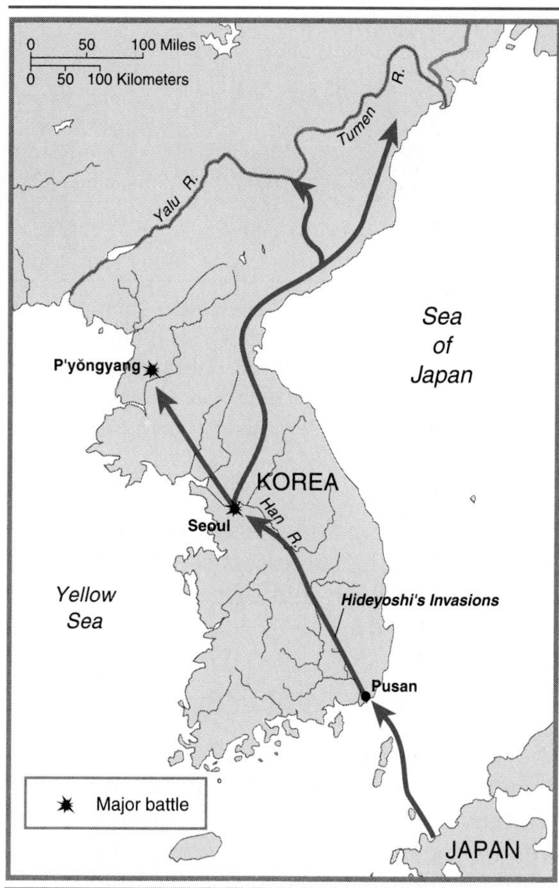

MAP 28.3 ***Hideyoshi's Invasions of Korea, 1592–1598.*** *Japan's unifier looked overseas for new realms to conquer. Since Korea stood in the path of the planned conquest of China, it suffered two massive and destructive invasions in the late sixteenth century. Korean resistance fighters and Chinese soldiers helped blunt the Japanese invasion, forcing Hideyoshi's successors to withdraw from the Asian mainland.*

THE EARLY TOKUGAWA SHOGUNATE: BUILDING MODERNITY, 1603–AROUND 1800

After the death of Toyotomi Hideyoshi, Tokugawa Ieyasu emerged as the main power in Japan when his forces defeated their opponents in 1600 at the Battle of Sekigahara.[14] Three years later, Tokugawa Ieyasu was proclaimed *shogun*, and his govern-

[14] **Sekigahara:** SEH kee gah hah rah

FIGURE 28.6 **Daimyo *Procession.*** Daimyo *regularly traveled to Edo and back home. Their entourages consisted of various* samurai *and servants. Lower-ranking* samurai *walked; their superiors rode on horseback. The* daimyo *himself was carried in an enclosed conveyance. Over time, the procession became more elaborate and costly, draining revenue from potential rivals to the* shogun. The Tokugawa Art Museum, Nagoya.

ment lasted for two and one-half centuries. Tokugawa Ieyasu and his successors permitted the continuance of local governments provided that the *daimyo* remained loyal.

Creating Political Stability

The Tokugawa *shoguns* were concerned about maintaining their rule and built a polity that thwarted alliances among their adversaries. All *daimyo*, for example, had to spend one out of every two years in the shogunal capital attending a variety of meetings called by the *shogun*. The other year they could return home but had to leave their wives and sons behind as hostages. All *daimyo* marriage alliances had to be approved by the *shogun*, and the size and number of castles in a province were strictly regulated. Shogunal spies also kept tabs on internal provincial administration and policies.

The shogunate had control of much economic power. Although taxes collected in the province stayed there, *daimyo* were sometimes called upon to contribute to expensive shogunal construction projects, draining monies from their treasuries. The *shoguns* and their allies controlled 60 percent of agricultural land, and the *shogun* administered the capital, Edo[15] (present-day Tokyo), and the two major cities, Kyoto[16] and Osaka.[17] In addition, mining and coinage were shogunal monopolies.

The other area of concern for the shogunate was international relations. Europeans had traded with the Japanese since the 1540s, but they had brought Christianity and gunpowder weaponry along with trade goods. As Christianity spread through Japanese society, shogunal authorities became uneasy, fearing that Japanese Christians were more loyal to their priests, some of whom were Europeans, than to their Japanese lords. This placed the whole political and social hierarchy at risk. After a major uprising of Japanese Christians in the late 1630s, the shogunate outlawed Christianity, closed Japan to European shipping (except for a tiny Dutch outpost), and forbade Japanese from going overseas. Korean and Chinese merchants were the only other foreigners permitted to do business in Japan. These policies, which were similar to those of the Ming Dynasty, turned Japan inward and ended outside threats to stability for two centuries.

Another consequence of Tokugawa rule was the creation of large urban population centers at the new capital, Edo; at Kyoto, a large city of around 300,000 people; and at Osaka, a major trading center, also with a population numbering 300,000 people. Urban growth included the emergence of large castle towns with merchants and artisans, among others.

Caste and Gender

The Japanese borrowed the Chinese four-class system and modified it to fit their own purposes. Instead of scholars at the top, the Japanese placed the *samurai*, many of whom became scholars in the Tokugawa period. As in China, below the *samurai* were the peasants, reflecting the agrarian

[15] **Edo:** EH doh
[16] **Kyoto:** KEE yoh toh
[17] **Osaka:** OH sah kah

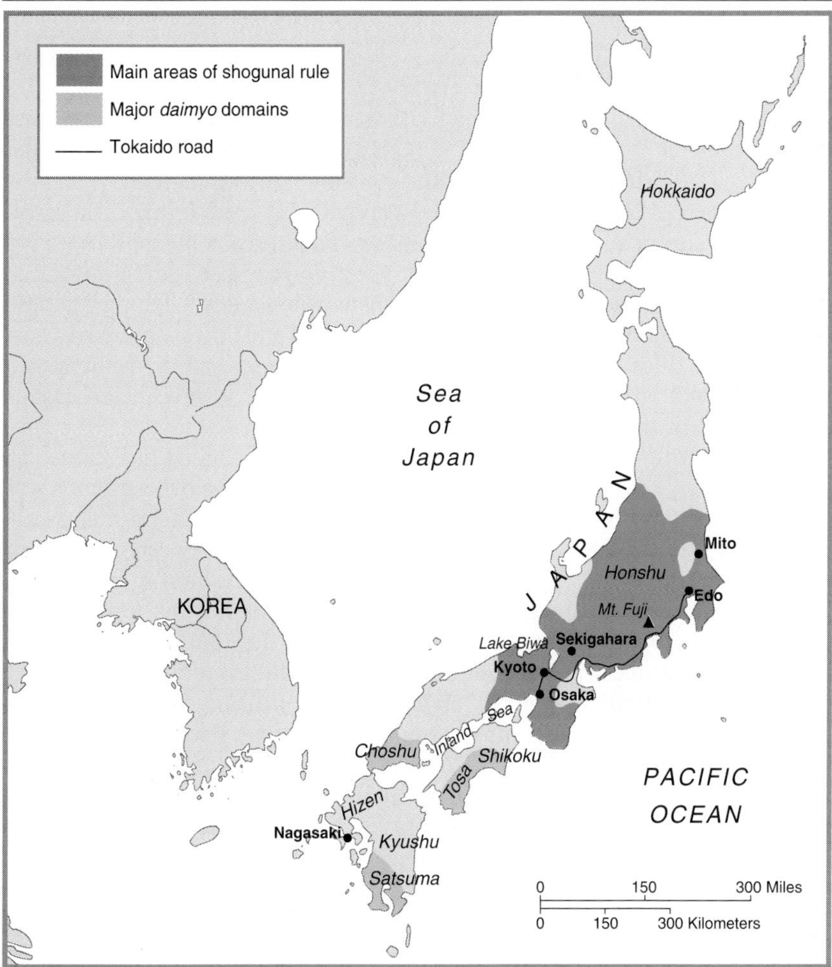

MAP 28.4 ***Tokugawa Japan around 1700.*** *By 1700, Japan's shogunal government had closed its doors to nearly all communication and commerce with Western diplomats and merchants. Trade with Asians was relegated to the southern islands off the coast of Kyushu. The inward-looking Japanese government had developed a political system of modest stability that lasted for over two centuries. The central government dominated the polity, permiting rival localities to survive provided they refrained from overt military challenges.*

FIGURE 28.7 ***Japanese Laborers in Edo.*** *Japanese woodblock art flourished in the cities of seventeenth-century Japan. Later, such work influenced European artists, especially the Impressionists. Here we see three workers sawing and stacking wood in a lumberyard. Mount Fuji sits quietly in the distance, oblivious to all human activity. Edo was an early name for Tokyo.*
The Japan Ukiyoe Museum.

UNDER THE LENS

Japan Turns from the Gun to the Sword

Most empires after the fourteenth century developed and maintained gunpowder weaponry. Although some, like the Mughals and the Safavids, did not keep apace of European improvements in cannons and firearms, only the Japanese deliberately turned their backs on these weapons. They banned rifles, sidearms, and cannons from being used and permitted only a few rifles in private hands for hunting or scaring off wild birds, which threatened to eat certain crops. All of these firearms, however, had to be registered with the appropriate authorities.

A component of the unification of Japan in the sixteenth century was the introduction and spread of firearms. Oda Nobunaga, who was among the first warlords to appreciate their use, developed musketeer units. Improvements in technology brought greater firepower to bear and made the large armies of *samurai* and commoners fearsome. Toyotomi Hideyoshi and Tokugawa Ieyasu relied on gunpowder technology in their successful unification efforts.

Once Japan was united, however, governments looked askance at rifles and pistols, not to say cannons, because they threatened to disturb the peaceful order. Stability and harmony became the values most appreciated by the Tokugawa *shoguns*. Therefore, shogunal decrees forbade the carrying of the new weapons except by specially sanctioned soldiers. The *daimyo* agreed with this policy. In fact, in the late 1630s, when a revolt among Japanese Roman Catholics erupted and the rebels seized a castle, the Tokugawa government had no cannons and needed Dutch ones in order to breach the castle's walled fortifications.

Another element in the banning of firearms lay in the nature of the *samurai* elite, whose status was distinguished and was symbolized by the sword. Indeed, when Toyotomi Hideyoshi wished to distinguish the *samurai*, he forbade non-*samurai* from wearing swords. A common saying in the warrior era was that the sword was "the soul of the *samurai*." These attitudes facilitated the various governments' policies about limiting firearms. With appropriate training, commoners might shoot firearms and threaten the military monopoly of the *samurai*. That could not be permitted. Most *samurai*, therefore, eagerly supported the ban and maintained their exclusive practice of wearing their treasured swords.

---

bias of Japan's rulers; then came the artisans and merchants. Because of their desire to maintain social stability, the Japanese transformed the Chinese system into a caste order of fixed social groups without social mobility.

Japanese society was actually much more complex than the four castes, however, and aristocrats, physicians, and accountants found themselves outside the ideal structure. In addition, various pressures soon undermined the social system, despite the rulers' attempts to maintain it. The prevention of social mobility at the end of the sixteenth century briefly kept most Japanese in some form of a fixed social position, but many *samurai* became farmers or merchants in order to make a living. Other impoverished *samurai* ignored laws forbidding marriage with people of artisan or merchant background. By 1800, one's position seldom reflected that of one's grandparents.

Confucianism traditionally supported males, who dominated females in all social relationships. In fact, when the Japanese government began to promote Confucianism as an ideology conferring ideas and values of stability, the social position of women began to decline. Japanese Confucians advocated keeping women at home and under tight control; these admonitions were often supported by the *samurai* and *daimyo*. Arranged marriages became increasingly common among all social groups, and women lost inheritance rights they had previously enjoyed. Some became common laborers, and others plied traditional women's trades as well as prostitution.

One exception was the growing number of educated women. Girls joined with boys in local schools, studied in all-girl schools, or learned from private tutors. Scholars have estimated that as many as 10 percent of Japanese girls in this period could read and write.

The rapid spread of education ensured a more effective tapping of available brainpower. Increasing numbers of *samurai* became literate, as did many merchants and peasants; both males and females went to local schools. Perhaps as many as 40 percent of boys in this period were literate.

Popular and Elite Culture

The intellectual horizons of the Japanese expanded considerably in the Tokugawa period. A significant number of Japanese, especially in the cities, became literate and supported a growing output of popular culture. At the same time, traditional intellectual pursuits, like philosophy, engaged the *samurai*, who became highly literate.

Popular culture of the Tokugawa era included new dramatic forms: Kabuki plays and puppet theater plays. Both developed in the cities, catering to commoners, who watched performances that lasted for much of a day. One playwright, Chikamatsu Monzaemon (1653–1724), wrote for both theaters and is considered Japan's greatest dramatist. His play *Forty-seven Ronin* dealt with a historical incident in which forty-seven *samurai* avenged their *daimyo*'s wrongful death and caused a problem for the authorities, who could condone neither the initial murder nor the act of retaliation.

Poetry, short stories, novels, and woodblock prints also flourished in the Tokugawa era. The *haiku* poem of seventeen syllables became a popular poetic form because of its brevity and apparent simplicity. Short stories appeared in the late seventeenth century and fascinated Japanese readers, who loved their often satirical themes. Woodblock prints developed in the seventeenth century, and Japanese artists mastered forms such as nature scenes, portraits of city life, and renderings of famous Kabuki actors, receiving acclaim and imitation by later European painters.

Arts continued to flourish, too. Although few Noh plays were written, many older ones were still performed for *daimyo* and various courtiers. Confucianism was studied and commented upon by Japanese scholars, and the ideas of Wang Yangming (Oyomei in Japanese) received widespread attention, especially in the nineteenth century. One group of intellectuals strongly criticized the amount of attention given to a foreign ideology and took it upon themselves to study early Japanese institutions and ideas, which were deemed "free" from Chinese influence. A monumental history of Japan was written during much of the Tokugawa era; scholars from all over the country participated in the project, inaugurating a cross-

FIGURE 28.8 ***Woman Reading.*** *This woodblock shows a woman at ease with a book in her hand. Although the adoption of Confucianism as the ideology of the shogunate brought a decline in the status of women, many elite women learned to read and write at home. By the mid–nineteenth century, about one in ten women was literate. Japanese manuscripts are read from top to bottom and from right to left.* The Japan Ukiyoe Museum.

fertilization of ideas and a self-conscious Japanese intellectual elite.

Buddhism and Shinto, two major religions of Japan, generally maintained an entwined existence, with Shinto shrines being protected by Buddhist deities and Buddhist temples having Shinto

IN THEIR OWN WORDS

Haiku Poetry and Commentary

Japanese *haiku* became a distinctive poetic form in the seventeenth century and grew very popular among commoners, who loved its simple and brief message. Although most Japanese people tried their hands at *haiku*, certain masters wrote poems that have been greatly admired. Two poets, Basho[a] and Kyorai,[b] teacher and pupil, conversed about the theory and practice of composing *haiku*, and the following is Kyorai's record (including poems) of some discussions.

> The departing spring
> With the men of Omi
> Have I lamented
>
> The Master [Basho] said, "Shohaku criticized this poem on the grounds that I might just as well have said Tamba instead of Omi or departing year instead of departing spring. How does this criticism strike you?" Kyorai replied, "Shohaku's criticism misses the mark completely. What could be more natural than to regret the passing of spring, when the waters of the Lake of Omi are veiled so enchantingly in the mist? Besides, it is especially fitting a poem for one who lives by the lake to have written."

The Master said, "Yes, the poets of old loved spring in this province almost as much as in the capital." Kyorai, deeply struck by these words, continued, "If you were in Omi at the close of the year, why should you regret its passing? Or if you were in Tamba at the end of spring, you would not be likely to have such a feeling. What truth there is in the poetry of a man who has genuinely been stirred by some sight of Nature!" The Master said, "Kyorai, you are a person with whom I can talk about poetry." He was very pleased . . .

Will the two-day moon
Be blown from the sky
By the winter wind?
–KAKEI

Kept by the winter wind
From falling to earth—
The drizzling rain
–KYORAI

Kyorai said, "I feel that Kakei's verse is far superior to mine. By asking if it will be blown from the sky, he makes mention of the two-day moon all the more clever." Basho answered, "Kakei's verse is built around the words 'two-day moon.' Take away the two-day moon and there is nothing left to the poem. It is not apparent on what you have based your poem. It is good all around."

[a] **Basho:** BAH shoh
[b] **Kyorai:** KEE yoh ry

shrines on their grounds. Shrines of highly venerated Shinto deities, like Amaterasu, the sun goddess, and those connected with the imperial institution became sites of pilgrimage in the eighteenth and nineteenth centuries. Millions of Japanese visited them in an outpouring of devotional passion. Fearing that many Japanese secretly continued to practice Christianity, the Tokugawa government decreed that all Japanese had to register with the nearest Buddhist temple. Authorities stamped out remaining elements of Christianity by crucifying priests and believers alike. Tens of thousands of Japanese Christians died in the ongoing persecutions. Despite these oppressive practices, a few Japanese secretly practiced the Christian faith throughout the Tokugawa period.

Consequences of Japan's Closing

The central government and the semiautonomous provinces either initiated or supported a series of efforts that led to Japan's growing economic and social integration. At the same time, significant private initiatives (often by merchants and wealthy peasants) supplemented or superseded state programs, thereby aiding agricultural productivity and accumulation of money. And although Japanese were aware of European developments in modernizing political institutions, the Japanese path toward modernity came from internal pressures and responses.

By the late seventeenth century, a small group of scholars persuaded the shogunal government to permit a few Dutch books to enter Japan. They became the basis for scholars who provided a window on the world. From the Dutch, the Japanese kept abreast of medical developments, learned about the European empires, and saw how gunpowder technology was improving. This group, by the nineteenth century, included many who urged Japan to become a colonial power.

During the seventeenth century and after, many governments took special interest in improving Japan's infrastructure. Major efforts were undertaken to build and improve roads linking Japan's major cities. Significant resources were expended to control Japan's rivers, irrigate farmlands, and reclaim lands from the sea as well as from disuse. By 1800, people easily and safely traveled to distant parts of the realm; some moved to cities, others visited sacred shrines, and a few observed how people farmed in different areas.

Between 1550 and 1650, urban growth stimulated additional changes in agriculture. By 1700, Japan had become one of the world's most urbanized societies, with three cities of 300,000 or more inhabitants and many more with populations in the tens of thousands. This development helped promote the commercialization of agriculture: Cash crops were grown specifically to sell to city folk. One of the first cash crops was cotton. Wealthy farmers enjoyed the financial security to experiment with growing cotton, and in a brief time consumer demand was driving the rapid conversion of grain fields to cotton planting. By the early 1700s, perhaps 50 percent of farmland in the Osaka area was given over to cotton fields. The seas began to be harvested on a large scale as well; drift nets were increasingly employed during the eighteenth century as sardines and other fish became increasingly commonplace in Japanese diets.

The Tokugawa era was a time of fiscal growth and maturity as the Japanese developed the basis of a modern financial system. Both the shogunate and *daimyo* developed alliances with merchant groups, giving them monopoly rights in certain trade items or protecting them from regional competitors. Despite this institutional support, many merchant groups took their own initiatives in developing markets, in seeking reliable supplies of raw materials, or in finding sources for raising money. Wholesalers, for example, fanned out in Japan to pay farmers in advance to produce specified crops or products, or they loaned money for production purposes. Some local producers gradually became shipping agents for urban wholesalers and used urban capital to purchase and ship goods to cities.

New ways of raising money helped finance commercial activity. Merchants held cash on deposit, made loans, and formed joint-loan groups to spread the risk. Promissory notes secured by real estate or current accounts also went into circulation. Collectible credit drafts due in sixty days were used as collateral for loans and helped fuel a dramatic expansion of available credit. Moneychangers entered financial markets to ensure transactions; maritime insurance developed by the late eighteenth century.

By 1800, self-sufficient villages long had been producing for urban markets, and there had been a general spread of agricultural technology so that production levels had improved by the nineteenth century. The central government's encouragement of blacksmiths to move into farm villages was significant because many improvements in agricultural tools came from the smiths. In addition, wealthy farmers kept journals as a record of successful experiments with tools and methods of growing crops: Some traveled to observe successful farming techniques and included them in the journals, many of which were published.

Resource Management

Human and material resource problems became serious in the Tokugawa period, and the Japanese developed a range of responses to these issues. The doubling of arable land (1550–1650) brought population growth from around 12 million people in 1650 to perhaps 28 million by 1730. Overcrowding reached severe levels and compelled the Japanese to respond. Women began marrying later and having fewer children, abortions became more commonplace, and infanticide was practiced more frequently.

Fertilizer use is another example of careful resource allocation. A trade in manufacturing by-products developed by the eighteenth century. Fish residues, along with pressed oil seeds, became fertilizers.

Clothing use illustrates another dimension of resource management in Tokugawa Japan. Japanese dress was centered on the ***kimono***,[18] a

[18] ***kimono:*** KEE moh noh

China	Japan		
		1300	
	Ashikaga Shogunate, 1338–1573		Ashikaga Takauji named *shogun,* 1338
Ming Empire, 1368–1644			Zhu Yuanzhang founds Ming Empire, 1368
		1400	Ashikaga Yoshimitsu builds the Golden Pavilion, c. 1400
			Japan's Warring States Period begins, 1467
		1500	Wang Yangming dies, 1528
			Hideyoshi dies, ending the invasion of Korea, 1598
		1600	
	Early Tokugawa Shogunate, 1603–c. 1800		Battle of Sekigahara, 1603
			Japan closes its doors to most Westerners, 1640
Early Qing Empire, 1644–1796			
		1700	Kangxi Emperor conquers Tibet, 1720
			Qianlong Emperor dies, 1799
		1800	

robelike outer garment. It was made of cloth that was cut into eight rectangular strips from a single rectangular piece. This meant that no material was wasted; children's *kimonos* were gathered at the shoulders so that they could be let out as the child grew. The sewing was by simple basting, which permitted the removal of the threads to wash the *kimono* and a quick rebasting later. When a *kimono* could no longer be worn, it was cut up for rags or diapers as needed. In a land with scarce resources, the Japanese developed techniques to conserve them efficiently.

SUMMARY

1. The Ming and Qing empires of China remained inward looking and indifferent to trade. The Qing emperors, unlike their predecessors, conquered surrounding peoples. Massive population growth based on New World foodstuffs undermined the state and led to major nineteenth-century uprisings.

2. The Hongwu and Yongle emperors set the basic patterns of the Ming Empire, including the use of eunuchs to carry out special tasks for the monarch. Moving the Chinese capital northward to Beijing intensified China's strategic focus on the Mongols and helped spur the rebuilding of the Great Wall.

3. Chinese urban life flourished and city folk often prospered. A major literary product was the novel; some novels clearly reflected social trends.

4. The Manchus of the northeast conquered and ruled China as the Qing Empire from the mid–seventeenth century. The Kangxi and Qianlong emperors ably ruled for more than a century, ordering the gathering of huge collections of scholarly works.

5. Chinese population growth in the eighteenth century created profound social strains that overwhelmed the system by the mid–nineteenth century.

6. Successive warrior governments ruled Japan. The last, the Tokugawa shogunate, ruled a unified state that coexisted with semiautonomous provinces.

7. Like the Chinese, the Japanese severely curtailed trade with Europeans and ousted Christian missionaries, who were perceived as subversive. The closing of the country enabled the uninterrupted improvement of the infrastructure.

8. Population growth helped spur the creation of large cities like Edo and Osaka. They in turn helped promote the demand for products from the agricultural sector. The commercialization of farming and the general improvement of agricultural technology and farming methods transformed the rural economy. At the same time, a whole range of financial techniques for raising capital emerged that underlay the growth of a modern commercial system.

SUGGESTED READINGS

Birch, Cyril. *Stories from a Ming Collection*. London, 1958. Representative short stories from the Ming era.

Hall, John W., ed. *The Cambridge History of Japan*. Vol. IV: *Early Modern Japan*. Cambridge, Eng.: Cambridge University Press, 1991. A history of Japan, reflecting Japanese and Western scholarship.

Ho, Ping-ti. *The Ladder of Success in Imperial China*. New York: Columbia University Press, 1964. A classic study of the Chinese imperial examination system.

———. *Studies on the Population of China, 1368–1953*. Cambridge, Mass.: Harvard University Press, 1959. A classic treatment of demographic issues in Chinese history.

Huang, Ray. *China: A Macro History*. Armonk, N.Y.: M. E. Sharpe, 1990. A thought-provoking examination of Chinese history, looking at the role of commercialization in China's modernization.

Ikegami, Eiko. *The Taming of the Samurai*. Cambridge, Mass.: Harvard University Press, 1995. A sociological examination of the transformation of the *samurai* from a warrior to a scholar caste.

Mote, F. W., and D. Twitchett, eds. *The Cambridge History of China*. Vol. VII: *The Ming Dynasty, 1368–1644*, Part I. Cambridge, Eng.: Cambridge University Press, 1988. A political examination of the Ming era by key scholars of China.

Totman, Conrad. *Early Modern Japan*. Berkeley: University of California Press, 1993. A history of the Tokugawa era, incorporating much ecological analysis.

China's Empress Dowager and Eunuchs. *The Qing Empire was dominated by the Manchus, and the Empress Dowager Zixi was the most important Manchu ruler from 1862 to 1908. In this photograph taken around 1900, she sits in her royal conveyance as it is transported by eunuchs. The Manchus continued the imperial practice of employing eunuchs (the great majority of whom were Chinese) in the inner court, where the emperor's wives, daughters, and concubines lived. Unlike many of the Ming emperors, who were often under the influence of powerful eunuchs, the Manchus kept their eunuchs under strict control.*
Courtesy of the Freer Gallery of Art, Smithsonian Institution, Washington. D.C.

ISSUE 6

Slavery around the Globe

In the mid–fourteenth century, King Kano Rumfa of the Hausa kingdom in what is now Nigeria appointed one slave as the head of the state treasury and another as the commander-in-chief of the military. In the mid–sixteenth century, Dutch slave owners in South Africa systematically mutilated their slaves' faces as warnings against misbehavior. How could slaves acquire so much power in Hausaland and so little in South Africa? The answer is simple: The institution of slavery has encompassed a great diversity around the world, unified only by the common fact that one person owns another. This issue explores some of that diversity, underscoring how the colonial slavery discussed in Chapter 26 is an atypical version of slavery.

The first documentary evidence of slaves comes from the Ur-Nammu tablet of Sumeria, around 2100 B.C. Most scholars believe that slaves probably were important one or two thousand years prior to this date. By 1000 B.C., slavery had appeared independently in Europe, Asia, and Africa; by A.D. 1000, it also was important in North America, Central America, South America, and the Pacific.

Slavery has been in continuous existence since its inception, and it continues today, though there are very few slaves now and institutionalized slavery is rare. Throughout this range of time and location, slavery has taken a wide variety of forms, and this section explores their areas of commonality and difference.

FIGURE I.6.1 ***Ur-Nammu Tablet.*** *This stone carving from Sumeria dates to around 2500 B.C. and may be the earliest depiction of slaves in the world. King Ur-Nanshe is shown twice, in oversized proportions, with his children and various attendants; the smallest figures are probably slaves.* Louvre © R.M.N./P. Bernard.

THE CONCEPT OF SLAVERY AND ITS VARIANTS

No matter where or when it occurs, slavery has some common features that relate directly to the philosophy of owning another human being. There are, however, several variable factors that differ from case to case and are critical in determining the treatment of a slave.

The Basic Concept

Slavery can be defined by its five fundamental characteristics:

— the slave is owned by a master;

— the slave provides involuntary labor for that master;

— the slave has a low, often the lowest, position in the social hierarchy;

— the slave is acquired by purchase, capture, or birth to another slave; and

— the slave is an outsider to the master's community.

Each of these characteristics warrants a bit more discussion.

Although ownership is central to the concept of slavery, different societies have viewed the relationship between slave and owner differently. At one extreme, slaves have been seen as nonhuman objects, mere pieces of property; this is chattel slavery. At the other extreme, slaves are simply members of the lowest stratum of society who owe labor to their masters; slaves of this latter sort retain their humanity and at least some of the basic rights accorded to all people in that society. No matter how benign the relationship between the slave and owner, however, the slave is required to carry out labor at the wish of (and for the benefit of) the owner.

The slave always is near the lowest rung of the status ladder for the society in question. Although Classical Greek slaves who served as tutors and scholars, such as Epictetus, occupied a rung higher than common slaves, they still were viewed with contempt. The plays of Sophocles usually depicted slaves as sneaky, playing on an ancient Greek stereotype. Greek and Roman families expressed concern whether it was fair to a child to hire a slave tutor, because the economic savings might be offset by the possible unspecified negative effects on the child, effects that presumably would grow purely out of contact with a slave. Slaves who held high positions in governments obviously ranked high in power, but they still carried a stigma that affected their overall social position.

Normally slaves have been acquired through purchase, capture, or birth to slave parents, but there have been exceptions. Criminals could be sentenced to slavery as punishment for their crimes in many societies, including those of China, imperial Rome, and parts of West Africa. These slaves, though, were sold by the state, so they came to their eventual owner through purchase. In many societies, debtors could sell themselves into slavery, in essence their new owners purchasing them by paying their debts. Debt slavery was especially prominent in ancient Greece and Rome, eastern Europe, Southwest Asia, and the Aztec Empire. In some cases, particularly in China, destitute parents could sell children into slavery, sometimes for a pittance. Here the primary aim was to reduce the number of mouths to feed, and the money paid for the children was secondary. Nonetheless, the children were purchased, and it probably was important that money change hands to emphasize symbolically the changed status of the children.

Usually a slave comes from a group other than that of the owner. Most of the slaves of Christian Europeans were Jewish, Muslim, or nonwhite. Many scholars believe that the degradation of slavery normally is imposed only on someone from the outside, someone who could be labeled inferior on the basis of differing ethnicity, religion, or race. Sometimes, however, slaves came from the same groups as the masters, as when Benin began trading its own citizens to Europeans in times of slave shortages. When this happened, the act of assigning a person the status of slave in itself differentiated that person from the rest of the society.

In practice, there rarely is any difficulty in deciding whether or not a particular practice is slavery, although there sometimes are overlaps with serfdom and indenture, which will be discussed later. The real purpose of this definition of slavery is to focus our attention on the common core of characteristics before looking at how slavery varies from place to place.

Factors of Variation in Slavery

The variations among different systems of slavery are practically infinite, but many of the differences relate to four factors. The four factors make up a continuum, and a system of slavery may fall anywhere along it.

First, slavery may be open or closed. **Open slavery** provides realistic ways by which a slave can be freed, while **closed slavery** maintains a slave in that status for life. Open systems of slavery often permit slaves to accumulate property to purchase their freedom or standard ways to distinguish themselves (as in battle) and be granted freedom. Consequently, manumission (the freeing of a slave) is moderately common in open slavery systems. In some open slavery systems, a slave automatically is adopted into the owner's kinship group, giving the slave a place in society and paving the way to his or her eventual full incorporation into the owner's family.

In contrast, a fully closed system has no provision for the freeing of slaves. Most systems have provided some mechanism of manumission, though in some cases it was difficult to implement and, therefore, rarely used. A Brazilian plantation owner's freeing a field worker for exceptional service, for example, was unlikely, because most owners rarely had contact with these slaves and didn't know anyone's personal record. Many scholars believe that closed slavery encourages fatalism and hopelessness in slaves, thereby discouraging rebellions and escapes.

Second, slavery varies in terms of whether it extends to the descendants of slaves. Under **hereditary slavery** systems, the children of slaves also are slaves; under **single-generation slavery** systems, the parent may remain a slave, but the child is free. Hereditary slavery is an extension of closed slavery, carrying slave status beyond an individual's death, and it presumably contributes to the fatalism and hopelessness discussed earlier.

Third, as discussed in Chapter 26, slaves may be viewed as chattel (mere objects), or they may be given personal rights. At one end of this continuum, slaves lose all humanity, because society treats them as inhuman, denying them the rights that society accords human beings. At the other end, slaves are simply low-status persons who retain their basic human rights.

FIGURE I.6.2 *Roman Gravestone for Former Slaves. This gravestone shows portraits of Demetrius and Philonicus (most likely father and son), freedmen who previously had been slaves of Publius Licinius, a magistrate. This elite-style gravestone indicates that they were able to achieve both social and economic distinction despite their former status as slaves. It is not known exactly how they gained their freedom, but it may have been purchased by accumulated wealth.* Courtesy of the Trustees of the British Museum.

Fourth and finally, slaves may be kept for various purposes, and slaveholding societies usually have different rules for the proper treatment of slaves doing different jobs. The most common distinction is between **domestic slaves** (performing household duties) and **agricultural-industrial slaves** (providing hard labor for commercial activities). Domestic slaves usually are fewer in number and higher in status than agricultural-industrial slaves. Although agricultural-industrial slaves often produce more than the cost of maintaining them, domestic slaves usually cost more to maintain than strict economics would justify. Domestic slaves usually are luxury items whose possession confers prestige on their owner.

There are some loose correlations among these factors. Most closed systems of slavery also are hereditary and view slaves as chattel; many open systems are single-generation and consider slaves to have personal rights. Many systems of slavery that have agricultural-industrial slaves also have domestic slaves, although the opposite is not always true. These correlations are only approximate, and historical cases of slavery have combined aspects of the positions along the continuum formed by these factors into unique systems.

Slaves, Serfs, and Indentured Servants

While slavery is the best-known system of involuntary labor, it has two principal cousins with which it sometimes is confused: serfdom and indenture. The features that differentiate these three systems are subtle but significant.

Like a hereditary slave, a **serf** is a worker whose labor is owed to someone else and whose status is inherited by children, but serfs have certain personal rights and are not thought of as "owned." Serfdom is essentially a relationship between a group of laborers and a lord that guarantees certain rights for the serf and certain expectations for the lord. It is usually a manifestation of feudalism—the hierarchic relationship between a lord and vassals—and often grew out of it.

The specific rights of a serf have varied from place to place, though the central philosophy behind serfdom everywhere has been that serfs had some personal rights and could not be owned. More practically, serfs often provided a portion of their labor for their own subsistence, so in a sense they shared the profits of their own labor with their lord. Truly, their share usually was low, but they had a stake in their own activities. The very fact that their share was small meant that they could ill afford to shirk their duties.

Most serfs have been attached to a plot of land. If the feudal control of that land shifted to another lord, so did the serfs' allegiance. This relationship often is considered central to the concept of serfdom, but some serfs in medieval Europe were attached to the lord directly and could be shifted from place to place.

Indenture differs from either slavery or serfdom in that it is temporary and entered into voluntarily. It is unclear how far back in history

FIGURE I.6.3 *East African Slave and Master. This photo from around 1900 documents the persistence of slavery in East Africa into the twentieth century. The slave (left) demonstrates his subordination to his master.* Keystone View Company/Library of Congress.

indenture can be traced, though it clearly existed in China in the first millennium B.C. Indenture became prominent during the era of European expansion and colonization, from about 1500 to about 1800, when individuals wanting passage to a colony but unable to afford it could sign a contract transferring rights to their labor to someone else for a specified term. In return, the person receiving the labor would provide funds for the soon-to-be-indentured servant to book passage to the colony. Indenture existed in various colonial areas, including North America, but it was most important on the islands of the Indian Ocean, where it was the primary means of obtaining labor.

In theory, slavery, serfdom, and indenture are distinct, but real cases can be remarkably murky. In the Seychelles (an island group in the Indian Ocean), for example, laborers were brought from India under indenture, but a series of laws made it difficult for indentured servants ever to complete their contracted service. Indentured servants were required to carry a ticket stating their status; if found without this ticket or in an area away from their work site, they could be jailed for a week for vagrancy. Annually, about 10 percent of indentured servants were jailed for this offense. If they were absent from work for more than six days—and, as noted, jailing was for a week—the month or sometimes the year in which they were absent was not deducted from their indenture. By accumulating offenses that prolonged servitude, an indentured servant might remain in that status for a lifetime, effectively little different from a slave.

REGIONAL SLAVEHOLDING TRADITIONS

A few examples cannot adequately represent the diversity that has existed within slavery. Nonetheless, the examples that follow, along with others in this text, will give an idea of how much variety there has been within slaveholding systems.

China

China developed slavery at least by 1200 B.C., and it was abolished only with the founding of the People's Republic of China in 1949. Chinese slavery was unique in focusing on children, usually under the age of ten years. Adolescents and young adults sometimes went into indenture to pay off debts, but entering slavery was rare. The only prominent adult slaves were concubines, whose purchase and exchange served almost as sport among the elite, and state slaves, who labored for the Han government in the early centuries A.D., making iron weapons and agricultural tools.

The reason for China's focus on children was related to the purposes to which slaves were put. There was limited agricultural-industrial slavery, and slaves usually were either domestic servants or designated heirs of the purchaser. Domestic slaves needed to be raised in an elite household if they were to be able to perform their duties with the proper polish, so they were acquired as young as was practical. Girl slaves usually were used as domestic servants, and occasionally they would be married to a son of the owner at their adulthood. Boy slaves, on the other hand, could be domestic servants or be designated as the heir of their owner. An elite man with no sons might make a slave boy his designated heir so that his line could continue, although he was more likely to adopt a relative. If a boy slave were designated as heir, he would assume virtually all the rights of a biological son. If not designated an heir by a legally prescribed age, a boy slave irrevocably became a domestic slave.

Those slaves who were not designated heirs or married to sons remained slaves all their lives, and their children also were slaves. Their tasks were not exceptionally taxing, and their lot in life was in many ways better than that of peasants. On the other hand, they were viewed as chattel, and their personal rights were highly limited.

Chinese slavery, then, was largely closed, with the exceptions of designated heirs and marriages to sons. It was hereditary and chattel-based, and it was almost exclusively domestic.

India

Slavery in India extends back at least 3,000 years and may well have existed before then. It was abolished under British colonial rule in 1844.

In North India, slaves were almost all domestic slaves, and they contributed relatively little to the physical well-being of the households in which they worked. Rather, their primary purpose seems to have been the aggrandizement of the slave owner. In South India, where most slaves were used for agricultural labor, their value rested more in economics and less in prestige. Slaves in both parts of India were considered chattel, and children of slaves automatically became slaves. Although owners could permit slaves to accumulate property in life, upon their deaths it reverted to their owners. Slaves normally could not buy their freedom, and owners rarely granted freedom as a reward for meritorious performance.

Owners were expected to care for their slaves, who were considered to be somewhat like dependent children. Owners were obligated to (and typically did) see to their general welfare, by providing appropriate living quarters and meals, health care, support and protection in old age, and funeral arrangements. Special concern was given the marriage of slaves, and owners were expected to provide spouses and to defray the costs of a wedding (much as parents were expected to do for their children). Slave owners had a strong interest in matchmaking, because the ownership of children of the match was at stake. Local rules stated whether the children would belong to the father's owner or the mother's, and special agreements could supersede the usual rule. For obvious reasons of self-interest, owners usually married their own slaves to one another, thereby reducing conflict over the children.

India's caste system, with its focus on the importance of high-caste persons avoiding tasks seen as ritually defiling, had profound effects on Indian slavery. Agricultural-industrial slaves were drawn primarily from the lowest castes, but domestic slaves had to come from higher castes because they performed ritually pure tasks like drawing water and interacting with the high-caste elite. This produced a paradox: Domestic slaves were ritually high-ranking yet socially low-ranking. A complex system of symbols and usages was developed in order to maintain this complex and seemingly contradictory status.

Also because of the caste system, outsiders were seen as unfit to handle food that was to be consumed by high-caste owners and were therefore unacceptable as domestic slaves. Consequently, slaves had to be drawn from the ranks of Indians themselves. This case is a significant exception to the general rule that slaves are drawn from different ethnic or tribal groups than those of their owners.

Slavery in India was very closed and hereditary. Although it was chattel-oriented, owners incurred a wide range of obligations to their slaves. It was primarily based on domestic slavery, though agricultural-industrial slavery was more important in the south.

The Muslim World

The areas that Islam dominated in the seventh and eighth centuries had been keeping slaves for centuries before, and the practice continued under Islam. Slaves were recruited through capture, purchase, or birth. In the first two centuries of the spread of Islam, war was common enough that capture accounted for a large percentage of slaves, but this source declined as Islam spread, because the Qur'an forbade the enslavement of fellow Muslims. In fact, the Qur'an expressly forbids the enslavement of any "people of the Book," that is, Muslims, Jews, or Christians. In practice, Muslims received the greatest protection by this proscription. Purchase of slaves was primarily through the trans-Saharan trade with West and East Africa, although a lesser trade with eastern Europe and Byzantium helped supply some areas with slaves. Law prohibited Muslims from entering slavery voluntarily to erase a debt, as well as from selling one's children into slavery.

The children of two slave parents were slaves. Marriages between slaves and free persons (usually slave women and free men), however, were common, and the resulting children usually were free. An entire dynasty of caliphs of the Mamluks (750–1258) married slave women for several centuries beginning in 1260, thereby avoiding the political entanglements of marrying women of noble families.

Slaves under Islam were used primarily as domestic servants. Enslaved women also might become entertainers or concubines, and enslaved men sometimes became business agents. Agricultural-industrial slavery was rare under Islam, with the significant exception of the sugar plantations of Southwest Asia, which were staffed by sub-Saharan African slaves through the Indian Ocean slave trade from around 500 (in pre-Islamic times) to around 900. The other major use of slaves under Islam was as military troops.

Slaves had no legal rights. They could not own property or give testimony in court. The only penalty a free person incurred for killing a slave was to provide suitable compensation to the owner. On the other hand, the Qur'an and folk sayings attributed to Muhammad preached that an owner should display kindness to a slave, and most owners probably did so. Many owners bent the rules, allowing slaves to accumulate property toward purchasing their freedom.

The freeing of slaves was fairly common. Captives could be freed by ransom, around which bargaining was considered normal. As noted previously, many slaves purchased their own freedom. Also, many owners freed slaves who showed especial loyalty, skill, or initiative.

Islamic slavery, then, was largely open. Although it was hereditary, the number of marriages between free and slave parents was great enough to reduce significantly the number of children born into slavery. Although slaves were thought of as chattel, most Muslim owners tempered that conception with kindness and relaxation of restrictions.

FIGURE I.6.4 *Kwakiutl Slave Killer. This carved stone club, commonly called a "slave killer," is of the type formerly used by the Kwakiutl to sacrifice slaves during rituals. Such events were designed to show that a wealthy individual could afford to destroy things of value; blankets, wood carvings, and other items were also sacrificed.*
Courtesy of the Royal British Columbia Museum, Victoria, B.C.

The Kwakiutl

Slavery, although most common in agricultural states, occasionally has thrived in chiefdoms with less complex political systems. A prime example of this is the Kwakiutl[1] of Canada's Pacific coast. There, abundant resources allowed hunters and gatherers to develop large, sedentary populations with marked class stratification.

Among the Kwakiutl, war captives often became slaves. Although the child of a slave and a free person would not be a slave, the child of two slaves would. It was considered debasing for a free person to marry a slave, so such unions were rare. As a result of capture and birth, there was a permanent slave stratum in Kwakiutl society.

Slavery for an individual among the Kwakiutl, however, was not necessarily permanent. A captive could be ransomed out of slavery by relatives at any point. Alternatively, because slaves were permitted to accumulate property, they could purchase their own freedom, essentially ransoming themselves.

Kwakiutl slaves performed a variety of labors for their owners. They were excluded from religious ceremonies, and they occasionally were sacrificed during rituals. Although there was no organized slave trade, slaves sometimes were exchanged along with other goods.

Kwakiutl slavery was very open, though hereditary. Slaves were chattel, but they retained certain personal rights, particularly those relating to property.

The Melanau

Slavery was prominent among the Melanau[2] of Indonesia. The Melanau chiefdom had at its apex a class of artistocrats who controlled the export of the sago palm upon which the commercial economy was based, and the labor-intensive production of sago was largely in the hands of slaves. Slavery began sometime before the eighteenth century and ended in 1948, long after Dutch law officially had abolished it in Indonesia.

Slaves among the Melanau probably were recruited by capture in earlier days, but by the late nineteenth century, when written records became common, most slaves either were born to that status or sold themselves into it in order to relieve debts. From the moment people became slaves, they were on the route to manumission. There was a fixed sequence of seven steps to manumission,

[1] **Kwakiutl:** KWAH kee oot uhl

[2] **Melanau:** mehl uh NOW

with increasing personal rights and autonomy as one progressed through the steps. Each step was gained by a complicated procedure involving gifts at the weddings of daughters, and the process accelerated in the later stages, as one's rights to accumulate property became greater. Slaves served as both domestic servants and agricultural laborers, and the passage from domestic to agricultural duties was an important marker of the fifth step, because the agriculturalist had greater opportunities for economic betterment. If individuals did not make it to the final step and freedom during a lifetime, their children would take up the process at the point their parents had reached before death.

Slaves had no right to regulate their own marriages, which were arranged by owners. Slaves often married free people, in which case the first child was free, the second a slave, the third free, and so forth. Slaves retained many personal rights and were not considered chattel.

Slavery among the Melanau was very open; indeed, slaves were on the track to freedom, although only some achieved it fully in a single lifetime. Slavery was hereditary, but, because children inherited the final step achieved by their parents, families moved steadily out of slavery. As with most slavery systems in chiefdom-level societies, slaves retained many personal rights.

THE SPECTRUM OF SLAVERY

Although slaves are rare in our time, they have been commonplace in human history, at least for the last five or six thousand years. Indeed, some scholars have considered slaveholding to be typical and societies without slaves as the aberration. The variety within slavery has meant that each system has had very different implications for the slave, the owner, and the society as a whole.

It is a quirk of history that we live in a time when the most well-known instance of slavery was that of the Americas in the sixteenth through nineteenth centuries, based on the African slave trade conducted by Europeans. No form of slavery is benign or beneficial to slaves, but this form was the most rapacious and brutal ever known, probably because of the huge numbers of persons involved. Almost completely closed, fully hereditary, and chattel-based, it encouraged harsh treatment, abuse, and brutality. It focused predominantly on agricultural-industrial slaves, who were considered expendable parts in a plantation machine. This system destroyed the lives and often the wills of millions of slaves. It was an extreme form of slavery, and we should not draw our picture of slavery in other periods and places from it.

SUGGESTED READINGS

Finlay, Moses I. "Slavery." In *International Encyclopedia of the Social Sciences.* Vol. 14. New York, 1968, 307–13. A brief but insightful article, the best single work on the theory of slavery.

Patterson, Orlando. *Slavery and Social Death: A Comparative Study.* Cambridge, Mass.: Harvard University Press, 1982. Argues that the essence of slavery is the alienation of the slave from any societal context.

Phillips, William D. *Slavery from Roman Times to the Early Transatlantic Trade.* Minneapolis: University of Minnesota Press, 1985. A good synthesis focusing on Europe.

Watson, James L., ed. *Asian and African Systems of Slavery.* Berkeley: University of California Press, 1980. An excellent collection of essays discussing historical systems of slavery in anthropological perspective.

PART SEVEN EXAMINES THE MULTIFACETED CHANGES that transformed Europe and other societies. Massive conflicts among European nation-states accelerated changes in society and compelled rulers to alter their polities. Later, an industrial revolution transformed economic and social systems in Europe, the United States, and Japan. And the drive for resources and markets by industrializing states led to the development of imperialism, in which Western and Japanese governments carved out empires from conquered lands in Africa, Asia, and the Americas.

Broader participation in political affairs burst forth, beginning in the seventeenth century. The English Parliament wrested power away from the monarchy and then ruled England jointly with the crown. The American and French revolutions significantly expanded the voting franchise and participation in government. These events encouraged Latin American and Asian countries to become independent. Nationalism developed in the nineteenth century and helped fuel the drive for colonies by imperialist powers.

Human beings also began to see themselves and their world in strikingly new ways. For example, people gradually saw the earth as but one planet in a vast universe, and they eventually viewed human beings as one of many species that evolved over time. Science became increasingly important.

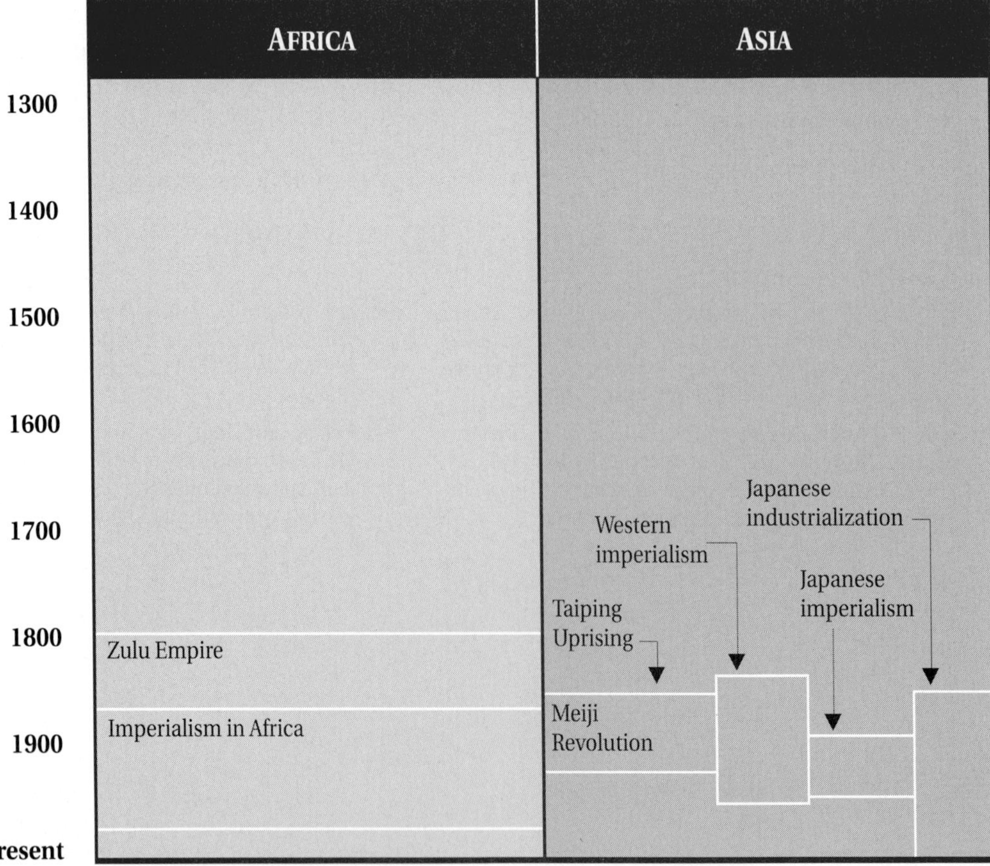

PART SEVEN

EUROPE'S GLOBAL REACH

Chapter 29 examines the Renaissance in Europe, a time of expanded economic and artistic development. It also explores the Protestant and Roman Catholic reformations, a time of religious ferment and conflict. Chapter 30 probes the growth of European absolutism, when monarchs centralized their governments and gathered new power for themselves. Chapter 31 develops the concept of revolution and analyzes revolutions around the world. Chapter 32 presents the Industrial Revolution, a transformative economic process that propelled Western countries and Japan into positions of political hegemony. Chapter 33 looks at nationalism as a political force in developing Zululand and many other nation-states. Chapter 34 examines imperialism—the modern form of colonialism—which uses industrialization and nationalism to build empires, especially overseas. Chapter 35 investigates the impact of Charles Darwin, Karl Marx, and others who changed the way human beings look at themselves and their environment. Issue 7 explores the relationship between science and the masses during a time when scientific discoveries and information excited common people around the world.

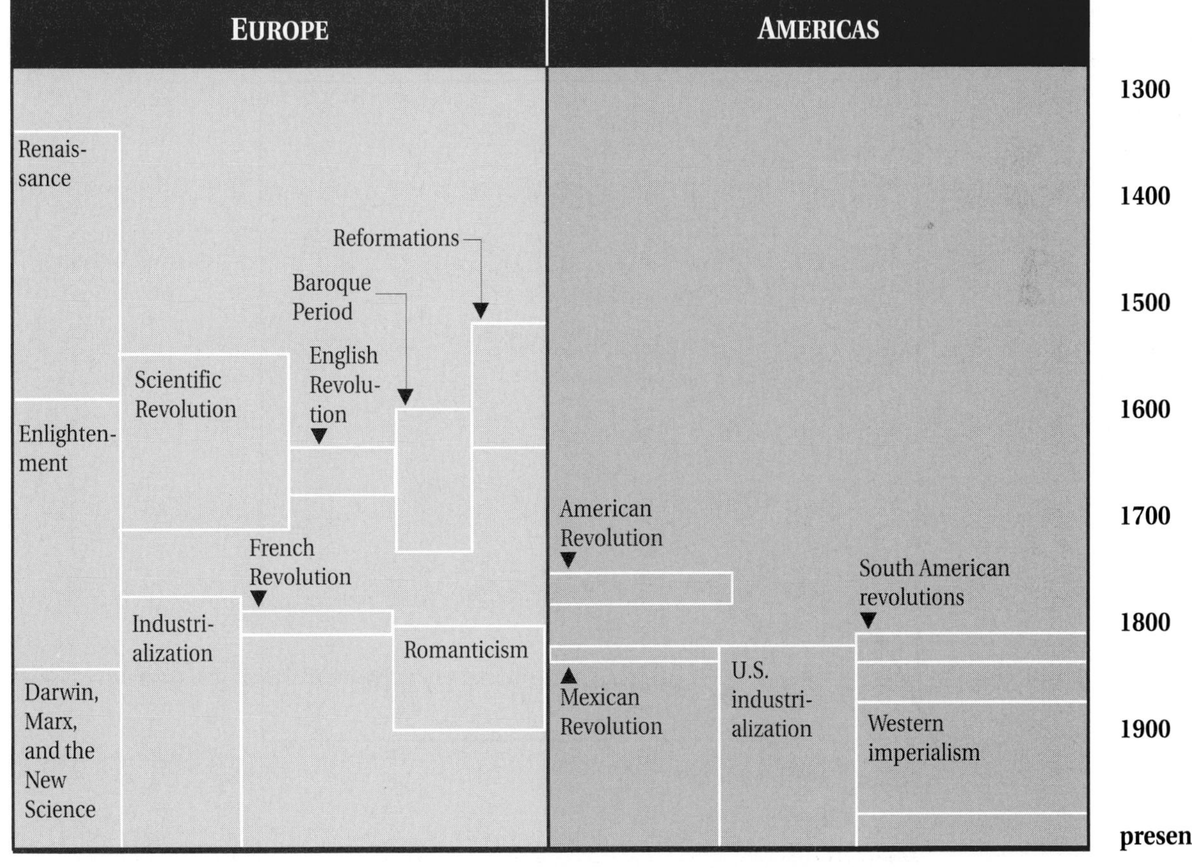

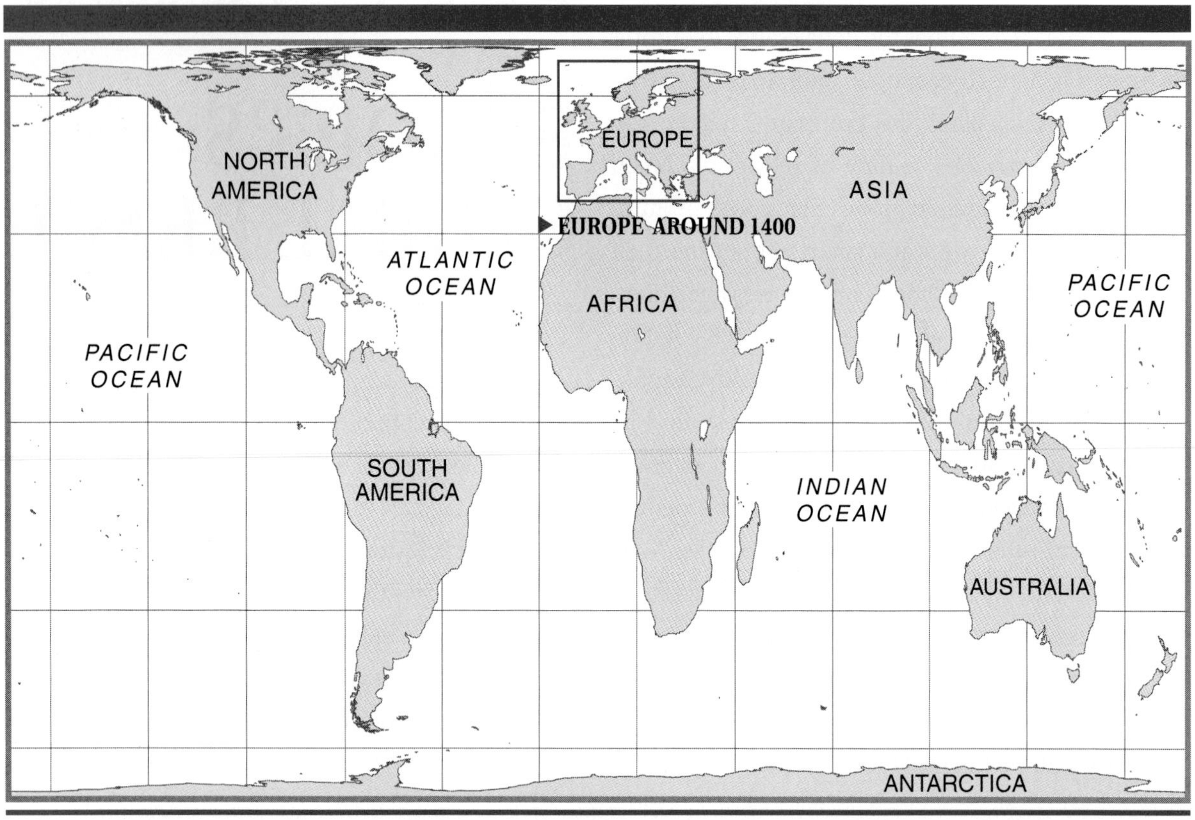

NORTH AMERICA
EUROPE
ASIA
ATLANTIC OCEAN
AFRICA
PACIFIC OCEAN
PACIFIC OCEAN
SOUTH AMERICA
INDIAN OCEAN
AUSTRALIA
ANTARCTICA
▶ EUROPE AROUND 1400

▶ **EUROPE AROUND 1400**

CHAPTER 29

European Cultural and Religious Upheaval

around 1350–around 1650

Ortelius, a late-sixteenth-century cartographer, carried an autograph book with him on his journeys throughout Europe. He called it his "Book of Friends," and in its pages were signed the names of lawyers, diplomats, historians, poets, printers, Protestant and Roman Catholic clergy, musicians, architects, antiquarian book dealers, and botanists. The geographical range of the signatories is impressive: Spain, Portugal, Italy, Germany, France, and England are represented. The diversity of Ortelius's friendships reflects the broad spectrum of European occupations and interests from the fourteenth to the seventeenth centuries.

Life in Europe in the late fourteenth century was fraught with complexities, uncertainties, and new opportunities. As a result of plagues and wars, the European population had suffered more than 20 million deaths. The legacy of this tragedy was economic depression for some, but it allowed opportunities for others. Many survivors seized the moment to advance their social positions or introduce new ways of thinking about the world. The voyages of exploration, beginning in the late fifteenth century, challenged Europeans to expand their worldview beyond their own neighborhoods; new markets opened for European products, and new goods arrived from distant exotic places.

The changes that occurred at this time helped usher in a new era in the fourteenth century in central, western, and northern Europe. Scholars call this era the **Renaissance**, meaning the rebirth of Greco-Roman culture as an authoritative model for society. Medieval intellectual and artistic attitudes had given way to perspectives that valued the Greco-Roman period more than the immediate medieval past. This reorientation in worldview was part of a broad sociopolitical and economic process that occurred at different times, in different places, and over several centuries, from the late fourteenth through the sixteenth centuries in Europe.

Questioning of religious ideology and calls for reform, which had already begun in the Middle Ages, took on greater urgency in the aftermath of devastation from plagues and wars. Many challenged the traditional social and political structures, and arguments over basic political theories, religious tenets, and procedures for change consumed European intellectuals. Religious self-examination and reform erupted in vehement disputes and protests and eventually in the schism of the Roman Catholic Church. This period of reform and schism is called the **Protestant Reformation** by scholars. Shortly after the Protestant Reformation began, the Roman Catholic Church initiated its own reform of lax practices and abuses of privilege; this reform is known as the **Roman Catholic Reformation**.

Renaissance and Reformation attitudes did not spread to all parts of Europe, especially not to eastern Europe. For example, the Ottoman Empire and the Russian state were little affected by Renaissance and Reformation trends. But, for much of Europe, the era of 1350 to 1650 was dynamic and destructive, innovative and incendiary.

THE EUROPEAN RENAISSANCE, AROUND 1350–AROUND 1600

Ideas that the ancient Greco-Roman past was superior to the immediate medieval past emerged in Italy in the mid–fourteenth century. At the same time, economic expansion brought increased wealth into Europe, spurring patronage of the arts. Social attitudes changed and new opportunities emerged for some people. With these economic and social changes came innovations in politics, philosophy, and the arts.

Economic Growth

Economies grew significantly in Europe during the Renaissance. Plague and war had greatly affected most of Europe, but financial devastation was not universal. Some regional commerce actually expanded because war and disease had wiped out competition. By the end of this period there were far fewer serfs throughout western Europe. Although many peasants continued to owe dues and labor services, a moneyed economy of rent payments and wages gradually supplanted the older manorial system. With tenant peasants and a growing middle class in the towns, lords tried to protect traditional rights of jurisdiction over markets and courts against the increasing power of monarchs.

European lands were sometimes reclaimed for commercial enterprises, causing a shift from farming to commercial activities. In England, for example, conversion of low-yield farms into pasturage for sheep because of a greater demand for wool brought higher profit to the lords but displaced many peasants because fewer of them were needed for animal husbandry than for crop production. Many of these dislocated peasants migrated to cities, where they became artisans and laborers or remained unemployed.

In some cases, such as that of the expansion of the wool market, commercial ventures brought increased controls on merchant activities and commercial alliances. In England, for example, the government regulated exportation of wool. All English wool had to be exported through a selected port by designated merchants, who had formed their own company. The government's payback came when the king borrowed heavily from this company to finance the crown's projects. Most of the older medieval guilds adapted to the growth in commerce by developing joint ventures. The result was the financial ruin of small, independent competitors who could not afford to match these larger capital investments.

Italian city-states had always been more commercially active than those in the comparatively agrarian areas north of the Alps because of their

MAP 29.1 ***Renaissance Italy.*** *Renaissance Italy was a patchwork of independent polities, many of which were fierce trade competitors. This competition sometimes resulted in aggression and warfare. Peace was usually achieved through hard-fought treaties that protected dominions over lands and trade routes.*

proximity to natural harbors and their vibrant traditions as areas of trade. Milan, for example, was known for its production of armaments and cloth. Several Italian cities became banking and insurance centers during the Renaissance. The trade network that had supported the medieval economy north of the Alps had expanded, and several major commercial centers now established financial ties with wealthy banking houses in Italy. As a result, most economies expanded rapidly. Although banking had developed in medieval Italy, standardization of policies and protection allowed for substantial economic diversity. Long and dangerous voyages led to new fiscal innovations to aid the growing commercial activities. For example, investors were encouraged by insurance that sheltered against crippling losses and by letters of credit that protected against monetary risk.

European commerce increased significantly through Jewish trade links with the vast networks of Muslim merchants in the Mediterranean. By the fifteenth century, Venice and Genoa dominated the European long-distance trade connection with Muslims in the eastern Mediterranean and acted as commercial conduits to the rest of Europe. When the Ottoman Turks disrupted eastern Mediterranean trade links and conquered Constantinople in the mid–fifteenth century, most Italian cities suffered temporary but significant revenue losses. Italian trade rebounded with new ties to Mediterranean trade and the New World trade.

Renaissance Society

Between the fourteenth and sixteenth centuries, European rural life continued as it had for centuries, with moderate changes. Cities had grown significantly. Several cities, including Venice, Milan, Naples, Paris, and London, could boast of populations totaling from 150,000 to more than 200,000. These populations created a demand for employment and goods. Most cities were divided into neighborhoods; sometimes the division was by profession, sometimes by wealth, and sometimes by religion.

European Jews had been forced to live in ghettos during the Middle Ages. Most Jews were subject to periodic acts of violence by Christians because of their religion. In many cases, authorities willingly participated in their deaths and destruction of their properties; in some cases, religious and political authorities tried to protect Jews from angry mobs. Persecutions by roaming gangs, particularly during plague years, accounted for thousands of Jewish deaths. During a plague in the city of Toledo, for example, rumors spread that Jews were poisoning the city wells, and many Jews were killed. As Renaissance trade developed in the fourteenth and fifteenth centuries, more restrictions closed many trade occupations to Jews in order to accommodate Christians. Heavy taxes kept most Jewish families in poverty, although some were able to gain funds through investments. Some Christians rejected anti-Jewish programs and supported Jews in their areas; the monarchs of the Kingdom of the Two Sicilies (southern Italy and Sicily) were recognized as tolerant rulers.

European Christians tolerated the presence of Jews in most areas and periods because of economic motives. Christians often let Jews absorb the financial burden of risky trade ventures by borrowing money and not repaying bad debts. Kings and merchants frequently confiscated Jewish wealth in fiscally lean times in order to replenish their revenues. Many Jews contributed to commercial interests with their artisan skills and merchant contacts. Others contributed to Renaissance society in the limited professions open to Jews, such as medicine.

FIGURE 29.1 ***Vanities.*** *This painting by the Italian artist Vittore Carpaccio depicts some of the "vanities" representative of worldly wealth that Girolamo Savonarola preached against. These Venetian women have bleached and styled hair and wear significant amounts of makeup, opulent clothing, and expensive jewelry. They are enjoying their leisure on a balcony with an attending servant and their various pets. These women happen to be prostitutes, but their attire and the setting reflect the aristocratic styles of the day. Savonarola's charismatic preaching attracted many followers who shared his abhorrence of extravagance and privilege.* Museo Correr, Venice/Art Resource, N.Y.

In all Italian Renaissance cities, important political families measured their power and influence by the number of families of lower status that supported and emulated them. Most lived near their patrons and copied their lifestyles as much as possible, leading to a pride in opulent living. Patronage of the arts was a direct result of increased economic activity.

The presence of such wealth in the face of poverty occasionally erupted in violent reaction. Girolamo Savonarola[1] (1452–1498), a preacher, led a revolt in the late fifteenth century in the city of Florence, establishing a democracy for a short period. He preached against what he saw as the immoral wealth and absurd vanities of wealthy Florentines. In huge bonfires, later given the collective name "the bonfire of the vanities," cosmetics, luxurious clothing, hundreds of pieces of art, and furnishings went up in smoke. Savonarola's radicalism eventually resulted in his arrest and execution.

Increased commercial activity certainly improved the standard of living for many in Europe, but the majority still lived meager lives. Traders in the thirteenth century could usually expect moderate growth in income, but, by the fifteenth century, competition stymied economic gains for the majority. It is tempting to assume that the grand living styles of the elite somehow raised the standard of living for everyone, but most wealthy patrons were little concerned with the plight of their poorest neighbors. To a large degree, innovations in education, philosophy, political theory, and the fine arts bypassed the poor.

THE LABOR FORCE. Labor in rural areas changed little for both men and women from the fourteenth to the sixteenth centuries. Many peasant women, however, worked in their homes as part of a cottage industry, carding, spinning, and weaving wool into cloth. Merchants then gathered the finished products for later sale in towns and cities.

Increased availability of capital through commercial activities led to an increase in paid professions in the cities. Two examples were soldiering and bookkeeping. Professional soldiers were in demand because long-distance commerce placed valuable cargoes in jeopardy. Hired by the highest bidder and given a contract, soldiers protected the banking and shipping companies' interests. Venice employed enough soldiers to secure its seaborne empire from the Adriatic Sea to Cyprus. Professional bookkeepers found more than enough employment in banking and commercial activities. Most merchants learned to read and write as children and then acquired the necessary skills in mathematics and bookkeeping to run their own family businesses or to keep records as employees of someone else. A young man might be apprenticed to a business as a bookkeeper or even sent on to law school so that he might hire himself out as a consultant in commercial law.

The laboring class in the cities worked at numerous professions, some old and some new. For example, the sixteenth-century city of Nuremberg, a hub for northern European trade, had 140 different craft occupations. Cloth makers, potters, oar makers, carpenters, blacksmiths, and arsenal workers, to name a few, represent the variety of urban laborers. Similarly to earlier artisans, groups of specialists protected the secrets of their crafts, as when Venetian glassmakers guarded their unique knowledge of adding enamels to glass.

Many laborers in the late fourteenth and fifteenth centuries earned low wages. They toiled in the mines or in cloth production, unable to defend themselves against the exploitation of merchants and investors. No guild or other organization existed to argue on their behalf, and new joint ventures focused increasingly on company management interests rather than on employee benefits. Miners, for example, rose early in the morning and worked long hours with only a short break for a little bread and ale before returning to the shafts to pick at the veins of ore. The life of a miner proved so difficult that many received exemption from military service or taxes as compensation. In some cases, criminals served on mining teams as punishment for their crimes.

The labor force in the cities included women. A few women in the city of Venice, for example, gained employment in manufacturing. Most women working outside of the home, however, became domestic servants. Some were personal maids who helped elite women adorn themselves with the newest styles of the day. Some poorer women supported themselves in the age-old employment of prostitution, and most cities had populations of female prostitutes and special taxes on them. Venice, for example, collected lucrative

[1] **Savonarola:** SAHV ah nah ROH lah

prostitution taxes and became financially dependent on them. Middle-class and elite women, however, typically remained in the home and managed their households.

LITERACY AND GENDER ROLES. Literacy was limited to members of the middle or elite classes. Conduct books, such as *The Book of the Courtier* (published around 1516), outlined the proper education for young men as physical mastery of swordplay, horseback riding, hunting, and games. A "Renaissance man's" education followed the Greek ideal of both physical and intellectual training to produce a well-rounded individual. Education for both men and women followed the axiom "a healthy mind in a healthy body." Conduct books for women taught young ladies household management and the arts of dancing, singing, playing instruments, and conversing so that they might properly entertain gentlemen. Although some women received formal training in the liberal arts, most education for women continued the traditional practices of needlework, embroidery, and the reading of religious literature.

It has been observed by scholars that, in some ways, Renaissance women actually lost some of the social status that had been gained in the previous medieval period. Many medieval women had enjoyed joint business partnerships with their husbands, and some merchant wives had become accountants and financiers for their husbands' commercial enterprises. Wives of lords usually ran the manorial properties and households for their husbands, who absented themselves for court activities and military obligations. Renaissance women, however, became social casualties in changing attitudes that accepted Greco-Roman literary figures as models. For example, an ancient Athenian gender distinction was adopted that categorized women's spheres of influence as inferior

FIGURE 29.2 ***Tennis.*** *Tennis originated in France and became a popular game for the wealthy. It was played with a small ball and rackets on a green enclosed by a walled and roofed courtyard. The physical exertion required by the rigorous sport helped to achieve a well-toned body, which was part of the Renaissance ideal. Tennis was imported to England, where Henry VIII had courts built at each of his palaces.* The Folger Shakespeare Library.

and domestic, while men's spheres were thought of as superior and public. Women who had exercised authority in businesses at the end of the Middle Ages found new Renaissance attitudes limiting their influence.

SOCIAL MOBILITY. One of the most important changes during the Renaissance was the expansion of opportunities for some gain in social advancement. In England, for example, only about fifty families held official titles of nobility; their position came from wealth based on traditional taxes, dues, and rents from extensive inherited landholdings. Below the nobility were the **gentry**, a new elite status that was not officially noble, yet was higher than the middle class; it was usually associated with rural property. The gentry controlled enough land to live comfortably without the need to work actively. Many small towns sought out members of the gentry to represent them in matters dealing with the nobility, and wealthy merchants often purchased country estates, becoming gentry themselves. This kind of social mobility reflected a shift from status gained through birthright to status achieved through wealth. In contrast to England, social mobility came more slowly in parts of continental Europe. Tenants or hired laborers, however, might achieve some improved status within their social class.

Renaissance Governments

The medieval legacy of the diverse independent political power of great lords and knights, of self-governing towns with powerful guilds, and of a universal Christian society gave way to emerging centralization during the Renaissance. Monarchs, strong regional princes, and independent cities tried to establish more centralized governments by slowly weakening customary financial obligations and multiple legal jurisdictions. Centralization under monarchs occurred in Spain, France, and England.

In part, the shift toward centralization occurred as a consequence of innovations in waging war. Mass armies and cavalry replaced medieval aristocratic knights on horseback, and men with muskets replaced bowmen. Navies protected commercial enterprises with decks of cannons mounted on gunships. Kings needed the support of their commoner subjects to wage war and, consequently, developed centralized policies to help govern and command them.

With this general move toward political centralization came theories that supported strong monarchies. In his essay *The Prince*, Niccolò Machiavelli[2] (1469–1527) explains that a good leader is not necessarily one who is the most virtuous. Machiavelli elaborated on the theory that an effective ruler must use any means necessary, even fear and deception, to govern. Many of Machiavelli's insights came from his astute observation of Italian politics.

Italian city-states always had strained against political control from kings, bishops, and popes, and they emerged in the thirteenth and fourteenth centuries as politically independent. These cities were commonly governed by powerful families, like the d'Medici.[3] Cosimo d'Medici (1389–1464) dominated Florence and, through an alliance with the cities of Milan and Naples, checked expansionist policies of the neighboring Papal States. Because many European ruling houses borrowed heavily from Italian financiers, several powerful Italian families extended their political tendrils into European courts. Fierce competition between cities later resulted in the emergence of five large regional polities, one of which was the Papal States under the Borgia family. By the end of the fifteenth century, the Borgias controlled the Papal States through a relative, Pope Alexander VI (reign dates 1492–1503), who used papal power against rival cities and local enemies. More a secular prince than a holy father, Pope Alexander led his family into a morass of murder plots and political intrigue that was scandalous even by Renaissance standards.

England, after the economic catastrophe of the Hundred Years War, suffered internal hostilities and civil war. One of the bloodiest contests in English history convulsed the country into a dynastic struggle. Finally, in 1485, a member of the Tudor faction became Henry VII (reign dates 1485–1509), king of England. The Tudor dynasty represents a change in English government because Henry diminished the power of the English parliament by building his power on a new royal council, whose members he handpicked from the gentry class. The royal council unequivocally established judi-

[2] **Machiavelli:** MAHK ee uh VEHL ee
[3] **d'Medici:** duh MEH dih chee

cial authority through the ruthless council of the Star Chamber, which arrested, tortured, and sentenced victims without benefit of trial. Local law was enforced through justices of the peace, who were appointed by the royal council. Henry rarely called Parliament to meet and centralized authority through his royal council, thereby keeping the nobility under control. Marriage alliances with Spain and Scotland, coupled with the support of the gentry and middle-class merchants, helped the monarchy consolidate power.

The French ruler Louis XI (reign dates 1461–1483) earned the nickname "The Spider King" because of his preference for intrigue and manipulation. A large number of the French nobility had been killed in the Hundred Years War, and Louis consolidated his power by outmaneuvering those who remained. His use of the new technologies of gunpowder and cannons blew apart the castles of the entrenched nobility. Upon his death, Louis left the area of France under the king's direct control nearly twice as large as when he inherited the crown. Louis supported middle-class interests by establishing lucrative trade treaties with other commercial centers. His interest in commercial activity brought new money into French territories and earned him the grateful support of the middle class. Succeeding French monarchs continued the policies of trying to control regional lords.

The Holy Roman Empire, consisting of most of Central Europe, was an anomaly. Consolidation there was occurring within regions rather than under the monarch. The Holy Roman Emperor since 1356 had been elected by seven major Germanic princes representing the three hundred confederated principalities and towns in the empire. By the end of the fifteenth century, however, Emperor Maximilian I (reign dates 1493–1519), a Hapsburg, exerted powerful leadership over the empire. He accomplished this task by enforcing imperial control over the assembly composed of the seven princes and representatives of the free cities of Germany. Although Maximilian waged war on Italian cities in order to reunify them with the Holy Roman Empire, he never gained political control over them. Marriage alliances, particularly with Spain, brought wealth and prosperity into the realm. The grandson of Maximilian inherited the Spanish throne (including its New World wealth and its holdings in Italy) from his mother; he also inherited the imperial crown and other lands from his father. The long history of princely power in the empire, however, limited his ability to establish long-lasting central authority.

Spain began as a patchwork of the kingdoms of Portugal, Castile, Aragon, and Muslim Granada. In the mid-1470s, the two principalities of Aragon and Castile united through the marriage between Isabella of Castile (reign dates 1474–1504) and Ferdinand of Aragon (reign dates 1479–1516). Although the realms remained separate entities, Ferdinand and Isabella were able to consolidate their power within each one. Both rulers limited the influence of the nobility in their respective assemblies. Royally appointed lawyers were members of councils that dealt with finances and justice, and royal officials replaced elected magistrates in governing cities. The expulsion of Muslims in the 1480s and Jews in 1492 from Christian-controlled areas attests to the intolerance of religious diversity by the Christians. The conquest of Muslim-held Granada in 1492 brought further religious and political unity to the peninsula. Spanish commercial interests in the New World, the expansion of previous interests into Naples and Sicily, and diplomatic marriage alliances with France, England, and the Holy Roman Empire helped to catapult Spain into European dominance.

The three kingdoms of Denmark, Norway, and Sweden were unified and ably administered by Queen Margaret of Denmark (1353–1412), who was named queen after the deaths of her husband and son. The kingdoms remained politically separate within a confederation called the Union of Kalmar but were unified under "the lady king's" authority. Although unrest plagued her successors, the Union of Kalmar lasted until 1523.

Renaissance Thought

The overwhelming social changes during the Renaissance brought intellectual and artistic change as well. Universities, which had operated since the twelfth century, shifted their emphasis to human areas of inquiry. **Humanism**, a system of thought based on the study of human ideas and actions, grew out of a developing focus on secular interests. Many of our modern colleges have schools of humanities, which are a result of the transition from the medieval focus on theology, logic, and metaphysics to a Renaissance focus on

PATHS TO THE PAST

Lorenzo Valla and Textual Criticism

The recovery of the Greco-Roman heritage meant also a recovery of ancient texts. Many had been diligently copied and preserved by studious monks throughout the medieval centuries, others had been brought into Europe in the twelfth and thirteenth centuries through Muslim contacts, and still others had come more recently through Renaissance trade networks. Many humanists became involved in the widespread search for manuscripts, while others took on the tasks of authentication and restoration of copies to their pristine condition. (Through the centuries, monks had translated texts into the Latin of their day, and the copying of copies had resulted in many scribal errors.)

Lorenzo Valla (1407–1457), an Italian humanist, attacked and criticized many medieval philosophers and historians for writing in a contemporary Latin style instead of the more formal Classical Latin style of the Roman Empire. This kind of criticism soon led to a focus on word usage, which in turn led to a study of words and their histories. This practice developed into **textual criticism**, the analysis and authentication of texts. Armed with new grammars and handbooks, critics began examining manuscripts. The most famous case of textual criticism is Valla's discrediting of the document titled *The Donation of Constantine*. In the eighth century, the papacy was threatened by the Byzantine emperor and surrounded by Germanic kings challenging papal independence. The papacy had turned to the Franks (a Germanic tribe) for aid. Upon the Frankish conquest of Italy and the liberation of the papacy from these threats, *The Donation of Constantine* was shown to the Frankish king, Pepin the Short. This edict of Constantine, the fourth-century Christian Roman emperor, placed all the western Roman territories under papal authority. In presenting this document to Pepin, the pope hoped that Pepin would not place Italy under the Frankish crown. Pepin issued an edict in his own name, establishing the independent Papal States.

In studying the document, Valla discovered that its language was not of the fourth century at all but was produced in the eighth century in order to influence Pepin. Therefore, Valla believed, the claims laid out in the document were insupportable. He called the document a forgery, and his methodology in authenticating Greco-Roman texts became a mainstay of historical analysis. Valla's discrediting of the document gave many reformers the ammunition they needed against papal authority in the Reformation period. Scholars today, however, note that an oral tradition telling of Constantine's donation had existed. This tradition was never written down until it was needed to assure papal independence from Pepin. In that sense, the document was not an intended forgery or a necessarily false statement but, to those who produced it, a transcription of a traditional belief. It was common in the Middle Ages to record folk memory and use it as legal evidence.

As a result of textual criticism, history became a discipline within the humanities that organized human events into a new narrative based on proper chronology and evidence. Later Protestant reformers used these same techniques to study biblical narrative and other Christian documents. They discovered that the apostles did not write the Apostle's Creed and that Jerome's Latin Bible had several errors in its translation from Greek to Latin. Examination of Greek texts also yielded new insights into and new Latin translations of Plato's works.

Greco-Roman subjects such as art, poetry, and philosophy. These latter subjects, concentrating on human endeavors, were considered to be more appropriate for study and became known as human studies or the humanities. The major focus of the early movement toward the humanities centered on Greek and Roman literature. Humanists believed that the Greco-Roman period was superior to the medieval era in thought and style, and they wanted to emulate ancient writers. To a certain degree, however, their emphasis on ancient Greek and Latin language and literature impeded the progression toward writing in the vernacular languages, such as French and Italian.

Petrarch[4] and Boccaccio[5] are examples of Italian humanists. Francesco Petrarch (1304–1374) studied law at Bologna and fell in love with the writings of ancient Romans like Cicero and Virgil. He wrote treatises and orations in the Greco-Roman style and attempted an epic poem. He wrote *Sonnets to Laura*, lyrical love poems to his one great love, who died in a plague. Petrarch's idealization of physical beauty and love earned him a mixed reputation: Some despised and ridiculed the new style, while others admired it. He searched out many manuscripts and encouraged other humanists to collect ancient literature, coins, and other antiquities. Giovanni Boccaccio (1313–1375) wrote the *Decameron*, which told stories about the Black Death through graphic descriptions of plague victims, in contrast to Petrarch's idealization of beauty. The focus on human experiences, shared by Petrarch and Boccaccio, caught on and became a favored topic of Renaissance literature.

Desiderius Erasmus (1466–1536), perhaps the most famous northern humanist priest, studied theology in Paris and wandered throughout Europe, quickly becoming recognized as a keen intellect. He popularized many Greco-Roman concepts in easily understood writings, and these helped to spread humanist ideas. In his 1509 work *In Praise of Folly*, Erasmus satirically exposed contemporary class pretensions. His most serious works, however, included humanist handbooks on education and interpretations of theologians of early Christianity.

Fine Arts

Renaissance attitudes inspired a new tradition of artistic support. Because the Renaissance value system expected people of wealth to sponsor the arts, Europe experienced unprecedented artistic production during the fourteenth to the sixteenth centuries. The growth of the middle class and increased wealth from commercial activities allowed all areas of the fine arts to find patrons and new avenues of expression.

LITERATURE. Michel de Montaigne[6] (1533–1592) epitomized humanist thought in his development of the literary style of essay writing. He wrote on education, friendship, skepticism, and the ideal of human beings living in a state of nature ("the noble savage"), helping to spread humanist ideas to sociopolitical theorists. He criticized certain historians: "The middle sort of historians, of which the most part are, spoil all; they will chew our meat for us." Montaigne clearly preferred to study history for himself, as any humanist scholar would. His skepticism regarding the lack of certainty in human knowledge led him to announce, "I know nothing." Consequently, his tolerance led him to decline support for either side of the religious quarrels of his day.

The Elizabethan Age in England bustled with artistic activity. The period gets its name from the influential reign of Queen Elizabeth I (reign dates 1558–1603). William Shakespeare (1564–1616) is perhaps the most significant writer of the period; his work still plays upon stages throughout the world. To a large degree Shakespeare's storylines included historical settings, but his comedic genius and psychological insight speak to the most basic of humanist issues: human nature, its emotions, and their role in comedy and historical tragedy. He captured the sentiments of many European intellectuals in these lines:

> Life is but a walking shadow, a poor player that struts and frets his hour upon the stage, and then is heard no more. . . . It is a tale told by an idiot, full of sound and fury, signifying nothing.

PAINTING AND SCULPTURE. Artists in Renaissance Europe emulated ancient styles and incorporated contemporary innovations. Lifelike statuary and painting resulted from artists' attention to the details of perspective and naturalism. The plethora of Italian painting and sculpture is perhaps best represented by two Italians, Leonardo da Vinci[7] (1452–1519) and Michelangelo Buonarrotti (1475–1564). Leonardo's numerous sketches reveal close attention to anatomical accuracy; he painstakingly duplicated human anatomy by sketching corpses and posed models. He believed that knowing the musculo-skeletal structure better prepared the artist to depict the human body realistically, even when it was clothed. Some of Michelangelo's most famous works are his frescoes in the Vatican's Sistine Chapel, restored in the late 1980s and early 1990s. These 350 biblical and Greco-Roman figures demonstrate Michelangelo's

[4] **Petrarch:** PEE trahrk
[5] **Boccaccio:** boh KAH chee oh
[6] **Michel de Montaigne:** mee SHEHL duh mawn TAYN

[7] **Vinci:** VIHN chee

FIGURE 29.3 ***Michelangelo's* Creation of Adam.** *This famous image, painted on the ceiling of the Sistine Chapel, depicts a scene from the Bible's Fall of Man. As with most Renaissance art, the focus is on the musculature of the figures. Adam is in repose, awaiting the spark of life (the soul) from God. He looks to God and beyond to Eve, nested under God's left arm and anticipating the moment of her birth.* Art Resource, N.Y.

artistry in depicting the human form. True to Renaissance ideals, Michelangelo examined ancient Greek and Roman works as he studied in Florence. His philosophy of art suggested that the sculpture lay encased in the marble, and his work as a sculptor was merely to free it by chiseling away the extraneous stone.

Like many Renaissance artists, Michelangelo also worked on religious topics. Art adopted and integrated Greco-Roman proportions, styles, and religious themes. Michelangelo's *David*, depicted as a young Hebrew warrior, could be mistaken for a heroic Classical Greek Apollo.

Renaissance artists' interests also led them to investigate technologies and the sciences. Leonardo was fascinated by many scientific principles, which led to his ingenious sketches of machines. He drew flying machines, submarines, and armored cars, some of which became realities only in later centuries. During this same period, circulatory systems and musculo-skeletal structures became the focus of those who studied the "art" of healing. Universities specializing in medicine increasingly used cadavers to examine the mysteries of the human body. Adoption of Muslim medical manuals also contributed to the knowledge of medicine.

Although other European artists were already experimenting with innovative techniques of their own, Italian art styles, like literary ones, crossed

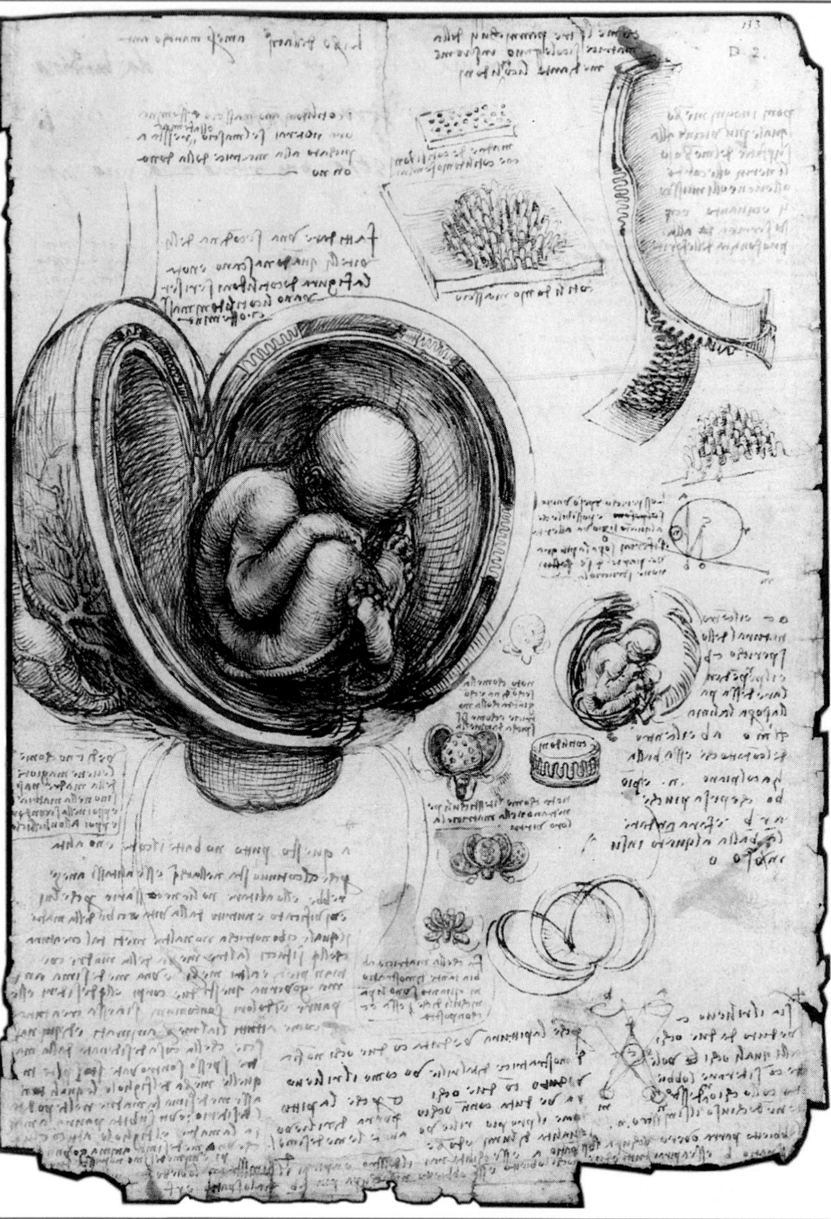

FIGURE 29.4 ***Da Vinci's Embryo Illustration.*** *Leonardo da Vinci was one of the first artists to employ his skills in scientific illustration. Da Vinci filled notebooks with sketches of human anatomy, rock formations, machinery, plants, and birds. His inspiration came from his desire "to learn the causes of things." In this example, he studied an embryo still in the womb and made notations on the embryo's condition and environment.* The Royal Collection, © Her Majesty Queen Elizabeth II.

the Alps. Albrecht Dürer[8] (1471–1528) traveled to Venice in 1494 and returned to his home in Nuremberg heavily influenced by Italian styles. He believed that an artist should be both a humanist and a gentleman.

ARCHITECTURE. Medieval Gothic architecture's spires and towers gave way to Renaissance building designs in the Greco-Roman style, incorporating domes and columns. Palaces and villas were commissioned, new churches were built, old ones were renovated, and building facades were updated. Filippo Brunelleschi[9] (1377–1446) dominated the field of architecture in Florence, Italy. Brunelleschi and a close circle of literary and artistic friends were in charge of several building projects that displayed the new Renaissance style. The dome of Florence's cathedral was the pinnacle of

[8] **Dürer:** DOOR uhr

[9] **Brunelleschi:** broon ehl EHS kee

FIGURE 29.5 ***Renaissance Architecture.*** *Designed by Filippo Brunelleschi, the church of Santa Maria del Fiore in Florence, Italy, is an excellent example of Renaissance architecture. It employs the classical Greco-Roman styles of arches and domes and introduces the innovative pattern of symmetric geometric spaces for which Brunelleschi became famous.* Alinari/Art Resource, N.Y.

their efforts. It was patterned on the circular Pantheon in Rome, and Brunelleschi modified the design to support the expansive weight of the dome. Brunelleschi and the sculptor Donatello designed the d'Medici family burial chapel together, using Greco-Roman antecedents. In addition to other architects (including Michelangelo), Brunelleschi used Greco-Roman columns, colonnades, and capitals in his plans. Andrea Palladio was the first architect to introduce the portico, a porch with two-story columns. The portico became popular in northern Italy and in plantation-house architecture in the southern United States and the Caribbean.

MUSIC. Renaissance music delighted both the wealthy and poor in courts, cathedrals, and common meeting areas. Medieval music had developed from Gregorian chant, the single-melodic line used in the monasteries of Europe. As time passed, the chants developed polyphony, multiple lines of harmony sung together. Secular music developed in the courts of medieval Europe, where polyphonic voice lines were accompanied by horns, stringed and wind instruments, and drums. Renaissance music continued the use of multiple instruments and voices, and the music of the pipe organ became an integral part of Christian worship. Medieval science had inherited the Greek philosophical notion that nature was essentially harmonic and that music represented the very essence of the natural order of the universe; the studies of science and music brought the seeker closer to the divine. Renaissance scientists and musicians continued to see the universe as the creator's composition and music as the creator's communication.

Renaissance music borrowed heavily from music traditions of neighboring peoples around the Mediterranean basin. Courtly fanfares for kings and the elite became popular with the advent of foreign instruments, such as Muslim quarter-tone instruments that added intriguing new sounds. Increasingly complicated rhythmic patterns influenced by African styles enlivened music at various gatherings.

THE PROTESTANT REFORMATION, 1517–AROUND 1600

The Protestant Reformation shared the stage of European human endeavor with the Renaissance. Most of the reform movements of the era ended in groups splitting off from the Roman Catholic Church; these splits, called schisms, resulted from differing opinions about Christian theology. The idea of reform did not originate in this period (the early 1520s), however. There had been reform movements throughout the previous centuries in the Middle Ages, but reform in the sixteenth century had greater impact because it was swept into the current of social and political changes already taking place. The torrent of debates for religious reform soon flowed out of the cloisters and halls of cathedrals and into the streets and palaces of Europe, eroding the unity of Roman Catholicism into islands of protest and resistance.

The Renaissance concept of returning to Greco-Roman styles and precedents led many Christians to believe the practices of the early church superior to those that developed in the medieval church. In addition to examining Greco-Roman texts and early church documents, many intellectuals focused on the study of Hebrew mysticism or the study of the Hebrew language. Discontent with real or perceived worldliness in the church, the buying and selling of church offices, and mandatory donations and taxes caused tensions between the Christian laity and the clergy.

The sale of indulgences became the issue that sparked a reformation of lasting consequence. **Indulgences**, cancellation of punishments for committed sins, began in the early church as simple prayers for the dead and pleas for leniency for those who could not complete penances. By the fifteenth century, professional "pardoners" held unrestricted power to sell indulgences like vegetables at the market. Their scandalous selling of "salvation" led to such caustic poems as the following, chanted by children in the street: "As soon as the coin in the coffer rings, the soul from purgatory springs." The ensuing fight over indulgences gave Martin Luther the occasion to find his reformer's voice.

Martin Luther

Martin Luther (1483–1546), a professor at the University of Wittenberg and a monk, unwittingly began the Reformation movement in 1517 by nailing a document listing ninety-five theses (topics) to the door of a Wittenberg church. This was a common practice when someone wanted to debate issues; it acted as an invitation to anyone who desired to come and speak or listen. The issue of selling indulgences in Wittenberg was only one of many that Luther wanted to discuss, and his arguments broke no new theological ground.

What, in the pope's words, began as a "monkish squabble" quickly accelerated into a widespread debate on reform. A medieval sociopolitical atmosphere would have limited Luther's arguments to intellectual, in-house debates, the path earlier reform movements usually had taken. Because of the new technology of printing and the growth of literacy in the vernacular, Luther's ideas spread like a wildfire across parts of Europe. Copies of Luther's ninety-five theses appeared throughout Germany within three weeks of his nailing them on the church door, resulting in widespread support of his ideas.

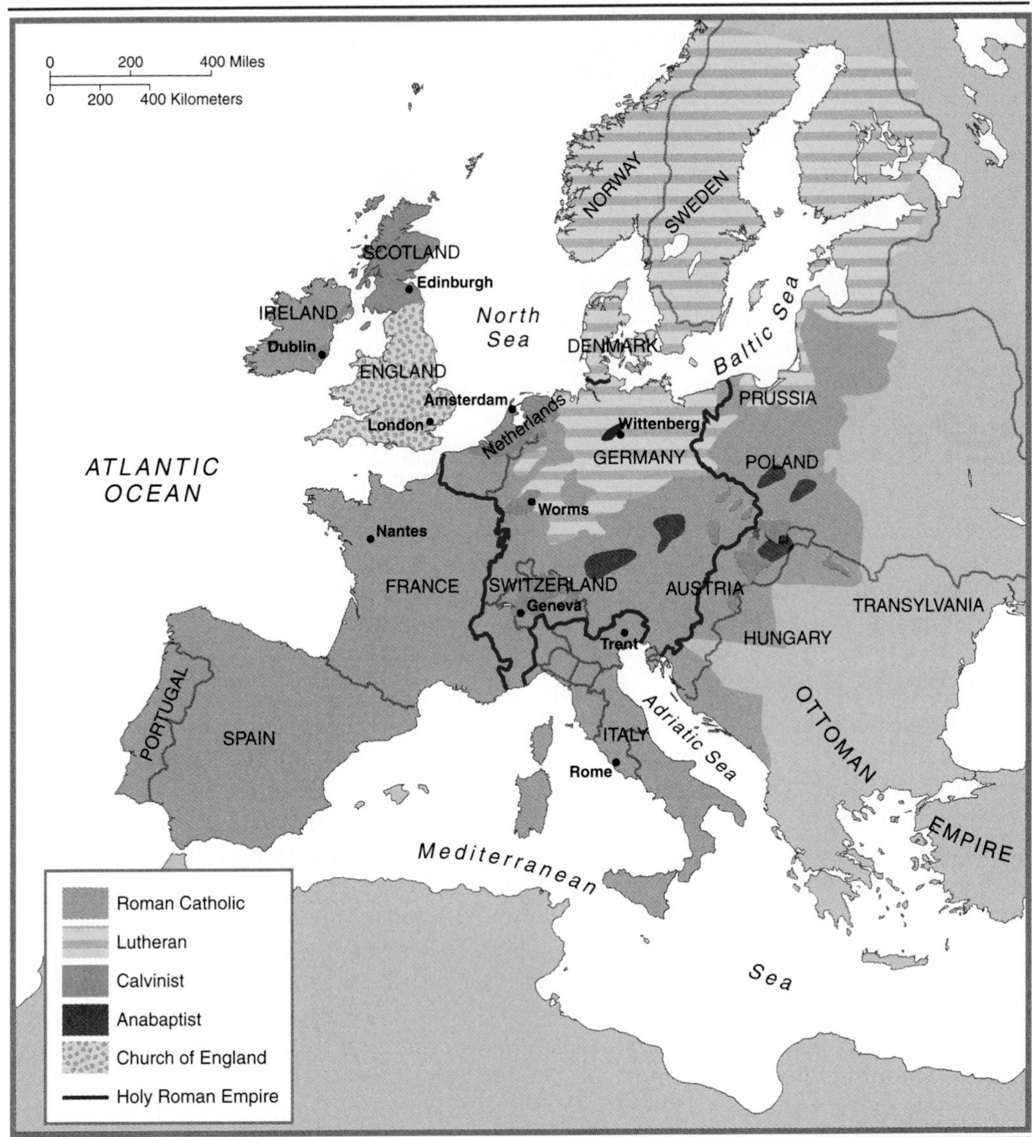

Map 29.2 ***Reformation Europe.*** *This is a general map showing the dominant Christian denominations in Europe around 1600. For example, pockets of Calvinism persisted in France, while in England practices of Roman Catholicism remained. The state policy on which religious denomination would be followed sometimes changed with the death of a monarch and the ascension of the successor.*

Luther engaged in several defenses of his reformist ideas in 1520 and 1521. In the city of Worms in 1521, Luther made a final stand in his defense, refusing to recant his positions. He was outlawed under an imperial ban and excommunicated (cut off from the church). The Reformation he had begun survived as Lutheranism; its two major tenets were justification by faith alone and the subordination of all traditional statements of doctrine to the authority of scripture. These tenets challenged traditional church practices and the authority of priests, bishops, and popes.

The arguments incorporated the new Renaissance way of thinking about the past that had swept over Europe. Like others before him, Luther believed that the early church was superior in authority to the contemporary church. Luther's reading of Lorenzo Valla led him to doubt the

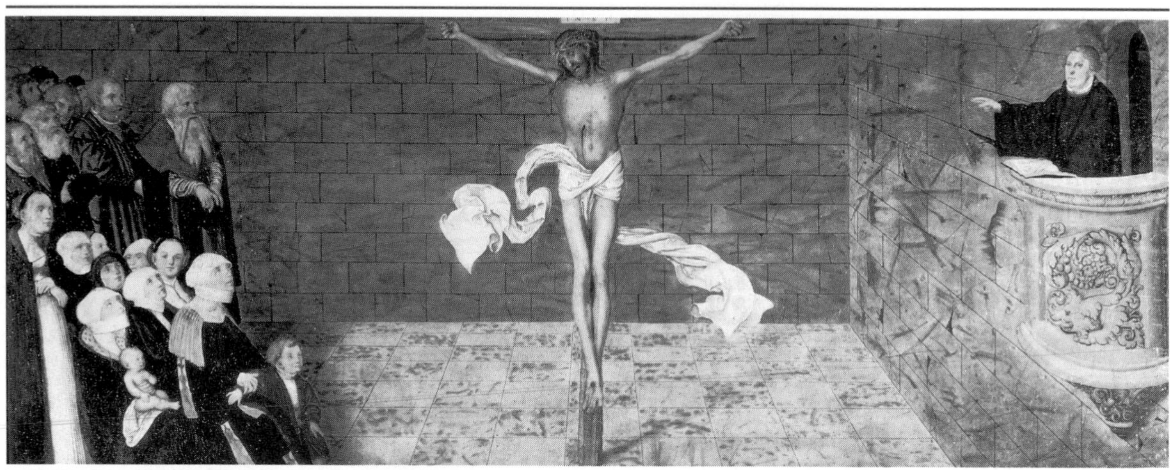

FIGURE 29.6 ***Martin Luther.*** *Martin Luther's theology focused on salvation as revealed through Scripture. Preaching, therefore, is a central part of Lutheranism, as opposed to the sacramental focus of the Roman Catholic Mass, in which preaching plays a lesser role. In Lucas Cranach's 1547 painting, Luther points to the crucifix, the vehicle for humanity's salvation; according to Lutheranism, belief in the sacrifice of Christ brings salvation.* Bridgeman Art Library, London.

validity of papal claims to supremacy over Western Christian society. His study of early theologians led him to question church practices that seemed to favor works or action over faith. Luther believed that faith, not action, led one to heaven. Luther called for major reforms, especially among the clergy.

John Calvin

Sweeping religious questioning inaugurated the rise of multiple Protestant reform movements in competition with Lutheranism. These movements developed their own theological structures based on Renaissance and Reformation attitudes. Individuals like Ulrich Zwingli (1483–1531) studied the humanist ideas of Erasmus and successfully challenged traditional theologies in Swiss territories. Humanist perspectives led to the practice of individual interpretation of scripture (regardless of educational level or ability), which challenged the role of priests as the interpreters of faith. In many areas, the Protestants fought with one another, as well as with Roman Catholics, over what constituted proper Christian belief and practice. The Anabaptists, for example, rejected infant baptism and insisted on rebaptizing all converts to their movement. Protestant dissension often led to violence and condemnation, sometimes resulting in the burning of dissenters at the stake. New reform movements sprang up all over central and western Europe.

A major figure in these new reform movements was John Calvin (1509–1564). Calvin was a French layman who had studied for the priesthood and who had continued his studies in the field of law. In 1534, Calvin left Paris to travel and speak in favor of reform. He became recognized as a reform theologian soon after his *Institutes of the Christian Religion*, a summary of Protestant theologies, found wide acceptance in 1536. Two theories were central to Calvinist theology. The first was the majesty of God (an omnipotent God in contrast to impotent humanity). The second was **predestination**, the idea that God preelects those who will receive salvation. These theories were not unique to Calvin's theology but became cornerstones of his reform doctrine. In Calvin's theology, God does not have to show any grace to humanity but magnanimously offers salvation to "the elect."

Calvin created a polity in Geneva that defined what he believed was the proper sociopolitical structure for a Christian community. The commercial city had become a refuge for Protestants fleeing France and Italy. He spelled out its political organization in the *Ecclesiastical Ordinances* of 1541. These ordinances established a mandatory public profession of faith and an oath to keep the city's Protestant-inspired laws. The city of Geneva

UNDER THE LENS

Printing and Propaganda

Printing techniques came later to Europe than to Asia. Wood-block printing, whereby text was laboriously carved into wooden blocks, had developed before the fifteenth century. By the mid–fifteenth century, Johannes Gutenberg produced one of the first European books printed with movable type, the Gutenberg Bible. Movable type consisted of a tray that held interchangeable letters that could be readily arranged and rearranged. About 3 million characters were used in Gutenberg's Bible, and about 200 copies were made. (Gutenberg purposely limited the number produced so the market would not be flooded, keeping the price high.) By the end of the century, more than 110 European cities had printing presses.

The new technology of printing made books more readily available and cut their costs. Before books were typeset, publication usually ran about 200 copies and took months to finish in wood-block formats. Most books printed by movable type, however, took considerably less time; some were printed in a matter of days. When Martin Luther published his New Testament in German, publication runs yielded about 3,000 copies. It cost roughly a week's wage for a top craftsman. This was considerably cheaper than medieval texts that would have cost hundreds of dollars in today's market, but it was still prohibitive for many.

Printed sheets, called news sheets, were posted or circulated, distributing information to an increasingly literate population in the cities. In 1493, a news sheet that was widely distributed in Rome described the voyage of Christopher Columbus. Rapid communication in the form of news sheets also disseminated reformers' religious ideas. During the Reformation, many unflattering cartoon images depicting both the pope and Luther accompanied narrative arguments. Luther specifically condoned mass propaganda techniques, especially cartoons, saying, "simple folk are more easily moved by pictures. . . ." Widespread distribution of his ideas helped fan the flames of German dissent that hastened the disintegration of Christian unity. In England, by the seventeenth century, London gentlemen sipped coffee or hot chocolate while gossiping and arguing over articles they read in *The Spectator*, a news sheet of the day.

Printing would not have had an impact on spreading either Renaissance or Reformation ideas, however, if there had not been consumers who could read the various news sheets and books. Literacy rates increased as more and more people tried to emulate elite lifestyles of opulence and the humanist appreciation of fine arts, especially literature. Latin classics, law books, and schoolbooks for teachers, doctors, and lawyers became part of the ever-increasing inventory of specialized books for sale. One publisher produced pocket-sized Greek and Latin grammars and Greco-Roman texts cheaply for the general population.

Seditious and reformist ideas could spread rapidly without a means for censure. Political and religious leaders reacted with edicts of censure against persons printing unacceptable ideas. In 1557, Pope Paul IV supported the prohibition of Protestant reform books. The *Index Librorum Prohibitorum* established the official list of books that Roman Catholics were forbidden to read or own. Protestant churches also limited the acceptable reading materials of their parishioners; Luther even presided over a book-burning. Censorship by churches and governments increased as the power of the printed word spread through mass printing.

---

was governed by a council consisting of pastors and twelve church elders. Secular powers enforced the council's decisions. Laws prohibited certain activities that were viewed as immoral, such as dancing and games. Serious doctrinal challenge could result in a death sentence; those who broke the law or denied church doctrines received severe punishment.

The city's school, established in 1559, offered the population of Geneva a Calvinist education. It taught students from elementary to advanced levels. Foreigners studied theology there and later acted as leaders for other Calvinist communities in Europe. One such reformer, John Knox, introduced Calvinism to Scotland. After building a constituency there, he established a Genevan

FIGURE 29.7 ***Calvinist Church.*** *Calvinist services and church buildings differed significantly from Roman Catholic ones. In contrast to the Catholic Mass, the Calvinist service (like most Protestant services) focused on the centrality of preaching the word of God from both the Old and New Testaments. Consequently, the pulpit was given a more prominent place so all could see the speaker and hear the sermon. The church interior was austere, with little or no decoration, and the congregation sat on wooden benches, sometimes segregated by gender.* German National Museum.

structure that in 1560 became known as the Presbyterian Church. Presbyterianism became the official denomination of Scotland by 1567. Through the focus on education, Calvinist reform soon spread widely, even resulting in colonies in the Americas.

Henry VIII

Protestant reform in England rode on the wave of dynastic crisis. Catherine of Aragon (1485–1536), the first wife of Henry VIII (reign dates 1509–1547), had not produced a son. Henry appealed to the pope for an annulment of his marriage to Catherine so that he might marry again in an attempt to gain an heir to the throne. Although Henry had heretofore supported Roman Catholicism against reformers, he challenged ecclesiastical authority when the application was denied by the pope (who was allied with Catherine's nephew, the Holy Roman Emperor). A royal minister convinced Henry that, as king and ruler by divine grace of God, he need not bow to the authority of the pope, even in spiritual matters. Henry convened the English parliament and used his influence to pass The Act of Supremacy of 1534. This act created the

Church of England, which recognized the monarch as its supreme head, and replaced Roman Catholicism with Anglicanism as the state religion. Henry never really wanted to break with Rome, however, and for the rest of his life he considered himself essentially Roman Catholic in theology. Nevertheless, all open opposition met with swift punishment. During Henry's reign, reform policies led to massive destruction of monasteries and churches that resisted reform and to the seizure of Roman Catholic church properties. As on the continent, the crown became the major beneficiary of confiscated church revenues.

English religious history continued to be volatile and closely associated with the political climate. Reformers in England resisted attempts by some to realign with Roman Catholicism. Henry VIII's two immediate successors alternately supported Anglicanism and Roman Catholicism between 1547 and 1558. Elizabeth I (reign dates 1558–1603) reinstituted Anglicanism during her reign but compromised on several issues of theology and church practices, shaping the development of a more tolerant Anglicanism. The queen did not allow significant changes once the compromises had been reached, and she demanded obedience. Roman Catholic and Protestant dissenters endured significant persecution, and many continued to voice their opposition to what became known as the Elizabethan Compromise.

THE ROMAN CATHOLIC REFORMATION, AROUND 1550–AROUND 1650

Reform ideas were not limited to Protestants; Roman Catholic laity and clergy also instituted the Catholic Reformation. Many within the Roman Catholic Church acted upon abuses they, too, had recognized and condemned but had not changed. By 1567, for example, Pope Pius V prohibited the sale of indulgences, but his prohibition proved too late to stem the tide of Protestant reform that the practice had set in motion. Some people who had joined Protestant movements, however, returned to Roman Catholicism because of the new reform policies. Roman Catholic reform took many paths. New emphasis was given to the private reading of scripture, for example, while many traditional practices, like confession, remained. In addition, secular power gained greater influence as Roman Catholic kings took on the role of "champions of the faith," as had the monarchs in Protestant states. Individuals concentrated on clerical education, devotional activities, and charity; many Roman Catholic women supported hospitals and charitable programs as they sought ways to put their faith into practice.

New Monastic Orders

Spiritual renewal swept through Roman Catholicism and is perhaps best represented by the popularity of new monastic orders during the sixteenth century, focusing on the ancient ideals of service to the poor and individual spirituality. The Spanish mystics are an example of this trend. Teresa of Avila (1515–1582) founded a reformed Carmelite order in 1562. After writing of her mystical experience of Christ in *The Way of Perfection*, she traveled around Spain establishing new reformed Carmelite monasteries. She went on to write several more books, including *The Interior Castle*, which enjoyed wide readership. The combination of mysticism and reform made her an especially successful model of Roman Catholic reform and spirituality.

Another new order, the Jesuits, or the Society of Jesus, came into being as the result of the efforts of Ignatius of Loyola (1491–1556) in 1540. Jesuits became active in teaching, founding schools, and widespread proselytizing in foreign missions. In Europe, the order fostered reform and placed itself at the disposal of the papacy. No Jesuit could accept any land or title, and all members of the order were to live on charity and rely on benefactors in order to check what was viewed as the corrupting influences of power and wealth.

The Institutional Church

Pope Paul III (reign dates 1534–1549) called a general council of bishops in response to Protestant attacks in 1545, initiating the Council of Trent. The council instituted reforms, many of them inspired by humanist thought and Protestant challenges. The Holy Roman Emperor and the French king supported the reforms and worked for conciliation with Protestants within their realms. With the help of both secular and religious leaders, the council's decrees were published and its recommendations were implemented, including those condemning the buying or selling of church offices, the holding of multiple bishoprics, and the misuse of authority. Succeeding popes began to reorganize education, governance of the church, and liturgy.

The Council of Trent's actions did not reunite Christianity. There was a general reluctance by secular rulers to reentrench papal authority within the realms or territories that had already broken with Rome. State churches had already formed or were in the process of forming. The changes initiated in society as a consequence of theological reform supported schism rather than discussion and reconciliation to end conflict.

Inquisition

The initial Roman Catholic reaction to Protestant reformers had been defensive, and many early reformers had been renounced as heretics. In some areas, Catholic reform led to fear of social and political instability. As a result, reform sometimes took on a violent defense of Roman Catholicism. Inquisition had precedent in the early church and had been used against individuals and groups of heretics in the Middle Ages. During the Reformation upheaval, however, the use of inquisition became increasingly common and severe in its tactics. Earlier inquisition relied upon the punishments of fasting, pilgrimage, or imprisonment as the most common forms of eradicating heresy. Those found guilty of the most grave charges were turned over to secular authorities for execution. As political interests became more involved with religious choice during the Reformation period, however, kings and officials worked with local church officials to stamp out unacceptable religious practices. Some monarchs used reform movements as a means to centralize their authority. Under secular influence, inquisitors' use of torture and execution became more frequent.

The Spanish Inquisition is perhaps the most notorious example of secular influence on inquisition. It began under Ferdinand and Isabella in 1479, and the numbers of persons tortured may have been in the hundreds of thousands. Current estimates of those burned at the stake are about 2,000 people. Ferdinand and Isabella used the inquisition for state purposes to bond the population into one obedient realm. The Spanish Inquisition became a formalized branch of their government, and renunciation of Roman Catholicism amounted to treason. The Spanish Inquisition first examined Jews and Muslims, who were forced to convert or be expelled, and then Protestants who sought to bring reform ideas into Spain. It was also exported to the Americas.

FIGURE 29.8 ***Inquisition.*** *Dominicans served as trained inquisitors at the court of Ferdinand and Isabella in fifteenth-century Spain. This painting by a court artist shows a scene from the life of Saint Dominic, who led an inquisition against a group of heretics in southern France. One of those charged, the man on horseback, recanted; others did not and met the fate of being burned at the stake. This image served as an inspiration to the defenders of the faith at the Spanish court and as a reminder to medieval heretics that dissenting views would not be tolerated.* Museo del Prado/MAS Barcelona.

THE RESULTS OF REFORMATION

Although sixteenth- and seventeenth-century reform movements heralded radical changes in religious expression and initiated numerous Christian sects, personal devotion to Christianity remained significant in European culture. In some cases, the search for religious truth often led to violence and religious wars. In other cases, reform brought renewed interest in basic Christian principles; religious devotion and personal piety continued to be the focus of Reformation literature. Men and women of all social classes found religious voices, and a plethora of pious works contrasted with mutual intolerance.

Social and Political Changes

One major reason these reform movements of the sixteenth century resulted in long-lasting change was the sociopolitical unrest that had been building since the fourteenth century. Church officials were associated with the aristocracy and held many revenue-gathering privileges based on medieval landholding patterns, which many commoners despised. Various social revolts had challenged the sociopolitical structures of Europe prior to the outbreak of Protestant reform. Often religious leaders, like Savonarola in Florence, rallied to the cause of social equality. Years before Martin Luther, John Ball had wandered around England preaching general social reform and had led a revolt in 1380–1381. He wrote:

> Oh good people, things do not go well in England and they will not go well until everything is held in common and there are no more serfs or lords. . . . Why should we be kept thus in bondage? We are all come from one father and one mother, Adam and Eve. How can they say or prove that they are greater lords than we are except that they make us work for what they spend?

Luther wrote treatises calling on the German princes to join the Reformation movement by breaking their ties with Rome and supporting Lutheranism in their territories. In some areas, from one-quarter to one-third of lands were under the authority of the church. Seizing the opportunity to control church lands and revenues, many of the German princes and the kings of Denmark and Sweden joined the reform movement. Eventually, each German prince chose which expression of Christianity—Roman Catholic or Lutheran—he and his subjects would follow. Subjects who did not conform could find themselves exiled.

Social Uprisings

The policies of repressive governments and self-interested lords and landlords had led to violent rebellions across many parts of central and western Europe. The only lasting changes restructured debts, from service owed to money payments; few real social reforms materialized. Social discord between the rich and the poor continued to intensify during periods of plague and war. Finally, several Protestant reformers preached open, violent insurrection, and the German peasantry revolted in 1525.

The Peasants' Revolt of 1525 exploded partly because German reformers—particularly Martin Luther—challenged the practices of Roman Catholicism. The peasants, spurred on by inspiring preachers, adopted reformist ideas. Mobs destroyed altars, crucifixes, and other furnishings and threatened the personal safety of those who resisted either social or religious reform. The leaders of the revolt put forward the Twelve Articles of 1525, which show the close interconnection of social and religious reform. The articles spell out the abolition of certain taxes and of serfdom; rights to fishing, hunting, and woodcutting; acceptable rent payments; and procedures to gain justice in the local courts. These social articles were included with religious articles, such as the right of peasants to elect the pastors of their churches and to control the use of donations made to their churches.

Martin Luther initially supported the Articles and even acted as arbitrator in the dispute. But lack of control in the movement led to random violence, and Luther withdrew his support as mobs indiscriminately burned and pillaged lords' and princes' lands. (Much of Luther's support came from the lords and princes being threatened by the mobs.) Luther wrote a pamphlet denouncing the peasants and supporting the retaliation against them. A union of princes stamped out the last remnant of the movement by 1526. Although the Peasants' Revolt was unsuccessful, many disillusioned commoners found expression for their sociopolitical grievances in the continuing reform movements.

In 1534, the French, too, endured internal religious upheaval, and persecution of Protestant reformers became increasingly severe. Massacres led to a meeting in Paris in 1559, when reformers drafted *The Articles of Faith for Reform Churches in France*, based upon Calvinist ideas. These French reformers, **Huguenots**, vowed to defend themselves if violence arose. By 1562, conciliatory gestures came from the regent of France, Catherine d'Medici, giving some freedoms to the Huguenots. Unfortunately, several massacres of reformers led to years of almost constant warfare in France (1562–1594). Claiming to foil a plot against her, d'Medici's troops and Catholic supporters killed most of the Huguenots in Paris during the Saint Bartholomew's Day Massacre of August 25, 1572. In the next few years, other French cities followed Paris's lead, resulting in the deaths of thousands of Huguenots. Restoration of peace finally came when King Henry IV (reign dates 1589–1610) signed the Edict of Nantes in 1598. Essentially a compromise for peace, the edict provided religious freedom, but with some restrictions. Henry IV and the realm remained Roman Catholic, but Protestants received guarantees of freedom of worship, the right to own property of their own, and the right to defend their property with their own troops.

Religious conflict did not end with the Edict of Nantes, however. Louis XIV tried to force religious unity in France through his perception of the state as the imperial self ("I am the State") and his idea of "one God, one king, one law, one faith." In 1685, Louis revoked the tolerant Edict of Nantes on the rationalization that no more Protestant reformers lived in France after years of restriction and forced conversions to Roman Catholicism.

Religious Wars

Religious wars seemed unavoidable as sovereigns led Protestant and Roman Catholic reformers toward state churches, and animosity toward perceived religious enemies heightened among subjects. Emotions ran high when German troops, mostly Lutheran reformers, sacked the city of Rome in 1527. More than 22,000 imperial troops, unpaid and without a commander, killed more than 13,000 Romans. After the attack, the devastation was so great and the fear so overwhelming that the remaining citizens hid in their houses, refusing to bury the corpses being gnawed by dogs in the streets. More than 30,000 houses and several hospitals burned to the ground or were left uninhabitable. The loss of manuscripts, fine paintings, and sculptures was incalculable.

War between Protestant England and Roman Catholic Spain erupted during Elizabeth's reign, which saw the defeat of the Spanish Armada (the so-called invincible navy) and the emergence of England as a maritime force. Elizabeth had no children, and her Roman Catholic cousin Mary Queen of Scots (1542–1587) was suggested as the legitimate heir to the English throne. When Mary sought asylum from Scottish political problems at Elizabeth's court, political and religious conspirators within England and Catholic Spain soon represented Mary as a potential usurper of Elizabeth's throne. Elizabeth had Mary arrested and, with great reluctance, ordered her execution. This spurred the Spanish to hurl 25,000 men and the Armada across the channel at England in 1588. The English navy under Charles Howard, aided by stormy weather, defeated the Armada. The rest of Elizabeth's reign was marked by increased prosperity at home and commercial activity abroad unhampered by the Spanish navy.

The Thirty Years War (1618–1648), involving most of central Europe, began as a result of the Holy Roman Emperor's desire to reestablish Roman Catholicism throughout his empire. Hostilities broke out when Bohemian Protestants revolted against the emperor's Roman Catholic policies. The conflict eventually turned into a struggle over dynastic claims to the imperial crown as several neighboring monarchs entered the fray. When hostilities finally ended with the Treaty of Westphalia in 1648, many church properties became secularized and were distributed among several involved states. The monarch of each area determined which faith subjects would follow.

Women and Reform

Some women played significant roles in religious reform movements, while most found that social reform of women's roles was not part of the general call for social change occurring during the Reformation period. Martin Luther's wife, Katharina, a former nun, spent much of her time practicing basic medicine for the poor. Later in England, Margaret Fell (1614–1702) argued that women should take leadership roles in the new church her husband, George Fox, had founded. Margaret's argument in support of women's roles was based on Old Testament precedents of women prophets, judges, and preachers. Margaret and John's church, The Society of Friends (the Quakers), had no priests, and both men and women could speak during services. Most reform churches, however, restricted the roles of women and settled into a patriarchal structure wherein men were preachers and women kept quiet in church.

FIGURE 29.9 ***Woman Preaching.*** *Some Protestant groups, such as the Quakers, encouraged women to teach and to preach in public. In many areas across Europe where social attitudes restricted women's religious roles, this practice was not met with enthusiasm. This English print satirizes a Quaker woman by showing a variety of reactions to her public speaking, ranging from amusement and skepticism to inattention.* Mary Evans Picture Library.

BAROQUE ARTS AND NEW PHILOSOPHIES

No artistic period is an island unto itself, and baroque art styles and philosophies mirrored the changes that had occurred in European society. Both the arts and philosophy reflected the Renaissance's emphasis on Greco-Roman classics, humanism, and religion and the Reformation's emphasis on sociopolitical and religious change. Artists during the baroque period (around 1550–around 1750) embraced complexity of design, paying significant attention to ornate detail. Absolutist monarchs employed the grandeur and opulence of the baroque style to demonstrate their supremacy over and superiority to their subjects. Resplendent palaces and grand halls awed and humbled court visitors. Printing technology and higher literacy rates made baroque literature more affordable and accessible. Painting and music, two examples of the fine arts, demonstrate the general changes of the period. The philosophies of Hobbes, Locke, Descartes, and Spinoza represent the influence of humanism in philosophical development.

Painting

Baroque painting shifted from the heroic grandeur of Renaissance style to a greater emphasis on ornate detail and emotion. The subjects of paintings, for example, were presented in more natural settings than in previous Renaissance presentations. Dramatic contrast of light and dark helped to focus attention on emotion. Perhaps the first baroque artist was a painter who called himself Caravaggio[10] (1573–1610), after his birthplace near

[10] **Caravaggio:** KAIR uh VAH jee oh

IN THEIR OWN WORDS

Martin Luther and John Calvin Define Women's Roles

Attitudes toward women during the Protestant Reformation continued to change. Just as women's roles shifted within the context of Renaissance admiration of Greco-Roman models, Protestant women's roles became more restricted under the increasingly literal interpretations of Christian scripture. Although many women were highly visible in the early reform movements, Saint Paul's writings became the litmus test for the proper behavior of wives, and other biblical references were used to illustrate acceptable roles for women in society. To some extent women continued to have informal influence within Protestant groups, but their roles were increasingly restricted to being helpmates to their husbands and vehicles for procreation.

Although Martin Luther did argue that women might be allowed to preach if no man were available, his general attitude toward women can be seen in the following passage:

> Now the ones who recognize the estate of marriage are those who firmly believe that God himself instituted it, brought husband and wife together, and ordained that they should beget children and care for them . . . [Luther here explains the duties of the father—including washing diapers if need be—and then continues with the duties of the mother.] A wife too should regard her duties in the same light, as she suckles the child, rocks and bathes it, and cares for it in other ways; and as she busies herself with other duties and renders help and obedience to her husband. . . . This is also how to comfort and encourage a woman in the pangs of childbirth . . . [say to her:] "Remember that you are a woman, and that this work of God in you is pleasing to him. Trust joyfully in his will, and let him have his way with you. Work with all your might to bring forth the child. Should it mean your death, then depart happily, for you will die in a noble deed and in subservience to God. If you were not a woman you should now wish to be one for the sake of this very work alone, that you might thus gloriously suffer and even die in the performance of God's work and will." . . . We see how weak and sickly barren women are. Those who are fruitful, however, are healthier, cleanlier, and happier. And even if they bear themselves weary—or ultimately bear themselves out—that does not hurt. Let them bear themselves out. This is the purpose for which they exist.

John Calvin also spoke about the role of women in Christian society. In a commentary on Genesis, Calvin explains that women should be helpmates.

> Now, the human race could not exist without the woman; and, therefore, in the conjunction of human beings, that sacred bond is especially conspicuous, by which the husband and the wife are combined in one body, and one soul. . . . Certainly, it cannot be denied, that the woman also, though in the second degree, was created in the image of God. . . . Now, since God assigns the woman as a help to the man, he not only prescribes to wives the rule of their vocation, to instruct them in their duty, but he also pronounces that marriage will really prove to men the best support of life. We may therefore conclude, that the order of nature implies that the woman should be the helper of the man. The vulgar proverb, indeed, is, that she is a necessary evil; but the voice of God is rather to be heard, which declares that woman is given as a companion and an associate to the man, to assist him to live well.

Milan. Not everyone liked the new style; Caravaggio's popularity waned in Italy, where many patrons preferred holy subjects to be depicted in the more idealized, heroic style. Slowly tastes changed, however, and artists found fame for their applications of the baroque style; two are Peter Paul Rubens and Rembrandt van Rijn.[11]

Peter Paul Rubens (1577–1640) incorporated baroque presentation in such works as *The Raising of the Cross.* The figures reveal muscled bodies straining to raise up their heavy load, while foliage and a dog are painstakingly detailed in the foreground. Landscapes were another venue for Rubens to create an imposing scene. His painting *Landscape with the Château of Steen* sweeps from the detailed hunter and cart, depicted in the lower left corner,

[11] **Rijn:** RYN

to a grand view of the countryside in all its vast splendor.

Rembrandt van Rijn (1606–1669) is a good example of the popular and influential Dutch masters of the baroque style. He was one of the most famous portrait painters in northern Europe by age 25. His religious topics have been described as vigorous and imaginative. By 1642, his fortunes had turned; his wife's death, his bankruptcy, and a paternity suit that caused him difficulty with Protestant reformers led him into depression. He began focusing on the Passion of Christ as a reflection of human suffering, producing at least ninety paintings and etchings on the theme. His work is perhaps best known for its intense realism and human emotion, often breathing life into biblical scenes that had previously been heroically idealized.

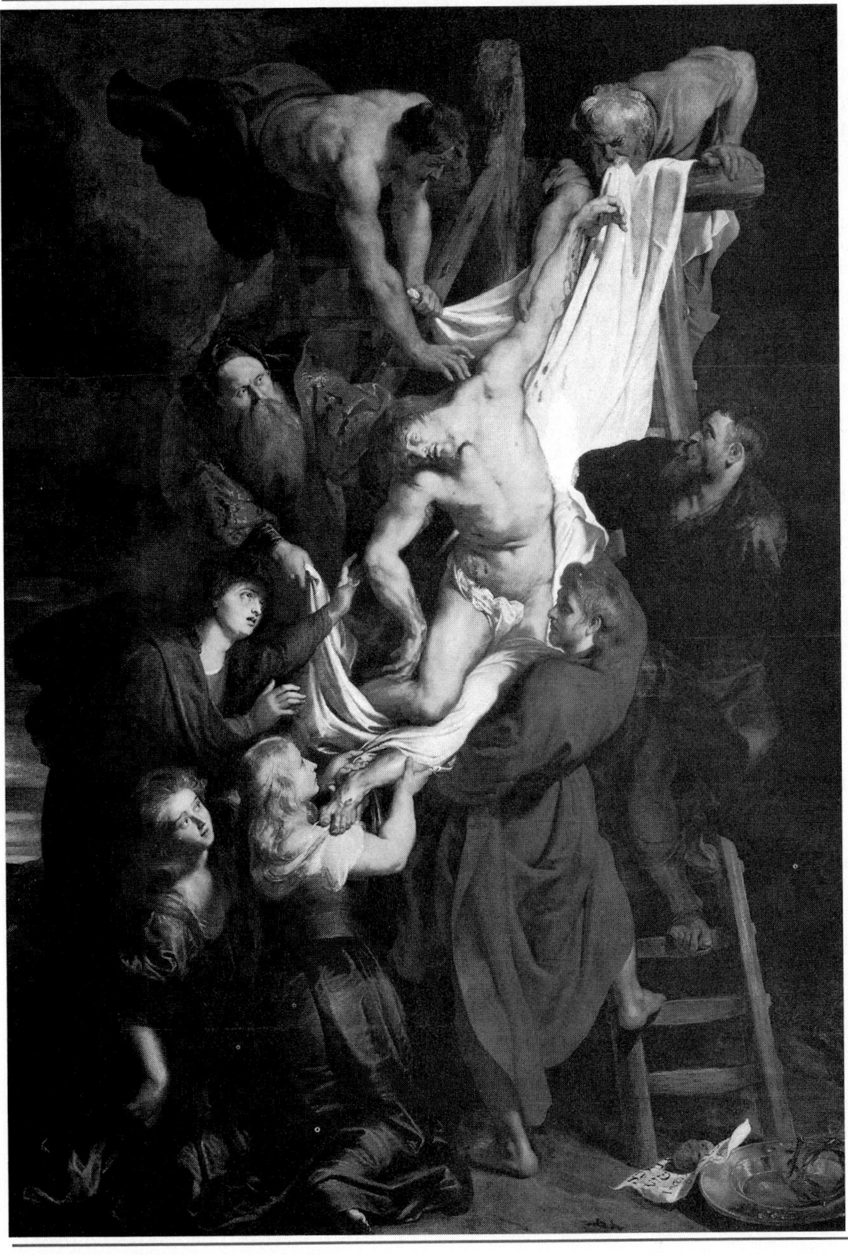

FIGURE 29.10 ***Rubens's* Descent from the Cross.** *In this seventeenth-century painting, Peter Paul Rubens uses light to increase dramatic effect; light focuses attention on Christ's body and plays on the expressive faces of the women, drawing the viewer into the painting and inviting an empathetic response. The poignancy of the scene is further enhanced by the straining of the men to lower the limp body from the height of the cross.* AKG London.

Music

Baroque musical styles evolved during the sixteenth and seventeenth centuries. Medieval and Renaissance musicians had introduced polytonality, complicated rhythmic patterns, and new instruments, but Reformation music applied new trends of scientific logic and complex mathematics to music. The hymns or chorales of the Reformation were at first based on Roman Catholic hymns but soon developed a style of their own. Statements of faith set to easily sung melodies (some even from easily recognizable bar tunes) gave voice to the religious passions of many reformers. The Roman Catholic composer Antonio Vivaldi (1675–1741) inspired communicants with dramatic emotion in his musical settings of the Mass. Four of his Mass movements exist today.

The baroque organ, a hybrid of previous organs, allowed for greater range of tonality and supported the congregational singing of reform churches. Its popularity grew under the genius of Johann Sebastian Bach[12] (1685–1750), who, with many other baroque composers, created musical masterpieces of mathematical logic that are still performed in churches and in concert halls throughout the world.

The complexities of baroque music also entertained patrons outside of the churches, in palaces and elite homes. In addition, those who frequented the theaters enjoyed the melding of music, drama, elaborate sets, and costuming in ballets, operas, and the less sophisticated but equally enjoyable stage shows. As musical entertainment became more widespread, increasing numbers of middle-class and noble patrons employed composers and performers on retainer.

FIGURE 29.11 ***Hobbes's* Leviathan.** *This engraving from the title page of Thomas Hobbes's 1651 pamphlet graphically illustrates his political philosophy. The individual subjects of the state comprise the "body politic." These subjects give their collective authority to the monarch, who rules on their behalf. The monarch holds the symbols of his secular and sacred powers, the sword and the shepherd's crook, an allusion to Jesus, the Good Shepherd.* Bibliothèque nationale, Paris.

New Philosophies

Political and social turmoil in the sixteenth and seventeenth centuries stimulated new theories in governance and reinforced old ones. Some theories challenged the older perceptions of political authority and the nature of humanity. New political philosophies influenced government policies concerning New World peoples and new polities and helped to inspire the theoretical changes of the Scientific Revolution, which will be discussed in Chapter 31.

Thomas Hobbes (1588–1679), an English tutor, wrote a controversial philosophical treatise, *Leviathan*, in which he outlined his political theory of absolutism. *Leviathan* essentially stated that sovereignty is ultimately derived from the people but then transferred to the monarch. The monarch, therefore, does not rule by divine right; yet, the monarch has absolute authority over law, revenues, military affairs, and justice. Hobbes rested his political theory on the belief that humans are driven by self-interest and fear. He theorized about how life would be lived in a purely natural state without benefit of social or political

[12] **Bach:** BAHK

EUROPE

Elizabethan Age, 1558–1603	Roman Catholic Reformation, c. 1550–c. 1650	Protestant Reformation, 1517–1600	Baroque Period, c. 1550–c. 1750	European Renaissance, c. 1350–c. 1600	Date	Events
				European Renaissance, c. 1350–c. 1600	1350	Petrarch dies, 1374; Cosmo d'Medici born, 1389
					1400	
					1450	Niccoló Machiavelli born, 1469; Jews expelled from Spain, 1492
		Protestant Reformation, 1517–1600			1500	Leonardo da Vinci dies, 1519; Council of Trent, 1545; Martin Luther dies, 1546
Elizabethan Age, 1558–1603	Roman Catholic Reformation, c. 1550–c. 1650		Baroque Period, c. 1550–c. 1750		1550	Teresa of Avila founds Carmelite convent, 1562
					1600	William Shakespeare dies, 1616
					1650	

controls and surmised that a condition of brutality would prevail, devoid of civilization; and to Hobbes, civilization meant European culture. In contrast to Montaigne's image of the "noble savage," Hobbes argued that natural human life would be "solitary, poor, nasty, brutish, and short." In order for people to live harmoniously and as civilized human beings, a "social contract" must be established, at least tacitly.

In opposition to Hobbes, John Locke (1632–1704) argued for constitutionalism in his *Two Treatises of Civil Government*, published in 1690. His work emphasized that the only legal government was government by consent of the governed; revolution was the natural outgrowth of a repressive government. Like Hobbes, Locke incorporated the concept of the natural state of humanity into his political theory. For Locke, a "blank slate" reflected the state of human nature. Unlike Hobbes, Locke believed in a state of nature wherein humans perform reasoned action and possess the natural rights of life, liberty, and property. Because occasional infringement of rights occurs, assent to a social contract for mutual protection is advantageous. Government, however, must be limited in its power over the governed.

In Locke's opinion, tolerance of minority opinion should be exercised for the good of all. He pleaded for religious freedom for all groups except **atheists**, people who do not believe that any deity exists, and Roman Catholics, who he believed threatened the sovereignty of the English state. Eventually his concept of freedom of speech for religious groups won wider application through those who adopted his political philosophy.

René Descartes[13] (1596–1650), a wealthy French intellectual, is often proclaimed the founder of **rationalism**, the philosophy that reason is the only valid basis for determining actions or opinions. This focus led to his axiom "I think, therefore I am," which became the cornerstone of his philosophy. According to rationalism, one's senses could delude and emotions could mislead; only the rational human mind could fathom reality. Descartes did not abandon religion; he agreed with some medieval philosophers who had argued the rationality of a creator God, but Descartes's deity did not intervene in human affairs. Because the deity had created a rationally organized universe, the human mind (seen as an attribute of God) could discover the laws of nature without the need of revelation. Thus, Descartes supported increased interest in mathematics and science and turned away from the speculative philosophies of the medieval and Renaissance periods.

Baruch Spinoza (1632–1677), a Jewish lens grinder turned philosopher, differed in his opinion of human rationality. Instead of only reason being an attribute of God, as in Descartes's philosophy, Spinoza argued that both mind and matter were infused with God. This philosophy is **pantheism**, the belief that God is present in all that God creates. It allowed Spinoza and other philosophers to view nature as worthy of scientific investigation. Like others of his day, Spinoza employed mathematical methodology to understand the rational order of the universe. Spinoza's philosophy, however, did not bode well with more traditional Jews, who did not merge God with the creation.

SUMMARY

1. Renaissance ideas had a profound influence on social attitudes, polities, and economic development. Italian cities were commercial centers and places of innovation in the fine arts. Renaissance attitudes centered on the revival of Greco-Roman culture, which became the model for Renaissance fine arts.

2. In some Renaissance urban centers, the middle class experienced rapid growth and social change, while other areas developed more slowly. Although most people were low-wage laborers, new and more lucrative professions developed. Because of the rebirth of Greco-Roman attitudes, many elite women lost social gains they had enjoyed in the medieval period.

3. Renaissance Italian city-states tended to remain independent polities, and monarchies became more centralized in Europe. The exception was the Holy Roman Empire, which experienced regional centralization under local princes.

[13] **Descartes:** day KAHRT

4. Intellectual and artistic development was influenced by Renaissance humanist philosophy. Adoption of Greco-Roman styles and humanism in religious and political treatises influenced attitudes about the past and inspired new ways of thinking. These ideas were imported to areas colonized by Europeans.

5. The Protestant Reformation was a combination of religious and sociopolitical reform. Many lower-class revolts added to the instability of Renaissance and Reformation Europe. Rulers adopted reformist ideas to aid in their centralization policies.

6. Protestant reform was spurred by Renaissance admiration of Greco-Roman culture, which led to the belief that early church practices and theologies were superior to those of the Middle Ages or Renaissance period. The repudiation of selling indulgences spearheaded initial reform under Martin Luther. Reform spread to many geographical areas. Protestants and Roman Catholics both employed execution as a means to defend their theologies. State responses to reform varied, and in some places, like England, state leaders vacillated between Protestantism and Roman Catholicism.

7. The Catholic Reformation implemented many of the reforms that Protestants had demanded. Finally, the Council of Trent's reforms were publicized and implemented, but the Protestant Reformation had moved beyond reconciliation because of its link with sociopolitical issues.

8. Religious wars kept Europe in turmoil in the sixteenth and seventeenth centuries. France was beset by internal warfare between Roman Catholics and Huguenots; the Thirty Years War (1618–1648) began when Protestant Bohemians revolted against the Holy Roman Emperor and ended with the Treaty of Westphalia in 1648.

9. Some women played significant roles in the early Reformation, but most remained in subordinate positions. Reformation led to the acceptance of violence and schism within Christianity as a means to settle disputes.

10. Artists brought new expression to the fine arts that paralleled the changes in society. Emotion and naturalism were the hallmarks of the highly ornate baroque style.

11. New philosophies synthesized Renaissance and Reformation ideas into new political theories that supported either absolutism or constitutional monarchy. Hobbes, Locke, Descartes, and Spinoza focused on the study of nature, human rationality, and proper forms of government.

SUGGESTED READINGS

Bainton, Roland H. *Here I Stand: A Life of Martin Luther.* New York: Mentor/New American Library, 1977. A standard in Reformation history.

———. *Women of the Reformation in Germany and Italy.* Boston: Beacon, 1974. Several biographies of women and their roles in the Protestant Reformation.

Bouwsma, William J. *John Calvin: A Sixteenth-Century Portrait.* Oxford, Eng.: Oxford University Press, 1988. The standard biography of John Calvin.

Breisach, Ernst. *Renaissance Europe, 1300–1517.* New York: Macmillan, 1973. A general but thorough review of the Renaissance.

Chadwick, Owen. *The Reformation.* New York: Penguin, 1972. An old standard by a church historian.

Hale, John. *The Civilization of Europe in the Renaissance.* New York: Atheneum, 1994. A thorough treatment of the Renaissance period.

Kohl, Benjamin G., and Alison A. Smith, eds. *Major Problems in the History of the Italian Renaissance.* Lexington, Mass.: D. C. Heath, 1995. A collection of essays and documents, focusing on major issues that shaped the period.

Ozment, Steven. *The Age of Reform, 1250–1550: An Intellectual and Religious History of Late Medieval and Reformation Europe.* New Haven, Conn.: Yale University Press, 1980. An introduction to reform movements, with a focus on intellectual history.

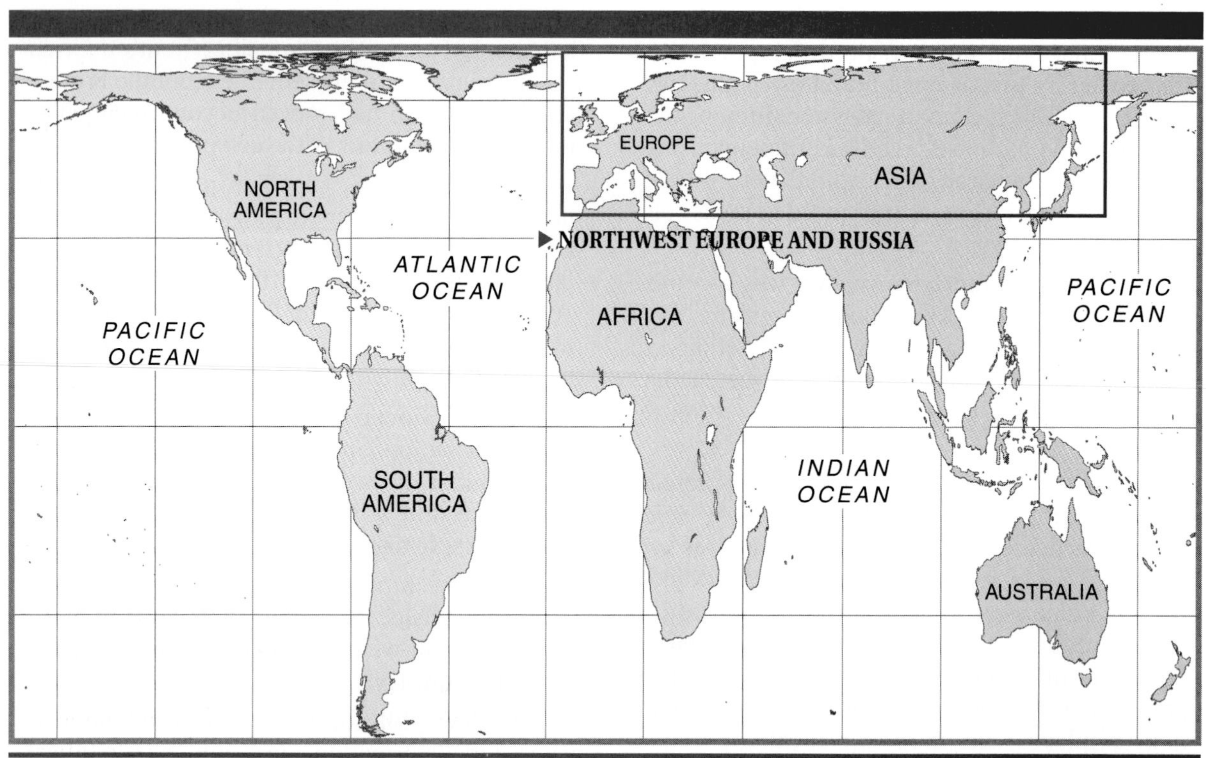

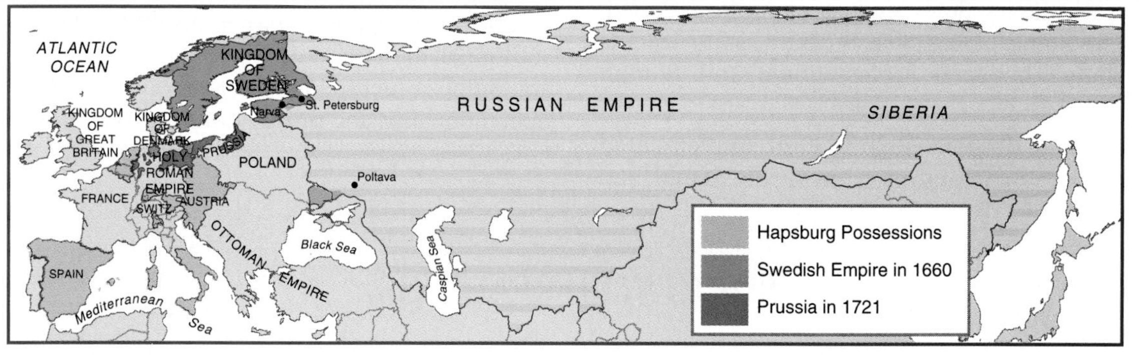

▶ **NORTHWEST EUROPE AND RUSSIA**

CHAPTER 30

European Absolutism

1611–1740

In the world is now none that is his equal, nor has there been for centuries such a one; and indeed I doubt the future will produce his peer. Yea, truly we may call him King Gustav the wise and great, the father of the fatherland, whose like never yet reigned in Sweden, as is acknowledged not by us alone, but by men of all nations, whether friend or foe.

—Axel Oxenstierna

Thus wrote Sweden's chancellor about King Gustavus Adolphus, one of the significant figures in Europe's seventeenth century. Gustavus Adolphus was the first of several monarchs who built absolutist states, which taxed their subjects most heavily in order to build strong centralized governments and large armies. It was a time of warfare and great suffering from battlefield losses, disease, and famine.

Absolute monarchs achieved varying degrees of success, because they were sometimes inhibited by long-established traditions, powerful social groups, or elite distaste for heavy taxes and the like. **Absolutism** is a system of government in which monarchs aim to achieve total control through a bureaucracy centralized along military lines. Major economic developments also accompanied the centralizing efforts of monarchs. Mining output increased substantially, metallurgical processes improved rapidly, and shipbuilding became increasingly efficient. The challenge of government was to harness these changes as efficiently and as completely as possible.

EUROPEAN ABSOLUTISM: THE BUREAUCRATIC-MILITARY MODEL

The development of absolutism in Europe was a process that often took decades to complete. It was often linked to the changing nature of European warfare, which forced governments to alter substantially their administrative systems, including tightening control of their subject peoples. Larger armies, often filled with drafted soldiers, gradually replaced mercenary forces. In order to pay and supply these military forces, monarchs gained control of their nobles and cities, which had traditions of autonomous rule. Absolutist governments grew significantly larger, extending central control over mining, arms manufacturing, and commerce.

We will define the features of the bureaucratic-military model of absolutism as:

—the adoption of a military-style chain of command for government wherein orders from the top must be promptly obeyed by all officials;

—the growing emphasis on central regulation of politics, economics, and society;

—the increasing stress on discipline, obedience, and duty in politics and life;

—the dominance of law and bureaucratic directives over customary practices; and

—the increasing use of mechanical terminology like "ship of state" to describe society and government.

Bureaucracies more successful in implementing this system were ones that harnessed social groups more fully to the all-powerful state. States that failed to implement military-style governments either exploited more intensely sources of revenue like colonies or resorted to funding ambitious strategic plans through massive loans and debt.

THE THIRTY YEARS WAR, 1618–1648

Beginning as a war defined largely in religious terms (Roman Catholic versus Protestant states) the Thirty Years War changed into a conflict pitting the armies and other national resources of the Danes, Swedes, and French against those of the Austrians and Spanish and their allies. As fighting persisted from one decade to the next, various contending governments devised means to finance and supply their armies. As bureaucracies grew in size, so did their control of economies and societies. Larger armies also meant that absolutist monarchs had the military might to cow their domestic rivals or rebels.

Central Europe had been the battleground between Protestant princes and Roman Catholic monarchs for about a century, and religious issues ignited the Thirty Years War. Conflict began when Protestant nobles of Bohemia (the present-day Czech Republic) agitated against their ardently Catholic king, Ferdinand, of the powerful Hapsburg family. The Catholic forces of Ferdinand crushed the Bohemian Protestant army, and a thoroughgoing reconversion of Bohemia to Roman Catholicism commenced. Continued successes by Catholic armies in Germany during the rest of the 1620s threatened Protestantism in Central Europe. Soon, the French perceived Ferdinand's successes as Hapsburg successes that threatened sovereign states like France, even though it was largely Roman Catholic.

While religious issues continued to be significant in the Thirty Years War, political issues assumed greater importance by the 1630s. France had begun funding Protestant armies and eventually pitted its armies against the Hapsburg forces. Fearing the growing power of Emperor Ferdinand, who threatened to dominate Germany completely, some Roman Catholic German rulers allied themselves with Protestant forces. Thus, dynastic and political concerns prevailed over religious questions in the minds of many.

France and Prussia began establishing absolutist systems in response to their need to fight wars. France's King Louis XIII and his chief minister, Cardinal Armand Jean Richelieu, jointly began devising the means to support a large French army by heavily taxing the French peasantry. Eventually, French victories over the Hapsburgs helped create the conditions for an absolutist monarchy under Louis XIV in the latter half of the seventeenth century. Although Prussia did not begin creating the conditions for absolutist rule until after the Thirty Years War, it gained new territory, and its ruler, Frederick William, needed a strong army to impose his will on the Prussians.

Three decades of warfare devastated parts of Central Europe. Some areas lost more than 50 percent of their population, and it took nearly a century for demographic growth to return to 1618 levels. Once-thriving cities and towns never recovered their prewar dynamism. Merchants and artisans, who were beginning to develop the financial and technological bases for industrialization, died from the fighting or disease. Mining and other industries, for example, declined during and after the conflict.

Political changes came through the negotiations that ended the Thirty Years War. Prussia and a few other states gained territory to offset the growth of Swedish and French power. Rulers of the surviving states determined the religion of their domains, and some states for the first time could conduct their own foreign relations. Perhaps most significant, the Thirty Years War demonstrated that ambitious monarchs needed large armies and the means to support them. With a powerful bureaucratic system, rulers could attain absolute power.

THE RISE AND FALL OF SWEDISH ABSOLUTISM, 1611–1718

Sweden became a major European power in the seventeenth century, establishing a Baltic Empire that included parts of Germany. But by the death of Sweden's monarch Charles XII in 1718, the empire lay in ruins and was never to be reconstructed. Swedish absolutism waxed and waned because it was heavily dependent on its monarchs.

Monarchs and Ministers

Because absolutism established itself gradually, we must examine it over the course of the reigns of several Swedish rulers. King Gustavus Adolphus (reign dates 1611–1632) commenced the construction of absolutist institutions, and Charles XI (reign dates 1660–1697) modified the system of government he had inherited to ensure that his wishes would be obeyed. Charles XII (reign dates 1697–1718) spent nearly two decades outside Sweden, campaigning against a variety of powers, and his prolonged absence severely undermined Swedish absolutism.

FIGURE 30.1 ***Portrait of Gustavus Adolphus.*** *This Swedish monarch, called by some "The Lion of the North," helped turn his country into an important European power. Gustavus Adolphus instituted numerous changes, including the establishment of an efficiently organized bureaucracy. He led his troops into Germany in 1630 and helped expand Swedish control of territories along the Baltic seacoast. The portrait conveys the sovereign's regal bearing and shrewdness.* Skokloster Collection, Styrelson, Sweden.

Gustavus Adolphus came to the throne as a teenager and developed an alliance with his chief minister, Axel Oxenstierna (1583–1654). The two men agreed that the monarchy must be strong but also that the king must rule in conjunction with Swedish nobles, especially those of the highest social ranks. Gustavus Adolphus agreed to consult regularly with the state council and the *riksdag*, an assembly of **estates** (groups of elites and other commoners). He also assented to the condition that the top bureaucratic posts should be filled with nobles who were Swedish-born. Although these limitations may have hampered other rulers, Gustavus Adolphus used his forceful character to mold institutions and people to his will. At the same time, he was committed to consultative measures by various deliberative bodies and went to great lengths to ensure a thoughtful decision-making process. This system worked well during Gustavus Adolphus's two-decade reign.

Another dimension of Gustavus Adolphus's rule was his successful military policies, which led to the foundation of a Swedish empire. Part of the reason that the king desired to have domestic harmony was to ensure stability for his intended military campaigns. In addition, Gustavus Adolphus took great pains to train and equip the Swedish army by the most modern methods. He had studied the works and methods of Maurice of Nassau, a Dutch strategist, and modified them in the course of Sweden's military campaigns. Gustavus Adolphus also gave much attention to building a military-industrial system to equip his troops with weapons and supplies.

Gustavus Adolphus's battlefield death in 1632 left the throne to his young daughter, Christina (reign dates 1634–1654), and the actual rule in the hands of Chancellor Oxenstierna and the nobles. In 1634, the bureaucracy issued a document, the *Form of Government*, proclaiming Lutheranism as the state religion, the legislative power of the *riksdag*, and the primacy of the nobles. This was an attempt by the nobles to wrest power from the monarchy. Neither Christina nor her successors ever formally accepted the document and its limitations on royal power. She took a moderate interest in government affairs once she reached adulthood but preferred engaging in intellectual debates, including some with René Descartes. Christina secretly harbored designs to surrender power and to embrace Roman Catholicism, both of which she did in 1654, to the shock of Sweden.

Charles XI completed the process of building absolutism. Shortly after he became king, Charles firmly took the reigns of power and had the *riksdag* declare the king the sole decision maker, who should consult with various councils and deliberative bodies. Ultimate lawmaking power belonged to the king, who was answerable only to God. Criticism of the king became a crime, effectively curbing freedom of expression.

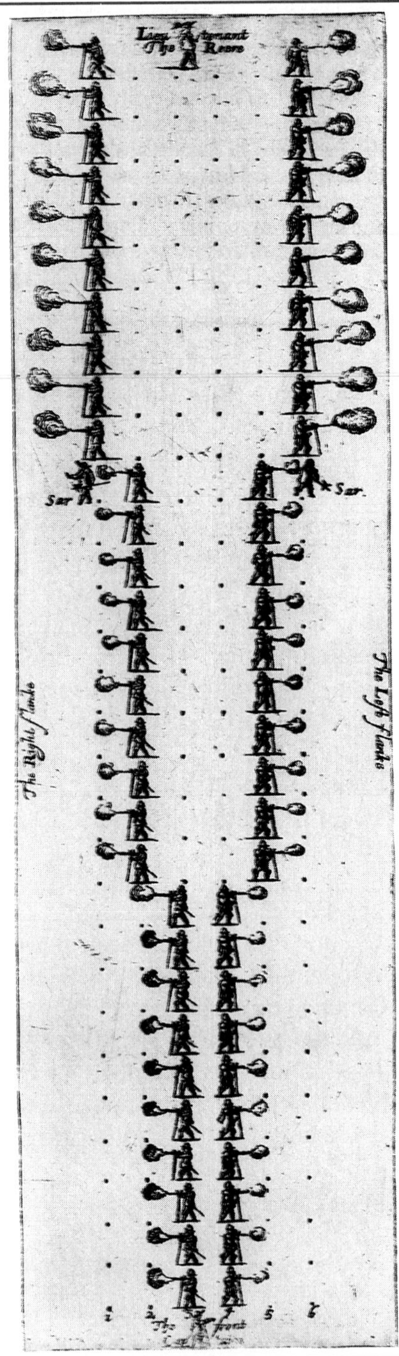

FIGURE 30.2 Military Firepower in the Seventeenth Century. *Maurice of Nassau helped transform military training through his writings, many of which were illustrated. This drawing shows how a particular massed formation gave a broad field of fire to the left and right. Careful and regular military training re737sulted in devastating barrages. Maurice's success on the battlefield made his writings popular with the rulers of Sweden and Prussia, as well as in the Netherlands.* Courtesy of the University of Illinois Library.

UNDER THE LENS
The Impact of Maurice of Nassau

One of Early Modern Europe's military strategists and tacticians, Maurice of Nassau, Prince of Orange (reign dates 1585–1625), offered rulers not only a means to create a superior fighting force but also a reliable way to maintain domestic order. This Dutch leader's ideas and methods spread throughout Europe in the seventeenth century; his famous manual appeared in a German edition in 1614 and by 1649 had been translated into Russian. Gustavus Adolphus carefully studied Maurice's ideas.

During his university studies, Maurice had become enamored of the ancient Romans, whose military methods he adopted. Essential to Maurice was keeping soldiers busy at all times to minimize problems of poor discipline and demoralization, especially during long siege operations. The army was divided into battalions of 550 men because this was the largest size that could respond to a single human voice. The squad of ten men acted as a single unit whether marching, deploying, or firing; soldiers became parts of a human machine that could be devastating on a battlefield. Maurice also insisted that the chain of command reach from himself down to the corporal who commanded the squad, and he established officer training schools where subcommanders learned their roles and duties.

Constant drill and weapons practice had additional advantages. Drillmasters constantly repeated the ways of using muskets, handguns, and pikes, ways that had been broken down into distinct muscular acts. Thus, when massed firing took place, the squad or battalion responded to voice commands with a minimum of error. The efficiency of the force soon became apparent on the battlefield. Later, Maurice printed an illustrated military manual for illiterates.

Political leaders realized that by using Maurice's methods, they could create a reliable and relatively inexpensive instrument for foreign and domestic needs. Constant drill and group activity established powerful psychological bonds within the units. This esprit de corps began to dominate the consciousness of the soldiers, who viewed themselves as brothers in a common cause. In addition, the soldiers saw themselves as distinct from the civilian society from which they came and could thereafter more easily follow orders to shoot their social peers or whomever their commanders chose to repress.

Because all social classes and individuals could be transformed, commoners were drafted into armies whose troops were paid at lower rates than upper-class people. These forces were inexpensive and reliable for maintaining the rule of absolute monarchs. They also facilitated the expansion of European colonies abroad.

An ongoing process of divesting land and income from the high nobles was accelerated, strengthening royal absolutism. During their heyday in power and influence in the middle decades of the seventeenth century, the high nobles amassed so much land and wealth that they became the target of criticism by the lesser nobles and commoners. In addition, these nobles and commoners allied with Charles XI to increase his power, partly so that he could carry out land reform. This land reform process undermined the power of the high nobles and brought significant revenues into the hands of the state.

Charles XII inherited the mantle of absolutism and affirmed his dominance of Sweden. His early battlefield successes maintained Swedish absolutism, but later defeats, loss of much of the empire, and Charles's death opened the gate for a time of rule by the nobles in alliance with city leaders and free peasants. The immediate cause of the dismantling of absolutism was the absence of a male or an unmarried female successor. The nobility soon filled the power vacuum.

Sweden enjoyed the services of excellent officials in the seventeenth century, and two of the best were Axel and Bengt Oxenstierna (1620–1702), father and son. The Oxenstierna family was one of Sweden's most venerable, and their kin had served Swedish monarchs for decades. Perhaps the most important official was Axel Oxenstierna, who achieved top administrative ranking about the time Gustavus Adolphus ascended the throne. The two men shaped Sweden's domestic and foreign policies through the seventeenth century. Axel

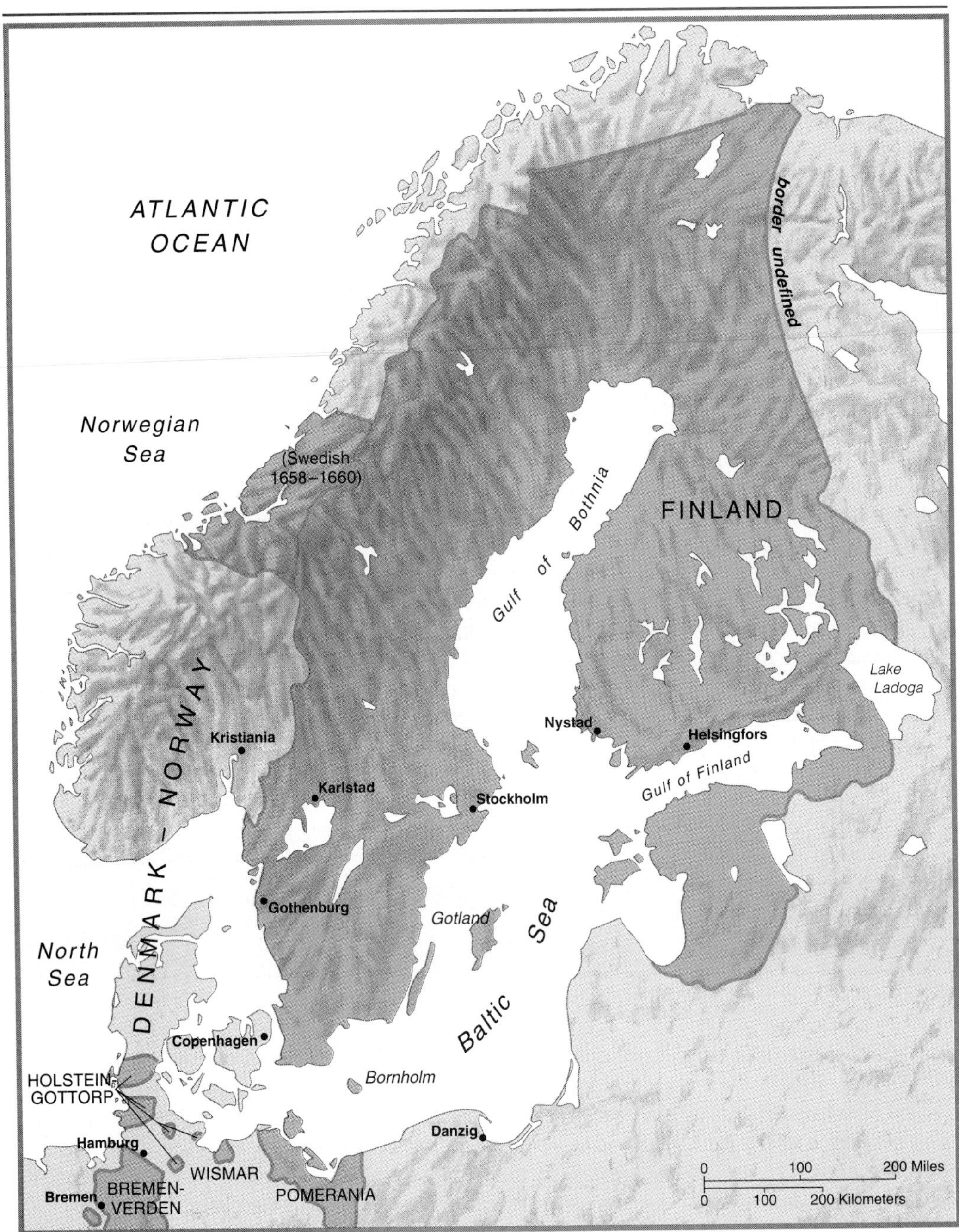

MAP 30.1 *The Swedish Empire in 1660.* *Sweden controlled much of the Baltic seacoast in the mid–seventeenth century. Gustavus Adolphus played a key role in expanding Swedish influence along the southern coast. Lands in Germany were lost by the eighteenth century, as were lands in the eastern Baltic region.*

Oxenstierna charted the course of alliance between high nobles and crown that prevailed in the first half of the century. His greatest contribution may have been holding the system together during the minority of Christina. Bengt Oxenstierna, architect of Sweden's foreign policy in the late seventeenth century, worked out a series of alliances that helped secure the empire. Yet, the great ambitions of Charles XII after 1697 unraveled this system during the eighteenth century.

The Swedish Model of Absolutism

Although various Swedish monarchs tinkered with their absolutist system, other Europeans, such as Peter I of Russia, admired and adopted parts of the Swedish bureaucratic model. Gustavus Adolphus and Charles XI fashioned an absolutism based on cameralism, a machinelike political structure that emphasized **subordination** (a chain-of-command system), **regimentation** (emphasis on discipline and obedience), and **differentiation**. The last idea was simply that each governmental bureau must concern itself with a single function; thus, finances, military affairs, or justice must each be the domain of a single department. Staffing and pay were uniform throughout the bureaucracy, and the system was grounded in a comprehensive set of laws and regulations.

This bureaucracy was fused with a national army based on conscription. The army drafted peasants who were regularly paid, highly trained, and well equipped; experienced officers, many of whom received formal educations, skillfully led this Swedish force. The combination proved formidable, as Gustavus Adolphus successfully fought the Russians and Poles to gain new territories along the Baltic seacoast. During the Battle of Lützen in 1632, Gustavus Adolphus was mortally wounded, but his soldiers rallied and carried the day against the enemy.

Socioeconomic Patterns of Swedish Absolutism

Swedish society and politics was dominated by the nobility, especially the high nobility, and they used their power to amass great amounts of land and other forms of wealth. Full-blown absolutism, however, did not develop until monarchs wrested control of land from the high nobility. Monarchs were supported by lesser nobles and by members of other estates who also allied with kings in most

FIGURE 30.3 ***Swedish Iron Manufacturing.*** *This eighteenth-century painting depicts a Swedish foundry where workers used simple techniques for making iron and steel. The low labor costs and exceptional quality of Swedish iron ore gave Sweden a competitive advantage in international markets. The British, especially, imported large amounts of Swedish iron, and the Dutch played a significant role in helping the Swedes develop their iron manufacturing.*
National Museum of Stockholm.

political matters. Thus, Swedish absolutism had a certain appeal to a broad spectrum of people.

Mercantilism was the cornerstone of Swedish economic policy beginning with the time of Gustavus Adolphus. Industry and commerce received much attention and resources for development in Sweden. Mining, for example, was a significant industry, and copper and iron were the two most profitable metals extracted. Copper became the major revenue source, especially after the bureaucracy made it illegal to export half-processed ore. Swedes built their own ships to carry exports and sought out their own markets, and Sweden enjoyed a favorable balance of trade until the early 1700s. To support the development of Swedish industry, the state subjected workers to their employers' rules forbidding workers to move. Strikes were considered mutinous, and those who did strike were treated with great severity.

Foreigners played a large role in the development of certain industries. Dutch artisans helped create the burgeoning Swedish military industry. Louis De Geer, a prominent Dutch industrialist, enjoyed Gustavus Adolphus's confidence and helped establish a variety of armament industries. De Geer eventually moved to Sweden and was made a Swedish noble in 1641. The city of Gothenburg was rebuilt as a Dutch-style city with a large export marketplace and a canal that ran into the heart of the city.

Swedish agriculture did not maintain the developmental pace of other sectors. Although individual landownership increased, Swedish farmers did not apply much of the new agricultural technology seen in other parts of Europe. Repeated famines plagued Sweden in the late seventeenth and early eighteenth centuries.

EARLY FRENCH ABSOLUTISM, 1625–1715

The French government grew significantly larger in the sixteenth and seventeenth centuries, increasing from 4,000 officials in 1515 to 46,000 in 1665, and the financial burden of maintaining the bureaucracy along with a standing army caused unrest and suffering, especially among the peasants. Internal unification needs and the successful conduct of an activist foreign policy drove French leaders to adopt centralizing policies. A major problem, however, was that the great majority of officials had purchased their positions and could not be dismissed without compensation. They could pass their offices to their sons.

The Rule of the Two Cardinals, 1625–1661

Much of France's recovery from religious dissent and near-anarchic conditions after 1610 was owed to the policies of two chief ministers who happened to be cardinals of the Roman Catholic Church. Cardinal Richelieu (1585–1642) and Cardinal Giulio Mazarin (1602–1661) ably served their sovereigns. The two cardinals began building the foundations for French power, which loomed over Europe from the 1660s.

Although Cardinal Richelieu had become a political figure early in the reign of Louis XIII (reign dates 1610–1643), he did not wield significant power until the mid-1620s. From that point, however, he dedicated himself to increasing the influence of the monarchy and fostering internal unity, as well as to increasing his personal fortune. One problem Richelieu faced was the continuing existence of Protestant stronghold cities and areas in France. Richelieu disarmed these cities to achieve greater political unity. He also expanded monarchical influence with the creation and dispatch of royal officials or **intendants** to various parts of the realm. These loyal representatives of the king corrected local abuses and extended state reach into distant regions.

The major foreign policy challenge facing France was the growing threat from the Hapsburg family. This situation resulted from Hapsburg control of the Spanish government, the Spanish Netherlands, territory in the Italian Peninsula, and lands near France's northeast frontier. From the French perspective, the Hapsburg encirclement constituted a mortal threat, especially after the successes of the Hapsburg armies in Germany. Thus, the French government supported Protestant powers that fought against the Catholic Hapsburgs in the Thirty Years War. Danes and Swedes received financial and diplomatic support from France until the death of the Swedish king, Gustavus Adolphus, in 1632. Then, France committed itself to direct combat against the Hapsburg forces, with the French prevailing in the 1640s. The costs

MAP 30.2 ***Hapsburg Possessions "Threatening" France.*** *In the seventeenth century, French leaders grew increasingly worried that the Hapsburg family, a dynastic rival, might isolate and strangle France. Thus, a key aim of French foreign policy was to ensure that Spanish and Austrian possessions near France's borders be reduced or eliminated, especially in Italy and Germany. By the end of the century, French expansion under Louis XIV made these concerns superfluous.*

of supporting the war effort and the growing government triggered major French social unrest in the 1630s.

Cardinal Mazarin succeeded Richelieu and continued his predecessor's policy of strengthening France. Rather than use the system of patron-client relationships of Richelieu, Mazarin created a parallel system of power, relying on intendants as local administrators. This change alienated many other officials who benefited from the old ways, and they rebelled against Mazarin. Compounding the threat was the alliance of officials with distressed commoners in cities and rural areas. One uprising by Parisians compelled King Louis XIV (reign dates 1643–1715) to flee Paris. Louis's palace complex and court at Versailles, located a moderate distance from Paris, became a symbol of the king's distaste for the Parisians. Cardinal Mazarin outlasted the various rebellious groups by using military commissioners and intendants to enforce obedience to royal commands. The intendant system survived.

Mazarin also taught statecraft to his young sovereign, Louis XIV. Careful schooling in the application of royal power well served the king, who ruled on his own after Mazarin's death in 1661. One of Louis XIV's first decisions concerned the personal assumption of the first minister position, as well as the royal reins of power. In addition, the overwhelming majority of top ministers

PARALLELS AND DIVERGENCES

Peasant Protests in the Seventeenth Century

The main cause of rural unrest in Europe lay in the growth of state bureaucracies, as well as in the means to fund them. New taxes, direct and indirect, triggered protests, especially when the fiscal assessments became systematic and regular. Taxes on salt, grain, and wine hit the poor quite hard, and French officials imposed a tax on each person, a tax that became a chief source of state revenue between 1630 and 1640. This assessment sparked massive peasant unrest. Quartering of soldiers also heavily burdened poor people, who deeply resented the arrogant ways of the soldiers.

Peasants had a strong sense of justice. They were convinced that their rights, going back generations, should be honored by the state and its rapacious officials. Peasants held a powerful belief in tradition and faith in the ruler's commitment to justice, so when new taxes were imposed, peasants revolted. They believed that the king was just but uninformed about the wrongdoings of his officials. Peasants also resented new obligations imposed by manorial lords who were often perceived as greedy; in addition, rural folk resisted duties proclaimed by new lords who moved into the area. In the peasants' minds, tradition had to be followed.

Even though peasant uprisings were suppressed, sometimes most brutally, the state recognized certain limits of bureaucratic power by canceling new taxes, reducing existing taxes, or abolishing restrictions on movement by peasants. Nobles, too, tread warily after a peasant outburst because the aristocrats feared for their lives, their families, and their property.

Peasant resistance centered on the village; it was their strength and also their weakness. Rural life was constantly threatened by bandits, soldiers, and officials, so village cohesiveness was a strength against outsiders. Villages were the main line of self-defense, the main taxpaying unit, the focal point of economic activity, and the center of social life for peasants. The parish church was often the village's sturdiest building, where locals gathered to resist predators. Because most farming tools could be used as weapons, a crude arsenal existed within the village community. And often it was but a short step from self-defense to rebellion. Peasant armies were also organized by village under local leadership; this gave some cohesiveness to a military force. At the same time, one village unit might refuse to fight under a commander from another village, causing disunity, especially when a defeat occurred. Thus, peasant armies were easily formed and easily dissolved.

served solely at Louis's pleasure and came from nonaristocratic origins. This was unlike Gustavus Adolphus but similar to Charles XI. Like Richelieu, Mazarin had amassed great personal wealth in feeding off the system he helped expand. Thus, the two cardinals played a vital role in strengthening France in the seventeenth century.

Louis XIV's Absolutism

French absolutism reflected the personality of the monarch who titled himself the "Sun King." Louis undertook a self-promotion campaign, including the creation of an image that, along with the dazzling court life at Versailles, awed French aristocrats. In fact, the courtliness of France was imitated across Europe. Yet Louis was not an innovator. He worked with the institutions available to him, including the bureaucracy, the courts of the nobility, and the estates of France. He controlled the patronage system and used that along with threat, persuasion, and bribery to compel obedience. Because the nobility was fragmented by the time of Louis's assumption of power, taming of the aristocrats was moderately easy.

The nature of absolutism meant that in the absence of a dynamic character such as Louis XIV at the helm, the ship of state might drift or flounder. Indeed, that happened in the eighteenth century as Louis's weaker successors failed to control

FIGURE 30.4 *Louis XIV.* *The "Sun King" set the tone for most of his fellow monarchs in the seventeenth century. Louis epitomized the absolute monarch; he commissioned artists to create impressive paintings, drawings, and tapestries as testaments to his god-like power. In this Gobelins tapestry, he sits astride his steed pointing forward while looking at the viewer. Such tapestries were an important export industry for France.* Musée de Versailles © R.M.N.

the disgruntled aristocrats. Absolutism needed a monarchical system that functioned smoothly with a strong ruler. The other legacy of Louis XIV was a firm commitment to an expansionist policy. Ultimately, this policy bankrupted France, playing a role in the unfolding French Revolution later in the eighteenth century.

In his campaign to foster French power and his own glory, Louis concentrated on dominating the internal administration. He selected capable administrators, insisting that they could be dismissed by him at any time. The great demand on resources owing to the major wars beginning in the 1660s accelerated the centralization process. Civilian militias were replaced by a central police force, and municipalities were brought under royal control, especially after the intendants gained access to and influence over municipal finances. The number of intendants was sharply increased.

By the late 1670s, the basic institutional framework and policies had been set, and Louis turned to foreign matters. His guiding principle remained the extension of French territory and influence throughout Europe and across the globe. The French army grew to a standing force of several hundred thousand; the navy swelled from a small coastal fleet to an oceanic armada of several hundred fighting vessels; and a vigorous colonization program commenced in North America, the Caribbean Basin, and India. Warring against the

Dutch, English, and others occupied nearly all of Louis's energy in his later reign.

A series of poor harvests and the heavy toll of taxation and service nearly wrecked France in the 1690s. Widespread starvation stalked the land, and the king grew unpopular. At the announcement of his death in 1715, many French subjects openly celebrated.

Financing French Absolutism: Colbert's Policies

The impetus to build a bureaucracy to enlarge and equip the military forces came from many officials, but especially from Jean Louis Baptiste Colbert (1619–1683). Although he would have preferred to create an even more centralized political system, Colbert used the intendants to double the tax revenues arriving in Paris. These funds helped build the Versailles palace complex, intended as a symbol of royal splendor that would awe the aristocrats and other subjects. The massive project took several years to complete and cost a significant fraction of the state's annual budget.

In addition, Colbert undertook a series of measures to improve the economy. He dispatched agents to hire artisans and experts in various sectors of the economy. Some came to France, although they barely offset the losses of Huguenot technicians and scientists who left France (see the discussion in Chapter 29 of the revocation of the Edict of Nantes). Colbert established the rudiments of an educational system, and he built a merchant marine force to transport French goods and to avoid tolls on Dutch and English ships. Colbert also began a modest effort to promote high-quality French export goods. The overall policy slightly improved France's economic position, but it could not forestall a serious economic crisis in the 1690s.

Social Unrest in the Age of Absolutism

The drive for a larger government and the revenues to support it triggered major outbreaks of French social protest. After taxes increased fourfold during the Thirty Years War, unrest exploded in mass actions. Dissidents maimed the livestock of

FIGURE 30.5 ***The Palace at Versailles.*** *Versailles symbolized Louis XIV's power and grandeur. At the same time, it represented his distrust of Parisians, who forced him to flee Paris in humiliation early in his reign. Versailles was located some distance from the French capital; Jean Baptiste Colbert, one of Louis's outstanding ministers, supervised the construction of the palace complex. The great cost of construction forced Colbert to improve tax collection and undertake revenue-raising projects.* Giraudon/Art Resource, N.Y.

Figure 30.6 ***Peasant Discontent.*** *This seventeenth-century painting shows peasants exacting revenge against their rulers. Soldiers who had abused peasants by eating their food, stealing their possessions, and insulting their families are caught off guard and succumb to the rage of rural folk. Although such incidents were sporadic, there were also eruptions of large-scale violence. The elite greatly feared challenges to their authority and responded ferociously to crush the unrest.* Rijksmuseum.

local aristocrats or beat local agents of the government. Haylofts and stacks burst into flame from torchings by agitated subjects, and in local carnivals people mocked members of the political and social elite by burning effigies of officials and singing ribald songs. Serious mass protests erupted in 1636 and 1637, and regional outbursts troubled the government in 1639. The most sustained unrest occurred between 1648 and 1652, when uprisings led by disgruntled officials coincided with riots by Parisians and peasants. These disturbances threatened the social and political fabric but were finally crushed.

During the 1690s, famine claimed many French subjects and consumed the attention of potential opponents of the regime. The hardest hit were peasants who were taxed to the point of desperation. Massive armed forces dampened rural unrest.

One method of co-opting potential dissenters was the elevation of talented members of the middle class into government positions. Office holding also meant rising into the aristocracy, despite efforts by the ancient noble families to divide sharply the boundaries between themselves and the new social elite. The resulting social mobility eased some tensions among the middle class, providing the state with talented bureaucrats.

The legacy of Louis XIV and the two cardinals was a centralized patchwork of contradictory parts. High taxes, large armies, and royally appointed officials increased the centralized power of the king. Yet the state's finances also depended on the sale of offices, which left sizeable portions of the government independent of the king's control. This tension between centralization and decentralization was an important structural feature of French absolutism. It was not resolved

FIGURE 30.7 *Prussian Militarism.* *Prussian absolutism depended heavily on the army. Some said Prussia was more an army with a country than a country with an army. Successive Prussian rulers built the military into an effective, well-trained instrument of power. This picture shows a training scene. Harsh discipline and constant drill were essential to effectiveness in combat. The wooden horse in the background was used as an instrument of punishment.* Bildarchiv Preussischer Kulturbesitz.

until the French Revolution did away with the sale of offices and allowed centralization to proceed unabated.

EARLY PRUSSIAN ABSOLUTISM, 1648–1740

Out of the Thirty Years War came an enlarged state, Brandenburg-Prussia (hereafter known as Prussia). A succession of three Hohenzollern sovereigns ruled Prussia between 1640 and 1740. Through shrewd statecraft and force they forged a powerful state system out of disparate and territorially disconnected parts.

Building Absolutism in Prussia

Prussian power came from strong-willed monarchs, a large army, and the building of a bureaucracy to maintain it. Frederick William, the Great Elector (reign dates 1640–1688), increased the army's size from 8,000 to 22,000 soldiers during the Little Northern War (1655–1660). Special wartime taxes had been wrung out of recalcitrant city administrations, and the fiscal levies became permanent after the victorious monarch refused to disband his army, turning it against his urban opponents. Frederick William also co-opted the **Junkers**, the impoverished landed nobility of East Prussia, by turning the peasants who worked Junker estates into serfs. This enserfment brought agony to peasants but loyalty from grateful aristocrats who staffed the bureaucracy and army.

To support the Prussian army, Frederick William needed an efficient means to collect taxes. Reorganization of the tax system began in 1667, and Frederick William soon heavily taxed peasants and urbanites. In addition, the monarch built a bureaucracy of officials and tax collectors who were directly responsible to him. By 1713, the army had grown to 39,000 soldiers and became more battle-seasoned during combat in the early 1700s.

Frederick I (reign dates 1688–1713) gained the title King of Prussia. A significant contribution of this ruler and his wife, Queen Sophie Charlotte, was the building of many princely palaces and a dazzling courtier life centered on intellectuals, like Gottfried Wilhelm Leibnitz, who joined the faculty at the newly created University of Halle.

Prussian absolutism reached its most complete form under the leadership of Frederick William I (1713–1740), the Soldier King. The army grew to more than 80,000 soldiers and consumed around 80 percent of state revenues. Between 50 to 65 percent of the nobles in the east served in the Prussian officer corps or the bureaucracy. A military reserve system had been fashioned by organizing and training peasants for service in the event of a general mobilization. In fact, the system avoided the problem of having a larger standing army and thereby saved significant sums. Military commanders played a role in developing and improving Prussia's roads and waterways because they wished to be able to move military units rapidly from one spot to another. One joke asserted that Prussia was more of an army with a country than a country with an army.

Frederick William I reorganized his bureaucracy along military lines. Taxing authority and material supply powers rested with the local officials who owed absolute obedience to the monarch. In addition, Frederick William I rewarded merit by permitting commoners to attain noble status through outstanding state service. He also kept officials' salaries low but augmented them with bonuses for good service. Another bureaucratic practice forbade nobles from serving as officials in their home territories to

Map 30.3 ***Prussia in 1721.*** *Disparate states had been welded into Prussia by the early eighteenth century. The Prussian army and bureaucracy had played key roles in forging that unity. In the process, Prussia emerged as a significant power in European affairs, especially after 1740, during the reign of Frederick the Great.*

FIGURE 30.8 ***Conscription of Jews.*** *Prussia, like many states in Europe, treated Jews with disdain and discrimination. This drawing shows the drafting of a group of Jewish men into the Prussian army. While forcible conscription was a common occurrence, certain groups, including the Jews, were treated more harshly both in the conscription process and later while in service. Beatings were common throughout the Early Modern Era.*
Courtesy of the Trustees of the British Museum.

avoid their becoming too tied to local instead of state interests.

The system worked tolerably well but needed additional safeguards to ensure efficiency and full compliance with the sovereign's commands. Inspectors widely traveled the realm to report on the conduct of appointees in local positions. Frederick William himself journeyed around the realm to remind local officials that they served at his pleasure.

Prussian monarchs welcomed a small Protestant sect, the Pietists. **Pietism**, which became a kind of state religion that helped centralize ideological loyalty, called for a renewal of direct religious experience. Pietists emphasized the significance of personal conversion and rebirth to a new life of active Christianity. Many areas in Europe expelled the Pietists for their refusal to submit to state laws regulating religion, but Prussia welcomed them to counter the influence of Lutheranism in the provinces: Lutherans often depended on the support of provincial nobles who might oppose state interests. Pietists became influential at educational institutions at all levels, including the universities of Halle and Königsberg. Through these intellectual centers Pietism exerted considerable sway over elite cultural life in other parts of Germany.

Social Issues in Prussia

Prussian rulers also actively encouraged the migration of numerous religious minority groups to Prussia in order to repopulate and rebuild its economy after the Thirty Years War. Perhaps 20,000 Huguenots settled around Berlin after their expulsion from France in the 1680s. Another 20,000 Protestants fled from Salzburg in 1731, and they were welcomed in Prussia. The proliferation of sects led to religious toleration in Prussia. The status of Jews remained uncertain, with some rights granted them only in the late eighteenth century. Full legal status for Jews in Prussia did not come until 1812. In many parts of Germany, Jews still experienced extreme forms of anti-Semitism and financial exploitation.

The Prussian state adopted many elements of absolutism, and its army dominated and altered the existing political and social systems. Until 1740, the army had seldom been used in extensive campaigns. In that year, Frederick II came to power and conquered the rich Austrian province of Silesia. The action embroiled Europe in a series of wars over the next twenty-three years, but Prussia survived great battle losses and emerged with enlarged territories and a full treasury. Prussian absolutism had passed a major test.

PETER THE GREAT BUILDS RUSSIAN ABSOLUTISM, 1689–1725

Peter the Great forged the basis of Russian absolutism. Within a century after his death, Russian troops helped drive Napoleon from power and secure a Bourbon restoration by Louis XVIII. Peter's legacy included a state apparatus of immense power that long outlived him, and he introduced the Western calendar, newspapers, a revised written script, and a whole complex of Western-style manners to Russia.

Peter's Youth

An examination of Peter's pre-adult years sheds light on his later actions. Peter witnessed terrifying court struggles between the families backing his mother and those backing his half-sister, Sophia. In a coup organized by Sophia, Peter and his half-brother assumed joint rule, with the actual power being placed in the regent Sophia's hands. After the ten-year-old Peter watched as soldiers murdered his relatives, he was moved into a safe haven away from Moscow.

Life outside the Kremlin's walls meant freedom from the stultifying rituals tsars performed and a chance to give free rein to his immense appetite for learning. War games fascinated Peter, and he held mock battles with real soldiers playing parts. Peter sailed local lakes, becoming enamored of naval matters. In addition, he conversed at length with Westerners, whose friendliness and knowledge excited him. In 1689, after military and policy failures by Sophia's political allies, forces loyal to Peter ousted her.

Two events, a trip to Archangel (1693–1694) and a military campaign near the Sea of Azov (1695–1696), particularly influenced Peter. In Archangel, the young tsar visited a bustling port with many ships and foreign merchants. Peter also sailed in dangerous waters, and that adventure strengthened his desire to learn more about shipbuilding and sailing. After returning from the north, Peter decided to attack the Ottoman Empire by capturing its strategic fort near an entrance to the Sea of Azov. The initial effort failed miserably, but Peter learned from the loss; after spending the winter building a new flotilla, he beat the Turks.

The Grand Tour, 1697–1698

Perhaps the most remarkable event of Peter's reign was his tour of Europe in the late 1690s. Peter traveled with a large party. This allowed him to be free in his intelligence-gathering activities. The embassy had three purposes: to collect information about how to improve Russia, to interact with top political figures in Europe, and to assess the possibilities for foreign-policy initiatives.

Peter lingered at the great shipyards of the Netherlands and England, taking the opportunity to participate in all phases of shipbuilding. Having delighted in the toil and in conversations with prominent artisans and engineers, he invited some of them to Russia to aid in a variety of technical matters.

Peter generally impressed his hosts and charmed monarchs and princes alike. The diplomatic contact afforded Peter better relations with a variety of sovereigns and a personal appreciation for the complex web of international relations in Europe. Prior to this journey, Russia's diplomatic corps often had been ineffective in representing Russia's interests. The tsar also learned that conditions seemed propitious for a dynamic diplomatic effort to strengthen Russia. Poland had become an ally, and Denmark looked north at Sweden, a great power of the seventeenth century and one that controlled much of the Baltic seacoast. In addition, Britain and France had begun to prepare for a major war over the succession to the Spanish throne. A Russian, Danish, and Polish alliance against Sweden was forged.

The Great Northern War (1700–1721): Testing Russian Absolutism

Determined to modernize Russia, Peter knew that the task demanded a long, taxing effort. When he returned from the tour in 1698, Peter began insisting that Russians break with their traditional manners and habits. Perhaps the most famous effort involved compelling Russian men to cut off their beards to look Western. These and other policies consumed the young tsar's days until a shattering military defeat at Narva (1700) forced a transformation of Russia's political system.

FIGURE 30.9 **Peter the Great.** *The equestrian pose in this picture is reminiscent of Louis XIV's portrait (Figure 30.4). Peter, unlike Louis, frequently accompanied his troops into battle, and his attire is suitable to a military commander. In many ways, Peter was leading his people in a campaign to Westernize themselves. To do so, he established a military-style system that bound his subjects like serfs or soldiers.* Novosti, London.

Sweden's monarch, Charles XII, although a teenager, proved to be an adept warrior. Once Russia, Denmark, and Poland declared war against Sweden, Charles swiftly attacked Denmark. After defeating the Danes, Charles turned on Poland and won a series of victories. Then the Swedes invaded Russia, and at Narva the larger Russian army fell to the firepower of the disciplined Swedes. Charles drily noted that fighting the Russians was like shooting geese. Nearly all of Russia's commanders surrendered, and Peter, anticipating defeat, left before the battle, wishing to salvage the surviving elements and to rebuild Russia.

The staggering losses compelled the tsar to accelerate the adoption of Russian absolutism. Peter usually dressed, acted, and thought like a soldier. From his youth, army life suited the tsar's character. Militaristic discipline, loyalty, and service in a hierarchical structure could accomplish a great deal with efficient dispatch. Men and materials were quickly raised and employed.

Peter also thought in orderly and systematic ways; he believed that using logic and rationally determined methods provided the best hope of attaining lofty goals. This trait caused him to see government as a machine. Peter took great interest in laws and rules. He understood that they acted like a skeletal structure underlying the sinews and tissue of government.

The absolutist model passed its test in the Battle of Poltava in 1709. Peter had confiscated treasured Russian church bells for their metal content; to the dismay of the church hierarchy, they were transformed into new artillery pieces. Recruiters scoured the frontier regions, and their harsh methods triggered a massive uprising (1707–1708) in

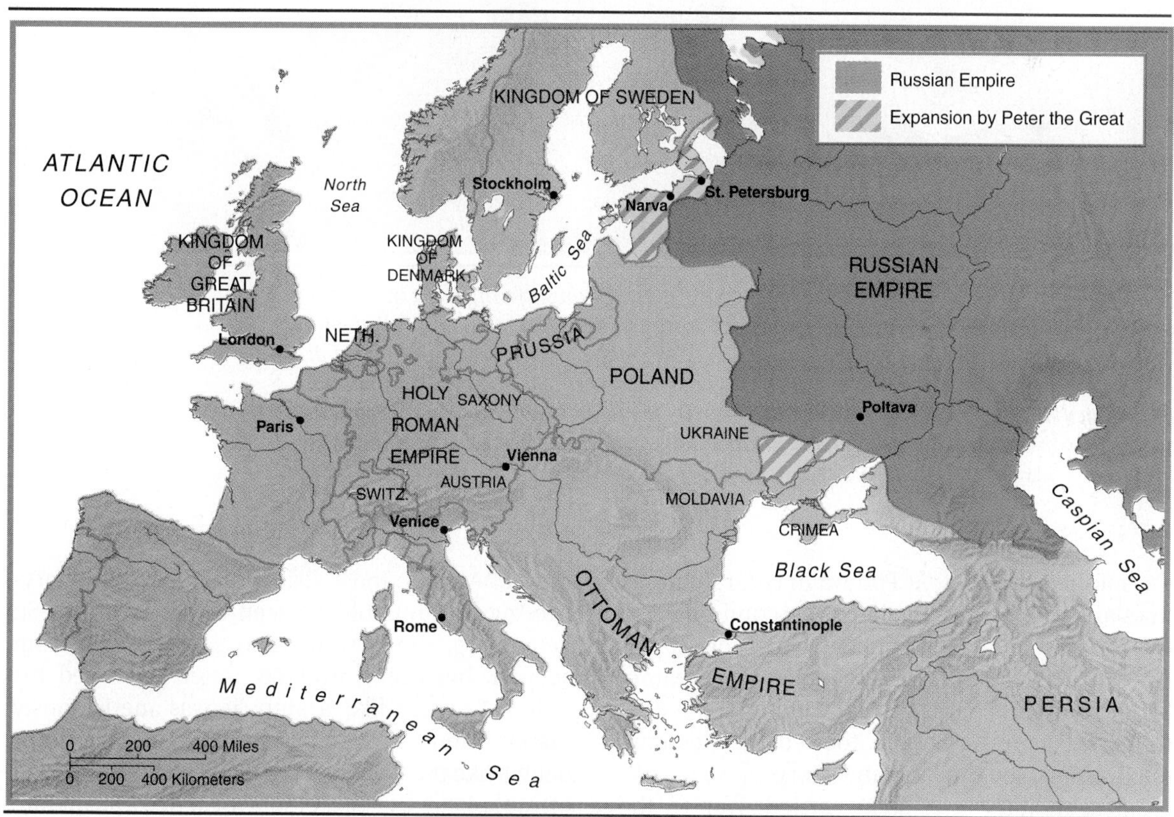

Map 30.4 ***Expansion of the Russian Empire under Peter the Great.*** *Peter laid the foundations of an expanded Russian Empire by annexing lands along the Baltic coast. He also led campaigns against the Ottoman Turks and the Safavid Persians. Russia's succeeding monarchs continued his foreign policy efforts, creating one of the world's largest empires. Much of Peter's success came at the expense of Sweden.*

FIGURE 30.10 ***Layout of St. Petersburg.*** *Great human suffering went into the building of St. Petersburg, Peter the Great's "Window on the West." Thousands of laborers died while toiling in the marshy environment of the city. This schematic, drawn around 1720 by J. P. Homann, indicates that early city plans envisioned the city being located on large islands in the Neva River. Peter was determined that the city would be built and would become a successful capital. To realize that dream, he invested considerable human and material resources.* Courtesy of the Trustees of the British Museum.

the southern steppes. At Poltava in central Russia, Russians and Swedes fought for a second time. On this occasion, Russians routed the army of Charles XII, who fled to the Ottoman realm. At a celebratory banquet after the conflict, Peter gathered the captured Swedish officers and toasted the "lessons" that had enabled the Russian victory.

The military style soon carried over to the civilian sector. Peter spent a great deal of time and energy writing and publishing a detailed code of military law. His ideas about the state found their clearest and most complete expression in military legislation. He sought to tame and correct society by extending to it the norms of military life. Perhaps one of the most visible products of military-like regulation could be seen in the layout of St. Petersburg, the new Russian capital, built from scratch, beginning in 1703. Peter fashioned his political center like a ship; it was meticulously planned and carefully regulated. Seemingly minor details like the dimensions of chimneys, the forms of roofs, and the placement of fences in private dwellings fell under governmental control.

Provincial administration also received the tsar's attention. There too, a military model dominated regional and local life. Each of the subnational administrative units had a military force stationed therein and attached to it. Officers assumed census-taking duties and eventually became tax collectors. In addition, military detachments were expected to assist local police forces when discontent reached major proportions. One feature of Peter's government was the large number of military figures who became bureaucrats. Discipline and obedience educated them to be loyal, hardworking officials.

Peter also revitalized the upper levels of government by applying Swedish-style hierarchies there. He created a ministry system, wherein each ministry had a specific function. The Admiralty Ministry, the War Ministry, and the Foreign Affairs Ministry constituted the first of a line of administrative structures. Peter believed that military regulation and discipline created soldiers who lived moral lives and followed modern practices. Similarly, the long-range goal of absolutism was to substitute regulation for coercion in political and social life. Peter hoped that ethical humans could emerge from his military-style system.

Transformation of the Russian Economy

Economic growth between 1695 and 1725 laid the foundations for a fiscal base that could support a major war. Mercantile policies also brought production levels to previously unimaginable highs. Once undertaken, the government's control and regulation of the iron industry conferred national self-sufficiency in iron production within five years.

Government funds and regulations helped build the factories and establishments; the state's needs for materials took first priority. Whole economic sectors came under military control, and there were factories for sail cloth, for rope, for saddles, for leather goods, and for wool. Peter insisted that manufactured products regularly be tested to ensure quality. State serfs were forced into factories as laborers, and criminals under sentences of hard labor were made to work off their sentences in manufactories.

The state, ever eager to develop strategic industries, recruited foreigners for mining and metallurgy. Indeed, an entire metallurgical complex was built in the Ural Mountains. Monopolies were frequently promised to prospectors if or when they found massive deposits of ores.

Cities like St. Petersburg were built or reoriented to meet governmental requirements. City managers collected municipal taxes, and troops lived in private dwellings in provincial cities and towns; urban centers often had to transport troops and supplies from their own resources. Horses were demanded as a kind of taxation in certain towns. The growing municipal burden forced many to flee the towns; depopulation became a major problem. Internal passports were issued in an attempt to inhibit free movement of people, and border guards turned back fleeing Russian refugees.

The merchant class was devastated by many of the tsarist policies. Peter commanded that the primary trade route from Russia to the West be shifted from Archangel to St. Petersburg. In addition, groups of merchants were forcibly moved from their hometowns to the capital. Also, as the state became more involved in the establishment of factories and other enterprises, merchants could not compete with the minimal costs of state peasant labor or with state monopolies. This expansion of state servitude doomed whole economic sectors.

Social Upheaval in Russia

Nobles were deeply affected by the new imperial laws. The main basis of the nobility was service rather than birth, and heredity was replaced by personal merit in determining social ranking. This new system gave Peter great power over the nobles; he even commanded that they could not marry until they had been educated. People from other social groups advanced into the nobility by achieving a certain level in the ranking system.

One category, state peasants, demands some consideration. This group was created by Peter to bring previously free social groups under state control and regulation. These groups included the peasants of the Russian north, the fur-tributary peasants, the single homesteaders of the south, Siberian peasants, and sharecroppers. The state peasantry, composed of more than one million adult men, became bonded to the state; their movements were curtailed and their tax obligations were increased. All too often throughout the rest of the eighteenth century, tens of thousands of these state peasants were given by tsars to their favorite courtiers. "Free" now meant fugitive or criminal, and police or army detachments regularly rounded up travelers for investigation and return to a bondage system.

IN THEIR OWN WORDS

Two Women Examine Education and Writing

Women continued to have limited opportunities for education and personal expression in writing or other forms of artistic activity, like painting or sculpture. And the overwhelming number of women who did write or paint came from the upper classes of European society. Margaret Cavendish, the Duchess of Newcastle (1623–1673), received an excellent education and was highly regarded as a playwright and author of other literary genres. In this passage, she defends her right to write an autobiography, *A True Relation of My Birth, Breeding, and Life,* by comparing herself with other famous authors.

> But as I hope my readers will not think me vain for writing my life, since there have been many that have done the like, as Caesar, Ovid, and many more, both men and women, and I know of no reason I may not do it as well as they. But I verily believe some censuring readers will scornfully say, why hath this lady writ her own life? Since none care to know whose daughter she was, or whose wife she is, or how she was bred, or what fortunes she had, or how she lived, or what humour or disposition she was of? I answer that it is true, that 'tis no purpose to the readers, but it is to the authoress, because I write it for my own sake, not theirs. Neither did I intend this piece for to delight, but to divulge; not to please fancy, but to tell the truth. Lest after-ages should mistake, in not knowing I was daughter to one Master Lucas of St. John's near Colchester in Essex, second wife to the Lord Marquis of Newcastle; for my lord having had two wives, I might easily have been mistaken, especially if I should die and my lord marry again.

Anna Maria van Schurman (1607–1678) earned a reputation as the most learned European woman of the seventeenth century. Her father insisted that she learn alongside her brothers, and she first focused on the arts. Later, she studied ancient languages like Syriac and wrote an Ethiopian grammar. Although she was permitted the rare privilege of attending the University of Utrecht, she was required to stand behind a curtain during classes. In the work The Learned Maid or Whether a Maid May Be Called a Scholar?, Schurman states that women should be educated.

> My deep regard for learning, my conviction that equal justice is the right of all, impel me to protest against the theory which would only allow a minority of my sex to attain to what is, in the opinion of all men, most worth having. For since wisdom is admitted to be the crown of human achievement, and is within every man's right to aim at in proportion to his opportunities, I cannot see why a young girl in whom we admit a desire for self-improvement should not be encouraged to acquire the best that life affords.

Townsfolk experienced similar if startling shifts in their status. Because of a sudden imperial decree, all townspeople might wake one morning to find themselves retained as members of merchant guilds or artisan corporations. By this judgment, the number of taxpayers in an urban area significantly increased. Thus, the tax assessment on towns grew sharply, with the wealthier people paying larger shares of the town assessments. Initially, state revenues increased, but soon people fled the urban areas for the safety of the southern frontiers or the anonymity of foreign countries.

Social unrest erupted as the government's noose around its subjects' necks tightened. Acts of violence increased; the most serious challenges took place in 1707 and later, when two massive uprisings erupted in protest of the controlling policies.

WOMEN UNDER ABSOLUTISM

For women, the age of absolutism brought little change to their lives; in a few ways, opportunities seemed to lessen. Most European men believed that women should remain under male control; marriage therefore was the natural state and laws generally insisted that widows remarry. One group

EUROPE

Period bars	Date	Events
	1600	
Swedish absolutism, 1611–1718		Gustavus Adolphus becomes king, 1611
Thirty Years War, 1618–1648		
Early French absolutism, 1625–1715		Battle of Lützen, 1632
		Cardinal Mazarin becomes First Minister, 1642
Early Prussian absolutism, 1648–1740	1650	Fronde begins, 1648
		Protestants flee French religious persecution, 1685
Early Russian absolutism, 1689–1725		Peter the Great's Grand Tour begins, 1697
	1700	Battle of Narva, 1700
		Battle of Poltava, 1709
		Death of Charles XII, 1718
		Protestants flee Austrian religious persecution, 1731
		Frederick I dies, 1740
	1750	

of German women who lived by spinning pooled their wages and lived together, but the town fathers forbade all unmarried women to have their own households, forcing these women to abandon their communal life. Jewish marriages were usually arranged with the understanding that love would come later. The Jewish ideal marriage was said to be predestined in heaven, and divorce was permitted for unsuccessful unions.

Many women found their opportunities for employment limited, and when they did find work, they were usually paid much less than male workers. A few guilds were limited to women who could bequeath their tools and property to others in the guild. Louis XIV and Colbert, concerned about the lack of opportunities for women needing work, created a guild of dressmakers exclusively for them. The growing trend to license members of certain occupations also caused problems for women, and women were effectively barred from becoming licensed physicians because they were forbidden from taking university classes on anatomy and related subjects. The same thing happened to women who were apothecaries (dispensers of medicines) and midwives. In many German cities, however, custom demanded that women be midwives.

Some places in Europe and some groups permitted more participation by women in economic activities. A few Polish cities allowed women to be active in commercial ventures in the urban marketplaces; one scholar estimated that around 75 percent of traders in Polish cities were women. One measure of their financial success can be seen in the fact that in the seventeenth century about half of the loans in Danzig and Warsaw were financed by women. Because regulations often forbade women from staying at inns and therefore curtailed their travel, Jewish women relied on networks of friends to provide housing for them.

SUMMARY

1. European nation-states of the seventeenth and eighteenth centuries experimented with absolutist forms of government that included a military-style chain of command. The central government regulated politics, economics, and society, imposing discipline, obedience, and duty on officials as well as on subjects. Absolutist monarchs promoted the reliance on law rather than custom and the use of mechanical terminology in political discourse.

2. Wars often accelerated the process of gathering power in the hands of the monarch, and the Thirty Years War was a factor in the development of Swedish and French absolutism.

3. Sweden began its absolutist course under King Gustavus Adolphus, who led a coalition of aristocratic officials. Although dominance by the nobles grew after Gustavus Adolphus's death, King Charles XI reasserted royal dominance of the political system, and an ongoing land reform undermined the economic and political base of the high aristocrats.

4. French central power was built on a tension between officials who purchased their positions and officials who served only as long as the king was satisfied with their job performances. Louis XIV, France's absolutist king, dominated the nobles, but his successors could not duplicate his success.

5. Prussia built an absolutist system based on the army. Successive rulers created a bureaucracy grounded in dedicated, loyal, merit-rewarded service. Junker nobles gave loyal work in exchange for full control of the peasants who worked on their estates.

6. Peter the Great channeled his youthful fascination with foreign experts and military life into building an absolutist state, where Russian subjects either served or paid heavy taxes. Nearly every aspect of public life was state regulated and disciplined. After the warring ceased, the militarization of civil life continued.

7. Women were still regarded as inferior to men and needing to be under some form of male control. They were also frozen out of jobs by a rising professionalism that excluded them from being licensed by governments.

SUGGESTED READINGS

Anisimov, Evgenii. *The Reforms of Peter the Great.* New York: M. E. Sharpe, 1993. A compelling interpretation of Peter's era and the tsar's role in it.

Herwig, Holger. *Hammer or Anvil? Modern Germany, 1648–Present.* Lexington, Mass.: D. C. Heath, 1994. A useful survey of major issues and personalities of modern Germany.

Major, J. Russell. *From Renaissance Monarchy to Absolute Monarchy.* Baltimore: Johns Hopkins University Press, 1994. A synthesis of scholarship concerning the development of French absolutism, emphasizing the role of the nobility.

Roberts, Michael. *The Swedish Imperial Experience, 1560–1718.* Cambridge, Eng.: Cambridge University Press, 1979. A standard interpretation of the rise of the Swedish Empire.

Rosener, Werner. *The Peasantry of Europe.* Trans. by Thomas M. Barker. Oxford, Eng.: Oxford University Press, 1994. A synthesis of research about the European peasantry.

Scott, Franklin D. *Sweden: The Nation's History.* Carbondale: Southern Illinois University Press, 1988. A standard survey of Swedish history.

Wiesner, Merry E. *Women and Gender in Early Modern Europe.* Cambridge, Eng.: Cambridge University Press, 1993. A major study of women's history and issues in the Early Modern Era.

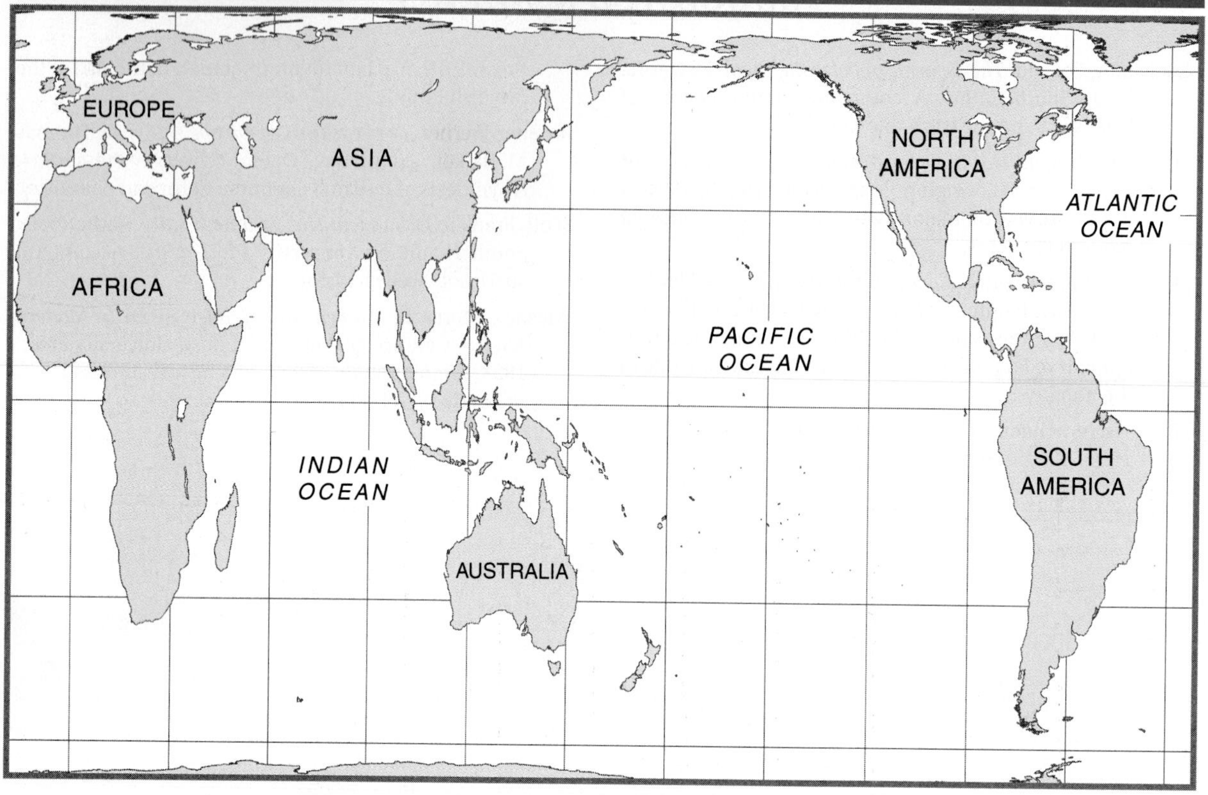

EUROPE
ASIA
NORTH AMERICA
ATLANTIC OCEAN
AFRICA
PACIFIC OCEAN
INDIAN OCEAN
SOUTH AMERICA
AUSTRALIA

NORTH AMERICA
EUROPE
ASIA
ATLANTIC OCEAN
AFRICA
PACIFIC OCEAN
PACIFIC OCEAN
SOUTH AMERICA
INDIAN OCEAN
AUSTRALIA
ANTARCTICA

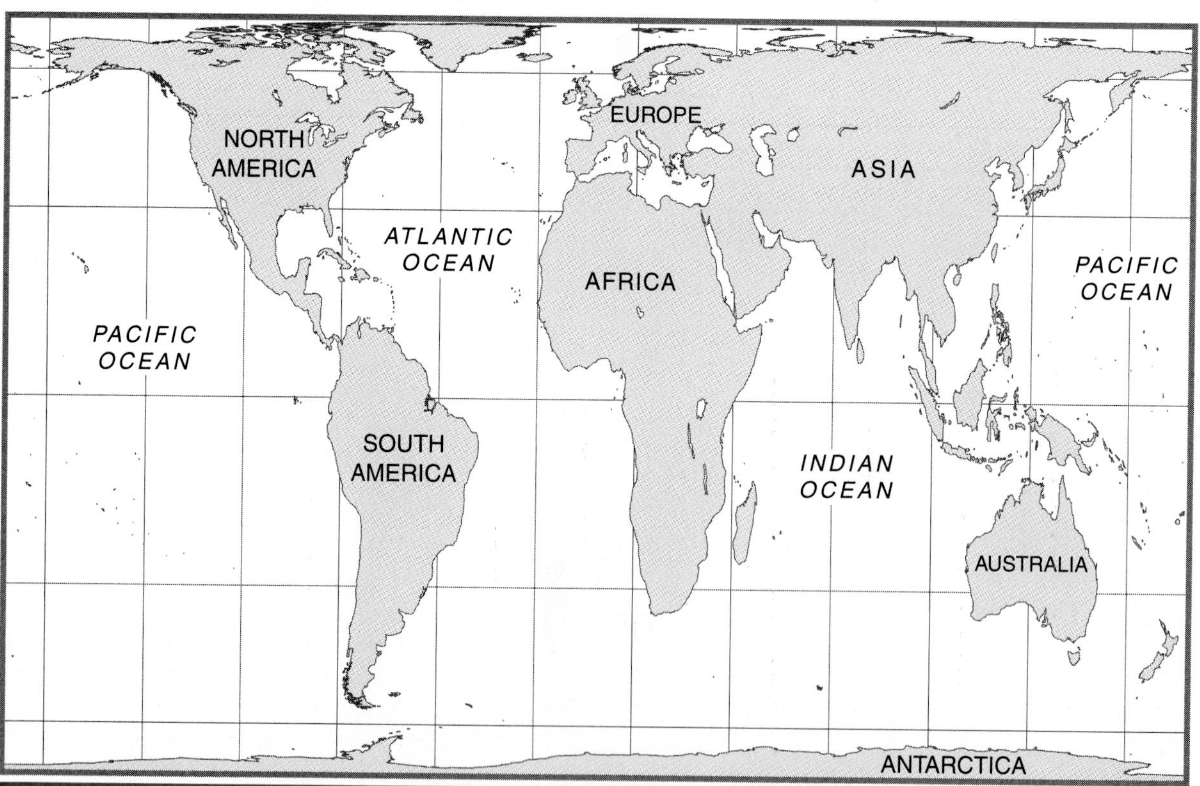

CHAPTER 31

Revolutions in Europe, the Americas, and Asia

1543–1895

Charles I of England, who had been on the throne since 1625, had blundered into a bloody civil war with Parliament in 1642 and had lost, but he still had managed to persuade most war-weary Parliamentarians to accept him once again as their monarch. Army commanders, among them Oliver Cromwell, purged Parliament and put the hapless king on trial for his life in early 1649. The English Revolution of 1640 to 1689 was a long era of often violent change. Charles's execution was a turning point in the English Revolution, one of many revolutions in the seventeenth and eighteenth centuries.

From the sixteenth to the nineteenth centuries, revolutions around the world transformed people's lives. During this period, local landed elite and urban middle-class members of society gained greater participatory roles in government as the electoral franchise widened. In certain cases, even the lower socioeconomic classes contended for power, but they usually succeeded only in uniting propertied people against them.

Revolutions can change political structures, social structures, economic structures, or intellectual views of the universe and the place of humans within it. Some revolutions caused great suffering, while others transformed institutions with only moderate upheaval. A few were implemented by existing rulers, and others resulted from opposition forces seizing power and restructuring the way in which power was exercised. Abortive revolutions, such as the Taiping Uprising in mid-nineteenth-century China, also severely traumatized societies.

DEFINITIONS AND TYPES OF REVOLUTIONS

A **revolution** is a process whereby rapid and fundamental structural change occurs. It may be relatively peaceful, like the Scientific Revolution of the sixteenth, seventeenth, and eighteenth centuries or the Industrial Revolution from 1770 to 1905. More often, however, revolutions that transform societies produce great unrest, major upheaval, and massive amounts of physical violence. Revolutions are processes rather than events. Because revolutions entail significant alteration in political and social structures, time is needed to complete the transformation. A revolutionary group's seizure of power is merely a single event in the revolutionary process rather than the process itself. In that sense, it is inappropriate to speak of a single year for the American Revolution or for the French Revolution.

Revolutions may be classified into several types. A revolution that changes mainly the political structure is a **political revolution**. A revolution that alters society is usually known as a **social revolution**. The Scientific Revolution was an **intellectual revolution**, a transformation of how human beings thought about themselves and the universe around them. The Industrial Revolution (discussed in Chapter 32) was an **economic revolution**, a transformation of a country's economic structure.

Another way of looking at revolutions is in terms of the agents bringing about the revolution. A revolution implemented by the ruling elite is called an **elite revolution**, and a revolution implemented by the common people seizing power is called a **populist revolution**. Thus, for example, a political revolution may also be an elite revolution or a populist revolution.

How do revolutions compare with rebellions? A **rebellion** is an uprising by people who seek to change the leaders rather than the political structure of a country. Rebellions are invariably political and may include large-scale violence. But the aim of a rebellious group is to replace the leadership, not a polity's institutional structure.

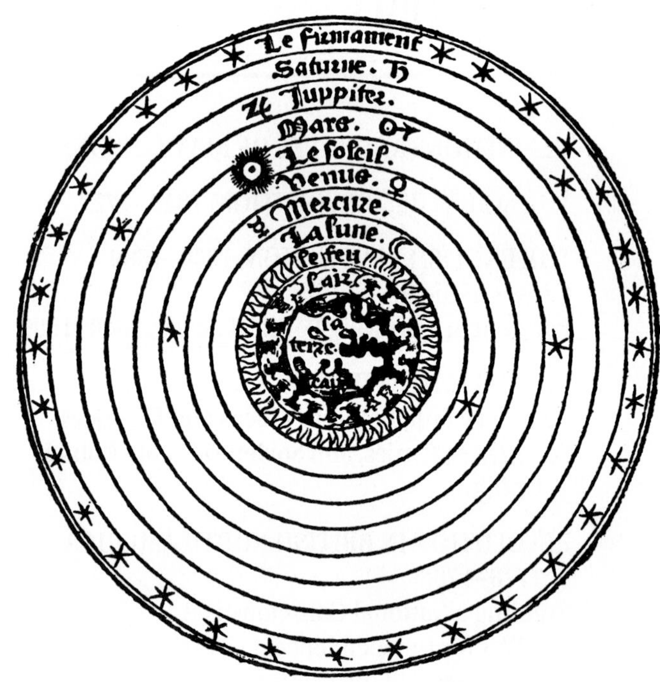

FIGURE 31.1 ***The Ptolemaic Universe.*** *This sixteenth-century diagram lays out the accepted interpretation of the universe as revolving around the earth. This system was elaborated by the Greek astronomer Ptolemy (A.D. 127–151) and later modified by others. Above the earth is air and then fire; above these spheres are the moon, the sun, and the five planets. If one accepts that the earth does not move, then a common-sense interpretation is that the stars and other bodies circle the earth.* Diagram from Oronce Fine, *Théorique de la huitième sphere et sept planètes.*

THE SCIENTIFIC REVOLUTION, 1543–1727

The Scientific Revolution fundamentally altered the human view of the universe and inspired new perspectives about people and ways to solve their problems. Although modern science owes much to Islamic, medieval, and Renaissance antecedents, the Scientific Revolution came when researchers abandoned the divine explanation for natural processes and explained the universe by general scientific laws. This process of secularization was a characteristic of modernity. Although important discoveries were made in most fields of science during this era, the focus in this chapter will be on two fields that experienced transformative change, astronomy and mathematics.

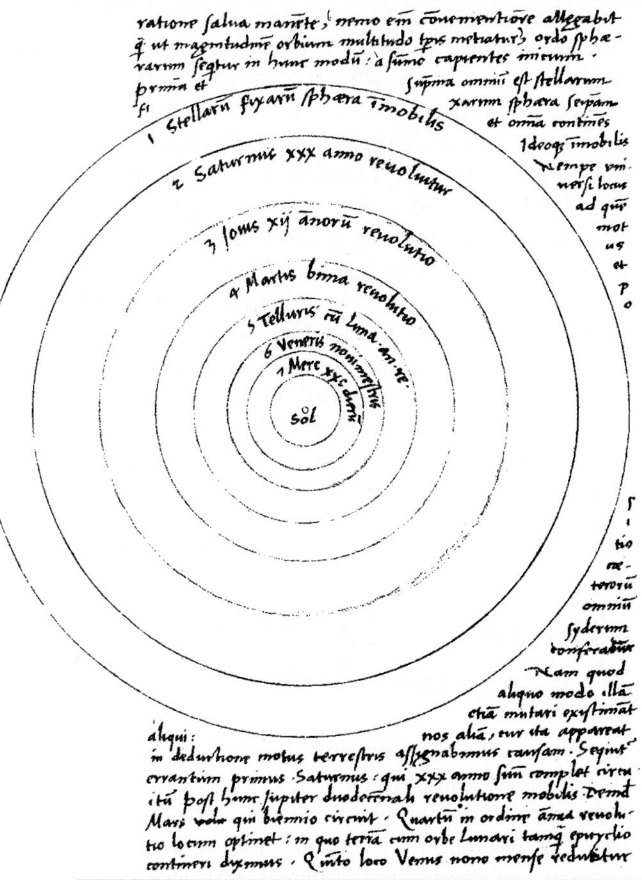

FIGURE 31.2 ***The Copernican System.*** *Nicolaus Copernicus's system shifted the earth from the center of the universe and placed an unmoving sun in the earth's stead. The moon circles the earth, while the earth, other planets, and stars move around the sun. Copernicus believed the orbits to be circular (they are actually elliptic). The Copernican system comes closer to representing the actual solar system than did the Ptolemaic universe, and its key achievement was to shift the earth away from the center.* Hulton-Getty/Tony Stone Images.

Nicolaus Copernicus (1473–1543) developed the first systematic critique of the Ptolemaic view of the universe, an earth-centered model of the cosmos that had held sway among European and Muslim scholars for over eight centuries. Copernicus, a Polish priest, used mathematics and logic to develop a sun-centered model of the universe, with the cosmos revolving around the sun. He believed that this more simple and elegant view was also more accurate. Much still remained to be investigated before an accurate picture of the universe emerged, but Copernicus's new perspective permitted others to think in different ways. Copernicus used different kinds of mathematics to formulate his model, and the intense use of mathematics became a feature of modern science.

Galileo Galilei (1564–1642), a professor of mathematics in Italy, improved the Dutch design of the telescope and made remarkable observations of the planets and their moons. Elaborating on fourteenth-century studies of velocity and acceleration, Galileo's research on the motion of bodies led him to conclude that heavier objects do not fall faster than lighter ones. He conducted careful experiments and helped develop the systematic and experimental method of investigating nature, using sophisticated mathematics to interpret the results. Other scientists replicated his experiments to verify the discoveries.

Advances in astronomy and other fields alarmed some members of the Roman Catholic Church. Given the religious wars of the period, new ideas were sometimes equated with heresies, and criticism of the prevailing view of the heavens might be construed as an attack on religious doctrine. For this reason, a few critics of traditional views, like Giordano Bruno, were burned at the stake for declaring that the universe was infinite. Later, when some church officials asserted that several of Galileo's teachings bordered on subversion, he yielded to the pressure and recanted certain views. More open-minded church leaders

FIGURE 31.3 ***Émilie de Breteuil, Marquise du Châtelet.*** *A mathematician, Émilie de Breteuil introduced Isaac Newton's work on gravity and the laws of motion to France and Europe. She translated the* Principia Mathematica *into French and thereby played a key role in the history of science and in the Enlightenment, as Newton's view of a universe run by laws deeply influenced many thinkers of the era.* Private Collection/Bulloz.

came to accept the changing views of the universe resulting from continued scientific probing and testing. Most scientists also professed devotion to God, and they hoped to create a system that validated God in a new universal order.

Isaac Newton (1642–1727) synthesized the ideas of his predecessors into the Newtonian model of the universe, which forever replaced the Ptolemaic model. One of the unifying elements in the new scheme, gravity, had been explained by Newton, who saw that the mutual attraction between two bodies applied to humans and the earth, the planets and the sun, and all of the stars. To help explain the forces at work in his grand scheme, Newton applied his newly developed calculus, a branch of mathematics that helped spur the development of modern science. Newton published the results of his synthesis in a significant work, *Principia Mathematica.* It stands as one of the great achievements of human intellect.

Newton's ideas, especially his elegant view of a universe run by natural laws, spread to the European continent and altered how humans thought about the universe and themselves. Émilie de Breteuil, Marquise du Châtelet, played a significant role in introducing Newton's concepts to French readers. A mathematician herself, de Breteuil translated Newton's *Principia,* making it intelligible to nonmathematical readers. Her writer friend Voltaire also played a key role in popularizing Newton's ideas, arguing that human behavior might also be governed by natural laws.

One belief system, deism, gained a following during the Scientific Revolution. **Deism** asserted that the universe functioned like a machine (a clock), which was constructed by its maker. According to this theory, after fashioning the universe, which ran by natural laws, God had nothing left to do. Many deists therefore believed that God had become unnecessary.

THE ENGLISH REVOLUTION, 1640–1689

A destructive political revolution swept England in the middle of the seventeenth century and concluded in 1689. Conflict between English monarchs and Parliament had been building for a long time. During the reign of James I (1603–1625) and at the ascendancy of his son Charles I (reign dates 1625–1649), the monarchy clearly enjoyed political supremacy. The monarchy could raise substantial sums of money, enjoyed significant influence in the House of Commons, and could count on the loyalty of the English people. By 1689, Parliament had ousted two monarchs from power and supported ones who agreed to limits on their authority, including Parliament's control of fiscal matters. Thus, Parliament had become a major partner in England's mixed governmental system.

Causes of the Revolution

Population growth played a key role in the crisis that precipitated the monarchy's collapse between 1640 and 1642. England's population doubled between 1500 and 1640, and the number of gentry landlords tripled. English commentators in the seventeenth century decried the huge population growth. This demographic increase contributed to long-term inflation, with rising prices steadily eroding the real wages of urban laborers. In addition, the costs of government sharply increased; one scholar estimated that in 1640 the English government would need twelve times the revenues of 1603 in order to keep pace with inflation. Stuart monarchs followed the aggressive foreign policies of their predecessors at a time when the costs of warfare were soaring.

Population pressures also increased tensions in English society. Localities became more factionalized, as seen in the rising numbers of civil litigations, heightened competition to get into college, and the growing number of contested seats for Parliament. Landlessness among the elite became more common because the growing number of male heirs in a family meant that more sons got less land or no land at all. In addition, the percentage of young people in the population grew, and males in their late teens and early twenties joined armies and demonstrated their support of the various political factions. Many turned to Puritanism, a Protestant movement that stressed discipline, sobriety, and morality to cure England's social ills.

Religion became a driving force in the English Revolution. The Stuart monarchs supported the Church of England (Anglican), including its archbishop, William Laud, who from 1637 began implementing policies that were binding on all subjects and seemed to the Puritans reminiscent of Roman Catholic practices. By restricting religious practices only to those of the *Prayer Book* of 1559, the Church of England effectively curtailed or abolished many Puritan observances. Archbishop Laud also promised to restore church lands confiscated and sold over the previous century and to curb lay control over tithes and clerical appointments. Thus, he challenged powerful secular interests. Charles I supported similar policies in Scotland, the land of his birth.

In the late 1620s, Charles I had amassed large debts and continually needed Parliament's sanction to raise new monies. He also antagonized Parliament with high-handed ways, including ruling for more than a decade without its approval. Like his father, Charles believed that kings had a God-given right to rule. In 1640, a Scottish invasion of England and the collapse of the royal army forced Charles to summon a new Parliament, one that inherited the cumulative resentments from previous years. The incompetence of the monarchy in the war against Scotland added urgency to the political crisis.

Parliament's Growing Political Power, 1640–1689

Between 1640 and 1642, Parliament constituted itself as a permanent branch of government and dismantled the monarchy's independent fiscal position and many of its institutions, including the court system that sustained the king's power. John Pym, a fiery orator, often led the debates and decisions against the monarchy.

Although political problems precipitated a dynastic crisis, religious issues also drove the political debate in the legislature. Key members of Parliament believed that England should be governed jointly by the king and Parliament. Thus, arbitrary actions by Charles were seen by these Parliamentarians as threatening the tradition of joint rule. From September 1641 to March 1642, Parliament imposed a Presbyterian form of governance on the Church of England, catalogued its view of the errors of Charles from his first days as king, and placed all military appointments under its own approval. These decisive measures split the legislature and helped catalyze a body of royal adherents who pressed Charles for military action against the Parliamentarians.

The English Civil War (1642–1649) broke out, resulting in the monarch's defeat and confirmation of Parliament's dominance. Yet it also brought into being an army of Parliament that was independent of royal control, a force that slowly emerged as the power broker in English politics. The first phase of civil war set the king against Parliament (he lost), and the second pitted Parliament against a few petty provinces (they lost). Charles I was executed, and a republic was declared in 1649, lasting until 1660. Several forms of rule were attempted, but real power remained in the hands of the army and its commanders, especially Oliver Cromwell

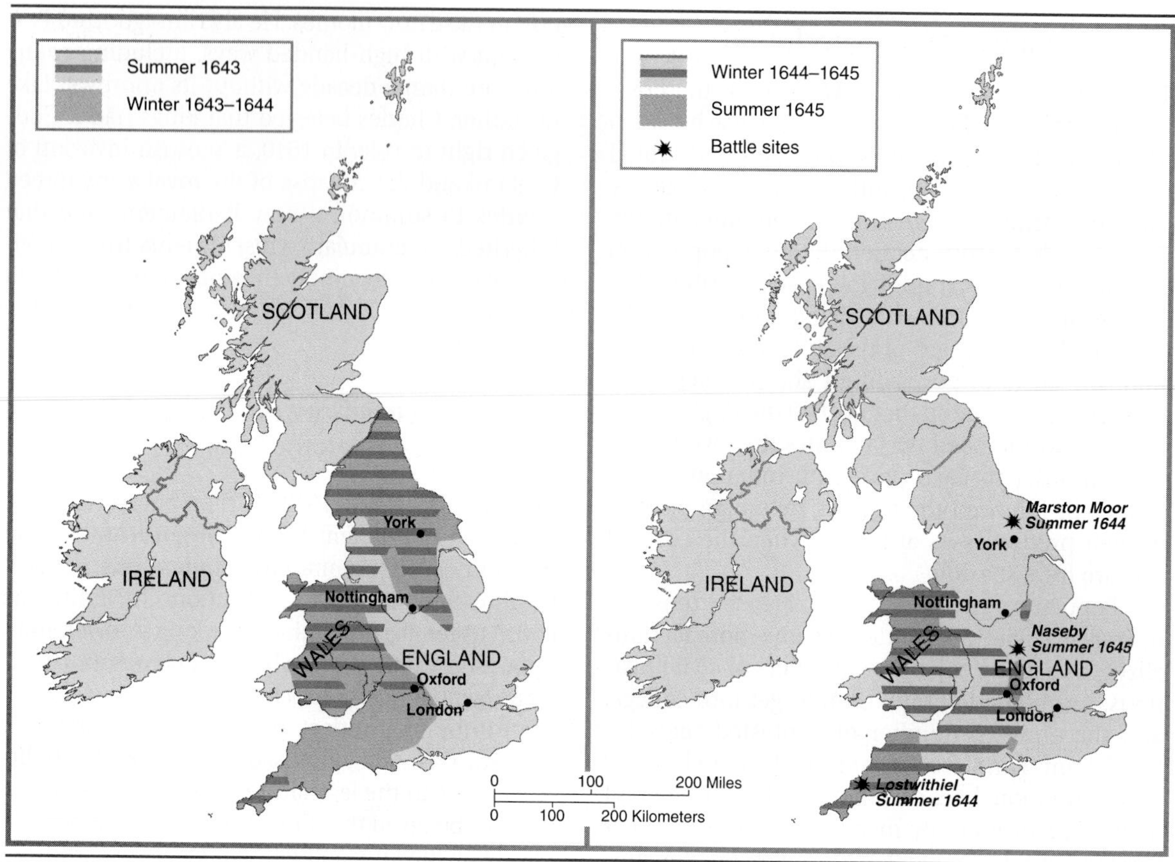

MAP 31.1 ***Royalist and Parliament Areas in the English Civil War, 1643–1645.*** *Eastern areas of England generally supported Parliament while the north and west supported the crown. Gradually the north was conquered by the parliamentary army, and, by early 1645, the areas under royal control had shrunk considerably. London remained in Parliament's hands throughout, depriving the crown of a major urban base and revenues associated with it.*

(1599–1658), who was essentially a dictator between 1653 and 1658. Cromwell tried a form of direct military rule that united most of the elite against him, and after Cromwell's death, members of the political elite began plotting a return of the monarchy.

The English political elite invited Charles II, son of the executed monarch, to rule. A quarter-century of peace commenced, during which James II succeeded his brother as king. Though a converted Catholic, James was viewed as more Anglican in his policies. The birth of a son, who would be raised Roman Catholic, ended the political calm. The English would not tolerate Catholic rule, and James was forced out by the ruling political elite. They turned to James II's Protestant daughter Mary and her Dutch husband, William of Orange. The peaceful change showed that Parliament made and broke monarchs, confirming the success of the political and elite revolution. (Members of Parliament had already been part of England's ruling elite.)

William and Mary became joint rulers of England, but they accepted further limitations on their sovereignty to do so. The Bill of Rights was written, replacing hereditary rights by the will of the nation as expressed through Parliament. The Toleration Act of 1689, which promised freedom of worship to non-Anglican sects, provided guarantees of legal security unprecedented in England. In 1694, Parliament issued the Triennial Act, designed to compel the monarchy to assemble Parliament every three years, and in the next year state censorship was ended. Thus, the English political revolution

FIGURE 31.4 ***William and Mary Being Welcomed to London.*** *Following the fall of James II, Mary and her Dutch husband, William, became the new rulers of England. They were invited to rule partly because they were Protestants and partly because they accepted Parliament's role as a key force in English politics, which helped bring the English Revolution to a successful conclusion.*
Mary Evans Picture Library.

resulted in a joint rule that favored Parliament and paved the way to the evolution of a constitutional monarchy with the king or queen as a figurehead.

THE ENLIGHTENMENT

The **Enlightenment**, a movement of intellectual change that inspired thinkers in Europe and North America, began largely in the eighteenth century. It aimed to emancipate human reason from what it saw as superstition, prejudice, and the assertiveness of established religions by applying rational thought to social and political reforms. Enlightenment thinkers gathered in salons, academies, universities, reading societies, and clubs to discuss and debate ideas like natural rights, laissez-faire economics, and freedom of the individual. In this process, alliances of like-minded people were formed across elite social classes; ultimately, these alliances played major roles in the American and French revolutions.

Some Key Enlightenment Ideas and Practices

Building on Newtonian ideas of natural laws regulating the universe, political thinkers argued that natural law was the universal foundation for all law. Natural law comes from human beings, growing out of their communal living. Such things as respect for property, honoring agreements undertaken, and the obligation to compensate for damage are elements of natural law. John Locke, one English thinker discussed in Chapter 29, used natural law to argue that the state rests on a contract between the ruler and the ruled, with each having duties to carry out to meet the needs of society. In the eighteenth century, thinkers added the idea that people have natural rights as well as duties: the right to ownership of property and freedom of

IN THEIR OWN WORDS

Enlightenment Thinkers Examine Racial Equality

Some Enlightenment thinkers used natural law to argue that all human beings are equal. They encouraged Europeans, especially explorers, to treat other peoples with dignity and respect. The following passages were written by a president of the Royal Society of London and a German naturalist and philosopher, both of whom pleaded for respectful treatment of indigenous peoples.

The president of the Royal Society recommended that members of James Cook's expedition around the world be peaceful.

> It should constantly be borne in mind that to shed the blood of these peoples is a capital crime, for we are dealing with human beings from the hand of the same almighty Creator, and are obliged to care for them as much as for the most polished European, in that they are possibly less warlike and more deserving of God's favor. They are the natural, and in a strict sense, the legal owners of the various territories they inhabit. No European nation has any right to occupy any part of that land or to settle there without their freely given consent. The subjugation of such a people cannot confer any convincing title in law, since they have not acted the part of the aggressor.

Albrecht von Haller, a German naturalist, used natural law to argue that

> Nothing is better calculated to dispel prejudice than an acquaintance with many different nations and their diverse manners, laws, and opinions—a diversity that enables us, however, with little effort to cast aside whatever divides men and to comprehend as the voice of Nature all that they have in common. However uncouth, however primitive the inhabitants of the South Seas islands may be, however remote the Greenlander may be from Brazil or the Cape of Good Hope, the first principles of the law of nature are identical in the case of all nations: to injure no man, to allow every man his due, to seek perfection in one's calling, this was the path to honor with the ancient Romans, and it is . . . the same for . . . the Hottentots [a South African tribe].

Despite these articulate and perceptive arguments for seeing a basic equality among human beings in Early Modern times, most Europeans did not follow this path. They viewed non-Europeans as inferior or even nonhuman and treated them accordingly.

conscience. By midcentury, Charles de Montesquieu[1] argued that the best government worked through a system of checks and balances, with no dominant branch.

Natural law was also used to promote the emancipation of women and ethnic groups, for instance Jews. As seen in Chapter 30, women had begun advocating the right to an education. Poulin de Barre[2] published a work on the equality of the sexes in 1673, and, in the seventeenth century, others began applying natural law to argue for gender equality and rights. Aristocratic women had already been elected to local governments in France, and they played prominent roles in salons. Jews also benefited from the application of natural law to their subordinate status. Works on Jewish political rights were written in 1714 and 1781, and Jews were given full civil rights in British colonies in 1740. In Berlin, Moses Mendelssohn, a Jew, was accepted into a circle of Enlightenment writers, and he soon became a dominant figure.

In both England and France, economists like Adam Smith (1723–1790) applied natural law to economic development. Smith saw the world as a global system and believed that it should become one vast free market that would be self-regulating. Smith asserted that state intervention in economic matters was bad and should be avoided. French economists followed some of Adam Smith's ideas and stressed the importance of agriculture to economic growth. Many of these economic thinkers favored **laissez-faire**—minimal governmental interference in economic development.

[1] **Montesquieu:** mon tehs KYOO

[2] **Poulin de Barre:** POO lahn day BAH ray

The French *Encyclopédie* presented Enlightenment ideas in essay form during the latter half of the eighteenth century. Although more attention will be given to this work in Chapter 32, a few things should be noted here. Denis Diderot became editor of the *Encyclopédie* in 1746, and the first volume of more than thirty came out in 1751. Initially, it was conceived to be a French edition of a British encyclopedia, but Diderot developed a different aim. He secured the best thinkers of his age to write essays on various subjects. Voltaire (1694–1778), perhaps the most brilliant if not the most prolific Enlightenment thinker, wrote essays for the *Encyclopédie,* as did Jean-Jacques Rousseau (1712–1778), who had a significant impact on many leaders of the French Revolution. Rousseau argued that human beings are born free but are held in servitude by despotic states. He advocated government based on the consent of the governed. Jesuits tried to have this encyclopedia banned in France, but they were thwarted by Madame de Pompadour, mistress of the king.

Salons, Academies, and Societies Create Public Opinion

Ideas were important, but they needed to be discussed and widely spread in order to have a significant impact. This happened in Europe and British North America during the eighteenth century in a variety of social groups. By 1789, there were around 150 such societies in Europe alone. Ideas were disseminated even further through journals and correspondence associated with some of these organizations.

Salons appeared in France and were organized by women beginning in late-seventeenth-century Paris. Aristocratic and middle-class women invited men and a few women to have discussions about literature. After the death of Louis XIV in 1715, fundamental issues of politics, society, and economics began to be debated in the salons. Gradually, salons had an impact on the public, as they spread to the provinces as well as to Switzerland and Germany. In Berlin, for example, one popular salon was presided over by Henriette Herz, a Jewish woman.

Academies and royal societies also played a role in disseminating ideas associated with the Enlightenment. France established a society for the cultivation of the French language in 1635 and later added a society for historical studies. The Royal Society of London was founded in 1660, numbering many of Britain's most famous scientists among its members. The Royal Academy of Berlin was founded in 1701 under the auspices of Queen Sophie Charlotte to promote the welfare and reputation of the German nation. The Royal Academy developed a network of correspondents both in Germany and abroad. Many academic societies held meetings at which papers were presented, and they published journals of their proceedings. Books were reviewed in these journals, too. Some others founded more practical societies, like the Dublin Society for the Improvement of Husbandry, Agriculture, and Other Useful Arts.

FIGURE 31.5 *Enlightened Intellectual Discourse.* *This nineteenth-century painting captures the spirit of the Enlightenment by showing Moses Mendelssohn discussing religion with two guests. Mendelssohn, a Jew, was accepted into some gatherings of Enlightenment leaders. This particular scene never occurred, but reflects a challenge presented to him in 1769 to debate the superiority of Judaism over Christianity.* Collection of the Judah L. Magnes Museum, Berkeley.

UNDER THE LENS
The Masons in the Enlightenment

The Masonic Order was one of the significant societies of the Enlightenment. It developed an international organization and a tolerant orientation toward other peoples and groups. Many Masonic lodges welcomed Jews as members. Indeed, a key characteristic of Masonry was equality among members.

Originally, the Masons grew out of craft guilds, especially when artisans were joined by nobles, scientists, and surveyors. Consequently, they had a broad social makeup from the beginning. Masons were committed to spreading ideas, and many of their lodges had libraries. In addition, regular correspondence was carried out among various lodges throughout Europe. In the spirit of the guilds and of the humanitarianism characteristic of the Enlightenment, Masons freely helped members in need of assistance. They nursed sick colleagues, provided burial insurance, and supported those burdened by debts.

Many early lodges were founded in England and spread rapidly across Europe in the 1720s and after. By the late 1730s, a papal decree banned Roman Catholics from being members of the Masons. A second papal decree in 1751 affirmed Catholic opposition to this society of free-thinking people. Many Masons also espoused a religion of nature that was later expressed in a song with the melody attributed to Wolfgang Mozart, himself a Mason.

> Let us, then, all hand in hand be joined!
> In this, our finest festive hour.
> Lead us up to lustrous heights,
> And banish all our earthly cares!
> That union of our brothers may
> Forever firm and splendid stay.
>
> Praise and thanks to God our Master
> Who our minds and all our hearts
> Inspired to join in endless striving
> To bring to earth His Justice, Light, and Virtue
> Through the truth our hallowed weapon
> May this be our godly task!
>
> You upon our planet here,
> The best of men in East and West
> And in North as well as South,
> Speak the truth and practice virtue,
> From the heart love God and man,
> Let this be our watchword still!

These organizations enjoyed success in bettering people's lives, but many people felt that more fundamental change was needed.

Reading societies became common in the latter half of the eighteenth century. These organizations were popular in Germany and France and concentrated on improving the general knowledge of the public. Members wanted to spread Enlightenment ideas through discussions and books; most had lending libraries.

REVOLUTION IN BRITISH NORTH AMERICA, 1776–1789

Like the English Revolution, the revolution in British North America brought a change of government; both were political revolutions. The first phase of this American Revolution was concerned with throwing off British rule, and the second phase dealt with the creation of a political system in the form of a limited republic. Much like the ruling class in England, wealthy landowners in America dominated politics.

Building a National Consciousness

In 1765, thirteen English colonies in North America had little in common, yet by 1776 they expressed a united resolve to declare independence from England. English colonies in what is now Canada remained loyal. Much of this nation-building effort came in response to real or imagined transgressions by England. The essential disagreement between the English and their American colonists centered on the massive debt accrued in securing the colonies from French dominion and the English government's desire to see that the settlers assumed a share of the burden.

The English government, including Parliament and king, passed a series of acts to raise funds. In addition, mercantilism supported the domination of the home country over its colonies. Goods shipped between England and the colonies had to travel on English vessels. European products destined for America first landed in England, and customs duties were collected, increasing their prices. This arrangement allowed England to profit from all trade in its colonies.

Americans found the restrictions unbearable when additional fundraising acts were passed by Parliament in the late 1760s. The colonists' cry soon became "no taxation without representation." They were unrepresented in Parliament and believed that they should not have to pay taxes they had had no say in imposing. American boycotts in response to the early acts disrupted trade, compelling England's merchants to pressure their legislators to repeal the acts. In addition, smuggling became a major and well-respected American enterprise.

One major development in the forging of an American identity was the establishment of committees of correspondence. This uniquely American development had kinship with European societies that had members who regularly corresponded with one another. Samuel Adams (1722–1803) formed an early committee during 1772 in Massachusetts, and, within eighteen months, most colonies had followed suit. These committees were clearinghouses for information about the anti-English effort.

Additional punitive acts by England drove some colonists to summon the First Continental Congress, which met for seven weeks in the late summer and fall of 1774. Delegates spent as much time socializing as debating. This proved invaluable because it helped overcome some intercolonial frictions. The First Continental Congress passed a document spelling out detailed plans to implement a general boycott against English goods. A second Congress met in May 1775 in response to hostilities that had broken out in Massachusetts during the previous month. Colonies sent representatives, who selected George Washington (1732–1799) to lead the combined colonial forces. This action consolidated the military effort because Washington, although not a military genius, possessed a flinty determination and projected a moral force.

The War for Independence, 1776–1783

The American Revolution consisted of two wars, an external war and a civil war. The external war initially involved the Americans and the English, but, in 1778, the French entered on behalf of the Americans, and Spain and Holland joined to avenge themselves on the British for earlier wars. The civil war pitted revolutionaries against loyalists, who represented perhaps 35 percent of the population but a much higher percentage of wealthy people. Conflicts occurred everywhere between the American colonists, but most seemed confined to the southern colonies. The result was

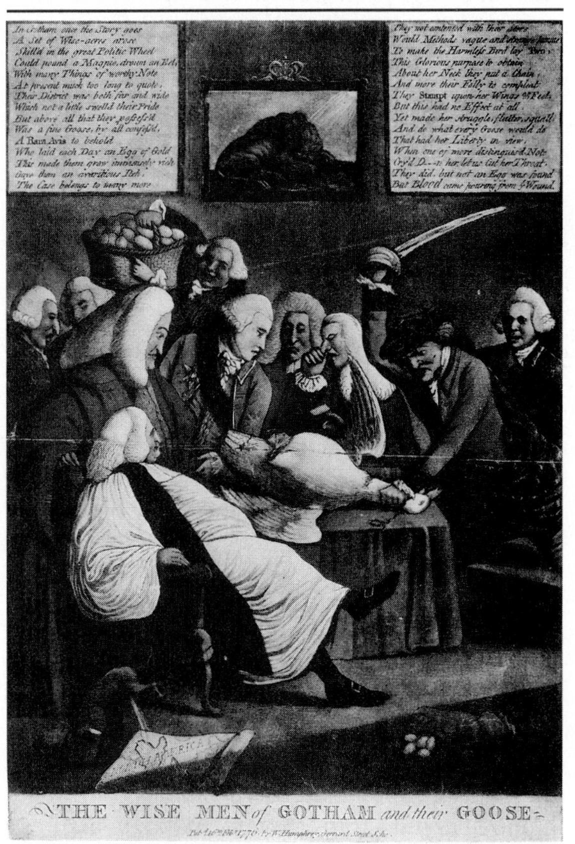

FIGURE 31.6 ***Portrayal of the American Revolution.*** *This British cartoon satirizes the greed of British cabinet officials who kill the goose (the non-Canadian American colonies) in order to get more than one golden egg per day. Some British were sympathetic to the cause of the American colonists.* The John Carter Brown Library, Brown University.

the expulsion of much of the loyalist population; confiscation of their property was one of the primary motivations behind their decision to relocate. This weakened the established social elite, increasing social equality.

Two writings in 1776 united many Americans in the cause of independence. Thomas Paine (1737–1809), an Englishman who recently had arrived from England, wrote *Common Sense,* a pamphlet that succinctly argued for independence. America's first bestseller, it reached a distribution of 120,000 copies. The second piece, the Declaration of Independence, has been called the most important document in American history. Largely written by Thomas Jefferson, it explained the American case for severing ties with England. Arguing from the natural-law philosophy that human beings possessed natural rights to life, liberty, and the pursuit of happiness, Jefferson put the Congress's position into a larger interpretative framework in tune with Enlightenment ideas. He showed how King George III of England violated these natural rights by a series of tyrannous misdeeds. After the Declaration was amended, it was finally adopted on July 4, 1776.

Fighting continued throughout the colonies. From 1775 to 1777, the main task of Washington and other commanders was to maintain armies in the field. With secret French assistance, the American military effort survived. Then, in the summer of 1777, an English campaign to take New York and sever New England from the rest of the separatist colonies failed, enticing the French to support the colonists openly. With the able diplomatic leadership of Benjamin Franklin, the American ambassador to France, the French committed their armed forces to the war.

Washington barely managed to keep his tattered army from disintegrating in the harsh winter of 1777–1778. He enjoyed some victories and suffered defeats in the north, while his colleagues participated in heavy fighting in the south. In 1781, the English commander, Lord Charles Cornwallis, blundered into a trap at Yorktown, Virginia. After a naval blockade by a French fleet and attacks by a combined American and French army, Cornwallis surrendered. Peace negotiations took place from 1782 to 1783, when the Treaty of Paris was signed. Independence was secured in a territory of the original thirteen colonies, including a region west to the Mississippi River, north to the Great Lakes, and south to Florida. The British firmly held on to their more profitable colonies in the Caribbean and India.

Social Aspects of the War for Independence

People of modest means and social position yielded to merchants and landowners in the war and nation-building effort. Men of property dominated the Continental Congresses and assumed leadership of the war effort. Common people assumed a lesser political role, and the mass of women and slaves exercised little influence.

The committees of correspondence and the Continental Congresses included those who could read and write or who enjoyed substantial financial means. Many people were literate, but most depended on others to decipher written materials. Schools remained the preserve of the well-to-do, and widespread education came some decades after the war for independence. Education became a great equalizing force for common folk.

Although the Declaration of Independence included the statement that "all men are created equal," most American leaders believed in the superiority of men and whites. They believed that white males of some property were a superior group. The right to vote, for example, was extended only to those who owned property. Jefferson himself owned slaves for his entire adult life, and many other delegates also had slaves, who did not enjoy liberty and the pursuit of happiness. Earlier, in 1774, the First Continental Congress had called for the abolition of the slave trade, and many states followed its lead. Some northern states either abolished slavery or provided for the gradual emancipation of slaves; Pennsylvania formed the first antislavery society in the Americas in 1775. Because of the need to maintain unity among the colonies, references to the liberation of African Americans were stricken from the final version of the Declaration. American Indians also received no mention in the historic document. Among the various tribes, the Iroquois remained staunchly loyal to the English, while the Algonquians and the Cherokees backed the Americans.

Women, too, did not enjoy equal rights. Abigail Adams chided her husband, John, a drafter of the Declaration, not to forget the women. But the pertinent words "that all men are created equal"

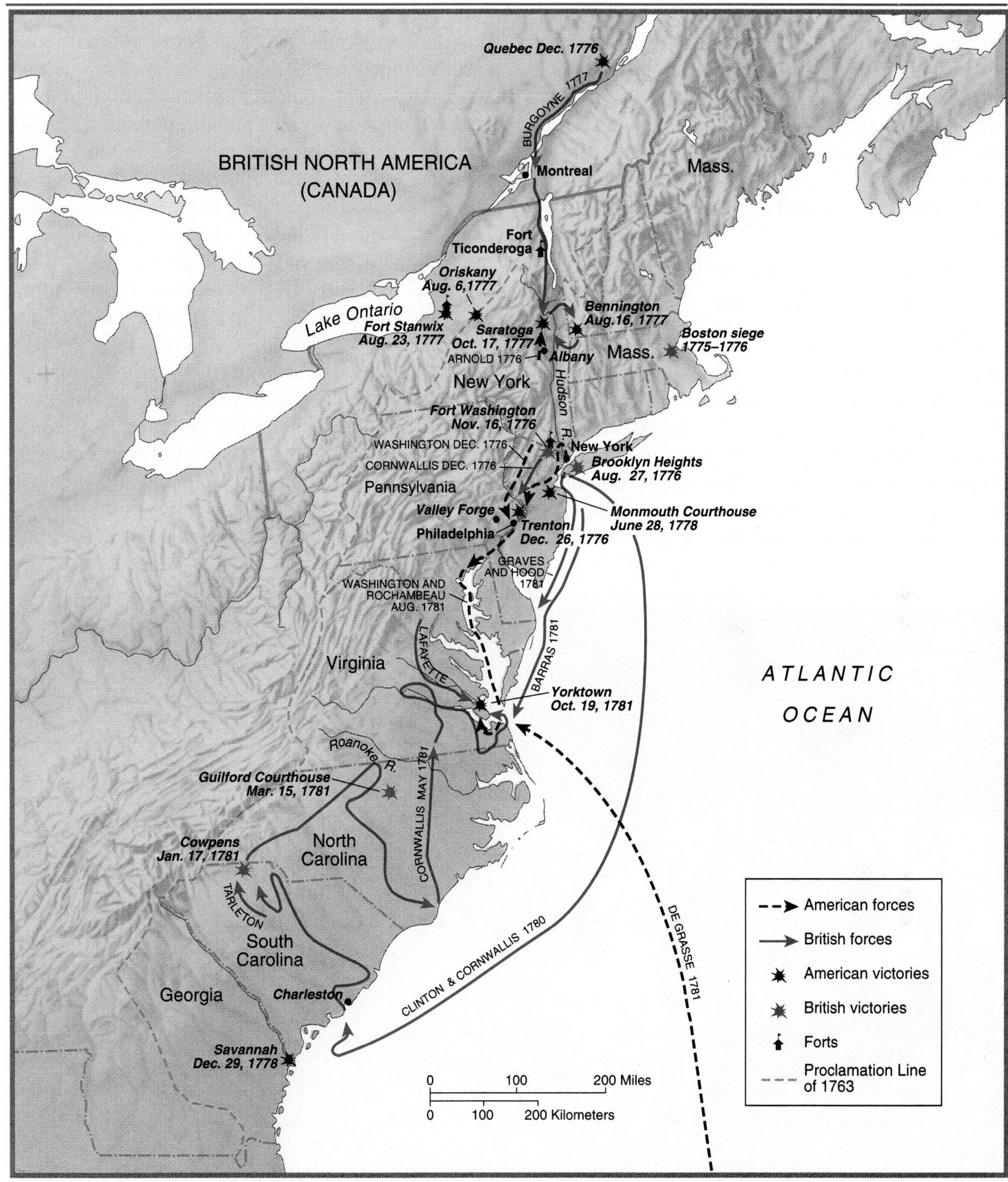

Map 31.2 ***Battles of the American War for Independence, 1776–1781.*** *Many battles were fought in the American colonies, both in the north and south. A key need of the rebels was to keep military forces in the field to avoid defeat. The Battle of Saratoga was especially significant because it thwarted a British effort to sever New England from the other colonies; in addition, France thereafter gave important aid to the rebels. Another campaign of major importance was the taking of Yorktown resulting in the surrender of the British forces there. French ships played a key part in the American victory by preventing the British navy from supporting British land forces.*

suggest that Mrs. Adams's advice was ignored. Women, however, were expected to teach the values of good citizenship to their children. Women played very little role in combat activities, though a few disguised themselves as men and served in the colonial armies. Others made saltpeter for gunpowder, hid soldiers, and supported their families when their husbands were away fighting.

Creating a Constitutional Government, 1783–1789

Winning independence was only the first step in a lengthy process of nation building. The national consciousness that emerged in the early days of the independence struggle dissipated after the war. The framework of government proved to be a troubling issue because the Articles of Confederation adopted by the Second Continental Congress in 1777 failed to gain unanimous approval until 1781. It provided for a congress along with thirteen independent states. Having control of commerce, taxation, and judicial matters, the states remained suspicious of a strong, national system. Problems in the 1780s, including a failed rebellion in Massachusetts, caused men of property to work for a stronger central government. They met in 1786 and persuaded the congress to approve the gathering of a group of delegates elected by the states to amend the Articles of Confederation.

In 1787, fifty-five delegates representing twelve states convened in Philadelphia and for seventeen weeks hammered out a new governmental framework. George Washington, Benjamin Franklin, James Madison, and Alexander Hamilton decided to abandon the old system and create a new one. They fashioned a series of compromises. One body of the legislative branch was the House of Representatives, and its representation was based on population. The other body, the Senate,

FIGURE 31.7 ***George Washington Addressing the Constitutional Convention.*** *In 1787, delegates gathered to improve the existing political system based on the Articles of Confederation—instead, they created the Constitution. George Washington, hero of the War for Independence, was chosen head of the convention. This painting by Junius B. Stearns captures the solemnity of the meeting, which was attended by many of the Republic's leading figures, including James Madison, Alexander Hamilton, and Benjamin Franklin.* Gift of Edgar William and Bernice Chrysler Garbisch. Photo by Ron Jennings © Virginia Museum of Fine Arts, Richmond, Va.

had two representatives per state. Representatives were elected by a direct-voting process; the senators were selected by state legislatures. An executive branch was formed with a president as commander-in-chief of the armed forces. The president also came to power by an indirect election process; voters selected electors (by state), who assembled and voted. A system of checks and balances like the one favored by Montesquieu emerged, so that no one branch could dominate the others. When the new system emerged from secret sessions, it was to take effect after ratification by nine of the thirteen states.

Americans were shocked by the result of this revolutionary process, and it took several months of debate before the Constitution was approved. Supporters of the new system were known as Federalists, those who contested the outcome as anti-Federalists. James Madison, Alexander Hamilton, and John Jay wrote the *Federalist Papers* to convince New Yorkers to support the Constitution, and the essays represented some of the most significant commentaries on the new document. In 1788, after New Hampshire became the ninth state to ratify the document, preparations commenced to implement the new system. Within a year, George Washington assumed the presidency and created the instruments of government, such as the Departments of State, Treasury, and War. The House of Representatives and the Senate convened and passed the Bill of Rights, the first ten amendments to the Constitution, completing the process of forging a government that had begun in 1776.

THE FRENCH REVOLUTION, 1789–1804

Unlike the English and American revolutions, the French Revolution triggered massive violence and more significant social and political change. In 1789, France had been bankrupted by its international diplomacy. This failure coincided with growing unrest, owing to a surge of population growth. Many French thinkers admired the American struggle against England and appreciated the ideas represented in the Declaration of Independence. They longed to create a French government with similar governing ideals and practices.

Global Causes of France's Bankruptcy

Louis XIV created an absolutist state and promoted French colonialism and France's domination of Europe. These policies continued under his two successors but became more difficult to sustain. Apart from the great expenses necessary to support a large army and navy and to build a palace, increasing failure reduced the confidence of the regime's supporters. Some officials who purchased their offices were forced to pay additional sums in order to stay in power, and they became demoralized and angry at the monarchy. Economic bankruptcy and a crisis of confidence undermined the legitimacy of the traditional system.

The determination of French monarchs to rule without much consultation created an atmosphere of social and political tension. The state, for example, used the craft guilds and peasant villages as agents of regulation and control of their members. Yet these bodies inhibited the commercial and agricultural growth necessary to underwrite government programs. Taxes grew, but the taxpayers, especially members of the middle class and rural landowners, refused to pay more until they were brought into the system of governing.

Demographic Problems

Population growth exploded between 1730 and 1789, causing severe problems. Inflation increased because the outmoded agricultural system could not produce enough food to keep prices low enough for the poor. A larger population threatened already fragile food supplies. Rising prices and rents combined with lowering wages to severely pinch the poor in cities and especially in rural areas. Inflation drove up the state's expenses, but agrarian problems kept revenues low. In addition, large numbers of aristocrats and merchants enjoyed tax-exempt status, limiting the state's revenue base.

The immediate economic situation from 1788 to 1789 intensified the regime's crisis. Intermittently poor harvests in the 1770s and 1780s culminated in a disastrous grain harvest in 1788. A glut in the wine grape harvest triggered a collapse of grape prices, ruining many peasants who depended on the wine industry for all their income. The grain shortage increased the price of bread by more than 50 percent between August 1788 and February 1789. This caused sporadic and increasing levels of violence.

Collapse of the Monarchy and Upheaval, 1789–1795

Between 1789 and 1795, France saw the demise of its monarchy and the onset of internal and external war. The antiroyal and antiaristocratic nature of the revolutionary changes caused most major European states to fight France, fearing that such ideas might spread. To fight a broad array of opponents, revolutionaries mobilized nearly all adult males. By 1795, the excesses of terror by both factions had been curbed, and a new time of peace and stability dawned.

In 1788, Louis XVI had been warned that France faced economic bankruptcy if he failed to reform the government, and he had haphazardly groped for a solution to the growing crisis. By the fall of 1788, Louis had called for elections to convene an Estates General, a representative body that had not been summoned in 170 years. The Estates General was composed of three estates. The First Estate included representatives of the clergy and had many factions; it generally agreed that the existing system no longer worked. The Second Estate representatives were aristocrats. A wide range of political opinion could be found in the estate, but most wished for political change. Members of the Third Estate, everyone else in French society, had factions that desired a larger political role and more access to government positions.

Political maneuvering in the fall of 1788 brought to the fore divisions within estates, as well as among estates. Two issues centered on how many members were to represent each estate and whether the voting on issues should be by estate or by representatives. After the judicial court of Paris, a bastion of aristocratic power, ruled that each estate should have equal representation, a loose alliance of members of the three estates argued that the number of Third Estate representatives should equal those of the other two estates. Using ideas discussed in salons, they wished to reconstruct the Estates General into a national assembly. Although the king disagreed with part of the alliance's argument, he doubled the Third Estate's number of representatives.

Elections took place in early 1789 with 326 clergy selected for the First Estate, 330 aristocrats for the Second Estate, and 661 members of the Third Estate. Most of this last group were landowners and lawyers, many of whom were most hostile to the existing government and to elite members of the estates. The political struggle ended with the formation of the National Assembly in June 1789, when members of the three estates agreed to meet as a single body. A feeble monarchical response failed, and the National Assembly emerged.

Elections also stirred up commoners, who began to take matters into their own hands. Parisians stormed the Bastille, a largely abandoned prison, on July 14, 1789, thereafter celebrated as France's independence day. Rumors in the rural areas incited peasants to burn aristocratic manors and kill nobles. This uprising sparked a response in the National Assembly, where on August 4 members of the nobility and clergy renounced their special privileges.

The following year, the National Assembly produced a raft of significant changes. On August 27, 1789, they presented the Declaration of the Rights of Man and the Citizen as a statement of political principles. Among the ideas it expressed, drawn from concepts of natural law, were

—that men were born free and equal in rights;

—that states existed to protect these rights;

—that political sovereignty resided in the nation and its representatives;

—that due process of law and presumption of innocence existed;

—that all had freedom of religion; and

—that property was a sacred and inviolable right.

These Enlightenment ideals became hallmarks of the revolution. As in the American Revolution, women and slaves were not considered free or equal to free men.

In a controversial decision, the National Assembly seized church lands and other property, putting them up for sale. This action raised revenue and created a group of landholders with a stake in the success of the revolution. In the summer of 1790, the National Assembly passed the Civil Constitution of the Clergy, whereby the clergy

Figure 31.8 ***The Tennis Court Oath.*** *Jacques-Louis David became a major figure in the French Revolution through his paintings capturing famous events. Here he shows the heroism exhibited on June 20, 1789, when members of the Third Estate, along with a few members of other estates, vowed to meet as the National Assembly—the legislature of France—in defiance of the king. Most figures are given dramatic poses; some clearly are overcome with emotion.* Musée Carnavalet/Giraudon/Art Resource, N.Y.

served at the government's pleasure and had to swear loyalty to the state. Many clergy opposed these measures and rallied their parishes against the revolutionary government.

A Legislative Assembly, composed entirely of new representatives, met between 1790 and 1792, embroiling France in an external war with Prussia and Austria. Turmoil and fear of invasion propelled many radical leaders to the forefront and undermined the moderates. Maximilien Robespierre (1758–1794), for example, became increasingly influential among the lower middle classes. Robespierre headed an organization of **Jacobins**, individuals who wanted the broadest male voting franchise, abolition of the monarchy, and price controls. Jacobin clubs followed a social pattern of the Enlightenment and evolved into a political movement.

The National Convention succeeded the Legislative Assembly in 1792 as the war worsened. The extension of the vote to most adult Frenchmen meant that the well-organized Jacobins elected many delegates. After Louis's failed effort to flee France in mid-1791, he was regarded as an enemy of the revolutionary government. He was eventually tried and convicted of treason. Louis XVI was executed in 1793, and his queen, Marie Antoinette, followed some months later.

Growing civil unrest and a poorly fought external war caused the National Convention to create a highly centralized government with much power resting in the Committee of Public Safety. This body of the National Convention instituted a national draft, implemented a merit system of military promotion, organized the supply of the army, implemented wage and price controls, and launched a reign of terror.

Terror, the deliberate use of massive force to cow or eliminate opponents, was used by revolutionists and antirevolutionists alike. It grew out of Rousseau's ideas of the general will of the people dominating the lives of individuals as well as from the French political practice of indivisible sovereignty (absolutism). Most absolutist governments had used terror to maintain control of the people. Because French absolutism had been toppled by the revolution and the revolutionaries had taken a doctrinaire political stand, control became important. In the face of the failure of state institutions to compel compliance with laws and decrees, revolutionaries resorted to terror. Fear helped discipline the army of draftees, intimidated many of the state's enemies, and furthered state control over rebellious regions. One area of western France launched a fierce resistance to the new order and suffered brutal atrocities at the hands of the revolutionaries.

In the face of terror, some people adopted grotesque forms of behavior in attempts to defuse the devastating psychological impact. A few donned human-skin clothing. A popular dance form included a peculiar drop of the head that mimicked a head falling from the guillotine. Some wore red bands around their necks, symbolizing cut throats.

In the summer of 1794, the crises had been surmounted, and the Committee of Public Safety ruled with power undreamed of a few years before. Robespierre gained power through purges sanctioned by the National Convention, but his frequent reprisals created enemies. In late July, he was voted out of office. He fell prey to the very policies he had championed and died by the guillotine after bungling a suicide attempt. The tide turned against the Jacobins and their supporters, some of whom were executed, exiled, or forced into hiding.

The revolution had fundamentally altered the political structure of France. The monarchy was abolished, feudalism was swept away, and the aristocracy was shattered; decision making resided with the people, the clergy lost their powerful political and social positions, and obstacles to central power had been swept aside.

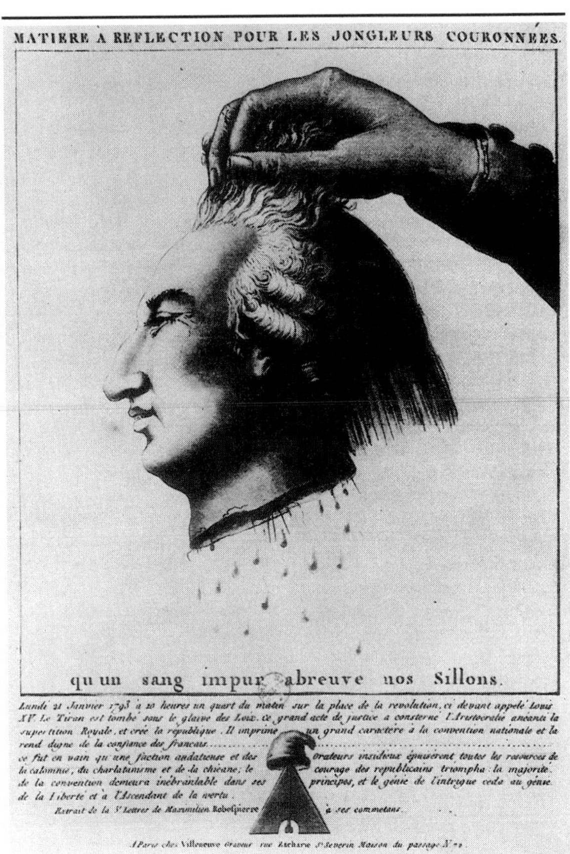

FIGURE 31.9 ***The Fate of King Louis XVI.*** *In this political cartoon, the severed head of France's former ruler is displayed over an inscription that carries a warning to the other monarchs of Europe—beware of the French example. At the bottom is an extract from a letter by Maximilien Robespierre to his constituents, saying that the execution proves the resolution of the French government and its worthiness to have the respect of the people.* Bibliothèque nationale, Paris.

Social Features of the Early Revolution

The opening stage of the revolution (1789–1795) brought many social changes and experiments, some of which endured. Revolutionaries followed Enlightenment ideas of reorganizing and of secularizing society. Another social consequence was the diminishment of the status of women. Finally, greater social equality among men emerged during the early revolution.

One rational innovation concerned time. The radical leaders of 1792–1794 decided to change the French calendar to show the newness of their sociopolitical experiment. They redesignated 1793 as the year 1 and renamed each of the months. The month of July, for example, was renamed Thermidore. Controlling one's reckoning of time was a powerful way to demonstrate dominance by the state. It also decisively broke with the traditional Christian numeration of years. This particular experiment did not endure and was abandoned later.

Another rational transformation concerned weights and measurements. The basis for the new system was the number ten; this was the decimal system. The meter became the standard linear measure, the liter became the standard volume measure, and the gram became the standard weight measure. This change facilitated trade because amounts and values could be easily and speedily calculated. Most of the world today uses the metric system.

Women suffered a loss of influence relative to that which they had enjoyed for decades. As early as the sixteenth and seventeenth centuries, some aristocratic women who owned property had been elected to provincial assemblies. And we have seen how some women of the aristocracy and middle class played a key role in leading salon discussions that developed French public opinion favorable to Enlightenment ideas. Jacobins and more radical revolutionaries believed with Rousseau that the eighteenth century was tainted by a "feminization" of society. A few feminists were executed by guillotine or publicly whipped as a warning to others. Women were forbidden to gather in groups of five or more, and they were banned from sitting in the galleries of the National Convention. Thus, the revolutionaries systematically drove women out of politics and back into the home to care for the young, educating their sons to be patriotic citizens.

The Directory, 1795–1799

The National Convention was transformed into a mixed government with two legislative houses and an executive branch that was elected from the upper house. The electorate was sharply reduced to around 20 percent of adult males. From 1795 to 1799, the **Directory**, a group of five men who ran the executive branch, ruled France in conjunction with the legislature. The policies of the new government favored the survivors of the elite groups; they also cut off the needy from state subsidies.

Challenges troubled the new regime, but the real threat turned out to be the army and one of its generals, Napoleon Bonaparte (1769–1821). By the end of two years in power, Directory members and local officials had become corrupt and ineffective. Finally, a coup by Napoleon toppled the Directory in November 1799.

Napoleon Bonaparte Builds a Modern State, 1799–1804

Napoleon rose to power and ruled ably until his fall in 1815. He came from Corsica and entered the French military as a teenager. By choosing artillery as a military career and by outstanding service, he became a general by his mid-twenties. The high number of battlefield deaths and desertions among officers opened the way for the rapid advancement of Napoleon and others. His alignment with the Jacobins aided his career, until their fall in the summer of 1794. Loyalty to the Directors in 1795 brought Napoleon command of the French army in Italy, where he brilliantly distinguished himself as a strategist. A campaign in Egypt in 1798, however, failed miserably and Napoleon abandoned his army in the Egyptian desert. Nevertheless, he was given a hero's welcome when he arrived back in France.

After the coup that brought him to power in 1799, Napoleon embarked on a program of stabilizing France by creating a centralized state and fashioning a hierarchical system whose officials were appointed from Paris. Bureaucrats enjoyed generous salaries and lofty status as representatives of the government in the administrative districts. Forty percent of Napoleonic high officials had been nobles under the former monarchy. Reenfranchising the aristocracy that had worked against previous regimes lent stability to the new government. A more efficient tax levy and collection system, coupled with a central bank, created a stable currency. The Code of Napoleon, a law code, fashioned a law-based government that accorded personal liberty, equality before the law, and the protection of property. It also codified the subordination of women to men. In 1802, an agreement with the pope provided for the preeminence of Roman Catholicism in France, but it insisted on state rather than papal control of the clergy. Napoleon also created a new social hierarchy based on state service. Officials were to be trained in schools, and top officials were permitted to enter the nobility. Nearly 60 percent of those who attained noble status were from the middle class, while 20 percent of the new nobles came from the lower class. To keep dissent under control, the state enforced censorship and built an effective police force.

Napoleon capped his achievements in 1804 by crowning himself emperor of France, launching a military campaign to control Europe. Despite several victories, Napoleon met major defeats in Spain, Russia, and Belgium. More than 500,000 soldiers from Napoleon's army perished in Russia alone. By 1815, Napoleon had consolidated the French Revolution, building a modern state in the process. The French Revolution was a social revolution with strong populist (early) and elite (late) elements.

FIGURE 31.10 ***Napoleon on His Throne.*** *This portrait captures the majesty of Napoleon Bonaparte, ruler of France, in full imperial regalia. As shown, he conveys a sense of power of person. The icy stare and smooth facial features seem more like sculpture than human flesh. Before the throne is an eagle—the "emperor" of the skies and symbol of Napoleon.* Musée de l'Armée/Laurie Platt Winfrey, Inc.

REVOLUTION IN LATIN AMERICA, 1810–1824

The Napoleonic Wars indirectly affected Latin America when Napoleon ousted the Spanish and Portuguese monarchs and placed his own brothers on their thrones. These actions by the French emperor sparked the **Creoles**, the Spanish elite in Central America and South America, to fight for independence. African slaves in the French colony of Haiti also revolted and successfully established an independent government. By 1824, nearly all of Latin America lay in the hands of independent governments that ranged from republics to monarchies.

Liberation Wars

Anger against Spanish mercantilism and other colonial policies had been building among the local elite during the late eighteenth and early nineteenth centuries (see Chapter 24). Spanish control of the Latin American colonies created an environment of trade that benefited Spain rather than the colonies. This caused resentment among the Creoles, much as similar policies had angered North American colonists. The local elite also resented the Spanish reliance on officials sent from Spain. These officials, considered interlopers from the local point of view, quickly monopolized many top positions that had formerly been filled by locals.

Ideas from the Enlightenment filtered into Latin America and encouraged the restive members of the elite to seek redress by self-rule. Only when Napoleon's brother sat on the throne of Spain did the Creoles act.

Two key leaders in South America, Simón Bolivár[3] (1783–1830) and José de San Martín[4] (1778–1850), spearheaded independence drives. Bolivár spent most of his time in Venezuela and Colombia fighting against the Spanish royalists and occasionally against rebellious slaves who wished to be liberated. Between 1810 and 1824, the effort experienced ups and downs, and opponents ousted Bolivár's government. Bolivár also conquered Colombia and additional lands later called Bolivia (named after Bolivár) by 1824. Unlike Bolivár, who favored republican government, San Martín leaned toward monarchy. San Martín began his campaign by liberating what came to be Argentina, and in 1817, his army crossed the Andes Mountains to help liberate Chile. San Martín moved northward and conquered Peru, over which he established a protectorate. By 1822, the joint forces of Bolivár and San Martín freed Ecuador, although the two leaders bitterly quarreled over what form of government to implement.

Generally, members of the social and economic elite favored a government akin to that found in contemporary England. These conservatives feared sharing power with the slaves and the few members of the middle class, so little changed politically. Soon, however, most Latin American governments abolished slavery or promised to do so in the near future.

FIGURE 31.11 ***Simón Bolivár.*** *Simón Bolivár helped to liberate many South American countries. In this painting, his uniform and his tight control of the horse clearly convey a sense of command.* Courtesy of the Organization of American States.

Brazilian and Mexican Independence

Brazil followed a different path. During the upheaval of the post-Napoleonic era, an uprising drove the Portuguese monarch from Portugal to Brazil. Because the Brazilian elite had few resentments against the monarchy, they preferred to retain a king until late in the nineteenth century. Only then did the elite topple the monarchy and implement a republic with themselves in power. In addition, because many members of the elite had plantations, slavery endured in Brazil.

Mexico saw a few abortive efforts to gain independence. The first attempts involved an uprising led by two priests. One was a Creole, Father Miguel Hidalgo y Costilla,[5] and the other was a *mestizo* (of mixed Spanish and Native American blood), Father José María Morelos y Pavón.[6] They fomented social as well as political unrest from 1811 to 1815, when the royalists and local elites finally crushed the revolutionary force of African slaves, Indians, and *mestizos*. This victorious alliance sup-

[3] **Simón Bolivár:** see MOHN BOH lee vahr

[4] **José de San Martín:** HOH zay day sahn mahr TEEN

[5] **Miguel Hidalgo y Costilla:** mee GEHL ee DAHL goh ee coh STEE yah

[6] **Pavón:** pah VOHN

MAP 31.3 ***Revolution in Latin America, 1804–1825.*** *Liberation in Latin America often came through military conquest. The Haitian Revolution began with a slave uprising against France, followed by a war of resistance. Argentina and Paraguay were liberated a few years later. Other states appeared in the aftermath of the Napoleonic wars which weakened Spain and gave hope to Latin Americans. Chile, Colombia, Peru, and Bolivia all fell to invading forces. By 1825, most of Latin America had become independent.*

ported the Spanish government until a monarch who favored the establishment of representative institutions ascended to the Spanish throne. Fearing a diminution of their political and social power, the elite supported a former royalist commander, Agustin de Iturbide,[7] who declared and won independence for Mexico. Although Iturbide formed a short-lived monarchy, rule by the social and political elite continued and dominated Mexico and much of Central America.

Thus, the revolutions in Latin America were political revolutions with an elite character. The exception was the populist social revolution in Haiti. Like the U.S. and English revolutions, most Latin American revolutions changed the political system and little else.

JAPAN'S MEIJI REVOLUTION, 1868–1895

Like Peter the Great of Russia, a group of Japanese *samurai* (warriors) forged an elite revolution. They transformed their political, social, economic, and cultural systems far more profoundly than did the revolutions in Europe and the Americas. The Japanese case involved more of a group effort,

[7] **Agustin de Iturbide:** ah GUS tyn dee ee TUHR bee deh

PARALLELS AND DIVERGENCES

China's Taiping Uprising (1850–1864): An Abortive Revolution

History's largest uprising convulsed China in the mid-1800s, forcing the gentry elite to mobilize all of its resources to defeat the revolutionaries. Whole sections of populous Central China were devastated by the titanic conflict, and one scholar estimated that more than 20 million Chinese perished.

The Taiping Uprising grew out of the teachings of Hong Xiuquan[a] (1814–1864), who believed he was the younger brother of Jesus Christ. Hong took and failed the imperial examinations five times. After his fourth failure, Hong had a nervous breakdown and became catatonic for forty days. Later, he interpreted the event as his being taken to heaven, meeting God, and being introduced to Jesus, his older brother. According to Hong, God gave him a sword and told him to exterminate the "demons," the Manchu rulers of China.

Hong formed the God-Worshipers Society and gathered poor people by promising them a kind of heaven on earth. Hong's ideas contained a crude mixture of Christian beliefs and traditional Chinese thought. The combustible combination exploded across southern and central China during a time of massive population growth that overwhelmed the traditional social system. Hong created a shared-property system and smashed Buddhist and Confucian temples, deeply angering the gentry.

Women were elevated in social standing in the Taiping movement. In contrast to traditional Chinese practices, they could own property, hold office, take exams, choose their own husbands, and fight. A Taiping female army marched with the main force, numbering perhaps 100,000 and obeying female officers.

The Taiping rulers decreed abstinence from tobacco, alcohol, drugs, and gambling. The Taipings also decreed gender separation for all but the leaders for the new government's first several years. The policy seems directed at protecting women from rapacious men, but it also may have aimed at breaking up the family, because husbands could not even visit their wives. The Taipings wanted the complete energy and loyalty of their followers.

The Taipings moved north and picked up strength in the populated areas of Central China. Major cities, including Nanjing, China's second most important city, fell to them. Control of a prosperous area corrupted the Taipings, who lost their revolutionary momentum. In 1851, the Manchu rulers of the Qing Empire mobilized armies against the Taipings, eventually crushing them. The Taiping effort drowned in a sea of blood, and the minor changes it wrought soon disappeared.

[a]**Hong Xiuquan:** HOHNG SHOO choo wahn

reflecting the longstanding Japanese cultural value of consensus. Finally, the Japanese fashioned a modern, Western-style state, one that was highly centralized.

The Western Model

Japanese *samurai* had ruled Japan since the twelfth century, and a group of them continued to dominate the political system until the early twentieth century. The desire to overthrow the Tokugawa Shogunate in 1868 arose in four disaffected regions, Satsuma, Tosa, Choshu, and Hizen.[8] The effort involved a group of lower-class *samurai* who had risen to prominence by their ability rather than by birth. This clique determined that the existing, discredited shogunal government needed to be thrown out and replaced by an imperial one. Both institutions had existed in the Tokugawa era, but emperors had been powerless. These *samurai* dissolved the shogunate and shifted power to the monarchy. The teenage Emperor Meiji[9] (reign dates 1867–1912) merely sat on the throne, while power transferred to the lower *samurai* and their court allies. Rule from behind the scenes had been a traditional feature of Japanese politics.

[8]**Hizen:** HEE zehn

[9]**Meiji:** MEH jee

FIGURE 31.12 ***Japanese Leaders Going Abroad.*** *This image reflects the determination of Japan's leaders to learn about the world. Between 1871 and 1873, over 100 Japanese leaders and students traveled the globe, especially the West. They brought goodwill and the hope of revising unfavorable treaties imposed on Japan by Western states. Despite their failure to win equal diplomatic status, the Japanese learned much about other countries, giving them a basis on which to Westernize their own. The dress of the people mixes traditional Japanese styles with Western attire, capturing the old-new dichotomy of mid-nineteenth-century Japan.*
ET Archive.

The new rulers embarked on a program of Westernization and industrialization aimed at strengthening Japan in the briefest possible time. Within the Charter Oath, a statement of principles of the new government, lay sentiments favoring studying the West and building a representative government. Behind these was the pragmatic realization that unless Japan strengthened itself, it might perish in conquest by Westerners. Another compelling force was a nationalism fed by the sense that tiny Japan lay as a mouth-watering prize to be gobbled up by Western powers. As the rulers saw it, only an imperial government that commanded the people's loyalty could accomplish societal transformation.

After abolishing the decentralized regional governments and fashioning a highly centralized polity in Tokyo, many top leaders left Japan from 1871 to 1873 on a grand diplomatic and learning tour of the West. Soon the government established new administrative areas and appointed officials answerable only to the central government to administer them. Then, about fifty top leaders departed Japan on a diplomatic mission whose purpose included the revision of a series of unequal treaties imposed on Japan by various Western powers. The diplomatic effort failed, but the leaders learned some reasons for the economic and political dominance of the Western countries. The Japanese visited factories, legislatures, shipyards, and museums, and when they returned they committed Japan to a rapid, elite-directed transformation. This mission closely resembled that of Peter the Great in 1697 and 1698.

Social and Cultural Changes

One of the most remarkable transformations involved society. For the previous two centuries or more, one's occupation was frozen and became the determinant of one's social position. At the top, for instance, the *samurai* ruled, while at the bottom, the merchants languished. Believing that this system inhibited the development of one's individual talent, the Meiji leaders abolished this caste system. By that action, they overturned the elite status of their own *samurai* group. All people, henceforth, had to exert their own energy to succeed, and adventuresome people could flourish in business, education, and the military.

Government leaders also created a system of universal education that built on the already high literacy rates of around 40 percent for males and around 10 percent for females. The education system welcomed students of both genders and provided for a trained population to undertake the tasks necessary for building a modern Japan.

Japanese culture underwent similar dramatic changes as a small group of government officials and private people ardently promoted Western

EUROPE	AMERICAS	JAPAN	Date	Events
			1500	
Scientific Revolution, 1543–1727				Copernicus dies, 1543
Enlightenment, c. 1600–c. 1780			1600	
English Revolution, 1640–1689				Galileo dies, 1642
				Charles I executed, 1649
				Newton publishes *Principia Mathematica*, 1689
			1700	
	American Revolution, 1776–1789			Adam Smith publishes *The Wealth of Nations*, 1776
French Revolution, 1789–1804				George Washington becomes president, 1789
			1800	Concordat with Rome, 1801
	Revolutions in Latin America, 1810–1824			San Martín helps liberate Chile, 1817
		Meiji Revolution, 1868–1895		Iwakura embassy departs Japan, 1871
				Japan wins Sino-Japanese War, 1895
			1900	

culture. Fukuzawa Yukichi[10] (1835–1901), a Japanese intellectual, traveled to Western lands and wrote a series of bestselling pamphlets and books. Indeed, he introduced whole generations of Japanese to Western ideas. The Society of Meiji Six (1873) included a mix of governmental and private individuals who met regularly and who popularized Western ideas. Translation of Western authors became a major occupation, and *Self Help*, an English work written by Samuel Smiles, sold around one million copies. Traditional Japanese works and practices experienced a temporary eclipse in the frenetic drive to Westernize.

Building a Modern State

The elite revolution unsettled many and sparked challenges to the new order. Assassination claimed a number of officials who had guided the Meiji transformation from 1873 to 1878. Planned revolts caused additional disturbances, and the most serious effort centered in Satsuma, one of the leading Meiji strongholds. Saigo Takamori[11] (1833–1877), a mighty Satsuma warrior who had led the imperial forces in 1868, became disaffected with government policy in 1873 and left politics. As the *samurai* suffered a series of blows that deprived them of elite identity, many rallied around Saigo. By 1877, the Satsuma Uprising erupted and was defeated by the new imperial army of peasant conscripts. The counterrevolutionary uprising failed.

In 1881, government leaders decided to create a constitutional system, modeled on the German Empire, and Ito Hirobumi[12] crafted a document that would keep power in the hands of the ruling elite. About the same time, outdated Japanese legal codes were rewritten to fashion a law-based society, again patterned after that of the Germans. The new system took effect in the 1890s, and a series of political struggles between the Meiji rulers and leaders of political parties erupted. The latter successfully inserted themselves into the ruling structure, proving the viability of the Western-style polity.

The Japanese industrial effort (see Chapter 32) provided an increasingly powerful armed force. One test of the Japanese achievement came in the Sino-Japanese War (1894–1895), in which the Japanese military simply overwhelmed the Chinese. And around a decade later, the Japanese military defeated the Russians in the Russo-Japanese War (1904–1905). These victories seemed to confirm the Japanese way of revolution and began the building of a colonial empire. Japan's social revolution transformed all aspects of Japanese life and was led by the *samurai* elite.

SUMMARY

1. Revolution is a process whereby fundamental structural change occurs. Occasionally a nonviolent transformation, like the Scientific Revolution, takes place, but most revolutions are violent. Types of revolution include political, economic, intellectual, and social. Another way to analyze revolution is to determine the character of the revolutionary leadership. Thus, there are elite and populist (mass-based) revolutions. Rebellions may involve widespread violence, but they differ from revolutions in that the rebels seek to change leaders rather than structures.

2. The English Revolution transformed the government by elevating Parliament and deemphasizing the monarchy through civil war and political upheaval, including the execution of King Charles I.

3. The Enlightenment was an eighteenth-century intellectual and social movement that stressed the use of reason to expose and reform presumedly outmoded political, social, and religious practices. Enlightenment ideas were spread through salons, academies, and associations in the development of public opinion.

4. The American Revolution involved the winning of independence from England and the building of a centralized republican government. This revolution was dominated by landowners and merchants.

[10] **Fukuzawa Yukichi:** FOO koo zah wah yoo KEE chee
[11] **Saigo Takamori:** SY goh TAH kah moh ree
[12] **Ito Hirobumi:** EE toh HEE roh boo mee

5. The French Revolution emerged from the collapse of the enfeebled autocracy and swept away feudalism. Various revolutionary governments were installed until the modern state was founded by Napoleon Bonaparte between 1799 and 1804.

6. Latin America had a series of political revolutions whereby the propertied elite groups wrested power from the home countries and created polities that they themselves dominated. Uprisings by lower social groups were crushed. The exception was Haiti, where slaves won their independence from France and built a revolutionary order. It was a social and populist revolution.

7. Japan used an elite revolution to modernize and Westernize itself. Fundamental changes took place in society, elite culture, and politics.

SUGGESTED READINGS

Goldstone, Jack. *Revolution and Rebellion in the Early Modern World.* Berkeley: University of California Press, 1991. A fruitful synthesis of revolutionary studies in a comparative framework, emphasizing the importance of demographic growth.

Im Hof, Ulrich. *The Enlightenment.* Oxford, Eng.: Blackwood Publishers, 1994. A work stressing the Enlightenment's social context and institutions.

Keddie, Nikki, ed. *Debating Revolutions.* New York: New York University Press, 1995. A series of discussions and debates about studies of revolution.

Morgan, Kenneth, ed. *The Oxford History of Britain.* Oxford, Eng.: Oxford University Press, 1988. Essays on various periods of English history.

Spence, Jonathan. *God's Chinese Son.* New York: Norton, 1996. A recent study of the Taiping Uprising.

Stone, Bailey. *The Genesis of the French Revolution.* Cambridge, Eng.: Cambridge University Press, 1994. An analysis of the breakdown of French absolutism in terms of its failure to compete globally in colonial and economic terms.

Tilly, Charles. *European Revolutions, 1492–1992.* Oxford, Eng.: Blackwell Publishers, 1993. A recent examination of revolutions in the past five centuries.

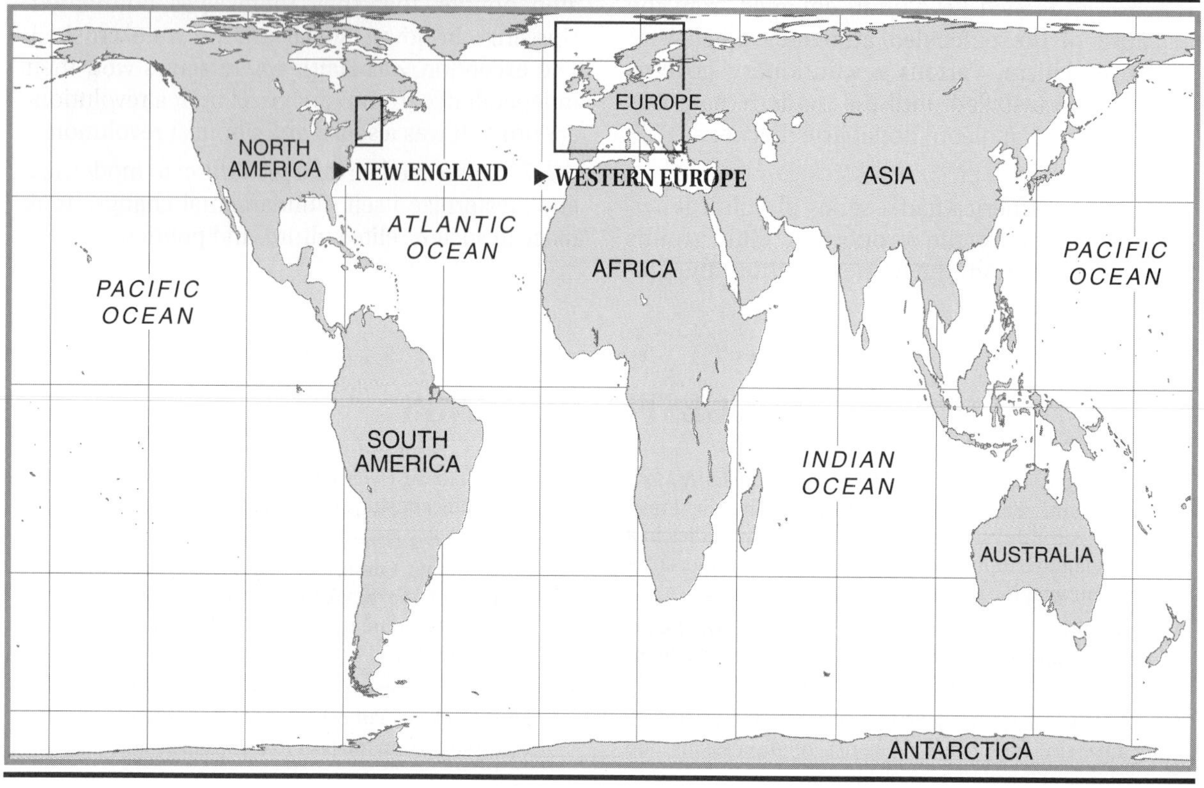

NORTH AMERICA
▶ NEW ENGLAND
EUROPE
▶ WESTERN EUROPE
ASIA
ATLANTIC OCEAN
PACIFIC OCEAN
AFRICA
PACIFIC OCEAN
SOUTH AMERICA
INDIAN OCEAN
AUSTRALIA
ANTARCTICA

Manchester, N.H.
Lowell, Mass.
Salem, Mass.
Pawtucket, R.I.
ATLANTIC OCEAN

▶ NEW ENGLAND

SCOTLAND
North Sea
ENGLAND
ATLANTIC OCEAN
FRANCE

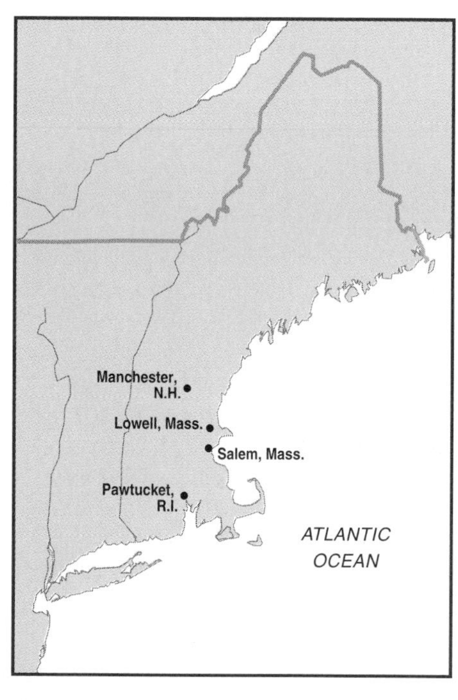

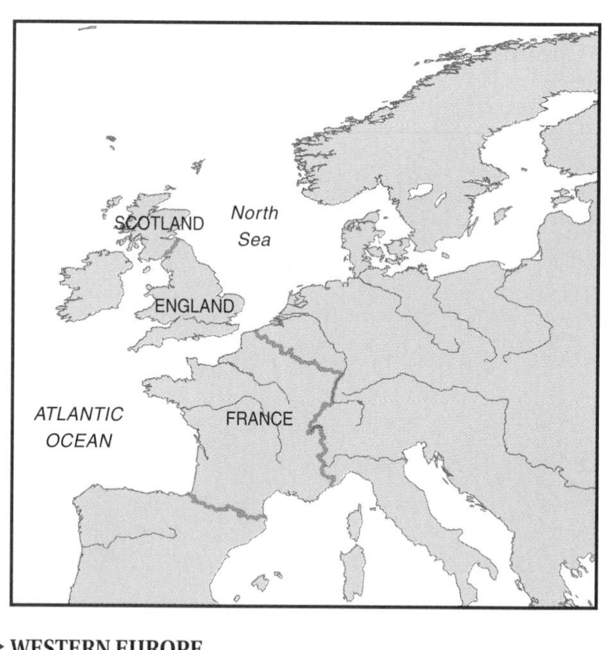

▶ WESTERN EUROPE

CHAPTER 32

The Global Industrial Revolution

around 1770–1905

In the summer of 1852, a young Mexican man began his job as a textile weaver in a crowded cloth factory outside Mexico City. Late that same summer, when water levels were at their annual lowest, a Polish farmer built a modest dam and a water-powered mill on his property; he began grinding grain and sawing lumber for his neighbors the following fall. Also in that summer, a teenage Irish woman moved to the tenements around the shoe factories of Salem, Massachusetts, and began her new job sewing soles to shoes.

Each of these lives was being transformed by a process set in motion in the eighteenth century: the Industrial Revolution. Prior to the mid-eighteenth century, goods in Europe were produced primarily by independent craftspeople. The businesses they ran, collectively termed **cottage crafts**, operated on a very small scale, used simple technology, usually employed family members for labor, and, as the phrase suggests, typically were located in the home. The vast majority of people were farmers, and the craft and service sectors composed less than 5 percent of the population. The material holdings of most people were few by today's standards, but this mode of production was able to supply society's needs.

In the mid–eighteenth century, however, Europe was on the verge of a change comparable in significance to the massive societal changes that the development of agriculture had caused. The **Industrial Revolution**, the shift to the manufacture of most goods in mechanized factories, and the changes that came in the wake of this shift, originated in England. There, around 1770, factories with large workforces of hired laborers began springing up. These factories used machines to produce far larger quantities of goods than had the earlier cottage crafts, and the wage earners employed in the factories formed part of the market that purchased these goods.

From England, the Industrial Revolution spread to western Europe and North America by the early decades of the nineteenth century. Once industry was established in a new region, it evolved along its own distinctive lines. Wages remained low in English industry, for example, while they were relatively high in the United States. Despite such differences, the Industrial Revolution had commonalities wherever it occurred.

Certainly the Industrial Revolution had roots in earlier times and was not an overnight phenomenon, but the pace of change was remarkably rapid. By 1830 or shortly thereafter, the core areas of England, western Europe, and northeastern North America had been transformed into industrial powers. Industrialization since has spread beyond these core areas, particularly to Japan and Russia.

In the core areas, the Industrial Revolution had two phases. In the first phase, lasting until about 1830, light industry dominated; textiles, shoes, and similar commodities were manufactured and sold to mass markets of consumers. While each item sold produced only a small profit, the numbers of items sold were large. In the second phase, beginning around 1830, heavy industry became important, particularly the manufacture of railroad engines, vehicles, and tracks. In part stimulated by the need to transport the products of light industry, the second phase of the Industrial Revolution shifted some of the industrial focus to expensive items that would be sold in smaller numbers. Because those large items were made mostly of steel, the expansion of the steel industry was part of the second phase. The development of the petroleum industry to fuel railroad and other vehicles also developed in the second phase.

The temptation is to see the Industrial Revolution as purely a technological development, but that temptation must be resisted. While it is true that mechanical inventions made industrialization practical, they were not really at the root of the process. Rather, intellectual and legal developments paved the way for the Industrial Revolution, while the crucial innovations were driven by economic and demographic factors. Mechanical inventions are best seen as improvements that helped the Industrial Revolution succeed, not its fundamental causes. The factories and mill towns are physical monuments to the changes that the Industrial Revolution brought, but the greatest changes were in organization, not hardware.

THE INTELLECTUAL AND LEGAL UNDERPINNINGS OF THE INDUSTRIAL REVOLUTION

Revolutions, especially economic and social ones like the Industrial Revolution, are processes, not events, and they unfold over time. Though the Industrial Revolution progressed rapidly once begun, it was preceded by several decades during which conditions gradually evolved to set the stage for the more dramatic developments that followed. Intellectual and legal developments in the core areas were critical in preparing the way for the Industrial Revolution.

Encyclopedias

Today's encyclopedias are rather bland affairs, with usually inoffensive descriptions and discussion. Early European encyclopedias, however, were politically charged and controversial, and they strongly promoted the Enlightenment ideas that were one of the driving forces of the Industrial Revolution. The Eurasian tradition of encyclopedias, discussed in Chapter 28, took root relatively late in Europe.

The first of the politically charged European encyclopedias was written by John Harris and published in 1704; it was followed in 1728 by one written by Ephraim Chambers. Both included some caustic social commentary but emphasized technical activities: how to blow a glass bottle, how to construct a cottage, how to bind a book. These early works profoundly influenced the editor of what was to be the most influential encyclopedia of all time.

Denis Diderot[1] (1713–1784) was editor of the *Encyclopédie*,[2] the massive French encyclopedia that grew out of the French Enlightenment. As editor, he had the tasks of deciding what articles to include, finding scholars to write those articles, and writing many of the articles himself. This mammoth work ran to more than thirty volumes of text and illustrations, and publication spanned the years between 1751 and 1780.

Diderot understood his task clearly, as he stated in his article on encyclopedias:

> The purpose of an encyclopedia is to assemble the knowledge scattered over the surface of the Earth, to explain its general plan to the men with whom we live, and to transmit it to the men who come after us . . . that our descendants, by becoming better instructed, may as a consequence be more virtuous and happier.

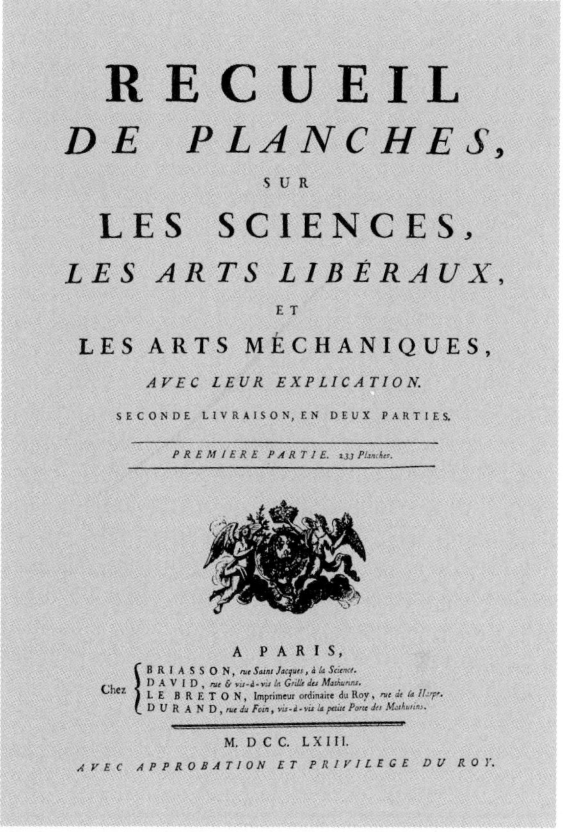

RECUEIL
DE PLANCHES,
SUR
LES SCIENCES,
LES ARTS LIBÉRAUX,
ET
LES ARTS MÉCHANIQUES,
AVEC LEUR EXPLICATION.
SECONDE LIVRAISON, EN DEUX PARTIES.
PREMIERE PARTIE. 233 Planches.

A PARIS,
Chez BRIASSON, rue Saint Jacques, à la Science.
DAVID, rue & vis-à-vis la Grille des Mathurins.
LE BRETON, Imprimeur ordinaire du Roy, rue de la Harpe.
DURAND, rue du Foin, vis-à-vis la petite Porte des Mathurins.

M. DCC. LXIII.
AVEC APPROBATION ET PRIVILEGE DU ROY.

FIGURE 32.1 ***Title Page of Denis Diderot's* Encyclopédie.** *The title translates to "Collection of Plates: Sciences, Liberal Arts, and Mechanical Arts, With Their Explanation." This book and its companion volumes revealed trade secrets that were once known only to specialized artisans. The general publication of this technical information paved the way for the Industrial Revolution.* Courtesy of Dover Publications.

His *Encyclopédie* was to unify and present knowledge—especially knowledge about the trades—for the good of humanity. He saw trade secrets as damaging and selfish, and he and his collaborators went into the streets, shops, and wherever else necessary to research their articles. The *Encyclopédie* included articles on glass manufacture, the making of fishing nets, the production of nails, and many other craft activities. The articles often were masterful and detailed treatments, providing sufficient information for the uninitiated to be able to learn the skill discussed. Equally important, the *Encyclopédie* was profusely illustrated, and the illustrations provided additional technical information. The secrecy associated with the trades in Europe was gone forever.

In addition to its technical articles, the *Encyclopédie* presented essays on social and moral subjects such as the clergy, the arts, marriage, and the proper role of government. Some of the articles produced minor furors, as when the article on Geneva criticized the Puritan ways of the Swiss Calvinists there. The encyclopedists were convinced that technical advancement had to proceed in step with social advancement; it was as important to

[1]**Denis Diderot:** day NEE dee duh ROH
[2]***Encyclopédie:*** ahn see kloh pay DEE

PARALLELS AND DIVERGENCES

Japan's Agricultural Manuals

In the late eighteenth century, about the same time that the encyclopedists of Europe were collecting and publishing information on crafts and technological skills, a parallel but independent movement was taking place in Japan. There, rich peasant farmers were producing agricultural manuals to improve agricultural practices and production.

These farmers recognized that various improvements in agricultural tools and techniques were being made continually throughout Japan. These refinements, however, usually remained local, because there was no established means of disseminating the information that would allow others to take advantage of them. Accordingly, many of these farmers undertook travels throughout Japan, visiting other farmers and observing their practices. They presented their findings in text and illustrations, had copies printed, and distributed them to their colleagues.

Such agricultural manuals were crucial in spreading technical information on agriculture across Japan. The improved techniques described in these manuals were widely adopted and were instrumental in increasing agricultural production. During this period, Japan's agricultural yield per unit of area, already high, rose to among the highest in the world.

While Japan's agricultural manuals differed from the *Encyclopédie* in that they focused exclusively on farming, they bore many similarities. Both were established to spread knowledge that otherwise was difficult to obtain; both were technical in nature, emphasizing practical knowledge; both were widely distributed; and both represented a progressive faith that the future could be improved by rational efforts. The agricultural manuals were precursors to Japan's Industrial Revolution, and the productive agriculture they promoted helped bear the financial burden of Japan's industrialization in the latter part of the nineteenth century.

---

banish superstition as it was to abandon outmoded methods of making shoes.

In these social and moral articles, the encyclopedists preached an Enlightenment ideology of progress, reason, and material betterment. Underlying that ideology was a concern for the welfare of everyday people, as Diderot stated in his article on art:

> It is for the liberal arts [represented by encyclopedists] to lift the mechanical arts from the contempt in which prejudice has for so long held them, and it is for the patronage of kings to draw them from the poverty in which they still languish.

Diderot and his colleagues were preaching the kind of egalitarian ideals that three decades later would inspire the French revolutionaries.

In keeping with its thrust for simultaneous technological and social improvement, the *Encyclopédie* was peppered with political and moral views, sometimes occurring in unexpected places. The article on salt manufacture, for example, discusses the royal tax on salt immediately after citing the biological need for salt. It then launches into a condemnation of any tax levied on a necessity of life. Social and moral commentary of this sort caused the French authorities concern (rightfully, as the French Revolution later confirmed), and Diderot spent three months in jail near the beginning of the project for expressing his nonconformist views in print. His publisher began removing especially controversial statements from later volumes without Diderot's authorization, but what remained was sufficient to fuel many a heated discussion.

The *Encyclopédie* and other encyclopedias paved the way for the Industrial Revolution. First, they presented practical information on how to manufacture items. France had the most advanced manufacturing techniques of the age, and the *Encyclopédie* in particular served as a catalogue of industrial secrets for entrepreneurs throughout Europe and North America. Second, the encyclopedists advocated improved material standards of living for everyday people and saw the "mechanical arts" as the route to that improvement. The *Encyclopédie* was only one voice in a rising chorus of like-minded scholars and others.

Other Intellectual Underpinnings

The rise of encyclopedias was probably the most important intellectual support for the Industrial Revolution, but there were others. Beginning in the seventeenth century, for example, there had been an increased exchange of information between scholars and technologists, two occupational groups that, prior to this time, had communicated remarkably little with each other. Scientists of the seventeenth century also became increasingly adamant in their commitment to testing their theories, and their work became more useful to inventors.

In addition, more narrowly defined and empirically grounded questions were supplanting the grand philosophical topics of inquiry that scientists of earlier times had considered important. More narrow (but more tangible) topics, such as the chemical-combining powers of different metals, were becoming more fashionable, and these subjects had the potential to provide an inventor with information necessary to devise a new manufacturing process.

Further, increasing literacy and the development of widespread and relatively inexpensive printing permitted inventors to read the scientists' tracts, something that would have been unlikely earlier. By the mid–eighteenth century, scholarly science and manufacturing technology had become firmly wedded, and the bond became stronger as time went on.

A final intellectual input came from the English philosopher Herbert Spencer (1820–1903). Writing in the mid–nineteenth century, Spencer obviously did not affect the beginning of the Industrial Revolution nearly a century earlier, but his ideas influenced its later years strongly. Spencer developed the concept of **social Darwinism**, the idea that human society operates by a system of natural selection, whereby individuals and ways of life automatically gravitate to their proper station. According to social Darwinism, poverty is the natural condition for inferior individuals, and an inferior society will be conquered or otherwise dominated by a superior one. Social Darwinism is very much out of fashion today, but it was quite popular in the century following Spencer, and it served as a justification for all sorts of exploitation of laborers and for the extinction or domination of indigenous communities around the world.

Legal Underpinnings

Few inventors are likely to devote their energies to technological innovations if they believe themselves unlikely to benefit from them. Yet the legal systems of Europe before the seventeenth century frequently forbade inventors from using their own inventions. Monarchs (and sometimes lesser royalty) had the right to grant **monopolies**, the rights to exclusive legal use of a device. Monopolies frequently were sold by the crown to the highest bidder regardless of whether that person was the inventor, and fraud was common; sometimes royal favorites would be given a monopoly as a reward for loyalty. In this legal environment, it is small wonder that most inventors considered secrecy the best protection for an invention.

England was the first European country to abolish the old system of monopolies in 1624 and replace it with a new patent system. Under that system, an inventor had only to register a new device with the government and pay a modest fee in order to receive exclusive rights to the use of the device for a stated period. The holder of a patent was permitted to license anyone else to use the device, negotiating whatever arrangement was mutually agreeable. Other western European countries followed suit in the seventeenth century, and the United States provided for patents in its Constitution in 1789. Many scholars believe that this legal change provided critical impetus to the development of the technology that supported the Industrial Revolution.

THE DEMOGRAPHIC AND ECONOMIC BASES OF THE INDUSTRIAL REVOLUTION

While intellectual concepts, law, and technology had their impacts on the Industrial Revolution, demographic and economic factors arguably were the most important. Certainly, the reason that England was the cradle of the Industrial Revolution had nothing to do with the technology there, because equivalent or more sophisticated technology was available elsewhere. But the demographic and economic conditions in England were especially conducive to the development of the Industrial Revolution.

The Demographic Basis

In western Europe—and England in particular—population was increasing very rapidly in the eighteenth century. Average annual population increase in England, for example, was 3 percent, leading to a doubling of the population every twenty-five years. Such population growth was unusual, not having been seen since the development of agriculture and perhaps not even then. This was all the more noteworthy because large numbers of people had been leaving England and western Europe for more than a century to go to the colonies.

The reason for this population explosion was not a greater birthrate but a lower death rate. Fewer infants and children were dying, and more adults were surviving into old age, permitting women to bear children through their entire reproductive life. Several factors were behind this longevity, including an improvement in diet with the adoption of New World crops, better sanitation and medical care, and a falloff in the frequency of devastating epidemics. In addition, because most western Europeans were farmers and farming benefited from the labor of large families, there were few voluntary efforts to limit family size.

This large population meant two things for the Industrial Revolution. First, there would be plenty of labor to fuel the factories. In fact, the abnormal size of farming families led to pressures on some of the younger sons to leave the farm upon reaching adulthood, because they had little chance of inheriting it later. Second, and equally important, there was a huge market to purchase the goods that eventually would be churned out by factories once the Industrial Revolution was under way.

Another important demographic issue was mobility. A large labor pool is of little use if it is scattered all over the countryside and unwilling to move. But in eighteenth-century England there was a great willingness to migrate. It manifested itself in those who left for the colonies and in those who left for the English cities to find employment.

A final relevant demographic factor was slavery. While slaves were not a significant source of labor in eighteenth-century England, they were in the colonies from which raw materials were sent to England. The slaves underwrote the procurement system that provided English factories with cheap raw materials, such as cotton. A less exploitative system would have raised the price of raw materials, jeopardizing the economic viability of certain industries.

The Economic Basis

The Industrial Revolution had two economic prerequisites. First, if great numbers of laborers were to be lured away from farms to become factory workers, then agriculture had to be efficient enough still to provide an adequate food supply. This requirement was easily met in England, where agricultural surpluses had been commonplace for decades and where the shift from subsistence agriculture to commercial agriculture was well under way. The second prerequisite, finding sufficient capital for investment, was more complicated.

Before the Industrial Revolution, the funds needed to establish a cottage craft typically were quite modest. A factory, on the other hand, was a major investment. A great deal of money had to be assembled in order to build the facility, purchase appropriate machines, and stock up on raw materials. Furthermore, all this had to be accomplished before hiring a worker and producing a single item.

Few people could afford individually to invest this amount of money, and those who could were wealthy already and usually had little inclination to risk a substantial sum on such a scheme. The money for the Industrial Revolution, therefore, came mostly from the middle class: petty merchants, craftspeople, and clerks who had saved a bit of money and were looking for an investment. The Industrial Revolution saw investment shift predominantly from a relatively few large shareholders to a broad base of smaller shareholders. Entrepreneurs sold shares in their companies, and investors received returns in proportion to the amount of their investments. The shareholding corporation, the mechanism through which most businesses are funded today, rose to prominence in step with the Industrial Revolution.

Industrialists in the first phase of the Industrial Revolution had the advantage that many of

UNDER THE LENS

"A Fine Stout Mill"

While massive urban factories dominated the economic scene during the Industrial Revolution, coexisting beside them was another institution: the rural mill. These rural mills were a hybrid form, drawing their organization and economics from the tradition of cottage crafts yet taking advantage of the technology of the Industrial Revolution.

A typical rural mill usually was located along a brook. A simple earthen dam created a pond, impounding enough water to run a waterwheel, while gears, levers, and pulleys transmitted the power into a small, wood-frame building. There it could be shunted to an impressive diversity of devices. After the harvest, great stone wheels ground grain into flour; in the winter, when wood was driest and farmers had the most free time for cutting it, saw blades cut logs into lumber; when a shovel needed repair, power bellows puffed a tiny forge into white heat. There were few jobs to which the rural mill could not be turned.

Typically, a rural mill could be built with materials and labor available to most farmers. The mill was made mostly from wood, and that was harvested from the land; the dam was made of earth dug from what would become the pond.

Other than appropriate land and a willingness to work, all that was required to build such a mill was a millwright's manual. The nineteenth century saw the publication of dozens of these millwright's manuals, guides giving information on how to build the mill, and they truly were spiritual descendants of Diderot's *Encyclopédie*. These manuals, usually about 100 pages long and costing a few pennies, provided sample plans, formulas for calculating the placement of the waterwheel and other elements of the mill, examples of devices for transmitting power, and hints of mistakes to avoid. They were down-to-earth and practical, and they could turn a willing reader into a competent millwright.

Few of these rural-mill operators were full-time specialists. More often, they were farmers who invested their spare time and energy in mill-building in order to supplement their income. A dollar for repairing a shovel was a bargain for both the owner of the shovel and the owner of the mill, and those dollars helped many a rural farmer rise to the respected middle class.

The owner of a rural mill usually was its sole operator, shifting attention from one task to the next, searching for clever ways to use the mill's equipment to perform new functions. Unlike the big factories, nothing was standardized here, and everything was a unique task. The rural mill truly was the heir to the cottage craft tradition, drawing on the Industrial Revolution only for its admiration of and reliance on labor-saving mechanical devices.

their facilities were modest, accommodating perhaps a few dozen workers and using relatively inexpensive machines. Still, the economic drain was substantial, and many factory managers developed ways to control their cash flow and keep the business afloat. Some companies, for example, abandoned the traditional practice of paying employees daily or weekly in favor of quarterly pay, hoping that some of the products they had made would have been sold by payday. In the meantime, workers were extended credit to buy necessities at the company-run store and be housed in company-owned tenements; in some cases, the amount owed would be deducted from the wages before they were given to the wage earner. The owners could make substantial profits on both the factory and the company store; rents usually were kept more modest as an attractant for workers.

THE TECHNOLOGICAL BASIS OF THE INDUSTRIAL REVOLUTION

If economics arguably was the heart and soul of the Industrial Revolution, machines were its bones. The day-to-day operation of a factory was dependent on those machines, and profits rose or fell with the effectiveness of the technology. Although virtually all of the machines of the

Industrial Revolution were based on principles that had been known for decades, sometimes centuries, great attention was now being given to their design and refinement.

Power Sources

Prior to the Industrial Revolution, most of the energy expended in producing goods came from human muscles. A major change came with the proliferation of a wide variety of power sources.

Simplest were the wind and water mills. With various arrangements of paddles or vanes, they were propelled forward by the current of wind or flowing water, and energy was transmitted through a central axle into a mill building. Water mills had been used in Europe since at least the first century B.C., and windmills were used there by the twelfth century A.D. Their primary use was to grind grain, but there are a few examples of mills adapted to manufacturing. A water-powered mill in France, for example, was producing felt by 1000, as were others in Sweden and England within the following two centuries. A French water mill was used for sawing lumber in 1204, and Italian, French, and German mills made paper in the late thirteenth and fourteenth centuries. These practices were out of the ordinary and noteworthy at these dates, but during the Industrial Revolution they became common.

Especially in the United States, where many of the prime regions for industrialization were along rivers at waterfalls, water power became the primary motive force for industry. For the most part, the technology remained quite similar to that which had been known for nearly a millennium. One significant innovation, however, was developed in the middle of the nineteenth century: Rather than using water to turn a large wheel, it could be directed through a narrow jet and into an enclosed drum, where it would squirt against vanes and turn a small rotor. This device, called a

FIGURE 32.2 ***Volta's Electric Battery.*** *Alessandro Volta demonstrated his electric battery to Napoleon in 1802. Volta was a theoretical scientist investigating previous conceptions of how electricity was produced. His research, however, led him to construct a device that had unexpected practical applications: the electric battery. This linkage between theoretical science and practical invention became prominent during the Industrial Revolution.* Private collection/Bulloz.

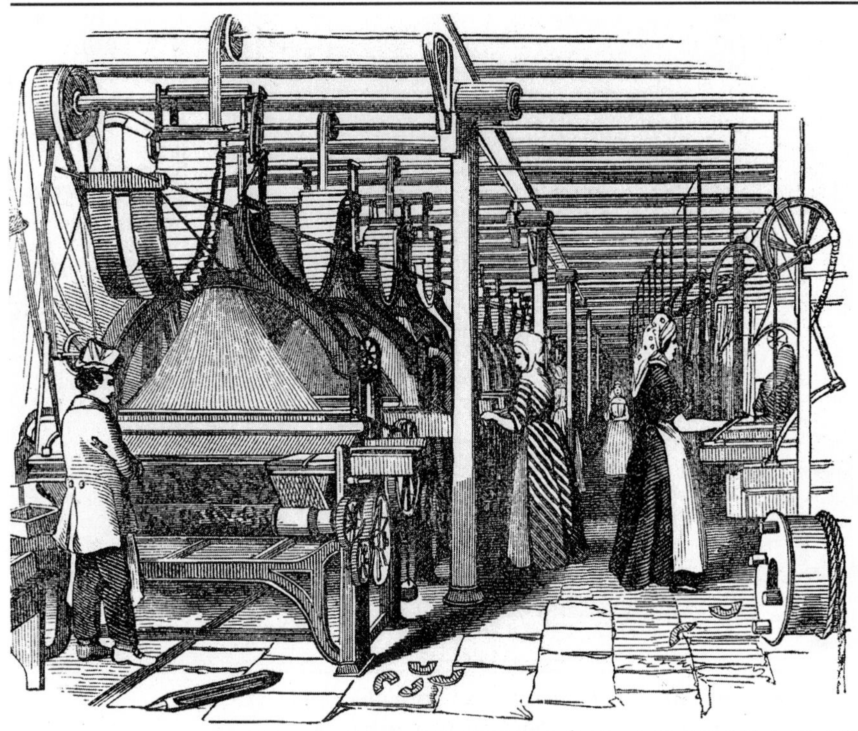

FIGURE 32.3 ***Jacquard Loom.*** *This 1847 illustration demonstrates how just a few workers managed machines that could produce large and complicated textiles rapidly. As documented by this picture, women were prominent in the factories of the nineteenth century.* British Library.

turbine, increased the usable energy output of the water by as much as 30 percent and was especially useful along small streams or in regions where rivers shrink in the summer.

The use of water or wind power, of course, is limited to locations with the proper geographical endowment. The steam engine, however, overcame that difficulty because it could be used anywhere, including in moving vehicles. The steam engine is simple in principle. Water is heated until it vaporizes, at which point it expands and drives a piston; levers or gears transmit the energy from the piston to wherever it is needed. Greek philosophers of the fifth century B.C. invented a steam engine, but they never applied it to any practical task. Various Europeans produced more or less practical steam engines in the seventeenth and eighteenth centuries, but it was the improvements made by James Watt that produced a truly useful power source in 1782. Steam engines were variously stoked with wood, coal, or even dry animal dung.

By the end of the nineteenth century, internal combustion engines running on petroleum fuels and electric motors were becoming efficient enough to be useful. They were the only truly new power sources to be invented during the Industrial Revolution, and it is notable that they were developed only at the end of the period. The revolution, so far as power was concerned, was not in the devices themselves but in how they were used.

New Machines and Inventions

New machines to support the Industrial Revolution were as varied as the tasks they were designed to complete. There were rolling mills for making oatmeal, cotton gins for separating cotton fiber from seeds and other waste, spinning jennies for making thread, bending machines for making paper clips, rotary steam presses for printing newspapers, and even Hercules dredgers for keeping canals clear of silt. Rather than catalogue hundreds of specialized inventions, we shall examine one as an example.

In the eighteenth century, weaving patterned cloth was very laborious. It had to be made by hand, because the power looms of that era could produce only plain fabrics, all of the same thread and with no raised designs. Joseph Jacquard,[3] a French inventor, solved this problem with the **Jacquard loom**, a device that could be attached to any existing loom. To produce patterns, it was

[3]**Joseph Jacquard:** zhoh SEHF zhahk AHR

FIGURE 32.4 ***Segregation of Tasks in the Industrial Revolution.*** *This illustration from Diderot's* Encyclopédie *shows how the manufacture of so simple an item as a button could be split into different tasks to improve efficiency. The pair of workers at the left cut wood or similar materials into blocks, which in turn were cut into button blanks by the pair in the foreground; the trio in the background used the wheel to polish and bore perforations in the buttons.* Courtesy of Dover Publications.

necessary to raise each thread at the right moment so that cross-threads could be passed beneath it. The Jacquard loom controlled each thread individually, allowing it to be lifted at the precise instant necessary. A series of cards with holes drilled into them programmed the loom to the desired pattern. Jacquard exhibited his loom at the French Industrial Exposition in 1801 and received a medal for it. He subsequently was decorated by Napoleon and was awarded a permanent stipend by his grateful government.

The Jacquard loom exemplifies the general pattern seen in many machines of the Industrial Revolution, although it was far more successful than most. The invention really did little that was new; it automated tasks that previously had been done by hand, but the process remained much the same. In fact, the Jacquard loom differed from its predecessor only in its treatment of individual threads, rather than groups. It embodied no new scientific principles and was dramatic only in that it accelerated the weaving process.

Organizing the Workplace

The new facilities and machines required a different organization of labor from that of cottage crafts, and, in this sense, the Industrial Revolution was something entirely new. In the cottage crafts before the Industrial Revolution, a single worker normally completed the entirety of a product. Work was largely at one's own pace, and an especially productive day could be followed by a light day or even a self-proclaimed holiday. Work usually was done by one or a very few workers, and all workers probably were family members.

In the factories, many unrelated workers labored together at a pace dictated not by their own consciences but by the foreman. Work began and ended by the clock, without regard for how near one was to completing a task. Early industrialists frequently commented on how difficult it was to maintain discipline in the workplace because the workers formerly employed in crafts were so entrenched in more free-form work habits.

A major innovation in the factories was the **segregation of tasks**. Each worker had one small task to complete, and that task was repeated over and again. Making a pin in England in 1770 required eighteen distinct tasks, one person making the wire, another cutting it, another grinding the point, another making the head, another attaching it, and so on. This arrangement, alien to cottage crafts, had the virtue of efficiency. The advantage of a point-grinding machine is largely lost if a worker goes to the machine to sharpen one pin, then walks to the head-making machine to perform the next task.

The segregation of tasks was made possible by another principle of organization in the Industrial Revolution: **standardization of parts**. In cottage crafts, workers made each part as needed and fitted it to the adjacent part; in the factories, all examples of a particular part had to be the same so that any one of them could fit into its appropriate place. This meant that machines had to be designed in such a manner that it would be difficult to produce variations in their products. While the British and French pioneered the standardization of parts, it was the Americans who perfected it and made it a major element of mass production.

Another American innovation, coming into practice around 1900, was the **assembly line**. Refined by Henry Ford in his automobile plant, it consisted of a conveyor system with workers standing along it, arranged in the order in which their tasks were to be performed. Workers completed their tasks on the automobile literally as it passed by, each one executing a single, simple operation. Before the institution of the assembly line, assembling an automobile body had required 748 worker-minutes; with the assembly line, it required only 93 worker-minutes.

New Modes of Transportation

As the Industrial Revolution rumbled into its second phase in the 1820s, a crisis was brewing. Factories were hungry for the raw materials that they processed, and they spewed out large quantities of goods. Bringing in materials and distributing products became major problems in the early Industrial Revolution, but technology came to the rescue.

Thinkers as early as Isaac Newton in 1680 proposed using steam to power a carriage, and several eighteenth-century inventors built working models, but it wasn't until 1801 that a working steam-powered railroad locomotive was produced. Richard Trevithick's "Puffing Devil" was largely a circus attraction, but working steam locomotives were in service by 1829 in both England and the United States. Railroads were critical in servicing

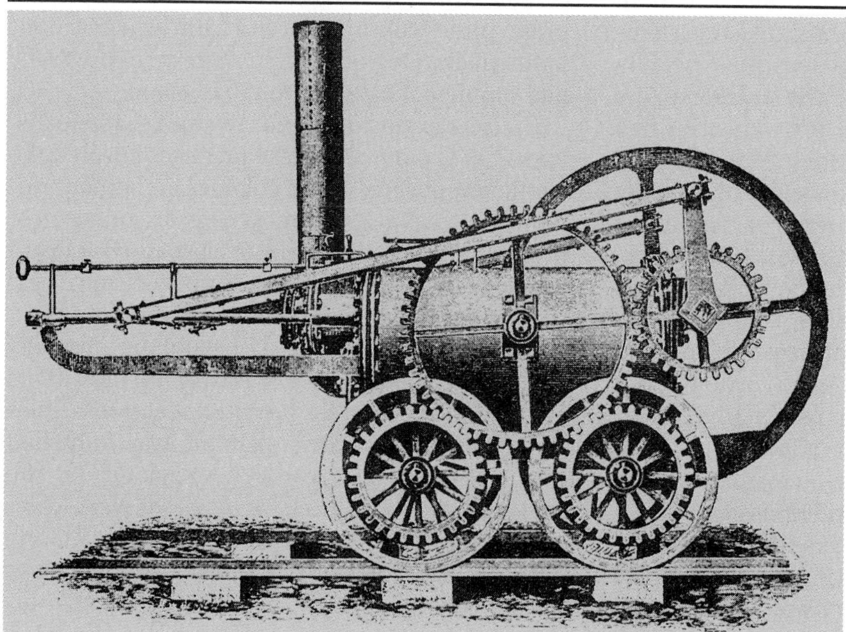

FIGURE 32.5 ***"Puffing Devil."*** *Richard Trevithick, an English inventor, designed and built the first successful railroad locomotive, which was capable of carrying seven or eight passengers at a breathtaking speed of three miles per hour. The first version, built in 1801, ran on the ground, but the difficulties of traversing uneven terrain led Trevithick to place it on rails in 1804.* From Edward W. Byrne, *The Progress of Invention in the Nineteenth Century* (New York: Russell and Russell, 1900).

many industries, especially the manufacture of iron and steel, whose raw materials and products were so heavy.

Less important, though prominent in the nineteenth century, were steamships. Working steamships were in service from 1801 on. These boats often were constructed with a very shallow draft that permitted them to operate in shallow water, so they were excellent for plying the rivers and navigation canals of Europe and eastern North America.

THE INDUSTRIAL REVOLUTION TRANSFORMS SOCIETY

The Industrial Revolution was an economic revolution whose effects were widespread and far-reaching. Economic conditions both in industrialized nations and elsewhere around the world were drastically altered, and society in industrialized nations veered in a new direction. Processes of environmental degradation that have proven difficult to reverse were also set into motion.

Economic Winners and Losers

Economically speaking, virtually all segments of society profited when a country industrialized. The investors, providing the business was managed skillfully, were likely to receive a healthy return on their investments; the entrepreneurs who established and directed the industries had the potential to become wildly rich. Many middle-class investors found themselves suddenly wealthy as the result of holding shares in a successful enterprise. Laborers, although hardly getting rich, typically found themselves in better economic shape than they had been before. Many of them had few other opportunities for wage earning, and a factory job was considered good fortune. Consumers benefited from lower prices and greater availability of previously scarce goods.

The system fed upon itself, creating increasingly favorable economic conditions for at least some of its participants. Workers who had left the farm for the factory now had more cash (though they forfeited the subsistence commodities available to farm workers), and that cash could be used to purchase goods produced by factories. The laborers for one factory were consumers of the products from all the other factories, and the growth of the labor force greatly expanded the domestic market for goods. Further, the substantial financial gains of the first phase of the Industrial Revolution provided investors with sufficient capital to fund the more expensive iron and steel factories that became prevalent in the second phase.

There were, however, economic losers in the Industrial Revolution, though the losers were predominantly not in the industrialized countries. Many of the industries of this period produced goods for a foreign market and depended on raw materials that were unavailable locally.

An excellent example comes from the cotton textile industry of England, the first major industry there and a major component of English industrial output throughout the Industrial Revolution. The climate of England, of course, cannot support cotton growing, so cotton was shipped to England, primarily from Brazil, the Caribbean islands, and southern parts of North America. Subsidized by slavery, cotton growing was lucrative for a very few growers but marginal (at best) for virtually all the laborers. Cheap raw cotton then came into England, where it was spun and woven in the factories, boosting the English economy. Two-thirds of English textile production in the first half of the nineteenth century was exported and sold at considerable profit, principally to India and Latin America, non-industrialized regions that in some cases originally had supplied the raw cotton to England.

A clear extension of the mercantile system discussed in Chapter 24, these practices ensured the continued poverty of the colonies and other non-industrial regions. Colonies were discouraged or prohibited from attempting to alleviate their destitution by developing industries of their own and thereby becoming competitors with England.

In at least one case, England purposefully destroyed a competing industry in one of its colonies. Long a major exporter of cotton textiles throughout the southern parts of Asia, India had begun exporting textiles to England in the mid–seventeenth century. A series of wars, carefully orchestrated by the British through shifting alliances, destabilized India in the early years of the nineteenth century, destroying its textile industry and removing it as an industrial competitor.

Classes and Class Conflict

The Industrial Revolution transfigured the structure of economic classes. Between 1730 and 1830, the overall standard of living in England had improved dramatically. At the beginning of that span, the vast majority of the English population were farmers, and by the end most worked in factories or service jobs: A huge, new class of workers had been formed almost overnight. Many small investors had made sufficient money to become quite comfortable, and the ranks of the middle class had swollen. A few spectacularly successful entrepreneurs, especially in the latter half of the nineteenth century, had gained incredible wealth, becoming richer than many aristocrats.

These changes created considerable conflict. Workers and owners often found themselves at odds over working conditions and wages, and work stoppages, lockouts, and violence became more common. Labor unions of the modern kind were formed in the nineteenth century to help workers act together in their opposition to owners, though it was not until the latter half of the nineteenth century that unions were sufficiently powerful to conduct major strikes. The swarms of political upheavals in both 1830 and 1848 in part reflected the difficulties Europe was having in adjusting to the new order.

Working Conditions

Factories of the Industrial Revolution usually evoke the image of wretched working conditions, but this was far from universally true. Particularly in the early decades of the Industrial Revolution in the United States, owners went to great lengths to try to establish healthful, stimulating, and morally uplifting conditions.

Lowell, Massachusetts, is a good example. There, several textile mills opened in 1822, attracted by the falls of the Merrimack River and the favorable terrain for harnessing their power. More than just a collection of mills, Lowell included churches, assembly halls for touring lecturers and musicians, schools, a hospital, and a

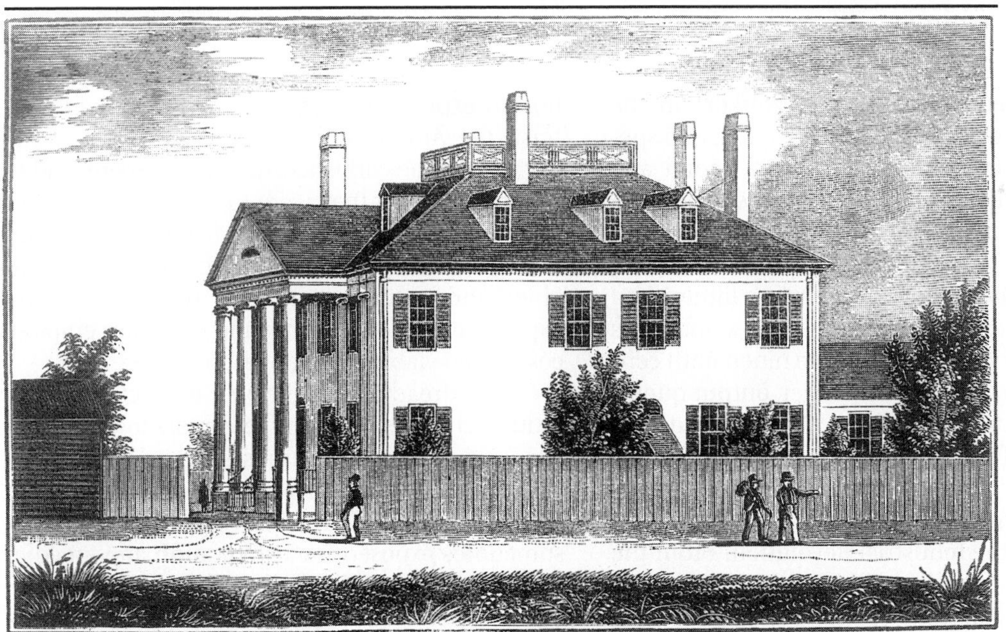

FIGURE 32.6 ***Lowell Hospital.*** *Many American industrialists in the first half of the nineteenth century felt obligated to provide services for the welfare of their factory workers. This hospital in the mill town of Lowell, Massachusetts, provided workers with better medical care than was available to most of their contemporaries, many of whom were more financially secure. Other services included schools, churches, and concert and lecture series.*
Courtesy of the Center for Lowell History.

IN THEIR OWN WORDS

An Interview with an Eleven-Year-Old Coal Miner

As the Industrial Revolution progressed and working conditions worsened, reformers on both sides of the Atlantic Ocean began agitating for laws and regulations to improve the workplace. The plight of women and children was especially important to these reformers, and various governments commissioned studies that interviewed women and children in factories, mines, and other work venues. The following testimony was collected in 1842 by investigators looking into the conditions in coal mines. Janet Cumming, at the time eleven years old, had been working in the coal mines of Scotland for two years when she gave this testimony. The testimony is largely a quotation of her own words, but there are occasional shifts to the perspective of the interviewer. Touching accounts like this led to a series of nineteenth-century laws that limited child labor in Great Britain.

> Father gangs [assembles with other workers] at 2 in the morning: I gang with the women at 5, and come up at 5 at night; work all night on Fridays, and come away at 12 in the day. I carry the large bits of coal from the wall-face to the pit-bottom, and the small pieces called chows in a creel [basket]; the weight is usually a hundred-weight [100 pounds]; does not know how many pounds there are in a hundred-weight, but it is some work to carry; it takes three journeys to fill a tub of 4 cwt [hundred-weight]. . . . The roof is very low; I have to bend my back and legs, and the water comes frequently up to the calves of my legs; has no likening [*sic*] for the work; father makes me like it. . . . Never got hurt, but often obliged to scramble out when bad air [poisonous gas] was in the pit.
>
> I am learning to read at the night-school; am in the twopenny book [beginning reading text]; sometimes to sabbath-school. Jesus was God; David wrote the Bible; has a slight knowledge of the first six questions in the Shorter Catechism.

variety of other public services. Workers in the early years were primarily young women, and special care was taken to provide them moral and practical instruction, courtesy of the company. Several other mill towns furnished comparable services.

As time passed, however, services diminished and finally were discontinued, and conditions generally deteriorated. By the late nineteenth century, work days had become longer, output quotas had increased, and safety often was sacrificed. This was the era of the sweatshop. Curiously, English factories never exhibited the good working conditions of their American counterparts, even in the early years of the Industrial Revolution. From the beginning, they were comparable to the later American sweatshops.

This pattern of benign and exploitative conditions may be explained by the geographical relationship of industry to the frontier. In England, there was no frontier to which a disgruntled worker could retreat, leaving the oppressive conditions of the factory. Workers had no alternatives, and their employers took advantage of the situation to exploit them as fully as possible. In contrast, the American frontier was within walking distance of the early factories, and workers had to be treated well if they were to stay. As the frontier advanced and the distance from the factories increased, that pressure valve no longer was available, and owners gradually turned to more exploitative practices, knowing that their employees had no viable alternatives to staying.

The dreadful conditions in factories and industrial towns led many reformers to clamor for laws regulating industrialists. Charles Dickens, himself briefly a British factory worker in his youth during the 1830s, wrote novels and stories that sometimes exposed the exploitation and greed of industry. Other social critics, such as Lewis Hine, used the newly developed technology of photography to expose the horrors of child labor in turn-of-the-century America. The combined weight of exposés and reform agitation led to laws and regulations regarding child labor, maximum length of work days, safety standards, and other aspects of labor in countries throughout the industrialized world.

The Special Role of Women, Children, and Immigrants

Especially in the early days of the Industrial Revolution, women were an important component of the workforce. A few decades later, children became a significant sector of labor, and after that, recent immigrants became important. Traditionally, none of these groups would have held a significant position in the labor force, but there were several reasons why they emerged in the Industrial Revolution.

First, these groups were considered more compliant than male, American-born adults. This was especially true of women and children, whose traditional social roles were subservient to those of adult men. All these groups were perceived as less likely to complain about conditions or to organize into labor unions, and there is some evidence that this perception was accurate. Further, in the early days of the Industrial Revolution, owners found it difficult to reshape the work habits of men accustomed to the cottage industries. By using laborers with little or no previous work experience, owners felt better able to mold them to the new requirements.

Second, these groups were willing to work for lower wages than men. In mills where both men and women worked, women's wages typically were from 40 to 60 percent lower than men's, and children's wages usually were lower still. Recent immigrants also would accept low wages, which often led to conflict with local-born workers who correctly believed that this practice undercut prevailing wage levels. A labor force willing to work for inferior wages was important in an entrepreneur's quest to extract the greatest profit from an industrial enterprise.

FIGURE 32.7 ***Child Labor in a Carolina Cotton Mill.*** *Lewis Hine, who photographed this scene in 1908, was a crusader against the exploitation of children in industry. Child labor was common in American factories, especially in the South, but Hine's photographic campaign drew Congress's attention to the problem and resulted in stricter and more aggressively enforced child labor laws.* Edward L. Bafford Photography Collection, University of Maryland Baltimore County.

Effects on Cities and Countryside

The most obvious immediate effect of the Industrial Revolution was the shift of population from the countryside to cities. Many factories were located in or near cities in order to take advantage of the labor pools there, and the majority of workers became urbanites. For every worker in the city, there was one fewer farmer, and contemporary writers commented on the noticeable depopulation of the countryside.

Another important result of the Industrial Revolution, while not so immediately obvious, was environmental destruction. Most industries produced waste along with their products, and those wastes sometimes seriously degraded the environment. A small cottage craft could safely dump the minimal volume of waste it produced with little damage, but large factories produced much more waste, and their sustained dumping was more likely to devastate an area.

Certain industries were especially polluting. Paper mills dumped dense effluents into rivers, killing fish and contaminating waterfowl. Hat factories, important in the nineteenth century, when hats were required of socially prominent persons, employed mercury to dress the fur used in top hats, and the runoff usually was dumped in a nearby stream. One community in the Merrimack Valley had the highest rates of insanity in Massachusetts for decades, until it was realized that its residents were suffering from mercury poisoning, the result of a water supply severely polluted by its hatmaking industry. When industries used coal for metal working or producing steam for power, the landscape for miles around was sooted with black grime. There were no environmental protection laws during the Industrial Revolution, and most countries realized only in the late twentieth century how serious the dangers of pollution were.

FIGURE 32.8 ***Rows of Factories in Industrial England.*** *This photograph of factories in Burnley shows the grim result of focusing exclusively on efficiency and profit: The environment suffered massively. Not only were such working conditions depressing to workers, but the buildings they occupied were also hotter in summer, colder in winter, and more oxygen-deprived than the more spacious, less efficient structures in which they were employed prior to the Industrial Revolution.* Aerofilms, Ltd.

INDUSTRIALIZATION BEYOND WESTERN EUROPE AND NORTH AMERICA

In the modern world, political, military, and economic power are in direct proportion to the industrial strength of a country. Countries around the world have realized this since the nineteenth century, and many far beyond the original core area of the Industrial Revolution have tried to stimulate their own industrialization. They have achieved success to varying degrees, and they have modified Western-style industrialization in various ways to fit their needs and resources.

Japan

When the Meiji rulers of Japan came to power in 1868, they inherited a country on the brink of being absorbed into an expansive American trade sphere. Their predecessors had attempted to isolate Japan from the outside world, but the United States had used its military strength to force Japan into an unequal treaty that gave American nationals a privileged position in Japan. Later, other Western powers also used their military might to extract humiliating and lopsided trade agreements with Japan. Japan's industrialization was, in large measure, an attempt to build national power to the point where outsiders could not compel such unfavorable agreements.

The Meiji rulers' program to modernize Japan was based on industrial strength. Prior to this time, manufacturing had been of the cottage craft sort similar to that of Europe, and Japanese leaders began actively promoting factory growth alongside cottage crafts. Basically, quality items for domestic consumption, especially traditional items like chopsticks, continued to be made by skilled craftspeople. To complement this, factories specialized in large-scale production of inexpensive items for export and domestic use (such as cotton textiles), silk fabrics (to fill the void left when Europe's silk industry was devastated by silkworm disease in the 1870s), and armaments and other items that could be used to build the political and military power of Japan. Because Japan was resource-poor, many industries manufactured finished products from raw materials purchased abroad.

The road to industrialization in Japan was carefully guided by the government. Many top Japanese leaders had traveled to the West between 1871 and 1873 and had been impressed by Western industry and its virtues; when they returned to Japan, they were eager to promote similar developments there. These leaders recognized that Japan already possessed the elements required to support industrialization: a strong base of commercial agriculture, financial institutions for loans and investments, and coal for use as a fuel.

Government support took several forms. When sufficient capital to start an enterprise was not available in private hands, the government financed factories. When technical expertise was unavailable in Japan, the government hired foreign experts to advise in the design and establishment of factories. More than 4,000 foreign advisors were hired, paid well, and shipped back home after they had trained Japanese in their specialties. Similarly, when the problem was industrial organization, foreign experts were brought to Japan to teach European approaches. Once the industries were established, the government sold them off at bargain prices to Japanese entrepreneurs, leaving their management in private hands.

To ensure that Japanese products were competitive on the international market, the government oversaw a quality-control operation that spot-checked exports for defects and encouraged manufacturers to install quality-control procedures of their own. In the 1880s, the finance minister, Matsukata Masayoshi, implemented a program of tax incentives and other measures to encourage Japanese export of finished products.

All of these measures helped produce a powerful industrial base for Japan. Japan's trade balance was very favorable, with exports considerably greater than imports, and the military strength produced through its armament factories was demonstrated in 1895, when the Japanese military easily defeated China and began establishing its Asian empire; Japan's power was confirmed with its defeat of Russia in 1905.

While the concept of industrialization came from the West and Japanese officials were eager to borrow ideas from the West, Japan was not merely an imitator of European industry. Japanese industry acquired its own stamp, and factories were organized along a model that took the Japanese character into account. Rather than focus on individual workers, production teams were stressed; the family was taken as the ideal model for factory organization after about 1900. Socialized into the values of teamwork and institutional goal achievement, Japanese workers adapted well to these work teams. As in the Western tradition, women workers comprised most of the labor force, again largely because they were seen as more docile and willing to accept low wages. Men began to outnumber women in most sectors of Japanese industry only in the 1920s.

FIGURE 32.9 ***Tomioka Silk Factory.*** *The massive factory shown in this contemporary Japanese print was an early creation of the Meiji program of industrialization in Japan. It was the first factory in Japan to apply mass-production techniques like segregation of tasks, and the first to employ women.* Tsuneo Tamba Collection, Yokohama, Japan/Laurie Platt Winfrey, Inc.

By the turn of the century, scarcely three decades after its beginning, Japan's Industrial Revolution was complete. Although Japanese industry was not as powerful as most of its European and North American counterparts, it was the strongest in Asia. In the second half of the twentieth century, Japan would become one of the greatest industrial powers in the world.

Russia

Russia did not participate in the Industrial Revolution very fully. By 1830, it was receiving imported industrial technology, primarily in the form of textile machinery. Industry had difficulty taking root, however, because there was so small a market for its products. Russian poverty was deeper than the poverty suffered by the poor elsewhere in Europe. The vast majority of Russians were impoverished serfs, and, even after emancipation in 1861, they remained too poor to purchase industrial products in quantities sufficient to support the factories. At the end of the Crimean War in 1856, Russian leaders were convinced that the lack of a strong industrial base was responsible for Russia's defeat.

Attempts were made to invigorate industry through state direction. The most successful of these began in the 1880s and lasted two decades. During that period, many armament plants were established, and a growing railroad system was used to transport raw materials and finished products. (The building of major railway systems, such as the Trans-Siberian Railroad, further stimulated industrialization.) The building of armament factories solved the market problem, because the state purchased the weapons, strengthening its international position in the bargain. Capital came partly from foreign investors but primarily from the government; high tariffs maintained the high prices of competitive foreign goods, protecting Russian products. The government monies were raised through increased taxes, causing considerable unrest, especially among the poor.

There were limits, however, to industrial growth in Russia in the early years of the twentieth century. Consistently poor agricultural yields made it imperative that attention and labor be directed to that sector, and the gap between Russian industrialization and that of western Europe continued to widen. Russian industry developed slowly until interrupted by the Russian Revolution, and the final phase of industrialization took place under socialism. As a result, it incorporated none of the entrepreneurial elements characteristic of the Industrial Revolution under capitalism.

Patterns of Industrialization outside the Core Areas

There were three patterns of industrialization outside the core area of the Industrial Revolution. Japan was successful at industrializing, probably in large part because of strenuous government intervention, astute private entrepreneurship, and the absence of neighboring industrial competitors. At that relatively early date, Western industrial powers were unable effectively to promote their

FIGURE 32.10 ***Russian Armament Factory, 1916.*** *This factory in Petrograd was devoted to the production of artillery pieces; the guns shown here are nearly completed. Factories like this one resulted from a government policy aimed at stimulating industry through the purchase of arms. For this reason, the Industrial Revolution in Russia followed a different course than it did in Western Europe.* RIA-Novosti/Sovfoto.

EUROPE AND NORTH AMERICA	JAPAN	RUSSIA		
Cottage Crafts period, to 1770			**1600**	
			–	British patent system established, 1624
			–	London Stock Exchange opens, 1697
			1700	
			–	Diderot publishes *Encyclopédie*, 1751–1780
Industrial Revolution: Phase 1, 1770–1830			–	Watt develops practical steam engine, 1782
			1800	Jacquard loom designed, 1801
			–	Railroads in use, 1829
Industrial Revolution: Phase 2, 1830–1905			–	American industrial working conditions begin to deteriorate, c. 1860
	Japanese Industrial Revolution, 1868–1905	Abortive Russian industrialization, 1880–1905	–	
			1900	Assembly line comes into use, c. 1900

products there, aiding Japan's success. Russia followed a second pattern. It was unsuccessful in establishing a capitalist industrial base and achieved full industrialization only through governmental involvement on the socialist model. The third pattern, that of colonies and other dependent regions, is one of little or no industrial development in this period. Home countries effectively stifled any local efforts to industrialize, maintaining the market for themselves. Industrialization would come to former colonies only a century or more later, and then it usually would be incomplete and faltering.

THE IMPACT OF THE GLOBAL INDUSTRIAL REVOLUTION

The Industrial Revolution was characterized by several elements wherever it occurred. These were:

- —the use of mechanized equipment to increase output and decrease labor costs of production;
- —the creation of large factories;
- —mass production and standardization;
- —a workplace that emphasized production, sometimes with assembly lines;
- —financing that often included shareholders and stock; and
- —an expanded labor force that included women, immigrants, and children.

These elements combined to form an efficient mode of organization and production that soon dominated much of the world. What made industrialization so attractive?

Above all else, industry gave individuals a chance to improve their lot. A middle-class investor might get rich by backing the right enterprise; a younger son with no future on the family farm might find an alternative career as a factory worker; a woman with few other options could support herself operating a machine. Industry gave hope for economic betterment, and for many that hope was realized, creating upward mobility in the class system.

Expansive governments, too, found industry attractive, because it went hand-in-glove with empire. An empire was an expensive business; industry could produce the wealth necessary to form and maintain it. Industry required raw materials to process; the colonies of an empire could provide them. Industry needed markets to sell its goods; empire provided colonies to expand industry's markets.

The Industrial Revolution also led to an increase in technological development. Each mechanical improvement in production processes gave its possessor an advantage over competitors, so industrialists found themselves supporting research and development in technology. Transporting goods also was a major problem for many industries, a problem that began to be solved only by the steam railroads of the second phase of the Industrial Revolution. Later, the development of internal combustion engines fueled with petroleum products led to more efficient railroads, to automobiles, and eventually to airplanes.

The cost of industrialization, of course, has been high. Nonrenewable resources are inexorably depleted; renewable resources sometimes are used faster than they can recover. Pollution has fouled our air, water, and soil. And human beings have suffered from the stresses and dangers of the factory. It is difficult to judge whether the Industrial Revolution has improved or worsened the human condition on balance, but it is clear that it has been a major force in shaping subsequent events and processes.

SUMMARY

1. The Industrial Revolution began in England around 1770; within the next fifty years it spread to the rest of western Europe and North America, where it evolved further. It was characterized by mechanization, large factories with mass-production techniques, and a reorganization of production. It largely replaced the earlier cottage craft tradition.

2. Encyclopedias laid the intellectual groundwork for the Industrial Revolution by disseminating trade secrets, advocating an improved standard of living for the working classes, and championing progressivism. Social Darwinism also played a role by providing a justification in the minds of many Europeans for exploiting colonial peoples and the poor.

3. The establishment of the patent system in Western countries encouraged inventors to focus on devising improved technology.

4. Abundant capital for investment, efficient agriculture to support industry, mushrooming population, and personal mobility all contributed to the initiation of the Industrial Revolution in England.

5. The technology of the Industrial Revolution relied on few new principles and consisted mostly of refined versions of preexisting technology. The greatest change was in the increased use of these machines, not in new technological concepts.

6. The factory required new forms of organization, including standardization of parts, segregation of tasks, and eventually the assembly line. It also required different attitudes and work habits.

7. Most segments of society profited economically from the industrialization of their countries. Colonies and other dependent regions that supplied raw materials to fuel industry, however, suffered from depressed economies as the home country thwarted their industrial development.

8. The early phase of the Industrial Revolution focused on light industry; the later phase (after 1830 in western Europe and northeastern North America) also included heavy industry.

9. The Industrial Revolution redrew class lines and intensified conflicts between classes in most places, especially between labor and management in the factories.

10. Working conditions in English and European factories were generally harsh and exploitative. Working conditions in American factories were relatively benign in the early period but became increasingly exploitative over time. This probably relates to the presence of the frontier as an escape valve in the early phase of the American Industrial Revolution.

11. Women, children, and immigrants formed major parts of the factory labor force, largely because they would work for lower wages and were considered more cooperative.

12. The Industrial Revolution hastened urbanization and created massive environmental pollution.

13. Industrialization outside the original core area has been spotty. Japan, building on a strong preindustrial base, successfully industrialized itself in the late nineteenth century under government sponsorship and through entrepreneurs. Russia's industrialization was slow until after socialism was established, so it experienced no major Industrial Revolution along capitalist lines. Most other areas did not industrialize in this era.

SUGGESTED READINGS

Chirot, Daniel. *Social Change in the Modern Age.* San Diego, Calif.: Harcourt Brace Jovanovich, 1986. A global treatment of modern industrialization, focusing on political and social impacts and written from the sociological perspective.

Dublin, Thomas. *Transforming Women's Work: New England Lives in the Industrial Revolution.* Ithaca, N.Y.: Cornell University Press, 1994. A current treatment of the role of women in the American Industrial Revolution and its effects on women's roles in society.

Fisher, Douglas. *The Industrial Revolution: A Macroeconomic Interpretation.* New York: St. Martin's Press, 1992. Examines the backdrop and consequences of industrialization in terms of economics.

Habakkuk, H. J. *American and British Technology in the Nineteenth Century: The Search for Labour-Saving Inventions.* Cambridge, Eng.: Cambridge University Press, 1962. An excellent comparative approach that presents the hypothesis of the frontier as a significant factor in shaping the Industrial Revolution on both sides of the Atlantic.

Kemp, Tom. *Industrialization in the Non-Western World.* London: Longman, 1983. Capsule summaries of the progress of industrialization in Japan, Russia/the Soviet Union, India, China, Brazil, Nigeria, and Egypt, as well as two synthetic essays. Written from the point of view of economic history.

Singer, Charles, E. J. Holmyard, A. R. Hall, and Trevor I. Williams, eds. Vol. IV of Singer, Holmyard, Hall, and Williams, eds., *A History of Technology.* Oxford, Eng.: Oxford University Press, 1958. The classic collection of synthetic essays on the technical and technological aspects of the Industrial Revolution.

Stearns, Peter N. *The Industrial Revolution in World History.* Boulder, Colo.: Westview Press, 1993. An excellent global treatment of the Industrial Revolution.

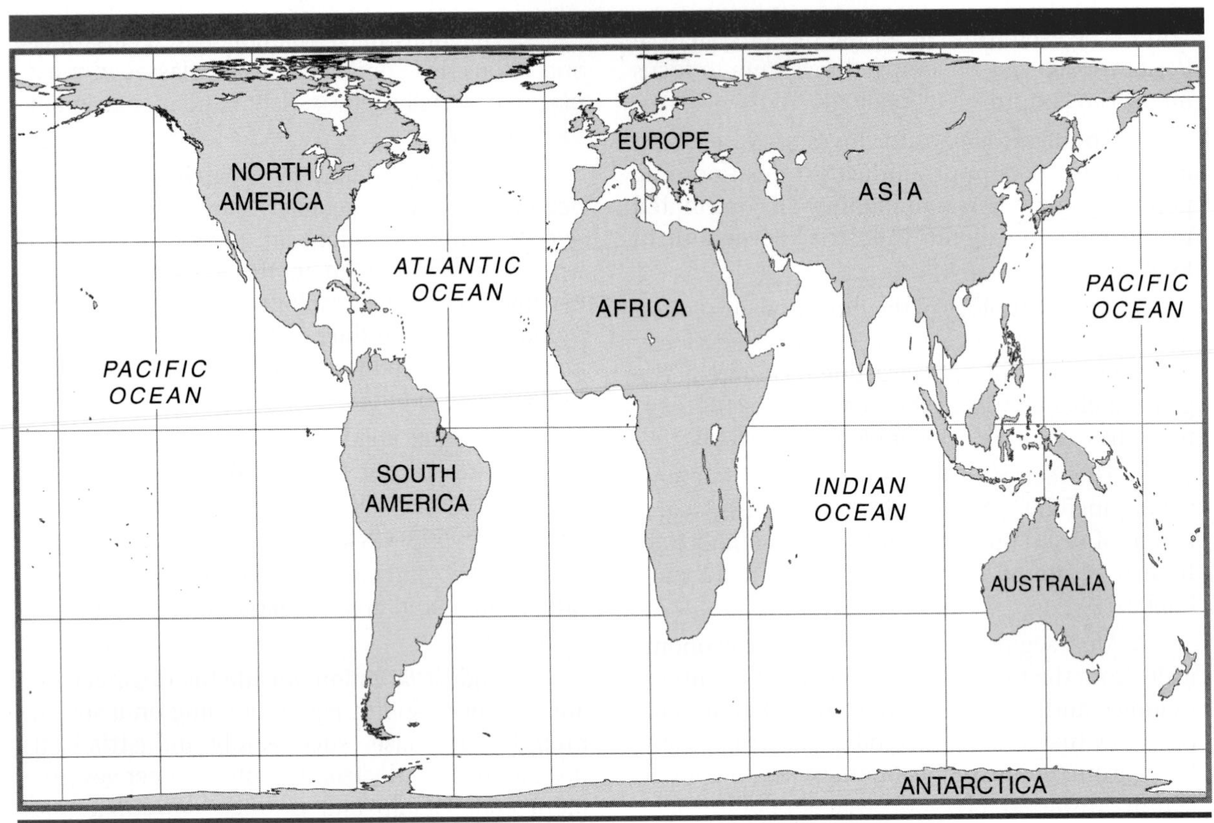
NORTH AMERICA
EUROPE
ASIA
ATLANTIC OCEAN
AFRICA
PACIFIC OCEAN
PACIFIC OCEAN
SOUTH AMERICA
INDIAN OCEAN
AUSTRALIA
ANTARCTICA

CHAPTER 33

Modern Nationalism around the Globe

around 1790–1920

In 1879, columns of Zulu warriors overran an English-led army invading Zululand. Although they were using the most advanced military technology, more than 1,500 of the invaders fell to the Zulu, who were armed generally with the signature stabbing spears developed a few decades earlier. After the killing of the survivors, one Zulu force moved to take Roark's Drift, a thinly defended outpost a few miles away. The Zulu had been united into a nation by Shaka in the early nineteenth century, and they remained nationalistic and militarily potent until the Zulu War of 1879.

Like the Zulus, many peoples began to identify themselves more strongly with their government or ethnic group in the latter part of the eighteenth century. This modern nationalism was fostered by intellectuals, especially writers and scholars, who collected folktales and wrote histories. They both discovered and recreated various national pasts and traditions that inspired elite and commoners alike. Political leaders promoted nationalist movements to enhance their political power in internal unification and expansionist foreign policies.

SOCIAL AND POLITICAL ELEMENTS OF NATIONALISM

Every person plays several roles in society. One person may be a parent, spouse, community member, member of a particular occupation, and so forth. While all these roles are held at the same time, they may not be felt equally strongly. **Nationalism** is an ideology that emphasizes one's social role as a member of a nation. The nation always is characterized by a sense of ownership of the government, the nation-state. In addition, the nation usually has several characteristics:

—a common language,

—shared historical experiences and institutions, and

—similar cultural traditions, including religion, at both elite and popular levels.

In some cases, nationalism can exist even when a people does not have its own state, as with the Bosnian Serbs in the 1990s. As the fighting in Bosnia showed, nationalism has both inclusive and exclusive characteristics: The Serbs united (inclusion) and warred against the Muslims and Croats (exclusion), who also fought against each other.

Modern nationalism emerged from intellectuals and members of other elite groups, who united to enjoy common cultural activities or to defend against a common enemy. Previously, many European intellectuals of the Enlightenment had seen themselves as members of an international community, members who may have been French, German, or English but who were united by a common desire to seek universal solutions to humanity's problems. French thinkers and the French language tended to dominate intellectual discourse. Nationalists reacted against this internationalism and French cultural influence. They focused instead on the nation and their national language.

Nationalism spread to other social groups through the development of institutions like national armed forces, educational systems, extended voting franchises, and transportation networks. Often, this process emerged from policies of government officials who wished to develop a citizenry passionately devoted to the state. Newly drafted soldiers, who had been taught to revere a national flag, anthem, and history, underwent further military indoctrination to ensure that they would sacrifice their lives in the national interest. Casting votes in national elections gave people roles in forming governments and a sense of ownership of their nation-states.

Nationalism also developed in highly charged political contexts. Zulus united against other tribes and fought against Europeans, who encroached upon Zululand. Japanese leaders feared European invasion and domination, promoting nationalist slogans like "revere the Emperor and expel the foreigners." American colonists who formed the United States unified against what they perceived as tyrannical rule by Britain. Canadians united partly in fear of conquest by the United States.

Modern nationalism emerged from global interactions among peoples. During the nineteenth and twentieth centuries, Westerners and Japanese ruled indigenous peoples in empires in which the nationalistic passions of the rulers triggered nationalist movements among their subjects. These movements toppled modern empires in the twentieth century.

MODERN NATIONALISM AS AN IDEOLOGY AND POLITICAL FORCE

Nationalism has been a potent ideology and catalytic force in the nineteenth and twentieth centuries. From 1859 to 1871, nationalism played a major role in the creation of two nation-states, Italy and Germany, drastically altering the European political scene. Later, at the end of World War I, nationalism helped bring Poland, Hungary, Yugoslavia, Czechoslovakia, Latvia, Lithuania, and Estonia into being. Eventually, nationalism sparked successful independence movements in the Pacific islands, Africa, and Asia. Nationalism helped to splinter Yugoslavia and Czechoslovakia in the 1990s and eased the reunification of Hong Kong with China in mid-1997.

Early Nationalist Thought

The most developed expression of early nationalism came through the writings of Johann von Herder (1744–1803), a German. During the 1780s, Herder argued that intellectuals alone could not create nationalism; rather, they should build on elements of the common folk culture. Herder believed that a nation's past should play a vital role in the understanding of the present and planning for the future. Further, he argued, the masses should be encouraged to play a part in developing a nation's greatness. Herder and his followers condemned the French ideas and language that dominated princely courts in German-speaking areas.

Not only were French intellectuals predominant in European intellectual discourse, but French military power controlled many Europeans from 1794 to 1815. Johann Fichte (1762–1814), a major intellectual and follower of Herder, initially welcomed the French Revolution as an expression of the emancipation of the human spirit, but after the French conquered and ruled many German-speaking domains, Fichte issued his *Addresses to the German Nation* to summon a latent German spirit that he believed superior to that of the French. German nationalism was forged in reaction to French domination.

Italian intellectuals responded positively to the ideas of the American and French revolutions, but they quickly became disillusioned with the terror in France and then with the repressive rule of the French. Some Italians welcomed revolutionary ideas, like the right of a people to determine its own laws, and championed the sentiment that a nation was a unit of humanity with the right to determine its own form of political rule. Napoleon Bonaparte twice invaded Italy, and French rule helped unleash early Italian nationalism.

Map 33.1 *Napoleon's Empire. Under Napoleon, the French ruled significant parts of Germany, Italy, and Spain. Their rule sometimes excited national movements of opposition to foreign domination. After the end of French control, some Germans, Italians, and Spaniards unsuccessfully attempted to establish national governments. By 1871, a united Germany and a united Italy emerged from wars of independence, wars that had connections to the national movements begun during the Napoleonic era.*

Imposition of the French language, however, provoked many intellectuals to promote cultural nationalism. Later, collapse of French rule brought in the Austrians, who opposed Italian unification as a threat to their empire.

Hatred of French tyranny captured the imagination of artists like Francisco Goya, who painted powerful scenes of Spanish patriots dying at the hands of their French rulers, conveying the horror of tyranny. Anti-French patriotic sentiments received a boost from such paintings, and they helped fuel a national mood that brought a return of the Spanish monarchy.

Gathering folktales became a way to recover and preserve the oral and written traditions of a nation, promoting nationalist identity and pride. The Grimm brothers, for example, spent many years traveling through German-speaking areas and collecting folktales and folk poetry. Wilhelm Grimm once wrote that "only folk poetry is perfect because God himself wrote it like the laws of Sinai; it is not put together from pieces like human work is." In 1812, the Grimm brothers' published endeavors began reaching a wide audience in Germany.

In a similar vein, Central European scholars followed Johann von Herder's idea that language was the glue holding a nation together. According to this idea, language was the essence of a national people and should therefore be purified by the excision of foreign words. Small groups of scholars developed grammars, compiled dictionaries, wrote literature, and edited journals. They created standard languages, like modern Czech, Slovak, Hungarian, Ukrainian, and Bulgarian, from the native tongues of peasants, servants, and shopkeepers. From these scholars also came the nationalist belief that the nation-state was the political framework for the fullest realization of the individual.

European Romanticism

Romanticism, an artistic movement of the period between 1780 and 1900, developed in Europe and spread to several countries, including those in the Americas. Romanticism, the elite artistic emphasis on feelings, imagination, and nature, often was employed as a vehicle to create national identity. European Romanticism began partly as a reaction to the Enlightenment's emphasis on reason, science, and humankind. Increasingly, Romantic writers and composers searched out their nations' folktales and folk songs to express love for the

FIGURE 33.1 ***Spanish Resistance to French Rule.*** *Francisco Goya made scores of etchings depicting the Spanish fight against the French from 1808 to 1813. In this scene, a Spaniard armed with a pitchfork drives away a feeble vulture. The vulture is a satire on the imperial eagle of Napoleon; the comical spectacle of its removal appears to delight the unarmed crowd in the background. Humor has often been an effective weapon against repressive governments.* Nimatallah/Art Resource, N.Y.

IN THEIR OWN WORDS

Friedrich Schlegel on Romantic Poetry

In 1798, Friedrich Schlegel and his brother often hosted gatherings of German intellectuals who criticized what they considered the bankruptcy of rationalism and championed a poetry of intuition and emotion. Among the people attending was Novalis (Friedrich von Hardenberg), who became a significant Romantic poet. Friedrich Schlegel wrote this fragment that outlined his conception of Romantic poetry:

> Romantic poetry is progressive, universal poetry. Its aim isn't merely to reunite all the separate species of poetry and put poetry in touch with philosophy and rhetoric. It tries to and should mix and fuse poetry and prose, inspiration and criticism, the poetry of art and the poetry of nature; and make poetry lively and social, and life and society poetical; poeticize wit and fill and saturate the forms of art with every kind of good, solid matter for instruction, and animate them with pulsations of humor. It embraces everything that is purely poetic, from the greatest systems of art, containing within themselves still further systems, to the sigh, the kiss that the poetizing child breathes forth in artless song. It can so lose itself in what it describes that one might believe it exists only to characterize poetical individuals of all sorts; and yet there is still no form so fit for expressing the entire spirit of an author; so that many artists who started out to write only a novel ended up by providing us with a portrait of themselves. It alone can become, like the epic, a mirror of the circumambient world, an image of an age. And it can also—more than any other form—hover at the midpoint between the portrayed and the portrayer, free of all real and ideal self-interest, on the wings of poetic reflection again and again to a higher power, can multiply it in an endless succession of mirrors. It is capable of the highest and most variegated refinement, not only from within outwards, but also from without inwards; capable in that it organizes—for everything that seeks a wholeness in its effects—the parts along similar lines, so that it opens a perspective upon an infinitely increasing classicism. Romantic poetry is in the arts what wit is in philosophy, and what society and sociability, friendship and love are in life. Other kinds of poetry are finished and are now capable of being fully analyzed. The romantic kind of poetry is still in the state of becoming; that, in fact, is its real essence: that it should forever be becoming and never be perfected. It can be exhausted by no theory and only a divinatory criticism would dare try to characterize its ideal. It alone is infinite, just as it alone is free; and it recognizes as its first commandment that the will of the poet can tolerate no law above itself. The romantic kind of poetry is the only one that is more than a kind, that is, as it were, poetry itself: for in a sense all poetry is or should be romantic.

nation and admiration for its heroes. German Romantics, for example, responded to calls by patriots to create a national culture that differed from French culture.

Friedrich von Hardenberg, also known as Novalis (1772–1801), was an important member of a group of German intellectuals who developed German Romanticism in the 1790s. Of these thinkers, Novalis perhaps best exemplifies the importance of the individual in Romanticism. In 1797, Novalis's fiancée died, an event that inspired him to write poetry that eventually brought him great popularity. Death became a central theme in Novalis's poetry, and he saw death as the purpose of life, a time of transcendent unity with God. Humanity and nature also became central themes of Novalis's writings, leading to a mystical vision of uniting human beings with nature.

Richard Wagner[1] (1813–1883) embodied a Romantic artistic image and also nationalist tendencies in his work and life. Wagner's operas served as musical dramas, uniting art, dance, music, and poetry. He exulted in the Romantic image of the individual as genius. In his grand artistic synthesis, Wagner followed the tradition of earlier Romantics like Novalis. German history fascinated Wagner, and it came to life for him in the works he read; like other German nationalists,

[1] **Richard Wagner:** ree KAHRD VAHG ner

Wagner took a keen interest in German folktales and legends, incorporating many into his operas.

Wagner saw himself as the living embodiment of the destiny of the German nation. In 1842, upon returning to Germany from France, Wagner wrote, "I saw the Rhine [River] for the first time; with tears swelling in my eyes I, a poor artist, swore eternal loyalty to my German fatherland." He gave the operatic theater a central place in German social life. The Wagnerian opera cycle, a set of related operas, lasted for more than ninety hours of singing, dancing, and acting on the grandest scale. This led Gustav Mahler to exclaim that "If the whole of German art were to disappear, it could be recognized and reconstructed from this one work."

FIGURE 33.2 ***Shaka.*** *Although this portrait titled "Chaka, King of the Zooloe" may not be an exact likeness of Shaka (few existed), it is an accurate rendering of a warrior of his time. The shield, however, may be somewhat larger than the shields carried into battle.* MuseuMAfricA, Johannesburg.

NATIONAL UNIFICATION EFFORTS, 1816–1877

Major unification drives occurred in Africa, Asia, Europe, and the Americas between 1816 and 1877. All were directed by ruling elites and enjoyed varying degrees of popular support in the form of nationalism. Three nations, Zululand, Japan, and the United States were challenged by external threats (invasion) or internal threats (civil war). By 1877, many countries around the world had strengthened or forged nation-states.

The Development of the Zulu Nation

In the nineteenth century, the Zulu nation had expanded into parts of southern Africa and had come upon European settlers who blocked further settlement. The confrontation helped maintain the Zulu nation by strengthening Zulu nationalism against their enemy. The Zulu spoke a common language and shared a variety of historical experiences, institutions, and cultural traditions. Conflict with Dutch and English settlers revealed the need to consolidate Zulu political and military systems for protection.

The architect of the modern Zulu nation was Shaka (reign dates 1816–1828), who assumed rulership of the Zulus when they faced the Europeans. Shaka's military genius flowered in a series of reforms. First and most important, he declared that the primary goal of warfare was to kill large numbers of the enemy. Previously, warfare had been a ritualized affair with a battle frequently ending upon the wounding of someone. Rarely would more than a few people be killed. Second, Shaka's armies were organized into formal regiments and drilled in formations and with coordinated actions. This forged a powerful bonding among the warriors, making them more likely to win large battles. Third, Shaka converted the throwing spear, a traditional weapon, into a shorter thrusting spear. His soldiers were able to advance on the enemy with shields locked, impregnable to thrown spears; then, when close enough, they rushed upon the now-defenseless

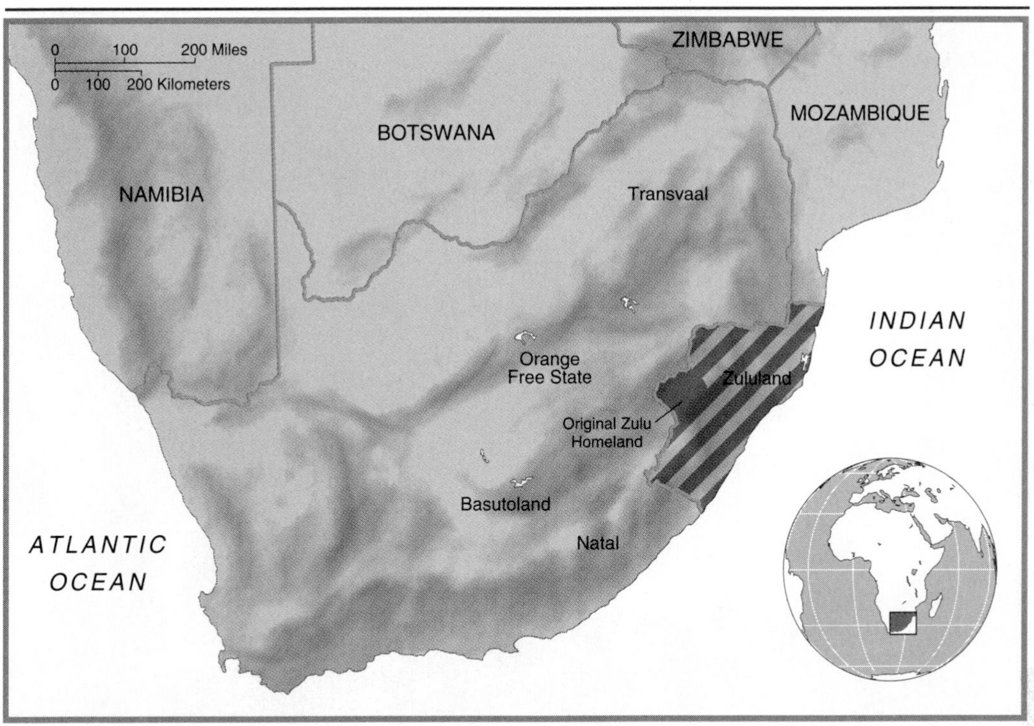

Map 33.2 ***Zulu Expansion, 1816–1879.*** *Under the leadership of Shaka and his successors, the Zulus conquered and united considerable territory, creating Zululand. Zulu nationalism helped spur this expansion, which came at the expense of other tribal groups, some of whom were assimilated by the Zulus. Zulu expansion came to an end with the defeat of Zulu forces by the British in 1879. Eventually, Zululand became part of the Union of South Africa.*

foe. Fourth, Shaka assimilated conquered peoples into his own nation, ensuring a stock of women to produce food for his soldiers and a supply of men for future replacement of battlefield losses.

These reforms strengthened the Zulu nation and made it invincible against other African peoples. Indoctrination of Zulu soldiers and captives ensured a cohesive nationalism, and success in warfare lured warriors from nearby tribes, who volunteered to join the growing Zulu nation. A powerful Zululand gradually emerged, one that outlived Shaka, who was assassinated by a half-brother, Dingane.

The Zulu ambushed and killed nearly 500 Dutch colonists in 1838, incurring the wrath of the Europeans. After decades of conflict, the British finally conquered the Zulu in 1879. The Zulu legacy as a model for nationalism inspired other African peoples to undertake nationalist movements.

The Development of Japanese Nationalism

Japanese nationalism emerged from elite fears that Japan's modest size invited foreign domination. The immediate threat began when ships of Western countries entered Japanese waters in the late eighteenth century in violation of the Japanese policy of closing Japan to most Western commerce and communication. News of China's defeat by the British in the Opium War (1839–1842) alarmed the Japanese emperor, who commanded the *shogun* to strengthen Japan's defenses. This order shocked the Japanese because the emperor had hitherto been a puppet dancing to the *shogun*'s tune.

Pilgrimages to imperial shrines by commoners also indicated the revival of emperor worship. Scholars who foresaw the decline of the Tokugawa Shogunate predicted that only the imperial system

FIGURE 33.3 *Satsuma* **Samurai** ***Fighting Imperial Troops.*** *During the Satsuma Uprising, a conscript army of diverse social groups fought for the Japanese government against the warriors of Satsuma. In this print, mounted imperial troops in Western-style uniforms charge traditionally attired Japanese women armed with long-handled swords, or* naginata. *Women, however, seldom fought in armed combat during this time.* Tsuneo Tamba Collection, Yokohama, Japan/Laurie Platt Winfrey, Inc.

could rally the Japanese to defend themselves against outside threats. By 1868, a coalition of *samurai* and court nobles wrested control of the imperial palace from shogunal troops, ending the shogunate in the next few months. These new Japanese leaders used an emperor-based nationalism to legitimize their policies.

Nationalism drove many of the revolutionary changes wrought in the emperor's name. Japan's new leaders transformed the shogunal system of central and local government into a highly centralized unitary state, luring local leaders to surrender their domains to the emperor. A national army was created by conscription, undermining the exclusive *samurai* privilege of wearing swords, and imperial shrines were brought under government control. National symbols and patriotic sentiments became an essential part of the Japanese educational system. Students began each school day with a salute to the flag and a bow to the emperor's portrait.

Samurai smarted from a series of blows to their financial, social, and political bases. One large group rallied around Saigo Takamori, a former government leader, in the Satsuma Uprising of 1877. The crushing of these insurgent *samurai* in the brief civil war preserved the Japanese union and permitted the nationalist transformation to continue.

By 1894, Japan's Westernization and modernization policies achieved success. Japanese leaders embarked on a program to build an Asian empire, and the Sino-Japanese War (1894–1895) and the Russo-Japanese War (1904–1905) intensified the Japanese nationalism that led to their military successes. In 1905, some patriots rioted against their government when they learned that Japan received less than had been expected from the Russo-Japanese War's settlement. During World War I, Japan won additional territory in China, and patriots in the Japanese military plotted a takeover of Manchuria between 1928 and 1931. The success of this plot in 1932 triggered an upsurge of Japanese nationalism that eventually helped unleash World War II in Asia.

Nationalism and the Unification of Italy

Italy had been divided for many centuries. In 1859, eight separate states ruled parts of the Italian Peninsula and the islands of Sardinia and Sicily. Most of these polities had existed since the Middle Ages, and some had become powerful governments during the Italian Renaissance. In addition, France and Austria controlled parts of the Italian Peninsula.

Nationalism played a role in the unification of Italy, but nationalists who favored a republic were outmaneuvered by Count Camillo di Cavour (1810–1861), who preferred an Italian monarchy. Cavour was a nationalist who initially believed that a united Italy was an impossible dream. Yet national unity did come, between 1859 and 1871. Prior to that time, much of the intellectual foundation for an Italian nation-state had been laid. A group of thinkers, including Giuseppi Mazzini (1805–1872), founded Young Italy, a secret society to promote unification of the Italian Peninsula. Mazzini's group ardently propagandized the cause of Italian nationalism, and operas by Giuseppi Verdi helped inspire a birth of the Italian spirit.

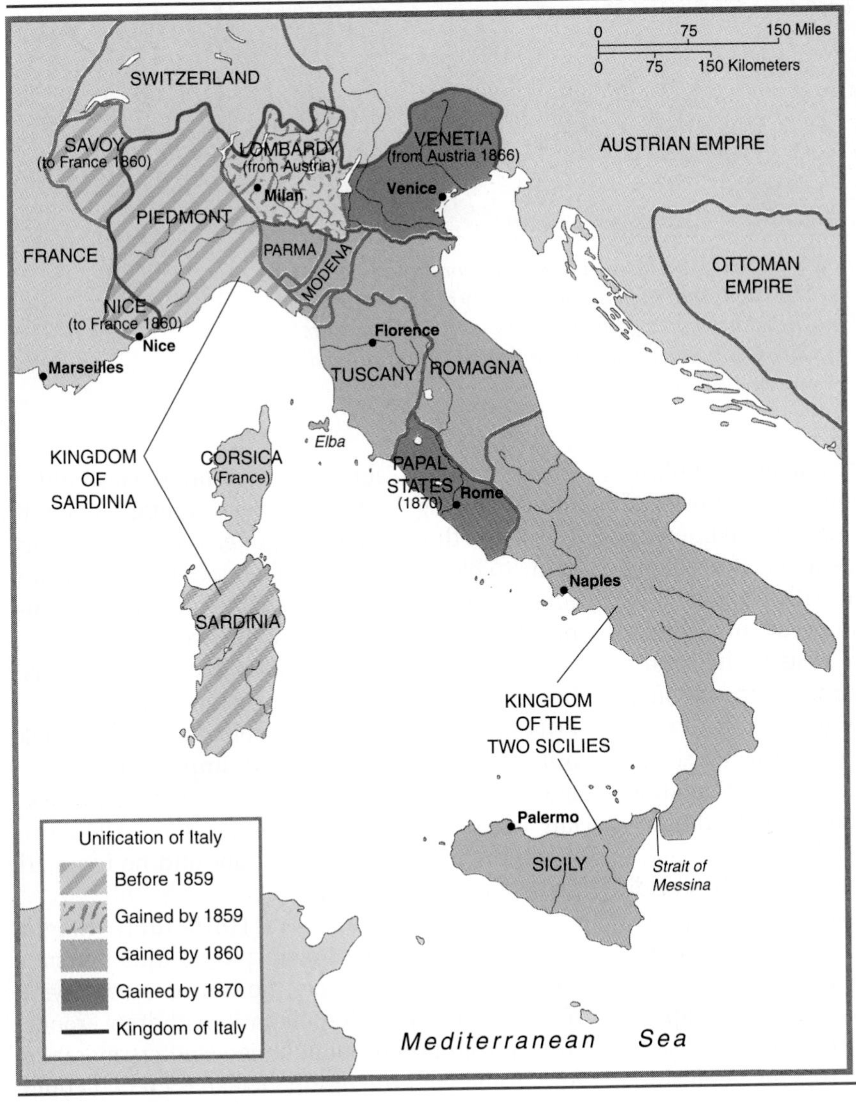

MAP 33.3 *The Unification of Italy, 1859–1871. The Kingdom of Piedmont-Sardinia unwittingly initiated the unification of Italy by seeking to expand its territories. Count Cavour allied with the French to wrest parts of northern Italy away from the Austrians. This partly successful effort spurred Italian nationalists who sought a wider unification of Italy. By 1871, all Italian territories, including the Papal States and Rome, were annexed. Sicily was added as well.*

FIGURE 33.4 ***Garibaldi Landing in Sicily.*** *Giuseppi Garibaldi, an Italian nationalist, formed a liberation army known as "The Thousand" to fight for the unity of his country. This scene depicts a larger-than-life Garibaldi exhorting his troops onward. His forces are welcomed and resisted. After taking Sicily, Garibaldi crossed to the Italian Peninsula and advanced northward.* Collection Bertarelli, Milan. Photo by Saporetti.

Count Cavour played a key role in the unification of Italy after he became the prime minister of Piedmont-Sardinia in 1852. Cavour planned to build Italy as an extension of his state. Efforts along those lines led to an alliance with Napoleon III (reign dates 1852–1870), emperor of France. Napoleon III desired to annex areas to the southeast of France, and Cavour managed to convince France to wage a joint campaign against Austria-Hungary in exchange for these provinces. Napoleon III's forces defeated the Austrians, liberating part of northern Italy and doubling Piedmont-Sardinia's size.

Another Italian nationalist, Giuseppi Garibaldi (1807–1882), independently led an army of patriotic soldiers to free southern Italy from foreign rule. After Garibaldi freed Sicily, middle-class Italian nationalists supported his march on Naples. Large-scale disturbances broke out there, and support for a united Italy spread across the peninsula. These popular activities facilitated Garibaldi's effort. Fearing French anger and military action if Garibaldi threatened the pope, Cavour used his army to block Garibaldi's liberation of Rome. After intense negotiations, Garibaldi offered his conquests to the king of Piedmont-Sardinia.

Venice, which was ruled by the Austrians, became part of Italy as a result of the Austro-Prussian War of 1866. The defeat of Austria took only seven weeks and had important consequences for Italy. After Prussia's victory, the Prussian leader, Otto von Bismarck, compelled the Austrians to cede Venice to Italy, and he initiated an alliance with the Italians.

The Franco-Prussian War (1870–1871) brought the last piece of the Italian puzzle under Italian control. In order to meet the German army with his forces amassed, Napoleon III withdrew French troops from Rome. Soon, Italian soldiers marched into Rome, and the utterly defeated French could do nothing about it. Less than a year later, Rome became the capital of a united Italy, and the Vatican, a tiny area of the city, remained independent under the pope's control. Losing Rome, however, turned the papacy against the new state, hampering the program of consolidating the new state's control over Italy.

Nationalism and the Unification of Germany

German unification was facilitated by several factors, including a common language, similar cultural traditions, and the growing economic integration of Germany. Although many Germans desired to form a German nation-state, they failed to attract the requisite support of a major state, particularly Prussia. That had to await the foreign policies of Otto von Bismarck, who had his own vision of the German nation-state.

Political factors became prominent in German unification efforts in the first half of the nineteenth century. We have seen how French rule of German areas turned German cultural nationalism into political nationalism. German nationalists, however, were thwarted by Austria's Prince Clemens Metternich, who helped create a German confederation of nearly forty states under Austrian influence in 1815. Efforts by German nationalists to promote national unification were crushed by Austrian repression. During political upheavals in 1848 and 1849, when Metternich fell from power, German nationalists again failed to create a united Germany.

Economic and social factors played a more vital role in Germany's unification. In the 1830s, many German states formed the Zollverein, a free-trade alliance that included Prussia but excluded Austria. This economic organization promoted trade and economic development, which mushroomed through the rest of the nineteenth century. Another unifying element was the Prussian army's building of an integrated transportation system centering on railroad lines to be used for military purposes in wartime. Through the middle decades of the nineteenth century, musical, sporting, and cultural associations effected German cultural awareness through festivals, shooting contests, and gymnastic events. A first-rate educational system also emerged in the nineteenth century and became a focal point for German intellectuals, many of whom were ardent nationalists.

The architect of German unity was Prussia's chancellor, Otto von Bismarck (1815–1898), who circumvented the Prussian parliament and built up Prussia's armed forces. Thereafter, he used a squabble with the Danes over disputed northern territories to create an alliance with Austria, and

Figure 33.5
Proclaiming the German Empire. *This painting captures the spirit of celebration that accompanied the founding of the German Empire in 1871. Jubilant officers hold their swords aloft, while Otto von Bismarck, who became the empire's first chancellor, dominates the foreground. Attired in white in a sea of black uniforms, von Bismarck is the painting's central figure despite his placement below the German monarch. Much to the dismay of the French, the German Empire was proclaimed on French soil, at Versailles, the palace of Louis XIV.*
Bismarck Museum, Friedrichsruh.

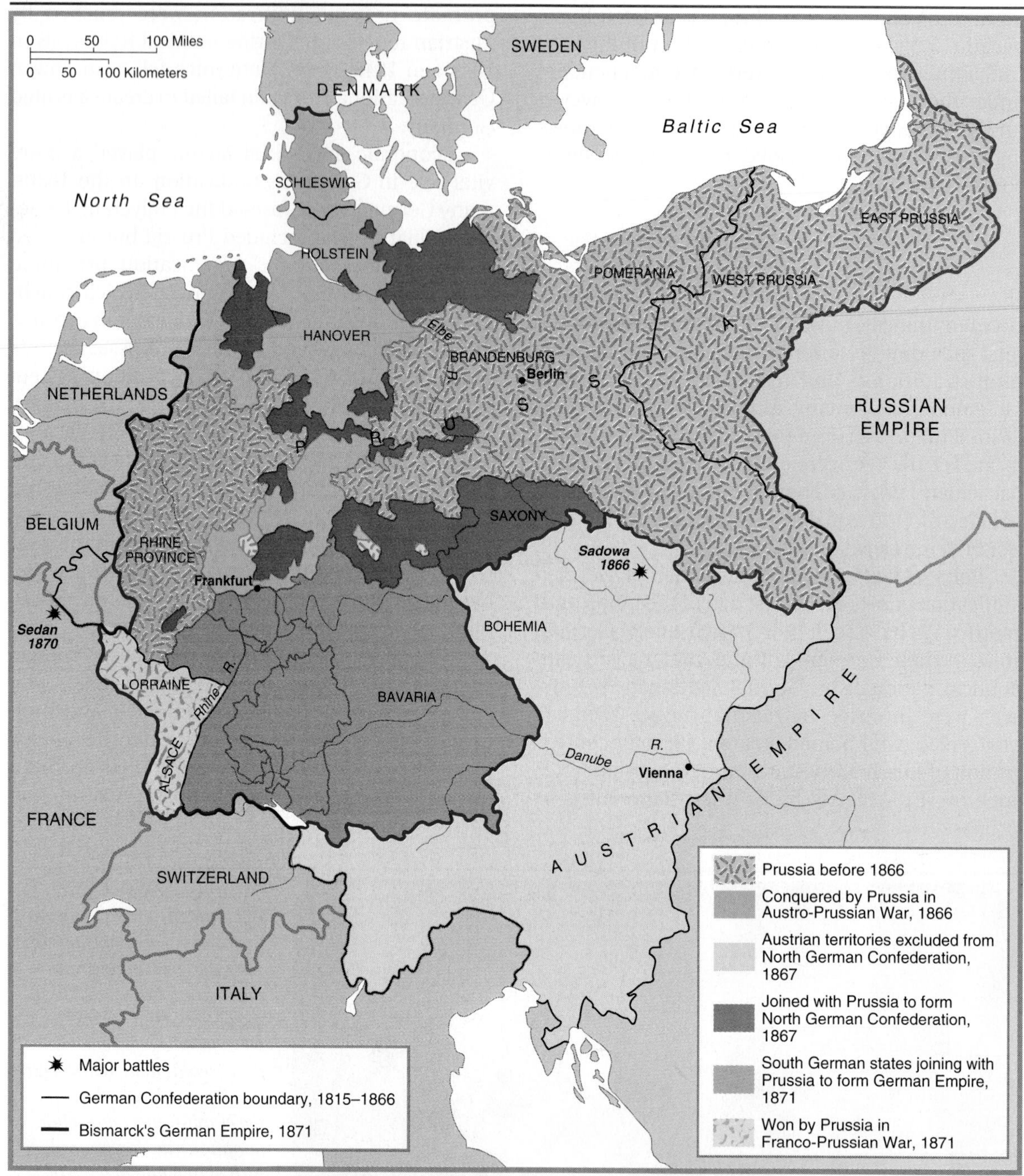

MAP 33.4 ***The Unification of Germany, 1863–1871.*** *Prussia, under the leadership of Otto von Bismarck, began a policy of territorial expansion that culminated in German unification. The disputed territories of Schleswig and Holstein were wrested away from Denmark in 1863. A few years later, Prussia defeated Austria, omitting the Austrians (many of whom spoke German) from a united Germany. In 1870, France and Prussia went to war. German nationalism generated during this conflict helped push the final unification of the German states in 1871. France also lost Alsace and Lorraine to Germany, a loss that rankled the French into the twentieth century.*

their combined forces compelled the Danes to cede the contested areas. Then Bismarck deliberately provoked a crisis between Prussia and Austria over who would get the disputed territories, eventually triggering a war with the Austrians in 1866 that ended with Austria's defeat.

A major issue in Germany's unification was the composition of the German nation. Some favored a broad definition that included all German-speaking peoples; others espoused a more limited interpretation that excluded the German-speaking Austrians. A major reason for keeping out the Austrians was their rule over non-Germans (e.g., Poles, Hungarians, and Czechs). As long as Austrians insisted on keeping these peoples subject, many opposed their inclusion in Germany. More of a Prussian patriot than a German nationalist, Otto von Bismarck wanted Prussia to dominate a German state, and he had to exclude powerful Austria from the union, fearing that it could effectively challenge Prussian dominance.

To achieve German unification, Bismarck believed he needed to provoke the French into declaring war on Prussia. This could animate German nationalism to drive the remaining German states into a Prussian-dominated union. French nationalists, succumbing to some provocative diplomatic maneuvers by Bismarck, demanded that Napoleon III declare war. The remaining German states joined Prussia, whose train-transported forces quickly overwhelmed the French. Napoleon III fell into Prussian hands at the Battle of Sedan in September 1870. In early 1871, German princes and states declared their allegiance to the German monarch, and the German Empire came into being. The hapless French ceded the provinces of Alsace and Lorraine to the Germans and also paid a substantial indemnity.

Zionism: The Development of Jewish Nationalism

Zionism grew out of a reaction to the pervasive anti-Semitism in Europe at the turn of the twentieth century. Richard Wagner was but one of many intellectuals and others who hated Jews, blaming them for a variety of misfortunes plaguing Europe. A long-term economic recession from the 1870s to the 1890s, for example, provoked hatred against Jews, who were imagined to be behind the trouble. This was a continuation of a centuries-old animosity against Jews.

Theodore Herzl (1860–1904) was a Hungarian-born Jew and journalist who covered stories involving Jews. After writing about the Dreyfus Affair, a famous French legal case that revealed deep-seated French anti-Semitism, Herzl wrote a pamphlet, *The Jewish State*, in which he argued that Jews should have their own nation-state. The

Figure 33.6 ***Theodore Herzl.*** *In this 1903 photo, Theodore Herzl greets people outside a synagogue. Herzl had become well known in the Jewish community for his advocacy of Zionism, the movement to create a modern Jewish state in Palestine.* The Central Zionist Archive, Jerusalem.

nationalist movement devoted to this cause, Zionism, developed, and it united Jews around the world. Zionism had a strong millennial component because some Zionists believed that the founding of a Jewish state would be the onset of the last days of the world.

Zionism flourished in eastern and central Europe in the twentieth century. Societies like the Lovers of Zion and the Jewish Colonization Association promoted Jewish settlement of Palestine, in Southwest Asia, which Jews considered to be their traditional homeland. Zionist aims grew in intensity because of the Nazi Holocaust, a deliberate extermination campaign by the German state that killed millions of Jews during World War II. Many survivors ardently believed that Jews deserved a homeland in Palestine. In 1948, the dream became a reality as the state of Israel, but the methods and passions of Zionists also helped spark Palestinian nationalism.

The U.S. Civil War

The United States underwent a major test of its unity during the Civil War (1861–1865), America's bloodiest and most convulsive conflict. Earlier, nationalism had aided in the formation of the United States, but, by mid–nineteenth century, many disagreements among states threatened the Union with dissolution. The central problem was states' rights versus those of the federal government.

Political and economic issues tied to slavery sharply divided Americans. Although many in the North morally objected to slavery and wished to abolish it, the central issue igniting the conflict was whether or not states might secede from the Union. Indeed, slavery remained in some Union states, like Maryland, until after the end of the Civil War. Southern states had long been upset by the federal government's economic policies favoring the industrialized northern states. The South's agriculture-based society needed high-tariff policies, which ran counter to the interests of other states. In addition, Southern leaders believed that the growing movement to abolish slavery in the United States could lead to an agricultural catastrophe, because they remained convinced of the need for slave labor in order to work their plantations and maintain their profits.

President Abraham Lincoln (1809–1865) strove ardently to maintain the Union. He told suspicious Southern leaders that he could live with slavery but not with disunion. These pleas fell on deaf ears, and war erupted. Northern states possessed superior material resources and industrial capabilities that gradually overcame the superior generalship of Southern generals like Robert E. Lee. At the same time, Lincoln began to conceive of a strategy for postwar rehabilitation and reconciliation. The main effort was to be victory tempered by charity, but Lincoln died from an assassin's bullet before he could implement his plans.

Nationalism sparked many Americans in the North to volunteer to fight for the Union's preservation. Soldiers in the Northern armies usually fought in state units, yet they shared a national purpose, to maintain a strong United States.

Many African American soldiers in the North had responded to the need to free their brothers and sisters from chattel bondage, and more than 186,000 African Americans served in the Union army. These African Americans played a critical role in the fighting that ultimately claimed more than a half-million lives in the North and South. Among famous African American fighting units was the 54th Massachusetts Regiment, which stormed Fort Wagner near Charleston, South Carolina.

Later, freed slaves in the South faced a difficult life with few resources to support themselves, and they benefited only slightly from the Thirteenth, Fourteenth, and Fifteenth amendments to the Constitution. These amendments officially abolished slavery throughout the United States and forbade discrimination based on race and other factors, yet the rights guaranteed by these amendments rarely were recognized after the Civil War.

Canadian Unification

Canadian political leaders decided to unite their country under British protection in the 1860s. The area of British North America had two dominant European groups, those who spoke English and those who spoke French. The latter had been brought under British control in the French and Indian War (1756–1763), and they maintained a separate identity that was encouraged by works like the *Histoire du Canada*, which was published in 1845. The author, François-Xavier Garneau,[2]

[2] **François Xavier Garneau:** frahn SWAH zah vee AY gahr NOH

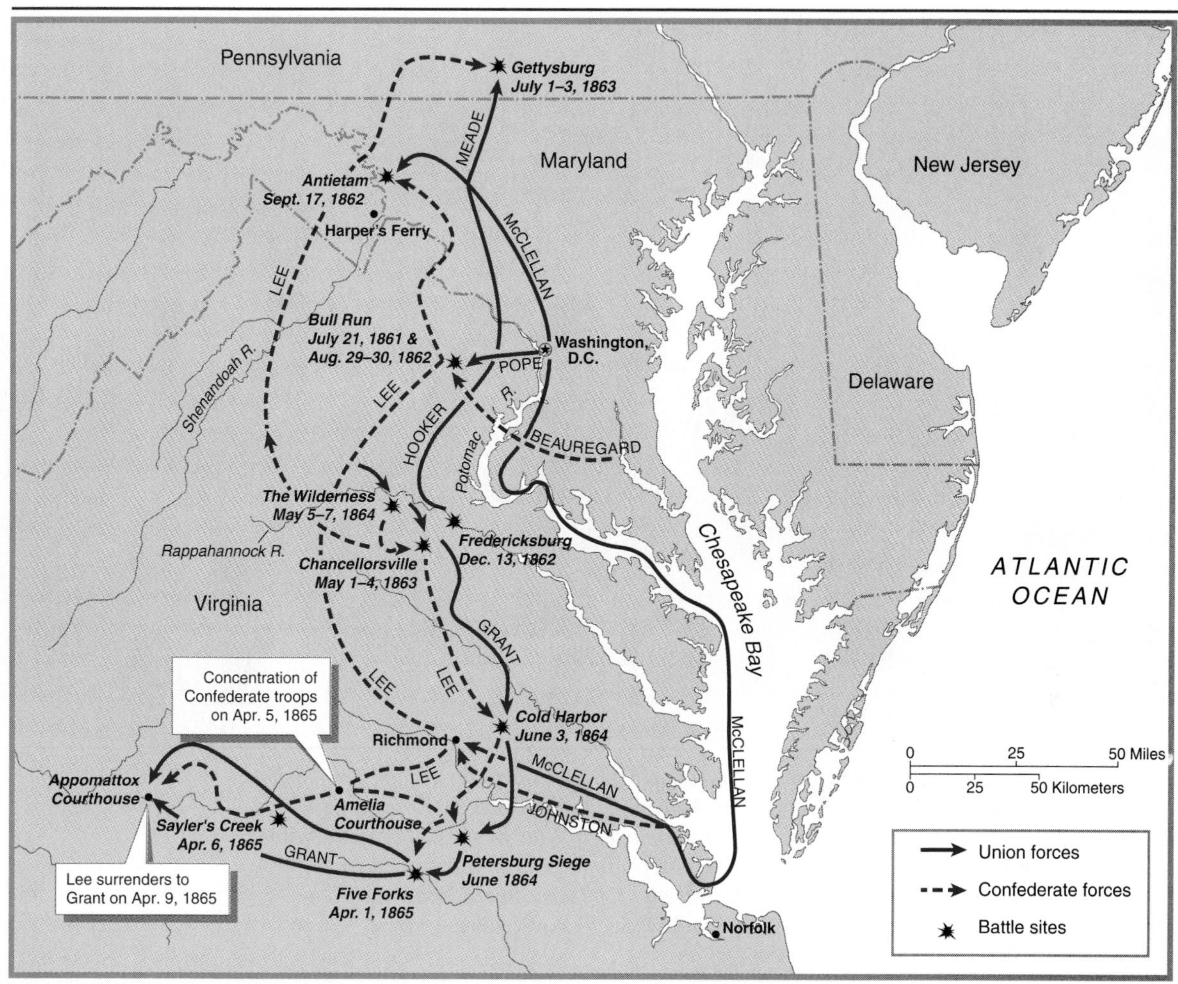

Map 33.5 ***The U.S. Civil War (East), 1861–1865.*** *A major challenge to the United States began in 1861, when several Southern states seceded from the Union. Ferocious fighting followed in the next few years, leading to the deaths of hundreds of thousands. Although fighting erupted in various parts of the South and West, many of the strategic campaigns took place in the East, where the capitals of the North and South were located. A major invasion of the North, begun in 1863, was stopped at Gettysburg by Union forces. Hard fighting occurred for another year and a half until the Southern forces surrendered in April 1865.*

proved that French Canadians had a history and literature, writing a bestselling book in the process.

Canadian political leaders had been stymied in their attempts to reform the government between 1858 and 1864. They slowly realized that political deadlock created the image of weakness, attracting expansionists in the United States, some of whom had even talked about annexing parts of British North America. Two Canadian politicians, George-Étienne Cartier (1814–1873) and John Macdonald (1815–1891), put aside their differences to forge a united Canada. The French-speaking Cartier and the English-speaking Macdonald fervently desired to create a Canada by persuasion rather than coercion because they saw the tragedy of the bloody U.S. Civil War to their south. Macdonald promoted a Canadian experiment in cooperative nationalism, while Cartier desired that English-speaking Canadians accept policies supporting a French Canadian cultural identity.

FIGURE 33.7 ***Canadian Delegates at the Charlottetown Conference.*** *In 1864, delegates from many parts of Canada met on Prince Edward Island to discuss forming a Canadian confederation. Just six weeks later, a second conference in Quebec agreed to federal union. Shown in the foreground (in front of the second pillar from the left) are George-Étienne Cartier and John Macdonald, two key delegates. Meetings at Government House played a key role in the peaceful process of Canadian unity.* Public Archives of Canada, Ottawa, Documentary Art & Photography Division (C-7333).

Canadian unity developed between 1864 and 1867. A key event was the Quebec Conference, which was attended by representatives from all provinces. The delegates agreed on a federal union having central powers and provinces having autonomy, all under British protection. Representatives went to London to get British support for the Canadian proposal. Sympathetic British leaders sold the idea as a relief to British taxpayers and as an opportunity for investment. From the deliberations came the British North America Act of 1867, which created the Dominion of Canada. Prince Edward Island's inhabitants did not join until 1873, and the citizens of Newfoundland waited until 1949 for entrance into the nation-state.

Canadians enjoyed considerable autonomy within the British Commonwealth of Nations. The governor-general of Canada was appointed by London and exercised executive power on advice from the Canadian cabinet. Canadians had created a continental federation of provinces despite sharp ethnic and cultural differences. In the 1990s, however, there has been an upsurge of Quebec nationalism, centered on separating from Canada.

NATIONALISM AND THE COLLAPSE OF EMPIRES

Five major empires—the Chinese, the Ottoman, the Austro-Hungarian, the German, and the Russian—collapsed in the period between 1911 and 1918. Nationalism among subject peoples accelerated the disintegration of these empires. Out of the

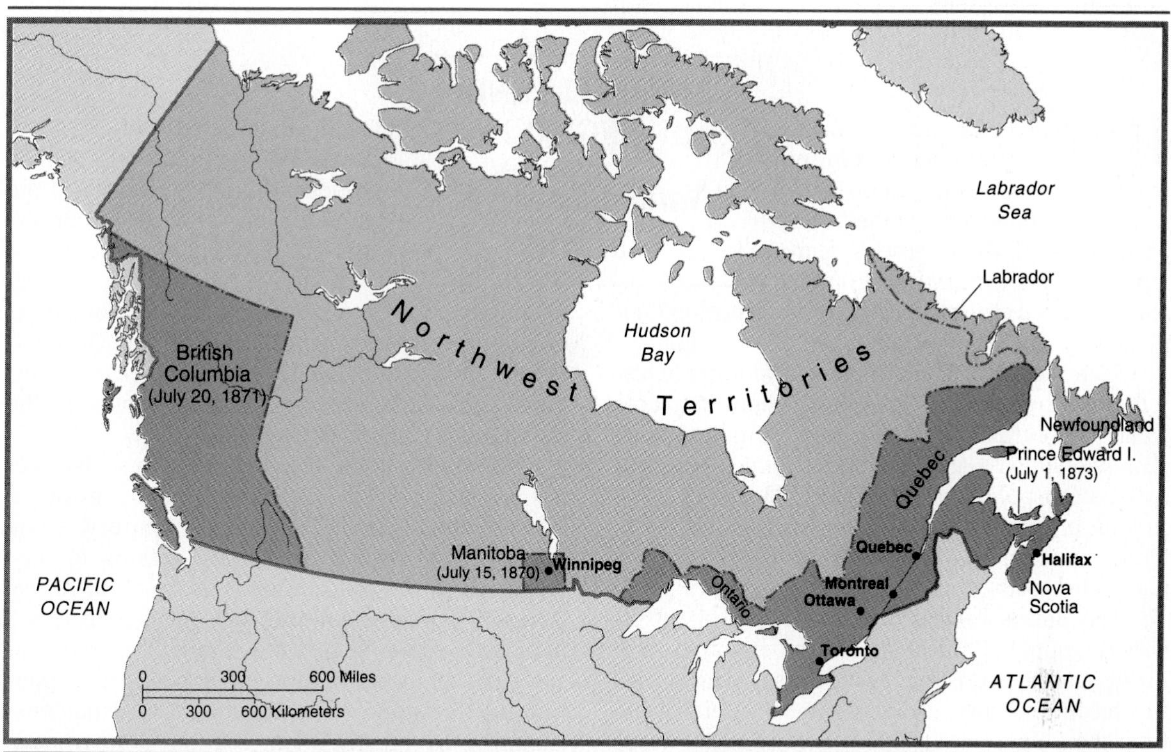

MAP 33.6 ***Dominion of Canada, 1867–1873.*** *Canadian leaders decided to seek union in the late 1860s. They wished to forestall what they feared might be a northward expansion of the United States. Key to a union of Canada was the uniting of Quebec and Ontario, the most populous and prosperous provinces. Soon, most of the eastern maritime provinces joined the union. The British were persuaded to support this effort, keeping considerable influence in Canadian affairs. The unification process was peaceful and relatively noncontroversial.*

aftermath of this disarray came the formation of national states, many of them founded by dominant ethnic groups. Thus, the global map was redrawn dramatically.

The Collapse of China's Imperial System

The Qing Empire had been ruled by the Manchus since the mid–seventeenth century. A few million Manchus controlled the hundreds of millions of Chinese, partly through maintaining the traditional political and social systems, as well as by portraying themselves as determined defenders of Confucian values. Adopting Chinese ways and using military force had kept the Manchus in power for more than two centuries.

During the last two years of the nineteenth century, the Manchu government, headed by the Empress Dowager Cixi,[3] formed an alliance with a secret society called the Boxers. This organization of Chinese commoners, which had been both anti-Manchu and anti-Westerner, dropped the former orientation to concentrate on the anti-Western aspect. In 1900, a Boxer terrorist campaign against Westerners provoked a brief war that ended in defeat, rendering China helpless. If the Western powers had not feared a war over the division of spoils, China might have been partitioned. Utter defeat opened China to increasing foreign control.

The Boxer crisis brought a rare but temporary unity between the Chinese government and its

[3] **Cixi:** soo SHEE

PARALLELS AND DIVERGENCES

Nationalist Secret Societies

In the nineteenth century, Asians, Europeans, and Americans formed secret societies, using nationalist or racist sentiments to incite their members. Most of these groups feared repression by the ruling governments, and they acted circumspectly in order to further their plans.

Secret societies have long been important in history, and they usually have been found in places where an autocratic polity permits no political expression other than its own. In the time of modern nationalism, political aspirants formed secret organizations of intellectuals and others who hoped to ignite national movements in order to achieve nationalist goals.

The Boxers came from a long line of secret-society groups in Chinese history. Underground organizing against an existing regime goes back to at least the second century A.D. The name "Boxers" came from the Chinese designation "Society of Righteous Fists." Members frequently mastered martial-arts techniques and led their followers in antigovernment activities.

The Boxers also developed a strong anti-Western and racist bias that stemmed, in part, from the arrogant and sometimes belligerent actions of Europeans living in China. Upon learning that a growing anti-Western movement flourished in China, the Empress Dowager Cixi (reign dates 1862–1908), who despised Western meddling in China's affairs, cultivated ties with the Boxers. She encouraged their anti-Western activities in exchange for the submergence of anti-Manchu themes. In mid-1900, she allowed Boxer groups into Beijing and hoped that they might oust the troublesome Westerners. The Boxers were defeated and disappeared.

A secret society of Turkish nationalists, the Young Turks, campaigned for a thorough reform and revitalization of the Ottoman Empire. When they finally achieved their constitutional aims, the Young Turks set about oppressing the non-Turkish subjects of the realm.

Muslim brotherhoods originated as societies of like-minded men who preferred the company of fellow Muslims. By the nineteenth century, some brotherhoods turned to politics, seeking to oust Westerners from Muslim lands in Asia and Africa. When they became political, they operated in secret, fearing detection and destruction by the state. For some of them the issue was religion as well as politics, and they opposed conversions by Christian missionaries. By the twentieth century, brotherhoods became politically powerful in Arabia, Egypt, and the Sudan.

Other secret societies formed in Europe and the United States. The Italian Carbonari issued proclamations demanding Italian unity, and one Carbonari member, Giuseppi Mazzini, formed his own secret society, Young Italy, which played a role in propagandizing for Italian unification. Following the American Civil War, disaffected Southerners formed the Ku Klux Klan to intimidate the newly freed slaves, whom they considered racially inferior. Success by this racist group fueled organizations across America.

---

subjects. From 1901 to 1911, Manchu rulers attempted a series of changes, some dramatic, to reform the system. Manchus established Western-style ministries and implemented a constitutional system. Ultimately, however, all efforts collapsed along with the imperial system in 1912.

Chinese nationalism grew as imperial changes provoked political, social, economic, and cultural opposition. The government, for example, attempted to recentralize tax collections. This sparked local and provincial resistance by elite groups that depended on the tax revenues. Most important was the abolition of the Chinese imperial examination system in 1905. This profound decision ended Confucianism as the state ideology and helped sever the cultural ties between the Chinese elite and the Manchu rulers. Ethnic Chinese increasingly blamed the "blood-sucking Manchus" for China's problems. Rising nationalism helped dissolve remaining bonds of legitimacy that kept the Manchus in power. Finally, an abortive uprising in late 1911 triggered the system's collapse. Mongolian nationalism also ignited in the imperial collapse, and the independent state of Outer Mongolia emerged in 1919.

Nationalism brought down the Manchus, but it could not overcome the formidable strength of local and regional interests. In 1928, the Nationalist Party temporarily reunited China, but political ineptitude and Japanese imperialism thwarted nation building. A more lasting result had to wait until 1949, when the Chinese Communist Party forged a new nation-state from the white heat of revolution and civil war.

The Decline and Fall of the Ottoman Empire

By 1800, the Ottoman Turks had ruled a vast empire stretching across parts of Africa, Asia, and Europe for nearly five centuries. They had provided effective rule for their subjects, who repre-

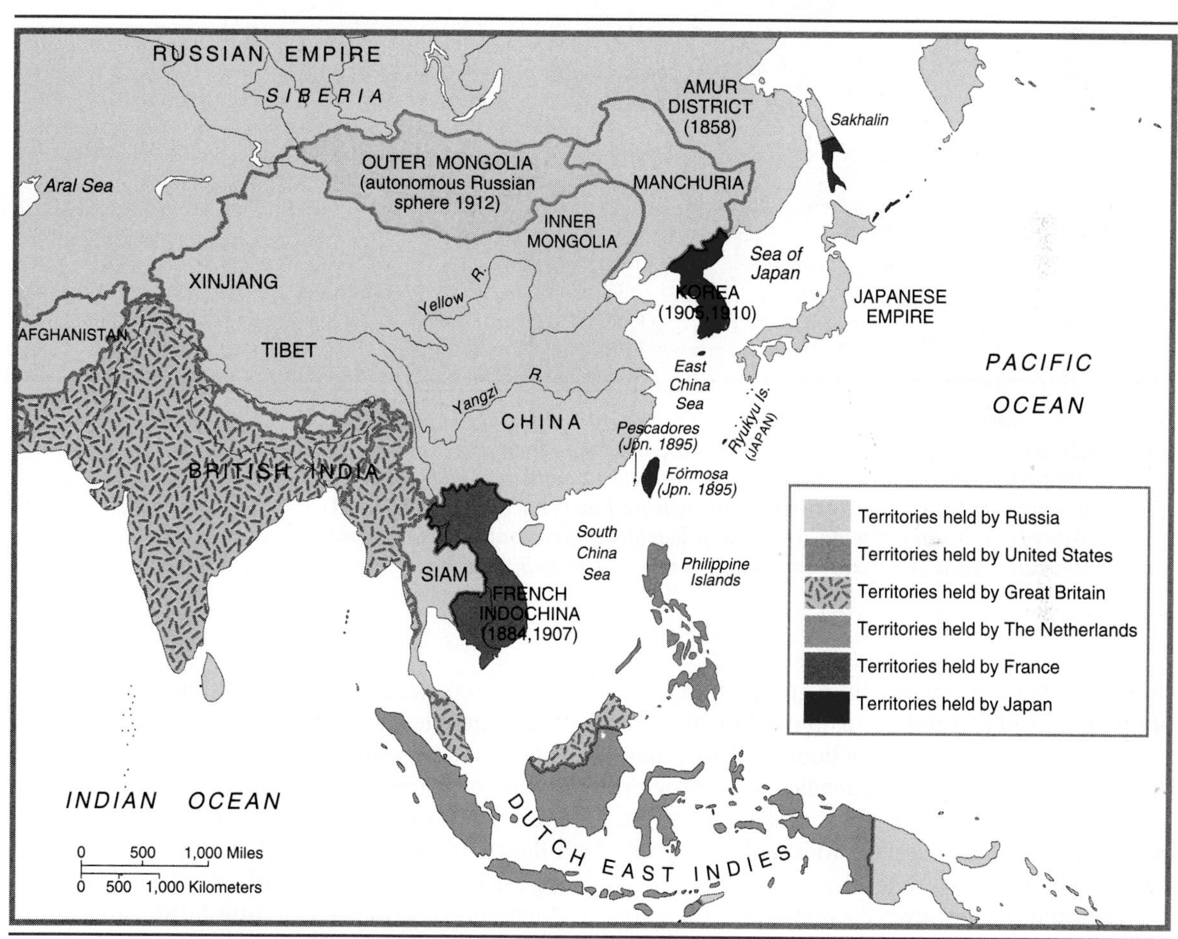

MAP 33.7 ***Nationalism and the Qing (Manchu) Empire to 1912.*** *The Manchus conquered and ruled China, beginning in 1644. They added Tibet, Mongolia, and Xinjiang as Chinese provinces in the seventeenth and eighteenth centuries. The Qing Empire collapsed early in the twentieth century, partly because of an upsurge in Chinese nationalism. In the collapse, Mongolia declared its independence, and Tibet and Xinjiang came under pressure from foreign powers to become independent. Both areas, however, remained under Chinese control.*

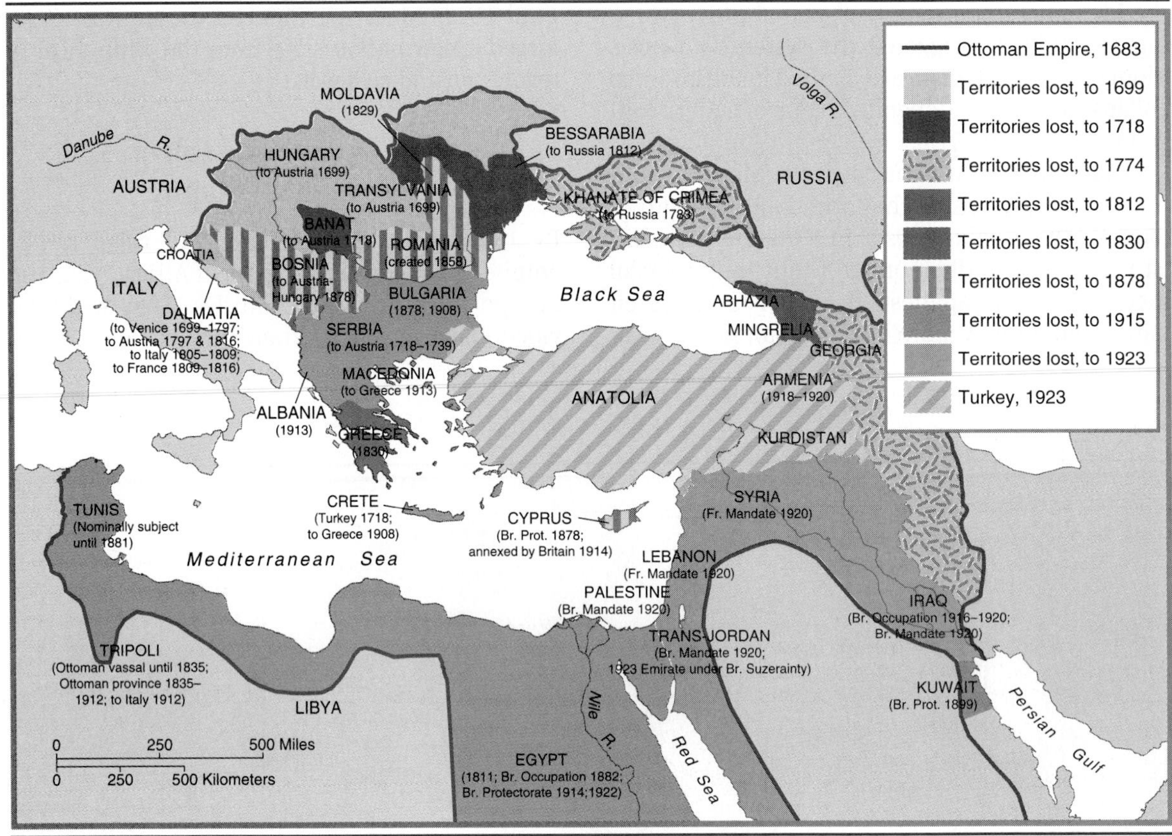

MAP 33.8 ***Nationalism and the Ottoman Empire, to 1923.*** *The Ottoman Turks conquered a vast domain, including parts of Europe, Asia, and Africa. They ruled a diverse group of ethnic peoples for several centuries. In the nineteenth and twentieth centuries, nationalists in the Ottoman Empire began to struggle for independence. By 1918, most of the territory ruled by the Ottoman Turks had fallen out of their control. Rising Turkish nationalism culminated in the creation of the Republic of Turkey in 1923.*

sented a diverse array of ethnic groups that were often organized like guilds. All enjoyed freedom of worship, access to their own schools and hospitals, and legal jurisdiction by the heads of their groups. Non-Muslims generally paid a special tax but were exempt from military service. Most subjects prospered under Ottoman rule.

Nationalism, however, hastened the breakup of the Ottoman Empire, especially in its European territories. Much of the nationalist pressure came in the Balkan Peninsula, which until 1829 had been controlled by the Ottomans. Balkan intellectuals began studying historical manuscripts, purifying national languages, and writing national histories. Soon, nationalists called for independence.

Russia's leaders acted as champions of the Balkan peoples, with whom they shared religious, linguistic, and ethnic ties. In the eighteenth and nineteenth centuries, Russian armies slowly wrested away control of Southeast Europe. Greeks, Bulgarians, Serbs, and Albanians revolted and appealed to the Russians and other states for assistance. At the same time, some European powers intervened to prevent Russia from assuming a dominant position. The Ottoman leaders were unable to resist the European powers, and nationalism developed in European parts of their empire.

The Ottoman Empire's decay also sparked nationalism among the Turks, a powerful ethnic group. Members of the Turkish elite despised the

FIGURE 33.8 *Young Turks Celebrating Victory. In 1908, a group of Turkish reformers wrested control from the Ottoman ruling elite. Inspired by similar movements in Europe, the Young Turk movement had been founded in the 1860s. Its activists declared that Turkey would survive only if it implemented a constitutional system. The Young Turks enjoyed a degree of success but collapsed under the challenge of nationalism.* Culver Pictures.

moribund Ottoman leadership and institutions. In 1908, one group, known as the Young Turks, forced the monarch to establish a constitutional government and ousted the ruling royalist group. They founded a state with a weak monarchy dominated by an elected parliament.

The Ottoman Empire supported the Austro-Hungarian and German empires in World War I, and it suffered the consequences of defeat: imperial collapse and territorial dismemberment. During the war, much of the empire had fallen to the British and French, and the Ottoman realm appeared near total collapse. British and French diplomats and agents had encouraged Arab nationalists, whose calls for independence were ignored after the war.

The Europeans also dictated a peace with the Ottoman ruler in 1920. This humiliating pact incited Turkish nationalists, who conquered the area of modern Turkey. In 1923, under the leadership of Kemal Atatürk (1881–1938), they declared a secular republic and negotiated a favorable settlement.

The Collapse of the Austro-Hungarian Empire

The Austrian Empire had emerged from the Napoleonic Wars with heightened influence in Central Europe. Austria, however, felt threatened by nationalism, which could undermine its multiethnic empire. Austria's foreign minister, Prince Clemens Metternich (1773–1859), led the effort to snuff out nationalistic fervor by ordering executions of or stiff jail terms for nationalists who stirred up people in Italy and Germany, areas of Austrian influence. Both the Italians and Germans, however, won independence and national unification by 1871.

Two other pressing concerns for Austria in the nineteenth century were Hungarian nationalism and the national tensions in the Balkan Peninsula. In 1867, the former problem was solved when Hungarians gained substantial autonomy, forming the Austro-Hungarian Empire. Hungarians won self-rulership with their own cabinet and administrative system, and Hungarian became the official language. Although this generous solution bought peace with the Hungarians, it became the model for other nationalities that demanded to rule

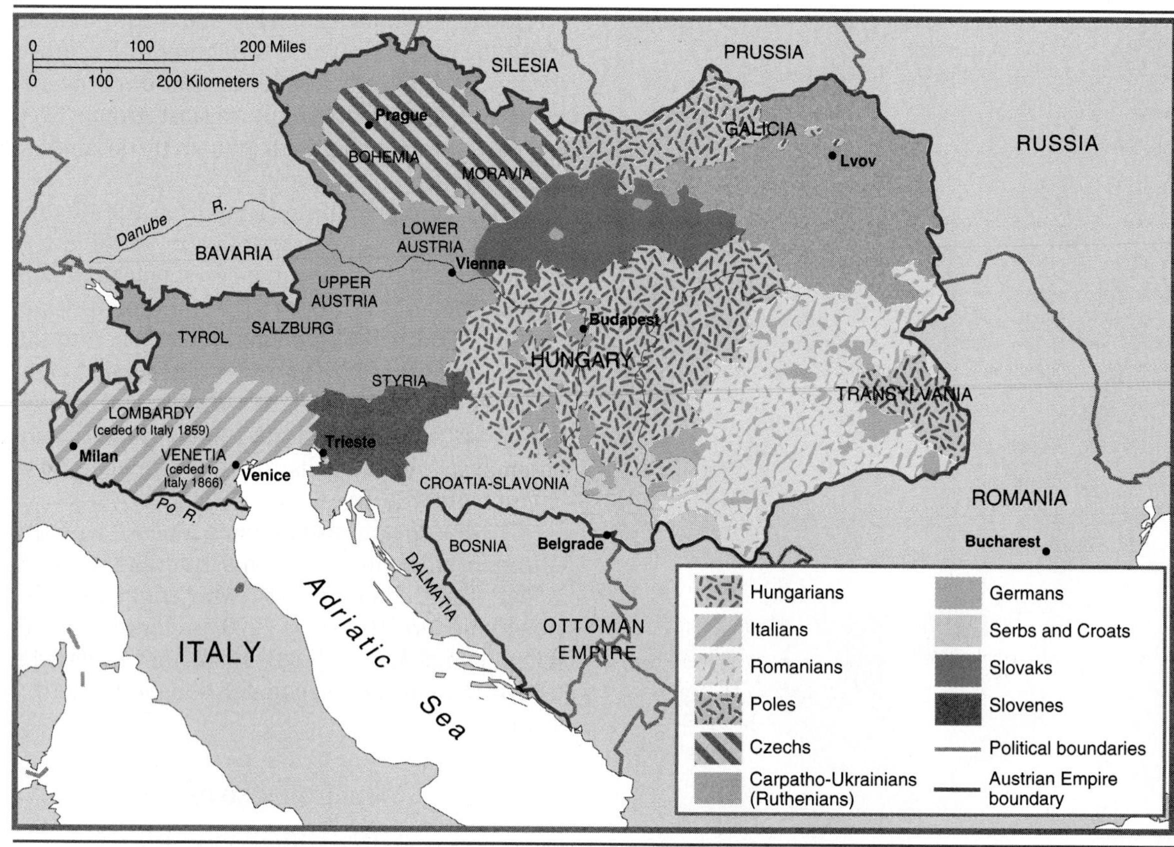

MAP 33.9 ***Nationalism and the Austro-Hungarian Empire, 1848.*** *Like many other empires, the Austrian Empire had been forged by the conquest and rule of diverse peoples. Nationalist agitation among the Hungarians in the latter half of the nineteenth century forced the Austrians to permit them considerable autonomy, within the new Austro-Hungarian Empire. Although this satisfied the Hungarians, many other ethnic minorities demanded similar treatment from the Austrians. Their refusal helped spark various expressions of nationalism, ultimately leading to the collapse of the empire in the aftermath of World War I.*

themselves. Thus, national tensions simmered until the outbreak of World War I.

Tensions in the Balkan Peninsula occupied the Austro-Hungarian Empire up to World War I and helped precipitate that conflict. Serbian nationalists outside the Austro-Hungarian Empire wished to destabilize the situation and provoke a war. They assassinated the Austro-Hungarian heir apparent, Archduke Francis Ferdinand, in mid-1914. After this killing, the Austro-Hungarian government demanded that Serbia give up its independence. The Serbs turned to their Russian allies for support. Soon the European alliance system came into play and eventually brought a series of declarations of war. The ensuing conflict saw the defeat of Austria-Hungary, leading to its dismemberment and the creation of Austria, Hungary, Poland, Czechoslovakia, and Yugoslavia. Nationalism had survived the war and led to Balkan tensions that endured into the 1990s.

Nationalism and Germany

Germany had managed to contain the forces of minority nationalism in its empire, but its support of the Austro-Hungarian Empire in World War I led

UNDER THE LENS
Paderewski and Polish Nationalism

Poland had been a powerful and sophisticated nation in the sixteenth and seventeenth centuries, earning the Poles the nickname "the civilized Slavs." The eighteenth century, however, saw the gradual dismemberment and destruction of Poland as a nation, and by 1795 it had been divided among Prussia, Russia, and Austria. In 1860, Ignacy Paderewski,[a] an important figure in modern Polish history, was born in the Russian part of what would again become Poland under his guidance.

Paderewski's initial inclinations were artistic. A largely self-taught pianist, he entered a music school at the age of twelve, where he was transformed into a trombonist. He loved the piano, and, despite warnings that he never would excel at that instrument, Paderewski took it up again. By 1884, he had undertaken a piano concert tour of Europe, and his magnetic personality and musical genius made him an instant success; later tours of America also were wildly applauded, earning him greater wealth than any contemporary performer. Paderewski's stage presence, enhanced by his shock of unruly, curly red-gold hair, made him the darling of the age. His stage routinely was rushed by young women wishing to touch the star; more than once he was attacked by a scissor-wielding adulator who removed a curl or two as a memento. Paderewski was once mobbed in a men's room when recognized by male fans, and the round of frenzied handshaking that followed left him unable to play for days.

In 1908, however, Paderewski's piano career was beginning to wind down because of persistent hand injuries that impaired his playing, and he commenced searching for alternative outlets for his energies. Paderewski turned to politics, because throughout his career he had inspired himself with the reminder that his success glorified Poland, his enslaved homeland. Beginning in 1912, Paderewski began a series of concerts and lectures—he also was a gifted orator—to raise funds to help support an independent Poland. His personal friendships with Woodrow Wilson (then president of the United States) and Herbert Hoover (later president of the United States) assisted his efforts, and the redivision of Europe following World War I restored Poland to nationhood. In 1919, Paderewski became Poland's first premier, representing his country in the negotiations at Paris that officially concluded World War I. Paderewski resigned his post under fire at the end of 1919 and returned to politics only briefly, in 1940.

Intensely patriotic, Ignacy Paderewski promoted national feelings through the arts, incorporating folk melodies and rhythms into his music and extolling Polish country life. When he turned his talents to the independence movement, his brief political career was marked by diplomacy and political acumen.

[a]**Ignacy Paderewski:** EEG naht see pahd ah REHF skee

to defeat. Earlier, repression and skillful statecraft by Otto von Bismarck helped keep German politicians in check and ethnic minorities like the Poles subdued. Military defeat in 1918, however, brought the collapse of the monarchy and the loss of territory at the Versailles Peace Conference in 1919. German nationalists despised the harsh peace and subsequent loss of territory, especially the loss of Alsace and Lorraine to the French.

While educational systems in Germany and Austria-Hungary promoted German nationalism, some of the ethnic minorities resented efforts to enforce German-only language policies. The attempted use of schools to encourage unification actually provoked nationalism among Serbs, Poles, and Czechs.

The Collapse of the Russian Empire

The tsarist Russian Empire suffered from many of the same problems that plagued the Austro-Hungarian and Ottoman empires. All presided over diverse ethnic groups and faced the growing desire of these groups for independence. Repression by the Russians, who were the dominant ethnic group, increased nationalism among the

MAP 33.10 ***Nationalism and the Russian Empire, to 1920.*** *The Russian tsars forged a multiethnic empire, beginning in the sixteenth century. This state, however, disintegrated during World War I, breaking into many states, among them Finland and Poland. After the Bolsheviks took power in late 1917, they began a reconquest of territories controlled by ethnic minorities. Many were retaken, becoming a part of Soviet Russia. Finland, Latvia, Lithuania, Estonia, and Poland, however, remained independent for some years.*

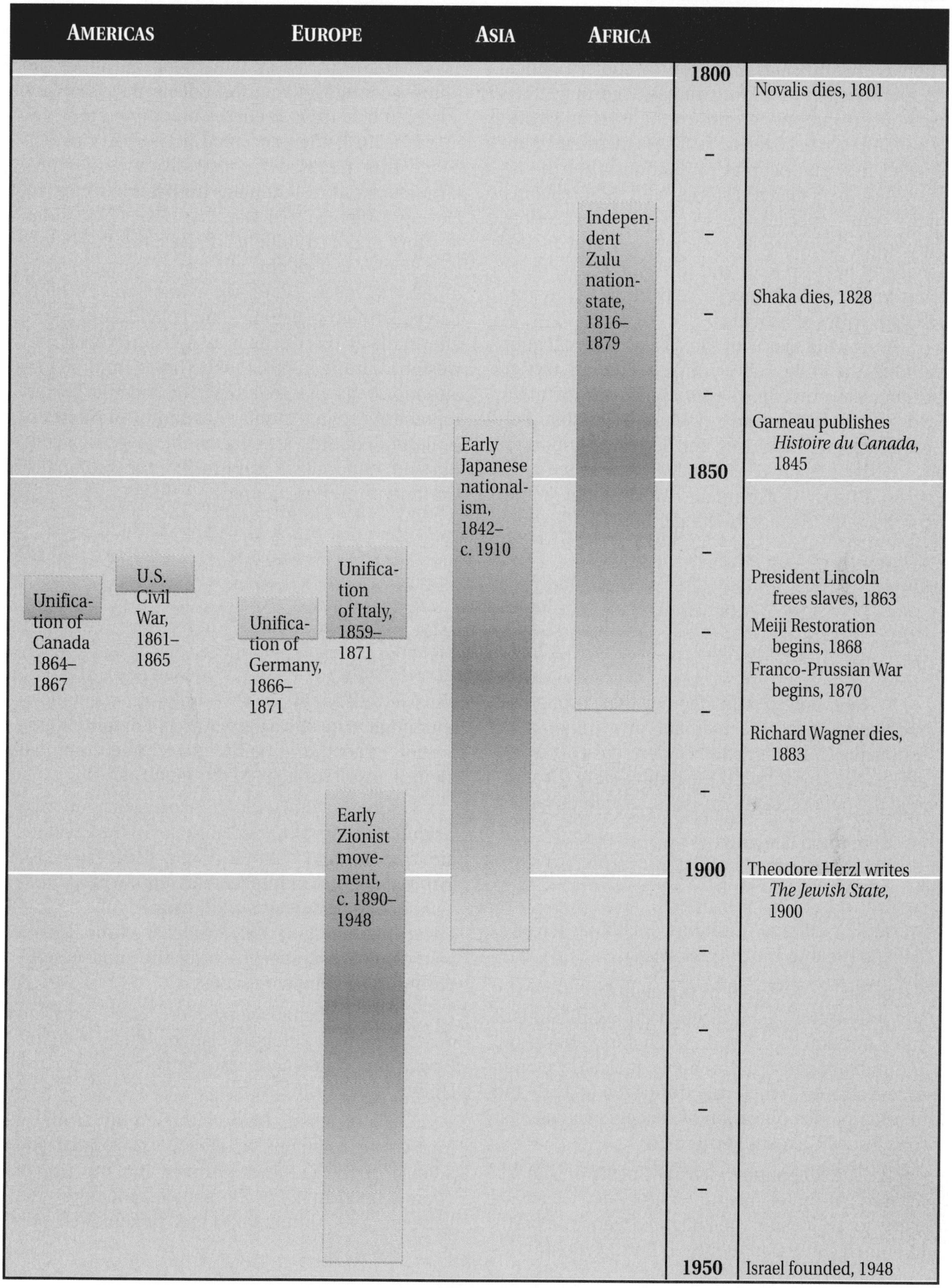

AMERICAS	EUROPE	ASIA	AFRICA		
				1800	Novalis dies, 1801
			Indepen-dent Zulu nation-state, 1816–1879		Shaka dies, 1828
		Early Japanese national-ism, 1842–c. 1910			Garneau publishes *Histoire du Canada,* 1845
				1850	
Unifica-tion of Canada 1864–1867	Unifica-tion of Germany, 1866–1871				President Lincoln frees slaves, 1863
U.S. Civil War, 1861–1865	Unifica-tion of Italy, 1859–1871				Meiji Restoration begins, 1868
					Franco-Prussian War begins, 1870
					Richard Wagner dies, 1883
	Early Zionist move-ment, c. 1890–1948			1900	Theodore Herzl writes *The Jewish State,* 1900
				1950	Israel founded, 1948

minority peoples, who had to use the Russian language in education and in government. In addition, ethnic Russians often got the choice political positions, even in minority areas. Vigorous efforts to convert minority groups to the Russian Orthodox faith increased tensions. These measures compelled minority peoples to abandon their native tongues, their shared histories, and their religions. Jews were especially persecuted in official riots, **pogroms**, in which bureaucrats led and incited mobs to beat up Jews and to destroy their shops and homes. All of these policies drove many into antigovernment activities.

A growing sense of Pan-Slavic identification among the ruling elite spurred Russian foreign policy. Slavs are those who speak one of many closely related languages, including Russian, Polish, Bulgarian, Ukrainian, and Serbian. Support for the Serbs remained especially important to the tsarist Russian government and brought it into conflict with the Austro-Hungarians. The Russians backed the Serbs, and the Germans supported Austria-Hungary.

After the tsarist system collapsed under the immense strain of war, the Bolsheviks, who took power in late 1917, needed a breathing space. So, in early 1918, they accepted a German-dictated peace that released Latvians, Estonians, Poles, Lithuanians, and Ukrainians from Russian control. During a bloody civil war that devastated much territory and cost millions of lives, the Bolsheviks won back most of the old tsarist domain. They failed, however, to regain control of Finland, Latvia, Lithuania, Estonia, and Poland. Only in the aftermath of the German assault on Poland and western Europe in 1940, when British and French attention was placed elsewhere, did the Soviets repossess Latvia, Estonia, Lithuania, and parts of Finland, Poland, and Rumania. A Soviet-style Russian nationalism suppressed the nationalist sentiments of these peoples.

SUMMARY

1. Nationalism is an ideology that emphasizes one's social role as a member of a nation. The nation always is characterized by a sense of ownership in the government, the nation-state. In addition, the nation usually has several characteristics:

— a common language,
— shared historical experiences and institutions, and
— similar cultural traditions, including religion, at both elite and popular levels.

Nationalism developed in the eighteenth century and was strengthened through the establishment and extension of the voting franchise, education, and military conscription pools. It also developed in response to French rule from 1794 to 1815 and to attempted suppression by leaders such as Austria's Prince Clemens Metternich.

2. The Romantic movement began in the latter third of the eighteenth century, as a reaction partly to the ideas of the Enlightenment and partly to French cultural influence in Europe. Romantics also viewed nature as alive in its manifestations and sought a mystical unity with it. Romantic composers, writers, and painters celebrated national themes, inspiration, and emotionalism.

3. Johann von Herder, Johann Fichte, and the Grimm brothers played major roles in the development of German cultural nationalism. They also inspired a group of intellectuals who believed that a national language was a key element of a nation. These people and their students standardized many modern languages of central and eastern Europe in the nineteenth century.

4. Nationalism became a force in the creation of nations like Zululand, Japan, Italy, Germany, Israel, and Canada. It also helped preserve the United States from disunion.

5. Nationalism helped the ethnic Chinese topple the Manchus in China; accelerated the demise of the Ottoman Empire and the rise of Turkey; freed many Baltic peoples, including the Latvians and Lithuanians; and precipitated two world wars.

SUGGESTED READINGS

Blum, Jerome. *In the Beginning.* New York: Charles Scribner's Sons, 1994. An account of the onset of the modern age, which Blum argues is the 1840s.

Duggan, Christopher. *A Concise History of Italy.* Cambridge, Eng.: Cambridge University Press, 1994. A recent synthesis of scholarship on Italian history.

McNaught, Kenneth. *The Penguin History of Canada.* London: Penguin Press, 1988. A standard interpretation of Canadian history.

Millington, Barry. *Wagner.* Princeton, N.J.: Princeton University Press, 1992. A recent history of Wagner's life and an analysis of his operas.

Pfaff, William. *The Wrath of Nations.* New York: Simon and Schuster, 1993. An interpretative general history of nationalism in the nineteenth and twentieth centuries.

Riasanovsky, Nicholas. *The Emergence of Romanticism.* Oxford, Eng.: Oxford University Press, 1992. An examination of the origins of Romanticism between 1796 and 1805.

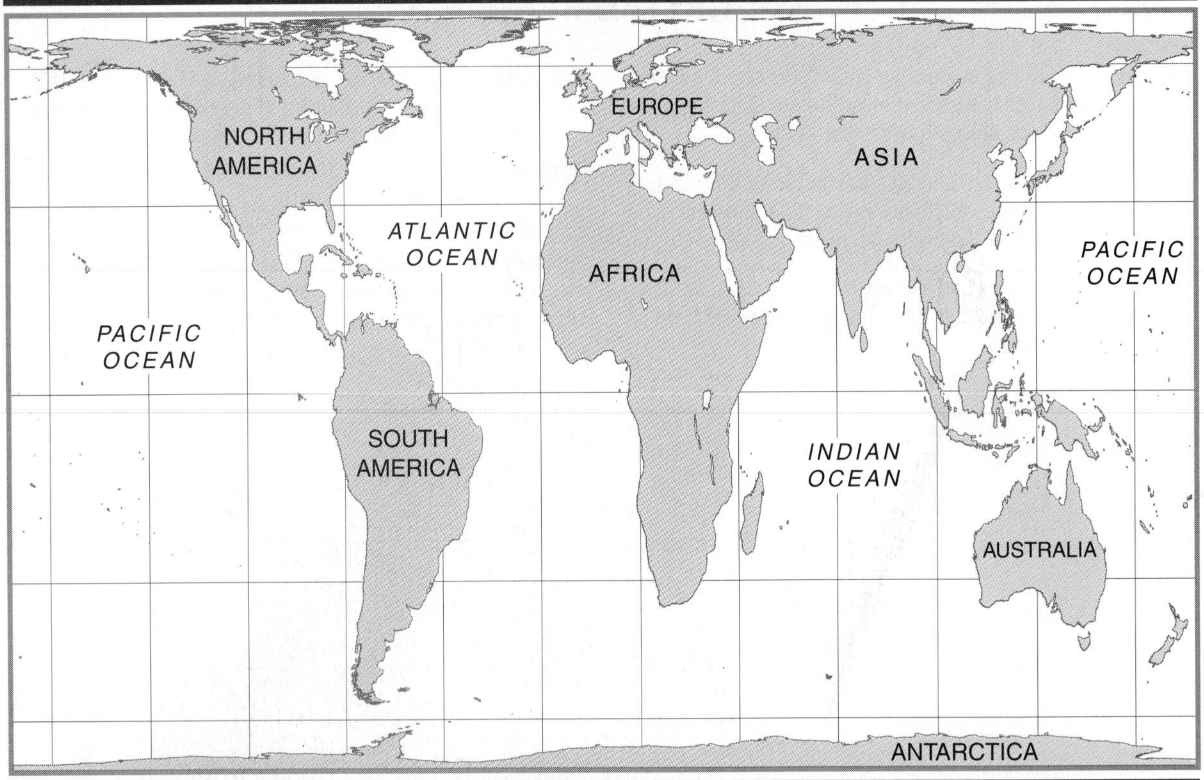

NORTH AMERICA
EUROPE
ASIA
ATLANTIC OCEAN
PACIFIC OCEAN
AFRICA
PACIFIC OCEAN
SOUTH AMERICA
INDIAN OCEAN
AUSTRALIA
ANTARCTICA

A Satirical View of China's Plight. *This cartoon depicts a prostrate Chinese dragon about to be carved up by Western powers and Japan. These imperialist countries seem ready to fight over the spoils of China's collapse, while a "noble" American eagle watches over the greedy beasts of prey. America's imperialist interests were elsewhere in Asia and focused on keeping trade open to all countries. As a consequence, the U.S. role in China was relatively passive.* From *Puck*, August 15, 1900. The Granger Collection, New York.

CHAPTER 34

Imperialism around the Globe

1803–1949

Government does not depend on consent. The immutable laws of humanity require that a people shall have government, that the weak shall be protected, that cruelty and lust shall be restrained, whether there be consent or not. . . . There is no Philippine people.

U.S. Secretary of War Elihu Root enunciated this sentiment to justify imperialist policies in the Pacific Ocean during the late nineteenth century. These words could have been uttered by nearly any official during the heyday of imperialism (1870–1914), when large sections of the non-Western world fell under Western and Japanese control. Imperialist arrogance characterized policies toward subject peoples in the nineteenth and twentieth centuries.

In this chapter, attention will be focused on imperialism, the modern form of colonialism. As was seen in Chapter 24, colonialism was the process of establishing and administering colonies in order to extract wealth from them in the Early Modern Era. **Imperialism** is an economic and political system of control by an industrial country needing raw materials and markets. Imperialism came later than colonialism and developed from the political leadership of industrializing nation-states. Imperialists used nationalism to garner popular support for their imperialist policies. The race to subjugate most parts of the globe intensified in the late nineteenth and early twentieth centuries, when nearly a quarter-million square miles of territory were added to empires each year. Diplomacy had averted a major war among imperialist countries until 1914, when rivalry and other factors exploded in global conflict. Many tensions and issues remained at the end of World War I, and imperialist ambitions helped ignite a second global conflict two decades later.

IMPERIALISM: INDUSTRIALIZATION, NATIONAL RIVALRIES, AND INTELLECTUAL JUSTIFICATION

Great Britain, France, Germany, Italy, Belgium, the United States, Japan, and Russia became imperialist powers in the nineteenth and twentieth centuries. The central factors behind their territorial expansion were their needs to obtain raw materials to process in their industrial machines, to find markets for the finished products, to compete successfully with rival imperialist nation-states, to control strategic places, and to drum up popular

MAP 34.1 ***Railroad Lines around 1900.*** *Building railroads often was a way for a country to promote industrialization. Russia and Prussia used this strategy in their industrialization efforts. For imperialist countries, building railroads in their colonies improved communications and facilitated resource extraction. Troops could also be moved quickly to crush resistance movements.*

support for overseas ventures. The nation-state became the vehicle for imperialism, and national leaders saw that they could gain widespread support among their citizens by publicizing their interest in territorial expansion.

Some imperialists did not seek direct control over other countries, preferring to exercise economic domination through **client governments**, local administrations that carried out the wishes of the imperialists. They also established spheres of influence in countries or contented themselves with gaining favorable trade agreements with local governments.

Industrialization's Need for Raw Materials and Markets

As seen in Chapter 32, Great Britain industrialized in the eighteenth and nineteenth centuries; France, Germany, the United States, and Japan followed suit somewhat later. Tsarist Russia commenced an industrial program in the 1890s. All became imperialist powers during their economic transformations.

Great Britain had an extensive colonial empire before it industrialized, but it intensified and extended its economic and political sway after its industrial revolution commenced. Britain became economically dominant in Latin America during the nineteenth century and added new imperialist domains in Asia, Africa, and the Pacific basin. The possessions of Britain on the Indian subcontinent became more closely integrated into the empire at the same time.

Germany had no colonies before 1871. The formation of the German Empire in that year and Germany's rapid industrialization helped promote an overseas empire in Africa, Asia, and the Pacific region. Tensions and imperialist rivalries between Germany and other imperialist countries helped start World War I. Germany's defeat and economic problems in the 1920s fueled the crisis that eventually brought the Nazis to power in 1933. Renewed economic growth under the Nazis in the 1930s seems to have influenced Adolf Hitler's successful efforts to annex parts of Central and Eastern Europe.

The United States and Japan industrialized in the nineteenth century, and both developed overseas empires. In fact, national rivalries in Asia and the Pacific region played a role in heightening tensions between the United States and Japan. One cause of World War II was an exploding imperialist rivalry between the United States and Japan.

After spurring a massive industrial revolution in the 1930s, the Soviet Union grabbed Latvia, Lithuania, and Estonia, along with parts of Poland, Finland, and Rumania, between 1939 and 1945. Additional territories in Central and Eastern Europe were incorporated into the Soviet Empire after World War II. Although some scholars see these expansions within the historical direction of Russo-Soviet strategic planning, the fact that these acquisitions came during and after the industrialization of the 1930s supports the view that socialist imperialism was at work. In addition, all new territory soon came within the Soviet economic sphere.

National Rivalries

National rivalries intensified the efforts to develop overseas and land empires. Japan, for example, decided to vie with China and then with Russia over Korea between 1894 and 1905. The rapid dismemberment of Africa was one significant consequence of the imperialist drive for territorial control. Certainly, competition in Asia (1890s and 1940s) and Europe (1940s) helped heighten tensions between nations and helped provoke World War I and World War II.

Perceived national interests played a special role in the fierce competition to grab some territories. Hawaii lay in the mid-northern Pacific Ocean, along vital trade routes from the Americas to Asia. Control of Hawaii and Pearl Harbor, with its marvelous potential as a naval base, became a driving concern for the United States in the 1890s. About a decade later, digging and controlling the Panama Canal obsessed U.S. strategic planners. Earlier, the British decided to take control of the Suez Canal in Egypt to protect the financial interests of British investors and also to safeguard Britain's strategic passage to India.

Intellectual Justification

A variety of intellectual concepts were employed to justify the imperialists' conquest and rule. Two of the most wide-ranging efforts were the "White Man's Burden" and "Yellow Peril" slogans employed in the early twentieth century. "White Man's Burden" was a commonplace idea in Europe

FIGURE 34.1 *"Dr. Livingstone, I Presume?" One of the most dramatic episodes in nineteenth-century newspaper reporting was the publicity surrounding the search by Henry Stanley for Dr. David Livingstone, a missionary in Africa. A self-publicist, Stanley developed the story that captivated British newspaper readers and sparked interest in Africa. Although Livingstone was not lost, Stanley had found a story by which to make himself famous.* Mansell/Time Inc.

and the United States, and it received popular expression in the writings of Rudyard Kipling, who wrote about the responsibilities of whites toward nonwhites, whom he saw as inferior and incapable of governing themselves. The concept of "Yellow Peril" came from writers and editorial cartoonists who warned about the uniting of Asians against Westerners, rationalizing the domination of Asian lands. Westerners had to conquer Asians before Asians conquered Westerners.

Even ideas about the nature of society were used to justify imperialist expansion. Both the Soviets and the Japanese, for example, argued that their expansions came from a need to develop defensive buffer zones against enemy nation-states. The Soviets couched their rule in terms of socialist brotherhood and alliance, yet they practiced atrocities against the subject peoples. The Japanese used the idea of one large Asian family system to argue for control of Koreans (younger brothers and sisters) and the idea of a Greater East Asian Co-Prosperity Sphere, a region under Japanese benevolent supervision, to mask their imperialist policies.

Newspapers played a significant role in the development of imperialist expansion. National education systems produced ever larger numbers of literate people, many of whom read newspapers on a regular basis. Some scholars call growth in this and other media the emergence of information capitalism because in order to sell papers, editors promoted stories that captured the public's imagination. An early example was the trek of journalist Henry Morton Stanley (1841–1904) through Africa on a search for Dr. David Livingstone. Stanley's account electrified his British readers and coined the immortal line, "Dr. Livingstone, I presume?" upon meeting with the missionary in 1871. This sensationalist account helped foster the image of deepest, darkest Africa as an alien place whose people needed to be saved.

COLONIZATION AND IMPERIALISM IN THE AMERICAS

The Americas had been colonized by various European countries beginning in the sixteenth century. By the nineteenth century, the United States and most countries in Latin America had won independence. As the United States industrialized, it became an imperialist power, focusing on territories in the Pacific Ocean and in Latin America. Britain also exerted imperialist control over countries in Latin America.

The United States and Imperialism

The United States expanded overland through the nineteenth century, establishing a network of overseas colonies from the 1890s. As the economy of the United States became more industrialized, the lure of markets and sources of raw materials attracted U.S. capitalists overseas. Capitalists have usually sought to exploit the cheap labor available in these territories.

After the War of Independence (1776–1783), the new area of colonization and settlement for the United States lay west of the Appalachian Mountains. Soon, American Indians suffered displacement by purchase, theft, and military conquest of their lands, actions of colonization by many people.

Purchase was a major means of territorial growth for the United States in the nineteenth century. The largest acquisition came in 1803 with the

UNDER THE LENS

Manifest Destiny

Well before the outbreak of the American War of Independence in the 1770s, American colonists desired to occupy the territories west of the Appalachian Mountains. Indeed, one of the causes of American anger was England's attempt to limit settlement in that region. **Manifest Destiny** was the nineteenth-century belief that the United States should expand until it controlled the Pacific coast and beyond. It became an almost religious belief for European Americans, who saw themselves destined to rule distant places and their peoples.

Manifest Destiny also related to the concept of the American frontier. Embedded within that perspective was the view that the frontier settlers must necessarily confront and overcome obstacles, including Native Americans and Mexicans. Such peoples might be killed, driven out, assimilated, or encapsulated as the need arose.

American Indian lands were often acquired through purchase, though the transaction typically was carried out through a tribal official who exceeded his authority by selling lands. In many cases, the concept of landownership was alien to the indigenous culture, and the consequences of the sale were comprehended only vaguely. Treaties also were a major route to acquiring Indian lands. Many treaties gave favorable disposition of lands to European-American settlers, and the less favorable ones were ignored by them. Relatively few lands were seized by simple force, but force often was used as an argument to encourage Indian leaders to accept purchase or treaty. The treaty system, established in 1824 but in wide use only after 1865, was designed to guarantee that some tribal lands remained for the Indian tribes.

Much of the territory in the West was purchased from various European states. The Louisiana Territory, the Florida Territory, part of the southwestern territory acquired through the Gadsden Purchase, and Alaska fit into that category. Other areas, like the Mexican Cession, were won by war. While the industrialization of the United States continued through the latter half of the nineteenth century and fueled overseas imperialism, the settling of the continental United States owed largely to more personal and less economic matters. Among the many elements persuading people to settle new places was the idea of Manifest Destiny.

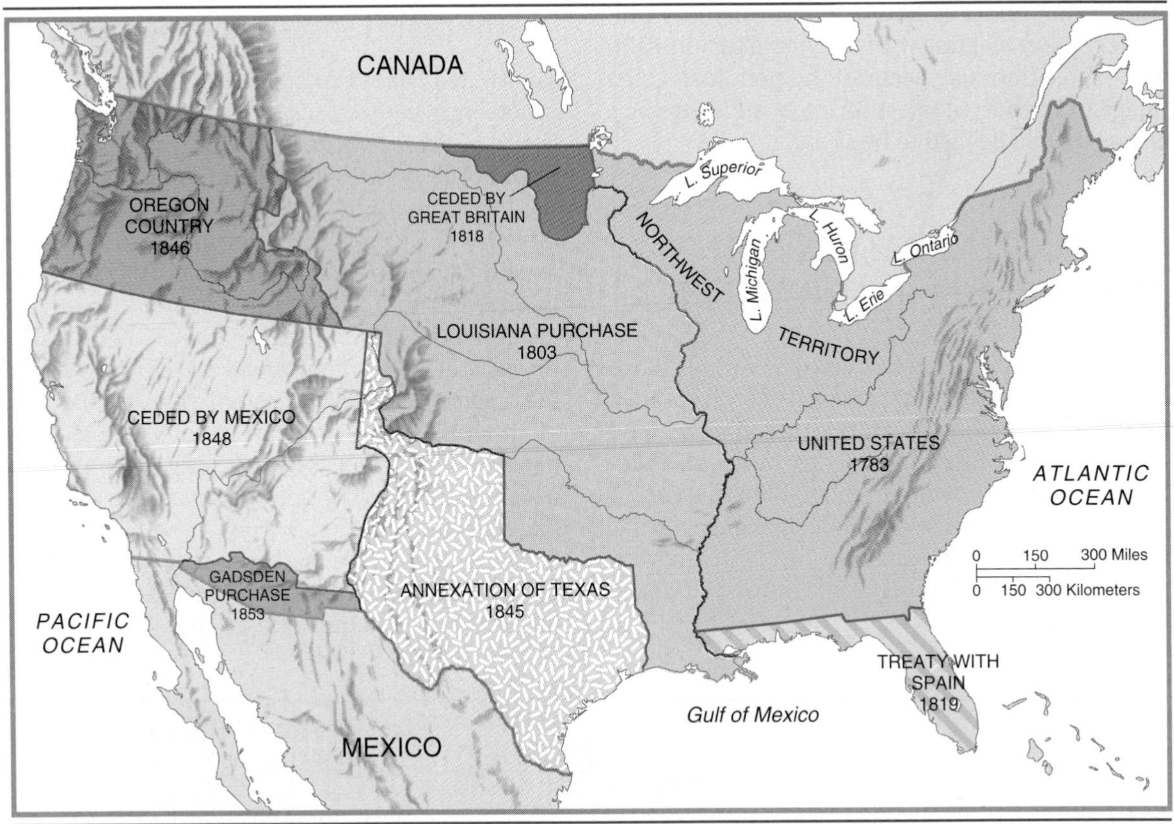

MAP 34.2 ***U.S. Territorial Expansion, 1803–1853.*** *The United States purchased great amounts of land during its westward expansion; two of the major acquisitions were the Louisiana and Gadsden purchases. U.S. leaders also won a significant part of the American West in a treaty settlement with Mexico after the Mexican War. These ways of expansion set the tone for the rest of the nineteenth century.*

Louisiana Purchase by President Thomas Jefferson. The French, who needed money to finance Napoleon's military schemes, sold the Louisiana Territory, which they in turn had acquired from resident American Indians by conquest and self-declaration. The United States also bought Florida from the Spanish in the early nineteenth century. That deal completed the acquisition of lands south of Canada and east of the Mississippi River. Mexico sold territory that made up part of Arizona and New Mexico, the Gadsden Purchase of 1853. In 1867, the Russians liquidated their remaining land in North America when they sold Alaska to the United States.

Conquest added more land to the United States. Most of the land from the Atlantic to the Mississippi River came to the United States from the War of Independence (1776–1783). The Mexican War (1846–1848) added the Mexican Cession, including the Texas Territory and parts of the western states of New Mexico, Oklahoma, Arizona, Colorado, Nevada, and California.

Most of the remaining lands came during the Spanish-American War (1898) and its aftermath. United States industrial pressure, combined with a surge of ardent nationalism fueled by sensationalist journalism in many newspapers during the 1890s, precipitated a successful war with Spain. The United States added the Philippines, Puerto Rico, Hawaii, and Guam to its territory. Aside from strategic interests, Hawaii and the Philippines also became sources of sugarcane and pineapples, once the local resistance forces had been crushed. A resilient Filipino guerrilla movement took more than five years to defeat, costing nearly a quarter-million Filipino lives.

FIGURE 34.2 ***Civilian Victims at Manila, Philippines.*** *In 1945, many Filipino civilians died in the crossfire as U.S. and Japanese soldiers fought for control of Manila during World War II. Some fifty years earlier, the Philippines had seen mass graves constructed for the bodies of Filipino resistance fighters who battled American forces intent on conquering and ruling the island nation.* Wide World Photos.

The United States gained territory after the end of World War II, when Japanese possessions in the western Pacific became the United States Trust Territories. The Japanese had taken these islands from the Germans in World War I, and the League of Nations recognized Japan's claims. Later, the United Nations approved the American occupation.

Other United States interests brought direct control of new territory in Colombia. As settlement of the west intensified during the Gold Rush in the 1840s and 1850s, sea routes from the eastern to the western United States seemed more important. During the years after the Spanish-American War, President Theodore Roosevelt, an ardent exponent of naval expansion, engineered a Panamanian revolt against the Colombians. The United States recognized and guaranteed Panama's independence in exchange for the ceding of territory in which the Panama Canal was built. American jurisdiction over the Canal Zone lasted until 1978, with a complete return scheduled for 1999.

Settlement of the continental territory followed the pattern established under the Northwest Ordinance of 1787. That decree provided for an orderly transition from territory to statehood, a process that proved highly successful. By 1912, forty-eight states had been created. Alaska became a state in 1958, and Hawaii entered the union in 1959. Puerto Rico, Guam, and the Trust Territory islands have remained outside the statehood ranks; the Philippines was granted independence in 1947.

Economic imperialism afforded the United States and other industrialized nation-states the means for indirect control of the assets of nominally independent states. Both the Monroe Doctrine of the early 1820s and the Open Door Policy of 1898 were unilateral policies by the United States with respect to Latin America and China. They asserted that these lands remain open for economic exploitation and development by all parties, especially the United States. Both gestures remained toothless, but they reflected the United States' growing economic interests in Latin America and Asia.

Economic Imperialism in Latin America

Latin America long endured the economic influence and domination of Western nation-states, especially Britain and the United States. While direct political rule remained only a short-term expedient, Western exploitation of natural resources occurred through the era. In the nineteenth century, the U.S. government increasingly considered the western hemisphere to be its special zone of influence and action. The overriding concern was the resolution of economic matters in favor of the United States.

Most Latin American countries won their independence from European colonial powers. Because wealthy members of the social elite became the ruling class of these newly independent states, they adhered to policies representing their interests. Latin American leaders struggled to revive economies that had been integrally connected with Spain and Portugal, and they decided to integrate Latin America into the burgeoning global economy.

During the nineteenth century, Britain played the most significant economic role in Latin America. The British navy ruled the seas, providing security for British ships that sailed between Latin America and Europe. Britain also possessed impressive capital resources, merchants, and insurance brokers. The philosophy of free trade stressed the importance of trade through open markets joined in a global network. This vision attracted many of the Latin American elite and offered the hope to Mexicans, Central Americans, and South Americans that they could integrate into a prosperous world structure.

The British dominated the financial exchanges in much of the western hemisphere, slowly exert-

FIGURE 34.3 ***European Influence in Nineteenth-Century Chile.*** *This photograph of Cape Street in Valparaiso, Chile, shows the bookstore and stationery shop of Thomas Purves, which catered to English-reading people. British economic influence was strong along the west coast of South America, and British capital dominated Latin American markets until World War I.* Courtesy of Ken and Jenny Jacobson.

PARALLELS AND DIVERGENCES

Olives, Bananas, and Sugar: Monoculture and Dependence

All farmers are faced with the same problem. On the one hand, they want to focus on the single crop that produces the best returns. On the other hand, depending entirely on one crop is risky business, because a disaster may wipe out their livelihood. Furthermore, it is not good for the soil. When farm produce is sold for cash, there is the added problem that prices rise and fall with the international market. When farmers resolve this problem by focusing on a single crop, it is called **monoculture.**

A classic case of monoculture comes from Greece of the fourth century B.C. Olive oil, the basis of much cooking in the eastern Mediterranean, was the primary export commodity of Greece, and its production was the quickest route to prosperity for farmers. Olive trees grew with little attention, rarely were there bad harvests, and the presses used to extract oil were inexpensive to construct and use. Thus, peasants converted huge land tracts into olive groves and reduced grain-growing areas. This shift vastly reduced the game population and led to erosion of the landscape but proved successful for decades. By the century's end, however, other places in the Mediterranean produced olive oil, and the market became unprofitable. Unfortunately, it was difficult for the Greeks to return the groves to grain production. Greece became dependent on expensive, imported food.

While the Greek experience was unfortunate, the problem had been self-induced. Many nineteenth- and twentieth-century monocultural disasters were fostered by imperialists. The banana industry in Central America, for example, began in earnest in 1899, when the first Honduran bananas arrived in New Orleans. Banana companies slyly tempted the newly established government of General Manuel Bonilla[a]: provide tax exemptions, and they would develop railroads, ports, and roads for Honduras. While Honduras gained an infrastructure, the main profits of the banana industry went to foreign investors, whose economic power permitted their domination of the Honduran government. Trade disruptions, such as in 1914, devastated Honduras, and fluctuations of world banana prices affected the economy immensely.

Cuba and other Caribbean islands had similar experiences with sugar. Introduced by sweet-hungry European colonial powers in the sixteenth and seventeenth centuries, sugar (and rum distilled from it) dominated all other products. This heritage persists today but with devastating results. Most Caribbean islands are politically independent, yet they import most of their food. Further, fluctuations in sugar prices severely affect their economic prosperity.

Imperialist powers fostered monoculture in their colonies, producing crops unavailable in the home country and often making huge profits. The greatest risks fell on the colonial peoples, while profits came to the investors in the home countries. The legacy of this monoculture, however, haunts now-independent countries whose economies are limited by these strategies.

[a] **Manuel Bonilla:** MAHN wehl BOHN ee yah

ing political control. The United States and France also had some influence in the nineteenth and twentieth centuries. Early financial efforts by Britain showed mixed results because, although the economic influence swelled, a large number of loan defaults rendered much of Latin America a high credit risk.

The economic influence of the United States rapidly increased in the latter half of the nineteenth century. While many Latin Americans appreciated the support of the United States in their independence struggles, others recoiled because the United States exercised much more control than Spain. Although U.S. investment grew about fivefold between 1898 and 1914, more than half of all foreign capital investment in Latin America still lay with the British. The United States accounted for around 15 percent of the total foreign investment in Latin America by the outbreak of World War I, but it was larger than the amounts of the French and the Germans.

From 1914 to 1949, the influence of the United States in Latin America became dominant. During this era, an inter-American system emerged and centered on the military and economic power of the United States. American military takeover of many governments in the Caribbean basin between 1912 and 1934 was justified by the need to protect the region's sea lanes. British influence sharply declined during World War I and never recovered, and when the European part of World War II erupted in 1939, the United States pressured Latin American governments into supplying war materials, basing U.S. soldiers, and signing alliances with the United States against its enemies. During World War II, the United States emerged as the dominant global power, controlling about half of the world's industrial production and two-thirds of its exports.

The political form of the inter-American system came in 1947 and 1948, when all states signed the Rio Pact, which declared that an attack on any American state was an attack on all. A year later, the Organization of American States was formed, committing its members to regular meetings, to ways of dealing with inter-American crises, and to the principles of democracy, economic cooperation, human rights, and social justice.

IMPERIALISM IN ASIA

East Asia suffered terribly from the ravages of imperialism. China and Korea fell under a Japanese imperialism, which cost millions of lives and immense loss of property. Freedom from the Japanese brought new problems and division of the Korean Peninsula and of China and Taiwan.

East Asia

Japanese leaders developed an empire in conjunction with an industrializing and Westernizing program; they believed that in order to be a modern power, Japan had to gain colonies. Fear of foreign domination also fueled Japan's imperialistic efforts. During the 1850s and 1860s, Western powers imposed a series of unequal treaties that humiliated Japan's leaders, who vowed to free Japan from foreign control. Only in the late 1890s did Japan begin to regain autonomy over its trade policies. In addition, Western imperialist threats to rule Korea and China spurred Japan's leaders to develop a long-range plan to dominate East Asia. After World War I, expansion in Manchuria and other parts of China caused Japan's leaders to protect these conquests by grabbing parts of Southeast Asia. Soon, most of Southeast Asia, East Asia, and the western Pacific Ocean had become part of the Japanese Empire.

Although the Japanese portrayed themselves as the elder brothers and other Asians as younger brothers, their policies fomented discontent among the peoples they ruled. Koreans and Chinese resented Japanese political and economic control, and Southeast Asians chafed under Japanese domination.

China had exerted political and cultural influence in East Asia through a tributary system that demanded that nations send diplomatic visits to China in exchange for trading privileges and Chinese protection. Both Korea and Japan had borrowed heavily from Chinese elite culture, especially education, family values, and hierarchical social structures.

Britain began significant trading with China in the early nineteenth century. Although the British sent diplomatic and trade missions to China in 1814 and 1834, both failed to open China to further trade and development. The Chinese sold the British large quantities of tea and other products but had little use for British imports. In order to offset this trade imbalance, the British East India Company, a private business, smuggled Indian opium into China. As a result, many Chinese became addicts. Eventually, the British government took over the company and its smuggling operation, and the British selling of opium to the Chinese continued well into the twentieth century. By the 1830s, China's drug problem mushroomed and began to cause severe economic problems for the Chinese.

These economic and social problems led to the Opium War (1839–1842) and China's defeat, commencing a long period of foreign influence and domination. Until 1894, the Chinese managed to contain the Westerners in a few treaty port areas, like Shanghai and Canton, but the Chinese government yielded to Western pressure to open more of its regions to trade. China lost control of its tariff rates, its power to try Westerners for crimes committed on its soil, and some of the revenues that had helped pay foreign debts. In the late nineteenth century, Western countries loaned the Chinese government large sums of money. The resulting indebtedness to imperialist powers formed a kind of economic imperialism shackling China.

Between 1894 and 1914, Korea and Vietnam were torn from the Chinese sphere of influence, and interior parts of China became foreign enclaves. Korea had been forcibly opened to trade by Japan in 1876, and the Japanese and Chinese governments signed an accord in 1885 to defuse tensions there. By 1894, a local Korean uprising provided the Japanese with an opportunity to extend their influence. The resulting Sino-Japanese War (1894–1895) brought China's defeat, Korean independence, and a settlement that gave Japan the island of Taiwan and a large indemnity. Other imperialist powers acquired Chinese territory in the next few years: Germany got a concession in Shandong province, Britain extended its Hong Kong lease (a prize taken in 1842) until 1997 and added new territory, Russia gained land in Manchuria, and France pressured China for a sphere of influence along the border with French Indochina.

World War I brought a reduction of Western influence in China and an increase in Japanese imperialism. The Japanese entered the war on the side of the British and the French, defeating the Germans in Shandong and adding that valuable sphere of influence. The German concession remained under Japanese control, thanks to secret deals with other imperialist powers and bribery of Chinese officials.

From 1931 to 1945, Japan launched a major effort to control Manchuria and China. Japan conquered Manchuria by 1932 and gradually expanded into China. Growing tensions provoked conflict between Chinese and Japanese soldiers in mid-1937, opening the Asian theater of World War II.

Korea gradually fell under the sway of Japanese imperialism; it was incorporated into the Japanese Empire in 1910. Harsh Japanese rule provoked intense Korean animosity. On March 1, 1919,

FIGURE 34.4 ***Korean Women Demonstrating for Independence.*** *March 1, 1919, was an important day in modern Korea: Around 1 million Koreans demonstrated for their freedom from Japanese rule. As this photo documents, many women were among the protesters. Though tightly constricted by custom and by the Japanese authorities, Korean women felt so strongly about their country's freedom that they took action. Overt Korean resistance, however, was ended by Japanese repression that brought numerous casualties and arrests.*
Courtesy of Yushin Yoo.

around one million Koreans demonstrated against Japanese rule, triggering brutal Japanese reprisals. Soon Koreans had to learn Japanese and to adopt Japanese names. At times, so many agricultural supplies left Korea that some Koreans went hungry. Later, numbers of Korean women were forcibly taken to serve as "comfort women" for the sexual gratification of Japanese soldiers.

After World War II, Korea was divided, filling Koreans with uncertainty. The North came under control of Korean communists who were supported by Russian advisors and equipment. The South fell under American occupation and remained in turmoil, although Syngman Rhee[1] gradually amassed considerable political power. The political troubles in the South invited an unsuccessful attempt at reunification by the North Korean communists in 1950.

Southeast Asia

Western imperialism extended its control across Southeast Asia in the nineteenth century, and Japanese imperialists contended with Western rivals in the twentieth century. Although the Japanese were defeated in World War II, their last-ditch efforts to foster national movements ignited indigenous anti-imperialist movements that won independence after 1945.

The British conquest and rule of Burma (present-day Myanmar) stemmed from Britain's position in India. Leaders in India and England sought to dominate the Irrawaddy and Salween river valleys in order to enhance their trading position in Southeast Asia. Conflicts with the Burmese monarchy commenced in the 1820s and continued sporadically through the 1880s, when the country fell completely under British control.

The British exploited Burma's natural and human resources. Wood products, including the much-valued teak, were shipped to Britain for manufacturing purposes. Ivory, rubies, and jade proved valuable resources for British jewelers. As in many other parts of the British Empire, the educational system in Burma taught members of the Burmese elite Western subjects, in English. Generations of Burmese learned to speak Oxfordian English, and some studied at British universities.

The British conquered Singapore and Malaya in the early nineteenth century, ensuring open British sea lanes from the Indian Ocean to the Pacific. A major naval base was built by the British in Singapore, and it was defended by massive guns. The British also developed Malayan rubber plantations and launched tin-mining operations.

The French had been interested in Vietnam as early as the seventeenth century, but the formation of French Indochina did not occur until the nineteenth century. A desire for imperial expansion drove the French emperor, Napoleon III. He curried favor with his Catholic subjects, who wanted to convert the Vietnamese, and began the conquest of Vietnam's Nguyen[2] Empire (1802–1955). The French navy also sought port facilities for its steamships. Between 1859 and 1894, the conquest of Vietnam, Cambodia, and Laos took place. The Vietnamese resisted the French effort, but the Cambodians generally favored the French Protectorate because Cambodia was being slowly dismembered by the Vietnamese and Thais. French rule ended the dismemberment. The French Indo-China Union was forged in 1894.

The French integrated the Union into the French Empire, ruling with a formidable police and military force. Wood products were harvested and sent to France along with rubber from the rubber plantations that sprang up in the region. Much as the Burmese and Malayan elite spoke English, the Vietnamese, Cambodian, and Laotian elite spoke French. Some studied at French schools in the Union, while a few went to France for further study. During World War I, tens of thousands of Vietnamese were shipped to France as laborers. Many who returned home after the war became disaffected members of the empire because they longed for Vietnamese independence.

Japan's interest in Southeast Asia stemmed from the devastation of western Europe in 1940–1941 and the prospect of exploiting the region's resources, especially oil and rubber. The Dutch controlled the East Indies, while the French administered French Indochina and the British controlled Burma and Malaya. The Nazi conquest of the Netherlands and France, along with the Battle of Britain, opened Southeast Asia for Japanese conquest. In mid-1940, Japan forced the French to permit the stationing of Japanese troops and sup-

[1] **Syngman Rhee:** SEENG muhn ree

[2] **Nguyen:** NUH yehn

plies in northern Vietnam, and a year later, the Japanese expanded into southern Vietnam.

The United States worried about Japan's expansion and its alliance with Germany and Italy. Japan's imperialist expansion prompted the Americans to announce an embargo on oil to Japan, threatening the Japanese navy's petroleum supplies. The oil fields of the Dutch East Indies loomed on Japan's strategic horizon, but the conquest of those islands meant that the Philippines, which dominated the South China Sea lanes, had to be taken. The United States controlled the Philippines, and the U.S. naval base at Pearl Harbor, Hawaii, dominated the Pacific Ocean.

Japan attacked Pearl Harbor and launched an invasion of most of Southeast Asia. The Philippines defense system collapsed within months, and General Douglas MacArthur fled to Australia. Singapore succumbed to a jungle campaign by a Japanese general who took the naval base from the rear, thus neutralizing the powerful coastal battery that could not be turned inland. Burma and the East Indies also fell under Japanese control by mid-1942. Thailand joined the Japanese alliance. The Japanese talked about permitting local autonomy, but they acted much as the European imperialists had. By 1944, Japan, facing imminent defeat, decided to grant its Asian subjects independence. When Western countries tried to regain control of their former colonies, they met widespread resistance. Burma gained independence in 1948, and Indonesia (formerly the Dutch East Indies) followed in 1949. Independence conflicts had also commenced in French Indochina. The Philippines was granted independence by the Americans in 1947.

South Asia

Imperialist control of South Asia grew out of economic influence there through the British East India Company. It gradually replaced the moribund Mughal Empire as the dominant force in the subcontinent. Britain's patchwork array of political relationships continued into the mid–nineteenth century, when native grievances exploded in the Indian Mutiny of 1857–1858. For a brief time, the widespread upheaval threatened Britain's domination, but the Muslims and Hindus could not unite, which enabled other Indian forces to aid the British in crushing the mutiny.

Many changes stemmed from the midcentury rebellion against British rule. In 1858, Britain took over the management of India from the East India Company and, to ensure the reliability of the army in India, increased the number of soldiers from Britain. British suspicion of the Indians intensified the segregation of imperialist rulers from their subjects. Harsh rule was supported by growing racist sentiments.

British imperialism significantly changed the ecological and social makeup of North India. Widespread deforestation denuded the northern lands and devastated the lifestyles of the nomads who lived there. Some migrated to the cities, where many lived beggarly existences, while others stayed behind, eking out livings as farmers.

Famines became a regular occurrence in British India. Sometimes the cause was drought. More often, the planting of tea, cotton, and opium crops in large quantities significantly reduced the land available for grain production.

Additional suffering resulted from the systematic destruction of the Indian cottage industries. To guarantee that British imports to India did not suffer from competition from local wares, British officials enacted measures that destroyed local manufactories. These policies threw Indians out of work and forced a large number to farm. By the late nineteenth century, Indian leaders began to seek local rule or the adoption of self-help measures.

The major drive for independence came in the early twentieth century. Although leaders like Muhammad Jinnah and Jawaharlal Nehru played vital roles in the freedom struggle, perhaps the liberation effort was best personified by Mohandas Gandhi[3] (1869–1948). A man of charismatic and spiritual stature, Gandhi became a major political figure, employing mass-action techniques of *ahimsa* (nonviolence) that originated from Jain and Buddhist traditions. Gandhi also used the ideas of Henry David Thoreau relating to civil disobedience. Political fasts and other symbolic actions ignited a growing Indian resistance to British rule, leading to the independence of Hindu India and Muslim Pakistan in 1947. The two new states, however, failed to overcome longstanding religious and sectarian differences, and war erupted several times. Following the Indian lead,

[3] **Mohandas Gandhi:** moh HAHN duhs gahn DEE

FIGURE 34.5 ***Indian Mutiny.*** *British rule in India was based on a sense of entitlement and the ignorance of Indian customs, which created tension between ruler and ruled. When Indian soldiers turned on their officers in 1857, they began a rebellion in which both military and civilian British were killed. This lithograph, "The Massacre at Cawnpore," shows one notorious event—the killing of British women and children—that fueled severe repression. The popular revolt that had started as military mutiny forced the British government to reexamine its policies in India.* National Army Museum/ET Archive.

the other modern states of the subcontinent—Bangladesh, Bhutan, Nepal, and Sri Lanka—eventually won independence.

Southwest and Central Asia

Much of the history of Southwest Asia in the nineteenth and twentieth centuries relates to the Ottoman Empire. As was seen in Chapter 33, European portions of this Islamic state agitated for independence, and some peoples gained freedom in the nineteenth and twentieth centuries.

During World War I, the Ottomans allied with the Germans. Thus, the British, the French, and some Arab groups formed an alliance to undermine the Ottomans. One example of this coalition building was the Husayn-McMahon correspondence of 1915 to 1916, in which British diplomat Sir Henry McMahon encouraged Arab hopes of independence. In 1916, Sharif Husayn[4] led an Arab revolt against the Ottoman Empire, and Arab forces fought alongside allied units thereafter. During the same year, the British and French negotiated an agreement that divided the Arab domain into a French-governed North and a British-administered South. This treaty showed that the two imperialist powers intended to control Southwest Asia long after the war's end.

The Ottoman rulers lost most of their Southwest Asian holdings, and the British and French assumed overlordship there. Various Arab leaders attempted to assert independence against the Europeans, but their efforts failed. During the 1920s, the British reduced their control over many

[4] **Husayn:** HOO sayn

parts of the South, but the French doggedly held on to their positions. The Saudis, one group of Arabs under Ibn Saud, conquered most of Arabia and established a monarchy. Oil discoveries in Arabia and other parts of the region highlighted its strategic importance for the oil-consuming nations in the West.

In 1917, the British government issued the Balfour Declaration, which promised a Jewish homeland in Palestine. This action recognized the importance of Zionism and the compatibility of British and Jewish interests in Southwest Asia. As early as 1865, sympathizers of the Jewish cause had established the Palestine Exploration Fund, and the Fourth Zionist Congress met in London in 1900, receiving extraordinary fanfare from the British press. World War II weakened France and Britain and transformed the political situation in Southwest Asia. By 1946, most states were either independent or soon became free. Relying on the Balfour Declaration, many Jews planned for the creation of Israel in the former area of Palestine. In 1948, they declared the existence of Israel, provoking Arab nationalists, who sent armies that failed to destroy the new country.

Russia developed significant economic and political interests in Southwest and Central Asia, beginning in the eighteenth century. Part of the expansion stemmed from Peter the Great's war against the Persians, but a significant development began when Georgia, a country in the Caucasus Mountains region, asked for Russian assistance against the Persian and Ottoman empires. The Russians defeated the Persians and Turks, expanding further into the Caucasus region and into the Balkans. By the 1850s, Russia's aggressive moves against the Ottoman Empire alarmed the British and French, who fought against the Russians in the Crimean War (1854–1856), temporarily halting Russian expansion.

FIGURE 34.6 ***Russian Troops on Patrol.*** *In the nineteenth century, Russia slowly made itself the imperial master of Central Asia, fighting and conquering various Muslim states. In this 1881 drawing, a group of Russian scouts surveys acquired territory. To the east, Russian troops reached the borders of the Chinese empire, securing a temporary hold on the strategic Ili River Valley, while forces to the south halted British conquests and developed a growing interest in Afghanistan.* L'Illustration/ Sygma.

During the nineteenth century, Russian imperialist interest in Central Asia precipitated an intense rivalry with the British. Part of the reason for Russia's push was the inability of Russian manufactured goods to compete in Europe, so Russians traded in Southwest, Central, and East Asian markets, where their goods were in demand. A Russo-Persian Bank and a Russo-Chinese Bank were founded to promote trade with Asian countries. Central Asian governments run by Muslim leaders opposed Russian interference. Conflicts erupted and led to Russia's conquest of much of Central Asia in the mid–nineteenth century.

Russian and British economic and strategic interests clashed in Afghanistan and Persia through the late nineteenth and early twentieth centuries. Both traded with the Afghan people. In addition, the British feared that Russian conquest would threaten their interests in India. On the other hand, the Russians saw Afghanistan as a step in their march through Central Asia. Russia and Britain, however, put aside their bitter rivalry in 1907, when they negotiated an alliance, assigning Russia a large sphere of influence in northern Persia and the British a smaller sphere in southern Persia. Russia also agreed that Afghanistan lay outside its Central Asian sphere of influence.

THE AFRICAN EXPERIENCE WITH IMPERIALISM

Between 1871 and 1912, Africa fell to European imperialism, and, by 1949, few African states had managed to regain their independence. During that time, Great Britain added nearly 4.4 million square miles of territory and 66 million people to its empire in Africa, while the French grabbed around 3.5 million square miles inhabited by 26 million people. Resistance to European domination took many forms; partially successful efforts pitted the Ethiopians against the Italians and the Zulus against the British.

North Africa

Much of North Africa fell to French, British, Italian, or Spanish domination. The French took Morocco, Algeria, and Tunisia, while the British dominated Egypt and Sudan. During the early 1900s, the British and French recognized each other's control of North African territories. The Italians added Libya to their overseas empire, while the Spanish increased their holdings in Northwest Africa (Spanish Morocco).

French influence in North Africa, based on a growing economic involvement, increased in the latter half of the nineteenth century. As France industrialized, North African markets attracted French manufacturers and financiers. In addition, many French settled in Algeria, Morocco, and Tunisia, becoming an important lobby in the French Parliament by promoting France's annexation of these territories. Another significant player promoting imperialist policies was the Roman Catholic Church, which wanted to increase missionary activities. Governments of the French republic supported overseas Catholic activities even though they pushed anticlerical policies domestically. By the 1880s and 1890s, French economic interests began seriously competing with those of the British in the eastern Mediterranean, especially in Egypt.

For much of the nineteenth century, Britain supported the Ottoman Turks in propping up their empire, and that meant maintaining a hands-off policy toward Egypt, which was in Ottoman hands. The prospect, however, of building a canal from the Mediterranean to the Red Sea meant that British ships sailing to India would not have to navigate around Africa. Although Egyptians played a major role in the Suez Canal's construction, the inflow of capital necessary to complete the work in 1870 caused severe financial problems for the Egyptians. In 1875, Britain purchased the Egyptian ruler's shares in the company that dug the canal, gaining a significant financial interest there. Political upheaval threatened British financiers in 1882, and Prime Minister William Gladstone ordered an invasion. Although never formally annexed, Egypt remained under British control until 1954.

The Sudan had often been closely linked with Egypt in the nineteenth century. In 1885, British troops commanded by General Charles Gordon were defeated by the Mahdi, ruler of the Sudan, but thirteen years later, an Anglo-Egyptian army under Lord Horatio Kitchener decisively defeated the Mahdi and his allies at the Battle of Omdurman. At the same time, French forces planted the French flag in the area of Fashoda[5] (Sudan), nearly precipitating a war between France and Britain.

[5] **Fashoda:** FAH shoh dah

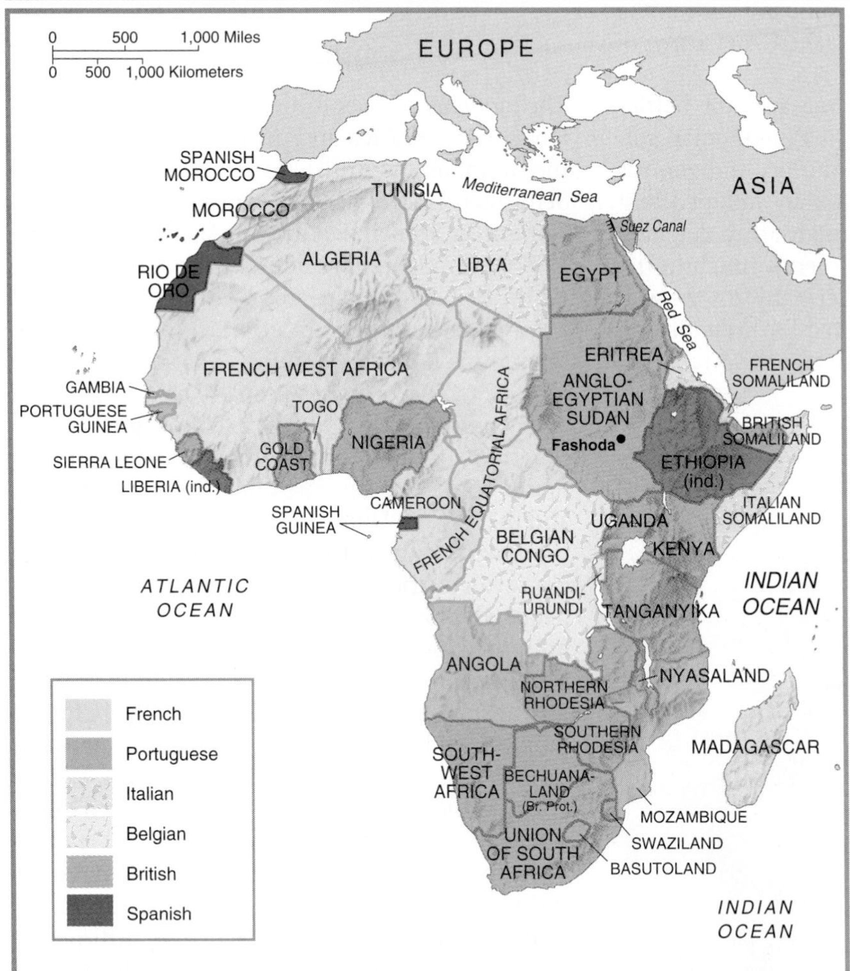

Map 34.3 ***Imperialism in Africa, to 1935.*** *Although the Portuguese had established African colonies prior to the 1880s, the greatest imperialist expansion in Africa occurred within the last two decades of the nineteenth century. Great Britain and France were the major players in this territorial grab. As a consequence of its defeat in World War I, Germany lost most of its African possessions to other European countries. Most African liberation movements began after World War II.*

The French army had marched west from Ethiopia, hoping to link up with another French force coming from east-central Africa. Lord Kitchener's detachment arrived in Fashoda and asked the French to leave. After the French refused, the two commanders sipped whiskey, waiting for their governments' instructions. British nationalist public opinion grew warlike. Seeing a miscalculation, the French abandoned their claims. In 1904, the French and British negotiated an alliance that divided their respective imperial interests, keeping conflicts to a minimum.

Italy developed significant financial interests in Libya. Partly to protect these investments and also to prevent other powers from seizing Libya, the Italian government sanctioned expansion of political influence in North Africa. Between 1913 and 1943, successive Italian governments supported this colonization, initially of the coastal areas and then gradually inland. Business leaders and Roman Catholic officials supported each other in the drive to make the Libyans fully subject to Italian rule and culture beginning in the 1920s.

East Africa

Imperialist rivalries precipitated a scramble for control of East Africa. The most intense activity came in the 1880s, when the Germans, Italians, French, and British all competed for land. The Italians had the most difficult time, losing 500 soldiers to the Ethiopians in 1887 and 5,000 more in 1896 at the Battle of Adowa.[6] The latter was the greatest defeat of imperialist forces in Africa. Full-scale

[6] **Adowa:** AH doh wah

defeat and annexation of Ethiopia came only in the 1930s, when the Italians smashed the army of Haile Selassie.

German East Africa became a major battleground during World War I. British-led Indian soldiers fought against German-led indigenous troops along with some German independent units. The mixed African-German army defeated and captured four Indian regiments, much to the shock of the British. Because Germany lost the war, however, these victories counted for little. Britain took over administration of the colony.

FIGURE 34.7 ***Belgian Rule in the Congo.*** *The Belgian king, Leopold, ran a private empire until the early 1900s in the Belgian Congo. Even by the brutal standards of other imperialist countries of the time, Leopold's domain witnessed many atrocities. In this British cartoon, a reptilian Leopold crushes a Congolese man—a stark representation of his policies toward the Congolese people.* Mansell/Time Inc.

West and Southwest Africa

The French took over the largest amount of African lands in West Africa and primarily competed with the Germans and British for influence there. Albert Schweitzer (1875–1965) became a medical missionary in French Equatorial Africa in the early 1900s. Although imprisoned by the French during World War I for suspected German sympathies, Schweitzer returned to Africa after the war to rebuild his hospital, winning a Nobel Peace Prize in 1952. The Portuguese, Spanish, and Belgians also controlled territories in the region, while Liberia, although nominally independent, fell under control of the Firestone Rubber Company and thereby the United States.

Belgian rule of the Congo territory was ruthless, even by the standards of the day. Many Europeans deplored Belgian rule, and the horrors prompted Joseph Conrad to pen *Heart of Darkness*, a telling critique of imperialist domination of Africans. International criticism eventually forced King Leopold of Belgium to surrender his personal control to the Belgian Parliament in 1909. Conditions gradually improved, but the Congo remained a Belgian colony until the early 1960s.

The German colonies of Togo, Cameroons, and German West Africa had been set up in the mad rush of the 1880s but fell into British and French hands after World War I. The British and French divided Togo and Cameroons, while the British administered Southwest Africa.

South Africa

British control of southern Africa came after a long campaign of fighting and several military defeats and political embarrassment. Tenacity and perseverance gave the British eventual victory, and the costs forced them into a reexamination of their foreign policy early in the twentieth century.

South Africa contained a diverse mixture of African tribes, Indians, and Europeans. As seen in Chapter 33, Zulu nationalism directed by Shaka and his successors precipitated an expansion of territory, threatening the British. The Zulu War of 1879 concluded a decades-long conflict between the Zulu and the British, who suffered a defeat at the Battle of Isandhlwana before eventually winning.

FIGURE 34.8 ***British Detention Camp in South Africa.*** *The Boer War (1899–1902) tarnished Britain's self-image as an enlightened imperialist power. Boers, including women and children, were interned in camps like this one; about one-fifth of the prisoners died. Britain's actions during the war brought international condemnation.* MuseuMAfricA, Johannesburg.

After subduing the Zulu, the British focused on the Boers, descendants of Dutch settlers, who had been in South Africa for centuries. In the 1830s, the Boers became disgusted with British diplomatic policies, trekking northward to colonize two regions, Transvaal[7] and Orange Free State. It was a remarkable saga of a people traveling great distances in wagons similar to those that carried settlers to the western United States. Discovery of gold and diamonds in the Boer-controlled area brought fortune seekers and growing conflict. In 1896, Cecil Rhodes, who was prime minister of South Africa, sponsored an expedition of a few hundred soldiers against the Boers, hoping to expand British influence and his own prestige. Defeat of Rhodes's expeditionary force compelled Rhodes to resign, but it also compelled Britain to avenge its loss. The Boer War broke out in 1899 and lasted nearly three years, to the shock of the British, who mustered 350,000 soldiers against a Boer population of 60,000 people. Outnumbered, the Boers successfully used guerrilla tactics until Lord Kitchener responded with a scorched-earth policy that burned down Boer farmhouses and herded Boer women and children into makeshift camps. The British outlasted the Boers but were stunned by the vehement international condemnation of their conduct of the war.

[7] **Transvaal:** TRAHNS vahl

SOCIALIST IMPERIALISM

Forces of nationalism and industrialization rocked the tsarist Russian Empire, bringing its collapse in 1917. The growth of a socialist state from the monarchical ruins brought a socialist imperialism. Most socialists followed Karl Marx in arguing that nationalism and imperialism stemmed from capitalism. To them, internationalism seemed more in line with the new socialist order, as expressed in the slogan "Workers of the world unite!" The experience of Soviet Russia, however, brought imperialist rule over many former Russian colonies.

Six months after the tsarist system collapsed, the Bolshevik Party under Vladimir Lenin's leadership seized power. Within months of gaining political control, the Bolsheviks blundered into a vicious civil war. During the conflict, the Bolsheviks reconquered most of the former tsarist realm.

In a related war with Poland, the Soviets expected their Polish worker brothers and sisters to join them. The Bolsheviks were surprised by the nationalism of the Poles, who threw out the Soviets.

Despite the professed internationalism of the Soviets, nationalism persisted after the civil war. Seeing themselves as surrounded by hostile capitalist states, communist leaders stressed the policy of "Socialism in One Country." In the mid-1930s, Josef Stalin permitted a more open celebration of past Russian leaders, including national heroes such as Ivan the Terrible and Peter the Great.

When the Nazis attacked Poland and diverted the attention of western European countries, Soviet Russia expanded its control of other former tsarist areas. Part of Poland was annexed, the Baltic states of Latvia, Lithuania, and Estonia were occupied, and Finland was attacked. Some have argued that Soviet Russia created a defensive barrier against possible attack by the Germans, but others have noted that the Soviets continued traditional Russian expansionist policies. The annexations followed Soviet industrialization, and the new lands were integrated economically into the Soviet Union.

By the end of World War II, Soviet armies occupied parts of East and Central Europe, and, although the Soviets did not rule directly, economic imperialism continued as the Eastern Bloc countries of East Germany, Czechoslovakia, Poland, Romania, Hungary, and Bulgaria all fell into the Soviet economic sphere. Socialist imperialism governed the relationships of Europe and even Mongolia in Central Asia (after 1919).

SOME SOCIAL CONSEQUENCES OF IMPERIALIST RULE

Imperialist states came into control of other countries and brought their own institutions, practices, and ideas into the colonies, conferring subjecthood rather than citizenship on indigenous peoples. In many cases, feelings of preeminence by the rulers were supported by claims of racial supremacy, whether disguised as "the White Man's Burden" or as the Japanese view of themselves as "older brothers."

Liberation of Indian Women?

Europeans examined the position of women in many societies over which they ruled and believed that customs such as footbinding, prohibitions against widows' remarrying, female circumcision, and *suttee*[8] (the burning of Indian widows along with their deceased husbands) were barbaric and proved the inherent "inferiority" of indigenous social and cultural practices. Thus, vigorous efforts were undertaken to abolish them.

Various rulers and individuals in India, for example, also spoke against *suttee* and the practice of forbidding widows to remarry. In the seventh century, the Indian emperor Harsha had condemned *suttee* but was unable to eradicate the custom. In the eighteenth and nineteenth centuries, some Hindu sects of the lower socioeconomic groups welcomed widows. The British undertook a concerted effort to abolish *suttee* and generally succeeded in the areas under their direct control. Success fed British attitudes of superiority along with their self-image of "civilizing" rule.

Education for women in Western colonies became another arena of imperialist policy making. Missionaries established coeducational schools in Asia along with a few strictly for women. Most schools founded by imperial governments were for males only, or the grade level for girls seldom went beyond elementary school. Indians founded single-sex and coeducational schools in Bengal, where classes were taught in the regional dialect. One reason was that men wanted women to read and write only one language, their own. Indian nationalists proudly pointed out that Indian women were graduated from universities before their sisters in Britain.

While many Indian men approved of the abolition of *suttee* and of the education of women, they also fervently believed that Indian women should remain unchanged in other ways. Indian nationalists, for example, accepted change mandated by imperialist rulers in the "outer world" of political and economic relationships. On the other hand, these nationalists rejected attempts of the imperialists to transform the "inner world" of the family, where the wife was sacred. In this view, the home was not to be colonized. Although idealized as goddesses, Indian women remained under the control of men in the "inner world."

[8] ***suttee*:** SUH tee

IN THEIR OWN WORDS

A Woman in Nineteenth-Century India

Many Indian men feared the Western education of Indian women, especially by Western teachers. The safest way, Indian men argued, was to create schools where Indian girls were taught in the local dialect. Then there would be control over what they learned.

Rassundari Debi[a] (1809–1900), a middle-class girl, first tasted education when she was eight years old by learning arithmetic and the Bengali alphabet. The experiment died with a fire that incinerated the school but left an inner flame that would not be snuffed out. At twelve years of age, Rassundari was married, ending her chances for study and self-improvement. When her mother died, Rassundari lamented being unable to visit her and being a woman.

> I tried in so many ways to go and see my mother, but I was not fated to do so. This is not a matter of small regret to me. Oh Lord, why did you give birth to me as a human being? Compared to all the birds and beasts and other inferior creatures in this world, it is a rare privilege to be granted a human birth. And yet, despite this privilege, I have failed grievously in my duty. Why was I born a woman? Shame on my life. . . . If I had been my mother's son and known of her imminent death, no matter where I happened to be, I would have flown to her side like a bird. Alas, I am only a bird in a cage.

Rassundari always dreamed of being able to read and prayed for that skill.

> One day in my sleep, I dreamt I had opened a copy of the *Caitanya-Bhagavat*[b] [a Hindu religious text] and was reading it. As soon as I woke up, my body and mind were filled with delight. I closed my eyes and again thought of the dream, and realized what a precious gift I had received. . . . Every day I had asked the Almighty, "Teach me to read. I want to read books." The Almighty had not taught me to read, but now had given me the power to read books in my dream.

One day, Rassundari's husband left a copy of the *Caitanya-Bhagavat* for her eldest son to read. Secretly, Rassundari learned to read the holy book.

> My mind seemed to have acquired six hands. With two of them, it wanted to do all the work of the household so that no one, young or old, could find fault with me. With two others, it sought to draw my children close to my heart. And with the last two, it reached for the moon. . . . Has anyone held the moon in her hands? . . . And yet my mind would not be convinced; it yearned to read the *purana* [holy teachings].

Rassundari's sons also helped her learn to read and write, and later she wrote her autobiography.

[a] **Rassundari Debi:** RAH suhn dah ree DEH bee

[b] ***Caitanya-Bhagavat*:** KAY tahn yah BAH gah vaht

Peasant Unrest

Imperialist policies disrupted the lives of rural peoples, especially peasants. The French in Vietnam and the British in India, for example, set tax rates on individuals rather than on village communities, upsetting traditional patterns of social interaction and responsibility. In addition, tax revenues had to be paid in money rather than in crops, causing some farmers to sell their lands and move to cities, where many became indigent and homeless. The Belgians needed laborers to work the rubber plantations in the Congo and forced reluctant farmers to contribute weekly or monthly *corvée* services. Indigo plantations in Bengal and sugar plantations in Cuba severely exploited workers, causing men and women to live in near-slavery conditions.

Rural unrest developed as living conditions deteriorated, taking many forms of rural violence. One common result of growing servitude was flight, and the early exploitation of the Belgian Congo led to widespread absenteeism on the part of peasants. Isolated sentry posts around rubber plantations were overrun by peasants in the Congo, and the guards were killed. Major uprisings by Indian peasants erupted in 1857 and again in 1942, when rural folk focused their hatred on the British government. It took months and many lives for the British to restore control.

AMERICAS		ASIA		EUROPE AND AFRICA		
U.S. continental expansion, 1803–1898	Economic imperialism in Latin America, c. 1800–1949				1800	Louisiana Purchase, 1803 (by U.S.)
					1850	Mexico cedes territory to U.S., 1848
			British imperialism in South Asia, c. 1850–1948			Gadsen Purchase, 1853 (by U.S.)
						Alaska Purchase, 1867 (by U.S.)
				German imperialism in Africa, c. 1880–1918		
U.S. imperialism, c. 1890–1959		Japanese imperialism, c. 1895–1945			1900	U.S. annexes the Philippines, 1898
						Anglo-Russian rivalry in Afghanistan relaxes, 1907
						Japan annexes Korea, 1910
						Germany loses African colonies, 1918
				Socialist imperialism, 1939–1989		Japan's Greater East Asia Co-Prosperity Sphere, 1940
					1950	Soviet occupation of eastern Europe, 1945

SUMMARY

1. Imperialism is an economic and political system of control by an industrialized country needing raw materials and markets. It developed out of the Industrial Revolution and the era of modern nationalism.

2. After the United States won independence from England, the Americans continued colonizing to the Pacific Ocean and beyond. Industrialization brought U.S. control of the Philippines and economic imperialism in Latin America.

3. Latin America gained independence from Spain, Portugal, Britain, Denmark, the Netherlands, and France but had to fend off imperialist efforts to gain direct control in later decades. Latin America long suffered from economic imperialism directed by England, France, and the United States.

4. China suffered growing humiliation at the hands of the British and other Western countries until 1894. Then, Japan entered the imperialist competition and eventually dominated China from 1931 to 1945. Chinese nationalism developed from the clashes with imperialists, benefiting the Chinese communists.

5. Japan's imperialism ended in utter defeat by 1945, and a wounded Korea lay prostrate under Soviet and American influence.

6. Southeast Asia fell under Western and Japanese imperialism. Although imperialism wrought havoc, it helped generate nationalism and brought defeat for the Europeans.

7. South Asia suffered under British rule, which left the subcontinent ecologically changed and highly fragmented. Under the leadership of Mohandas Gandhi and Muhammad Jinnah, India and Pakistan gained independence.

8. The decline of the Ottoman Empire afforded the European imperialists the opportunity to replace the Turks as imperial rulers. Arab nationalism, which helped bring the change, was frustrated by the change of masters. Eventually, most Arab states won independence, but Arab nationalism was provoked by Zionism and the formation of Israel in the territory of Palestine in 1948. Russia expanded into Central Asia, seeking markets and raw materials.

9. Africa was dismembered by the imperialist powers between 1871 and 1912. Germany lost its African territories in World War I, and Italy lost its lands there in World War II. Much of Africa lay under imperialism in 1949.

10. Socialist imperialism grew out of the nationalist fervor employed in the Russian Civil War (1918–1921), and it reappeared at the end of the Stalinist industrialization effort.

11. Women in countries controlled by imperialists gained some freedoms, but they remained under male domination. Peasants often suffered under foreign rule and revolted against it.

SUGGESTED READINGS

Chatterjee, Partha. *The Nation and Its Fragments: Colonial and Post-Colonial Histories*. Princeton, N.J.: Princeton University Press, 1993. An examination of British imperialism and Indian responses to it.

Duus, Peter. *The Abacus and the Sword: The Japanese Penetration of Korea, 1895–1910*. Berkeley: University of California Press, 1995. An analysis of Japan's conquest and annexation of Korea in the context of imperialism.

Gallager, John, and Ronald Robinson. "The Imperialism of Free Trade." *Economic Review*, 2nd series, 6 (1953): 1–15. A classic argument of a creeping Western imperialism through free trade policies and treaties with Asian and African states.

Hobson, J. A. *Imperialism*. Ann Arbor: University of Michigan Press, 1971. A reprint of a classic study (1902) and critique of imperialism, one that influenced Lenin's *Imperialism*.

Kiernan, V. G. *Imperialism and Its Contradictions*. New York: Routledge, 1995. Essays from the past few decades by an important scholar of imperialism.

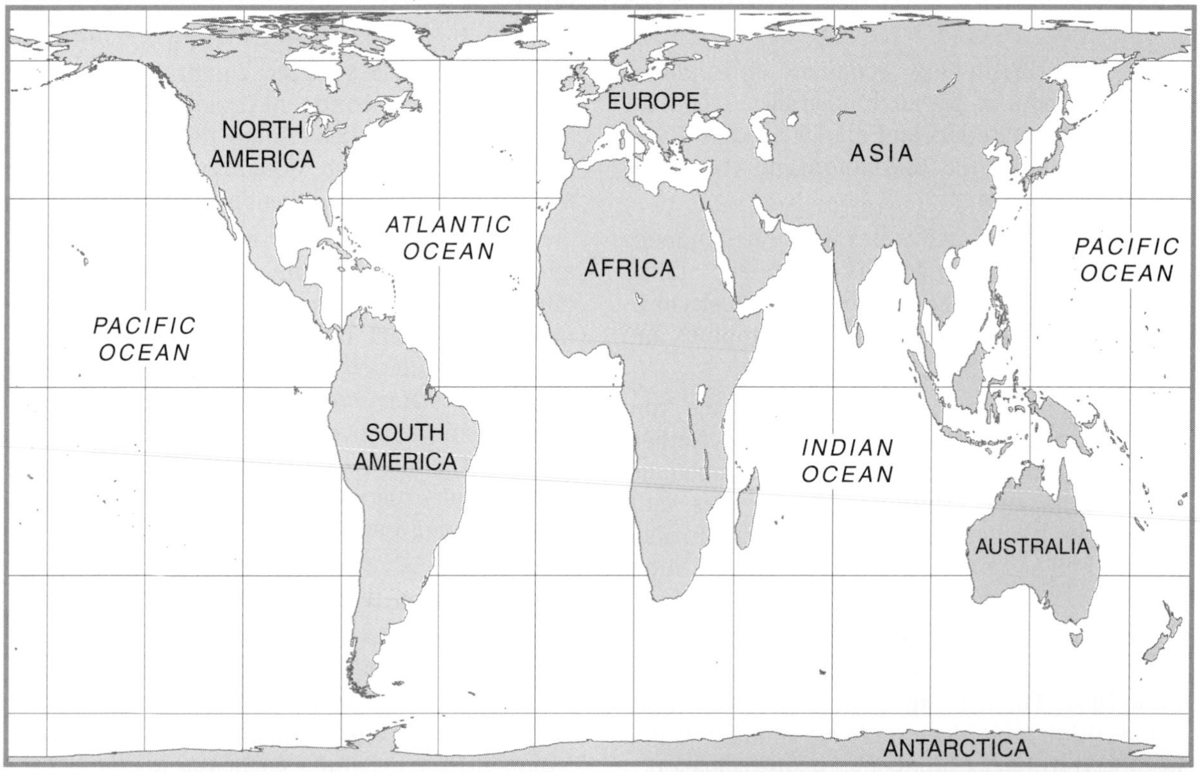

John Speke and Richard Burton. *These British geographers-explorers were fierce competitors in the European race to discover the source of the Nile—the place where its headwaters arose. Newspapers of the time closely followed the exploits of both men. Though his methods were less rigorous than Burton's, Speke (left) was ultimately successful.* *Left*: Illustrated London News Picture Library; *right*: Trustees of the National Portrait Gallery.

CHAPTER 35

Darwin, Marx, and Others Transform Our Views

1837 Onward

Human history is in essence a history of ideas.

This quotation from H. G. Wells reflects the pivotal position that many scholars accord intellectual history. If we accept this position, then the nineteenth century must be granted a special place in history. During that century, basic conceptions were changing in many or most academic fields, and our vision of the universe and our place in it was changing at a rate that arguably was faster than ever before or since. Certainly most intellectual disciplines can trace their modern forms directly to ideas developed in the nineteenth century.

During the nineteenth century, the fruits of the Scientific Revolution two centuries before led to drastically new ways of viewing the world. This period saw major shifts in the basic outlook, assumptions, and underlying theories in many branches of science and other scholarly fields; our understanding of how nature and people operate was elaborated into patterns that largely persist today. These new ideas, developed and debated by scholars, in turn were passed on to the general public as discoveries and theories were disseminated through books, newspapers, and other media.

INTELLECTUAL FERMENT IN NINETEENTH-CENTURY EUROPE

By the nineteenth century, the intellectual scene in Europe had become dynamic and exciting. Forces set in motion centuries before had wrought major changes in the ways that intellectuals conducted their scholarship, and more recent social changes had led scholars to question some of their most basic assumptions about the world and humanity. It was in this setting that the basic paradigms of many fields of study were reoriented.

Of considerable importance was the sheer increase in the number of professional scholars in the nineteenth century. Colleges had been around in Europe since the ninth century, but they were few and served only a small group of elite students training for particular fields, largely law, theology, and medicine. By the nineteenth century, however, higher education was expanding to include larger numbers of students and a greater variety of fields of study. Population increases of the period and the rise of the middle class fueled the upsurge in the numbers of students, and colleges and universities proliferated. In France, for example, the number of colleges and universities increased by more than 500 percent between 1750 and 1850, and there were similar increases in England, Germany, Italy, and elsewhere in Europe. This meant that more scholars were hired as professors and that more research was conducted.

At the same time that academia was expanding, it was reorganizing. In Renaissance Europe, scholars were expected to be versatile, making contributions in diverse fields. (The modern phrase "a Renaissance man" refers to someone who is knowledgeable or skilled in many areas.) Many students in the eighteenth and nineteenth centuries selected the more general liberal arts education, but increasingly large numbers chose to specialize more narrowly, focusing their study on only biology or history or mathematics. Universities began organizing into departments that reflected these academic specializations, encouraging scholars to study a more narrow field intensively. Compared with earlier times, nineteenth-century Europe had huge numbers of scholars, delving intensively into their specialized fields.

At the same time, these scholars had available to them the scientific methodology of the Scientific Revolution. The interim had seen tremendous advances in scientific knowledge, the accumulation of an impressive legion of scientific facts, and refinements in scientific method. The time was ripe to use these tools and raw materials to build new intellectual frameworks for looking at the world and society.

These scholars did not live in a vacuum, and they were profoundly influenced by the events that transpired around them. The French Revolution had spawned a new era of secularism that the succeeding decades had legitimized. Other political revolutions added to the perception of world instability, and the Industrial Revolution was in full swing, radically transforming the lives of everyone caught up in it. The pace of technological change was such that those of each generation grew up with everyday devices unknown in their parents' childhood. Omnipresent change encouraged scholars to look to new ways of seeing their disciplines, and the older tradition of looking to ancient scholars for inspiration had largely faded away. Scholars came to see progress and new ideas in a far more favorable light than had their predecessors.

Out of this setting developed a number of scholars who profoundly changed our ways of looking at ourselves. They certainly were major forces in world intellectual history, founders of the modern intellectual traditions of Western civilization.

DARWIN AND THE PLACE OF HUMANITY

Charles Darwin (1809–1882) was born into an elite, intellectual English family. Initially, he was a great disappointment to his family, who complained that he cared for nothing but "shooting, dogs, and rat-catching." His life was transformed, however, in 1831, when a family friend obtained for him a position on HMS *Beagle*.

This British vessel was setting out on a five-year voyage around the world to explore and collect scientific information, and Darwin was to be its naturalist. While he had no special training in that field, he had read widely and had always been interested in nature, and he threw himself into his position. The information Darwin gathered, coupled with his copious spare time aboard the *Beagle*, led him to formulate revolutionary ideas about the development of the various plant and animal species.

FIGURE 35.1 *HMS* **Beagle** ***at the Strait of Magellan.*** *The* Beagle *carried Charles Darwin around the world, carefully navigating the dangerous waters at the southern tip of South America en route to the Galapagos Islands. There Darwin studied local plants and animals, collecting much of the information that shaped his theory of evolution.* Corbis-Bettmann.

Pre-Darwinian Beliefs

At the beginning of the nineteenth century, most scientists believed that species were immutable—that is, that they could not change or evolve from one to another. This belief was founded on the everyday observation that a species always bore young of the same kind, and that there were no intermediate forms of known creatures, such as hybrids between dogs and cats. The biblical aphorism that "like produces like" was part of the fund of knowledge commonly taken for granted in the Western tradition during this period, leading most contemporary scientists to accept the immutability of species.

Another commonly held belief was that the world had been created relatively recently. There was no pressing evidence in this era to compel a scientist to believe the world was significantly older than the indications from the earliest historic documents. While only a minority of scientists at this time accepted the chronology derived from the Bible by Bishop James Ussher in the seventeenth century, which placed earthly creation at 4004 B.C., most allowed only a few tens of thousands of years for all of earthly events. A rising group of geologists (discussed later in this chapter) championed a much greater age for the earth, but they were opposed by most scholars in the early decades of the nineteenth century.

Such a short period between the beginning of the planet and the earliest historical accounts (which describe modern species of plants and animals) permitted insufficient time for the gradual development of modern species. Therefore, proponents of the short earthly chronology argued, evolution could not explain the development of species.

There was, however, a significant dissenting view, popular particularly in France. There, such scientists as Jean Baptiste Lamarck (1744–1829) and Georges Buffon[1] (1707–1788) had championed theories of **evolution**, the concept that each species developed by modification from an earlier species, now extinct. While some scientists were fascinated with this idea, neither Lamarck nor Buffon could suggest a satisfactory mechanism by which this evolution might have taken place. Rather, they suggested that new forms developed in direct response to needs. For example, if an antelope-like animal needed access to the tops of trees in order to eat the leaves growing there, individuals would strive to reach them, thus stretching their necks; these acquired traits, according to Lamarck, were passed on to offspring, and the result was the giraffe. While Lamarck and Buffon were wrong in their assumptions—experiments showed that acquired characteristics could not be passed on to offspring—they drew attention to the fact that animals and plants were adapted to the particulars of the environments in which they lived. Darwin used this insight as a crucial element in his theory of evolution.

Darwin's Theory of Evolution

As Darwin began observing plants and animals wherever the *Beagle* went, he began formulating his theory of evolution. He was particularly intrigued by the finches he found on the Galapagos Islands, off the western coast of South America. Each island was isolated from the others by winds and currents that would have made it difficult for a bird as small as a finch to have crossed from one to another, and the finches on each island were somewhat different from those on all the other islands. Yet, they all shared basic anatomy and characteristics. How could Darwin account for this?

To explain it, Darwin borrowed a concept from economics. While reading the influential *Essay on Population* by Thomas Malthus[2] (1766–1834), Darwin had been struck that every individual is in competition with every other individual. As Malthus argued, people (and animals) are such efficient reproducers that the population has the potential to grow sufficiently to outstrip its food supply. At that point, as Malthus saw it, individuals were condemned to a miserable struggle for survival, pitted against one another in a competition that invariably would result in the death of some. According to Malthus, the struggle for scarce resources by individuals is inherent in nature.

Using this as his starting point, Darwin took the crucial next step. He argued that individuals who survive are permitted to do so by certain traits that aid their survival, perhaps greater strength or the ability to eat a broader range of foods. These traits are inherited by the offspring of the survivors and are passed on to future generations. On the other hand, animals that die out do so because they possess less advantageous traits, and those traits are weeded out of the population with their deaths. In this manner, less successful characteristics are culled from a population, and the population becomes ever better adapted to its circumstances. Darwin used the term **natural selection** to describe this notion of the most adaptive traits' persistence and others' elimination.

As applied to the Galapagos finches, for example, Darwin's theory postulated that there was a single species of finches that colonized the islands, perhaps accidentally, as a few individuals survived the rigors of traveling there from the South American mainland. As time passed, however, the peculiarities of each island shaped the finches on it. An island with very hard-shelled seeds, for example, would favor finches with stout, rugged beaks able to crack them; an island where finch food was secreted in hollows in plant stems would favor a long, slender bill, and individuals with that characteristic would be most likely to survive. The founding population of each island would have some individual variation, and natural selection would favor some variants and weed out others, leading to considerable differences between the finches on different islands.

Darwin's theory of evolution differed from all evolutionary concepts that preceded it in a crucial way. Lamarck, Buffon, and the other evolutionists before Darwin had believed that evolution was headed in some particular direction, that it was somehow improving things. Darwinian evolution, on the other hand, was not directed toward any consistent goal. As conditions changed, adaptive traits changed, and creatures that once were numerous and well adapted might become extinct

[1] **Georges Buffon:** ZHORZH boo FOHN
[2] **Malthus:** MAHL thoos

as selective pressures changed. While Darwin carefully avoided linking evolution to progress, this was atypical of scientists of that day, and most popular interpretations of Darwin's theories saw evolution as progressive improvement.

As he developed his theory of evolution, Darwin saw that this single concept could account for the development of all the plants and animals in the modern world, as well as all the extinct forms he argued must have existed in earlier times. This theory solved two vexing biological problems.

First, if each species had been created independently of all the others, why were there so many similarities among modern species? A giraffe, trout, parakeet, and human being are all built about the same way. They have four limbs that intersect the torso at the same skeletal points, a comparable layout of sensory organs on the head, and very similar internal organs. Other animals, such as insects, followed a different plan, but they resembled one another equally strongly. Many scientists of the day thought these unlikely to be mere coincidences; instead, they argued, somehow all vertebrates had descended from a common ancestor and all insects from another common ancestor at some time in the very distant past.

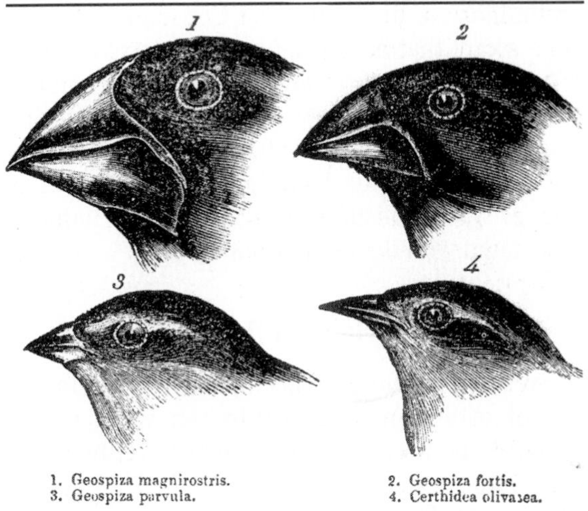

FIGURE 35.2 ***Four Species of Finches.*** *Though all of the finches on the isolated Galapagos Islands are descended from the same species, they followed different evolutionary courses that adapted them for different lifestyles. The heavy-beaked species (top) ate foods that required the breaking of an outer shell or kernel, while the fine-beaked species (bottom) used their narrow beaks to pull food out from narrow crevices. Evidence like this helped Darwin to formulate his theory of natural selection.* Bibliothèque nationale, Paris.

Second, geologists were unearthing a disturbing array of **fossils**, the remains of ancient creatures. Some of these fossils were quite like modern creatures, but others were very different, though still falling into general body plans comparable to those of modern creatures. Earlier scholarship had dismissed these creatures as monsters, aberrations, or failed experiments in creation, but their numbers by the nineteenth century were too great to ignore. Darwin's theory considered these fossils the remains of earlier life forms, successful for a while, yet gradually being transformed into modern species or dying out.

There were, however, difficulties with Darwin's theory of evolution. The first was time, because evolution would be a very slow process. While some scientists clung to the older idea that the earth and its creatures were less than 6,000 years old, geologists under the lead of James Hutton and Charles Lyell were demolishing it, and Ussher's chronology posed little serious impediment to the acceptance of Darwin's theory of evolution.

The second difficulty was the one that swayed most of the scientists who argued against Darwin's theory. Natural selection could explain how forms could die out, but it could not explain how new forms could come about. Darwin's explanation of the Galapagos finches, for example, could explain how delicate-beaked finches could die off on an island with hard seeds, but it did not explain how that same island could develop finches with more rugged beaks than those in the founding population. Darwin recognized this shortcoming of his theory, but he never was able to devise a suitable solution. Only in the early twentieth century would theories of heredity and genetics, pioneered by Gregor Mendel and J. B. S. Haldane, finally unravel this problem. They developed the notions of heredity and genetics that underlie the modern conception of **mutation**, a spontaneous development of a new trait as a result of an error in copying the biochemicals that carry the genetic code during reproduction.

A shy person, Darwin had put off publishing his ideas. In 1858, however, another scientist, Alfred Russel Wallace, came up with the same theory. While Darwin had not published his theory, he had discussed it with colleagues and written preliminary drafts of papers. Consequently, they were aware that each scientist had developed the theory independently and that Darwin actually had collected and analyzed far more supporting evidence. Darwin and Wallace presented a joint paper in 1858, but Darwin's *On the Origin of Species* was published in 1859, and his name is associated with this influential theory.

The Scholarly Reaction to Darwin

Many scientists flocked in support of Darwin's theory of evolution, and within ten years it was accepted by most scholars. There were, however, dissenters, some troubled by the lack of a clear mechanism for the formation of new characteristics and a few concerned that evolution seemed to contradict biblical revelation. Darwin was a Christian, and he felt a certain remorse at developing a theory that he thought might undermine confidence in the spirit (if not the literal truth) of the Bible. He expressed this concern in a letter in which he detailed his agonizing over the theory, finally surrendering to its logic, at which point he noted that he felt as if he were "confessing to a murder."

Darwin's shy personality tended to shrink from controversy, and he rarely defended his theory against the attacks of critics. An early convert to evolution named Thomas Huxley, however, stepped in to defend Darwin and his theory from its earliest presentation. Huxley's strongest supporters never professed him to be shy, and he was famed for his aggressive defenses of Darwin, earning him the nickname "Darwin's bulldog."

In his early work, Darwin avoided direct discussion of human evolution. In fact, he waited to the last pages of *On the Origin of Species* to predict timidly that through evolution, "much light will be thrown on the origin of man and his history." Scientists, as well as the public, were quick to see the ramifications of Darwinian evolution, however, and much of the controversy over Darwin's theory arose out of the implication that human beings evolved from some monkey-like animal, a less than appealing notion to most nineteenth-century readers. In 1871, Darwin attacked this problem head on with his *Descent of Man*. In this book, he provided a detailed analysis of similarities between the anatomy and behavior of human beings and those of other mammals. He concluded

FIGURE 35.3 ***Charles Darwin as Ape.*** *Nineteenth-century cartoonists had a field day with the controversy that developed over Darwin's theory of evolution. This artist placed Darwin's own likeness on the body of an ape, in a parody of the author's work.* From *The Hornet*, March 22, 1871.

that "Man, with all his noble qualities . . . still bears in his bodily frame the indelible stamp of his lowly origin." The probable human ancestor, Darwin said, was "a hairy, tailed quadruped, probably arboreal in its habits, and an inhabitant of the Old World." He even went on to speculate on the way that such a creature might evolve the sentiments and morals of human beings.

Before Darwin, the European scholarly tradition had viewed human beings as noble creatures, set off from the animals by knowledge, morality, and sentiments. After Darwin, scholars were forced to see human beings as another animal, surely ennobled by intelligence but still an animal with a heritage bequeathed by its beastlike ancestors. The effects on philosophy and thinking after Darwin have been many and profound, throwing into question concepts that previously had been

ENCOUNTERS
The Lay Reaction to Darwin

Rarely in the history of science has there been such a reaction to a scientific theory among nonscholars as there was to Darwin's theory of evolution. By the mid–nineteenth century, a high percentage of people in Europe and North America could read, so word of Darwin's ideas spread fast. Magazines and newspapers presented simplified versions, often coupled with editorials or guest essays by opponents, and cartoonists had a field day. Usually basing their opinions purely on these secondhand accounts and commentaries, schoolteachers and members of the clergy sometimes found themselves squaring off in sermons, lessons, debates, and letters published in newspapers.

The public debate over Darwin's ideas usually was framed very differently from the scholarly debate. Most scholars of the era were primarily concerned with Darwin's failure to propose a suitable mechanism for the development of new traits in a species or to produce an unequivocal sequence of fossils that supported evolution. When these obstacles were overcome, academic opposition evaporated.

The public debate, on the other hand, was more likely to revolve on emotional issues. Those who supported Darwin often did so because of a general faith in science: Darwin's theory allowed for an orderly universe to elaborate itself without the need of divine assistance. Many opponents rejected evolution because it was contrary to the literal biblical interpretations that were current in many nineteenth-century circles; others, while not necessarily wedded to a biblical account of creation, simply disliked the idea of so noble a creature as a human having descended from the pathetic monkey or from—even worse—pond scum.

Perhaps the most dramatic confrontation of lay proponents and opponents of evolution was in the "Scopes Monkey Trial." In 1925, John Scopes, a schoolteacher in Dayton, Tennessee, was arrested for teaching Darwinian evolution in violation of a Tennessee statute. The trial attracted the best legal talent, with Clarence Darrow defending Scopes and William Jennings Bryan prosecuting him. It also attracted national attention through the press, which gave it prominent and extensive coverage. Eventually Scopes was convicted, though he was released on a technicality. The negative reaction to the statute and his conviction, however, deterred other states from enacting similar laws and led to the eventual repeal of Tennessee's statute.

the foundation of most Western thinking, such as divine will and the existence of the human soul. The public, too, has been greatly influenced by Darwin, some in accepting his ideas and others in criticizing them.

MARX AND THE NATURE OF SOCIETY

Within a century of Karl Marx's death, one-third of the world's people lived in countries dominated by political systems derived from his theories, and the remaining two-thirds were profoundly affected by them. Even if no other criterion were considered, Marx would have to be judged one of the most influential thinkers of the nineteenth century.

Karl Marx (1818–1883) was born in Germany to middle-class parents. He studied law and philosophy at various German universities, where his reading included the works of earlier socialists like Claude Saint-Simon[3] and Pierre Proudhon,[4] writers who had championed workers, class struggle, and the abolition of private property. He completed his doctorate in 1841, but his radical political views kept him from an academic appointment, forcing him to enter journalism as an alternative career. He wrote several articles discussing politics in the next few years, but his first important publication came in 1848, when he (along with Friedrich Engels) published *The Manifesto of the Communist Party*. From that time on, he published extensively

[3] **Claude Saint-Simon:** clohd san see MOH
[4] **Pierre Proudhon:** pee AYR proo DOH

on politics and economics, in outlets ranging from newspapers to academic journals.

Marx's ideas on society, history, politics, and economics are collectively labeled "Marxism," but that simple term belies their complexity. Not only were the ideas themselves often difficult or complicated, but they changed over time. Sometimes Marx was ambiguous, presenting conflicting ideas in different places and never reconciling them. Further complicating matters is the fact that many people have interpreted Marx since his death, sometimes producing conflicting versions of his theories. It is possible, however, to reduce Marxism to a few essential ideas that convey his main points.

1. *Historical change takes place in regular patterns determined by economics.* Marx argued that changes in ways of life are not random but are the logical outgrowths of economic systems. In particular, the **means of production**, the way that people earn a livelihood, shapes the form of government under which people will be ruled. Marx produced a scheme of cultural evolution that began with hunter-gatherers in prehistory and ended with hypothetical stages yet to come, and for each he discussed the type of government that logically would accompany the means of production.

2. *Under capitalism there is a division into antagonistic classes based on wealth.* Marx saw the major economic system of his time to be **capitalism**, that in which ownership is private and individuals compete to increase their wealth, little hampered by governmental restriction. In such a system, as Marx saw it, some individuals naturally would succeed and others would fail, leading to classes made up of individuals with similar levels of economic wealth and with common concerns. Marx was unsure how many classes there were, but he was sure that there were at least two: the **bourgeoisie**[5] (wealthy investors and their middle-class allies) and the **proletariat** (poor factory workers). The nature of society, according to Marx, ensured that these classes would be in conflict with each other, because their interests were different. In particular, the workers, having nothing to gain from their production, were alienated from their jobs; consequently, workers resented the wealth that others accumulated through their efforts. This class conflict was the driving force behind change.

FIGURE 35.4 ***Karl Marx.*** *Marx, the primary founder of communism, was one of the most influential thinkers of the nineteenth century. His ideas have influenced intellectuals in their writings and sparked revolutions that have profoundly affected world society, economics, and politics.* Corbis-Bettmann.

3. *Over the long run, the profits of the bourgeoisie must decline, as must the standard of living of the proletariat.* Marx developed a complicated economic theory of constant and variable capital (items of value) that few people today accept. The logical consequence of his theory, however, was that there would be less and less material of value over time. This meant that the competition for limited capital would become greater over time, leading to increased class conflict.

4. *The state serves as an instrument of class domination.* Marx observed that the body of laws

[5]**bourgeoisie:** boor zhwah ZEE

serves largely to protect the interests of the capitalists and the bourgeoisie, tilting the odds in their favor in the inevitable class conflict. As he saw it, the main purpose of all states is to protect the status quo, hence protecting the monied ruling classes.

5. *The overthrow of capitalism and the establishment of a more fair system will have to be accomplished through revolution.* Because the legal system serves to support the current status, Marx reasoned, it will be necessary to go outside the law to change the system. Marx saw this as usually entailing a violent revolution that would replace the legal system. The new type of society would be characterized by a **socialist** economy, wherein property of all sorts would be held by everyone as a whole, and a **communist** political system that would serve the people but not support class domination. This new socialist state would be a classless system with a more equal distribution of wealth. It would be a society ruled by Marx's famous maxim: "From each according to his abilities, to each according to his needs."

6. *The revolution will need to be international and led by a communist party.* Recognizing the need for organizers, Marx argued that a communist party would need to be developed in order to lead the revolution. The revolution would need to be international, at least eventually, because national interests invariably are geared to the

IN THEIR OWN WORDS
The Communist Manifesto

The following excerpt is the beginning of *The Manifesto of the Communist Party*, jointly written by Karl Marx and Friedrich Engels in 1848. It introduces the factor they saw as underlying all history: class struggle.

A spectre is haunting Europe—the spectre of Communism. All the Powers of old Europe have entered into a holy alliance to exorcise this spectre: Pope and Czar, Metternich and Guizot, French Radicals and German police-spies.

Where is the party in opposition that has not been decried as Communistic by its opponents in power? Where is the Opposition that has not hurled back the branding reproach of Communism, against the more advanced opposition parties, as well as against its reactionary adversaries?

Two things result from this fact:

I. Communism is already acknowledged by all European Powers to be itself a Power.

II. It is high time that Communists should openly, in the face of the whole world, publish their views, their aims, their tendencies, and meet this nursery tale of the Spectre of Communism with a Manifesto of the party itself.

To this end, Communists of various nationalities have assembled in London, and sketched the following Manifesto, to be published in the English, French, German, Italian, Flemish and Danish languages.

The history of all hitherto existing society is the history of class struggles. Freeman and slave, patrician and plebeian, lord and serf, guild-master and journeyman, in a word, oppressor and oppressed, stood in constant opposition to one another, carried on an uninterrupted, now hidden, now open fight, a fight that each time ended, either in a revolutionary reconstitution of society at large, or in the common ruin of the contending classes.

In the earlier epochs of history, we find almost everywhere a complicated arrangement of society into various orders, a manifold gradation of social rank. In ancient Rome we have patricians, plebeians, slaves; in the Middle Ages, feudal lords, knights, vassals, guild-masters, journeymen, apprentices, serfs; in almost all of these classes, again, subordinate gradations.

The modern bourgeois society that has sprouted from the ruins of feudal society has not done away with class antagonisms. It has but established new classes, new conditions of oppression, new forms of struggle in place of the old ones.

Our epoch, the epoch of the bourgeoisie, possesses, however, this distinctive feature: it has simplified the class antagonisms. Society as a whole is more and more splitting up into two great hostile camps, into two great classes directly facing each other: Bourgeoisie and Proletariat.

monied classes. Communist and capitalist societies cannot coexist indefinitely, so the revolution would need to spread around the world.

7. *All states will wither away after the establishment of an international communist system.* Given that states existed primarily to support the interests of the bourgeoisie, there would be no need for them once classes were eliminated. Rather, the communist party, communes, and collectives would manage themselves. Marx expressed some ambiguity on just how such a system could operate without the guidance of a state.

These ideas, taken together, constitute the core of Marxism. In modern usage, "Marxism" can refer to two quite different ideologies. On one hand, it can designate an intellectual-philosophical system, wherein scholars examine historical events in terms of Marxist ideas, such as class conflict. On the other hand, it can refer to an activist political movement advocating revolution to establish a communist system. Clearly, Marx envisioned both. While most of his own writing was devoted to the intellectual ends of Marxism, he was very excited by the political upheavals of 1848, which he thought might be the beginnings of the anticipated revolution that eventually would establish communism. The government leaders who expelled Marx from France and Belgium as a subversive were correct in their assessment of his revolutionary intentions.

Marx's significance cannot be divorced from his period in history. *The Manifesto of the Communist Party* appeared scarcely fifty years after the American and French revolutions, and it was still a fresh idea in Western society that an established elite could be overthrown by a revolution and a new system could be created to replace the old one. The American and French revolutions drew the outlines of a new concept of government, and Marx's ideas colored them in.

At the same time, mid-nineteenth-century Europe was dominated by uncontrolled capitalism. Government regulation of industry and business was minimal; labor unions were yet to become potent political and economic forces; and institutions such as the graduated income tax, whereby those with greater income pay greater tax and ease the burden on the poor, had not yet been proposed or adopted. Only in later years would these responses to capitalism appear.

Marx and his period, therefore, lay in between. Philosophers had created ideas of government as a means of creating greater fairness, yet the application of most of those ideas in the economic world was still decades away. Marx and his theories provided a plan attractive both to the worker, feeling oppressed and resentful of the economic elite, and to the intellectual, attracted to the idealistic philosophy they embodied. The intellectual also saw in Marxism the first modern theory systematically to posit broad principles of regularities in history. It was this dual attractiveness that made communism a major intellectual and political force around the globe in the twentieth century.

OTHER INTELLECTUAL REVOLUTIONARIES

Darwin and Marx were not the only significant intellectual figures of the middle and late nineteenth century. Rather, every discipline had its share of seminal figures whose ideas changed their fields radically and set them in the directions that would lead to today. Just a few of those whose significance was particularly wide ranging are discussed here.

James Hutton and Charles Lyell

The biblical account of creation, with its Great Flood and other catastrophic events, was widely held to be essentially accurate by Western scholars in the seventeenth and early eighteenth centuries. This acceptance had accustomed them to the idea that events in the past were on a grander scale than the events of the modern world and led them to assume that the world had been shaped largely by such catastrophes. The school of thought that sees the past as shaped primarily by such grand events is called **catastrophism**, and for a while it dominated thinking in the geological and biological sciences.

The counterargument came from two British geologists, James Hutton (1726–1796) and Charles Lyell (1797–1875). Hutton presented many of his most important ideas in his *Theory of the Earth*, published in 1785 and revised in 1795. There, he presented **uniformitarianism**, the idea that the forces at work in nature today are similar to and on

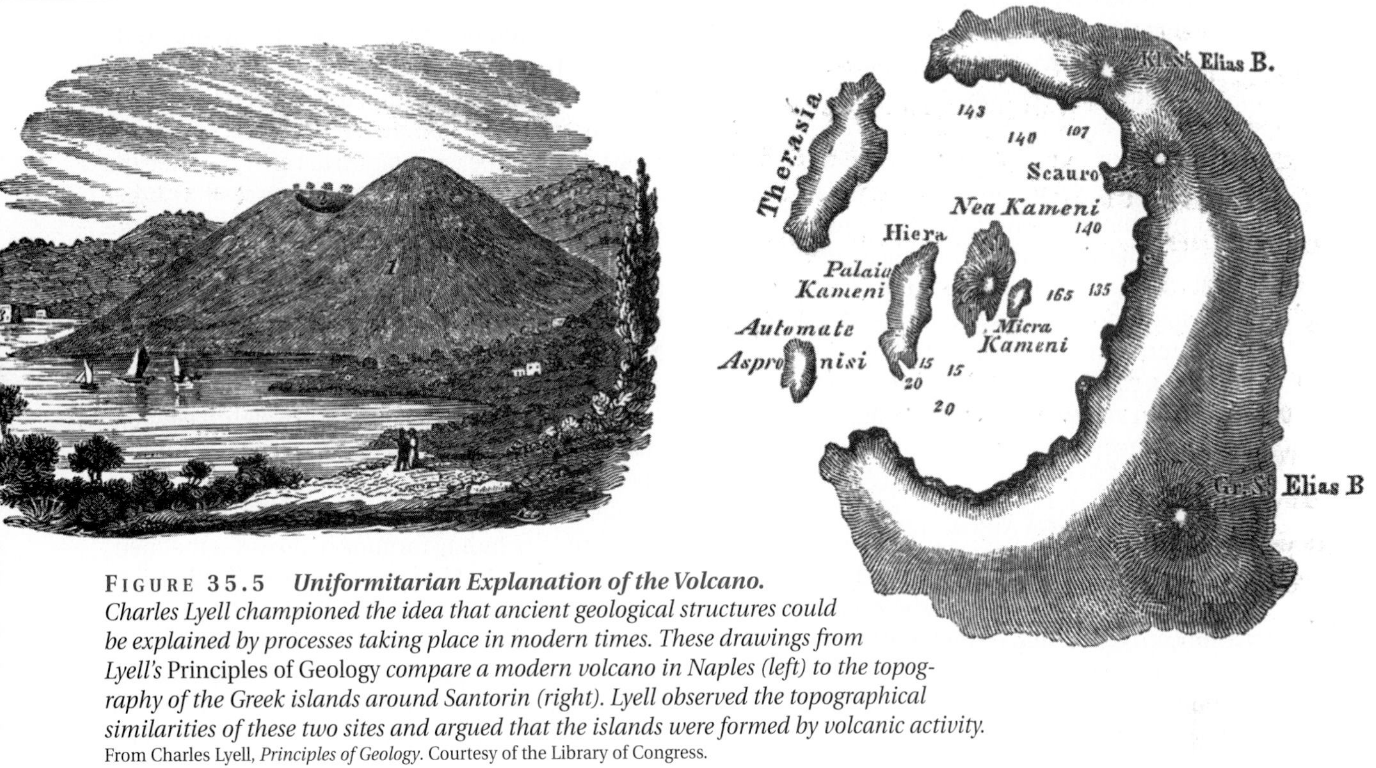

FIGURE 35.5 *Uniformitarian Explanation of the Volcano.* *Charles Lyell championed the idea that ancient geological structures could be explained by processes taking place in modern times. These drawings from Lyell's* Principles of Geology *compare a modern volcano in Naples (left) to the topography of the Greek islands around Santorin (right). Lyell observed the topographical similarities of these two sites and argued that the islands were formed by volcanic activity.*
From Charles Lyell, *Principles of Geology*. Courtesy of the Library of Congress.

a scale comparable to those that operated in the past; accordingly, because gradual processes dominate the modern scene, Hutton argued that the same sorts of processes must have been the primary shapers of the earth. Like Darwin, Hutton was reticent to become involved in academic battles, and he convinced few colleagues of his ideas. Lyell, however, enjoyed scholarly arguments, and he served as the popularizer of uniformitarianism, especially in his *Principles of Geology*, published in three volumes from 1830 to 1833. Lyell was active several decades after Hutton, and he benefited from a wealth of evidence that had come to light after Hutton's death.

Hutton and Lyell carefully examined geological deposits and realized that their structures and compositions were the same as those of deposits being formed in their own day. When they examined the evidence for ancient catastrophes put forward by the catastrophists, they found it weak and put forward uniformitarian explanations.

Archaeological evidence also played a role in the support of uniformitarianism, especially for Lyell. Ancient stone tools had been found throughout Europe, and there was increasing evidence of their great age. French scholars reported the finding of flint tools with the bones of extinct animals at Grotte de Bize[6] in 1828. At Brixham Cave in England, similar tools and bones were found together in 1858, and these were sealed off by a cap of dripstone, limestone redeposited by the evaporation of mineral-rich waters that dripped onto the cave floor. The deposition of dripstone was well known to geologists, and it would have taken thousands of years—far more time than available with the catastrophist chronology—for the cap to have formed.

In the absence of sound evidence for massive floods and cataclysmic earthquakes as the primary forces shaping the earth, Hutton and Lyell argued that the slow processes of erosion, deposition, and the like must have been responsible. If uniformitarianism were correct—and Lyell convinced most scientists of its correctness—then the earth must be far older than the earlier scholars had calcu-

[6] **Grotte de Bize:** GROHT duh BEES

lated. Lyell was considered radical when he suggested that the earth was hundreds of thousands of years old, maybe even a million years old. Today we know that his guess was too low by a factor of several thousand, but in the 1830s it opened up a new vista for geology. Suddenly there was a great deal of time for natural processes to have produced our modern world, and new mechanisms could be entertained for those processes.

Hutton and Lyell presented a new paradigm for geology and set the stage for the development of the modern discipline. Perhaps even more important, they paved the way for Darwin's theory of evolution and the changes it brought to humanity's self-conception.

Dmitri Mendeleyev

While it had been recognized for thousands of years that different substances existed, the modern concept of elements—materials that could not be broken down into more basic substances—became part of science only in the eighteenth century. In the century following, dozens of these elements were found, and scientists began wondering whether there was any predictable relationship among them. In 1866, J. A. R. Newlands, an English chemist, presented a paper on what he called "the octave theory" of elements. He noted that if one arranged the elements from lightest to heaviest, sometimes every eighth element shared similar characteristics. Unfortunately, Newlands used an analogy to the piano keyboard and suggested bizarre chemical relationships analogous to European musical harmony; his ideas were ridiculed or ignored by his colleagues.

The next step in establishing the relationships among elements was taken by Dmitri Mendeleyev[7] (1834–1907), a Siberian-born chemist in Russia. Mendeleyev was an indefatigable worker and had established a solid reputation on diverse research concerning petroleum, egg whites, and other organic compounds. His professional life, however, was dominated by the search for order among the elements.

Mendeleyev began his study by organizing the sixty or so elements then known into a sequence based on the relative weights of one atom of each. (While he was unable to isolate a single atom, of course, techniques were available in the mid–nineteenth century for inferring its weight.) Unlike Newlands, he assumed that this sequence was neither complete nor completely accurate. He undertook years of experimentation to verify or refine the existing data on atomic weights, as well as other characteristics of the elements. He also scoured the international literature to take advantage of work done by his colleagues, sometimes corresponding with them by the newly invented telegraph. When he felt he had adequate data, he constructed a new sequence and looked for patterns.

For the lighter elements, every eighth element shared traits. For example, the third (lithium), eleventh (sodium), and nineteenth (potassium) elements were alkali metals that had similar characteristics, including forming hydroxides that neutralized acids. As Mendeleyev moved further into the heavier elements of his sequence, he found that the similar elements were separated by various multiples of eight. Mendeleyev recognized this and compiled rules for figuring where in the arrangement each element should fall. This scheme left Mendeleyev with a table of elements arranged in order of their relative weights and with columns possessing similar characteristics; this table eventually came to be known as the **periodic table**.

Some positions in the periodic table, however, were blank, because no element then known fitted them. In 1869, when Mendeleyev first presented his ideas publicly at a meeting of the Russian Chemical Society, he suggested the existence of these missing elements. In 1871, he took the bold step of predicting not only the existence of the elements but also their natures. By following the patterns he saw among the known elements, he could predict such characteristics of these unknown elements as atomic weight, color, melting point, and ability to combine with other elements in predictable proportions to form compounds. He even went so far as to name many of these unknown elements.

Mendeleyev's 1871 paper created a sensation around the world. While many scholars were skeptical, they read the paper and were impressed with the careful work that underlay it. Soon, however, skepticism was swept aside as Mendeleyev's predicted elements began to be discovered and to conform to the characteristics he had predicted. In

[7] **Mendeleyev:** mehn duh LY ehf

ПЕРИОДИЧЕСКАЯ СИСТЕМА ЭЛЕМЕНТОВ												
		ГРУППЫ ЭЛЕМЕНТОВ										
ПЕРИОДЫ	РЯДЫ	I	II	III	IV	V	VI	VII	VIII			0
1	I	H 1 1,008										He 2 4,003
2	II	Li 3 6,940	Be 4 9,02	5 B 10,82	6 C 12,010	7 N 14,008	8 O 16,000	9 F 19,00				Ne 10 20,183
3	III	Na 11 22,997	Mg 12 24,32	13 Al 26,97	14 Si 28,06	15 P 30,98	16 S 32,06	17 Cl 35,457				Ar 18 39,944
4	IV	K 19 39,096	Ca 20 40,08	Sc 21 45,10	Ti 22 47,90	V 23 50,95	Cr 24 52,01	Mn 25 54,93	Fe 26 55,85	Co 27 58,94	Ni 28 58,69	
	V	29 Cu 63,57	30 Zn 65,38	31 Ga 69,72	32 Ge 72,60	33 As 74,91	34 Se 78,96	35 Br 79,916				Kr 36 83,7
5	VI	Rb 37 85,48	Sr 38 87,63	Y 39 88,92	Zr 40 91,22	Nb 41 92,91	Mo 42 95,95	Ma 43 —	Ru 44 101,7	Rh 45 102,91	Pd 46 106,7	
	VII	47 Ag 107,88	48 Cd 112,41	49 In 114,76	50 Sn 118,70	51 Sb 121,76	52 Te 127,61	53 J 126,92				Xe 54 131,3
6	VIII	Cs 55 132,91	Ba 56 137,36	La 57 * 138,92	Hf 72 178,6	Ta 73 180,88	W 74 183,92	Re 75 186,31	Os 76 190,2	Ir 77 193,1	Pt 78 195,23	
	IX	79 Au 197,2	80 Hg 200,61	81 Tl 204,39	82 Pb 207,21	83 Bi 209,00	84 Po 210	85 —				Rn 86 222
7	X	87 —	Ra 88 226,05	Ac 89 227	Th 90 232,12	Pa 91 231	U 92 238,07					

* ЛАНТАНИДЫ 58-71						
Ce 58 140,13	Pr 59 140,92	Nd 60 144,27	61 —	Sm 62 150,43	Eu 63 152,0	Gd 64 156,9
Tb 65 159,2	Dy 66 162,46	Ho 67 164,94	Er 68 167,2	Tu 69 169,4	Yb 70 173,04	Cp 71 174,99

FIGURE 35.6 ***Mendeleyev's Periodic Table of the Elements.*** *Mendeleyev recognized the patterning of characteristics of elements with progressively higher atomic weights, and in 1869 produced this periodic table that predicts the existence of elements then unknown (see numbers 61, 85, and 87). Although today's periodic table is slightly larger and reflects elements discovered and synthesized since 1869, it follows Mendeleyev's essential form.*
Sovfoto.

1875, a French scientist discovered gallium (Mendeleyev's "eka-aluminum"); in 1879, a Swedish scientist isolated scandium (Mendeleyev's "ekaboron"); and in 1886, a German scientist found germanium (Mendeleyev's "ekasilicon"). The discoverers of these new elements ignored Mendeleyev's names in favor of ones honoring their own nations; each of these elements' names was based on an ancient name for the country of the discoverer. Nonetheless, they all paid homage to Mendeleyev's insight. On the basis of incomplete and sometimes faulty information, he had drawn a blueprint for all the elements. Eventually the periodic table included more than one hundred elements, neatly corresponding to virtually all of his predictions.

Although the periodic table became standard fare for chemistry students, Mendeleyev remained obscure most of his life, partly because he worked in Russia, a backwater for science at that time. During one visit to the United States, he actually was introduced to a senator as Gregor Mendel, the Austrian monk who had researched the heredity of peas! His achievement, however, remains one of the most remarkable examples of pattern recognition in science.

UNDER THE LENS

Einstein's Seminal Year

Albert Einstein (1879–1955) had a very good year in 1905. He had been working in the Swiss patent office while finishing the dissertation for his doctorate in physics, which he completed in 1905. In addition, he was able to publish six papers in professional journals, three of which established his reputation as a major thinker. Recognition was not immediate, however, and he was forced to remain in the patent office until 1909, when the University of Zurich offered him his first academic appointment.

The first paper dealt with the photoelectric effect, the production of electricity by the exposure of certain substances to light. Einstein built on the theoretical work of Max Planck, demonstrating that the electric current was formed by a stream of electrons bounced out of the substance by the impact of light. This explanation, in turn, clarified the nature of light, showing that it acted both as waves and as particles.

The second paper related mass to energy in the famous equation $E=mc^2$. Prior to this time, energy and substance were conceived of as different things, but Einstein was able to demonstrate theoretically that they were aspects of the same thing. This meant that there were enormous amounts of energy locked within the atom, and this finding laid the groundwork for nuclear weapons in the 1940s.

The third paper developed the special theory of relativity, a revolutionary theory that requires considerable mathematical background to appreciate fully. Stated simply, it posits, among other things, that space and time are not separate entities; instead, they are aspects of the same thing, forming a space-time continuum. The implications of this theory are enormous, suggesting that the speed at which something moves actually affects the passage of time. Experimental verification of Einstein's theory of relativity came only in the latter half of the twentieth century.

Each of these papers had a major impact on physics. Einstein soon was honored throughout the world and was awarded a Nobel Prize for physics in 1921. He was offered prestigious posts around the world and accepted a position at Kaiser Wilhelm Institute in his native Germany. Einstein was Jewish, and his property was confiscated by the Nazi government in 1933. From that time forward he lived in the United States, becoming an American citizen.

Einstein's intellectual legacies are enormous, because he revolutionized thinking in several fields of physics. His ideas may have had their most profound effects, however, in the invention of nuclear weapons. An ardent pacifist yet determinedly opposed to the fascism of Germany in World War II, Einstein was in the grip of a dilemma. Ultimately, he urged the U.S. government to investigate how nuclear energy could be harnessed in weapons, though he later advocated restraint in the use of those weapons.

Franz Boas

Although Franz Boas[8] (1858–1942) did not found the discipline of anthropology, his effect on it was so great that he rightfully could be said to have reformulated it. Born in Germany, Boas received his doctorate in physics, but he spent his life studying people and cultures around the world.

Before he entered anthropology, Boas had been struck by the complexity of human behavior. In fact, it was the challenge of understanding this complexity that stimulated him to switch his attentions to anthropology. Boas was always distrustful of authority and cherished beliefs, and this trait fit well with the modern role of scientist as one who questioned existing ideas. Boas devised a radical revision of anthropology's assumptions, and his immensely successful teaching career at Columbia University passed his ideas along to many of the most influential anthropologists of their generation, effectively reorienting the discipline.

When Boas entered the field of anthropology in 1883, it was dominated by scholars whose ideas today would be considered racist and ethnocentric. Most anthropologists of that period believed

[8] **Boas:** BOH az

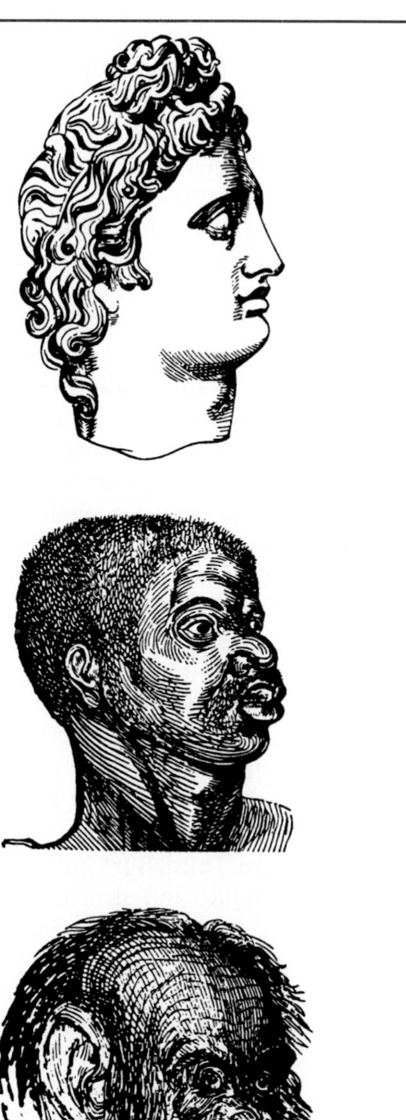

FIGURE 35.7 ***Nineteenth-Century Example of Racist Science.*** *This illustration dating to 1868 was designed to show a hierarchy surmounted by the idealized European; the African is relegated to a status below the European, and the chimpanzee is placed at the lowest level. The African's features have been distorted, presumably to make him appear more like the chimpanzee. Orderings of this sort were common in Western science during this period; the anthropologist Franz Boas was influential in discrediting them.* From Stephen Jay Gould, *The Mismeasure of Man* (New York: W. W. Norton & Company). Reproduced with permission.

that there were significant differences in human potential that were inborn and that race was a primary determinant of intelligence, morality, and worth. University students studying anthropology at that date read the writings of Count Joseph Gobineau[9] (1816–1882), particularly *The Inequality of Races.* This book classified humanity into four races, a relatively innocent exercise, but went on to rank these races in terms of their characteristics. Africans, for example, were described as lazy, stupid, and improvident; Asians were considered intelligent but crafty and ruled by tradition; and American Indians were said to be proud, shiftless, and only slightly intelligent. Europeans, particularly northern Europeans, contrasted with all these others: They were described as intelligent, noble, moral, and advanced.

The intellectual doctrine of racism was popular in European and American academic circles throughout the nineteenth and early twentieth centuries, though there always were dissenters. The doctrine was particularly cherished by many politicians who saw it as a moral justification for the oppression of other peoples through imperialist conquest and rule; in addition, it was invoked as a defense of the oppression of Jews, blacks, Gypsies, and other minorities at home. Given their political importance, it is little wonder that racist ideas became entrenched in intellectual tradition.

In addition to racist ideas, anthropologists of the late nineteenth century were taught that human societies could be ranked in order, from primitive to advanced—with their own society at the pinnacle of advancement, of course. The fact that an Australian Aborigine wore no clothes and had no writing was seen as the logical consequence of a faulty and childlike mind, and the culture of the Aborigine was seen as inferior to that of the civilized European. The double stigma of biological and cultural inferiority, as envisioned by these scholars, justifiably destined non-Europeans to a second-rate status. Boas was to challenge and vanquish these ideas in anthropology.

Running counter to the Eurocentric and racist ideas prominent in the anthropology of the day, Boas's ideas were rooted firmly in a conviction that all human societies had equal intelligence, creativity, talent, and potential. He conducted a wide range of studies, many of which today would be

[9] **Joseph Gobineau:** ZHOH sehf GOH bih noh

considered part of sociology or even clinical psychology, examining the intelligence of children and adults from different races. His results indicated that race was unrelated to intelligence, morality, or any other such trait. He supported this conclusion further with his field studies of other societies, concluding that they included geniuses and artists in proportions comparable to those in Western society.

But Boas went further. Not only is race unrelated to human creativity and potential, he argued, but different societies and cultures also should be viewed as equally advanced. This was a logical consequence of his first conclusion, because people of equal potential should be expected to create cultures of equal sophistication, but it challenged the long-held European assumption that Western civilization was somehow better than all other ways of life.

FIGURE 35.8 ***Franz Boas in the Field.*** *An anthropologist, Boas spent years with the Kwakiutl tribe of western Canada. Posed like a tribesman, he wears a bark-fiber blanket made by women of that tribe. Boas's experiences in the field led him to recognize the inherent equality of all peoples and to reject the predominant racist ideas held by the academia of his time.*
National Anthropological Archives, Smithsonian Institution.

Boas's argument for the equality of cultures was based on three supports. First, he contended, anthropologists came from Western society and had so thoroughly accepted its cultural values that they could not easily recognize its biases. Moral judgments of other societies' behavior based on Judeo-Christian precepts were, according to Boas, one of the major factors underlying these biases. For example, Western scholars found it hard to accept that the Aztecs, who practiced human sacrifice, could have produced art as great as any in Europe. Second, he argued, societies select different emphases for their greatest efforts. The Australian Aborigines, for example, have very complex and sophisticated mythological cycles and kinship systems, while they have relatively simple technology; Germans, in contrast, have relatively simple mythological and kinship systems but complex and sophisticated technology. The high value placed by Western society on technology and military-political power assured that most other societies, judged on those criteria alone, would be deemed primitive. Third, Boas indicted anthropologists for inflexibility and arrogance in assuming that their own culture was superior to all others. These ideas encompass Boas's concept of **cultural relativism**, the notion that all cultures should be viewed as equal in sophistication and value. In the year of Boas's birth, anthropology was the staunchest scholarly advocate of inequality, both of individuals and of societies; by his death more than eighty years later, it had become the strongest proponent of equality and relativism. Anthropology's embracing of these concepts has provided intellectual justification for egalitarian policies, and the publication of popular books by such anthropologists as Ruth Benedict and Margaret Mead has brought the concepts into public consciousness.

Sigmund Freud

In 1881, a woman known to history only as "Anna O." invented what today is known as psychoanalysis. She was troubled by irrational fears of various everyday things, and she consulted Josef Breuer, a prominent Vienna physician. Anna O. was graced with a forceful personality, and she insisted that Breuer listen to her recount in detail events and imaginings she had experienced since her previous visit. She called this technique "the talking cure" or "chimney sweeping," and she derived great relief through it. While Breuer was unimpressed by this case and found it merely odd, he mentioned it to a colleague who found it fascinating and exciting: Sigmund Freud.[10]

Sigmund Freud (1856–1939) was an Austrian physician who specialized in mental problems, and he believed that Anna O. had discovered a method of exploring the individual's mind. He began using her method, modifying it through the use of hypnosis or other techniques. He came to believe that patients' experiences had some strong bearing on their current mental difficulties; discovering those past events seemed to relieve the problems, yet those very events were the ones patients were most reluctant to discuss. Gradually, he developed a series of methods and concepts that formed the basis for modern psychology. While many of Freud's findings are no longer accepted, five of his basic conclusions endure as fundamental assumptions of psychology.

Figure 35.9 ***Sigmund Freud.*** *Freud founded the discipline of psychoanalysis in the nineteenth century and lived long enough to see it become a respected and influential field in the twentieth century. He believed that his ideas could be used to better understand historic figures and other cultures as well as contemporary patients.* Mary Evans Picture Library/Sigmund Freud Copyrights.

1. *There are hidden forces in the mind.* Previous to this, physicians had no clear explanation for phobias, manias, and other mental aberrations. Some considered them physical problems and prescribed sessions with electric machines designed to "restore mental vitality"; these machines later became a symbol of quackery in medicine. Others considered mental problems a sign of personal weakness or perversity, a behavior that could be overcome simply by the force of the patient's will. Still others were mystified by the whole phenomenon. Freud recognized that these problems were real to the patient and that they were beyond the patient's conscious control.

2. *Mental problems develop from outmoded adaptations to stress.* As Freud saw it, the mind develops ways of coping with unpleasant circumstances, and these become habitual. For example, a child who is subjected to stress will develop coping mechanisms that may be carried forward into adulthood. Once valuable, they become maladaptive for the adult and are the source of mental problems. A child, for example, might be extremely submissive to a demanding parent in an attempt to gain the love the child craves; as an adult, that same person might continue submissive behavior that becomes a serious obstacle to the establishment of conventional adult relationships.

3. *The primary factor underlying mental problems is sex.* Freud saw the need for sexual gratification as the strongest instinctual urge in human

[10] **Freud:** FROYD

beings, and he believed that it developed very early. A child, as he saw it, inevitably formed a sexual attraction to the parent of the opposite sex, yet society's disapproval produced a sense of shame. This conflict could be coped with in various ways by the child, many of which would create deep psychological problems in later life. Many modern psychologists believe that Freud overestimated the importance of childhood sexual desires; nonetheless, this aspect of his theory has been very influential.

4. *The forces in the mind can work against one another.* The fact that patients were reluctant to discuss the things that Freud felt were most important led him to postulate that there were conceptual divisions of the mind and that they could work at counter-purposes. Eventually he elaborated this notion into three main divisions of the mind, but his great contribution was the general notion of contradictory elements within the mind.

5. *A person is likely to use a preestablished pattern to meet new circumstances.* Freud believed that people meet new challenges with old responses, ones that have proven themselves effective before. A child, for example, establishes a way of relating to its parents; as an adult, that child may continue that same way of relating to other authority figures, such as a boss, a political leader, or even a religion. Freud called this **projection** and viewed it as a complicating factor that made it difficult to trace the path from an original cause to a current problem.

Freud's historical importance lies less in the details of his specific theories than in his basic conceptions. He devised a way to look at individual human behavior that recognized the individual's past yet saw patterns of general behavior. He invented the scientific study of the human mind and provided tools for investigating it. His influence in psychology obviously was enormous, but his work also was incorporated into the studies of scholars in other fields. Anthropologists like Margaret Mead searched for evidence of Freudian processes among the Samoans and others; art historians like Arnold Hauser sought European Romanticism's Freudian roots; Freud himself devoted his last book to a Freudian analysis of Moses and the analysis's implications for theology. And finally, Freud's influence made its way to the lay public, largely through the writing of others who popularized his ideas. The fact that terms like "mania," "neurotic," and "ego" are so widely known throughout the world is a tribute to the legacy of Freud and Anna O., the woman who devised the psychoanalytic method to heal herself.

THE COMMON THREAD

The mid- and late nineteenth century was a period of incredible intellectual activity in Europe and America, and the few scholars mentioned in this chapter were chosen from the many who could have been discussed. Indeed, during this period scientists developed the ideas underlying the modern understanding of such diverse issues as thermodynamics, electromagnetism, and probability; scientific engineering, statistics, and nutrition also came into being as modern fields of endeavor.

Above all else, the scholars who transformed our understanding of these various fields reflected **scientism**, the faith that the world was predictable, that it operated according to rules and principles that could be discovered. Whether considering natural or human phenomena, these thinkers argued for patterning; this patterning, they argued, reflected processes that inexorably produced predictable results. Accident, serendipity, the unknowable—these were replaced with a confident expectation that all would eventually be unraveled and understood by science. Mendeleyev summed up the scientistic position when he wrote:

> It is the function of science to discover the existence of a general reign of order in nature and to find the causes governing this order. And this refers in equal measure to the relations of man—social and political—and to the entire universe as a whole.

While not all scholars agree so confidently that human behavior can be reduced to principles in the same manner as natural phenomena, Mendeleyev's confidence certainly was shared by Marx, Freud, and many other thinkers in the nineteenth century. The optimistic expectation of science's ability to subject nature to human control through technology has extended into the twentieth century and still is shared by many today, both scientists and the public. Faith in the natural workings of the world has encouraged an increasingly secular worldview.

EUROPE

Great expansion of European universities, 1750–1850	**1750**	
	–	
	–	
	–	Hutton champions uniformitarianism, 1785
	–	
	1800	
	–	
	–	
	–	Voyage of HMS *Beagle*, 1831
	–	Marx and Engels publish *The Communist Manifesto*, 1848
	1850	
	–	Darwin publishes *On the Origin of Species*, 1859
	–	Mendeleyev deduces periodic table, 1869–1871
	–	Boas leaves physics for anthropology, 1883
	–	Freud first publishes on psychoanalysis, 1893
	1900	Einstein's three great papers, 1905
	–	
	–	Scopes trial, 1925
	–	
	–	
	1950	

From the late eighteenth century onward, Western society was becoming increasingly enamored of progress, and scholars were no exception. Marx made progress a hallmark of his theories, because he saw humanity naturally progressing toward a more just society. Even Darwin, who tried to avoid the notion of progress, was interpreted popularly as arguing for the improvement of species.

Most nineteenth-century thinkers in the Western tradition, particularly those studying social subjects, were quite Eurocentric in their theories. Freud believed that his findings about Europeans were directly applicable to other peoples, although he believed that some "primitive" societies had arrested development, making them permanently like European children. Marx was sure that the European sequence of historical development was applicable to the rest of the world, even when there were apparent difficulties in making it fit with known facts. One of the more extravagant Eurocentrists was J. A. R. Newlands, the British physicist who believed that the chemical elements were arranged in octaves; he argued that they would combine according to laws parallel to the conventions of European music, apparently unaware that other peoples had developed radically different systems of musical harmony. The one light shining against Eurocentrism in this era was Boas, who was joined by his many students and converts.

SUMMARY

1. The nineteenth century saw the revision of many fields of scholarship in light of new methods and concepts. The greatest changes in intellectual outlooks during this period originated in Europe.

2. Charles Darwin developed the theory of biological evolution that forms the basis of the current understanding of evolution. It was based on the concepts of natural selection and the inheritance of traits from parents. The phenomenon of mutation and its importance to evolution was realized only after Darwin's death. Darwin's work inspired scholars and others to regard human beings as less separate from other animals than they had previously.

3. Karl Marx, in his writings on communism, argued that class conflict based on economic factors was the basis for political and social change. He further argued that capitalism would be overthrown by a proletarian revolution and that international communism would be established. Marx's ideas were in reaction to the unbridled capitalism of his time and the simultaneous recognition in Europe that traditional elites could be toppled by popular revolution. His ideas, though extensively modified, have remained important in many places around the world through the late twentieth century.

4. James Hutton and Charles Lyell reacted against catastrophism (the notion that massive upheavals dominated the formation of the landscape) and argued for the new paradigm of uniformitarianism (the idea that the landscape had been formed predominantly by more gradual processes similar to those at work in modern times). Their successful advocacy of uniformitarianism meant that the earth was now seen as very ancient, providing the time required for the evolutionary processes Darwin envisioned.

5. Dmitri Mendeleyev recognized the patterns inherent in the chemical elements and produced a periodic table that predicted the existence and characteristics of dozens of previously unknown elements. Subsequent research located these elements and showed his periodic table to be accurate.

6. Franz Boas argued for the equality of individuals of different races in terms of intelligence, morality, and human potential. He also contended that different cultures and societies were equally sophisticated and valuable, and condemned ethnocentric arguments to the contrary. This turned anthropology from a judgmental discipline to a champion of cultural relativism.

7. Sigmund Freud founded the fields of psychology and psychoanalysis, arguing that hidden forces in the human mind can create mental problems when outmoded patterns of behavior are continued and that many problems are caused by the conflicts surrounding sexual desires and behavior.

8. These and other scientists embraced scientism, the general philosophy that the natural and human worlds are predictable and understandable and that they follow basic principles. They sought secular laws of nature through scientific observation and experimentation.

SUGGESTED READINGS

Gillespie, David. *Genesis and Geology*. New York: Harper & Row, 1965. An excellent treatment of Hutton, Lyell, and Darwin.

Kardiner, Abram, and Edward Preble. *They Studied Man*. New York: World Publishing Co., 1961. A collection of relatively brief critical biographies of major figures in the social sciences, including Charles Darwin, Franz Boas, and Sigmund Freud. Kardiner worked with Freud, and the section on him is both extensive and authoritative.

McLellan, David. *Karl Marx*. New York: Penguin, 1982. A brief, lucid, informative summary of Marx's life, writings, and thought, as well as interpretations of Marx by political figures.

Posin, Daniel Q. *Mendeleyev: The Story of a Great Scientist*. New York: Whittlesey House/McGraw-Hill, 1948. A popularized biography of Mendeleyev, valuable because so little is available in English but frustrating because of the bulk of fictionalized dialogue diluting the historical material.

A REMARKABLE ENGLISH INVENTION

THE LONDON GALVANIC GENERATOR,

A ROYAL REMEDY!

Now offered to the American Public by

THE PALL MALL ELECTRIC ASS'N: OF LONDON

FRONT VIEW THIS SIDE IS HANDSOMELY CARVED & RESEMBLES A LOCKET OR PENDANT. IT IS HIGHLY POLISHED AND MADE OF A BEAUTIFUL MATERIAL RESEMBLING EBONY.

EXACT SIZE

A great revolution in Medical Practice has spread throughout England. It has been discovered that most remarkable cures attend the application of a newly invented Galvanic Generator to diseased parts of the body. Experience has shown that they act immediately upon the blood, nerves and tissues producing more relief in a few hours than medicine has given in weeks and months. There is no shoc' or unpleasant feeling attending their use, and they can be worn day or night, interfering in no way with the dress or occupation of daily life. Full directions accompany each one. Every mail brings us most gratifying letters from those using them.

THE GENERATOR QUICKLY CURES

Stomach, Liver and Kidney Complaints, Constipation, Gout, Debility, Heartburn, Rheumatism, Neuralgia, Weak Stomach, Dyspepsia. Aches and Pains, Weak Back, Malaria, Chills & Fever, Nervous Troubles. Sciatica, Vertigo, Indigestion, & all their Complications,

THERE IS NO WAITING, IT ACTS IMMEDIATELY!!

A Guarantee goes with every Generator,

OUR MOTTO BEING "NO CURE, NO PAY."

WARRANTED FOR FIVE YEARS

BACK VIEW SHOWING THE SURFACE OF THE METALLIC BATTERY OR GENERATOR WHICH SHOULD ALWAYS BE WORN NEXT TO THE BODY.

LONDON GALVANIC GENERATOR

PALL MALL ELECTRIC ASS'N OF LONDON. N.Y. BRANCH 842 BROADWAY.

From a Rail Road Contractor.—BOSTON, Mass., January 28th, 1881.
Bad digestion and dyspepsia, caused by hurried eating while traveling, has made me a sufferer for years. Your Generator has made me a well man, and I would advise others to try it. Please send me three more to General P. O., Galveston, Tex. Enclosed is 3 dollars. R. H. SANDFORD.

From a Naval Officer.—PHILADELPHIA, Pa., February 5th, 1881.
Your Generator has proved a blessing to me. I have been a great sufferer from liver trouble and constipation, but am now relieved entirely. I was doubtful at first as I had tried all sorts of batteries and pads without effect. There is no trouble in wearing it and it certainly is more agreeable than drugs. E. T. CRAWFORD, U. S. N.

From Reverend C. Q. Huntington.—ASTOR HOUSE, N. Y. City, Thursday.
While visiting your city, attending a meeting of our clergy, I was induced to buy your Generator for indigestion and dyspepsia, from which I have suffered for years. Nothing hitherto tried did me any good; but believing in electricity and having found an infallible cure for headache in Dr. Scott's Electric Hair Brush, I determined to buy a Generator, which, I am glad to say, relieved me at once, and I now feel entirely cured. I shall lose no opportunity to recommend it, and take this method of thanking you. (REV.) C. Q. HUNTINGTON.

From Major A. H. Townsend.—CHICAGO, Ill., December 17th, 1880.
Your Generator is a wonder. It stopped my rheumatic pains in two hours and it has not returned now in 5 weeks. I suffered for years and am truly grateful. The second one has also relieved the pain in my wife's back, and she says it is worth its weight in gold. Enclosed find $2.00, please send two more for a friend. (MAJOR) A. H. TOWNSEND.

Many more could be printed, did space permit.

Having purchased the sole right to introduce them in America we will **send them on trial, post paid, on receipt of $1.00,** which will be returned, if they fail to relie after a reasonable time. Remittance can be made in Check, Draft, Post Office Order, Currency, or Stamps, and should be made payable to **GEO. A. SCOTT, No. 842 Broadway, New York,** (*Mention this Paper*), or we will send them by Express, C. O. D., with the privilege of opening and examitning, but the Express Charges will add considerably to *your* cost; or ask your Druggist to obtain them for you. Agents wanted in every town.

You have been imposed upou if you have bought a 'Battery,' 'Pad,' or 'Medal', thinking it was the Generator. Its great Success in England has Caused the Market to be Flooded with Cheap, Worthless Imitations. See that the Name "Pall Mall" is Stamped on the back.

London Galvanic Generator. *Science became fashionable in the late nineteenth century, and products such as this purported medical aid sold better when touted as scientific breakthroughs.* Culver Pictures.

ISSUE 7

Science and the Masses

Carlos Alvear, a vaquero *driving cattle on the remote grasslands of Argentina, huddled over a magazine. Reading by the light of a campfire, he learned of Louis Pasteur's success in vaccinating against anthrax in far-off France. It was 1883, and the magazine was a little over a year old.*

The nineteenth-century development of Western science was unique in world history. Never before had there been so wide a literate audience and such inexpensive means of disseminating information through the printed word. In addition, the Industrial Revolution was in full swing, the notion of progress was ascendant, and the public was receptive to many of the new findings of science. Science was seen as important in its own right, but it took on greater significance because of the technology that grew from it. Under these conditions, science had a profound effect on the basic patterns of Western thought, including the sorts of explanations that everyday people found satisfying. Still, the science that made its way to the public often differed in fundamental ways from the science that was debated by scholars.

SCIENCE, WESTERN THOUGHT, AND THE WORLD

Nineteenth-century science was the product of European scholarship, but it percolated throughout Western society and into societies beyond. On the one hand, lay persons in Western society came to accept the assumptions and views of science as part of their worldview; on the other hand, many educated people outside the Western tradition came to accept these ideas as they were presented through European colonial institutions.

Faith in Science Comes to Permeate Western Thought

Most Europeans and North Americans of the nineteenth century were confronted with the fruits of science in their everyday lives. The steam engine and its derivatives, the railroad locomotive and the steamship, had revolutionized transportation. Medicines, some truly efficacious and others merely making astounding claims, were heralded as scientific remedies. Mineral deposits that previously had been impractical to exploit were being mined and refined by new scientific techniques. The more colorful adventures and discoveries of scientists traveling to the far corners of the earth were reported in the newspapers and magazines of the day. These conspicuous successes brought three major changes to how everyday people saw the world.

First, faith in rational explanation increased. Science was built on the premise that everything happens for a reason and that the same cause should consistently produce the same result; the fruits of science were seen as the proof that this premise was sound. Miracles, the inexplicable, and things that happen for no apparent reason are abhorrent to the scientist, and the public increasingly came to share this scientistic view. In earlier eras, it might have been acceptable simply to throw up one's hands and declare a problem insoluble or an event the will of God, but nineteenth-century people increasingly preferred to seek a scientific explanation.

This does not mean, however, that religion was on the run in the face of the troops of science. Certainly some intellectuals argued for atheism and against organized religion, but many others found ways to integrate science and religion in their personal beliefs. In any case, few common people became embroiled in these philosophical debates. Instead, many religious people simply moved slightly more toward the pole of secular rationalism, either by explaining more things by science and relegating religion to the narrower realm of the spiritual or by developing religious views compatible with the findings of science. Perhaps miracles could happen, many nineteenth-century people suggested, but they certainly were rare and seemed to have happened more in the distant past. God created the world, they felt, but it continued to operate by itself on scientific principles, a notion similar to that of the "clockmaker God" of the eighteenth-century Deists. Literal interpretations of the Bible often were in conflict with the findings of science, and everyday people more and more came to accept the scientific explanations, considering the biblical accounts metaphorical or figurative.

Second, the position of humanity became less central. Over the centuries, the European notion of the human place in the universe consistently had been eroded by science. The earth once had been thought of as the center of the universe, around which everything else revolved; in the sixteenth century, Copernicus had proved the earth merely a planet orbiting around a star. Human beings once had been the focal point of all creation; in the nineteenth century, Darwin had made them one of many creatures that had evolved from humble beginnings, the product of luck as much as any divine plan. While still extraordinary in their cultural capabilities, human beings were being forced into a less prominent position in the worldview. This line of thinking would culminate in the twentieth century with ecological activists arguing that human beings are merely one of many species and must modify their behavior to accommodate all the others.

Third, science became the new authority, the yardstick by which things were measured. The great scientific and technological successes of the Industrial Revolution could not be denied, and it is little wonder, then, that other, less lofty accomplishments tried to bask in the light of science. Lash's Blood Purifier and Laxative, an American patent medicine of the 1870s, presumably was more effective because it was "scientifically compounded." The first Jewish cookbook published in the English language was published in London in 1846, and it described itself as a treatise on "Culinary Science." Karl Marx distinguished his ideas from their predecessors by labeling them "scientific socialism." Mary Baker Eddy founded the Christian Science Church in Boston in 1879, fusing health science and religious ideas. Even French cloth was marketed as being manufactured "according to the most scientific standards."

In one sense, this worship of science was merely the invoking of a trendy word in support of one's commercial product. But there also was a deeper reverence for science, probably an outgrowth of the ideal of progress that permeated the Industrial Revolution. Many folk beliefs were decried as mere superstition, and ruralites who believed in the evil eye were held up as examples of ignorance and backwardness by writers and others. Those who persisted in these nonscientific beliefs often kept that information to themselves for fear of being ridiculed.

Sophisticated urbanites also were subject to attack, as in the case of Sir Arthur Conan Doyle. The author of the Sherlock Holmes mysteries and a physician by training, Conan Doyle was intrigued by the occult and held seances at his London home. His beliefs earned him public attacks by prominent scientists of the day, especially Sir Arthur Keith, who published a series of scathing letters to the editors of London newspapers, leaving Conan Doyle humiliated and bitter. Others used science as a weapon with which to attack religion, as when Karl Marx and his followers described religion as "the opiate of the masses," a spurious doctrine serving to provide false hopes to the workers and peasants, making them more docile and easier to control by the state.

FIGURE I.7.1 ***Sir Arthur Conan Doyle.*** *The author of the Sherlock Holmes mysteries was a trained physician who was also intrigued by the occult and held seances in his London lodgings. This caricature in* Punch *lampoons Conan Doyle's beliefs, bearing a rhymed caption: "Your own creation, that great sleuth / Who spent his life in chasing Truth— / How does he view your late defiance / (O ARTHUR!) of the laws of Science?"* Mary Evans Picture Library.

In nineteenth-century Europe and North America, science assumed a dominating position in society, not just for the intellectual elite but also for everyday people. The products of technology that proliferated with science during the Industrial Revolution had profound effects on everyday life, but they also served to validate the position of science as the final authority. While these objects certainly changed people's lives, it may be that the faith in science that accompanied them had even more profound effects.

Faith in Science Spreads around the Globe

The popularization of science described in the previous paragraphs was restricted largely to Western society, where the Industrial Revolution had carried the banner of science and where literacy and publishing helped spread scientific ideas. The rest of the world, however, soon was to be swept along as Western society exported its ideas abroad.

The nineteenth century was the era of European expansion, and European agents were scurrying over the globe. Governors and their agents were administering colonial governments, seeing that children were educated, because this was the first step to what they considered civilizing them. That education attempted to inculcate Western values and ideals, including science, rejecting native ideas as "primitive superstition." Missionaries, too, traveled to the colonies, attempting to convert the local people to Christianity, and that meant convincing them of the "correctness" of Western thinking, including the expunging of native magic and superstition.

Often, however, non-Western people actively sought this new scientific knowledge. Many coun-

Figure I.7.2 ***Guyanan Missionary School.*** *This school in Guyana (in northeastern South America) was run by the London Missionary Society and was designed to inculcate British values and a British-style education. On the chalkboards are maps of India and Australia—parts of the British Empire.* Archives of the Council for the World Mission, London.

tries, especially in Asia, began sending students to Western universities to receive their higher educations, and these students spread the Western findings of and attitudes toward science in their homelands. Western education and acceptance of its worldview often were viewed as signs of sophistication and actively were sought by the native elite. Some Chinese intellectuals, for example, became part of the New Culture Movement, which began in 1915. These intellectuals saw science as a hallmark of Western worldview (and therefore modernity) and welcomed it. While their viewpoint was not universal around the world, it was one reaction to Western science.

Western society had embraced science wholeheartedly, and peoples abroad came to embrace it, too, either through force or through choice. Typically, rural people were more resistant to accepting scientific thinking, often clinging tenaciously and clandestinely to their traditional beliefs. People in cities and towns, especially the elite, usually received more rigorous Western education and often became strong advocates of science and scientific thinking. To a greater or lesser extent, Western science and the faith in it spread throughout the world.

POPULAR SCIENCE

In the early part of the nineteenth century, many scientific discoveries were relatively basic, and they usually could be comprehended moderately easily by the public. As scientific knowledge accumulated and scientific theories became more complex, however, the significance of a discovery often was more difficult to appreciate. By the latter half of the nineteenth century, there were great differences between science as it was understood by scientists and science as it was understood by the masses.

Science Sells Newspapers

Newspapers and magazines were the primary means by which most people in Europe, North America, and beyond learned about new discoveries of science. Most of these publications originated in the late eighteenth or early nineteenth century as literary journals of sorts, dominated by high-toned letters on philosophy, the arts, and politics. Gradually they came to include more notices of current events and assumed a form similar to that of modern newspapers. By the mid–nineteenth century, most major cities and many smaller communities had several newspapers, all competing for readership. In order to attract that readership, newspapers emphasized topics they believed would interest their readers. The intellectual pieces often were jettisoned and replaced with sensational ones, often reporting new scientific discoveries.

But not all discoveries were equally interesting to readers, so they were not equally newsworthy. Mendeleyev's creation of the periodic table, discussed in Chapter 35, was a major advance for science and was lauded by scientists around the world, yet it never received even a mention in most newspapers. The complexities of the creation of the periodic table and the somewhat arcane nature of its significance would have made it difficult for readers to follow even a simple discussion, and they most probably would have skipped the article. Instead, the discovery of a tribe of purported cannibals or of a new planet caught the editorial eye and became known to the general public. There were three main criteria for whether a scientific subject was newsworthy.

First, the subject had to be romantic and exciting. Among the most romantic and exciting were archaeological finds of lost cities and ancient knowledge, such as Hiram Bingham's 1911 discovery of Machu Picchu in the Peruvian jungles, widely reported in the contemporary press as "the lost city of the Incas." The prediction and subsequent discovery of a new planet, Neptune, in 1846 also was a great sensation, as was the competition in 1858 among Sir Richard Burton, John Speke, and others to find the source of the Nile in East Africa. Louis Pasteur's development in 1881 of inoculation as a means of preventing anthrax was followed closely by newspapers because of its practical significance, and Pasteur was portrayed as a scientific warrior fighting disease.

Second, the scientists had to have dramatic personalities. Science was seen as a heroic enterprise, and popular sentiment demanded that it be pursued by heroic figures. Few scientists met this requirement, though those who did were lionized. Burton, for example, was a colorful scholar who spoke dozens of languages well enough to pass for a native, and he did so in order to gain access to Mecca, the holy city of Islam otherwise closed to non-Muslims; the scar from a Maasai spear that passed through his cheek only added to his reputation as an adventurer.

When scientists failed to project sufficiently robust personalities, circumstances might come to their aid. The discovery of the Egyptian tomb of Tutankhamen in 1922 was popular on the basis of the incredibly rare and valuable artifacts found

WE WILL BUY YOUR CAR FOR CASH AND PAY SPOT CASH ON SIGHT

100 Cars Wanted At Once.

GEORGE NEWMAN & Co.
319-321, Euston Road, London, N.W.1
'Phone Museum 1568, 1569 & 6675.

PALL MALL

GAZETTE AND GLOBE

London's Most Influential Evening Paper.

PALL MALL GAZETTE.
Subscription Rates
The Prepaid Subscription Rates for Copies sent by post anywhere:
Three Months - - 13s.
Six Months - - - £1 6s.
Twelve Months - - £2 12s.

No. 18,045. [REGISTERED AT THE G.P.O. AS A NEWSPAPER] THURSDAY, APRIL 5, 1923. ONE PENNY.

LORD CARNARVON'S FATE.

EXPERTS AND A LUXOR "POISON TRAP."

SUPERSTITIOUS BELIEFS RIDICULED BY WELL-KNOWN EGYPTOLOGISTS.

TRAGEDY OF HIS DEATH.

EARL WHO FOUND TUTANKHAMEN'S TOMB, BUT NEVER SAW THE MUMMY.

The death of Lord Carnarvon, coming swiftly upon the heels of his great triumph—the discovery of the tomb of Pharaoh Tutankhamen in the Valley of the Kings—has created widespread controversy.

There will probably be thousands who see in the Earl's fate the "black arts" of the ancient Egyptians, while on the other hand the theory of a poison trap in the tomb is advanced.

Below, the "Pall Mall Gazette" publishes the views of well-known Egyptologists and pathologists, who ridicule, without exception, the theory that poison was left in the tomb for the purpose of dealing death to intruders.

Lord Carnarvon died peacefully in the early hours of

THE NEW LORD AND LADY CARNARVON

A HITHERTO UNPUBLISHED PHOTOGRAPH OF LORD PORCHESTER, WHO SUCCEEDS TO THE EARLDOM, AND HIS WIFE.

LORD CARNARVON'S LAST HOURS.

DEATH AFTER HOPES OF RECOVERY.

CHEAPER BEER

ACTION BY CHANCELLOR AND BREWERS.

NOVELIST AND CHILD.

PATHOS AT INQUEST ON FATHER.

"SHE WAS TAKEN AWAY."

DRAMATIC APPEAL TO SEND HER BACK.

THE GIRL'S CHOICE

Remarkably pathetic statements were made at the inquest at Hammersmith this afternoon on Mr. Alfred Sandells Baines, the engineer who was found dead with his head in a gas oven at his flat in Clanricarde-gardens, Bayswater, on Tuesday morning.

Mr. and Mrs. Baines' seventeen-

FIGURE I.7.3 *"Lord Carnarvon's Fate." The death of Lord Carnarvon, a member of the team that discovered the tomb and mummy of "King Tut," made front-page headlines in 1923. The drama of his death and the deaths of several co-researchers led newspapers to focus on rumors of an ancient curse rather than on the archaeological significance of their find.* Courtesy of John and Andrew Frost.

intact there, but its popular acclaim skyrocketed when various members of the expedition began dying, leading to the assertion—first put forward by the press—that a curse would kill all the members of the excavation party. (The press did not stress the facts that only a small proportion of the party died shortly after the opening of the tomb or that most of the members who died were elderly.) The incredibly well-publicized search of Henry Stanley, a reporter for the *New York Herald*, for Dr. David Livingstone in Africa in 1871 is an even more telling example. Although the *Herald* painted the picture of Livingstone as an explorer lost in the jungles of deepest Africa, he actually was resting along the shores of Lake Tanganyika following a bout of fever and was not lost at all; the "rescue mission" was prompted purely by the urge to improve newspaper circulation.

Third, and perhaps most important, a scientific discovery must be simple enough for people with limited scientific education to understand it. A more difficult discovery might be acceptable if it could be simplified by the reporter, sometimes at the expense of accuracy. Albert Einstein's theory of relativity in physics, published in 1905, was widely heralded in the press, but reporters were faced with the difficulty that most of their readers were unable to understand the theory; probably most of the reporters also failed to grasp its complexity. As a result, press coverage often praised the discovery, described it in a sentence or two with no real discussion of why Einstein believed it to be true, then proceeded to discuss the implications of "relativity" as a social concept, something Einstein never had intended.

In a real sense, the press has determined the popular reputations of scientists since the mid–nineteenth century. Those whose research or personalities led to good entertainment were the subject of extended reportage. Those whose research actually was more significant but less entertaining had to be content with the recognition of their peers.

FIGURE I.7.4 ***Armageddon.*** *Atlantis may have been the ancient Mediterranean island of Thera, or it may have been a literary invention of Plato and other ancient Greeks. In either case, it caught the imagination of nineteenth- and twentieth-century writers such as Ignatius Donnelly. They envisioned Atlantis as a massive and sophisticated island-state somewhere in the Atlantic, where people held lost secrets and were wiser, stronger, and better looking than anywhere else. This vision of Atlantis emphasized its demise in an apocalyptic upheaval, borrowed in part from the biblical prediction of the end of the world as depicted here. Such romantic conceptions of Atlantis have been far more popular than the more realistic (and less exotic) interpretations of scholars.* Culver Pictures.

Electrical Rejuvenation and Shocked Wheat

Many journalists of the nineteenth and early twentieth centuries saw their job as selling newspapers, not necessarily educating the public. If exotic science would sell newspapers, then maybe even greater sales could be achieved by stepping beyond the bounds of mainstream science and publicizing ideas on the fringes of science.

The past two centuries have produced hundreds of bizarre ideas claimed by their originators as scientific breakthroughs, though rejected by the scientific community. The originators often have derided the professional scientists as too jealous to admit the worth of these new ideas, but the professionals usually have considered them simply too outlandish to merit comment. Some of the supporters of these odd ideas have been simply naïve, too poorly educated in science to recognize the weaknesses of their ideas; others have been professional con artists out to make a great deal of money; and still others have been psychologically unstable. But their ideas sometimes have appeared in seemingly reputable outlets, and they have seemed to some members of the public to be of equal stature with the findings of mainstream science.

In the 1920s in the United States, for example, the nationally distributed *American Weekly* had a column devoted to lurid pseudoscience, including arguments that the earth was flat and that electrical current fed into the body with a complicated device could prevent a person from aging. Other newspapers also publicized such exotic but peculiar findings by self-styled scientists, including a way to produce hardy wheat by "shocking" the wheat seeds with cold, the production of microscopic fish by the melting of metals, and a new theory of physics based on the mutual suction of all tangible things.

Many of these pseudoscientific ideas sound like the stuff of science fiction: the creation of life, the existence of various monsters, visits from outer space, chemicals from comets passing near the earth that affected human personalities, and the like. But they often were presented plausibly and with evidence that—if legitimate—would be persuasive. The reader with limited background in science and with a great urge to believe was likely to be taken in by at least some of these preposterous ideas. The incredible success of tabloid newspapers in the twentieth century is potent evidence that many readers are more interested in an exotic account than in scientific accuracy.

SUGGESTED READINGS

Cooter, Roger. *The Cultural Meaning of Popular Science: Phrenology and the Organization of Consent in Nineteenth-Century Britain.* Cambridge, Eng.: Cambridge University Press, 1984. A discussion of popular science, oriented around phrenology, the pseudoscientific practice of appraising personal characteristics from bumps on the head.

Daniels, George H. *Science in American Society: A Social History.* New York: Knopf, 1971. An excellent treatment of the place of science in American popular and intellectual culture.

Gardiner, Martin. *Fads and Fallacies in the Name of Science.* New York: Dover, 1952. A classic anthology of brief articles on some of the more exotic crank scientific theories. Entertaining, easy reading.

Holton, Gerald, and William A. Blanpied, eds. *Science and Its Public: The Changing Relationship.* Boston Studies in the Philosophy of Science, vol. 33. Dordecht, Holland: D. Reidel Publishing Co., 1976. Largely devoted to contemporary conditions but includes some historical material.

Nelkin, Dorothy. *Selling Science: How the Press Covers Science and Technology.* New York: W. H. Freeman, 1987. Primarily concerned with the modern situation, but contains some useful historical perspective.

IN THE FIRST HALF OF THE TWENTIETH CENTURY, there was a close interrelationship between war and revolution. World War I helped bring about the collapse of the Russian Empire and the onset of the Bolshevik Revolution. Once in power, the Bolsheviks fought a civil war and later endured World War II. The Chinese Communist Party benefited from the chaos launched by World War II. Later, it won a civil war against the Nationalist Party.

The Great Depression devastated the economies of most industrialized countries. It also helped pave the way for the German National Socialist Party (Nazis) to gain power. The success of the German and Italian national socialists encouraged other leaders to develop similar movements. Global wars, revolutions, and the Great Depression brought tens of millions of deaths in the first half of the twentieth century, causing many to despair of the future.

Chapter 36 explores the causes and the social and economic consequences of World War I. Chapter 37 analyzes revolutions in Russia and China, where two

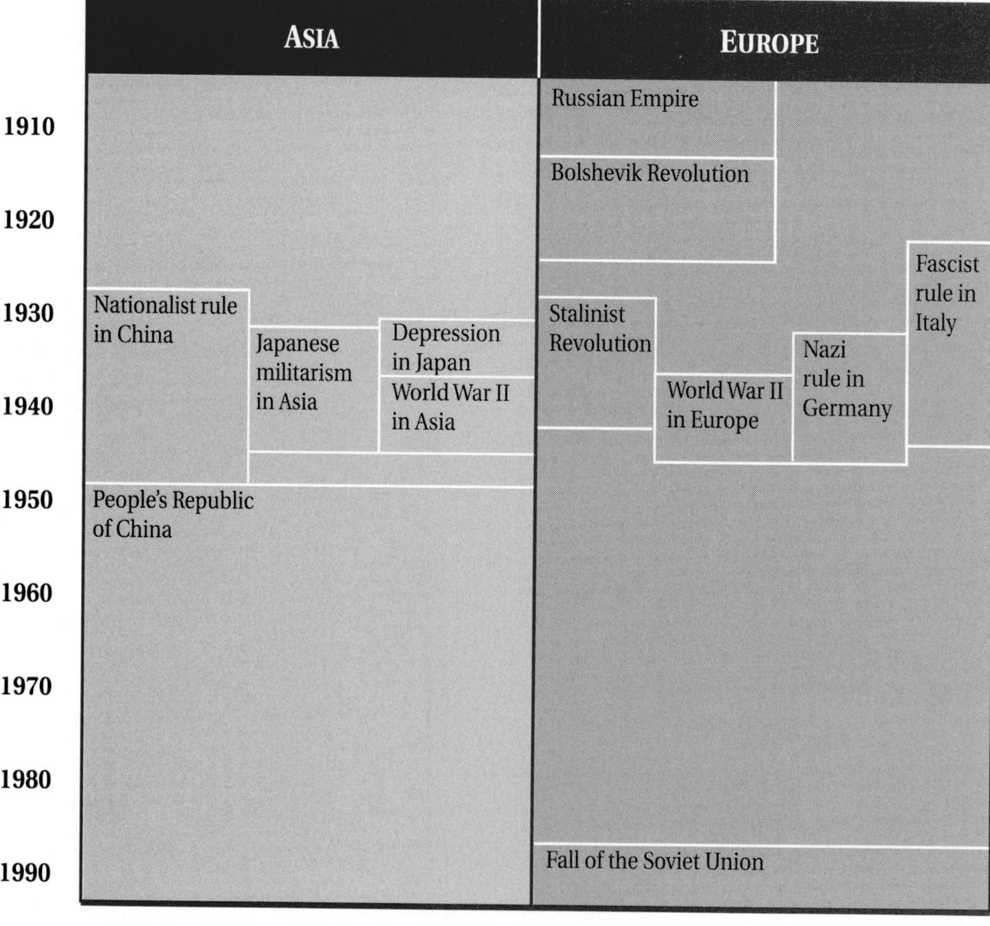

PART EIGHT

GLOBAL WAR AND REVOLUTION

empires collapsed. Workers and peasants benefited from revolutionary governments, although many died in the collectivizations of agriculture. Chapter 38 discusses the Great Depression and the growing power of the nation-state. In many countries, periods of depression ended as states began preparing for war. Chapter 39 looks at the rise of national socialist parties. Mussolini and Hitler led the two most successful national socialist parties that set up totalitarian states. Chapter 40 examines World War II, the most destructive war in history. Coupled with the war was Hitler's determination to exterminate Europe's Jews and many other minority groups. Issue 8 examines new modes of transportation and communication that unite the world.

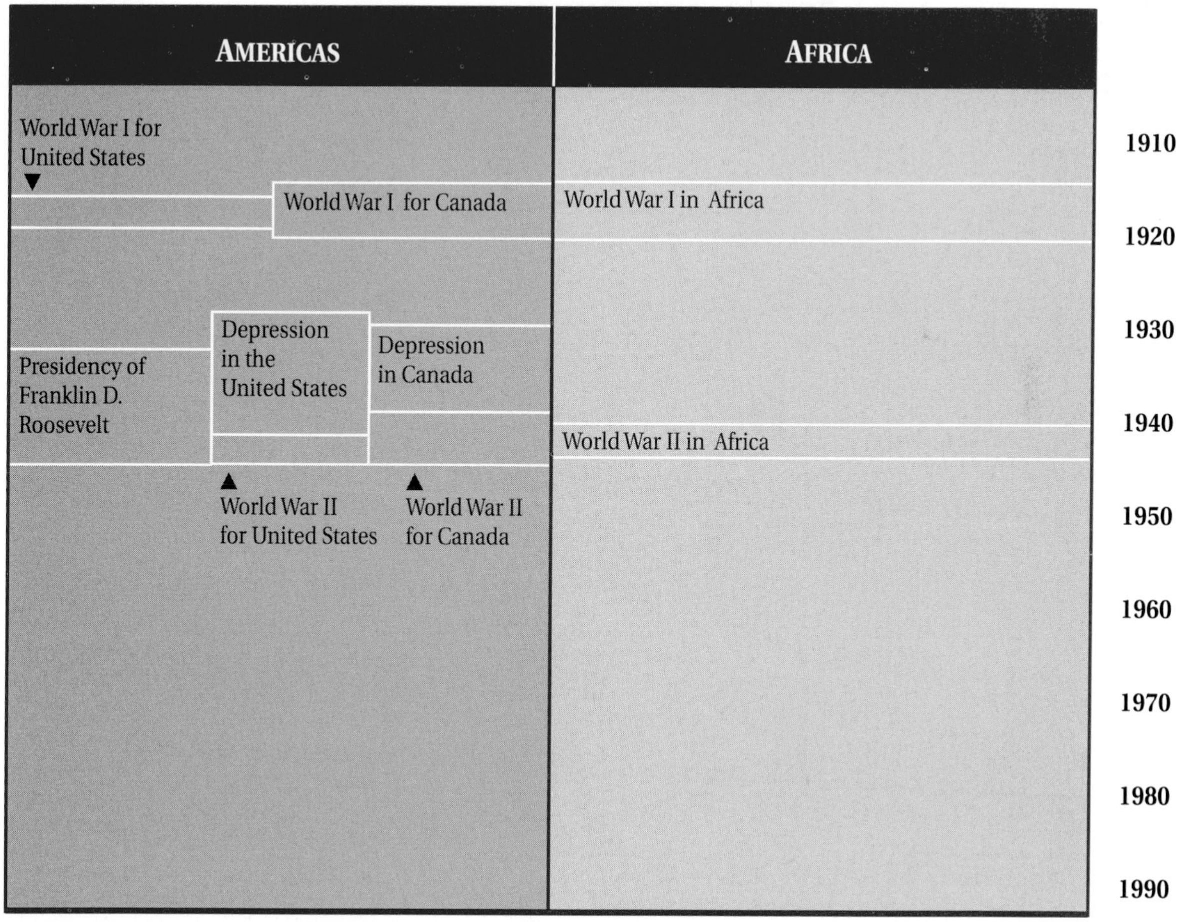

AMERICAS

World War I for United States ▼

World War I for Canada

Depression in the United States

Depression in Canada

Presidency of Franklin D. Roosevelt

▲ World War II for United States

▲ World War II for Canada

AFRICA

World War I in Africa

World War II in Africa

1910
1920
1930
1940
1950
1960
1970
1980
1990

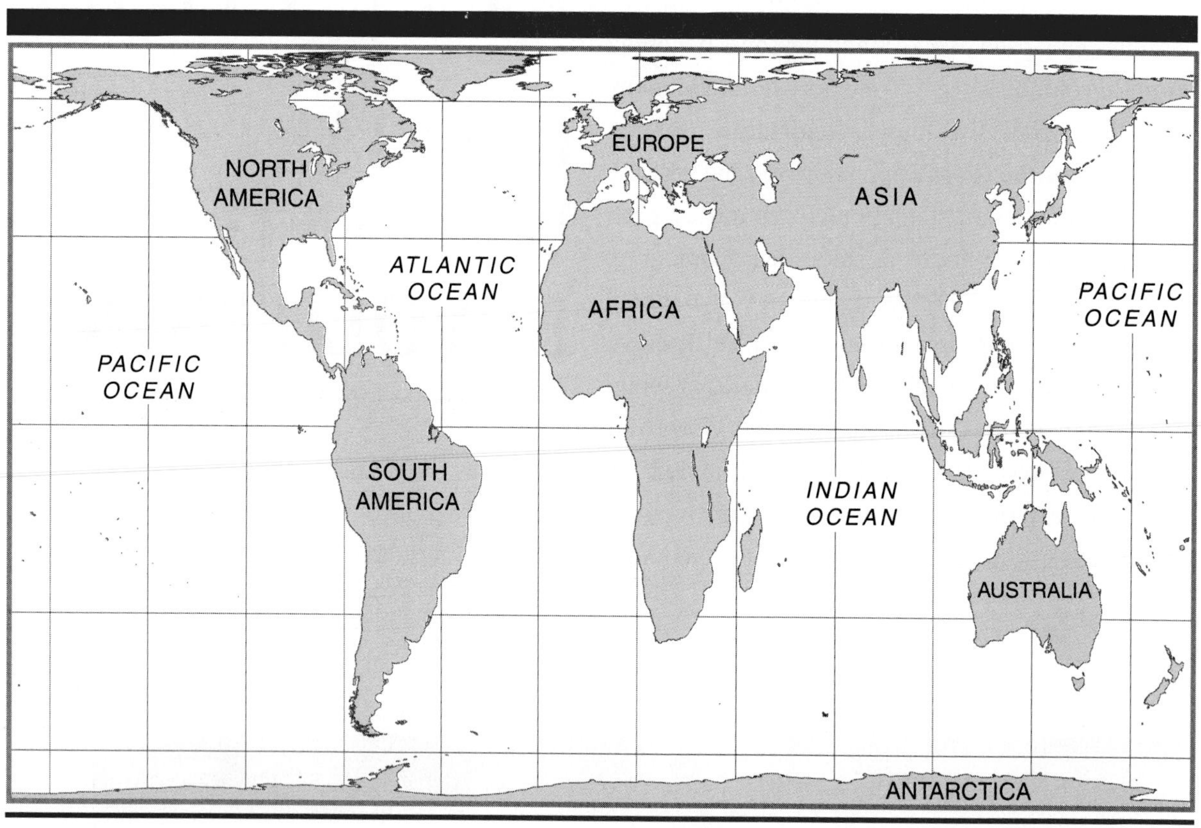
NORTH AMERICA
EUROPE
ASIA
ATLANTIC OCEAN
AFRICA
PACIFIC OCEAN
PACIFIC OCEAN
SOUTH AMERICA
INDIAN OCEAN
AUSTRALIA
ANTARCTICA

CHAPTER 36

World War I and the Versailles Peace
1914–1919

In August 1914, the rectors of southern German universities issued a joint appeal about the unfolding war:

> Students! The muses are silent. The issue is battle, the battle forced upon us for German culture, which is threatened by the barbarians from the East, and for German values, which the enemy in the West envies us. And so the *furor teutonicus* [German fury] bursts into flame once again. The enthusiasm of the wars of liberation flares, and the holy war begins.

This nationalistic manifesto of 1914—tinged with racial and cultural innuendo against the Russians to the east—excited many collegians, who enlisted in the German army. The young men formed two army corps and went to the western front to fight British combat veterans in October. A ferocious battle in Belgium killed 36,000 young Germans, who were buried in a common grave in the Langemarck cemetery. This slaughter was but one among many over the next four years.

World War I (1914–1918) saw the service of 65 million soldiers from thirty-five nations around the globe. The British Empire alone raised 8.5 million combatants. Although the number of war deaths may never be accurately tabulated, most agree that perhaps 30 million people perished, about half of whom died from war-related diseases. At the same time, the German, the Austro-Hungarian, the Russian, and the Ottoman empires collapsed, and the map of Europe was redrawn by the victors at the Paris Peace Conference in 1919. Furthermore, the United States and Japan suffered little damage and earned great profits from supplying the Europeans with munitions and other materials. Because of their significant economic power, Japan and the United States emerged from the war as major players in international politics.

CAUSES AND CONTEXTS OF WORLD WAR I

Many factors played roles in the buildup to World War I. Nationalism and imperialism, for example, had promoted a brutal global competition among European states, the United States, and Japan to divide the world into empires and protectorate zones. Clashing national interests ultimately exploded in Europe in 1914, and existing alliance systems helped turn a European war into a global conflict. Japan, for example, used its alliance with the British, French, and Russians to expand into China and the Pacific Ocean region.

Nationalism and Imperialism

Nationalist rivalries created great tensions among the imperialist states in the decades leading up to 1914 and helped precipitate World War I. The industrializing nation-states competed vigorously to impose their wills on less powerful states. Imperialist activities in Asia and Africa helped submerge

FIGURE 36.1 ***Imperialist Rivalries in Africa.*** *By 1905, European rivalries in Africa had begun to emerge as Germany competed with France and Britain, especially in North Africa. In this 1905 photo, Kaiser Wilhelm II leads German troops through Tangiers in a show of force. In the following year, an international conference challenged Germany's claims to Morocco. Germany's imperialist threats prompted Great Britain to ally more closely with Russia and France, laying the foundation for the Triple Entente.* L'Illustration/Sygma.

many tensions in Europe proper, and once the African and Asian states succumbed to outside domination, latent imperial rivalries erupted.

Germany felt impoverished by its lack of exploitable lands and peoples. National pride for the Germans meant competing with the British, who dominated the high seas and who had built a formidable empire that encircled the globe. One counterpressure to the increasing hostility toward Britain came from a loose coalition of German bankers, merchants, and shippers who understood that the loss of the British market for their goods and services could prove to be financially disastrous. At the same time, internal politics intensified because of the demands for greater power sharing by underrepresented groups. Many of the German elite felt that a brief and successful war might silence the internal conflict between the haves and the have-nots. Thus, the rising tide of nationalism and the monarch's determination to achieve a military settlement silenced the voices of those who wished to resolve the conflict by peaceful means.

Some German leaders favored a foreign policy that emphasized **pan-Germanism**, or unity among German-speaking peoples of all nations. Nationalist and racist ideas encouraged the interpretation of global competition in terms of racial rivalries. Not only did the Germans have to keep the Asians and Africans in their subordinate places, they also had to subdue rival Slavic groups like the Serbs and the Russians.

French nationalists sought revenge for the loss of Alsace and Lorraine to the Germans during the Franco-Prussian War (1870–1871). Alsace and Lorraine had caused trouble between the French and the Germans since the ninth century. Although France vigorously competed with Britain around the globe, fear of German power tempered French antipathy toward Britain. France did ally with Germany and Russia in the scramble for territory and influence in Asia, but the clash of French interests with those of the Germans in North Africa forged a closer relationship between France and Britain.

Britain had rarely involved itself in continental politics in the late nineteenth century, but growing German power and competition for control of the high seas compelled the British to rethink their diplomatic isolation. By 1902, they agreed to an Anglo-Japanese alliance that permitted a restationing of British naval forces in Asian waters. Britain signed an alliance with the French in 1904 and reached an understanding with the Russians in 1907.

The Russians and Austro-Hungarians feared the rising tide of nationalism in their domains. While the Russians promoted pan-Slavic policies and support for the Serbs, the German-speaking Austrians welcomed the pan-German assertions and the promises of support from Germany.

The Balkan Peninsula seethed with national tensions and plots. Serbia had gained independence from the Ottoman Empire in the late nineteenth century, but Serbs in other regions still lay under the Austro-Hungarian yoke. Other national rivalries exploded in the Balkan wars of 1912 and 1913. The settlements following these wars satisfied only a few states; the rest schemed for revenge and national aggrandizement. These tensions exploded in 1914.

The Alliance System

The global nature of World War I came partly from the alliances formed in preceding decades. Germany, France, Russia, Britain, Japan, the Ottoman Empire, Austria-Hungary, and other states formed alliance blocs that entangled the world.

The Franco-Prussian War created the German Empire in 1871 and brought German leaders new fears. Chancellor Otto von Bismarck formed his diplomatic policy around the need to isolate a vengeful France and the desire to keep close ties with tsarist Russia. Thus, Bismarck signed a treaty of alliance with the Austro-Hungarians in 1879 and another with the Italians in 1882, creating the Triple Alliance (Germany, Austria-Hungary, Italy). At the same time, he worked out a diplomatic agreement with the Russians. Things proceeded relatively smoothly until 1890, when the new German kaiser (emperor), Wilhelm II, dismissed Bismarck. The headstrong monarch had desired to conduct his own foreign policy, and his personal direction soon permitted the Russians to drift away. The kaiser never suspected that the democratic French and autocratic Russians could overcome their political differences and ally with each other.

The Triple Entente (France, Russia, Britain), allying the three major European powers, emerged from each nation's strategic insecurity and their wish to offset Germany's increasing military might. France and Russia lay on Germany's western and

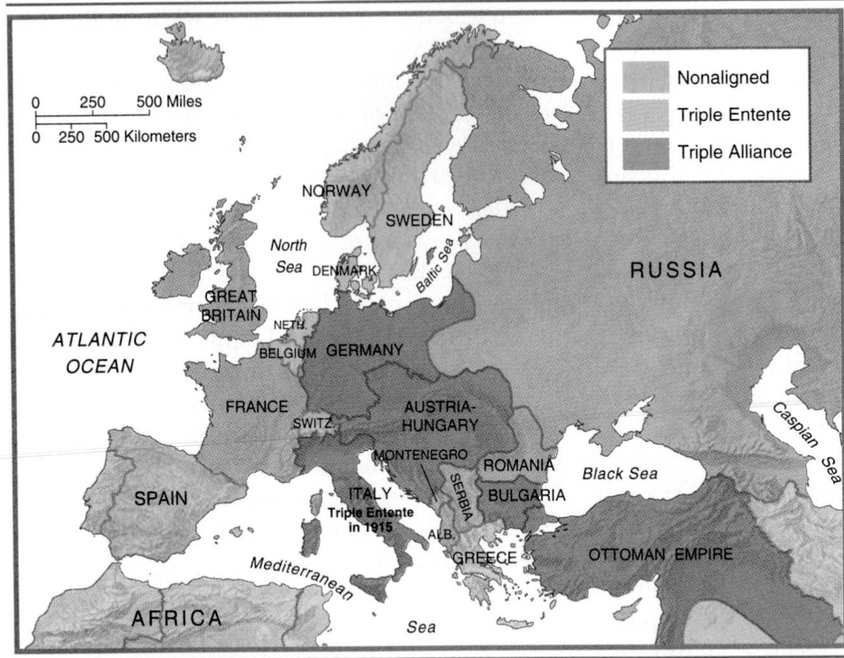

MAP 36.1 *European Alliances in 1914. The major European powers were knitted together in two separate alliance systems. Great Britain, France, and Russia formed the Triple Entente, members of which agreed to support each other in the event of war with other powers. Germany, Austria-Hungary, and Italy formed the Triple Alliance, although Italy refused to go to war in 1914 and switched to the other side in 1915. Other countries joined one side or the other, ensuring that the European theater would engage millions of soldiers in 1914.*

eastern borders, and, in 1890, neither had an alliance. Beginning in 1891 and concluding in 1894, France and Russia forged an alliance, despite their political differences. A significant factor in the alliance was the lure of French financing for Russia. The British and French also worked out an alliance in the early years of the twentieth century, settling their many differences. In addition, the British worked out an agreement with the Russians in 1907; the two sides resolved their imperialistic differences and agreed to cooperate against aggressive third parties.

As the Germans faced encirclement by hostile states, they drew closer to the Austro-Hungarians. After 1894, the Franco-Russian alliance threatened a two-front war, which was exactly what the German General Staff feared. To counter such an eventuality, German military planners came up with a plan to first defeat the French (as in 1870) and then turn against the Russians, who they assumed would take much longer than the French to mobilize. Timing became a critical issue for Germany's planners, who increasingly feared the Russian buildup of railroad lines and military supplies, allowing for more rapid mobilization.

Japan developed a system of alliances with various European states in the years leading up to World War I. In 1895, Japan had faced a coalition of France, Germany, and Russia that had forced the surrender of some Japanese war gains. Thereafter, Japanese leaders endeavored to gain allies and win military and diplomatic backing for Japan's foreign policy initiatives. Japan and Britain signed an agreement in 1902 that promised mutual support in a major war, and the Russians and French later negotiated separate agreements with the Japanese. German-controlled territories in China and the Pacific tempted the Japanese, who saw them as ripe for picking in a war.

Armament Buildups in Europe and Asia

One element resulting from the Napoleonic wars, the modern military state, contributed both to the arms race before World War I and to the heavy casualties in it. Although the arms race included the massive buildup of land-based weapons and railroad networks to get them to battlefield staging areas, a striking example of armament competition came in the British and German naval race from 1900 to 1914. In the late 1890s, the German naval command decided to challenge Britain's maritime domination. This effort entailed the rapid building of a modern armada. The plan failed because Britain kept a close eye on naval competitors, and when the Germans had constructed the third-largest navy in the world the

British Admiralty accelerated its own shipbuilding schedule. British strategists embarked on a policy of forging alliances and drawing elements of their global navy home to the North Sea.

WORLD WAR I'S OUTBREAK AND COURSE, 1914–1918

Many European leaders expected the war to be brief, as the Franco-Prussian War (1870–1871) had been. Unfortunately for the millions of European combatants, World War I was more akin to the United States Civil War (1861–1865). Both wars were anticipated by the participants to be short-lived, both quickly reached stalemates, and both accelerated into wars of material and human attrition. Once the forward momentum of the German armies halted, weapons like the machine gun turned combat into a war of attrition that cost millions of lives.

The War's Outbreak

In June 1914, the heir to the Austro-Hungarian throne, Archduke Francis Ferdinand, fell to a Serbian assassin's bullets; this cause of World War I was linked directly to nationalism. Gavrilo Princep, the assassin, belonged to a Serbian secret society

UNDER THE LENS
World War I and Disease

World War I stands in a pivotal position in the history of disease. Inoculation had been invented some decades before, and its benefits were beginning to be recognized in industrialized countries. Further, effective medicines to halt the advance or spread of disease had been developed and distributed. Finally, the significance of germs and sterilization had become well known in Western medicine, and sickroom infection was becoming far less common. As a result of all these factors, the era of epidemics (the temporary, extensive spread of a disease) and pandemics (the prevalence of a disease in most members of a population) seemed to be coming to an end.

Ironically, the years between 1917 and 1921 saw dozens of the most devastating worldwide epidemics and pandemics, many of which claimed huge losses of life. The most devastating of these was the Spanish influenza pandemic that began in the spring of 1918. At first, its death rate was low, and it attracted little attention. By August, however, the disease had spread around the globe, and its virulence had increased. Death rates doubled and tripled in the United States, and in places like Samoa, where natural resistance was low, as many as one out of every five infected died. In the war zones of Europe and Southwest Asia, infection and death rates were high, and huge numbers of soldiers were sheltered in makeshift hospital tents. Worldwide, several million people died in a matter of two or three months. One respected historian of disease has called this pandemic probably the greatest demographic shock ever to have been suffered by the world's population.

Why was the influenza so devastating? Probably it was caused by a combination of two agents, one bacterial and one viral, that acted to produce illness far more extreme than either could alone. The tens of millions of persons who moved long distances to perform wartime service before returning home would have served as excellent carriers for these agents, and the chance encounter of the two agents would have been all that was needed to instigate the disaster. Another element in the disease's profile was its attack on young adults, who are usually spared from high mortality rates. Significant deaths among this fertile group also affected the numbers of births later.

World War I saw unprecedented numbers of people moving great distances, thanks to the advance in transportation technology. With the moving of people came the spread of germs, and many diseases spread like wildfire. Diphtheria ravaged much of North America, Britain, France, and Germany in 1917 and 1918; it probably struck other places whose medical systems were not sophisticated enough to recognize it. Cholera afflicted millions in southern Europe, Southwest Asia, and India, spreading eventually to East Asia. Anthrax had a final resurgence in Great Britain, France, and Belgium in 1919 before immunization controlled it.

FIGURE 36.2 ***Trouble in the Balkans, June 1914.*** *A key precipitant of World War I was the assassination of the Archduke Francis Ferdinand and his wife, Sophie. Heir to the Austrian throne, Francis Ferdinand loomed as a target for Serbian patriots. This photo, taken shortly after the killing, shows the arrest of the assassin. With Germany's full support, Austria-Hungary issued an ultimatum to Serbia that eventually led to the outbreak of hostilities.* Gernsheim Collection, Harry Ransom Humanities Center, University of Texas, Austin.

that was directed by the head of Serbia's intelligence apparatus. The murder was designed to ignite an uproar that could lead to the liberation of Serbs under Austro-Hungarian rule.

During the weeks that followed the assassination, the alliance systems sprang into play. Austrian leaders pondered a reply to the daring assault and consulted with German leaders, who listened sympathetically. As early as December 1912, the German monarch had declared himself in favor of immediate war. After securing German backing, the confident Austrians delivered an ultimatum to the Serbs, who in turn sought support from Russia, a kindred Slavic state. The Russians supported the Serbs, bringing their French allies with them. By late July 1914, Austrian troops began shelling Serbian positions, instigating a Russian mobilization. This action alarmed German leaders, who had counted on a slow Russian mobilization. Ultimatums and war declarations followed along the alliance systems in the next days, and soon most major European states were mobilizing for war. Most scholars agree that although all belligerents should be held accountable for the war, Germany bears the greatest responsibility for precipitating World War I because German leaders had advised the Austrians to engage in hostilities rather than seek a diplomatic resolution of the conflict.

Some European countries remained neutral at the beginning of the war. The Scandinavian countries of Norway, Sweden, and Denmark refused to become involved because they were near Germany and were unprepared for war. The Dutch stayed neutral for the same reasons. Italian leaders decided that, because they had not been consulted by Germany or Austria-Hungary, they need not honor their commitment to the Triple Alliance. Debate within Italy's leadership continued until May 1915, when Italy finally entered the fighting, but against Germany and Austria-Hungary. Significant consideration was given to the fact that Italy would not be able to win new territories in the Balkans if they did not fight. By 1918, more than 600,000 Italians had died, and Italian industry had produced more than 20,000 machine guns and 6,500 airplanes. Italy put more and more artillery pieces in the field, and Italian war industries grew enormous. The Italian aircraft works alone employed 100,000 workers.

Many of Europe's able-bodied men carried identity cards that told them where to assemble, while their regimental depots had long been stocked with supplies. In July 1914, around 4 million soldiers stood ready to fight, but by September, 20 million Europeans had been called up. The Germans, who depended on mobility because their war plan demanded that they first defeat the French, called up more than 4 million soldiers and transported 1.5 million equipped troops to the western front, all in less than three weeks. The French, fearing a replay of the disaster of 1870, swiftly shifted troops to the north and northwest; even French taxis transported soldiers. The Russians surprised everyone by quickly assembling two armies at the eastern front through a railroad system built for that purpose. Ironically, when the troops and supplies reached the designated areas, human beings and horses toted most of the war material because of a dearth of transport vehicles.

Early Stalemate and Life at the Front

Desperate fighting erupted on western and eastern battlefronts, and stalemates soon resulted. On the western front, stiff and unexpected Belgian resistance delayed the German timetable and afforded the French time to organize a defensive plan. The succeeding fight in northern France stopped the

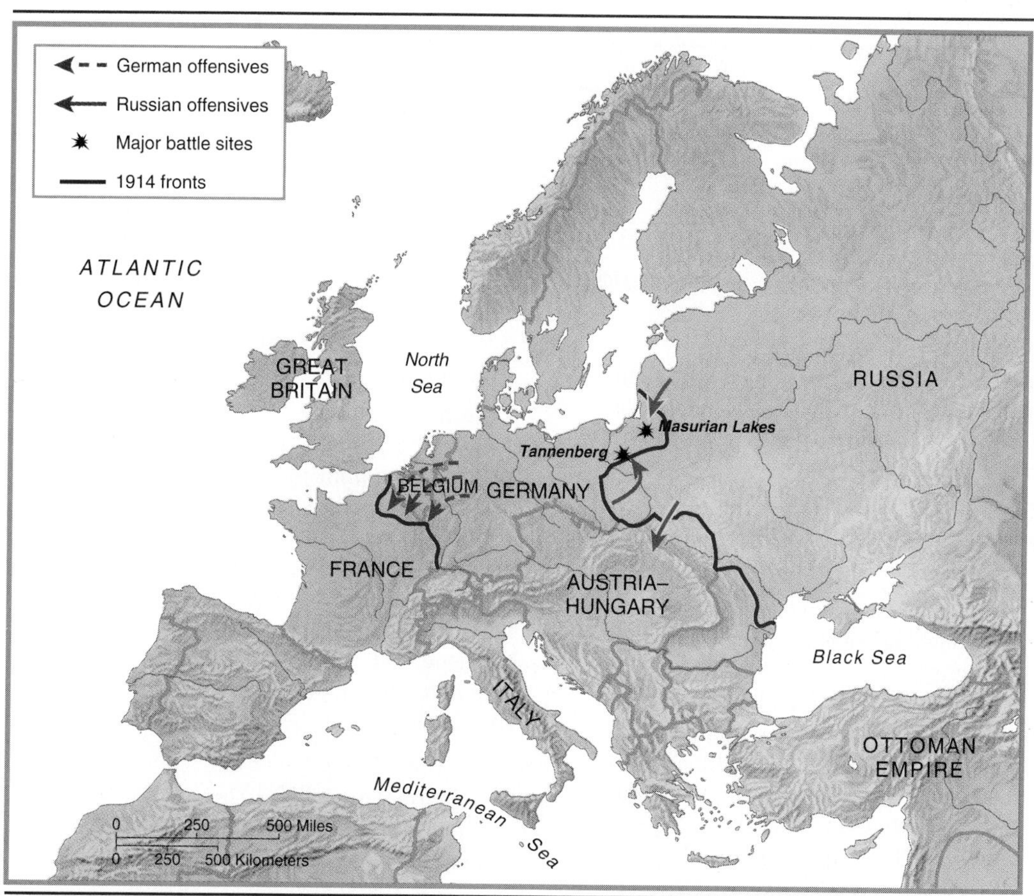

Map 36.2 ***Eastern and Western Fronts, 1914.*** *The Germans attacked the French and British, while the Russians hammered the Germans. The fighting, which began in August 1914, quickly stalemated on both fronts, the Germans being stopped in the west and the Russians in the east. Although both fronts saw trench warfare, the eastern front saw more widespread territorial movement in succeeding years.*

German advance, and both sides barricaded themselves in a complex of trenches and bunkers that soon snaked across the war-scarred French countryside.

Stalemate on the western front evolved into a war of attrition that consumed masses of human beings and materiel. The machine gun greatly strengthened defensive lines, while the rifle afforded the infantry troops individual protection. All, however, quavered before the artillery bombardments that rained metal destruction everywhere. Whole units could be wiped out in a few hellish minutes of awesome firepower. Gas was another terrifying battlefield weapon, and among the worst of these was mustard gas. Chlorine, the principal compound in mustard gas, gave a sea-green color to the deadly mist covering the battlefields.

The slaughter continued. By September 1915, the French alone had suffered 1 million killed and wounded, and, by 1917, 1 million French had died and hundreds of thousands more were wounded. At Verdun, a heavily fortified city near the German border, the German army tried to inflict large-scale casualties upon French defenders. Earlier, German soldiers had been stopped by a spirited defense led by Henri Pétain, who declared, "They shall not pass." In 1916 and 1917, however, the French suffered more than 600,000 casualties and the Germans a similar number. Verdun's image shifted from heroic to hellish. After many of these slaughters, half of France's fighting divisions refused orders to go on the offensive, although they did agree to defend their positions. A crisis of morale threatened to engulf the combatants and bring peace through desertion rather than negotiation.

IN THEIR OWN WORDS

A British Soldier Looks at War

Life at the front frequently traumatized soldiers who faced primitive conditions with few comforts. They suffered regular artillery barrages, intermittent assaults, and gas attacks. The British war poet Wilfred Owen (1893–1918) graphically captured the terrors of war that ravaged the flower of European youth. One memorable poem by Owen, "Dulce et Decorum Est," evokes the mood of soldiers, many of whom had studied the poet Horace, to whom the Latin lines are attributed. Horace alleged that it was sweet and appropriate to fight and die for one's country.

Bent double, like old beggars under sacks,
Knock-kneed, coughing like hags, we cursed through sludge,
Till on the haunting flares we turned our backs,
And towards our distant rest began to trudge.
Men marched asleep. Many had lost their boots
But limped on blood-shod. All went lame; all blind;
Drunk with fatigue; deaf even to the hoots
Of disappointed shells that dropped behind.

Gas! GAS! Quick, boys!—An ecstasy of fumbling,
Fitting the clumsy helmets just in time,
But someone still was yelling out and stumbling
And flound'ring like a man in fire or lime . . .
Dim, through the misty panes and thick green light,
As under a green sea, I saw him drowning.
In all my dreams, before my helpless sight,
He plunges at me guttering, choking, drowning.

If in some smothering dreams, you too could pace
Behind the wagon that we flung him in,
And watch the white eyes writhing in his face,
His hanging face, like a devil's sick of sin,
If you could hear, at every jolt, the blood
Come gargling from the froth-corrupted lungs,
Obscene as cancer, bitter as the cud
Of vile, incurable sores on innocent tongues,—
My friend, you would not tell with such high zest
To children ardent for some desperate glory,
The old Lie: Dulce et decorum est
Pro patria mori.[a]

Owen earned the Military Cross for gallant action on October 4, 1918, and was killed in battle a month later, one week before the war ended.

[a] **Dulce et decorum est/Pro patria mori:** Latin for "There is no greater honor than to die for one's country."

On the eastern front, the Russians honored their commitment to the French and British by attacking East Prussia, part of Germany. Although Russian generals planned eventually to mobilize 5.3 million soldiers, military planners failed to calculate the need for massive numbers of rifles, machine guns, and artillery pieces as well as their ammunition. Consequently, poorly trained Russian soldiers invaded Germany with woefully inadequate supplies when they marched into a territory whose inhabitants systematically destroyed things that could have been used by the Russians. Commanders had few modern means of communication, relying on wireless machines over which were dispatched uncoded messages. German officers intercepted these messages and knew as much about Russian troop movements as did Russian leaders. Airplanes might have helped the Russians learn about German troop movements, but a lack of spare parts kept most of their 250 airplanes grounded. The few that flew on reconnaissance missions were mistakenly shot down by uninformed Russian soldiers who thought these flying machines must have been German. Lacking sufficient supplies and general strategic plans, the Russian armies lost nearly a quarter-million soldiers in the war's first month.

Russia's commanders achieved success against the Austrians farther south but then fell back before the Germans, who reinforced their Austrian allies. The overconfident Austrian generals had sacrificed 300,000 of their soldiers in a futile campaign against the Russians. Seeing the possibility of a Russian breakthrough into Germany, the German commander, General Paul von Hindenburg, moved an army force into the conflict and stopped the Russian advance. Heavy fighting that continued into December 1914 claimed more than 1.5 million Russian casualties and prisoners of war.

The next two years brought similar losses and a deepening crisis. Russia simply could not replace the officers killed in the early months of the war. In 1915, the Russians launched a spring offensive against the Austrians. Initially successful, it broke under a German counterattack that struck deep into Russian territory. Refugees began to flood over the land, a massive wave of humanity surviving under appalling conditions.

Soldiers on the eastern front suffered from many of the privations of their allies to the west, and they often endured horrible conditions. Most lived in trenches year-round, and some had no overcoats during the war's first autumn. Others had no boots or marched with their toes sticking out of their footwear. Wounded soldiers faced operations by surgeons who often left their charges permanently crippled because of the woe-

Figure 36.3 ***Trench Warfare.*** *In this World War I photo, French soldiers haul the body of a dead soldier from the trenches. The morale of the stationary troops began to plummet, especially by 1916. By this time, millions of soldiers in the trenches on both fronts had endured such scenes of carnage for months, if not years.* Library of Congress.

FIGURE 36.4 ***Putting One's Comrades to Rest.*** *During World War I, millions died on the eastern front—perhaps as many as 10 percent of Russia's mobilized troops perished in battle. In this photo, a group of Russian soldiers prepare to bury their dead.* Hoover Institution.

ful state of military medicine. Nearly one in four who survived convalescence was mutilated for life. One official encountered 17,000 wounded Russian soldiers in Warsaw, lying in the cold rain and mud without even straw matting. In the late winter of 1915, German gas attacks caught the Russians unprepared and gasping for gas masks.

World War I's Last Years, 1917–1918

Momentous events shook politicians and soldiers in 1917. Russia faced a systemic collapse of the tsarist autocracy and then the seizure of power by the Communist Party under the leadership of Vladimir Lenin. This left an unstable situation on the eastern front that was resolved in 1918 by the Treaty of Brest-Litovsk, ceding major parts of the former Russian Empire to the Germans and freeing German soldiers for duty on the western front.

German planners saw the effectiveness of submarines in sinking British merchant ships and weakening Britain. After earnest debates at the highest levels, the reluctant German monarch agreed to a policy of unrestricted submarine warfare. In February 1917, a vast increase in British naval losses and the sinking of several United States ships crystallized United States public opinion in favor of war. British survival was ensured by forming convoys of merchant ships shepherded by United States and British warships. That new effort stymied the Germans and permitted massive resupplying.

The major powers in the Americas entered the war on the side of the British, French, and Italians. This brought the western hemisphere directly into the global conflict and provided a venue for a demonstration of North American power, headed by the United States. Armament factories in the United States had supplied the Russians and others since the outbreak of the war and now expanded production to accommodate American soldiers. Canadians had already fought alongside troops from other parts of the British-led Commonwealth of Nations. More than 600,000 Canadians served in the war and 60,000 died in battle, earning a reputation for bravery.

In 1918, the Germans made a final effort to overwhelm the Allies on the western front and fell back before the counterattack, suing for peace in November. The German commanders, Hindenburg and Erich Ludendorf, gambled on a spring offensive, before the United States could bring significant numbers across the Atlantic Ocean. German troops from the eastern front also fought on the western front, but they could not break through the French and British lines in a decisive manner. Momentum turned to the Allies, who in the summer had begun receiving large amounts of supplies and soldiers from the United States. Hard fighting began to wear down the Germans, whose army barely remained intact. When the war ended, however, Germany had been spared the devastation of other front-line countries, like France and Italy.

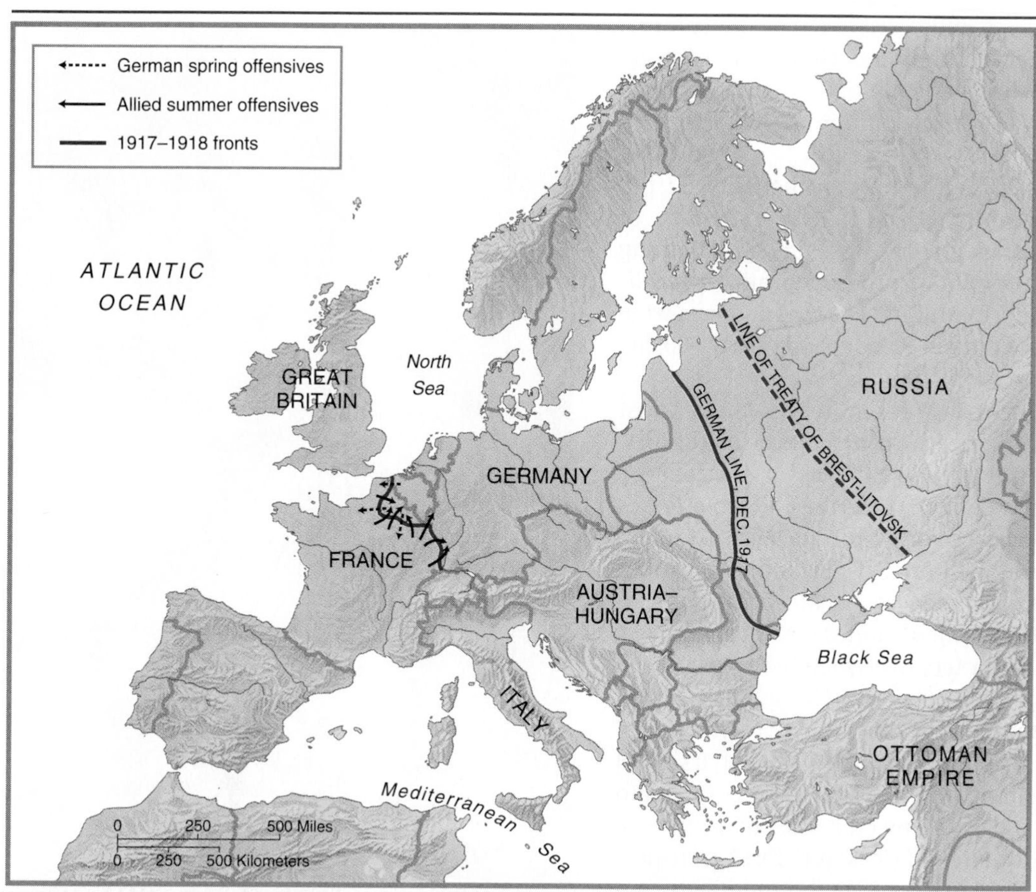

MAP 36.3 ***Eastern and Western Fronts, 1917–1918.*** *The eastern front began to deteriorate in 1917, when the tsarist government fell and the Bolsheviks took power with the slogan, "Peace." Fighting halted in March 1918 after the Bolsheviks ratified the Treaty of Brest-Litovsk, ending the war for Russia. The western front remained fairly static until the Germans launched a spring offensive in 1918. This campaign was halted in the summer, and the British, French, and Americans counterattacked, reaching the borders of Germany by November 1918, when an armistice was signed.*

THE HOME FRONT

As the battlefield slaughter continued, people in rear areas endured privation and suffering while contributing mightily to the war effort. Although massive amounts of supplies had been stockpiled to wage a limited war, the carnage that extended over weeks and then months compelled various countries to mobilize their human and material resources more fully. The resulting centralization efforts created governments that were taking on more control of their citizens' lives.

France

Although the outbreak of war surprised many in France and the mobilization brought a mixture of responses, patriotism blossomed in the veneration of Saint Joan of Arc, the heroine of the Hundred Years War. She became a popular symbol of French heroism in the face of defeat and suffering. Churches and schools played a growing role in rallying support for the war effort. Continued enthusiasm for the war, however, waned with defeats in 1915 and 1916. As the death toll passed

1 million persons, more despaired of the conflict. Yet most believed that the Germans must be driven from French soil, and French citizens adapted to wartime conditions over which they had little control.

The French Empire brought benefits for the French during World War I. Raw materials, of course, continued to flow to France, benefiting military and nonmilitary production alike. In addition, more than 1.9 million colonial subjects were conscripted for duty in France, and nearly 700,000 of them became combatants.

A coalition government representing most political constituencies ruled France for the first three years. In many cases, however, the military dominated the political planning. Terrible losses and worker sacrifices drove the socialists from the coalition by September 1917. Then, in November 1917, Georges Clemenceau became prime minister and restored civilian control over the army.

Economic matters overwhelmed much of the war's early decision making. The initial German onslaught captured nearly half of France's coal production and almost three-fifths of its steel capacity. To survive, French leaders were forced to intervene in the economy on a scale unseen since the French Revolution. Prices were fixed, transport systems were reorganized, and production and distribution networks were rebuilt. Shortages of labor, fertilizers, and farm machinery caused the 1917 harvest to fall 40 percent below prewar levels.

Loss of key industrial regions compelled the French government to develop a highly centralized economy. Financial investment came through loans and the printing of money, but the latter expediency fueled inflation. Although most workers supported the war, they increasingly resisted the militarylike regimentation in the factories. As living conditions deteriorated, strikes broke out around Paris. Rising prices for foodstuffs particularly incensed factory workers, who accused farmers of greediness. Workers also complained of managers' efforts to improve productivity at their expense and lengthen the work day, arguing that profits increased but not wages. Several work stoppages came in January 1917, while more erupted a few months later. Most were spontaneous, and the largest totaled around 100,000 workers.

Women formed a major component of the labor force. As men were called to the battlefields, women moved into agricultural and industrial production. They soon began to dominate certain economic sectors; ordnance factories lured women from other jobs by offering higher wages. Women played a key role in the spontaneous strikes of May and June 1917 that were led by munitions and fashions-trade workers.

FIGURE 36.5 ***Call to Patriotic Frenchmen.*** *This poster evokes the French government's renewed commitment to the war under prime minister Georges Clemenceau. The figure of the armed French woman recalls both Joan of Arc and the female personification of Liberty leading the French people in a nineteenth-century painting by Eugène Delacroix. Prior to efforts by Clemenceau to raise his country's morale, the French had nearly dropped out of the war—especially when the death toll exceeded 1 million.* Trustees of the Imperial War Museum.

Human labor needs grew dramatically during the war and forced the French to recruit many foreign workers. Vietnamese from French Indochina were hired to work in France, and, by war's end, more than 100,000 had labored there. By 1918, tens of thousands of Vietnamese had served in the French armed forces, including at least one who flew with the French air force. Some Vietnamese dug and repaired trenches, while others worked on farms or in French industry. Tens of thousands of Chinese also came to France. Most Asians left after the war, but a few stayed on and became involved in political and social issues. Many Africans, especially Senegalese, came to France, either to fight or to work as laborers. Some stayed in France after the war.

The Clemenceau government vigorously pushed the war effort. Clemenceau had a cabinet minister arrested for "defeatist" attitudes and forged the discipline necessary to prosecute the war. Renewed nationalist enthusiasm provided the energy that overcame defeatist attitudes. The arrival of large numbers of soldiers from the United States bolstered the morale of the French people and troops. They helped stop the final German push in the spring of 1918 and played a key role in the counterattack that broke the German resistance. Peace came in November 1918 and was universally celebrated by the French.

Germany

Despite Wilhelm II's optimism that the coming war would be brief, the immense expenditure of resources and the years of warfare taxed the energies of the German bureaucrats. The unpreparedness of the government caused problems with food distribution that led to deteriorating living conditions and food riots as early as 1915. Two years later, large numbers of German workers began to strike, asking for better pay and improved working conditions.

German women joined the labor force in industry and agriculture to replace men who had been drafted. Adolescents, too, entered the workforce in large numbers. By 1917, more than 700,000 women toiled in armaments factories, a fivefold increase in four years. In the succeeding year, more than 100,000 women worked for the German railroads, a tenfold increase since 1914. Many of those employed by the chemical industry were women. As in France, some of these female laborers played key roles in strikes. Sociocultural attitudes against women holding regular jobs vanished under the powerful need to ensure victory.

The German Supreme Command assumed rule in the summer of 1917 as a virtual military dictatorship. The tightening of central control temporarily staved off economic collapse, but many thoughtful Germans realized that defeat loomed ahead. The military tried to forestall a major social upheaval by yielding to a representative government. The deployment of the remaining naval units in October provoked a mutiny of the sailors. By early November, workers, sailors, and soldiers set up self-governing committees, the ruling government collapsed, and Wilhelm II fled to Holland.

The Weimar Republic (1918–1933) was founded in the war's dying days, promising an open political system with a welfare state. Germany's defeat and the harsh peace that followed hampered the governing process, as did an unstable economy. At the same time, the army, bureaucracy, judiciary, educational establishment, and religious institutions from the imperial system survived. These elements inhibited the radical changes planned by many.

Around 2 million Germans died in World War I. They had valiantly served their country but participated in a losing cause. This fact led to resentment in the immediate postwar era, when politicians like Adolf Hitler played on the combined resentments and humiliations to forge an electoral base of veterans and others.

Great Britain

Large numbers of British served in World War I, including members of the empire recruited from Canada, New Zealand, Australia, Africa, and India. David Lloyd George (1863–1945) directed the British war effort. An ammunition crisis in 1915 triggered a reorganization of British industry under the leadership of Lloyd George. He implemented a military-style chain of command and promoted a policy of negotiating long-term supply contracts with factories, solving the problem for the war's duration. This approach militarized much of British industry.

Most countries imposed some form of rationing on their people, but Great Britain's need to ration was unusually acute. An island country, Britain imported many things, and German submarines blockaded the British. Thus, goods were rationed, including foodstuffs. Ration coupons were distributed and had to be taken to stores to

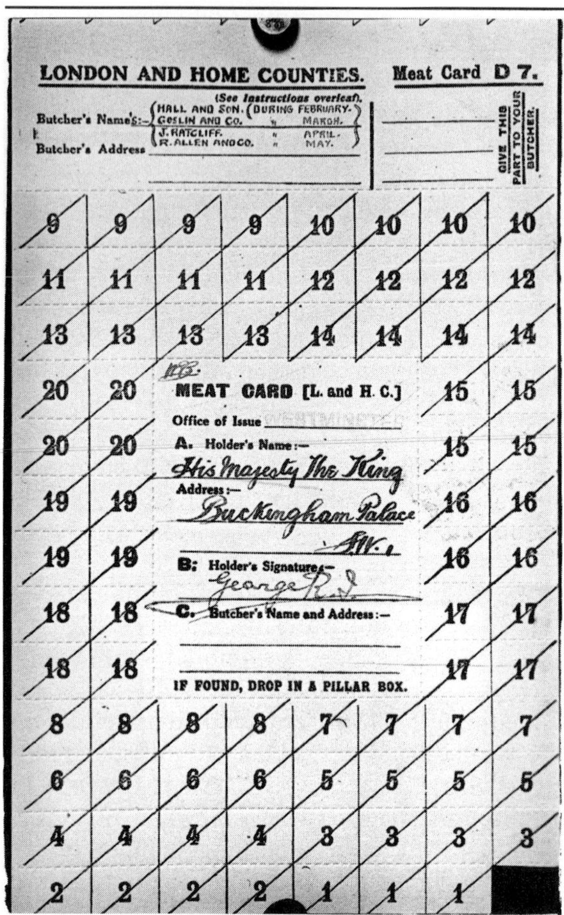

LONDON AND HOME COUNTIES. Meat Card D 7.

(See instructions overleaf.)

Butcher's Name's:— HALL AND SON. (DURING FEBRUARY. GESLIN AND CO. " MARCH. J. RATCLIFF. " APRIL. R. ALLEN AND CO. " MAY.

Butcher's Address

GIVE THIS PART TO YOUR BUTCHER.

9 9 9 9 10 10 10 10

11 11 11 11 12 12 12 12

13 13 13 13 14 14 14 14

20 20 MEAT CARD [L. and H. C.] 15 15

Office of Issue

20 20 A. Holder's Name:— His Majesty The King 15 15

19 19 Address:— Buckingham Palace S.W. 16 16

19 19 B. Holder's Signature— George R.I. 16 16

18 18 C. Butcher's Name and Address:— 17 17

18 18 IF FOUND, DROP IN A PILLAR BOX. 17 17

8 8 8 8 7 7 7 7

6 6 6 6 5 5 5 5

4 4 4 4 3 3 3 3

2 2 2 2 1 1 1

FIGURE 36.6 ***Scarcity on the Home Front.*** *All of Europe, and eventually the United States, faced wartime rationing. The island of Great Britain, dependent on supplies carried by ship, faced much deprivation. Shown here is the ration card used by King George V. Morale improved when the royalty endured the same hardships as other Britons.* Trustees of the Imperial War Museum.

FIGURE 36.7 ***British Women at Work in a Munitions Factory.*** *Thousands of women replaced men in the labor force as World War I wore on. Many women, like the factory workers pictured here, worked under extremely dangerous conditions, sometimes at the cost of their lives and their health.* Trustees of the Imperial War Museum.

be exchanged for various goods. Although a black market existed in Britain, most Britons loyally supported the rationing system.

Women were drawn heavily into manufacturing sectors of the economy. Their role was to replace the men who had been conscripted, killed, or severely wounded on the European mainland; Britain lost nearly 750,000 soldiers and suffered more than 1.5 million wounded. Around 1 million women worked in the munitions industry. Additional women served in paramilitary units in France. Yet, in the postwar era, these patriotic women found themselves increasingly displaced by the returning soldiers, many of whom enjoyed prior claims on jobs. Traditional social patterns were slowly reestablished.

Lloyd George presided over the early postwar era, when Britain's former position of global domination was altered. Britain lost ships with a capacity of nearly 8 million tons, and the national debt soared twelvefold. These and other factors changed Britain's strategic outlook. No longer could it afford massive naval armaments races with the powerful United States and Japan, which had emerged from the war with few losses and with large foreign-exchange surpluses. Thus, arms-limitation treaties in the early 1920s and early 1930s helped relieve some of the financial burden. Skillful diplomacy and political flexibility managed to slow the breakup of the British Empire and preserve British power in the postwar era.

OTHER WAR THEATERS

While the overwhelming bulk of fighting and casualties from World War I occurred in Europe, other regions saw conflict or change resulting from the war as well. The German imperial realm outside Europe totaled around a million square miles, and its ally, the Ottoman Empire, possessed significant holdings in Southwest Asia.

East Asia and the Pacific Region

When the war broke out in the summer of 1914, Japanese planners looked to China and the Pacific. Meeting their alliance commitments, the Japanese mobilized and attacked the German holdings in Shandong Province of China. Fighting was moderately costly in lives, and the German fortifications fell. Additional action in the Micronesian islands of the Pacific brought those German territories under Japanese occupation.

That Japan had larger imperialist aims may be seen in its subsequent diplomatic actions. To ensure a permanent hold on the new Asian and Pacific territories, Japanese leaders negotiated secret treaties with the British, French, and Russians. The Versailles peace talks validated Japan's claims, and continued domination resulted. The retention of areas in Shandong Province ignited Chinese popular opinion against the Japanese in 1919, helping spur Chinese nationalism.

The vulnerability of Germany's Pacific colonies invited the Australians and New Zealanders to seize those not already in Japanese hands. The German resistance proved light, and possession came with little difficulty.

Southwest Asia

While the positions of Germany's far-flung colonies limited its resistance to attack by the British and French, the Ottoman Empire's control of Southwest Asian lands was a different matter.

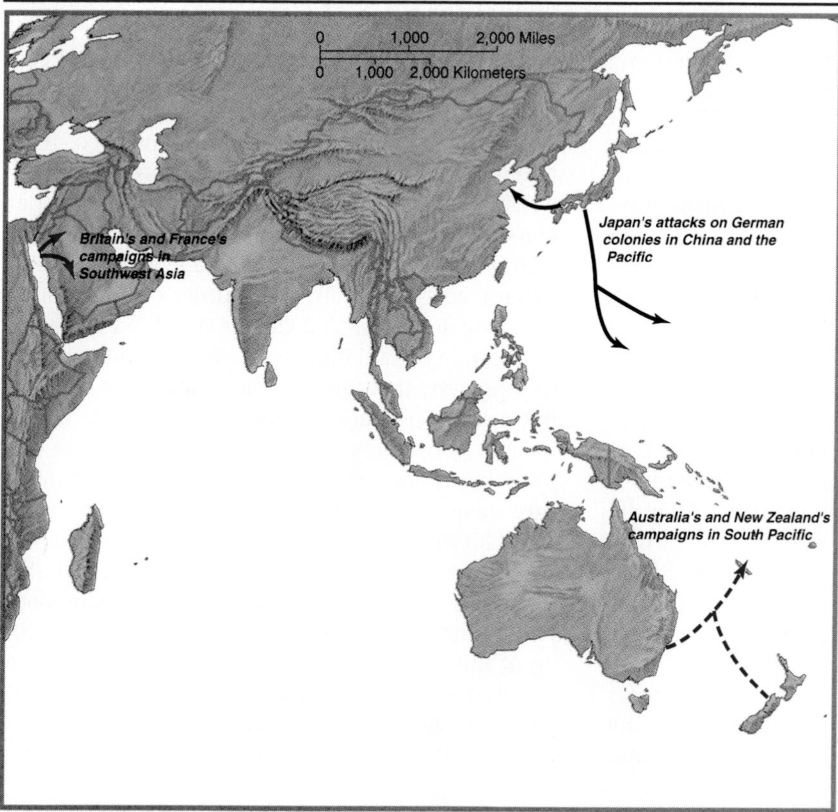

MAP 36.4 *The Asian Theater in World War I.* *The fighting in Asia and the Pacific was relatively brief, being largely over by 1915. The Japanese attacked German colonies in China (Shandong Province) and the North Pacific. Australian and New Zealand forces attacked German colonies in the South Pacific. Both land and sea operations were conducted in Asia.*

The Ottoman leaders joined the Germans and Austro-Hungarians in warring against the French, British, and Russians. Although the Ottoman soldiers sometimes lacked the firepower of the European forces, they were fierce fighters who fought off many advances by the European forces.

Tenacious Ottoman defensive actions held off the Russian conquest of Armenia, threw back a British attack on Mesopotamia, and limited an Arab uprising in Arabia. A major defeat for the British came in 1915 and 1916, when their forces, along with major Australian and New Zealand contingents, attacked the Gallipoli Peninsula, which was held by the Ottoman soldiers. Conceived by Winston Churchill, the campaign aimed at capturing Constantinople and driving the Ottomans from the war. Poor leadership, however, contributed to more than 150,000 casualties. By 1917, the British had assembled an army that numbered nearly 750,000 troops in the area, upsetting some who argued that Britain's primary strategic focus should be Europe rather than Southwest Asia. David Lloyd George ignored these criticisms and forged ahead on both fronts because his imperialist ambitions remained unshaken through the war years.

In 1918, the allied forces seized the offensive, and, in less than a year, the Ottoman Empire collapsed. As seen in Chapter 34, Arab support was garnered with vague British promises of Arab self-rule. By 1918, Mesopotamia had been wrested from the Ottoman Empire, Palestine had been conquered, and the Arabs of Arabia had seized their independence with significant aid from the British. In the Arabian campaign, the British adventurer and romantic T. E. Lawrence (Lawrence of Arabia) played a key role in aiding the Arabian rebel forces.

PATHS TO THE PAST
Turkey and the Armenian Genocide

Genocide is the mass killing of individuals in a deliberate attempt to extinguish a racial, ethnic, or religious group. One instance of genocide in the twentieth century was the action of the Ottoman Turks against the Armenians. Similarly to the denial of the genocide of European Jews by the Nazis, the Republic of Turkey and various organizations have, for their own purposes, discounted events that took place under the Ottoman Empire. Thus, the issue remains controversial.

When the Ottoman Empire joined with Germany in World War I, the empire had been ruled for some years by a group known as the Young Turks, who largely came from the military. An Ottoman campaign in the Caucasus Mountains against the Russians in 1914 failed miserably. Soon, the western part of Anatolia, home to perhaps 2 million Armenians, was deemed by the Turks as an area needing to be "cleansed." A complex set of actions in which hundreds of thousands of Armenians were evicted from their homes followed. Guiding the policymakers was a combination of factors, including religion (the Turks were Muslim and the Armenians were Christian), racism (the Turks strongly promoted a Turkism that was ethnically based), and wartime needs (the Turks feared an alliance between the Armenians and the Russians). Whatever the reasons, Armenian men were usually killed first and then women and children were forcibly marched to distant places. With little or no food or water, many perished along the way, and others were killed.

In the resulting carnage, several hundred thousand Armenians died. The Turkish government resettled the evacuated area with Turkish and other refugees, and many surviving Armenians were forced to convert to Islam. In a war filled with all forms of barbaric acts, the deliberate murder of a people by starvation and organized killings stands out.

Despite the attempts by apologists and revisionists who deny that this genocide took place or argue that it can be rationalized as necessary under wartime conditions, the historical memory of the Armenian Holocaust must be preserved, as all holocaust memories should be. Openness to different historical interpretations of an event does not mean that one must accept all versions as equally true. What is required is a careful examination of the relevant documents and other evidence as well as an understanding of the biases inherent in them. One might also note that Adolf Hitler confidently planned the genocide of the Jews, knowing that the world had seemingly forgotten about the Armenian genocide.

British and French imperialist ambitions determined the postwar makeup of Southwest Asia. Imperialist designs resulted in a conflict fueled by national ambitions and ethnic hatreds.

Africa

Most of the limited fighting in Africa took place in the sub-Saharan areas controlled by the Germans. In West, Central, and Southwest Africa, German resistance was limited by the small number of troops available to defend vast territories. African armed forces from Nigeria and Gold Coast helped round up Germans in Cameroon. Later, these and other armies fought in East Africa and Europe.

One region where a small, determined force held on was in Tanganyika, which remained under German control until a week after the end of the European fighting in 1918. In all, the German-led Africans occupied the attention of nearly 400,000 allied forces of Africans, Asians, and Europeans. Four Indian companies, along with their British officers, were captured by these German-led East African soldiers. Indeed, African valor and energy often lifted sagging German morale. After the war, Britain was awarded the East African territory previously held by the Germans.

Several hundred thousand Africans served in a variety of capacities during World War I. The French, for example, conscripted nearly a quarter-million sub-Saharan Africans, 157,000 of whom fought outside Africa. Some died under the most appalling conditions in Europe when French commanders neglected to provide them with winter uniforms. Large numbers of Nigerians ably fought for the British, and nearly 46,000 Kenyans died in wartime fighting.

FIGURE 36.8 ***East African Troops at War.*** *The British who commanded Indian troops in East Africa believed that their forces could easily defeat African soldiers led by the Germans. The British were shocked when their forces were captured. In this photo, a German officer directs two African soldiers.* Trustees of the Imperial War Museum.

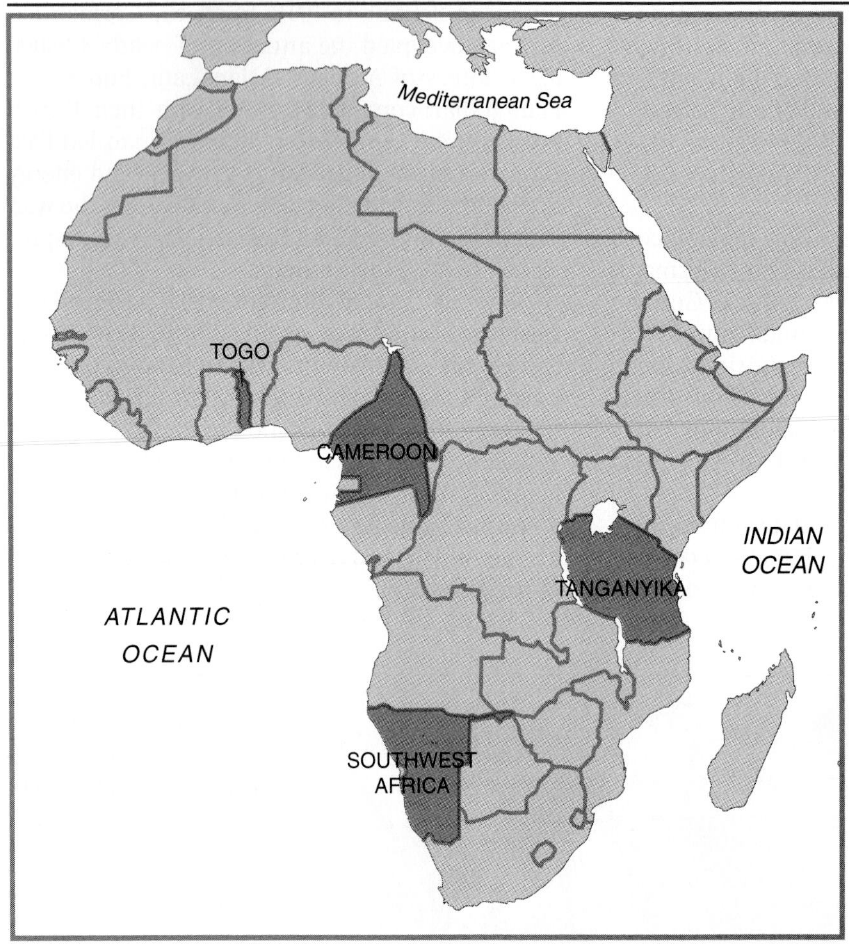

MAP 36.5 ***The African Theater in World War I.*** *Germany had several colonies in Africa. Those in the west were lost soon after the war began, but a stalemate emerged in East Africa until a week after the armistice in Europe. African troops—under the command of the British and French on one side and of the Germans on the other—did most of the fighting. Both sides fought well in the various campaigns, demonstrating that Africans could fight as well as Asians and Europeans.*

For the great majority of Africans, World War I meant little. Significant changes occurred in areas controlled by the Germans, but to the local peoples the war merely meant the exchange of one imperialist power for another. In some of these territories, however, tribal groups rebelled unsuccessfully against the new rulers. While the efforts failed, they foreshadowed uprisings against Western imperialism after 1945.

The Americas

The United States developed into a dominant military and economic power during World War I. The United States government followed the lead of its president, Woodrow Wilson, who advocated a nonaligned stance, even though he personally favored the British and French. Isolation worked until 1917, when unrestricted German submarine warfare helped compel the United States to enter the conflict. Wilson had become convinced that the loss of American lives and ships signaled a call for military action.

The Germans had calculated that the United States might enter the war, but they remained confident of victory before the Americans could make a significant impact. German strategists failed to consider that the United States navy could immediately play a role in helping to defeat the submarine. It became clear to the Germans that their strategy had failed.

The United States began producing vast amounts of war materials and shipping them east. This compelled the Germans to pressure the faltering Russians to sign an agreement on the eastern front. The prospect of large numbers of United States troops on the western front made the timing of a German move vital. By early 1918, United States soldiers were arriving in Europe at the rate of 250,000 a month. These numbers weighed heavily in the fighting and accelerated the eventual German collapse.

The United States suffered little destruction or dislocation because of the war. America's economic might also increased during the war years, and Bernard Baruch, a savvy politician, played a major role in reorganizing American industry for the war effort. Not only did U.S. factories increase their industrial production, but armaments and other industries that supplied the Europeans earned large profits. In addition, the withdrawal of European countries from Latin America and other places opened new financial opportunities for United States merchants.

Latin America was little affected by World War I. Certain commodities like nitrates from Chile were traded to the combatants, spurring economic production throughout the country. Brazil, Cuba, Costa Rica, Guatemala, Haiti, Honduras, Nicaragua, and Panama declared war for political advantage and to maintain their alliances with the United States. Five others broke off diplomatic relations with the Germans, and other states remained neutral.

Canada experienced great changes from its active participation in World War I. Although the country was not physically harmed by the war, well over a half-million Canadians served, including 24,000 in the British air services and another 8,000 in the navy. Canadians suffered more killed than the U.S., and the high conscription rate heightened intra-Canadian tensions among the English and French Canadians, leading to draft riots in Quebec. Canada's prime minister insisted on and won from Britain Canadian control of the Canadian units stationed in Europe, as well as a Canadian role in wartime and peacetime issues. Indeed, Canadian nationalism grew significantly during the war and laid the foundation for an autonomous Canada.

The Canadian economy experienced major growth during the war and became more closely tied to the United States economy. Prior to the war's outbreak, Canada seemed on the verge of an economic depression. Demand created by Europe's wartime needs, however, quickly ended the downturn. Prices rose and Canada's industries developed robustly. New York City gradually replaced London as the financial center for Canadian industrialists, and United States investors significantly increased their holdings in Canada.

World War I brought the United States increased economic prosperity and growing dominance of the Americas. Before the war, the British had played the dominant financial role in Latin America and Canada. During and after the war, British investment sharply declined, while United States economic influence mushroomed.

The Germans had briefly negotiated with the Mexican government to attack the United States. In return, the Germans promised to support a return of parts of the southwestern United States to Mexico. The diplomatic effort produced no results except a heightening of tensions between the Mexican and U.S. governments. Raids by Pancho Villa across the Mexican border into the United States brought a U.S. military response that quieted the border region.

THE PARIS PEACE CONFERENCE AND THE TREATY OF VERSAILLES

The forces that haunted the outbreak of the war—nationalism, imperialism, and revolution—were in evidence at the Paris Peace Conference during the first half of 1919. During the negotiations, delegates met at many sites around Paris, and the final major settlement was signed at Versailles Palace outside Paris. All of the countries had paid a great price in lives and material; many victorious elected governments heeded their constituents' demands for revenge and compensation. Few cool-headed diplomats presided in these talks.

War Aims

France sought severe punishment of Germany and won acceptance of many of its aims, including a treaty clause blaming the war on Germany. The German army was to be severely reduced, parts of prewar Germany were to be demilitarized, and large war reparations were demanded. Having suffered hundreds of thousands of casualties and massive destruction in its territory, the French government insisted that Germany be defanged and punished. Unfortunately for French long-term interests, the domestic industrial base of Germany had been little affected by the war, nor was it reduced by the treaty.

Britain was less eager to punish Germany severely, but it also insisted on certain restraints on German power and an indemnity to help pay for the war costs. Lloyd George had been reelected

FIGURE 36.9 *Delegates to the Paris Peace Conference, 1919. The settlement of World War I affected many parts of the world. Among these delegates from Southwest Asian and African lands is Prince Feisal (front, center), a representative of the Arabs. Behind him and to the viewer's right is T. E. Lawrence, "Lawrence of Arabia." Except for Arabia, most of Southwest Asia and Africa remained under imperialist control.* Trustees of the Imperial War Museum.

prime minister on the promise of "squeezing the German lemon until its pips squeaked." An amusing word play, this slogan reflected a vengeful attitude that tainted the British negotiating position.

To many diplomats, U.S. leaders appeared to be "honest brokers" because they desired no territorial gains. They also led the most powerful state surviving the war, and their voices received a hearing. Most delegates listened favorably to President Wilson of the United States, who restated his three broad goals as the basis of a peace settlement. First, he hoped to eliminate trade barriers, interference with freedom of the seas, imperialist tensions, arms races, and secret diplomacy. Second, Wilson desired to settle European problems relating to territorial integrity, national boundaries, and nationalism. Finally, Wilson believed that an international assembly should be formed to preserve the peace won at Paris. The treaty called for the United States and the other victors to give up their own imperialist domains, but the victors' justice unmasked naked power politics.

Peace Settlements

Under the Treaty of Versailles, imperialistic control of overseas colonies simply passed from one state to another. The territories gained from Germany were mandated to the various winners. Japan got German concessions in China and Micronesia. Other Pacific islands went to Australia and New Zealand, while Germany's possessions in Africa were parceled out to a variety of states.

Europe experienced the greatest change in terms of national self-determination. Poland was re-created after more than a century. Yugoslavia was amalgamated from Serbia and other lands and peoples in southeastern Europe. Some of these groups, like the Croats and Slovenes, feared Serbian domination but were pressed into accepting the new union. Czechoslovakia was formed from territories where Czechs and Slovaks predominated, although certain German-speaking peoples also lived there. A whole string of Eastern European countries came into existence or reemerged, including Latvia, Lithuania, Estonia, Hungary, and Romania. They were supported by the war victors, forming a kind of buffer between Soviet Russia and Central Europe.

Germans felt betrayed by the treaty they were forced to accept. They were prepared to sign agreements based on Wilson's three broad proposals for peace but resented the large indemnity and the war-guilt clause. Wilhelm II and hundreds of German officers were to be tried for offenses, including war crimes. Germans disliked the fact that they were forced to withdraw to the eastern bank of the Rhine River, and they hated the loss of territory to France, Belgium, Czechoslovakia, and Poland. Germany also had to surrender the bulk of its navy, including submarines, and it had to turn over most of its machine guns, artillery, air force, and motorized transport.

The Weimar Republic leaders who had been forced by the victors to accept the peace accord became the objects of popular hatred for the betrayal. Ultranationalist groups in Germany called for a repudiation of the Versailles Treaty. When Adolf Hitler gained power in 1933, he set about scrapping the treaty's provisions and putting the German people back to work. These acts restored German pride, and Hitler benefited from German nationalism.

The League of Nations

The League of Nations suffered from the nationalist and imperialist ambitions of its most powerful members. The failure of the United States government to ratify the treaties ending the war and thereby to accept the League of Nations as an international organization undermined the League's effectiveness.

The Japanese were allocated a prominent seat in the League of Nations. At the Paris Peace Conference, however, the Japanese failed to insert in the League of Nations Covenant a racial equality clause stating that all races are equal. Australians and Americans blocked the effort, and the racist sentiment behind the objection deeply offended the Japanese. Ironically, Japan's control of the Pacific islands captured from the Germans was predicated upon the racist idea that these Pacific islanders could not govern themselves. The Japanese did not seem to have minded this racist double standard.

In the two decades following the end of World War I, the League of Nations proved unable to deal with crises. Japanese aggression in Manchuria and Italian aggression in Ethiopia in the 1930s received condemnation by the League, but these diplomatic setbacks did not deter either country. In 1931, Japanese soldiers staged a violent incident, blaming it on the Chinese and using it as a pretext to conquer Manchuria. A League commission found that the Japanese had initiated the action and blamed them for the conquest of Manchuria. Similarly, Italy's conquest of Ethiopia roused the League's ire, but its condemnation had no real practical effect. Because of these and other failures, the League could not prevent the disintegration of international diplomacy and the outbreak of World War II.

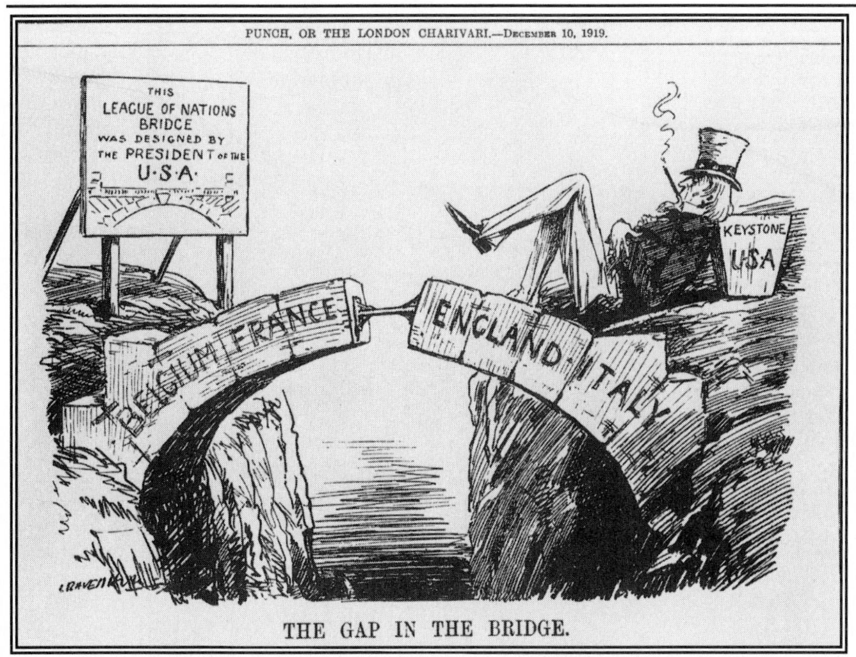

FIGURE 36.10 ***U.S. Reluctance Hampers the League of Nations.*** *This British cartoon conveys the Allies' frustration when the United States opted out of the League of Nations, an organization developed by President Woodrow Wilson. Uncle Sam, looking a bit like Wilson, lazes on the keystone block for the bridge. U.S. reluctance to honor its president's commitment to the League undermined the international organization.* Library of Congress.

EUROPE	ASIA	AFRICA	AMERICAS
Stalemate on western front, mid-1914–early 1918	Japan wins German colonies in China and Pacific, mid-1914–1915	Allied campaigns in west and southwest, late 1914–mid-1915	Unrestricted submarine warfare in Atlantic, 1917–1918
Stalemate on eastern front, mid-1915–mid-1918	Campaign in Gallipoli, mid-1915–mid-1916	Stalemate in East Africa, mid-1915–early 1919	
Paris Peace Conference, 1919	Campaign in Jordan, Palestine, and Arabia, early 1917–late 1918		
	Japanese navy patrols Mediterranean, late 1917–1918		

1914

- Assassination of Francis Ferdinand, June 1914
- Russia mobilizes, July 1914
- Battle of Langemark, Oct. 1914

1915

- Italy joins Allies, spring 1915

1916

- Easter uprising in Ireland, Apr. 1916
- Lloyd George appointed Prime Minister, Dec. 1916

1917

- Romanov dynasty collapses, Mar. 1917
- U.S. enters the war, Apr. 1917
- Bolsheviks take power, Nov. 1917

1918

- President Wilson's 14 Points, Jan. 1918
- Treaty of Brest-Litovsk, Mar. 1918
- Wilfred Owen dies, Nov. 4, 1918
- Armistice, Nov. 11, 1918

1919

SUMMARY

1. Nationalism, imperialism, revolution, and alliance systems combined to create the conditions favorable for war in 1914.

2. Germany rose in 1871, created an overseas empire, and competed with the British in a naval armament race. To protect itself from a "vengeful" France, the Germans worked out the Triple Alliance with the Austro-Hungarian Empire and Italy.

3. The German treaty system and the permitting of Russia to drift away from an alliance helped push the Russians and French into a military agreement that complicated Germany's strategic problems.

4. Germany's naval armament policy caused the British to reconsider their strategic priorities. Alliances with the Japanese, French, and Russians were formed between 1902 and 1907, permitting the British to pull home elements of their navy.

5. War broke out after the assassination of Archduke Francis Ferdinand, heir to the Austro-Hungarian throne. The Germans backed their Austro-Hungarian ally, while the French supported the Russians and the Serbs. Soon, various threats and maneuvers broke into armed conflict, and, after some spectacular shifting of human beings and arms, a deadly stalemate grew into a war of attrition.

6. Each warring state became highly centralized. The unprecedented social control and war costs created severe political tensions. Russia collapsed in 1917, and Germany and her allies fell in the second half of 1918.

7. The home fronts in Europe and the Americas saw many women taking industrial jobs. Some of these women spearheaded strikes in France and Germany. Many people under colonial rule also came to France to replace the human losses in the economy.

8. Warfare also took place in Asia, the Pacific, and Africa, with the Germans losing territory while its enemies expanded their control of the new lands. The Ottoman Empire collapsed, and the Japanese Empire expanded.

9. Canada entered the war in 1914, and the United States and parts of Latin America entered three years later. With the decline of European power, the United States became dominant in Latin America and influential in Canada.

10. The great human and material losses incurred in the war heightened national desires for revenge by the winners. These pressures affected the powers who gathered in Paris during the first half of 1919.

11. The Versailles Treaty awarded German and Ottoman lands to the victors and redrew Europe's map to give the Poles, Serbs, Czechs, Slovaks, and Baltic peoples independence. The loss of territory and German-speaking peoples to other states angered many Germans and helped fuel postwar resentments.

12. A League of Nations was created, but the international organization did not easily function in a time of heightened nationalism. The absence of the United States from the organization also severely crippled it. The Japanese deeply resented the lack of a racial equality clause in the League Covenant.

SUGGESTED READINGS

Fischer, Fritz. *War of Illusions.* New York: Norton, 1975. A summation of a revisionist interpretation, blaming World War I's outbreak on the Germans.

Keegan, John. *A History of Warfare.* New York: Knopf, 1993. A general history with an excellent overview of the situation in Europe before and during World War I.

Lincoln, W. Bruce. *Passage through Armageddon.* Oxford, Eng.: Oxford University Press, 1986. An account of Russia during World War I.

Sholokov, Mikhail. *And Quiet Flows the Don.* New York: Random House, 1966. A major war novel.

Woollacott, Angela. *On Her Their Lives Depended.* Berkeley: University of California Press, 1994. A significant treatment of women in the British munitions industry during World War I.

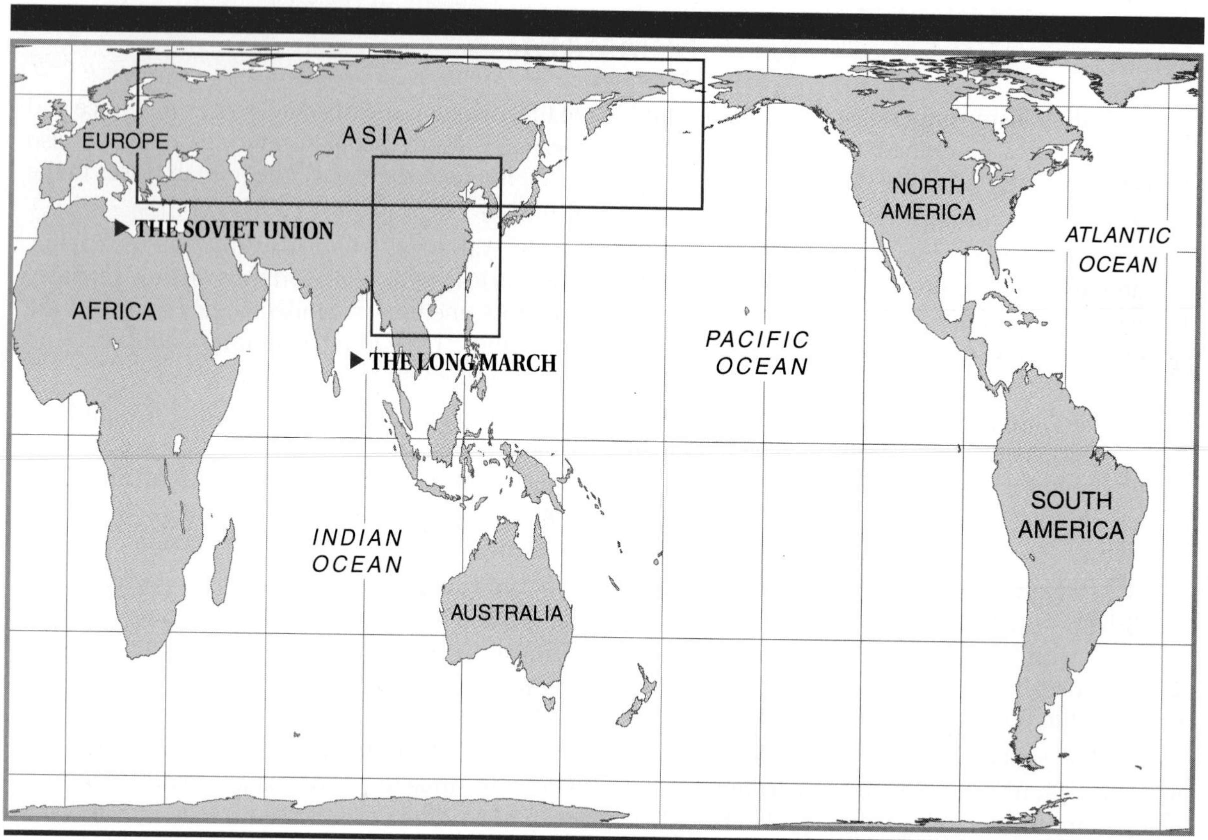

EUROPE

ASIA

NORTH AMERICA

ATLANTIC OCEAN

▶ THE SOVIET UNION

AFRICA

PACIFIC OCEAN

▶ THE LONG MARCH

SOUTH AMERICA

INDIAN OCEAN

AUSTRALIA

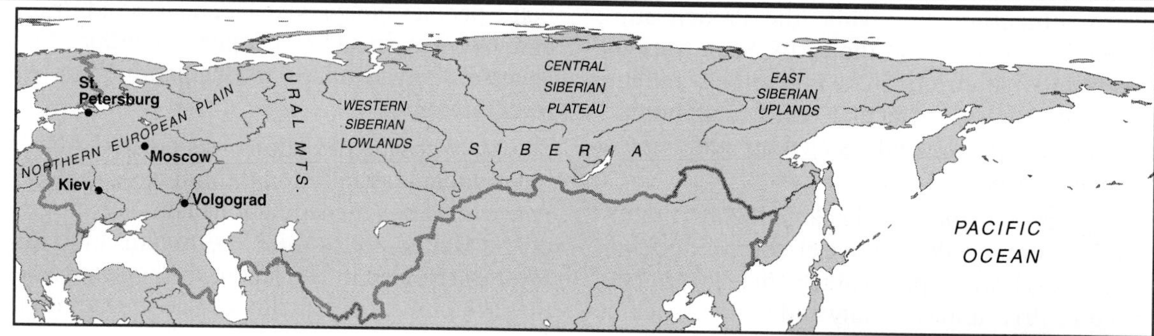

▶ **THE SOVIET UNION**

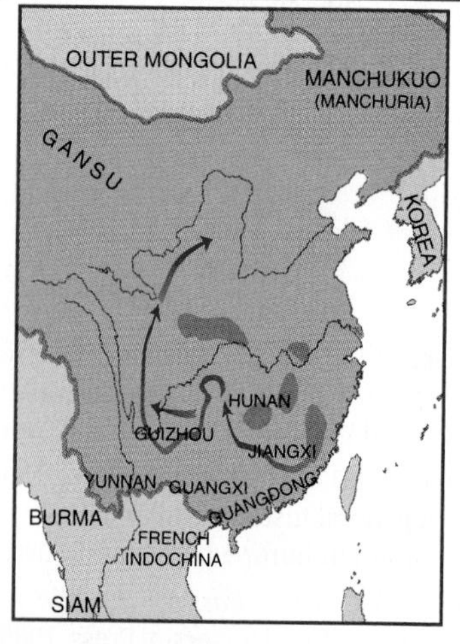

▶ **THE LONG MARCH**

CHAPTER 37

Transformation of Russia and China

1905–1989

Elena stared at her charred house in the smoldering ruins of her Russian village. Only a month before, the bountiful harvest had been gathered, and she and her husband had been happy. Their debts had been paid, and they could afford a milk cow. Then the local Communist Party leader came along with a police official, saying something about moving onto a state collective farm. Yuri, her husband, and most of the others argued against Stalin's directive. Last night, they were taken away, and a scuffle between the Red Guards and the village men had caused the fires. Snow fell. What was she to do?

The tragedy of this Russian village was repeated often during the Stalinist revolution. Russians and Chinese experienced revolutions that profoundly transformed their societies. Both imperial systems collapsed because they could not adapt to the challenges of industrialization and political modernity.

UNREST AND TRANSFORMATION IN RUSSIA AND THE SOVIET UNION

War and revolution became linked processes in twentieth-century Russia. The Russo-Japanese War (1904–1905) and World War I (1914–1918) fomented massive unrest that ultimately triggered the collapse of the tsarist system in 1917. Members of the Russian Bolshevik Party under the leadership of Vladimir Lenin seized power and had to fight a civil war while creating a revolutionary government. In 1941, Soviet Russia was attacked by Nazi Germany and managed to defeat the Germans, exporting revolution to Eastern Europe during and after World War II (1937–1945). Finally, the Cold War between Soviet-bloc and U.S.-allied countries led to Soviet-style revolutions in additional countries, ending in 1989, when the Soviet Empire collapsed.

Russian Unrest, 1905–1917

The tsarist system's collapse in 1917 was precipitated by many factors, not the least of which was the inflexibility of Tsar Nicholas II (reign dates 1894–1917). Serious unrest erupted in 1905, while Russia was losing the Russo-Japanese War. People lost enthusiasm for the expensive and distant war, industrial workers longed for better working conditions, and peasants desired tax relief and more land to farm. These elements unleashed a decade of unrest and trouble for the tsar.

The massive unrest of 1905 nearly toppled the government but brought little political change. Upheaval began when a large number of unarmed petitioners met armed resistance by the government. A few people were killed at the event known as Bloody Sunday in January 1905, and the attack on peaceful subjects ignited strikes and demonstrations across the empire. Recent military defeats at the hands of the Japanese had already weakened the state's popular support. Although Nicholas finally agreed to peace talks with the Japanese and a settlement a few months later, Russia's people demanded change at home. Some wished to end the monarchy, and most wanted representative government.

FIGURE 37.1 ***Russian Women Protesters.*** *This photograph, taken in Petrograd in March 1917, shows hundreds of women marching for better living conditions, specifically for increased rations. Women took active roles in the political events of 1917; later, in the winter of 1918, riots by women helped bring about the collapse of the tsarist system.* VA/Sovfoto.

MAP 37.1 *Territories Lost by the Russian Empire in 1917–1918.* *The defeat of the Russian army in 1918 by the Germans resulted in the Treaty of Brest-Litovsk. Territories lost to the Germans were a significant part of European Russia, including parts of Poland, Lithuania, Latvia, Estonia, Bessarabia, Byelo-Russia, and portions of the Ukraine. These lands were heavily populated and productive for the Russian economy.*

Peace failed to stave off a confrontation between the tsar and his people, but it allowed army units in Asia to be called back to deal with the civil unrest. In October 1905, a workers' strike ignited a general work stoppage and demonstrations by laborers, students, and government officials. Within a few days, most of the empire lay idle, and the tsar contemplated his reaction. Brief consideration of a military dictatorship to drown the unrest in blood gave way to a compromise that promised an elected legislature coupled with guarantees of personal liberties. The government's offer persuaded the moderates of the opposition to compromise, and they urged the strikers to return to work. Hardliners among the workers fought back but succumbed to the massive force of the state. Workers' administrative councils, ***soviets***, led the antistate effort.

Nicholas's refusal to surrender his dominant position in the system portended trouble. It took three elections before a legislature able to work with the tsar could be seated. Worker unrest resumed in 1911 and continued to plague Nicholas until the outbreak of World War I in 1914.

Wartime stresses finally unraveled the tsarist system. The initial patriotic euphoria of the mobilization evaporated with the serious defeats of Russian forces in 1914 and 1915. Nicholas foolishly assumed direct command of the Russian army, leaving the home front in the hands of Tsarina Alexandra, who was an inept administrator. In addition, she had been born in Germany, an enemy state of Russia, and the ensuing mismanagement eroded the government's remaining credibility, causing one legislator to question whether her actions reflected stupidity or treason. The hard winter of 1916–1917 and the breakdown of the transport system left a bread shortage in the capital, and a riot by irate women mushroomed into a massive protest against the tsarist system. When the government lost control of its metropolitan garrison, Nicholas abdicated and the Romanov Dynasty ended.

The next several months were a time of anarchy as the police and other agencies of control vanished. Two quasi-governmental agencies attempted to step into the power vacuum. Legislators formed the Provisional Government, which claimed to rule Russia until an elected government could be seated. A *soviet* modeled on the one of 1905 reappeared in the capital, Petrograd, and asserted that it acted in the interests of the workers and soldiers, who were mostly peasants. The Petrograd Soviet promised to support the Provisional Government, so long as the workers and soldiers received fair treatment. By August 1917, this system of dual government furthered the breakdown of authority, causing Alexander Kerensky (1881–1970), a socialist leader of the Provisional Government, to seek dictatorial power. Kerensky failed, opening the way for others to seize power.

Russia's rapid collapse had surprised everyone, including Vladimir Lenin (1870–1924), a Marxist living in exile. Lenin plotted his return to Russia upon learning of the government's demise, and he persuaded the Germans to permit him and his party to travel across Germany to Sweden. The Germans appreciated Lenin's talent for fomenting unrest, which weakened the Provisional Government. Upon arriving in Russia in April 1917, Lenin gave a speech to his Marxist supporters, known as the **Bolsheviks** (majority group). Much to the surprise of his old comrades, Lenin favored the immediate overthrow of the Provisional Government, an end to Russia's participation in World War I, the granting of seized land to the peasants, and adequate bread supplies for the cities. These proposals became central issues for the Bolsheviks, permitting them to profit from the growing peace sentiments, peasant unrest, and anarchical conditions. The Bolshevik Party swelled in size to become a major player in Russian politics. By September, majorities supported the Bolsheviks in the *soviets* of the Russian cities.

For Lenin and other Bolshevik leaders, the central question was when to seize power. If the attempt came too early, the opposition forces might easily crush the revolutionaries; if the takeover came too late, the revolutionary situation might not sustain a Bolshevik government. In September, Lenin opted for immediate power, but his cohorts refused. After weeks of acrimonious debate, Lenin's view prevailed. On November 7, 1917, the Bolsheviks staged a coup d'état and took power.

The Bolshevik Revolution, 1917–1924

The Bolshevik Revolution transformed Russia's society, economy, and government in the midst of a terrible civil war. Much of the Bolshevik effort centered on the destruction of the tsarist socio-political-economic system and on the building of a workers' state. As counterrevolutionary groups amassed military forces, the Bolshevik government organized an army of workers for self-defense.

DESTRUCTION OF THE TSARIST SYSTEM. Among the Bolsheviks' earliest acts was the elimination or suppression of the political and economic elite. Although most aristocrats fled Russia during 1917, some remained behind. Many lost their remaining status when the Bolsheviks abolished the system of social ranks developed by Peter the Great. Some were arrested and perished in Soviet ***gulags***,[1] labor camps in Siberia and northern Russia. During the civil war, fearing that the former tsar and his family might be captured by the anti-Bolsheviks, Lenin ordered the royal family's execution. Members of the middle class who enjoyed some social prominence and many clerics of the Russian Orthodox Church found themselves in the *gulags* or were shot as suspected counterrevolutionaries. Monasteries and most churches were closed or confiscated for state use. Indeed, the Bolsheviks openly avowed atheism and attacked religious beliefs of all kinds as supporting the capitalist status quo.

[1] ***gulags:*** GOO lahgs

FIGURE 37.2 ***Lenin Speaking at May Day Rally.*** *Lenin played a key role in overturning Russia's tsarist government in October 1917. In a speech made shortly after his return to Russia in 1917, Lenin laid the foundation for Bolshevik power; later addresses, such as this 1918 May Day speech, furthered the establishment of socialism. During Stalin's regime, photographs were doctored to remove people who had fallen out of political favor. Despite Lenin's criticism of Stalin, photos of Lenin were also altered to include Stalin at his side.*
Culver Pictures.

Some workers and a few peasants joined the new government, which proclaimed itself a Marxist "dictatorship of the proletariat." Because the Bolsheviks had little or no administrative experience before November 7, 1917, they retained some tsarist officials. These, however, were supervised and controlled by Bolshevik managers. Similarly, a dire need for experienced army officers forced the new regime to grant tsarist officers army commands. Paired with each of these commanders was a party official who had the power to execute those suspected of being traitors.

One problem for the Bolsheviks concerned national elections scheduled for late November 1917. After heated discussion, elections were held, and the Bolsheviks won somewhat less than 40 percent of the vote. Later, the National Assembly held a single meeting, which was terminated by the Bolsheviks.

Protection of the Bolshevik state fell to the **Cheka**, a police force that grew to hundreds of thousands of members and undertook such responsibilities as guarding the *gulags* and frontiers. A policy of state terror instituted in September 1918 afforded the Cheka great power over the people of Russia.

The state increased enormously in size and scope during the Bolshevik Revolution. Political ministers were renamed commissars, and they gradually took charge of foreign affairs, defense,

FIGURE 37.3 ***Women Being Sent to Siberia.*** *Imprisoned by the tsarist regime, the women in this 1905 photo are en route to Siberia. The Bolshevik government continued to use Siberia as a vast prison camp. Conditions deteriorated and larger numbers of women inmates were dispatched to Siberia under the Bolsheviks.* Ullstein Bilderdienst.

and the arts. During the civil war, survival of the state necessitated an extreme form of centralized rule. The **Politburo** (political bureau) became the command center of the Bolshevik Party, numbering a half-dozen of the top party leadership, who handled daily matters. The **Orgburo** (organization bureau) handled administrative matters concerning the state apparatus, and the **Party Secretariat** dealt with organizational issues relating to the Bolshevik Party. When Soviet Russia's top administrator, Jacob Sverdlov, died during the swine flu epidemic of 1919, Josef Stalin (1879–1953) succeeded him and began to amass influence in the party and state.

CIVIL WAR AND LEADERSHIP. After coming to power, the Bolsheviks opened peace talks with German military commanders. Directing the Soviet effort were Lenin and Leon Trotsky (1877–1940), Commissar of Foreign Affairs. Because they had an extremely weak hand, the Bolsheviks realized that they had to give up land for peace, and they decided to delay negotiations, hoping that the German proletariat would topple the German government. A twelve-day German advance had threatened the capital and the revolution. Finally, the Treaty of Brest-Litovsk (March 1918) was negotiated and presented to Bolshevik leaders; some denounced the document, which surrendered large parts of Russia's land and resources. Nonetheless, Lenin convinced a majority of party leaders to ratify the treaty.

Although the Treaty of Brest-Litovsk saved the Bolsheviks, it helped precipitate a tragic civil war. The Soviet government surrendered to the Germans more than 2 million square kilometers of land that housed 62 million people and produced a third of Russia's crops. In addition, the Soviets lost 80 percent of their sugar refineries, 73 percent of their iron mines, and 75 percent of their coal fields. One socialist faction that formerly had supported the Bolsheviks turned against them, and many opponents began to take up arms against Lenin and his party.

The Bolsheviks fought against two major groups during the Russian Civil War (1918–1921). One opponent, the Whites, was a diverse set of military commanders and their armies, representing the aristocrats and some wealthy people. The other contending group, sometimes called the Greens, included socialists and democrats, who agreed that the land should be divided among the peasants and that there should be peace. They opposed the Bolshevik refusal to share power and the dissolution of the National Assembly. Fighting between the Bolsheviks (Reds) and Greens broke out in

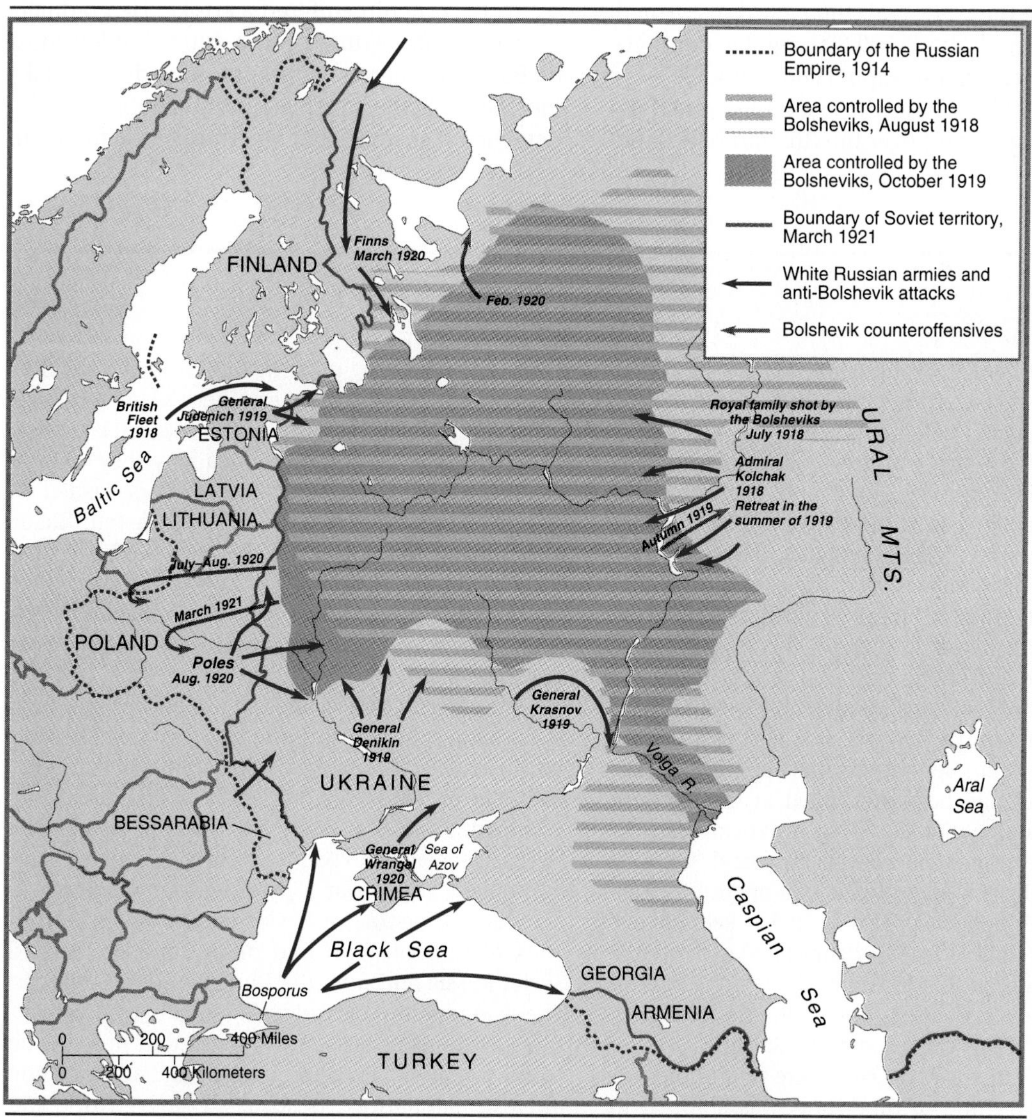

MAP 37.2 ***The Russian Civil War.*** *The Bolsheviks fought a civil war with their opponents between 1918 and 1921. During that period, the Bolsheviks lost and regained much land, many times. By the end of the civil war, however, the Bolsheviks had won back most territory lost at Brest-Litovsk. Only Poland, Latvia, Estonia, and Lithuania remained independent of Russian control.*

mid-1918 and continued for months. The Green forces collapsed after a White commander seized their political capital and their leadership. Thereafter, the civil war became a contest between the Whites and Reds. Although relatively small armies fought one another, civil war raged across Russia, claiming 7 million lives.

The Red Army was built by the Bolsheviks. Trotsky became the Commissar of Defense in 1918, traveling from front to front in an armored train. On one occasion, after a Red Army unit ran from battle, he ordered every tenth soldier shot for desertion. By the war's end, the victorious armed forces numbered about 500,000 regular combatants and several million support personnel.

Bolshevik victory was the result of several factors, including control over the Russian heartland and industry, nationalism, and the disunity of their opponents. Domination of central Russia meant an integrated transportation network, command of vital factories and supplies, and an easily defended territory. At the same time, foreign assistance (by fourteen countries) to the anticommunist forces permitted the Bolsheviks to stoke Russian nationalism. Patriotic feelings and Cheka terror silenced internal opponents, bringing cohesiveness to the war effort. By early 1921, much of the former tsarist empire had been reclaimed by the Soviet state.

In 1922, Lenin suffered a stroke. He gradually recovered and resumed some duties but left most affairs in the hands of others, including Trotsky and Stalin. Stalin's ruthless style troubled Lenin. Just when it seemed that Stalin might be forced to

UNDER THE LENS

U.S.–Soviet Relations, 1918–1922

The onset of U.S.–Soviet relations was marked by hostility and humanitarianism, elements that characterized the two countries' ties in the twentieth century. The United States intervened against the Bolsheviks in the Russian Civil War (1918–1921) and also played a major role in providing famine relief in the aftermath of that great conflict. Many of America's allies wished to see the radical Bolsheviks lose the civil war, and Japan wanted control of Siberia.

In 1918, U.S. soldiers found themselves in northern Russia late in World War I, as a part of an Allied action. They were sent to secure supplies of war materials that had been stockpiled at the ports of Murmansk and Archangel. This American expeditionary force numbered several thousand soldiers, serving with British soldiers in a joint operation. Certain American politicians also wished to keep an eye on the Soviet forces to see how they fared in the fierce civil war raging in Russia. Many U.S. troops had no idea why they had been sent to Russia, and they refused orders to fight against the Bolsheviks. After much confusion, the Americans were sent home.

A second group of Americans was shipped to Siberia in 1918; this time, they were to keep an eye on the Japanese, as well as the Soviets. Japan claimed that its forces were protecting civilians who were caught up in the civil war, but they really coveted Siberia's land and mineral wealth. Again, the American soldiers had no idea why they were in Siberia. Japanese soldiers clashed on several occasions with the Bolsheviks before finally withdrawing. Support given the anti-Bolshevik Russians by the Allies afforded the Bolsheviks the chance to use nationalism against their foes, who were derisively called "puppets of foreign imperialists." That slogan helped fuel the Bolshevik victory.

After the civil war ended, it rapidly became clear to Soviet authorities and international relief organization leaders that widespread famine stalked Russia. Calls for relief went out, and the American Relief Administration, a private organization headed by Herbert Hoover, who had performed a similar operation during World War I, provided significant aid to the starving people of Soviet Russia. By 1922, millions of tons of grain and other supplies reached Soviet Russia and were distributed with few hitches. The cooperation between Americans and Soviets saved millions of lives and showed that much good could result when both countries had common interests. Similar results occurred during World War II, when the United States supplied hundreds of thousand of trucks and gasoline to the beleaguered Soviet armies.

return some of his considerable power, Lenin suffered a new series of strokes and died in early 1924. Scientists preserved Lenin's body, which was displayed for decades as a symbol of the Bolshevik Revolution.

ECONOMIC CONTROL AND EXPERIMENTATION. Soon after taking power, the Bolsheviks had commandeered the financial institutions, key industries, and transportation system. In certain factories, the Bolsheviks attempted worker-management programs by replacing the owners and managers with laborers. These utopian efforts lasted until a decline in factory output compelled their abandonment. During the civil war, regime survival demanded an extreme form of state control of factories. Workers were given production quotas and paid by the item, a policy they hated. After the civil war's end in 1921, strikes forced the policy's abandonment.

Agricultural production declined during the Bolshevik Revolution. Keeping their campaign promise of granting land to the peasants, the Bolsheviks decreed that lands seized by the peasants should remain in their hands. This ensured peasant support for the Bolsheviks during the civil war, because the Whites demanded that these lands be returned to the former landowners. On the other hand, the Bolsheviks seized grain from peasants during the civil war. This policy was partly dictated by declining grain supplies in cities, which were strongholds of the Bolsheviks. Armed detachments of workers fanned out into the countryside to seize grain, and these desperate measures yielded enough to feed the urban folk. The oppressive policies, however, angered the peasants, some of whom retaliated by planting less grain in succeeding years. The actions exacerbated the famine of the early 1920s. In 1921, the civil war ended and peasant uprisings compelled the state to relax its control of agriculture.

The peacetime period from 1921 to 1929 was characterized by the **New Economic Policy**, relaxation measures taken by the Bolsheviks to permit economic recovery from the ravages of warfare. Control over some factories ended, workers' wages increased, and peasants regained control of production. By 1927, most economic measures showed a return to the production levels of 1913, the last full year before World War I. The complete transformation of agriculture and industry came with the ascendancy of Stalin in 1929.

The Bolsheviks finished the destruction of the tsarist system and its social support groups. They reshaped the economy and built a modern state in the midst of a civil war. In the process, they sowed the seeds of a new revolution, one that completed the transformation of Russian life.

The Stalinist Revolution and Its Aftermath, 1924–1953

The second revolution in the Soviet Union lasted from 1924 to 1941, setting the foundation for Soviet society until 1991. Josef Stalin's shadow loomed over Soviet Russia and world affairs for much of the twentieth century. He built a powerful state by industrializing, organizing the peasants, and fashioning a massive state apparatus. By 1941, Russia was the second most powerful state in Europe after Germany, and, by 1945, it was the second most powerful government in the world after the United States. Stalin's programs and failures cost tens of millions of lives. Indeed, he may have been responsible for more deaths than any other human being.

STALIN'S PERSONAL RULE. Between 1924 and 1929, Stalin struggled for power against top Leninists, like Trotsky. Although he was the least charismatic among Lenin's subordinates, Stalin held a great deal of power in the Politburo, the Orgburo, and the Party Secretariat. In each body, he built a faction of loyal supporters and with shrewd political maneuvering emerged triumphant in 1929 from the leadership struggle.

The Stalinists consolidated their hold on the party, although a leadership crisis developed in 1934, when a group of top Stalinists attempted to curb their leader. Later that year and until 1939, Stalin unleashed a terror against the party and other elite groups. The instrument of repression was the NKVD, a successor to the Cheka. Ruling elite members lost their lives or went to the *gulags*. The army, for example, saw the death or imprisonment of most of its top officers. As the elite echelon disappeared, a new group advanced and sometimes "claimed" the residences and even wives of the former elite.

Stalin's personal control of Soviet Russia dramatically increased. In fact, the dictatorship of the proletariat evolved from party dictatorship under Lenin to a personal dictatorship under Stalin.

IN THEIR OWN WORDS

Remembering the Stalinist 1930s

Fear stalked Soviet Russia in the 1930s. Josef Stalin collectivized agriculture, killing millions, and turned against Communist Party members and intellectuals, terrorizing them into silence. Anna Akhmatova (1889–1966) had been a published poet since 1914, writing lyric poems that charmed her readers. Marxist critics, however, disparaged her as a vestige of the past. She remained silent until 1936, when she resumed writing.

How was one to compose poems free from Stalin's security police? Her son and husband had been arrested and jailed. With a few trusted friends, Akhmatova memorized *Requiem*, her poetic portrait of the 1930s in the spirit of Dante's *Inferno*, a poetic journey into hell. She once wrote that if alive, the "late Dante would have created a tenth circle of hell." The prose-like "Instead of a Foreword," written in 1957 after much of the rest of *Requiem*, aptly sets the hellish scene.

> In the terrible years of the Ezhov terror [mid-1930s], I spent seventeen months in the prison lines in Leningrad. Once someone "identified" me. Then a blue-lipped woman standing behind me, who had, of course, never heard my name, came to from the torpor characteristic of us all and asked me in a whisper (everyone spoke in whispers there), "But can you describe this?"
>
> And I said, "I can."
>
> Then something like a smile slipped across what had once been her face.

Earlier, in 1940, Anna Akhmatova had written the poem "Dedication," which she later published with "Instead of a Foreword" to form a powerful evocation of the Stalinist terror.

> Before this woe mountains bend down,
> The great river does not flow,
> But strong are the prison bolts,
> And beyond them are the "convicts' holes"
> And mortal anguish.
> For someone there blows a fresh wind,
> For someone a sunset luxuriates,
> We do not know, we are the same everywhere,
> We hear just the fateful gnashing of keys
> And the soldiers' heavy tread.
> We would rise as if for early mass,
> Walk through the capital turned savage,
> Meet there, more breathless than the dead,
> The sun is lower and the Neva more misty,
> But hope still sings in the distance
> The sentence . . . And immediately the tears pour,
> She's already separated from everyone,
> As if the life had been painfully torn from her heart,
> But she walks . . . Staggers . . . Alone . . .
> Where are now the involuntary friends
> Of my two hellish years?
> What appears to them in the Siberian blizzard,
> What seems visible to them in the lunar circle?
> To them I send my farewell greetings . . .

Stalin's domination of the Soviet Union continued until 1953, assuming the form of a personal bureaucracy that operated outside the regular party and state channels, and only people he personally trusted worked for him there.

STALIN'S REVOLUTION: COLLECTIVIZATION AND INDUSTRIALIZATION. According to the Marxist perspective, socialism could not be achieved until Russia had been fully industrialized. Control of the peasants became a top state priority, and the effort to subdue them merged with the harnessing of agriculture to industry. For centuries, governments of Russia feared the peasants, who constituted well over half of the population. Peasant anger had been triggered by Soviet blundering and policies favoring cities over the countryside in the 1920s. Marxists often had focused their attention on the industrial working class of the cities and treated the peasants like nascent capitalists, the enemy.

As the New Economic Policy began to break down in the mid- to late 1920s, peasants withheld their grain from the markets. Armed detachments again roamed the countryside seeking grain, and force again provoked determined peasant resistance.

The state targeted rich peasants, ***kulaks***,[2] attempting to use the poorer peasants against

[2] ***kulaks:*** KOO lahks

them. When elements of the army and police began to surround peasant villages to force them onto state farms, peasants fought back. Soon, the label *kulak* was applied to anyone opposing collectivization. Peasants died defending their farms; others slaughtered and ate their farm animals rather than permit the state to seize them. Tens of millions of animals perished, and the animal husbandry sector of the Soviet economy did not recover from these losses until the 1950s. Peasant families were split up and parents were sent off to the *gulags*; gangs of homeless children wandered the countryside in search of food and shelter.

By 1934, agriculture had been collectivized at the cost of millions of lives. With control over the peasants and their grain, the state could purchase machinery for the industrial effort, and excessive grain requisitions starved more peasants. The Ukraine was particularly hard hit, and NKVD guards sealed off that area to prevent refugees from escaping. One scholar has estimated that 14 million people died in the human-made famine.

The Stalinist model of industrialization changed Soviet Russia. Heavy industry (like metallurgical plants) dominated the economy, receiving more than 80 percent of state capital. Planners set lofty production goals for five-year plans, and the eventual execution of 90 percent of plant managers sent the message that results were expected. In some areas, trains carrying vital raw materials for manufacturing were hijacked by factory desperados hungry to meet their quotas. *Gulags* became major work centers, their inhabitants erecting factories on and digging canals in inhospitable landscapes.

Cities were transformed during the 1930s as millions of peasants fled the countryside to work in the new factories. Later, however, the state became uneasy about all the free-wandering people, and it issued internal passports regulating movement. Once a worker found a job, the factory provided living quarters and other amenities, such as health care. Change to a new job was limited by the loss of benefits. Within a few years, most laborers in the Soviet Union worked in factories rather than on farms; most lived in cities rather than in the rural areas. The Soviet Union had developed an industrial society by 1936.

The Soviet Union avoided most early fighting in World War II but experienced catastrophic losses, beginning in 1941. Significant fighting began when Nazi Germany invaded in June 1941. Fierce combat occupied the next four years, ending with Nazi Germany's utter defeat and the Soviet occupation of Eastern Europe. More than 30 million Soviets died, and it took years for their ruptured society and economy to recover.

As noted in Chapter 34, industrialization fostered the development of Soviet imperialism. Between 1939 and 1940, the Soviet Union seized

Figure 37.4 ***Sentries for the Soviet State.*** *Collectivization reduced peasants to living at near-starvation levels, and millions of people perished in the ensuing famine. To guard harvests, the government adopted severe measures of repression. These young party members are on the lookout for desperate peasants who try to steal some grain or corn from the state.* Endeavour Group U.K.

FIGURE 37.5 ***Stalin Celebrating the Constitution.*** *In late 1936, the Soviet state presented a constitution to its people. The constitution promised many freedoms, from improved civil rights to a new electoral system. Despite the fanfare organized by Stalin, the mandates of the constitution were never fulfilled, and many Russians continued to die at the hands of the Soviet police or languish in the* gulags. David King Collection.

Latvia, Lithuania, and Estonia, as well as parts of Poland and Finland. After 1943, when Soviet troops counterattacked the Nazi forces and pushed into Eastern Europe, a series of satellite governments there made up a part of the emerging Soviet Empire. The integration of the economies of these states completed the classic imperialist pattern.

STALIN'S CULTURAL INTERESTS AND IMPERATIVES. When the Bolsheviks seized power in 1917, they began suppressing elements of the traditional elite arts, and some artists and writers eagerly supported the effort to create a new culture. The new rulers took charge of the libraries and museums, and Lenin's wife, Nadezhda Krupskaya,[3] took a personal interest in cultural matters. She oversaw, for example, the suppression of the writings of Feodor Dostoyevsky. In addition, important Russian figures, like Peter the Great and Ivan the Terrible, were interpreted in Marxist historical categories or ignored. At the same time, avant-garde poets and painters put their talents to use in service of the new revolutionary state. Over time, however, their cultural visions were censored as examples of bourgeois-decadent art.

Stalin continued some of the policies that devalued traditional art and literature. A key element of Stalin's cultural focus was in the development of **socialist realism**, a movement that stressed culture's ties to socialism. Stalin declared that literature must reflect socialist themes and arts must be more accessible to the common folk.

At the same time, Stalin promoted a revival of interest in Russia's past. A major idea behind this effort was a fear of German Nazism and the need to stress themes of Russian patriotism. One movie, *Alexander Nevsky*, focused on the thirteenth-century warrior who defeated Teutonic knights (Germans) seeking to invade and destroy Russia. The movie portrayed Germans as evil baby killers and the Russians as brave heroes repelling all enemies. The stirring musical score of Sergei Prokofiev[4] underlined the patriotic mood of the film. The titanic struggle of Soviet Russia in World War II also brought appeals to Russian nationalism.

Soviet authors and composers suffered from political persecution in the postwar era. A widespread campaign engulfed Jewish writers in the late 1940s, fomenting an anti-Semitism reminiscent of that in tsarist days. Dmitry Shostakovich[5] and Sergei Prokofiev endured alternate vilification and praise, depending on how the political winds were blowing. On one occasion, Andrei Zhdanov,[6] a top Soviet leader, summoned the two world-famous composers and proceeded to give them lessons on the piano.

[3] **Nadezhda Krupskaya:** nah DEHZ dah KROOP skay ah
[4] **Sergei Prokofiev:** sayr GAY proh KOHF ee ehf
[5] **Dmitry Shostakovich:** DEE mee tree SHAHS tah koh vihch
[6] **Andrei Zhdanov:** AHN dreh ZHDAH nohv

Stalin's Legacy, 1953–1989

Soviet Russia's industrialization, along with its victory over Nazi forces, propelled it to the forefront of global politics. Control of most of Eastern Europe and parts of Central Europe enhanced the Soviet Union's power. At the same time, the Stalinist system boasted a huge bureaucracy and an authoritarian policy that punished dissent. Could the Soviets adapt to the wide-ranging and rapid changes to come?

Stalin died in March 1953, and Nikita Khrushchev[7] (1894–1971) succeeded him and served as the leader of the Soviet Union until 1964. Among Stalin's successors, Khrushchev struggled mightily to dismantle Stalinism's worst features. He opened the *gulags* and released millions of survivors, breaking decisively with the Stalinist terror. Khrushchev promoted writers like Alexander Solzhenitsyn, who criticized Stalinist excesses. In 1956, Khrushchev gave a secret speech laying bare some of the worst features of the terror, hoping thereby to discredit Stalin and Stalinists, many of whom were Khrushchev's opponents. He also attempted a series of ill-conceived economic reforms that failed. A series of foreign policy gaffes further undermined Khrushchev, who fell from power with the dismantling of Stalinism incomplete.

Leonid Brezhnev (1906–1982) succeeded Khrushchev and implemented an era of neo-Stalinist policies. Massive resources accelerated the buildup of the Soviet armed forces, aiming at the projection of Soviet power. On the other hand, Brezhnev helped develop ***detente***, an easing of international tensions through goodwill gestures and negotiated arms-limitation treaties, in the 1970s. The armament buildup, however, severely weakened vital parts of the Soviet health care system. By the early 1980s, the Soviet Union was in serious demographic, economic, and political decline.

Mikhail Gorbachev[8] (b. 1929) came to power in 1985 and presided over the collapse of the Soviet system. Realizing that the Soviet Union could not survive with its aging Stalinist system, Gorbachev attempted to transform the state he inherited. Although a skilled politician who knew when to compromise, Gorbachev lacked the administrative talents and the vision to bring transformative change. He implemented policies of ***glasnost*** (openness and discussion), as well as ***perestroika*** (restructuring). Gorbachev intended to create a more humane communism and use the talents of the Soviet people to renew their system but failed. The beginning of the end came in 1989, when Eastern European states broke free from the Soviet Empire. Two years later, the Soviet Union itself collapsed after a failed coup by elements of the secret police, the army, and the party. Nationalism triumphed over imperialism. Economic collapse left unemployment and suffering in the 1990s.

CHINA'S IMPERIAL COLLAPSE AND THE TRIUMPH OF COMMUNISM

Much of the twentieth century was a time of turmoil for the Chinese people, who suffered from wars, revolutions, famine, and natural disasters. The Qing Empire collapsed in 1912, leaving unrest and political disorder. Warlordism caused havoc for Chinese society for more than a decade, and Japanese troops conquered vast regions. Later, the Chinese communists killed the gentry landlords, condemning millions. Since the late 1970s, however, the material well-being of the Chinese has improved significantly.

Imperial China's Systemic Collapse and Warlordism, 1905–1928

The gentry had long dominated Chinese life. Its position was owed to education, especially to a Confucian-based ideology that stressed hierarchical organization in the family and society. Yet China needed to modernize in order to survive in the intense international rivalries of the early twentieth century. In fact, much of China lay under foreign influence at the turn of the century, and many of its financial assets came under foreign control. To adapt, the Qing Empire decided in 1905 to abolish the imperial examination system, because its Confucian ideology seemed incompatible with the needs of modernity.

The elimination of Confucianism as the state value system brought many consequences. Confucianism supported an agrarian economy and

[7] **Nikita Khrushchev:** nih KEE tah KRUH shahv

[8] **Mikhail Gorbachev:** MEEK hayl GOHR bah shahv

despised the merchant class, retarding industrialization. Young people and women who were devalued in the Confucian system now had fewer restraints on their efforts to improve themselves.

Other Manchu reforms undermined the central government's legitimacy and hastened its collapse. One program directed more local tax monies to the national capital. This angered some provincial authorities, who took advantage of an uprising against the Manchus to secede from the empire. The Manchus also promised to implement a constitutional government, but their ineptness at handling the program spurred Chinese nationalism. Anti-Manchu forces toppled the Qing Dynasty in 1912.

Efforts to reunite China failed in the next decade or so, highlighting the profound nature of the collapse of the imperial system. Twice, ambitious individuals failed to reestablish imperial rule.

The military nature of Chinese politics from 1912 to 1928 has caused scholars to name it the Warlord Period. Militarization of Chinese politics had begun in the mid–nineteenth century. After 1912, however, force became the primary determinant of Chinese politics and was reflected in the phrase "political power grows out of the barrel of a gun." Numerous warlord regimes in various parts of China worsened the living conditions of the Chinese people. Taxes grew very heavy with burdensome special levies. Some warlords demanded that taxes for future years be paid early, and others compelled peasants to grow and harvest opium poppies. Starvation became common, and a famine from 1929 to 1932 took 3 million lives.

Peasant anger seethed in the 1920s and 1930s, fueled by gentry disinterest in traditional practices of promoting welfare policies. Landowners who previously might have aided destitute people had moved to the cities and left management of their estates to people who cursed rather than helped poor folk.

In 1915, a few intellectuals initiated a movement that helped transform the traditional elite-based culture. The New Culture Movement aimed at incorporating Western ideas, like science and democracy, into a different Chinese culture. Many of these people were given positions at Beijing University, spreading ideas through teaching as well as through writing.

On May 4, 1919, news that the Chinese delegation to the Versailles Peace Conference had agreed to Japanese demands for territorial concessions in China sparked demonstrations. Angry Chinese students, merchants, and other city folk vented their frustration against Beijing's warlord government. The resulting May Fourth Movement unleashed Chinese nationalism and political activism, and some of the New Culture Movement leaders became key figures in the May Fourth Movement.

The Bolsheviks of Soviet Russia founded the Communist International (Comintern) in 1919 to promote nationalist and socialist parties in colonies around the world. Comintern agents helped found the Japanese, Indochinese, Indonesian, and Chinese communist parties. In China, Comintern activists met May Fourth Movement leaders and others, creating the momentum to found the Chinese Communist Party in 1921.

Comintern agents also aided the reorganization of the Nationalist Party under the leadership of Sun Zhongshan (Sun Yat-sen, 1866–1925). Sun had been a leader of the movement that helped bring down the Qing government in 1912 but grew disenchanted with politics. In the early 1920s, he worked out an alliance with Comintern agents, who provided money, experts in organizational techniques, weapons, and the means to found the Whampoa Military Academy, where many of China's future leaders and military officers were trained.

By 1926, the Nationalists opened a military campaign to defeat the warlords and reunite China. Within two years, the effort commanded by Jiang Jieshi[9] (Chiang Kai-shek, 1887–1975) succeeded, and he ousted communists from his ranks and launched a terror campaign against them. Jiang used military force, and the communists did not have the means to defend themselves. The Warlord Period ended, but military affairs continued to dominate Chinese politics until 1949.

Mao Zedong and the Peasants, 1928–1947

Mao Zedong[10] (1894–1976) grew up in the Chinese countryside, the son of a well-to-do peasant. He became an intellectual and taught briefly, but his main talent was for politics. During Mao's college

[9] **Jiang Jieshi:** JEE yahng JEE yeh shur
[10] **Mao Zedong:** MOW zeh DONG

FIGURE 37.6 ***Jiang Jieshi Assuming Sun Zhongshan's Mantle of Leadership.*** *At the top of this poster is a likeness of Sun Zhongshan, China's leader who died in 1925. Below Sun, Jiang Jieshi raises his sword and leads his troops off to war. As commander of communist and nationalist troops, Jiang carried out Sun's dream of uniting China by force during the Northern Expedition of 1926–1928. Posters like this one helped Jiang to become the most powerful leader in the Nationalist Party.* R. B. Fleming.

days, China experienced a cultural flowering that stressed Western ideas. Mao himself was strongly influenced by these ideas and practices, helping to found the communist movement in China. As the direction of the party came from Moscow, Soviet leaders insisted on China's proletariat as the favored revolutionary class. Despite the fact that Chinese workers constituted only a tiny percentage of the population, the Chinese communists successfully developed an urban movement of workers, students, intellectuals, and women. Yet Jiang Jieshi's purge of 1927 severely crippled the communists, especially in the cities. During the mid-1920s, Mao saw that the peasants' difficult lives and their willingness to listen made them a revolutionary force. He began organizing them and was ordered to lead them in an uprising in September 1927. It failed, and Mao with about 1,000 followers fled to eastern mountains.

THE JIANGXI REVOLUTIONARY BASE AND THE LONG MARCH. Mao joined with a group of talented military and political leaders in the local mountains. There, he formed his plan: build a base area of peasant supporters, create a revolutionary army, and seek widespread popular support. The mountains held few people, so Mao moved into Jiangxi[11] Province, where he established a base area.

Mao's land program showed key elements of his revolutionary strategy. He involved peasants in

[11] **Jiangxi:** JEE yahng shee

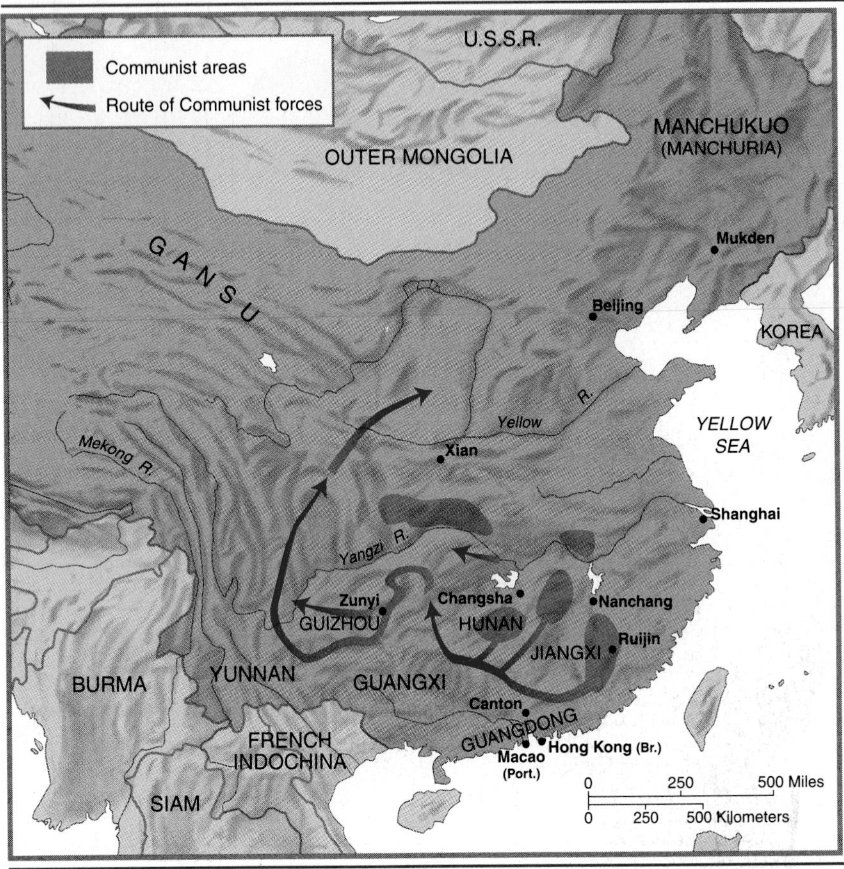

MAP 37.3 *The Long March.* *The Chinese Communist Party fled the Nationalist army led by Jiang Jieshi. The Long March, an epic event that lasted a year, traversed several thousand miles. The communists crossed many remote parts of China, some controlled by ethnic minorities. They also passed through difficult terrain, including rugged mountains and seemingly forbidding marshlands. Only a few thousand people survived, but they became the party elite.*

transferring land from the gentry landlords to the rural poor. In addition, the army played a key role in securing territory within which to work. After an area became secure, the communists organized the have-nots into land committees that directed the process. Communists surveyed the land and property in a village and published the results, showing who owned what. After a period of adjustment, a land committee published a list of who was to receive land and other kinds of property. Another period of adjustment followed, and then property changed hands. Each person received something, according to formulas based on age, and a family might accumulate more or less depending on its size. One section of land was reserved for the army, and its proceeds assisted war widows and orphans, as well as crippled veterans. This, of course, rooted the army firmly in the rural communities. Land transformation procedures varied somewhat over the area the communists controlled, but the general program remained intact.

Mao controlled the Jiangxi base for a few years before he was overthrown by a party faction backed by the Soviet Union. For the remaining several months of the base's existence, Mao was a kind of exile with little to do. From 1930 to 1934, the Nationalist Army, commanded by Jiang Jieshi, attempted to destroy the Jiangxi base area. Mao successfully led three campaigns against the Nationalists, and two more were commanded by Mao's Soviet-backed opponents. In the summer of 1934, the Nationalist assault on the Jiangxi base area had severely reduced the area controlled by the communists, and the land-shifting program was undone. A few months later, the whole area fell to the Nationalists. Fortune smiled on Mao because the Nationalist conquest of the base area discredited the Soviet-backed faction.

The communists broke out of the encirclement and began the Long March (1934–1935). The epic trek lasted for about a year, and the communists traversed around 6,000 miles of difficult terrain on foot. Perhaps 90,000 people began the march and fewer than 20,000 finally arrived in North China, but those who survived became a special elite in the communist movement. Top leaders formed a close-knit alliance that lasted for more than two decades. Finally, Mao Zedong became the head of the Communist Party and remained its leader until his death in 1976. He emerged from the Long March ordeal convinced of his leadership abilities and certain that with his leadership the Chinese Communist Party could accomplish anything.

The march's first phase lasted until January 1935 with many battles against the pursuing Nationalists. Heavy casualties were borne by the communists, and the capture of a district capital in a remote province gave them a brief respite. There communist leaders debated the events of the past year and the destination of the marchers. During these meetings, a consensus emerged that gave Mao party control.

Mao led the marchers through remote parts of China to get away from the pursuing Nationalists. The communists crossed rugged mountains and a marshland 90 miles long. The marsh was dotted with treacherous bogs and a corrosive soil that inhibited sleeping on the ground. Haggard survivors emerged at their destination in the fall of 1935.

WAR AND REVOLUTION. From 1936 to 1949, the communists built a formidable movement and conquered China. In the process, they benefited from the chaotic conditions unleashed by warfare and came to power with support from China's peasantry. Indeed, the success of the Chinese Revolution depended in large part on World War II

FIGURE 37.7 ***Mao Zedong.*** *From 1935 on, the Chinese Communist Party came increasingly under the control of Mao Zedong. In this 1938 photo, Mao speaks to a group of party and army leaders in Yan'an. Following the defeat of Japan in 1945, the northern Chinese city became the communists' headquarters during their war against the nationalist government. It was during the Yan'an years that Mao wrote his major works and developed his style of mobilizing and educating the people of China.* Wide World Photos.

(1939–1945) and the ensuing Chinese Civil War (1946–1949).

On July 7, 1937, Japan and China went to war after a firefight between their forces at the Marco Polo Bridge in North China. During the war, the Chinese Communist Party refined its land policies and encouraged anti-Japanese nationalism among China's peasants. Thus, the communist movement grew from a tiny size to major dimensions largely because of active peasant support. By the war's end, the Communist Party and its army numbered about 1 million members each, and the population under their control totaled in the tens of millions.

The Chinese Civil War erupted in 1946 with heavy fighting across China. In that conflict, the communists enjoyed superior leadership, effective intelligence operations, excellent military strategy, and active peasant support. Most of this support came through the Land Law of 1947, which guaranteed peasants land and targeted the landlord class for destruction. The Nationalists fell from power, partly because inflation devastated their urban support base. During the decisive campaigns of 1948 and 1949, the Nationalists lost more than 1.5 million soldiers and never recovered.

The Chinese Communist Party and government in North China went through a program of thought reform in the early 1940s. Although an intellectual, Mao distrusted his educated peers; he identified more closely with peasantry, which he believed harbored much wisdom. To Mao, academics seemed snobbish and distant from the common people, those who could effect a revolution. In addition, Mao distrusted bureaucrats, who often tyrannized people coming to them for assistance. These beliefs lay behind the thought reform campaign of 1942 to 1944, when Mao and other top officials remolded the thinking of communist elite group members.

The thought reform process involved a painful self-examination and ultimately resulted in the release of powerful psychological forces. Small groups read and discussed common writings (mostly by Mao). Then, in an orchestrated campaign, one group member endured a session of criticism by peers. These meetings severely upset people, who feared losing face. Usually self-criticism resulted, and after verification of the sincerity of the "confession" and rehabilitation, attention shifted to the next member. Some behav-

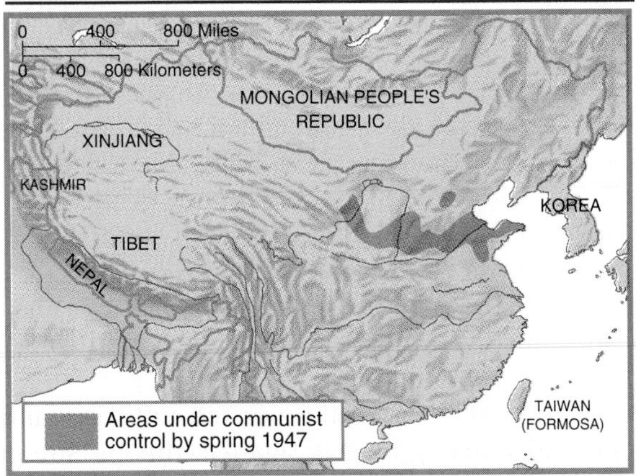

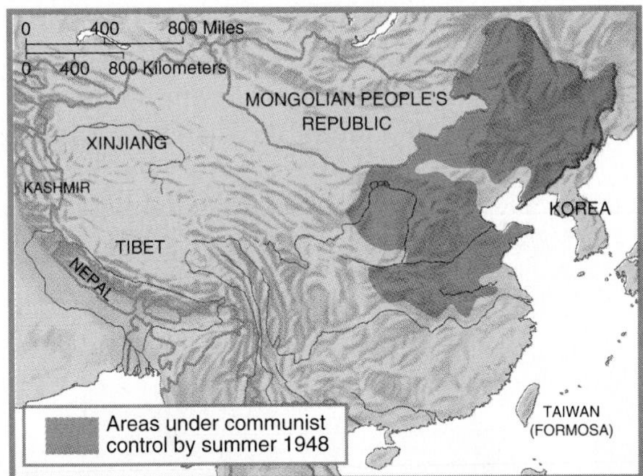

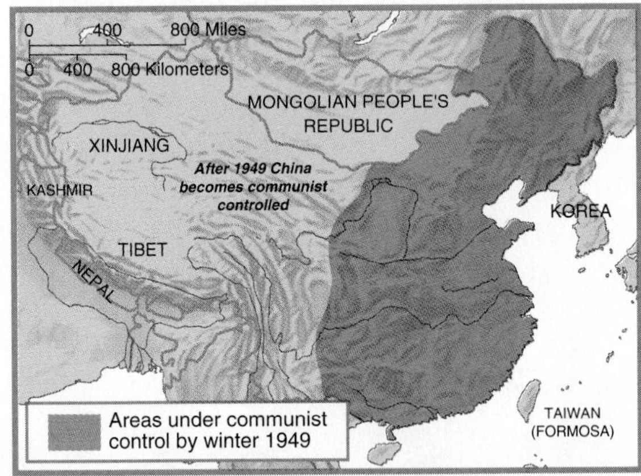

MAP 37.4 ***The Chinese Civil War.*** *The nationalists and communists fought a war that lasted from 1946 to 1949. Millions died and millions more were injured. The communists often controlled rural areas in Central and Northeast China. The nationalists controlled the major cities until 1948. Over time, peasant support and skilled leadership by the communists brought a victory over the nationalists. Only Taiwan remained under nationalist control after 1949.*

Figure 37.8 ***Chinese Socialist Realism.*** *After the communists established the People's Republic of China, they encouraged artists to depict examples of the tyranny of the previous government. A remarkable series titled "The Rent Collection Courtyard" appeared. In this lifesize sculpture, peasants line up to pay rent to a local landlord. Clothed in traditional garb, the peasants are observed by a figure dressed in Western clothing. While the peasants are weighed down by their burdens, the watcher, flanked by a well-fed dog, carries nothing heavier than a fan.* Sovfoto/Eastfoto.

ior modification occurred, and a kind of commonality of elite behavior emerged.

At the same time, Mao grew upset with intellectuals, who criticized the communists. Ding Ling[12] (1907–1985) was a writer who enjoyed a literary reputation before she came to the communist base in the late 1930s, where she worked in the propaganda division. By 1942, Ding Ling became uneasy about the conditions under which she worked, and she wrote literary pieces critical of male criticism of female activists and their lifestyles. The writings became controversial and helped spur Mao to deliver two addresses on literature and art. In these talks, Mao expressed the Marxist belief that art must serve the revolutionary cause. Accordingly, literature and art must be optimistic in tone and critical of noncommunists rather than of communists. "Art for art's sake" and such ideas as the "intellectual as critic" could not be tolerated by the communists. Ding Ling underwent criticism and self-criticism before mass audiences until she was "rectified."

[12] **Ding Ling:** DIHNG LIHNG

Elimination of the Gentry and Collectivization, 1947–1961

Beginning in 1947, the Land Law implemented a program of taking gentry property and distributing it to the poor. Although the effort ensured active peasant support of communist programs, its other aim was to wipe out gentry influence. The gentry had dominated China for centuries, and it lay in the path of the communist power hopes. Land campaigns strongly resembled those in the Jiangxi base area more than a decade earlier, except that violence occurred more often. Aroused villagers criticized and frequently killed their landlords, many of whom had tyrannized them. The process lasted into the early 1950s. Precise figures are not available, though the communists themselves admit to more than 2 million deaths. Landlord domination of society, agriculture, politics, and elite culture disappeared. Survivors of the onslaught usually had enough to live on, but their descendants were seldom permitted to forget their class origins. Destruction of the gentry left a vacuum in the countryside that was soon filled by the communists. Imperial governments had needed a few thousand officials to rule China because gentry landlords served as "unofficial officials." Communists now needed millions of **cadres**, officials and activists under party direction, to rule China.

As in Soviet Russia, the land transfers were the onset of a lengthy process to increase production. Unlike the Stalinists, however, the Maoists treated the peasants with more persuasion and less violence. The first stage of collectivization involved mutual-aid teams composed of around five families each. These units kept their family property but shared labor and draft animals. The next stage melded groups of perhaps village size (cooperatives). Land remained in private hands, though labor was shared. As labor resources increased, wells were dug and small irrigation systems were constructed. By the mid-1950s, cooperatives were merged into larger units of hundreds, if not thousands, of families. At that stage most private property was turned over to the cooperative, but peasants were permitted to keep garden plots. The massive labor pool also enabled large-scale construction projects.

In 1958, Mao became disenchanted with the pace of collectivization and the dearth of financial resources committed to agriculture. The Stalinist industrial model used by China exploited agriculture and brought into being a massive, centralized bureaucracy. In addition, Mao, who visited a rural collective that resulted from merging many cooperatives, believed that this gigantic unit of tens of thousands of people could solve many of China's economic problems. The new organization was called a **commune**, and it became the model for rural China. Mao envisioned communalism as the first stage of communism and asserted that China could move directly into communism instead of going through socialism. In other words, China—not Russia—had the potential to lead revolution on a global scale.

China's leaders backed Mao and drove the peasants into a frenzied campaign of mergers. Remaining private land was turned over to the commune, mess halls and nurseries were constructed to free women from some of their domestic duties, and top officials promoted the idea of peasants producing iron and steel in backyard foundries. Peasants melted down their iron pots and pans and bedsteads in an attempt to make steel. The effort failed, and the scrap proved worthless.

Cadres bent to the enormous pressures of their superiors, compelling peasants to work long hours to attain production targets. When lofty goals could not be reached, cadres fudged the data. As the inflated figures reached the national planners, exuberant officials proclaimed that China had reached self-sufficiency in grain output. Later, checking uncovered the deception, and the resulting embarrassment spurred bureaucrats to keep quiet and not divulge production statistics.

The policy of sparrow control best symbolizes the human failure of the Great Leap Forward, an attempt to increase industrial and agricultural production rapidly. Some communist officials decided to eliminate five types of pests, including grain-eating sparrows. People banged on metal at night, causing the panicked birds to fly until they died of exhaustion. Truckloads of sparrows were carted off by the state. What the communists learned, of course, was that the sparrows ate insects that consumed grain—and without the natural environmental check, much more grain was lost to insect pests.

Combining with human error was a rare spate of bad weather. Three years of natural calamities brought China to the brink of massive starvation by 1960. In recent years, scholars have estimated that more than 20 million people perished. As young people are more vulnerable to the afflictions of malnutrition, they suffered disproportionate losses in the early 1960s. The government finally admitted defeat and disbanded the communes. It took years for peasants to recover.

Industrialization and the Intellectuals, 1949–1978

Communist control of urban China came in 1949, and, because of the lack of personnel to run large cities, the new government retained a high percentage of Nationalist Party officials. The communists also established committees, organized city block by city block, to help control people.

The block committees gradually controlled China's cities. Composed largely of women who had adult children, these organizations informed their block members of hygienic and safety measures, helped identify prostitutes and enemy agents, and aided the government in educating people about political matters. Once in place, the committees helped eradicate prostitution, drug use and sales, various diseases, and so on. In the 1980s, they became a major part of the state effort to ensure a one-child-per-family policy by keeping tabs on the menstrual cycles of the women in their blocks. If a female became pregnant, the block committee members pressured her (if she already had a child) to seek an abortion.

The early years of the new government were spent in rebuilding war-ravaged China. Inflation was controlled until the late 1980s. Facilities were repaired, and roads and railroads were built or rebuilt as necessary.

By 1953, the state decided to industrialize. Officials followed the Stalinist model of concentrating on heavy industry, relegating agriculture to a minor economic role. After five years, China had achieved impressive production results, but problems troubled Mao and helped him decide on the Great Leap Forward program. An economic disaster, it idled about one-half of China's factories by the early 1960s. Production improved by the mid-

PATHS TO THE PAST

The Use of History for Political Ends in China

Chinese scholars and artists have often turned to China's past to criticize policies and monarchs who initiated them because they dared not attack their own autocrat lords. In the mid–eighth century, the poet Du Fu[a] (710–770) wrote an antiwar ballad criticizing two early Chinese rulers who had warred until their soldiers and people became destitute. Du Fu could not criticize his own sovereign, who was following similar policies.

In the early 1960s, Wu Han,[b] a playwright and deputy mayor of Beijing, wrote a play, *Hai Rui Dismissed from Office.* It concerned an honest official who lived in the sixteenth century and who had been fired because an emperor listened to Hai Rui's corrupt enemies rather than to the exemplary official. The play performed to packed houses in the capital, and rumors circulated that it was a veiled attack on Chairman Mao Zedong, who had fired his defense minister, Peng Dehuai, two years earlier. Mao had launched the Great Leap Forward (1958–1961), a disastrous policy that had been strongly criticized by Peng. Mao retaliated against his critic by firing him, just as the emperor had fired his honest official in the sixteenth century.

The play was performed in the early 1960s until a critic launched a broadside attack against it in late 1965. The critic accused the dramatist of criticizing Mao by using a historical event to make his point. Mao himself supported the charges and ordered an investigation. Nothing happened, and Mao surmised that a plot involving the deputy mayor, the mayor of Beijing, and others protected the playwright. These actions began the Cultural Revolution, which would convulse China for a decade.

Deng Xiaoping, who had been an ally of the mayor and deputy mayor, also fell from power in the Cultural Revolution but survived to head the People's Republic of China after Mao's death in 1976. The critic of the deputy mayor went on trial, accused of helping launch the Cultural Revolution and causing the deaths of many innocent people. He was convicted and given a life prison sentence. The play resumed production in the capital and once again played to packed houses.

[a] **Du Fu:** DOO FOO
[b] **Wu Han:** WOO hahn

1960s but slumped again in the late 1960s. A working class also emerged, with each worker controlled by a work unit that governed one's housing, food, education, and social benefits, like health care. The state also controlled the movement of its people and shifted millions of Chinese to the border regions in order to secure the areas inhabited by minority peoples.

Intellectuals suffered periods of tension at the hands of a government that needed their talents but distrusted their views. In 1956 and 1957, Mao grew troubled by the large number of bureaucrats and what he felt were their arrogant ways. He decided to use the intellectuals in a campaign to criticize officials, encouraging the intellectuals to speak out. The event known as the Hundred Flowers Campaign of 1957 slowly elicited a response by intellectuals. Although Mao believed that sharp criticisms could be exposed and blunted through debate, most institutions and practices suffered from a withering commentary. In early June, Mao turned against the intellectuals and ordered a campaign against "rightists," those who had criticized. Around 500,000 people lost their jobs and were ordered to undergo reform through manual labor. Ding Ling was charged with various crimes and subjected to a twenty-year sentence at hard labor in Northeast China.

A second major upheaval involving intellectuals erupted about a decade later. This time Mao used young students to attack officials and elite groups who held anti-Mao sentiments. The Cultural Revolution (1966–1976) convulsed China; schools closed and government offices were taken

FIGURE 37.9 ***Red Guards Parading a Victim.*** *During the Cultural Revolution, the Red Guards roamed China's cities, looking for enemies of Mao Zedong. This 1967 photo shows an official, accused of being an antirevolutionary, who has been forced to wear a dunce cap detailing his crimes against the people. Many officials and intellectuals were paraded and beaten by the Red Guards. By early 1967, many of China's cities were in chaos.* Wide World Photos.

Figure 37.10 *Deng Xiaoping and the Military. Like many of his contemporaries, Deng Xiaoping fought in China's wars of the 1930s and 1940s, gaining the respect and loyalty of many military commanders. During the Tiananmen days of May–June 1989, Deng called on some of these leaders to help crush the student-led protests.* Wide World Photos.

over by Red Guards claiming allegiance to Mao's dictates. Anarchic conditions led to the army's being used to restore order. In the process, Mao purged many of his enemies in the party and government, and hundreds of thousands of people died. After that time, the state took a milder view of intellectuals until 1989, when it crushed the student-led demonstrations centered on the square at Tiananmen[13] (Gate of Heavenly Peace).

Economic Growth, 1978–1989

Deng Xiaoping[14] (1904–1997), a victim of the Cultural Revolution purges, reascended the political summit in 1977 and directed an economic recovery that lasted into the 1990s. The extent of Deng's power may be measured by the fact that during the 1980s and early 1990s, he held no official position yet wielded decisive power on critical matters.

[13] **Tiananmen:** TEE yehn AHN mehn
[14] **Deng Xiaoping:** DUHNG SHEE YOW peeng

Mao's death in 1976 afforded Deng the opportunity to revive his political fortunes. Deng built a team dedicated to loosening controls over the economy. Peasants received plots of land and a state guarantee of noninterference with their use of the land. By 1985, these measures helped transform Chinese agriculture to produce more than 400 million tons of grain, an amount sufficient to feed its people. Soon special economic zones dotted China's coast, where private factories operated. China encouraged foreign investment and promoted trade, and since 1978 it has enjoyed one of the world's fastest economic growth rates, becoming one of the world's largest economies.

At the same time, Deng permitted the Chinese little political freedom. Indeed, two of his successors were replaced after tolerating individual expression and student criticism of the state. Massive gatherings in the square at Tiananmen provoked memories of the Cultural Revolution's anarchistic upheaval, and Deng ordered the Chinese army to crush the demonstration movement.

	Russia	China		
Russian Empire, 1725–1917			1900	Upheaval in Russia, 1905
	Russian Civil War, 1918–1921	Warlord Era, 1912–1928; New Culture Movement, 1915–1919	1910	Qing Empire collapses, 1912; Bolsheviks take power, 1917; May 4, 1919, Incident
	New Economic Policy, 1921–1929		1920	Stalin in power, 1929
Industrialization, c. 1930–1941	Collectivization, 1929–1936	Japanese militarism in China, 1931–1945	1930	Long March begins, 1934
Soviet Empire, 1940–1989		Chinese Civil War, 1946–1949	1940	Communists take power in China, 1949
	Political thaw, 1953–1964	Great Leap Forward, 1958–1961	1950	Treaty of Moscow, 1950; North Korea invades South Korea, June 25, 1950; Stalin dies, 1953; Great Leap Forward begins, 1958
	Neo-Stalinism, 1964–1985	Cultural Revolution, 1966–1976	1960	Khrushchev falls, 1964
		Market socialism, 1978–present	1970	*Detente* begins, 1973; Mao Zedong dies, 1976; Deng Xiaoping in power, 1977
			1980	Mikhail Gorbachev in power, 1984; Tiananmen massacre, 1989

SUMMARY

1. The Russian tsarist system could not survive the wars of the early twentieth century and the incompetence of Nicholas II. It collapsed in March 1917, ushering in a time of anarchistic chaos that the Bolsheviks exploited.

2. Vladimir Lenin provided the strategic vision that carried his communist party, the Bolsheviks, to victory in the Bolshevik Revolution of 1917–1924. He and his fellow party members destroyed the remnants of the tsarist system and began building a socialist state. Civil war taxed the Bolsheviks and their subjects, who intensified a drive to centralize the state. After victory in 1921, Lenin relaxed state controls.

3. Lenin's death brought a party crisis of leadership that ended with Josef Stalin's victory in 1929. Stalin collectivized the peasantry and industrialized the economy. Both measures gave Soviet Russia great-power status at a cost of tens of millions of lives. Terror also purged Stalin's rivals.

4. Soviet industrialization led to socialist imperialism as the Russians claimed several Baltic states and controlled many in Eastern Europe. All economies were carefully integrated into the Soviet economy.

5. Stalin's death brought to power two reformers, Nikita Khrushchev and Mikhail Gorbachev, neither of whom successfully transformed the Stalinist system.

6. In China, Manchu rulers undermined their government by abolishing the examination system. The Qing Empire collapsed and left China in chaos with warlord rule.

7. Early efforts to create a communist movement in China's cities failed under the terrorist onslaught of the Nationalist forces commanded by Jiang Jieshi. Mao Zedong organized peasant groups to promote revolution and undertook land reform as well. He developed a successful communist strategy that led to victory.

8. The communists destroyed the gentry and collectivized China's peasants at the cost of millions of lives. The communists also gained control of China's cities, partly through the establishment of block committees dominated by women.

9. Intellectuals had been harnessed for state purposes. Mao, in particular, distrusted them, although he used them against the officials in the Hundred Flowers Campaign and in the Cultural Revolution.

10. Deng Xiaoping survived two purges and emerged as China's leader in 1977. He promoted policies of permitting individual initiative for the peasants and entrepreneurs. These programs launched China on a course of economic change.

SUGGESTED READINGS

Fairbank, John. *The Great Chinese Revolution.* Cambridge, Mass.: Harvard University Press, 1986. A classic history of modern China.

Ferro, Mark. *Nicholas II.* Oxford, Eng.: Oxford University Press, 1991. An excellent recent biography of Russia's last tsar.

Fitzpatrick, Sheila. *The Russian Revolution.* Oxford, Eng.: Oxford University Press, 1994. A social history of the Bolshevik and Stalinist revolutions.

Swain, Geoffrey. *The Origins of the Russian Civil War.* London: Longman House, 1996. A provocative study of the Russian Civil War.

Wolf, Margery. *Revolution Postponed.* Stanford, Calif.: Stanford University Press, 1985. An examination of the fate of Chinese women under the Chinese communists.

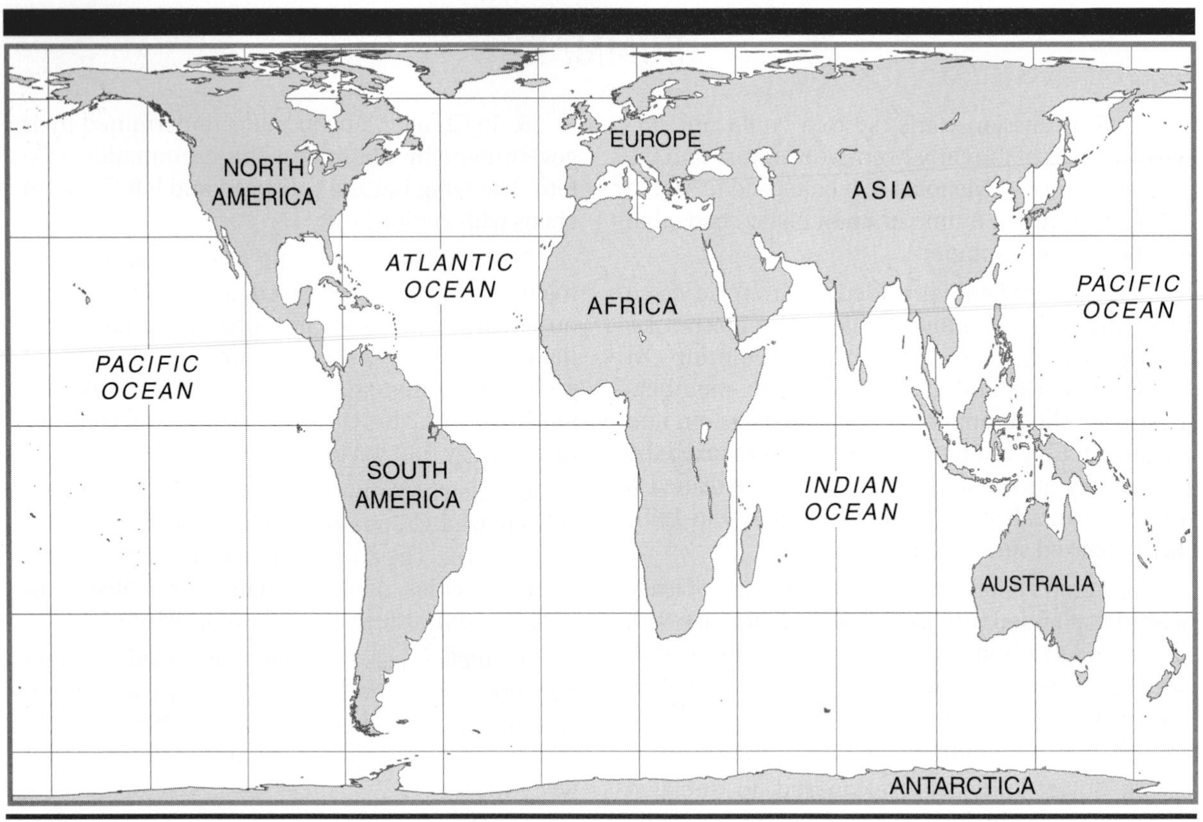

NORTH
AMERICA
EUROPE
ASIA
ATLANTIC
OCEAN
AFRICA
PACIFIC
OCEAN
PACIFIC
OCEAN
SOUTH
AMERICA
INDIAN
OCEAN
AUSTRALIA
ANTARCTICA

CHAPTER 38

The Great Depression

1929–1941

Reiko Yamanaka had survived, barely. Her son, Jiro, had died in Asia during the last war, and her daughter, Keiko, perished from consumption (tuberculosis) and venereal disease; she had been a prostitute in Osaka, after having lost her job in a silk-spinning mill there. Last week, Reiko's husband passed away from some fever, but she knew he died of a broken heart.

So many people were out of work, and farmers suffered from falling prices. Orphans wandered silently, and old people lay in their homes, hungry like her. Japanese politicians promised help but did nothing, while a new war loomed. As a schoolgirl, she had bowed to the emperor's portrait. What could he do for her now?

In the 1930s, a worldwide depression devastated economies, governments, and societies. While some individuals prospered, many more suffered as jobs became scarce and economic return on investments plummeted or disappeared. When the economic crisis unfolded, the instinctive reaction of some countries was to protect themselves, even if that meant harming the interests of other countries. Along with the dire nature of the depression came general ignorance about its causes and how to get out of it. In fact, many early policies caused more economic problems than they solved. Only the governments of the Nazis and Soviets managed to avoid the dire consequences of the depression. While various policies in other countries made inroads against the depression, most countries emerged from the depression only during World War II.

THE DEPRESSION'S CONTEXT AND CAUSES

A **depression** is an economic downturn involving long-term production drops, widespread unemployment, and **deflation** (a steep drop in prices and wages). In many ways, the Great Depression from 1929 to 1941 was unprecedented because, while there had been business downturns in the past, they had not combined with general production losses, massive unemployment, social unrest, and a steep drop in prices. In fact, the Great Depression was a significant contraction of industrial capitalism that reached crisis proportions.

An Integrated Global Economy

Prior to 1500, regional economies had existed in different parts of the world, but when Europeans began trading overseas, economic interconnectedness grew. In the late eighteenth century, the Industrial Revolution transformed economies, bringing them into close contact with client states and colonies. Indeed, by 1929 there was an interrelationship of production and commerce with great volume and complexity that constituted a different global economic order. Unfortunately, neither political leaders nor economic experts understood this.

The Industrial Revolution brought periodic downswings and upswings in the nineteenth century. While these depressions had been recognized and commented upon as early as the 1860s, no one knew precisely what caused them or how they might be avoided. One global downturn lasted from 1873 to 1896. This deflation accompanied general increases in production with sporadic surges and drops in industrial output.

By the twentieth century, the global economy offered prospects and problems for world leaders. The integrated international economy increasingly meant that there were few independent economies. In addition, economic problems in one country affected other countries, and economic policies in one country had repercussions throughout the world. Because neither economists nor policymakers realized these relationships fully, they often followed policies that benefited their own countries at the expense of others. These leaders failed to understand that they were facing a global problem.

Connections with World War I

Although the Great Depression hit more than a decade after World War I ended, the war contributed to the depression's onset. Immense war destruction, especially in France and other parts of Europe, took many years to repair. Financial costs of the war also hindered economic recovery in Europe. Britain failed to recognize the significant losses incurred by its wartime policies. Seeking to recapture some of Britain's prewar reputation, banks returned their country to the gold standard in 1925. An artificially high value placed on British currency severely hampered exports until dire financial conditions forced the abandonment of the gold standard in 1931.

Another war-related factor involved agricultural production. Because many countries heavily committed to the fighting took resources and laborers from agriculture, they had to rely on imports of grain and other commodities. The United States, Canada, and Australia, among others, significantly increased their own production levels to supply their allies and to make profits. After the war's end, the European combatants resumed grain production without a corresponding decline in the other countries. Surpluses accumulated and drove down agricultural prices through the rest of the 1920s. Various government schemes to decrease production and raise prices failed, and between 1925 and 1929 prices for key agricultural goods dropped by 40 percent on a global scale.

Raw materials suffered similar gluts and price declines in the 1920s. Some came from shifts in wartime production and the return of traditional producers after the war; others stemmed from different factors, such as general overproduction by exporting countries.

Both Japan and the United States benefited from the industrial production vacuum owing to the war. They suffered no major war losses at home, and their healthy industries became major suppliers to the world. Prior to 1914, Japan and the United States had had unfavorable trade balances (the difference between the amount of goods a country exports and imports in a year). If the amount of exports is greater than the amount of imports, the trade balance is favorable, a condition national leaders strive hard to promote.

During World War I, Japan and the United States became major arms exporters, and they loaned money to European nations. One major development of World War I was the United States' emergence as a world power. In fact, the United States was by far the dominant economic power; it produced 40 percent of the world's industrial products, a figure more than twice the combined production of Germany and Britain. Yet the United States failed to realize that its dominant global trade position meant economic leadership and responsibility. Many U.S. policies exhibited economically nationalist tendencies, harming other nations and worsening the depression.

FIGURE 38.1 *"Black Thursday." This print by William Gropper starkly depicts the panic and horror of stockbrokers as they face the 1929 collapse of the stock market. Beside the tumbling ticker-tape, one man prepares to take his life rather than face further news of his ruin.* Library of Congress.

Policy Inhibitions

Political leaders around the world had little economic training and tended to be ignorant about the causes of the Great Depression and what means should be employed to end it. Even economists did not agree on the causes and remedies of the Great Depression. Furthermore, the prevailing political wisdom perceived that **inflation**, a period of sharply rising prices, was the chief cause of economic devastation. Most leaders believed that Germany's severe inflation of the previous decade had wrecked German society. Consequently, politicians and economists fought inflation in the 1930s, though deflation was actually occurring. This misperception exacerbated the economic downturn.

Another government imperative was to balance annual budgets by cutting expenditures and raising taxes. Few realized that tax increases reduced disposable income that normally might purchase products. Governmental deficits might be the price of putting people back to work.

NORTH AMERICAN, EUROPEAN, AND ASIAN DEPRESSIONS AND RESPONSES

The Great Depression affected many countries, but we will focus on the examples of a few countries in North America, Europe, and Asia. They attempted in various ways to end their depressions and rehabilitate their societies.

The Depression's Onset

Two events, the stock market crash and the passage of the Hawley-Smoot Tariff, triggered the Great Depression, and they both highlighted international ramifications of the economic collapse. The crash of the U.S. stock market in October and November 1929 ushered in psychological and financial factors of the Great Depression.

The stock market crash resulted from speculative investing and helped lead to a crisis of economic confidence. Many U.S. investors played the stock market in the late 1920s. They were lured by the general surge in stock prices and indulged in buying stocks with borrowed money, taking great risks that share prices might drop sharply. When the market declined precipitously in October, many could not pay their losses and went bankrupt. A drop of stock share prices by 40 percent between September and November 1929 also dampened consumer confidence. Because much of the United States economy was driven by the spending of private citizens, cautionary buying seriously hurt economic growth.

Passage of the Hawley-Smoot Tariff by the U.S. Congress in 1930 gravely affected foreign economies. Goods from abroad were hit by high tariffs that made them more expensive than American products. While this policy of economic nationalism may have benefited U.S. workers, it harmed America's consumers, who paid more for the goods they purchased. More important, it severely harmed those countries that relied heavily on exports for economic well-being. At the same time, this economic shortsightedness sparked similar actions by America's trading partners.

The U.S. Federal Reserve banking system, which supervised the U.S. economy, also had a role in worsening the early effects of the depression. The Federal Reserve policy of raising interest rates was designed to attract foreign investments in the United States, but it also brought deflation. As a side effect, Federal Reserve actions weakened European currencies, harming European banks and deepening the world depression.

Canada, which depended on exports of grain, raw materials, and semifinished goods, suffered from the U.S. stock market crash and the implementation of the Hawley-Smoot Tariff. Canada's maritime provinces experienced a sharp decline in the fishing industry and coal and steel manufacturing centers. The shrinking demand for Canadian grain devastated prairie states, which were later hit by drought and swarms of grasshoppers. By 1933, around 23 percent of Canada's labor force was unemployed, a staggering increase from the 3 percent unemployment rate in 1929.

Germany's Weimar Republic (1919–1933) came to power and weathered crises, many of

FIGURE 38.2 ***Unemployed Workers Riding the Rails.*** *Canada suffered a heavy loss of jobs during the Great Depression, and in the summer of 1935 unemployed workers organized a protest ride to Ottawa. In this photo, the riders change trains at Kamloops. The government forced the riders off the train in Regina, ending their ride with bloodshed.* Photo by the Toronto Star Syndicate.

which were economic. Part of World War I's peace settlement forced upon Weimar Germany was the payment of war reparations determined in 1921. News of the reparations triggered a massive inflation, wherein payments had to be made by wagonloads of nearly worthless money. Germany had worked its way out of the severe inflationary times of the early 1920s and relied on short-term loans to underwrite public works programs that reduced social tensions and helped economic welfare. When U.S. sources of credit dried up in 1929, partly because of the American stock market's upheaval, the main source of German money evaporated. With economic downturn and loss of external credit, German banks began to fail, and the public works programs shut down. Between 1930 and 1931, German unemployment rapidly grew by 4 million people, and a general crisis rocked the Weimar Republic.

France endured a relatively mild but prolonged depression. A devaluation of the franc (the French monetary unit) in the late 1920s kept French products competitive into 1930, a prosperous year. Furthermore, French producers were less dependent on exports than their counterparts in other countries. Thus, only about 2.6 percent of French workers were unemployed during the depression. Social unrest, however, in the form of strikes and demonstrations by political factions, festered.

Japan suffered from the economic troubles in the United States. The United States had been a major market for Japanese exports, and when economic problems hit the United States, Japan's exports plummeted. Particularly troublesome was the reduction of raw silk purchases by U.S. manufacturers. This factor brought on the Japanese depression, sparking labor unrest and terrorism by paramilitary groups that threatened the political system.

China was less hard hit by depression than Japan. In 1928, the Nationalist Army under com-

FIGURE 38.3 ***Japanese Labor Unrest.*** *The Great Depression hit Japan hard. In the face of mass unemployment, some workers and leftist leaders organized protest. In this 1930 photo, angry leftist workers unfurl outlawed red flags to give symbolic emphasis to their demands.* The Mainichi Newspapers.

FIGURE 38.4 ***Franklin Roosevelt Speaking to Americans.*** *President Roosevelt skillfully employed the radio as a means of communicating his message to Americans; his "fireside chats" helped bolster morale and educate people about the New Deal. Like his contemporaries, President Roosevelt sought to boost his popularity, thereby ensuring his reelection (three times) and the stability of his continuing programs.* Corbis-Bettmann.

mand of General Jiang Jieshi unified China by military conquest. Although the drop in international trade and available credit resources hurt some Chinese exporters and producers, the Chinese economy depended heavily on agriculture, a sector more sensitive to domestic than international prices. General Jiang concentrated on helping promote commercial and industrial enterprises rather than agriculture. His problems were more political than economic.

The Depression's Influence on Leadership

Franklin D. Roosevelt (1882–1945) and Adolf Hitler (1889–1945) dominated the depression years, but other leaders, like Canada's R. B. Bennett (1870–1947), played important roles in fighting the Great Depression. Although they used different means to stay in power, these three politicians possessed similarities of style and substance. The British, French, and Japanese did not have a single dynamic politician to grapple with the domestic crises brought by the depression.

Hitler, Roosevelt, and Bennett appreciated the political value of new technological developments. Hitler used airplanes in a dramatic campaign swing when he visited nearly two dozen cities in a week during national elections, and Roosevelt insisted on flying from New York to Chicago to accept the Democratic Party's presidential nomination in 1932. In a 1930 election campaign, Bennett employed his bombastic rhetorical skills to attack his opponent as timid and vacillating. After winning, Bennett played a major role in creating the Canadian Radio Broadcasting Corporation, a national radio network. Roosevelt became famed for "fireside chats" by radio, and Hitler used the radio more than fifty times in his first year in office to reassure the German people. Early in their administrations, these leaders' messages employed powerful modes of expression about the suffering of people in collective and individual terms.

Bennett's, Roosevelt's, and Hitler's management styles usually permitted their subordinates to handle specific issues. Frequently, lower officials competed against one another for the ears of the top man; and all three leaders preferred to have people and bureaucratic sectors vying with one another. In that sense, they gained unusual control over their governments.

Aid to unemployed people occupied the attention of Canada, the United States, and Germany. In 1930, Bennett summoned a special session of Parliament to vote $20 million to put people back to work. The Canadian radio network also employed writers and actors. The United States budgeted around $3.4 billion to put people to work building roads, schools, and bridges. Hitler spent even more on a per capita basis in order to fund massive public works programs that built railroads, navigation centers, and a network of highways. The Nazis used public funds for loans and tax rebates to small companies. They undertook measures to encourage consumer spending.

Economic Programs of the Depression

The United States, Canada, Germany, France, Japan, and the Soviet Union devised a series of economic programs to combat the ravages of the depression. In the process, they created more highly centralized polities that delivered welfare and other social services to their citizens.

THE UNITED STATES. Franklin Roosevelt came to power in 1933, promising a "New Deal" for Americans, a depression-fighting program of public works projects. The U.S. government preferred a loose network of management-worker alliances. The regulatory codes were more voluntary in industrial compliance, but through the Presidential Re-employment Agreement, the U.S. government set minimum wages and maximum hours. The United States also permitted the growth of unions because that brought more workers under control.

Among the American agencies created in the depression era was the Civilian Conservation Corps (CCC). It was founded to employ people in a variety of projects related to conservation issues. Men were drawn to the CCC and lived in camps governed by a military-style discipline that regimented their lives. Officers in the U.S. armed forces directed these civilians, who built bridges, repaired roads, and constructed a variety of water control projects. One major CCC effort involved planting trees by the millions, reforesting large areas of the United States.

Another agency, the Farm Security Administration (FSA), employed many people to support farmers. One of these employees was the photographer Dorothea Lange (1895–1965), who became famous for her photographs of depression scenes. Before getting the FSA job, Lange had taken sensitive and emotionally affecting photographs of the unemployed, especially white-collar workers who never expected to be out of work. A major exhibition of this work brought Lange an FSA contract. Lange photographed farm families, capturing the misery and privation of these people while giving human faces to the plight of women and children in agriculture. Many Lange photographs of the depression era have been acclaimed as masterpieces of the medium.

Roosevelt stressed the bedrock nature of rural farm life and the positive values associated with it. Like Germany, the United States organized agriculture to increase farm income. Both countries made credit easier and less expensive in the countryside. The United States tried to reduce farm production and curtail agricultural surpluses, while the Germans maximized production.

Rearmament by the United States in the 1930s provided significant funds for industry and workers. The United States spent about one-third of the initial public works budget, about $1 billion, on military projects, like aircraft carriers, cruisers, airplanes, and military airports. In response to Japanese military expansion in China and Germany's expansion in Europe, American military spending escalated to nearly $9 billion in 1939 and $34 billion in 1941. President Roosevelt believed that it was prudent to prepare for possible war.

CANADA. R. B. Bennett tried but failed to improve the lot of Canadians, especially workers, between 1930 and 1935. He got Parliament to agree, apart from the emergency funds to put people to work, to raise tariff rates by 50 percent. This policy reversed a negative trade balance and raised nearly

FIGURE 38.5 ***Plight of a Migrant Family.*** *In the 1930s, the American photographer Dorothea Lange was commissioned by the state of California to document the migrant farmers' way of life. Lange's photographs convey the dignity of the laborers and their families despite the harshest poverty; her work led to the creation of state-funded camps for migrants. This 1936 photograph of a worn-looking migrant mother and children was taken in Nipomo, California, during the period that Lange worked for the Farm Security Administration.* Corbis-Bettmann.

$200 million. It saved Canadian industries from bankruptcy and kept Canadian workers from losing their jobs. On the other hand, keeping prices high worsened the lives of people living on relief or on reduced incomes. Bennett created the foundations of a national bank, a national broadcasting system, and a national airlines system.

Despite these measures, the economic lot of Canadians still worsened, driving Bennett to drastic measures. In January 1935, Bennett announced a Canadian New Deal without informing his own party. The central features included a national unemployment and social insurance system, minimum wages and maximum hours in industry, a federally sponsored farm credit system, and a natural products marketing board. All were enacted by Parliament despite serious misgivings of his party members, and their enactment gave the opposition a key election issue.

GERMANY. The German economy was starting to recover from the depression when the Nazis assumed power in 1933, quickly bringing industry, labor, and agriculture under state control. The

IN THEIR OWN WORDS

Canadians Look at the Depression

Canada's leaders grappled with the problems and issues of the Great Depression in the 1930s. They put forth visions of suffering Canadians and developed analyses of the causes of the misery, as well as critiques of policies proposed to end it.

J. S. Woodsworth, member of the Canadian parliament, spoke movingly about the human catastrophe:

> In the old days we could send people from the cities to the country. If they went out today they would meet another army of unemployed coming back from the country to the city; that outlet is closed. What can these people do? They have been driven from our parks; they have been driven from our streets; they have been driven from our buildings, and in this city [Ottawa] they actually took refuge on the garbage heaps.

Prime Minister R. B. Bennett led the fight against the depression-caused suffering and offered a vision of a moribund capitalism lying in ruins:

> In the anxious years through which you have passed, you have been witness of grave defects and abuses in the capitalist system. Unemployment and waste are proof of these. Great changes are taking place about us. New conditions prevail. These require modifications in the capitalist system to enable that system more effectively to serve the people.

With these words as a preamble, the prime minister began outlining the reforms that he intended to pass before new elections were held. Inspired by the U.S. New Deal, the Canadian New Deal came into being without much consultation with his cabinet or fellow members of Parliament.

The main opposition leader, Mackenzie King, sensed an opportunity to make political hay of Bennett's seeming authoritarian manner by asking Bennett to

> tell this House whether as leader of the government, knowing that a question will come up immediately as to the jurisdiction of this Parliament, and of the provincial legislatures in matters of social legislation, he has secured an opinion from the law officers of the Crown or from the Supreme Court of Canada which will be a sufficient guarantee to this House to proceed with these measures as being without question in its jurisdiction.

King had framed the constitutional issue without having to discuss the merits of the New Deal programs. In the process, King raised questions about the prime minister's integrity in going first to the people and then to Parliament. During the ensuing campaign and election, Bennett's party lost, and most of the Canadian New Deal was repealed or called into question. Canada stumbled on to economic recovery by the end of the 1930s, especially after entering World War II.

Germans developed a state-run economy, establishing thirteen gigantic agencies that governed all sectors of industry. In addition, the Nazis broke independent unions and organized all workers into one large federation. Nazis insisted that businesses provide better housing, sports programs, and working facilities for the laborers. Slogans like the "beauty of labor" and "strength through joy" created a sense of community in factories.

Hitler and the Nazis were concerned about German consumers and their standard of living. The Nazis, for example, planned the Volkswagen (people's car) as a car that the workers could afford to own and drive. By the end of the 1930s, German citizens associated the Nazis with a secure income and an improved living standard, especially when compared with the Weimar Republic.

The German farm program resettled large numbers of farmers. In later years, plans were formulated to move huge numbers to the east (Poland and Russia). Propaganda promoted the idea that agricultural production was vital to the nation. Documentaries were made showing happy farm workers toiling in their fields.

FIGURE 38.6 ***Hitler and the Volkswagen.*** *The Nazis promoted the idea of producing and selling a "people's car," an inexpensive car that would improve standards of living and also create jobs. On May 1, 1938, Adolf Hitler unveiled the prototype; within a year or so, factories that manufactured autos had also begun to turn out tanks and armored cars.* Ullstein Bilderdienst.

FRANCE. The Great Depression in France polarized society and politics, leading to a general breakdown of effective rule and prolonging the economic crisis. The French political system lodged power in parliament rather than in the presidency. In times of general turmoil, this led to legislative deadlock. Between 1932 and 1935, for example, there were eleven different parliamentary coalitions developing fourteen separate plans to fight the depression. These legislative measures only intensified economic stagnation.

Political deadlock pressured a group of parties to form a Popular Front coalition, uniting political groups claiming to represent workers and peasants. The Popular Front governed for two years. Coalition leaders implemented a program akin to the New Deal. They encouraged workers and employers to agree to modest wage hikes and enacted legislation guaranteeing two weeks' paid holiday per year and a forty-hour work week. A price-stabilization agency was created to raise cereal prices for farmers. In addition, the Bank of France and armaments industries were taken over by the government.

JAPAN. The Japanese established and administered bureaucratic agencies that controlled whole industrial sectors and used methods similar to the Germans'. Japanese leaders also implemented a major armament program in 1931, somewhat improving the nation's economy. Japan began to enter a wartime economic environment when it conquered Manchuria in 1931 and 1932. Thereafter, larger percentages of the budget went to military needs. The Japanese government broke up unions and oversaw the general regimentation of workers for the emerging warfare state. Because Japanese nationalism became the dominant ideology in the 1930s, most workers agreed with the regimentation, and those who disagreed kept silent.

The Japanese military focused the nation's attention on farmers and their difficult plight because many officers came from the countryside. They pushed the government to offer price supports, easy credit, and other means to encourage agricultural production. When Japan annexed Korea and Taiwan, it obtained two important rice-producing areas; production of rice and other foodstuffs increased, feeding the growing Japanese military machine.

Japanese leaders encouraged migration of Japanese to Hawaii, Peru, and Brazil. During the depression, some talked of sending farmers to newly conquered Manchuria, but that proved impractical; still, large numbers of businesspeople, clerks, and laborers moved there to work in the growing number of Japanese factories.

THE SOVIET UNION. While most of the world suffered from the Great Depression, Soviet Russia industrialized, and its industrialization developed outside the global capitalist system. Between 1929 and 1941, Josef Stalin determined to industrialize the Soviet system no matter the cost. As seen in Chapter 37, he took grain from the peasantry to sell in international markets. In 1929, for example, slightly more than 1 million tons of grain was sold, and, a year later, the Soviets sold 5.4 million tons abroad. These figures, of course, underlie the Stalinist famine of the early 1930s in which millions lost their lives. Soviet Russia's industrial success invited favorable commentary from observers who traveled to Russia. In certain respects, the Soviet model highlighted the importance of industrial planning, although the great cost in human lives gave imitators pause.

The Growth of Central Power

One notable trend of the depression era was the increase in state power. Expanded governmental control over citizens during World War I had been largely undone in the postwar period. The extreme conditions of the 1930s, however, revived military-style administrations, as politicians recalled the results gained from the concentration of political power.

The U.S. presidency changed dramatically in the years of Franklin Roosevelt, who set the model for an activist presidency that achieved results through public relations and carefully crafted speeches. The White House staff grew much larger after 1933, and the executive became the strongest of the three branches of government. Indeed, Roosevelt invented the modern presidency. President Harry Truman, Franklin Roosevelt's successor, wielded much greater power than did President Herbert Hoover, Roosevelt's predecessor.

As governments took more active roles in their economies, new economic regulations and laws appeared. The combined effect, which did not fade away after the depression, was to maintain strong governmental control of certain economic sectors.

NONINDUSTRIAL COUNTRIES' PROBLEMS DURING THE DEPRESSION

Countries supplying raw materials to industrial states suffered economic losses, too. Raw materials experienced a general deflation in prices during the 1920s, making life difficult in countries dependent on income from these sources. When the depression hit, industrial states sharply reduced their purchases of raw materials. Chile, for example, went from an export trade in copper and nitrates worth 2.3 billion pesos in 1929 to one worth only 282 million pesos by 1932. This catastrophic drop devastated the Chilean economy.

Similar blows staggered other Latin American countries. The purchasing power, for example, of citizens in Argentina, Brazil, Cuba, Ecuador, Mexico, Peru, and Venezuela dropped by at least 40 percent between 1929 and 1933. Brazil, however, benefited from some fortunate circumstances that turned its economy around. Coffee production and exports played a major role in the Brazilian economy. When coffee-bean prices dropped sharply, the government and coffee growers tried various means to raise the prices. Finally, the government agreed to buy surplus coffee beans and pay some growers not to produce. These combined expenditures put more money into the economy, and because of import controls and other factors, funds were spent on local goods. This stimulated Brazilian businesses to produce and sell clothing, housewares, furniture, paper, glass, steel, and cement. By 1932, industrial production surpassed 1929 levels, and the economy grew by a healthy 8 percent a year through the rest of the 1930s.

Most countries in Latin America did not have Brazil's manufacturing base, nor did they have the raw materials to accomplish its feats. Many Latin American countries adhered to the practice of **import substitution**, relying on local businesses to fill the gaps left by the withdrawal of foreign imports. Although these measures had limited

FIGURE 38.7 ***Brazilian Coffee Plantation.*** *Brazil suffered moderate damage from the Great Depression. Coffee prices held steady for a time, then dropped. The government intervened and bought up the surplus coffee beans, injecting the additional money into the economy. This kept Brazilian coffee workers on the job and plantation owners out of debt. Overall, Brazil worked its way out of the economic and social dislocation.* Popperfoto/ Archive Photos.

utility in sparking economic turnaround, they did make Latin American economies more balanced in what they produced for local consumption.

The price of rubber dropped steeply before the depression. Most rubber was produced on plantations in Southeast Asia; the French oversaw output in French Indochina, the Dutch controlled the plantations in the East Indies, and the British managed rubber-producing areas in Malaya. Some rubber was also produced in Ceylon in South Asia. British plantation managers and owners responded to the low prices for rubber by striking a voluntary agreement to reduce production. This plan received support from the Dutch growers, and it worked for a time. One major problem came when the Indians in Malaya and Ceylon tapped trees outside the plantations. These indigenous entrepreneurs filled the production vacuum, much to the chagrin of Western imperialists. During the depression, price drops once again produced an agreement to reduce production. Again, Indians ignored the "tapping holiday" and increased production to make up for the price drop. The combined effect was a drop in the price of rubber from 22 cents to 3 cents per pound; British owners complained that the business was going "local." A similar government-inspired drop in cotton production in the United States to maintain world price levels saw delighted Egyptians filling the gap by increasing their production.

SOCIAL CONSEQUENCES OF THE DEPRESSION

The great upheaval wrought by the Great Depression had several social consequences. In the United States, common suffering often drew families and people closer together. Houses where tramps might find a meal were marked by those who passed through earlier. People shared what little they had, especially farm families, which always seemed willing to take in cousins or other relatives down on their luck. This seemed to happen regularly in many parts of the world. One depression-era news story told of a group of men who had been arrested for vagrancy. Rather than be troubled by the jailing, they delightedly looked forward to regular meals and a warm place to sleep.

Women responded differently to their particular needs in bad times. In many countries where women constituted a sizeable fraction of the workforce, managers kept them on because they worked for lower pay than men. In households where women were the sole wage earners, tensions rose as men found it hard to cope with role reversals.

In Germany, the Nazis took various measures to take women out of the workforce. They paid women to marry and to leave the workforce, thus opening jobs for men. Nazis also propagandized German women to stay at home and build their nests.

Divorce rates also declined significantly in many countries, as families felt forced to stay together for survival. The downside was that women and men more often remained in dysfunctional marriages and suffered the consequences.

In Asia, women suffered disproportionately from the depression. Chinese women in poor households might find themselves sold by their husbands, and Chinese children in economic deprivation faced sale to Christian missionaries for conversion, Muslims for conversion, or wealthy people for sexual gratification. Female infanticide, the killing of female infants, increased during hard times in much of Asia. Peasant girls in Japan also

FIGURE 38.8 ***Peasant Girls Sold into Prostitution.*** *During times of financial hardship, peasant fathers in Japan sometimes resorted to selling their daughters to prostitution houses. Money and the thought of having one less mouth to feed were powerful inducements. This practice became more commonplace during the Great Depression. The girls in this 1934 photograph have just been rescued by social workers.* The Mainichi Newspapers.

faced sale into prostitution houses or factory work by their parents.

Minority groups also bore a heavy burden in the depression years. Migrant workers, especially those of an ethnic minority, experienced discrimination because they were perceived as taking jobs away from the majority group. One reason that the Jews, whom the Nazis tried to deport from Germany in the early years of their rule, were refused welcome in Western countries was the fear that they would compete for the few existing jobs. Anti-Semitism, of course, was another reason for the rejection of Jewish immigrants.

Some American Indians in the United States were relatively better off during the depression. Life on their reservations had always been meager, so when the depression hit, the falling prices for goods permitted their money to stretch further. New Deal programs that gave relief were extended to Indians for the first time. The Navajo tribe, for example, came out of the depression in somewhat better circumstances than it had entered it.

Birth rates declined in many countries, signifying that people deferred marriage until later age. Suicide rates increased during the difficult times, and, in Japan, whole-family suicides were not

UNDER THE LENS

First You Steal a Chicken

There is a story that goes around in historical circles about a cookbook written in a time of great privation. A stewed chicken recipe, according to this story, begins, "First you steal a chicken. . . ." French historians believe the cookbook was from the siege of Paris (1871), American historians think it was from the Great Depression, and Russian historians think it was from the siege of Moscow. It may well be that this recipe was written only in the mind of an imaginative historian and that it has entered into academic folklore.

The truth remains, however, that the Great Depression was a difficult time for many Americans to eat adequately. In 1930, there were eighty-two bread lines distributing food to the needy in New York and eighty in Philadelphia; in the next three years, conditions actually worsened. Citizens in New York, St. Louis, and other cities developed orderly systems of pillaging garbage cans and dumps for edible scraps. Many rural poor were reduced to a diet consisting entirely of wild greens and berries, and the absence of these foods in winter was disastrous. At the same time, President Hoover was sticking to his philosophy that the government should not distribute handouts, leaving that chore to private philanthropy. His decision to grant $20 million to feed livestock in the southwestern drought led a U.S. representative to complain, "The administration would feed jackasses, but it wouldn't feed starving babies."

One of the ironies of the situation was that there was plenty of food in America. The federal government had been buying food to keep farmers solvent and had stockpiled huge quantities of it; in later years, surplus food would be destroyed in order to maintain price levels. Norman Thomas, a prominent socialist leader, decried the system that spawned "breadlines knee deep in wheat." The food problem of America had nothing to do with production, merely with economics and distribution.

One of the problems of the historical assessment of the crisis is that there is little agreement on its magnitude. President Hoover declared in 1931 that no American was "actually starving," yet ninety-four deaths by starvation were reported in New York City alone in that year. Prominent health specialists quarreled, some arguing that the problems with diet were due to ignorance of proper nutrition, not lack of access to food. Any examination of the problem was politically charged, and no adequate study of national health as it related to diet ever was conducted during the depression. We will never truly know even the basic facts.

One point, however, was made very clear by the depression: Whatever the dietary effects, they were being felt only by the poorest citizens. Restaurant dining, a commonsense measure of economic well-being, remained steady through the stock market crash and the years of depression, actually increasing in some places. And, while the poor struggled to get food for the table, fad diets for weight loss were the rage among the well-to-do.

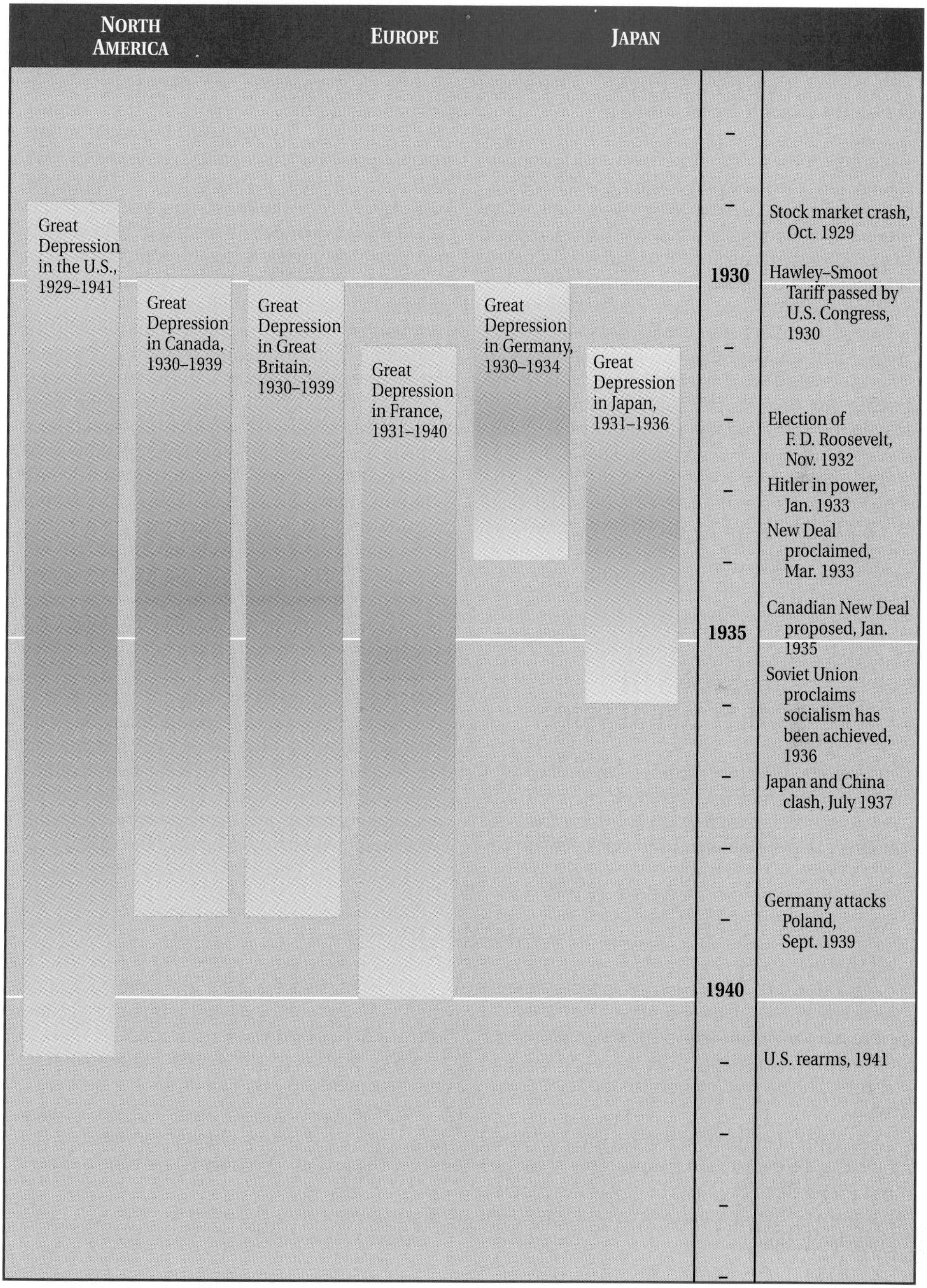

NORTH AMERICA		EUROPE			JAPAN		
Great Depression in the U.S., 1929–1941	Great Depression in Canada, 1930–1939	Great Depression in Great Britain, 1930–1939	Great Depression in France, 1931–1940	Great Depression in Germany, 1930–1934	Great Depression in Japan, 1931–1936		

	Stock market crash, Oct. 1929
1930	Hawley–Smoot Tariff passed by U.S. Congress, 1930
	Election of F. D. Roosevelt, Nov. 1932
	Hitler in power, Jan. 1933
	New Deal proclaimed, Mar. 1933
1935	Canadian New Deal proposed, Jan. 1935
	Soviet Union proclaims socialism has been achieved, 1936
	Japan and China clash, July 1937
	Germany attacks Poland, Sept. 1939
1940	
	U.S. rearms, 1941

uncommon. In the United States, life expectancy actually increased significantly between 1929 and 1939. Six years were added to the average American's expected life span. Improved medical care accounted for some of that growth.

Some states began to see their social mission as caring for their citizens in new ways. European nation-states were moving toward a social welfare system, and the depression era accelerated this tendency. Britain already had an unemployment insurance system and provided basic needs for the homeless and helpless. The United States prided itself on having private charities substitute for the public dole. Many Americans also espoused a rugged individualism that shrugged off charity in difficult times. The family filled a gap by taking in people. The Great Depression, however, caused a shift in thinking. President Hoover did little to help struggling people, but President Roosevelt committed the government to aiding the needy. The United States, for example, passed the Social Security Act in 1935 to pay for the retirement needs of employed people. The country thereby agreed to aid eligible workers who paid into the retirement system.

LESSONS OF THE GREAT DEPRESSION

The lessons-of-history concept sometimes is a useful teaching tool. Usually people are not sure of what might be learned from an event or a crisis. Yet the Great Depression seemed to teach economists and politicians that a quiescent, Hooverian approach to economic downturn courted disaster.

The greatest economist of the depression years, John Maynard Keynes[1] (1883–1946), actually accomplished little to alleviate the Great Depression's suffering. The ideas of his central monograph on governmental policy, published in 1936, were later followed by many leaders. During the half-century after the book's publication, Keynesian[2] policies (like deficit spending) held sway in many political circles. It might be said that no later depression of equal magnitude appeared because of these perspectives and efforts.

Another restraint on most countries was the realization that, while some mild form of protection for economic sectors might be necessary, return to the economic nationalism of the 1930s was a recipe for disaster. The Hawley-Smoot Tariff remained a symbol of protectionist stupidity to be avoided. Since World War II, international trade relations have been remarkably cooperative because more is to be gained from cooperation. Not only is there a global market, something only belatedly realized, but international trade agreements have been signed during the second half of the twentieth century to take advantage of it.

The Great Depression traumatized global societies for much of the 1930s. It followed World War I and helped prepare the way for World War II, and ferocious economic competition naturally emerged from the first and led comfortably into the second conflict. At the same time, political leaders gradually learned that massive military spending increases put many to work, alleviating the widespread unemployment of the 1930s.

SUMMARY

1. The Great Depression reflected a unique downturn in the global economy. Not only did prices plunge significantly, but production levels also sank dramatically. The crisis intensified because of economic nationalism and poor leadership.

2. Some of the problems and legacies of World War I, like the devastation it caused, the economic decline of Britain, and the recovery of the combatants' raw materials production, helped lead to the Great Depression.

3. From 1929 to 1932, government leaders tried to balance budgets and raise taxes at times when other measures were needed. In Canada, however, tariff increases raised substantial sums and kept many workers employed.

4. The stock market crash and the Hawley-Smoot Tariff helped precipitate and intensify the Great Depression. President Franklin Roosevelt

[1]**Keynes:** KAYNZ
[2]**Keynesian:** KAYN zee uhn

implemented most of the actions that helped end the depression, which lingered into the early 1940s.

5. Germany's economic collapse helped bring the Nazis to power. They and the Americans followed many similar policies to alleviate the negative effects of the Great Depression.

6. Japan devalued its currency. This policy, along with a major armament effort, pulled Japan out of the Great Depression. Both Germany and the United States also spent large sums on arming their nations.

7. Nonindustrial nations suffered in the 1930s. Many had supplied the industrial nation-states with raw materials that were no longer purchased in the 1930s. A few, like Brazil, successfully turned to production for the internal market. Local production also benefited Indian rubber producers and Egyptian cotton manufacturers.

8. The system of social welfare grew in many industrial states in the 1930s. It also played a role in the increase of political power of the nation-state.

9. The U.S. presidency became powerful during the Great Depression because of President Roosevelt's policies. A more powerful presidency is one example of the increasing centralization of industrial states.

10. Two lessons, the value of deficit spending in economic downturns and the need for international cooperation in trade matters, derived from the Great Depression and have contributed to the period of relative economic prosperity since 1945. Another lesson was that massive armament buildups helped bring countries out of their depressions.

SUGGESTED READINGS

Nakamura, Takafusa. "Depression, Recovery, and War, 1920–1945." In Peter Duus, *The Cambridge History of Japan: The Twentieth Century*. Cambridge, Eng.: Cambridge University Press, 1988, pp. 451–93. An examination of the depression in Japan.

Peukert, Detlev. *The Weimar Republic*. New York: Hill and Wang, 1992. A history of the Weimar Republic, including the depression.

Terkel, Studs. *Hard Times*. New York: Pantheon Books, 1970. An oral history of the depression in the United States.

Tint, Herbert. *France Since 1918*. New York: St. Martin's Press, 1980. A history of modern France and the Great Depression.

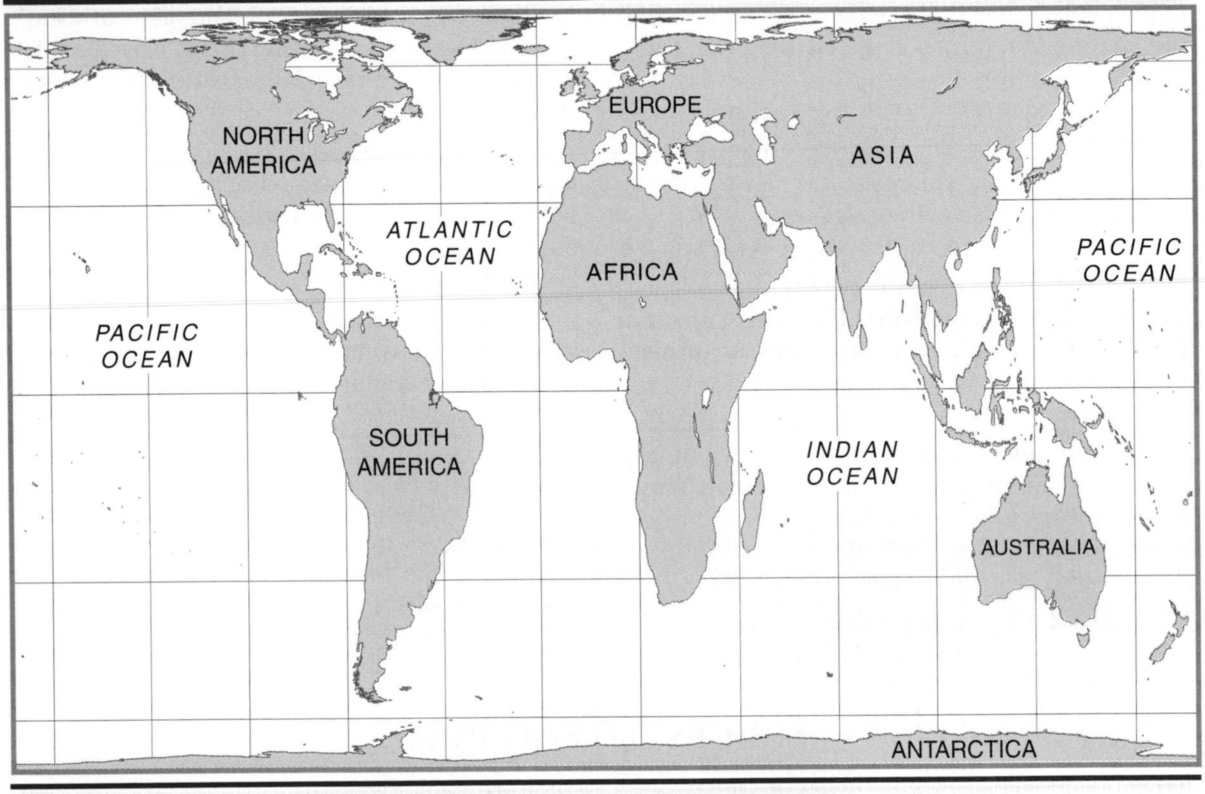

Hitler and Mussolini. *Adolf Hitler and Benito Mussolini represented the two main national socialist powers, Germany and Italy. Although the Italians were the first to adopt a national socialist government, the Germans led the movement in Europe. Hitler and Mussolini met often to discuss political and military matters; here they meet in München in 1937.* Ullstein Bilderdienst.

CHAPTER 39

National Socialism around the Globe

1919–1945

On the night of November 9, 1938, Germany's Nazi government organized the destruction of thousands of Jewish-owned shops and houses. Scores of Jews were killed and hundreds more were injured. Many were arrested and shipped off to jail or concentration camps. This came to be known as the "Night of Broken Glass" (Kristallnacht) and represented the policy of the German national socialist government to eradicate Jews, first in Germany and later in Europe.

National socialism arose out of the consequences of World War I and was energized by the sociopolitical upheavals of the Great Depression. It spread globally and was one of the dominating ideologies in the European theater of World War II. National socialists desired a powerful nation-state to control the nation's economy and army in order to expand national socialism by conquest.

THE MESSAGE AND CONTEXT OF NATIONAL SOCIALISM

National socialism appealed to disparate groups through a program of great persuasiveness. **National socialism** has the following elements:

—nationalism,

—socialism,

—imperialism, and

—totalitarianism.

Of these, the first two, nationalism and socialism, are primary. National socialists believed that the nation was holy and harmonious; therefore, class conflict was evil. They were passionate nationalists, and their sense of superiority fostered racism.

National socialists were quite unlike the socialists who followed Marx's ideas. Nonetheless, national socialists shared with socialists the idea that the state should control the means of production. National socialists believed in **corporatism**, the practice of combining owners, managers, and workers in a unitary whole within a business, factory, or industrial sector. Cooperation among all business components was paramount in the national socialists' economic vision.

National socialists were ardent imperialists. They believed that the nation-state should expand. In addition, national socialists argued for colonies to reflect national glory and to provide labor and raw materials for the nation's economy.

National socialists also favored **totalitarianism**, the belief that an all-powerful nation-state should control every aspect of its citizens' lives. In national socialist ideology, the nation's unity assumed paramount importance, and everyone was subordinate to it.

National socialists condemned certain aspects of modernity. They decried what they saw as the manipulative and corrupt politics of democracy and preferred an authoritarian regime. National socialists criticized elements of modern science's view of the world, and they despised the environmental degradation and poor working conditions created by capitalism. National socialism came into existence in part as a reaction to Marxism, out of fear of Soviet Russian dominance over Europe. Marxists' espousal of atheistic ideas and their stress on class warfare and the dominance of the working class ran counter to national socialist ideology.

NATIONAL SOCIALISM IN EUROPE

Europe became and remained the primary center of national socialism in the period from 1919 to 1945. Italy and Germany developed movements that took political control and carried out national socialist policies. Other countries had minor national socialist movements.

Italian National Socialism

Italy had been a victorious power in World War I, yet its political system did not long survive the war's end. Part of the problem came with the disintegration of its ruling coalition after the war and the inability of a succession of leaders to build viable coalition governments. By 1920, political activities by new parties had become more successful.

Italian national socialism gained influence in this era partly because of the breakdown of effective government and a corresponding upheaval in the cities. The Italian Fascist Party began in the urban industrial areas of northern Italy. With a strong component of World War I veterans (57 percent of the early party members), the early Fascists fought Marxist workers in city streets in order to establish themselves as a major political movement.

Benito Mussolini (1883–1945) was the leader of the Fascist Party. Mussolini's father, a socialist, named his son after Benito Juarez, the famous Mexican revolutionary. The young Mussolini became a Marxist, calling Karl Marx his father and teacher, but broke away from Marxism because he believed it to be unpatriotic. Despite his leaving Marxism, Mussolini's movement retained strong socialist features.

Given the sociopolitical chaos of the day, Mussolini's movement grew rapidly, and its demands became more aggressive. In October 1922, he declared a march on Rome to highlight the party's power. This dramatic action paralleled the march on Rome and seizure of the government by Julius Caesar nearly 2,000 years earlier. Around 50,000 activists arrived in the capital and greatly strengthened Mussolini's bargaining position. Within weeks, he was appointed the new leader of Italy. Once he was in control, Mussolini's example inspired imitators elsewhere.

By the time the national socialists came into power, their focus shifted to the conquest and monopolization of state agencies, especially those that controlled sources of information. Soon the party found support for its program of subordinating all of Italy's problems to nationalism. That is, the Fascists created a totalitarian state. They tapped into powerful nationalist feelings among those Italians who abhorred the warring of class against class.

Over time, national socialists developed full control of the political system. Corporatism

FIGURE 39.1 ***Mussolini and the "Roman Sons of the Wolf."*** *By 1938, Benito Mussolini had ordered Italy's armed forces to imitate the German army's goose-step marching. Here he reviews a corps of fascist youth patterned on its German counterpart. Marching played an important part in national socialist movements, especially in Europe, and parades were used to train soldiers and to energize the country's population.* Brown Brothers.

became the guiding principle for Italian businesses and workers. Mussolini directed the takeover and the transformation, bending Italy ever more to his will. In the mid-1930s, Mussolini formed a diplomatic alliance with the Germans and later with the Japanese, countries that had influential national socialist movements of their own.

The National Socialist Movement in Germany

Germany lay in ruins after World War I. Wilhelm II had fled to the Netherlands, and the Weimar Republic was created in place of the former German government. Hampered by a war-devastated economy and a punitive peace settlement, Weimar leaders struggled to maintain power. The German Communist Party decided to take advantage of the chaos. Workers fought in several cities and briefly managed to hold on to the local governments. In the aftermath of this violence and upheaval, the Nazi Party was formed.

Within a brief time after its founding, this national socialist group came under the leadership of Adolf Hitler (1889–1945). Born in Austria, Hitler had spent his youth as an unemployed painter of dubious talent. When World War I exploded, Hitler joined the German army, serving with distinction. After the war, he languished in southern Germany (Bavaria) until he joined and took over the leadership of the National Socialist German Workers Party (Nazi Party). For the next few years, the party was confined to southern Germany. In the period from 1920 to 1923, the party lost its military identity and began to recruit from all social groups and to establish small cells outside the south. The Nazi program also became more eclectic as the national socialists tried to appeal to many groups. Central to the platform was a virulent nationalism that placed the blame for Germany's problems on foreign countries.

Anti-Semitism became another central theme in German national socialism. From the beginning, Hitler cunningly paid lip service to rumors blaming Jews for Germany's problems, including the idea that they had been behind the severe inflation of the early 1920s. Hitler increasingly offered more radical solutions to the "Jewish question," and, when the Nazis gained control of the government, they confiscated Jewish property and intimidated Jews. Most scholars agree that these measures were calculated to produce the greatest possible effect on German popular opinion.

Franco-Belgian occupation of the Ruhr industrial region in Germany was an event that greatly increased membership in the Nazi Party. France and Belgium asserted that the Germans had failed to pay their war indemnity, and French and Belgian soldiers took control of valuable German property to support their claims. Germany's humiliating acquiescence to the seizure undermined the Weimar Republic and afforded the Nazis a potent political issue to exploit. Party membership grew manifold in little more than a year, and even industrial workers and miners in the Ruhr Valley supported the antiforeign policy of the national socialists.

The Nazi Party's spectacular growth persuaded Hitler to attempt a coup, which failed miserably. He planned a march on Berlin similar to Mussolini's march on Rome, but Hitler's influential allies deserted him, leading to his arrest, trial, and brief jailing. The party disintegrated in his absence. While in prison, Hitler wrote *Mein Kampf* (*My Struggle*), a book in which he outlined his political and racial beliefs.

Following his release, Hitler began rebuilding the party in the latter half of the 1920s. At the same time, the Nazis began to perfect their propaganda machine and to tailor their program to specific regions and social groups. This chameleonlike process did not seem to upset party members, although there was constant turnover in membership.

FIGURE 39.2 ***Anti-Semitic Propaganda.*** *Nazi leaflets like this one portrayed Jews as the source of worker and peasant servitude, thus making the Jews scapegoats for an economically depressed Germany. The left panel shows a caricatured Jewish businessman holding workers in bondage; the hammer and sickle below suggest a hidden communist agenda. The right panel promises economic freedom for workers when the Nazi Party is brought to power. Anti-Semitism was central to the Nazi ideology and culminated in the 1940s with the Holocaust, a massive attempt to exterminate Jews.* Library of Congress.

PARALLELS AND DIVERGENCES

The Roots of Nazi Racism

A prime organizing principle of Nazi ideology was its racial doctrine, which drew on a tradition of European racism and pseudoscience, serving as a justification for Nazi policies. Most peoples believe that they are the most advanced and moral, and Europeans' self-satisfied attitudes were common; the elaborate scientific edifice designed to defend them, however, was unique.

In the latter half of the nineteenth century, most German scholars were followers of Charles Darwin and his notions of biological evolution. Many also believed that his ideas could be translated directly into the social realm, following the ideas of Herbert Spencer and the social Darwinists. One influential group of German scientists, the **Monists**, carried this argument one step further, maintaining that ethnic groups were distinctive both biologically (racially) and socially, and that not all peoples were equally fit. Consequently, the most fit would naturally profit at the expense of the less fit. Some respected scientists, like Ernst Haeckel, were Monists, and the movement was highly esteemed in the German scientific community.

When this doctrine was translated into twentieth-century German political thought, it posited that Germans were the most fit of all races, and that they naturally would overwhelm the lesser races around them. Because to many Monists this was simply an application of Darwin's idea of survival of the fittest, public policies of extermination were seen as merely humane ways of speeding along the inevitable process. The Jews and Slavs, in this view, were the nearest of these lesser races, but Africans, Asians, and all non-Germanic races were thought to be inferior and eventually would become extinct. This argument had the ring of science, and it was ready-made for Nazi theorists like Alfred Rosenberg, who drew strongly on the Monist position.

The Monists borrowed their ideas from respected scientists, but they also took from branches of science that were no longer in good repute. In particular, most used **phrenology**, the now-discredited field that purported to relate physical characteristics to intellectual and moral worth. The best-known branch of phrenology claimed that the bumps on one's head revealed a person's character, but other branches made equally wild claims. Cesare Lambroso of Italy argued that careful measurements of the face could disclose criminal types; Richard Fletcher, a little-known Scottish physician, insisted that the shape of the collarbone was an indicator of one's moral nature as it related to sexuality; and Paul Broca, a biologist, claimed that brain size was a direct indicator of intelligence.

It was only a short step for Nazi theorists to turn these ideas into practical guidelines for recognizing "degenerates and inferior sorts." Nazi scientists devised formulas based on head measurements to identify Jews, Slavs, and other "undesirables." Anthropology thrived under the Nazis, largely because its practitioners devised seemingly scientific ways of recognizing targets for elimination.

Between 1930 and 1933, the Nazis achieved electoral success and power. A major factor in this era was the Great Depression. By inflaming the unrest caused by the depression, the Nazis transformed themselves from an irritant in German politics to a major political force. In January 1930, party membership numbered around 125,000; eight months later it had grown to 300,000, and by early 1933 had reached 1 million. Its increasing working-class appeal began to benefit the party in significant ways. During the election campaigns of this time, party members elected to national office increased from a handful to more than 100; in addition, the national socialists garnered around 37 percent of the national vote.

Adolf Hitler, more than Mussolini, defined national socialism. He had transcended his Austrian origins and poor education. During the years until 1930 Hitler honed his political skills, using radio and airplanes to create a flashy political product. More than one voter exclaimed that Hitler seemed to descend from the sky, like a deity. He also skillfully used the media of radio and motion pictures to dramatize the Nazi message.

UNDER THE LENS

Politics and the Media under National Socialism

The Nazis fully appreciated the power of the media in conveying the message they wished the German people to hear. Adolf Hitler himself called the radio a precondition to his victory, and he played a major role in the development of the important movie *Triumph of the Will* (1934). Less than two months after coming to power, the Nazis established a Ministry for Popular Enlightenment and Propaganda.

The radio assumed a valuable role for the National Socialist Party, both in its rise to power and in its building of a revolutionary system. Hitler wanted Germany to have the largest possible number of radios, and the number in the country increased from 4.5 million in 1933 to 16 million by 1942. Thus, Germany became blanketed by receivers carrying the Nazi message. Radio wardens were established to ensure that people had their sets on during significant radio speeches. Hitler gave about fifty radio broadcasts to the people in his first year of power, and his interpretation of events became the approved view. During parades, special microphones were stationed close to the marching soldiers in order to carry live the sounds of their goose-step footfalls. Everything was carefully choreographed.

During the normal "radio week," much time was given to musical performances, especially to light classical music by German composers. Because the somewhat soothing effect seemed satisfactory, more air time was allocated over the succeeding five years, so that around 70 percent of a weekly schedule included soothing music. Operettas by Franz Lehar and Johann Strauss led the selections played. Karl Maria von Weber's Romantic music also found a wide audience in the Nazi era. For more serious occasions, the Nazis preferred to play musical works by Richard Wagner, one of Hitler's favorite composers.

Movies, like radio, attracted the Nazi politicians, who admired propagandists in other countries. Josef Goebbels, the propaganda minister, personally paid tribute to *The Battleship Potemkin*, a Bolshevik movie directed by Sergei Eisenstein. Goebbels noted that its well-made character conveyed a powerful message likely to convert its viewers to Bolshevism.

Perhaps the most significant Nazi movie was *Triumph of the Will*, directed by Leni Riefenstahl. The idea came from Hitler's desire to present a film biography of Nazism and its leader, and he selected the title. The movie focused on a massive Nazi Party rally in Nuremberg and used it to convey the message of Nazism. Riefenstahl wrote a book about the making of the movie, detailing the immense effort that went into it. To obtain special visual effects, the city of Nuremberg had bridges, towers, and tracks constructed. The director controlled a unit of 120 people, including 16 cameramen, 22 chauffeurs to drive cars, and bodyguards. In all, well over 60 miles of film was shot. To create an overall effect, Riefenstahl chose to capture a mood rather than present a story chronologically. The impressionistic effect had a symphonic quality in which the different parts merged into a whole of sight and sound without a distracting narrative commentary. The movie received critical acclaim, even by enemies of the Nazi regime, and showed Nazi mastery of the media.

Finally, Nazi propagandists, led by Josef Goebbels, organized massive and spectacular Nazi rallies in major cities like Nuremberg.

Oratorical skill was perhaps Hitler's greatest asset. He perfected his speaking techniques in the smoky bars of Bavaria. Then he worked patiently to eliminate flaws in his delivery. He sensed an audience's mood and played to it. One film shows him standing in silence before a gathering of supporters, who chat amiably until a growing silence stills the hall. Hitler waits until he has measured them, then launches into a powerful address. He played to crowd responses by modulating his voice and using dramatic hand gestures to keep audiences enthralled.

In January 1933, the German political elite decided to manipulate Hitler and the Nazis into the government because the officials mistakenly believed that the Nazis could be easily controlled. President Paul von Hindenburg appointed Hitler to the chancellorship in 1933, but Hitler fooled the ruling politicians, who had hoped to use him for

Figure 39.3 ***Nazi Rally.*** *Nazi leaders became expert in staging rallies and events. This picture shows Hitler amidst the party faithful, accepting their salutes on September 1, 1939, the day Germany invaded Poland and drew the rest of Europe into war. This carefully staged show of nationalism included officers from all branches of the armed forces displaying their faith in Hitler as their supreme commander. Little was left to chance in these images.* Ullstein Bilderdienst.

their ends. Within months after taking power, Hitler and the Nazis had destroyed the other parties and turned state organizations to their benefit. Hindenburg's death in August 1934 facilitated Hitler's consolidation of power, permitting him to combine the presidency and chancellorship into one position, that of *führer* (leader). Chapter 38 explained how the Nazis developed their economic program and began the rearmament program after 1935. Hitler planned to shed the Versailles Treaty's controls on Germany because he realized that many Germans hated the treaty's humiliating conditions and because it limited German expansion. In violation of the Versailles Peace Treaty, Hitler unilaterally rebuilt the armed forces and reoccupied the east bank of the Rhineland. He soon began calling for the return of German peoples and former territories. Many of these efforts were tolerated by other European states, which did not wish to precipitate a confrontation. In fact, some European leaders felt that the Germans had been too severely punished.

In 1938, Germany occupied and annexed Austria, the country of Hitler's birth, and Hitler began an expansionist foreign policy. Soon after, he insisted that the Sudetenland, an area of Czechoslovakia inhabited by German-speaking people, be annexed. Germans there were provoked by Hitler to demand reunification. At the Munich Conference, attended by Mussolini, Neville Chamberlain (Britain), Edouard Daladier (France), and Hitler, the parties agreed to permit German occupation and annexation of the Sudetenland, despite the objections of the Czechs. Chamberlain and Daladier believed in appeasing Hitler and the Germans. Neither the British nor the French wished to fight another European war like the one that had devastated their countries and had killed or crippled millions of their men.

Within the following year, Hitler demanded the return of parts of Poland. Because Hitler feared the possibility of a two-front war, he carried on negotiations with the Soviets and with the British and French. The British and French were treaty-bound to fight alongside their Polish allies, and, when they refused Hitler's demands for further appeasement, he turned to the Russians. The Nazis and the Soviets inked the Non-Aggression Pact in

MAP 39.1 ***Hitler's Annexations in Eastern Europe, 1936–1939.*** *Adolf Hitler came to power vowing to revise the territorial settlement imposed on Germany at the Versailles Peace Conference of 1919. Accordingly, in 1938, he annexed Austria and the Sudetenland of Czechoslovakia (with British and French acquiescence). The rest of the Czech territories and parts of Poland were annexed in 1939. Poland's fate was decided by a Soviet-Nazi pact in August 1939 and the subsequent invasion of Poland by Germany and Soviet Russia in September 1939. The latter event precipitated the European theater of World War II.*

August 1939 and attacked Poland soon after. Britain and France declared war, one that they had tried to avoid. World War II in Europe had begun.

National Socialism in Iberia

The Spanish and Portuguese national socialist groups never won significant followings. Both states saw parties come to power that co-opted their national socialist rivals. Some Spanish national socialist groups received funding from wealthy landowners and bankers, and they often received inspiration and support from Italy and Germany. One Portuguese group, the National Syndicalist Organization, preached anticapitalism and the importance of attracting young people to the cause. About 20 percent of its membership came from students and intellectuals.

During the Spanish civil war (1936–1939), elements of the Spanish army led by General Francisco Franco (1892–1975) launched a coup against the Spanish government. Soon the Germans and Italians backed Franco, while the Soviets supported the ruling government. The Spanish civil war became a testing ground for a European war, as the Italians, Germans, and Soviets sent substan-

FIGURE 39.4 ***Poster of the Spanish Civil War.*** *The Spanish civil war (1936–1939) became a testing ground for national socialist armies and weapons. There they faced the forces of Spanish leftists, some of whom owed loyalty to Soviet Russia. This collage offers a leftist perspective that shows airplanes bombing the Spanish city of Madrid, taking the lives of children and destroying property. This "culture" of the national socialists is equated with fascism and terror.* Victoria & Albert Museum / Fotomas Index.

tial military aid and advisors. Although Franco's victory should have meant that the national socialists would rule, Franco refused to allow them into power. The national socialists in Spain were quickly relegated to political obscurity.

Other European National Socialist Movements

Other European countries harbored national socialist movements, but none gained a mass following. Racism proved a major theme of these parties, with the Jews and Gypsies suffering criticism and violence directed against them.

In Britain and Ireland, army veterans comprised a major element of the various national socialist movements. In both countries, national socialists adopted a variety of campaign slogans that had a constantly shifting appeal. In Britain, young people and lower aristocrats supported the British Union of Fascists. In Ireland, the rural community, especially cattle ranchers and farmers, gave the Army Comrades' Association the most support. Some Irish joined national socialist groups as a means of opposing the British, who had long been involved in Irish affairs.

Sir Oswald Mosley (1896–1980) went from England to Italy and Germany to study national socialism. Upon his return, he directed the British Union of Fascists to espouse a vitriolic anti-Semitism. He also stressed violent action, corporatism, funding of public works programs, and imperial self-sufficiency. By 1934, the British Union of Fascists had attracted around 50,000 members from most social groups and regions of Britain.

French national socialists built on conservative traditions from the nineteenth century. After World War I, the Action Française developed a program of intense nationalism that took an anti-German tone. It preached strong militarist values. Action Française was anti-Nazi, although it did favor corporatism and many Italian and German economic policies. It never assumed an important role in French politics.

The activities of the Italians and Germans helped inspire similar movements in the Netherlands and in Belgium. The dislocations caused by the onset of the Great Depression inspired change as well. Nationalism was strongly emphasized, especially in the development of an authoritarian state. Attention was given to veterans and young people. There were many national socialist groups in the Netherlands and in Belgium, and two of the largest numbered between 50,000 and 115,000 members. The Netherlands' main party received financial support from wealthy people. It grew rapidly until the Nazis became aggressive, and, during World War II, many in the party collaborated with the Nazis.

Central and eastern Europeans not only saw the devastating effects of World War I, but they also witnessed the collapse of the Austro-Hungarian and German empires. There had been no democratic traditions in the region, and corrosive ethnic tensions predominated. There were rivalries between the Czechs and Slovaks, between the Romanians and Hungarians, between the Croats and the Serbs, and between the Jews and gentiles. Again, national socialist movements there stressed violence, appealed particularly to veterans and young people, especially students, and often strongly felt the influence of the German and Italian national socialists.

The Austrian National Socialist Party was founded in 1919 and followed Hitler's lead in most areas after 1925. Following the collapse of the Austro-Hungarian Empire in 1918, Austrian nationalism was identified with Germany and was supported by the Germans to the north. It also appealed to groups in the chameleonlike manner of the Nazi Party and attracted support from professionals in public and private businesses. Although the Austrian National Socialist Party supported union with Germany, many Austrians preferred to remain independent.

Populist attitudes predominated in national socialism in both Hungary and Romania, and students and soldiers played a critical role there. The Romanian Legion of the Archangel Michael and the Iron Guard were established in the late 1920s. They appealed to the nationalist sentiments of college and high school students, and they violently criticized and attacked the Jews for being alien to Romanian culture and values. The Hungarian Arrow Cross Party, which espoused strong anti-Semitic views, was led by army officers. In 1937 and 1938, the Arrow Cross Party gained a mass following. In 1939, the Nationalist Alliance garnered 900,000 votes and appealed to the uprooted people in urban and rural sectors.

NATIONAL SOCIALISM IN EAST ASIA

At the other end of the Eurasian landmass, active national socialist movements developed in China and Japan in the 1930s. The Chinese movement represented an effort by the Nationalist Party leader, Jiang Jieshi (Chiang Kai-shek, 1887–1975), to imitate the methods of the Italians and Germans. The Japanese developed two movements: one that appealed to army officers and soldiers, containing an element of anti-Western sentiments, and another that openly copied Italian and German models.

China's National Socialism

The primary group of national socialists in China was connected with Jiang Jieshi, head of the Nationalist Party and the leader of China. Dissatisfied with his party, which had become riddled with corruption and torn by factions, Jiang helped bring into being the Blue Shirts, an organization directly modeled on the Italian and German national socialists. The Chinese organization, however, remained a secret group in the mold of China's secret societies. Despite the clandestine nature of the movement, its influence became pervasive in the few years of its existence in the 1930s.

The military played a vital role in China's national socialism. As early as 1928 and continuing thereafter, German military missions to China were led by people with close ties to Nazi Party leaders, including Hitler himself. Because these German officers influenced the educational system of China's military academies, they indirectly inculcated the ideas of national socialism in their fellow Chinese. In addition, Chinese officers who exhibited exceptional leadership capabilities went abroad to study. Most studied and trained in Italy and Germany and witnessed national socialist rule there.

Jiang Jieshi founded the Blue Shirts in the spring of 1933. Top leaders were graduates of the Whampoa Military Academy, especially from the first three graduating classes. The first class of cadets considered themselves bound to Jiang, the commandant of the academy, as disciples to a sage. Of the survivors of the 1920s unification wars, many considered themselves a separate elite.

National revival meant everything to the Blue Shirts, who despaired at the daily reminders of China's enfeebled state. They believed that the best way to energize people was through promoting Chinese nationalism. And the best symbol for China was Jiang Jieshi. The Blue Shirts took secret vows of absolute obedience to Jiang and his commands. To create the totalitarian state, the group had to prevail over the individual and even the family. This model, of course, was adopted from the Italians and Germans.

Although foreign models were followed, the Chinese rejected many values and practices of the West. Perhaps the idea most despised by the Chinese national socialists was individualism, a term that translates into Chinese as "selfishness." The Blue Shirts violently attacked individualism, democracy, representative government, and capitalism, all of which were linked to the West. The Chinese cultural program stressed the reanimation of many positive values from China's past, to be inculcated through social institutions like schools, the National Boy Scouts Association, and special summer camps where students received three to four weeks of military training. These organizations were led by the Blue Shirts and became major recruiting grounds for them.

The New Life Movement and the Special Movement Corps also had strong Blue Shirt connections. The New Life Movement developed in the mid-1930s and stressed four main virtues: propriety, justice, honesty, and self-respect. To guide the people, Jiang issued ninety-five rules governing behavior, embodying these four virtues. The Special Movement Corps, organized in mid-1933, had about 20,000 members and was led by Blue Shirts. Central to their task in Jiangxi Province, where the Chinese communists were embedded in the Jiangxi Soviet base area, was the effort to win back people to the Nationalist Party. Local people were given small arms and limited military training. To improve their chances of gaining popular support, the Special Movement Corps investigated and rooted out local corruption and sedition. They were generally successful in Jiangxi and drove out the communists. Later, they gained some ground in Sichuan[1] Province, farther west.

Many other nationalist organizations had top leaders who came from the Blue Shirts. One of the

[1] **Sichuan:** SEE chwahn

FIGURE 39.5 *Mass Marriage Ceremony in China.* *President Jiang Jieshi sponsored the New Life Movement, a program designed to improve the lives of Chinese citizens by promoting moral conduct. This mass ceremony highlighted marriage as an institution especially sanctioned by Confucianism, a value system supported by the nationalist government. Identically attired men and women stand before a Chinese temple. Jiang used symbolic ceremonies to enhance his claim to be father of the nation.* L'Illustration/Sygma.

most crucial was the Special Services Department of the Blue Shirts. This agency acted as a counterintelligence organization and carried out assassinations. It was headed by Dai Li[2] (1895–1946), a Whampoa Military Academy cadet who developed a talent for identifying and informing on communists. He caught the attention of Jiang and joined the Blue Shirts. Soon he was put in charge of overseeing special tasks, including assassination. Dai Li's organization became greatly feared, and some likened him to Heinrich Himmler, the infamous head of Hitler's Gestapo (political police). Dai believed that the leader should be safeguarded, that corruption should be punished, that counterrevolutionary forces and international spies should be destroyed, and that national reconstruction should be assisted. Like the Gestapo, Dai's group terrorized many, guilty and innocent alike.

[2] **Dai Li:** DY lee

The Blue Shirts numbered only about 10,000 members and prided themselves on their elite nature. Through various organizations, however, they influenced hundreds of thousands of people. When Jiang fell into the hands of his enemies in late 1936, he negotiated with the communists and others for his release. Some have argued that one condition of Jiang's freedom was the disbanding of the Blue Shirts. Whatever the reason, the organization and many of its subagencies were abolished in 1938. Thus, Jiang lost a key support group. The Nationalist Party declined further and lost control of the Chinese mainland.

National Socialism in Japan

Although there were numerous nationalistic organizations in Japan during the 1920s and 1930s, small national socialist parties developed. Two different but related programs generated by intellectuals appeared, one in the early 1920s and the other in 1940. The first, led by Kita Ikki[3] (1883–1937), influenced a large number of young Japanese army officers and others to stage a coup in order to bring down the hated Meiji system and usher in an age of national socialist rule. The second, developed by the Showa Research Association, an elite think tank that was cultivated by Prime Minister Konoe Fumimaro,[4] enjoyed a brief influence upon Japan's elite but was overturned by key political figures.

Kita Ikki developed his brand of national socialism from native Japanese traditions and from Western socialism. Kita came from one of Japan's small islands and was born into a wealthy family with a *samurai* lineage. By the early twentieth century, he had come to appreciate socialism, writing a book that sought to bridge the gap between an emperor-oriented nationalism and socialism. After that venture, Kita twice visited China and became friends with men who had participated in the overthrow of the Manchus between 1911 and 1912.

In 1923, Kita's most important book, *A Plan to Reorganize Japan*, influenced many Japanese, especially army officers. The political program advocated a military-led coup and a period of martial law to topple the Meiji constitutional system and its ruling elite. This program offered the direct unity of the emperor with his people without the intervening layer of bureaucrats and power brokers. After three years, a representative government would be established based on universal male suffrage. Imperial lands and properties would be nationalized and given to the needy.

The economic program envisioned the retention of private property and government regulation of the economy. The purpose was to ensure efficiency and effective planning. Seven special ministries (Banks, Maritime, Mines, Agriculture, Industries, Commerce, and Railroads) would be established. They would supervise businesses that came into state hands and sell agricultural and industrial merchandise produced by state concerns. Kita urged worker profit-sharing programs and worker participation in management. There would be an eight-hour work day, binding arbitration to resolve labor disputes, and other benefits for laborers. Peasants were to enjoy a land redistribution from imperial and wealthy landowners' lands.

Kita's social program advocated treating women favorably and called for the establishment of a welfare state. Women were to have equal opportunity in the workplace and to be treated with respect. The state would punish adulterous husbands. The state also was to provide for the welfare of orphans, widows with children, people over the age of sixty, disabled people, and others who could not provide for themselves or who did not have families able to support them.

Kita's ideas profoundly influenced young soldiers, many of whom had lived in rural areas and knew of the difficult life there. Some of them were involved in assassinations of prominent leaders in the 1930s, but the event that riveted Japan's attention was the attempted coup by the First Division of the Imperial Army on February 26, 1936. Around 1,400 soldiers took over government buildings in downtown Tokyo, assassinating political and naval leaders. Emperor Hirohito's refusal to support the coup doomed it. No officials joined the effort, and the rebels were persuaded to surrender. Several leaders and Kita Ikki, who had no direct role in the coup, were tried and executed. Members of an army faction that favored the overthrow of the Meiji system were purged.

[3] **Kita Ikki:** KEE tah EE kee
[4] **Konoe Fumimaro:** KOH noh ay FOO mee mah roh

Another national socialist movement developed among a small group of Japanese intellectuals in the late 1930s. They had been socialists early in their academic careers, but they had moved away from Marxism and toward nationalistic positions. All of them argued for a single mass party, a powerful nation-state, government control of the economy through corporate systems, and the inculcation of an ethic that promoted service to the nation. Their proposals built on examples in Germany and Italy. These systems impressed the Japanese thinkers who viewed national socialism as the ideology of the future. They discounted the role of violence in bringing systemic change and eschewed the racist programs found in Europe. The members of the Showa Research Association wanted to establish a society that was more just, less conflict-ridden, and more efficiently administered. Unlike Kita Ikki, they did not harken back to Japan's past for models or ideas. Rather, they postulated an elite national socialism that was comprised of components from the most current ideologies. Their ideas proved to be too revolutionary and were rejected.

IN THEIR OWN WORDS

Japanese National Socialism

Japanese intellectuals were alternately attracted by or resistant to Western ideas and influences in the 1930s. While some admired Hitler and Mussolini and their movements, they also believed that Japanese national socialism had to be unique.

Members of the Showa Research Association flirted with national socialism. They wished for a single party based on occupational units, leading to a Japanese form of "one nation, one party." As in Nazi Germany, the economic order would limit profits, implement economic planning, create regional and industrial cartels, and emphasize national goals:

> The new economic structure of the . . . national defense state aims at the competition of military preparations, expansion of productivity, and . . . a mobilization of the entire personnel and material resources of the country.
>
> This means an epoch-making development not only in the munitions industries. Such a rapid and large-scale reorganization of the industrial structure is practically impossible under the old liberal economic structure without causing disturbances to the entire national economic structure. Therefore it is essential first of all to intensify thoroughly planned economic control.

The trend of some Japanese extremists working toward a common goal in the 1930s elicited commentary from Ryu Shintaro, a member of the Showa Research Association:

> The Social Mass [Party] now seems to stand above the contradictions [of espousing both peace and national defense]. This is a [tactical] "necessity" and it is not an earth-shaking change for Japanese social democracy. We will not argue whether [this condition] depends on the special historical and economic character of the Japanese army or on the special nature of Japanese social democracy. We cannot, however, ignore the fact that a distinct social force has newly formed. This is very different from the attitudes that European social democratic parties have taken in their antifascist movements. We will not discuss here which historical and social conditions are causing these special Japanese developments. Also we cannot judge whether these trends will lead to fascist control or social control [by the masses]. . . . At any rate, the form and shape of the "international" character of the labor movement within Japan has disappeared.

Although Japanese national socialism never developed into a full-fledged movement like those in Italy and Germany, the Showa Research Association provided the idea of a totalitarian Japanese system of one party and one nation.

NATIONAL SOCIALISM IN THE AMERICAS

National socialist ideas had a limited impact in the Americas. In North America, a few intellectuals and business leaders were attracted to the personalities of Hitler and Mussolini, and others were attracted to the economic success of the national socialists. In Latin America, military officers and soldiers became enamored of the warlike nature of the Italian and German national socialists.

North American National Socialism

U.S. imitators of the Nazi and Fascist parties could raise only a few supporters in the 1930s. The Khaki Shirts and American Vigilantes formed but were unable to attract large followings. They were led by common people who sought personal power and influence rather than the implementation of programs. Veterans had little part in these outfits, which vehemently attacked the New Deal and President Franklin Roosevelt.

Ezra Pound, the poet, and a few other intellectuals found national socialism attractive. Perhaps the most sustained and articulate espousal of such views came from Lawrence Dennis, a diplomat and financier. Dennis published *The Coming American Fascism*, wherein he rejected communism as a viable option for America because it focused on class warfare. National socialism, he felt, had the best chance of success because it promoted class harmony in the sense of corporatism found in Europe; in addition, massive public works programs could put people back to work. Dennis also reflected the common view that women should not work because marriage, he felt, was a woman's best option.

Huey Long, a U.S. politician with presidential ambitions, seemed to many to be a latent national socialist. He professed admiration for some of the European programs of national socialism and promoted large public welfare programs. Dennis believed that Long had the charisma to lead the masses in the manner of a Hitler or a Mussolini, but Long's assassination in 1935 ended that possibility. No one else developed the ideas and program to become a major U.S. political figure in the national socialist movement.

Except for a few isolated people, Canadians did not espouse national socialism. In 1935, the Social Credit Party swept to power in the Province of Alberta on a platform of mortgage relief for farmers and ranchers who suffered from the Great Depression. The party grew more anti-Semitic and restrictive of civil liberties in the 1930s. In Quebec Province, the Union Nationale came to power in 1936. It appealed to Quebec nationalism and attacked communism, gaining the support of local trade unions and religious leaders.

Latin American National Socialism

Between 1932 and 1938, there developed in Brazil a movement similar to those in Italy and Germany. This national socialist party, the Integralists, received significant funding from the Italian embassy, especially in its formative months. Integralists espoused a strong nationalism tinged with a craving for traditional values and institutions. Catholicism became a key part of their party program, as in the Iberian national socialist movements. Integralists repudiated Marxism's internationalism, its scorn for tradition, and its atheistic ideology.

Integralists vehemently fought and helped destroy a Brazilian communist movement that was funded and directed by the Comintern (Communist International). The communists in turn dominated a coalition of parties, the National Liberation Alliance. The communists and the national socialists battled each other in the streets of Brazil's major cities. The Integralists adopted the symbol of the green shirt and held highly disciplined street rallies. In crushing the communist movement in the latter half of 1935, Brazil's president declared a state of siege and ruled by decree. Mass arrests, summary trials, tortures, and executions doomed the attempted communist uprising.

The Integralists were elated by the communists' defeat. They expected to play a role similar to that of the Fascists in Italy and of the Nazis in Germany, but there was no mass movement, and, following a feeble coup attempt, the Integralists themselves faced a state crackdown. The party disappeared.

Chile and Argentina were influenced by European national socialism. Chileans formed a small National Socialist Party that clearly imitated the

FIGURE 39.6 ***Interrogating a Leftist in Brazil.*** *The Brazilian Integralist Party, which had national socialist leanings, regarded socialists and Marxists as enemies of the state. In this 1936 photo, a communist leader is held in restraints and guarded by a member of the security forces. Examples were made of the socialists and their allies to deter others from political activism; many were harshly punished.* Iconographia / Pulsar Images.

German Nazi Party. It had little electoral success and mainly served as a target of vehement opposition by socialists. Argentina had many paramilitary groups organized along the lines of their European national socialist counterparts. The strongest influence in Argentina was found in the military. In secret lodges, the Italian model of national socialism received some praise and imitation. The Argentinian movement, however, did not develop a powerful ideological and organizational framework.

SOCIETY UNDER NATIONAL SOCIALISM

In Italy and Germany, most groups supported the national socialists, especially when they ruled. One social phenomenon was the predominance of men in the early national socialist movements. Soldiers and veterans seemed especially drawn to the national socialist message of the use of violence to solve problems. Many veterans from World War I could not find jobs and longed for the camaraderie and thrills they had experienced on the battlefield. Battling for national socialism seemed attractive to them.

Young people dominated the early national socialist movements in Italy, Germany, and elsewhere. War veterans, most of whom were in their twenties, were concerned about inflation and sociopolitical unrest. Young people, who had few chances to better themselves and felt cheated by circumstances, feared that the Great Depression was the start of a downward spiral that could be halted only by radical action.

The leadership core in Romanian, Hungarian, and Slovakian national socialism came from university students and from some high school students. They seemed more receptive to the relatively simple party messages and were more idealistic in seeking to bring about radical sociopolitical change. Proponents of national socialism in Japan were young army officers and their youthful soldiers. While some older people, like generals and Kita Ikki, served as models, the bulk of the activists were younger men.

Some women joined national socialist parties, but they seldom sanctioned the avowed use of violence. Significant numbers of women joined the German Nazi Party during the last years of World War II, when their percentage grew from 5 percent (1933–1936) to around 35 percent (1942–1944), or more than 2.1 million. This high percentage certainly reflects the number of men killed in wartime, but it also shows the growing influence of women on the home front, especially in businesses and industry.

While the Italian and German parties had a high proportion of middle-class elements among the core leaders, the Fascists and Nazis recruited from all social classes and all geographic regions, before and after they came to power. In that sense, they broadly represented the social makeup of their respective nation-states.

FIGURE 39.7 ***On Their Way to a Book-burning.*** *These Nazis and their supporters are carrying books and other papers for destruction. A favorite method was through incineration, which sent a fiery message to intellectuals to censor their works or have them turned to ashes. Book-burnings have occurred throughout history, and the Nazi Party celebrated the destruction of literature and the diminishing of ideas they hated.* Corbis-Bettmann.

Europe

Europe			Year	Events
			1910	
			–	
			–	
			–	
			–	Austrian National Socialist Party founded, 1919
			1920	Italian Fascist Party formed, 1919
	Italian national socialism, 1922–1943		–	Mussolini takes power, 1922 Kita Ikki publishes *A Plan to Reorganize Japan,* 1923
			–	Hitler writes *Mein Kampf,* 1924
			–	
			–	
			1930	
			–	Blue Shirts founded in China, 1933
		German national socialism, 1933–1945	–	British Union has 50,000 members, 1934 Social Credit Party wins power, 1935
			–	Kita Ikki executed, 1936
Austrian national socialism, 1938–1945			–	Blue Shirts disbanded, 1938 National Alliance gains 900,000 votes, 1939
			1940	
			–	
			–	Mussolini executed, 1945 Hitler commits suicide, 1945
			–	
			–	

SUMMARY

1. National socialism has four components: nationalism (focus on the nation), socialism (state control of the economy), imperialism (national expansion), and totalitarianism (subordination of all other elements to the nation-state). Central to many national socialist movements were the attraction of young people, veterans, and active soldiers, and resort to racist slogans, policies, and programs of violence.

2. National socialism was sparked by the aftermath of World War I and by the Great Depression. It was spurred by soldiers and young people who feared falling into poverty, as well as the Great Depression's devastation of workers and farmers.

3. Italian national socialism (fascism) owed much to Benito Mussolini. He led the party to power in 1922 and ruled a coalition of political parties afterward.

4. The Nazi Party achieved modest success up to 1923, when its leader, Adolf Hitler, attempted a coup and was briefly jailed. A second upsurge came with the Great Depression. In 1933, German leaders appointed Hitler chancellor of the Weimar Republic, and he eventually transformed Germany into a national socialist state. Hitler rebuilt the German economy and began a massive rearmament program that helped precipitate hostilities in the European theater of World War II.

5. National socialist movements were less successful in Hungary, Austria, Romania, Belgium, and the Netherlands. These national socialist organizations followed the lead of Italy and Germany, though they also had national variations.

6. Chinese national socialism came when Jiang Jieshi became enamored of the German and Italian movements. His Blue Shirts developed as an elitist Chinese-style secret society that influenced Chinese politics until they were disbanded in 1938.

7. Japan saw two movements of national socialism, one developed by Kita Ikki and the other by the Showa Research Association. The former followed many Japanese patterns and did not receive impetus from the European movements. The latter developed with Europe as a model but did not become significant in terms of government policy.

8. Latin American national socialist parties remained small and politically unimportant. They attracted some middle-class support but remained closely tied with military groups in Brazil and Argentina. They grew in imitation of European models and often were financed with European money.

9. The national socialists attracted different social groups, especially in their successful state governments. Women generally played minor roles in the national socialist movements. In some countries, intellectuals and professionals were particularly attracted to the parties.

SUGGESTED READINGS

Bracher, Karl. *Turning Points in Modern Times.* Cambridge, Mass.: Harvard University Press, 1995. A historical analysis of modern Germany, focusing on the totalitarian component of German national socialism.

Carsten, F. L. *The Rise of Fascism.* Berkeley: University of California Press, 1980. A classic treatment of fascism.

Fletcher, W. M. *Intellectuals and Fascism in Prewar Japan.* Chapel Hill: University of North Carolina Press, 1982. A look at the intellectual origins of Japanese national socialism.

Hsü, Immanuel. *The Rise of Modern China.* Oxford, Eng.: Oxford University Press, 1995. A standard history of China, emphasizing the 1930s.

Mosse, George. *Nazi Culture.* London: W. H. Allen, 1966. An important treatment of the uses that the Nazis made of culture in order to promote their message.

Mühlberger, Detlef, ed. *The Social Basis of European Fascist Movements.* London: Croom Helm, 1987. An examination of social class and national socialism.

Sternhell, Zeev. *The Birth of Fascist Ideology.* Princeton, N.J.: Princeton University Press, 1994. A look at the socialist elements in national socialism.

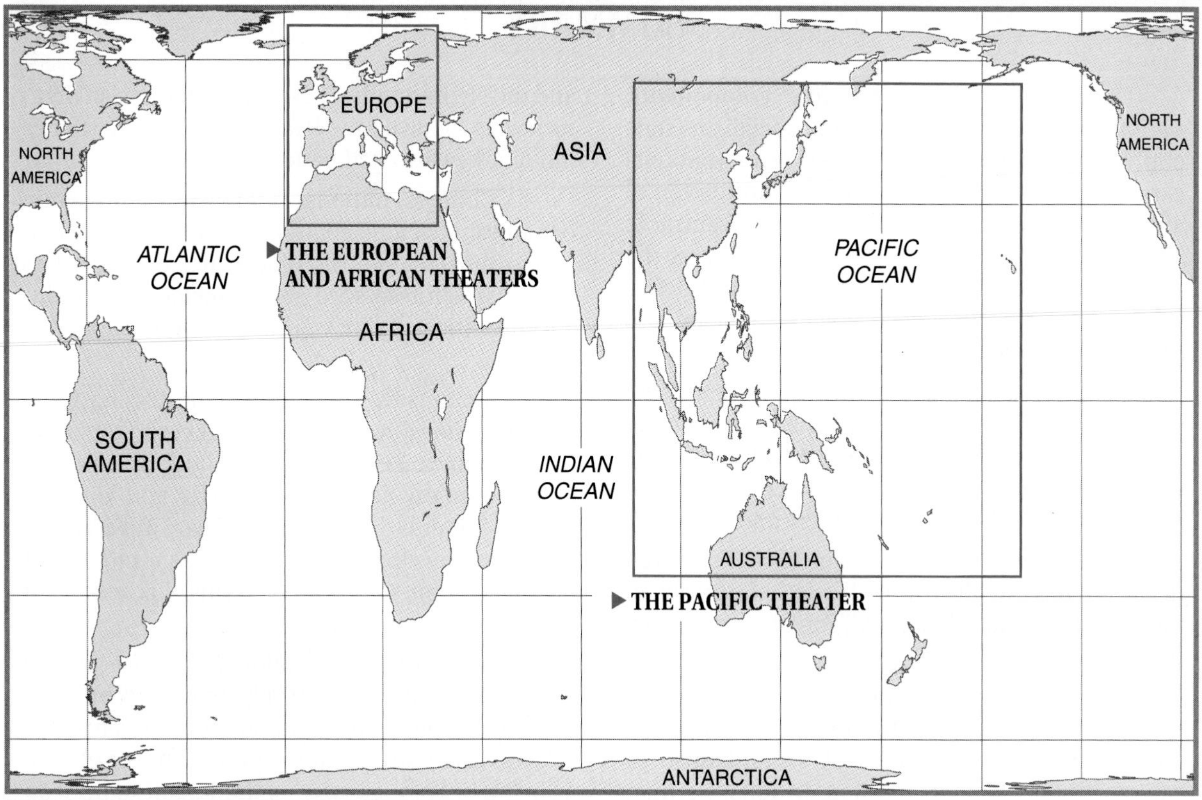

NORTH AMERICA
EUROPE
ASIA
NORTH AMERICA
ATLANTIC OCEAN
▶ THE EUROPEAN AND AFRICAN THEATERS
PACIFIC OCEAN
AFRICA
SOUTH AMERICA
INDIAN OCEAN
AUSTRALIA
▶ THE PACIFIC THEATER
ANTARCTICA

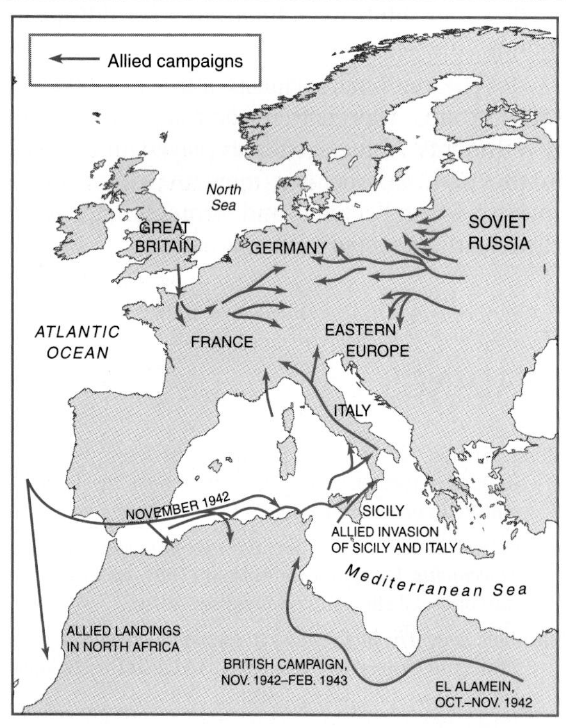

▶ **THE EUROPEAN AND AFRICAN THEATERS**

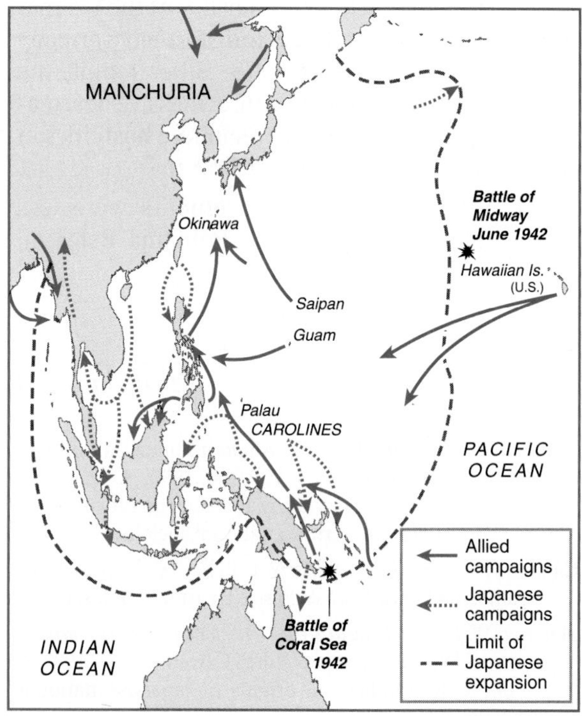

▶ **THE PACIFIC THEATER**

CHAPTER 40

World War II and Holocausts

1937–1945

A stench hung in the air over the ash-covered concentration camp. Today, a Gypsy lad of barely twenty was shot and killed for joking during the work detail. His crumpled body lay in the pit where charred human remains lay in smoldering piles. Among those killed had been homosexuals, Jews, disabled people, and senile folk. Why?

In terms of human suffering, World War II dwarfs all other human wars. Calculations of the loss of life, limb, and property scarcely begin to measure the scale of this global conflict. The number of dead and missing double the corresponding figures for World War I and may have reached more than 60 million people. Apart from that total, wartime destruction uprooted millions, some of whom moved to distant places in search of peace or opportunity. Millions were forcibly evicted from their homes by conquerors, paving the way for others to resettle. Isolated examples of racist actions involving humiliation, injury, and death abound, but these pale in comparison to the deliberate and systematic mass murder of around 11 million Jews, Poles, Russians, Gypsies, and others deemed unfit or troublesome.

CAUSES OF WORLD WAR II

Two main blocs fought each other during World War II. The **Axis** included Germany, Japan, and Italy, although other states gave minimal support to this group. The **Allies** comprised Britain, the Soviet Union, China, the United States, and Canada, as well as less powerful countries. When France fell to the Germans in 1940, the succeeding puppet government that cooperated with the Germans was known as **Vichy France**. A group of French who were antagonistic to the Germans later formed the **Free French**, a government-in-exile. Italy was an Axis power until it fell to the Allies in 1943.

Interlocking Wars

There were three interrelated war theaters in World War II—Asia, Euro-Africa, and the Pacific. The Asian theater erupted in July 1937, when Chinese and Japanese soldiers engaged in a firefight. Although this was a small-scale engagement, hostilities soon spread until much of East and Southeast Asia became embroiled in combat.

Fighting in the European and North African theater began when Germany attacked Poland on September 1, 1939, and the loss of life in the European theater exceeded the numbers of those in the Asian theater. The Italians and Germans made North Africa a battle zone and fought with the British and Americans for control there. The United States entered the war on December 8, 1941, the day after Japanese planes carried out a devastating attack on the Pearl Harbor naval base in Hawaii. Of course, the Germans had already conquered most of Europe by then. The Euro-African theater received much attention from U.S. planners, and the American effort in the Pacific was significant. In fact, the U.S. economy sustained a two-front global war.

War Aims

Each of the major participants in World War II had its particular war aims. Many wished to expand their control of adjacent territories, while others desired to maintain their political positions. Some war aims changed as the ebb and flow of combat opened new vistas for expansion.

JAPANESE WAR AIMS. In Japan, several groups were involved in policy formulation and there was no commander-in-chief; war aims therefore often reflected a consensus derived from complex and time-consuming negotiations. At times, the army and navy could not agree on a common strategy, which limited Japan's success. The army often drove Japan's foreign policy in the 1930s and 1940s, and members of the army's high command sought to negotiate a military pact with the Germans and Italians. In contrast, Japanese naval officials feared that this foreign policy initiative might antagonize the Americans and British, both of whom had significant naval fleets in the Pacific region. Thus, until 1941, top naval leaders blocked army plans to secure that military alliance.

Germany's conquest of the Netherlands and France and isolation of Britain by late 1940 forced the Japanese to rethink their war aims. French Indochina and the Dutch East Indies enticed Japanese strategic thinkers, who desired access to the rubber and oil produced in these Southeast Asian colonies. In addition, British-controlled Malaya, Burma, and even India seemed to be vulnerable to Japanese attack. Of its potential enemies, only the United States remained strong, but Japanese leaders believed that conquest of Southeast Asia was worth risking a war with the United States. The opportunity was too significant to let pass. When Japan attacked the United States, Japanese naval and army planners intended to use the blow to negotiate a favorable settlement with the Americans. They did not wish a sustained war, because they understood that the United States possessed formidable resources.

Justification for the expansion of Japan's empire came with the idea of "Asia for the Asians." According to this view, Japanese expansion and control in Asia was a way to "help" other Asians. Although some Japanese viewed their overlordship as a tutelage effort, most scholars see it as another form of imperialist domination and exploitation.

GERMAN WAR AIMS. Adolf Hitler wanted Germany to expand to the east, but in order to do that he had to defeat and destroy Poland. Then he planned to defeat the countries of western Europe and thereafter conquer the Soviet Union. Each phase of war was to be of Hitler's choosing and timing, and each would pave the way for the next. Ultimately, Hitler intended to harness Europe's resources to defeat the United States and dominate the world. His vision was clear and closely followed.

At the same time, Hitler believed that these conflicts would deflect attention from a major war aim of cleansing Germany, Poland, and the Soviet

Union of "undesirable" racial and other groups. Not only were Jews and Gypsies to be exterminated, but many Slavs also were to be killed. A massive demographic revolution was planned.

SOVIET WAR AIMS. Josef Stalin used the various conflicts of World War II to expand Soviet power and influence. Between 1939 and 1941, he annexed Latvia, Lithuania, and Estonia, along with parts of Finland, Poland, and Romania. Although these areas were lost to German conquest between 1942 and 1944, they came back under Soviet domination when Russian armies pushed the Germans back. After 1945, the Soviet Union controlled much of Eastern and Central Europe, and Stalin took advantage of the favorable situation to expand the Soviet Empire.

"Ethnic cleansing" became a major Soviet war aim as German armies fanned out over Soviet Russia beginning in 1941. One reason for the early success of the Nazi forces was the favorable reception given them by various ethnic minorities. Recognizing this, Stalin ordered his secret police to round up and deport "unreliable" groups in the path of advancing German soldiers. Several hundred thousand Germans who had lived in the Volga River Valley for nearly two centuries were shipped to Siberia. Tatars living in their Crimean homes for centuries were deported eastward, as were many Chechens of Chechniya.

BRITISH WAR AIMS. Winston Churchill led Britain through the war years as prime minister, and his primary aim was to defeat Germany, no matter the cost. To that end, Churchill allied with Stalin, even though he hated what Stalin stood for. Churchill's other major aim was the preservation of the British Empire, and, if possible, Britain's dominant global position.

Another of Churchill's war aims was to maintain a close relationship with the United States. Both he and President Franklin Roosevelt worked hard to ensure a smooth wartime alliance. In 1940, before the United States entered the war, Churchill and Roosevelt met in the Atlantic to hammer out a United States aid package to the British. They also met several times during the war.

U.S. WAR AIMS. President Franklin Roosevelt changed his aims as situations developed. He tried to keep the United States out of the war, but when that became impossible he directed the effort to defeat Germany and Japan. Even before the United States entered the war, Roosevelt warned the Japanese against expanding into Southeast Asia, desiring to preserve the sagging European empires there. He assumed the mantle of leadership of the "Free World."

The United States insisted on "unconditional surrender" by Germany and Japan as a prerequisite to ending the war. That would free the hands of the victors to take drastic measures, if necessary, to prevent future wars.

Racism

Most countries practiced racial discrimination during the war. The United States had segregated armed forces, with African Americans, Japanese Americans, and others in separate units. In addition, Japanese American citizens were rounded up in 1942 and shipped off to camps where they were interned for the war's duration. Japanese brutally lorded it over the Koreans, Chinese, and Filipinos during their occupations. Japanese doctors carried out medical experiments on living subjects from those countries. European and North American prisoners of war suffered from sometimes barbaric forms of treatment by Japanese soldiers.

Some of the most virulent forms of racism came from the national socialists in Germany and Yugoslavia. In Germany, the Nazis aimed to systematically murder whole population groups. Reflecting longstanding animosities, Croats used national socialist policies to murder, oust, or dominate more than 350,000 Serbs. These wartime atrocities reverberated into the 1990s, when some Serbs avenged themselves on the Croats.

THE ASIAN THEATER, 1937–1945

Japan launched invasions of Manchuria, China, and Southeast Asia and made small naval forays into the Indian Ocean. For a time, the Japanese fought the Soviets and briefly considered an invasion of Siberia. They also battled United States forces in the Pacific Ocean and in the Aleutian Islands off Alaska.

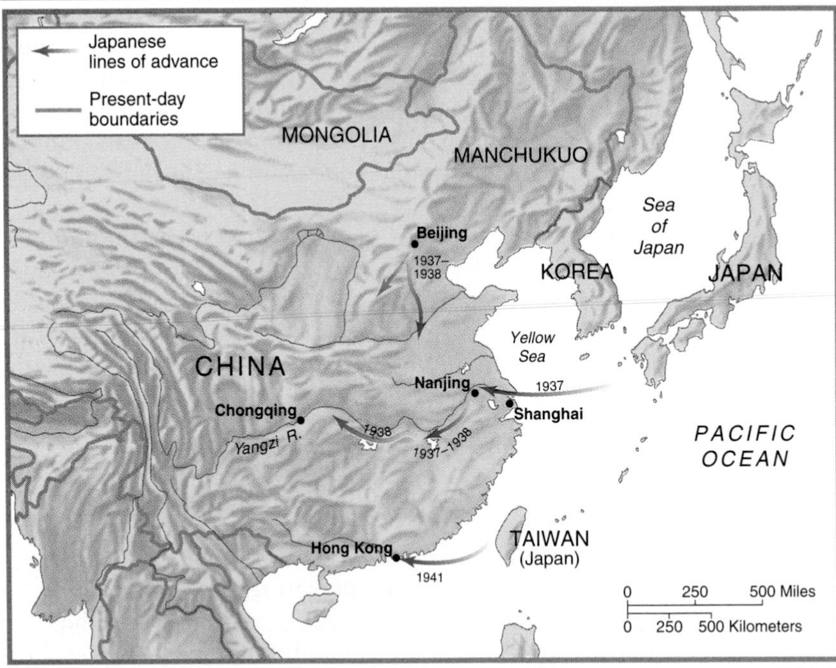

MAP 40.1 *Japanese Expansion in China, 1937–1941.* *Japan gradually expanded its influence in East Asia during the twentieth century. It annexed Korea in 1910 and took control of Germany's colonies in China in 1914. In 1931, the Japanese army began taking over territory in Manchuria. By the summer of 1937, Japanese control of China had extended into the North China Plain. Beginning in mid-1937, large-scale warfare broke out between Japanese and Chinese forces, with the Japanese expanding their control of China's cities, especially along the Yangzi River. Much of eastern China lay in Japanese hands by late 1941.*

The Japanese army directed a thrust into Manchuria, Inner Mongolia, and other parts of China from 1931 to 1937. Knowing that their government might oppose military action in China, elements of the Japanese army in Manchuria planned and executed a surprise attack on September 18, 1931. Chinese forces did not respond, and, in 1933, Japan renamed the region Manchukuo, ruling it as a puppet state. The Japanese government reluctantly supported its army and faced severe but futile criticism in the League of Nations. Japan ultimately withdrew from the League in 1933, showing it to be useless as a means of stopping aggression by a determined power.

Subsequent military campaigns brought Japan into Central China by the mid-1930s and set the stage for the beginning of World War II. China had been steadily retreating from Japanese advances because President Jiang Jieshi knew that resistance might be fatal to him. The withdrawals, however, caused Chinese nationalists to criticize Jiang so severely that by 1937 he had to resist the Japanese. When a firefight erupted on July 7, 1937, Jiang's response was to deliver a strong rebuke to the Japanese, who felt they could not back down, despite some desire to seek a negotiated settlement. Full-scale fighting broke out and continued for eight years, although the Japanese expected a quick victory, their feelings of racial superiority causing them to miscalculate resistance in China.

In 1938 and 1939, the Japanese and Soviets fought two major battles that caused great Japanese losses and a need for regrouping by their army. In the spring of 1941, Japanese and Soviet diplomats negotiated a nonaggression pact that remained in effect until August 1945.

Between May and June 1940, Nazi Germany defeated the Netherlands, Belgium, and France, opening the possibility of Japan's invasion of Southeast Asia, where the Dutch and the French had empires. Japanese planners jumped at the prospect of taking rubber plantations, tin mines, oil fields, and other Southeast Asian raw materials crucial for Japan's war machine. In July 1940, the Japanese pressured the French to permit them into northern French Indochina. This allowed the Japanese to sever key supply routes to China in hopes of compelling the surrender of the Chinese Nationalist armies. Eventually, Japanese troops moved into the southern part of the French colony, developing a base from which to threaten much of Southeast Asia, including the Philippines, a U.S. colony. At that point, the Americans announced that they intended to shut off oil supplies to Japan, making the Southeast Asian oil supplies even more valuable.

U.S. citizens watched with growing sympathy for the Chinese during the opening years of the Asian theater. Monies were raised through collections among movie theater audiences. U.S. and Canadian pilots served in China as volunteers as the famed "Flying Tigers." The U.S. government hoped that a combination of naval buildups, economic threats, and negotiations might force the Japanese to reconsider their Asian policy. Once Japan's key leaders decided on taking Southeast Asia, however, they refused to yield to pressure. The United States could avoid conflict only by accepting all of Japan's gains and its future plans.

Planning for the Japanese thrust southward took part of 1940 and most of 1941. The Japanese intended to invade Thailand and use it as a base from which to attack Malaya and Burma. To secure their sea-lanes, the Japanese had to neutralize the Philippines, bringing themselves into conflict with the United States. The initial planning aimed at attacking the Philippines itself, but the Combined Fleet's commander, Admiral Yamamoto Isoroku (1884–1943), insisted on hitting Hawaii first. The initial plan might have left open a chance for negotiations, but attacks on United States ships almost guaranteed an all-out American response.

FIGURE 40.1 ***Casualty of World War II.*** *This famous 1937 photograph shows a wounded Chinese baby amid the wreckage of a Shanghai train station after a Japanese bombing raid. The image of the crying infant underscored the war's horrors. Japan's war on China set the stage for the Asian theater of World War II, in which tens of millions would lose their lives.*
UPI/Corbis-Bettmann.

FIGURE 40.2 ***Catastrophe at Pearl Harbor.*** *Japan's surprise attack on Pearl Harbor devastated much of America's military firepower in the mid-Pacific region and immediately drew the U.S. into World War II. Beyond the wreckage of these airplanes, smoke billows from the battleships burning in the harbor. Although most of America's battleship fleet was disabled during the attack, the Japanese missed the aircraft carriers because they were out at sea.* U.S. Navy.

On December 7 and 8, 1941, military actions unfolded over a wide front, initiated by an attack on American fortifications in Hawaii, including the naval base at Pearl Harbor. Over the next six months, Japan conquered the Philippines, Burma, Thailand, Malaya, and Indonesia. Their losses were not costly, and they gained access to vital supplies of oil, tin, and rubber. The victories also brought an overbearing arrogance, reflected in the conquerors' brutal treatment of conquered peoples. The Japanese believed that they could easily defeat the Americans and British. At the same time, the British and Americans, whose own racial prejudices had kept them from regarding the Japanese as a real threat, now saw them as almost invincible warriors. Both perspectives smacked of racial stereotypes and inhibited successful planning. Soon, however, U.S. planners began to learn from their mistakes, revising their strategies and tactics.

In 1942, the Japanese sent a fleet into the Indian Ocean. Its purpose was to defeat the British navy there and to sever naval supply lines to the Soviets as well as to the British in North Africa. After some limited successes in Ceylon and along the Indian coast, the Japanese withdrew. The British conquered the Axis-held island of Madagascar off the African coast and used it as a base to safeguard the western and central Indian Ocean.

By and large, the remainder of operations in Asia assumed a secondary nature as focus shifted to the Pacific theater. In August 1945, the Japanese army in Manchukuo faced a massive assault by Soviet troops and collapsed quickly. Surviving Japanese officials in Harbin, a city in North Manchukuo, departed after releasing toxins from chemical and biological warfare facilities, killing large numbers of Chinese in the city. Japan's surrender in mid-August 1945 left large numbers of defeated Japanese soldiers in China.

In Southeast Asia, the Japanese had long boasted that they were better rulers than the Europeans. The Japanese did not allow their Asian colonies to rule themselves until 1945, after it had become clear that Japan was losing the war.

THE EURO-AFRICAN THEATER, 1939–1945

Adolf Hitler was the architect of the battle plan that dominated the Euro-African theater. He had come to power in 1933 and had consolidated control of the German government. At the same time, he had established a program for building the economy and rearming Germany. Hitler's determined effort propelled Germany ahead of its adversaries in Europe, and he adhered to his goals of expanding east and west. Hitler also had to be certain that the

PARALLELS AND DIVERGENCES

Military Codes and Ciphers

Codes have been used by military forces at least since the time of the Roman Empire to disguise the meaning of a message that might fall into enemy hands. With World War II, however, ways of making messages unintelligible to the enemy became far more important. Because radio broadcasts could not be hidden from the enemy, some means of scrambling the messages had to be devised.

Strictly speaking, a message can be rendered unreadable by two methods. With a **code**, symbols are substituted for other symbols. If "red" means to attack and "marmoset" signifies an enemy position, "red marmoset" might mean to attack that position. A **cipher**, on the other hand, manipulates the letters of the message, scrambling it so that only someone who knows the rules of manipulation can reconstruct it. A simple cipher might substitute the next letter of the alphabet for each letter of a message; with this cipher "history" would become "ijtupsz."

As military forces relied increasingly on radios, more and more effort was devoted to making codes and ciphers more complex. Their enemies, of course, devoted more and more effort to the cracking of those codes and ciphers. The German **Enigma machine** automatically produced a complex cipher of any message that was typed into it, and the Germans relied on it for much of the war. The Poles had begun to break this cipher and had produced a rough copy of an Enigma machine by the eve of the German invasion. With the invasion, the Polish machine and information on the German cipher were spirited away to Britain, where British intelligence officers refined the Polish device and decipherment rules. One German Enigma message described the date and plans for the bombing of the English town of Coventry. Winston Churchill believed information gained by deciphering Enigma messages to be so important that he permitted the devastating bombing to go forward uninhibited, rather than reveal to the Germans that their cipher had been cracked.

The most successful of all codes in World War II was an American code used in the Pacific. It consisted of Dine,[a] the language of the Navajo Indians of the American Southwest. There were very few speakers of that language outside the United States; among the Axis powers, probably only a single German anthropology professor knew the language, and he, a Jew, had been placed in a concentration camp. The complexities of the language eluded the Japanese intelligence officers who tried to decode it, and the Navajo "code talkers" continued to operate successfully throughout the war.

Codes and ciphers remain critical to military and diplomatic communication today, especially given the sophistication of "bugging" devices. Following the lead of the Enigma machine, most ciphers today are created by computers, and their complexities are so great that only other computers can break them.

[a]**Dine:** DEE nay

German people supported his efforts, and that meant avoiding too harsh a demand on the German economy and people.

Germany's Conquest of Europe

To implement his plan, Hitler fomented trouble in the Sudetenland, a German-populated area of Czechoslovakia. After German threats, the British, who wished to avoid war, convinced the French and Italians to negotiate. The British and French ignored previous diplomatic pledges of support for the Czechs. Soon, eastern Czechoslovakia (Slovakia) was formed into a German puppet state, and the rest was annexed to Germany. Hitler turned to Poland next.

As Hitler told a conference of his generals in 1939, the aim of the Polish campaign was Poland's destruction, not merely the defeat of its army. To ensure victory, however, Hitler had to ally Germany with the British and French or with the Soviets. Britain and France refused to succumb to his wiles, so an agreement with the Soviet Union became more attractive. Both Germany and the Soviet Union had longed to dismember Poland and extend their power in other parts of eastern Europe, so they favored an alliance. In addition, the Soviet Union promised to supply Germany with raw materials to offset a British naval blockade. A nonaggression pact was worked out along with an economic agreement in late August. The Soviets and Nazis agreed to a division of territories for exploitation, with the Soviets promising to attack Poland after an initial pause.

THE POLISH CAMPAIGN. On September 1, 1939, Germany invaded Poland and swiftly crushed its army. The German combination of air strikes and

FIGURE 40.3 ***World War II Poland.*** *The German army struck Poland with swift, massive air attacks and mobile army units. In this 1939 photo, a German supply convoy and motor unit (right and middle) proceed toward the eastern front. While motorized units carried the vanguard to victory, horses carried much of the materials necessary to feed and rearm Germany's soldiers. On the left, Polish refugees flee the conflict on foot, carting their belongings on bicycles and horse-drawn wagons.* Wide World Photos.

MAP 40.2 ***Germany's Campaigns, 1939–1940.*** *After a brief but bloody conquest of Poland (with Soviet assistance), the Germans turned to western Europe, home of their enemies, France and Great Britain. Before attacking these foes, the Germans struck at Denmark and Norway, then moved west against Belgium and the Netherlands. Finally, major German forces converged on France, nearly destroying a combined Anglo-French army. All of these countries, with the exception of Britain, surrendered by June 1940.*

rapidly moving army ground vehicles (including tanks) was called ***blitzkrieg*** (lightning war). *Blitzkrieg* dominated the European theater until early 1940, when large numbers of antitank weapons began to offset Germany's military advantage. Poland collapsed under the onslaught, especially after the Soviets invaded from the east.

Both victors settled into massive campaigns of violence directed against civilian and military groups. The Soviets massacred several thousand Polish officers and other leaders at the Katyn Forest; the Germans slaughtered tens of thousands of Poles and expelled others from their homes. The purpose was to create places for Germans to settle and to begin the demographic revolution through the extermination of designated population groups. As some German army officers objected to this use of their forces, Hitler decided to transfer control of the demographic revolution to the Schutz Staffeln (SS), Germany's secret police, and to other special extermination squads.

Soviet and Nazi officials met at the end of September to redraw their original plans. The Soviets exchanged part of central Poland for a free hand with Lithuania, a state previously considered under German protection. In 1939, Latvia, Estonia, and Lithuania agreed to allow the Soviet Union to station troops in their territories. Annexation soon followed. And in November, the Soviets launched an attack on Finland. Much to the Soviets' surprise, the Finns fought them off; 200,000 Soviets died, about eight times the number of Finnish casualties.

HITLER'S CAMPAIGN IN NORTHERN AND WESTERN EUROPE. Hitler then turned his attention north and west. Preparations took months and led to the invasions of Denmark and Norway. Both fell to German troops in early 1940; by May 10, Hitler had attacked the Netherlands, Belgium, and France. Central to the German success in most of these campaigns was *blitzkrieg*. After five days, the German tanks broke through Allied defenses and raced to the sea. This effectively divided the Allied forces, and the Germans turned to surround major British and French armies. Only a massive sea-lift rescue at Dunkirk prevented a total disaster for the

FIGURE 40.4 ***Execution of Resistance Fighters.*** *When the Germans defeated France in 1940, some French joined resistance forces fighting against German rule. When caught, the French patriots could expect no mercy; they were shot or otherwise executed. Resistance movements sprang up in many parts of occupied Europe.* Lapi-Viollet.

FIGURE 40.5 ***Germans Surrender in Winter.*** *Expecting a quick victory in Soviet Russia, German commanders had not prepared their soldiers for winter fighting. When "General Winter" struck, some freezing German troops surrendered to the better-prepared Soviet forces. This photograph shows one such result outside Moscow in the first year of the German attempt to invade Russia.* Sovfoto.

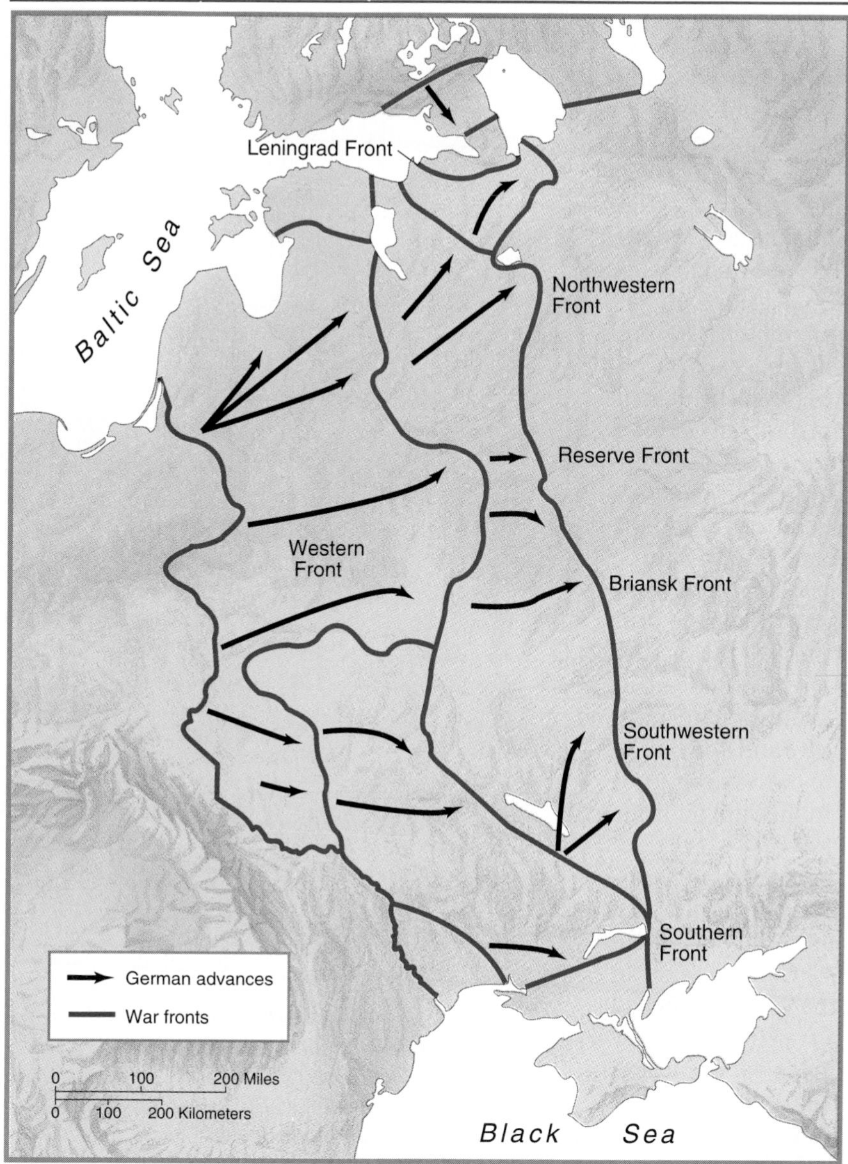

MAP 40.3 ***Initial Attack on Russia, June–September 1941.*** *Hitler turned his attention to Soviet Russia in late 1940, planning to strike in the spring of 1941. Despite a delay of some weeks, the Germans and their allies hit the Soviet Union with a three-pronged attack, north toward Leningrad, east toward Moscow, and southeast toward the oil fields of the Caucasus Mountains. By September, many divisions of the Soviet armed forces had surrendered. As the Germans consolidated their gains and struck anew in each sector, it was only the vastness of the territory to be conquered that gave the Soviets time to regroup.*

British. Britain mobilized all available vessels, including rowboats, sailboats, and ferries, to evacuate the defeated Allied soldiers. France surrendered in the latter half of June. Britain remained free but feared an invasion. Their fears were well founded, but Hitler's planned attack was called off because German troops lacked equipment and support services. Instead, Hitler concentrated on air attacks to defeat the British.

HITLER'S CAMPAIGN IN SOVIET RUSSIA. Because of their relative ease in winning the early campaigns, Hitler and the German High Command expected a brief war in the Soviet Union. Despite Germany's agreements with the Soviets, Hitler had decided that expansion farther east was critical to German security. German planners underestimated their Soviet adversary, because they believed the Slavs to be racially inferior. The western Russian area also appeared to give *blitzkrieg* forces ample opportunity for free movement to encircle and annihilate the enemy. What the Germans failed to consider was road conditions.

On June 22, 1941, Germany's invasion of the Soviet Union commenced. Stalin had ample warning that something major was about to happen because he had received countless intelligence reports about German troop movements. However, Stalin preferred not to believe the growing evidence—he felt that Germany had no reason to attack a country that already provided many of its raw materials.

The Axis army and air force attacked, and within hours the Soviet air force was virtually destroyed. Desperate Soviet pilots resorted to ramming German fighter planes with unarmed trainer aircraft. Soon, prisoners by the millions surrendered to the Germans. Although the Germans won victories, the Soviets kept fighting, and the dust of summer and the rains of autumn disabled German mechanized vehicles.

A winter counteroffensive by the Soviets threw the poorly clothed Germans back, sparing Moscow from enemy occupation. Other German forces, however, arrived at the gates of Leningrad (formerly Petrograd) and laid siege to it. For the next 900 days, the two armies contested the battleground, but the Soviets refused to be dislodged. In Leningrad, city folk bore devastating hardships, including the burning of their city and starvation. Farther south, the Ukraine fell to the Nazis in 1941, and German units drove hard to the vital oil fields beyond.

In 1942 and 1943, fronts expanded and contracted. One decisive conflict concerned the Kursk-Orel sector of south-central Russia, where the Soviets destroyed nearly 600 German tanks in one day. During the next year, the Soviets launched a massive attack all along the war front, and, by autumn, they pushed the Germans out of most of Soviet Russia and into parts of eastern Europe. By the spring of 1945, Soviet forces had entered Germany and were soon fighting in Berlin.

FIGURE 40.6 ***Serve Mother Russia.*** *This wartime poster shows a stern Motherland exhorting her sons to fight. Despite a communist ideology that condemned nationalism as a relic of the past, Soviet Russia employed all kinds of nationalistic messages to spur its citizens to defeat the invaders. Millions responded to the call to fight for victory.* Poster by I. M. Toidze, 1941, from David M. Glantz and Jonathan M. House, *When Titans Clashed* (Lawrence: University of Kansas Press). Reproduced with permission.

The Allied Campaign in the Euro-African Theater

North Africa became a battleground for several years during World War II. The British had defeated the Italians in Northeast Africa in 1940 and 1941 to secure the Red Sea and the Indian Ocean. Most large-scale engagements, however, came in North Africa, with the Italians and Germans fighting the British, Free French, and Americans. The British took the brunt of the earlier fighting as the Axis forces headed by General Erwin Rommel of Germany in June 1942 routed the British and pushed into Egypt toward the strategic Suez Canal. The German forces were stopped and thrown back by the British, led by General Bernard L. Montgomery. Later, U.S. soldiers landed in Northwest Africa and pushed east in their first major combat of World War II. The combined forces destroyed the Axis forces in Africa by early 1943. A few

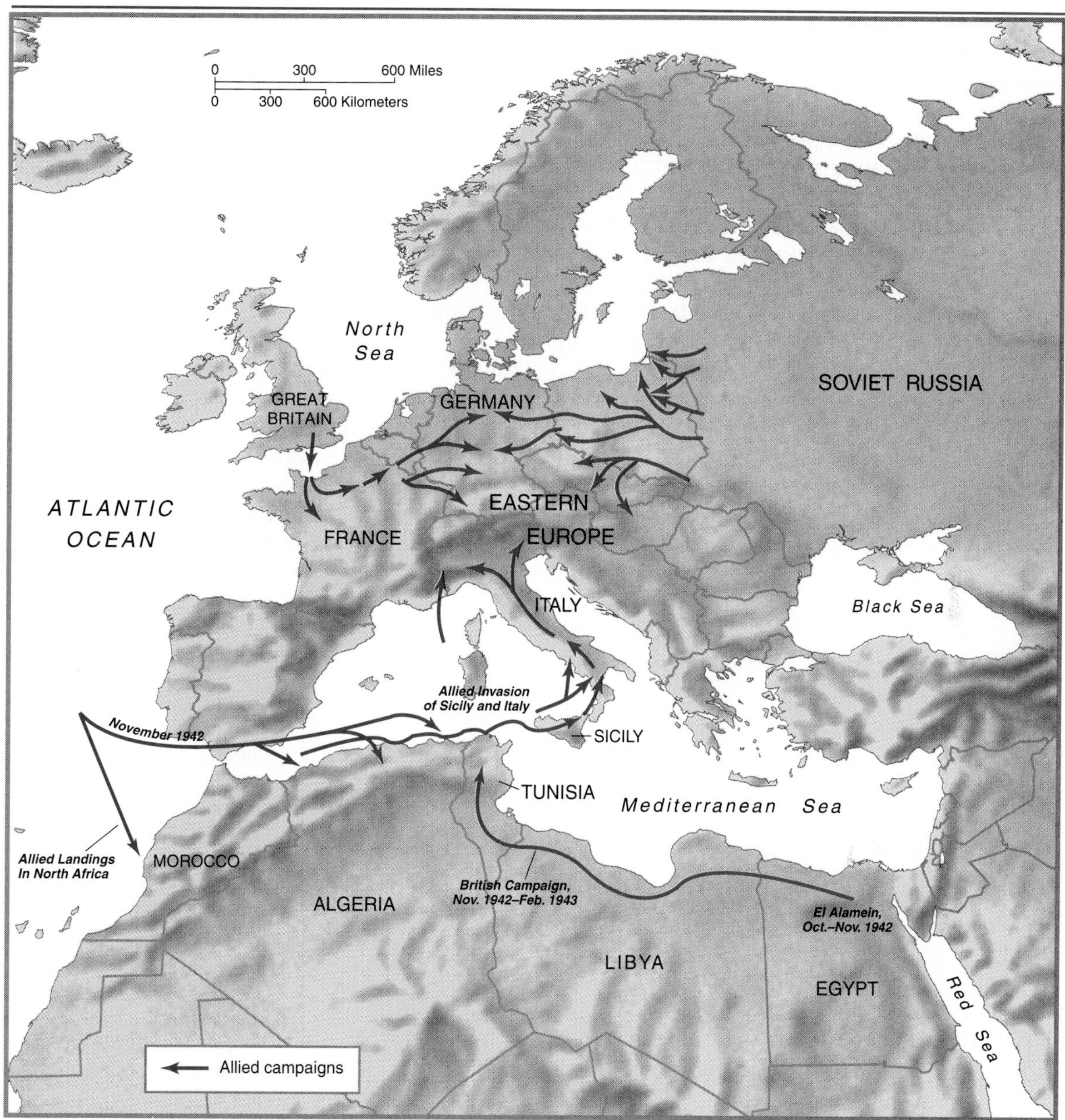

Map 40.4 ***The Euro-African Theater, 1942–1945.*** *Under command of General Erwin Rommel, German and Italian forces attacked British troops in Egypt. While advancing through Egypt toward the Suez Canal, the German soldiers were stopped at El Alamein in July of 1942. Then in October, the British counterattacked and began to push back the Germans. At the same time, U.S. forces landed in northwestern Africa. By early 1943, the British and Americans had defeated most of the German and Italian forces in North Africa; they resupplied and prepared to attack Sicily and the Italian Peninsula.*

In Europe, Britain and the United States combined their forces in 1943 to attack Italy through Sicily. In 1944, they opened a second front in western Europe with an attack on German forces in France. The Soviet armed forces began a sustained push in mid-1944, and threw German forces out of Soviet Russia, pursuing them into parts of eastern Europe. By 1945, Germany was being attacked from the west and the east; resistance collapsed in May with the surrender of all German forces.

months later, the Allies invaded Italy; the Italians surrendered, but Germans in Italy resisted the Allied forces.

After a long buildup in Britain, Allied forces attacked German-occupied France on June 6, 1944, and its liberation came in the late summer. The drive on Germany commenced, and following a brief but fierce German counterattack (the Battle of the Bulge) the Allies resumed their offensive, linking up with the Soviet army at the Elbe River in April 1945. Hitler committed suicide in late April, and Germany's military leaders surrendered in May.

The fighting had been long and extremely costly throughout Europe, and the Allied powers had decided that Germany should be divided into spheres of influence to prevent another war from beginning there. At Allied conferences, Roosevelt, Churchill, and Stalin laid out the framework for the preservation of peace.

THE PACIFIC THEATER, 1941–1945

When the Japanese attacked Pearl Harbor, they inflicted great damage, but the shallow water permitted the raising and salvaging of all except one battleship, the USS *Arizona*. The United States was determined to fight rather than negotiate, and it entered the war, contrary to Japanese planning assumptions.

The swift fall of Southeast Asian countries to Japan's forces was paralleled by the Japanese conquest of island chains in the South Pacific. Here, the effort combined both army and navy personnel. A major naval strategist was Admiral Yamamoto Isoroku, who respected America's industrial might. Yamamoto had planned the Pearl Harbor attack and many other Japanese naval campaigns.

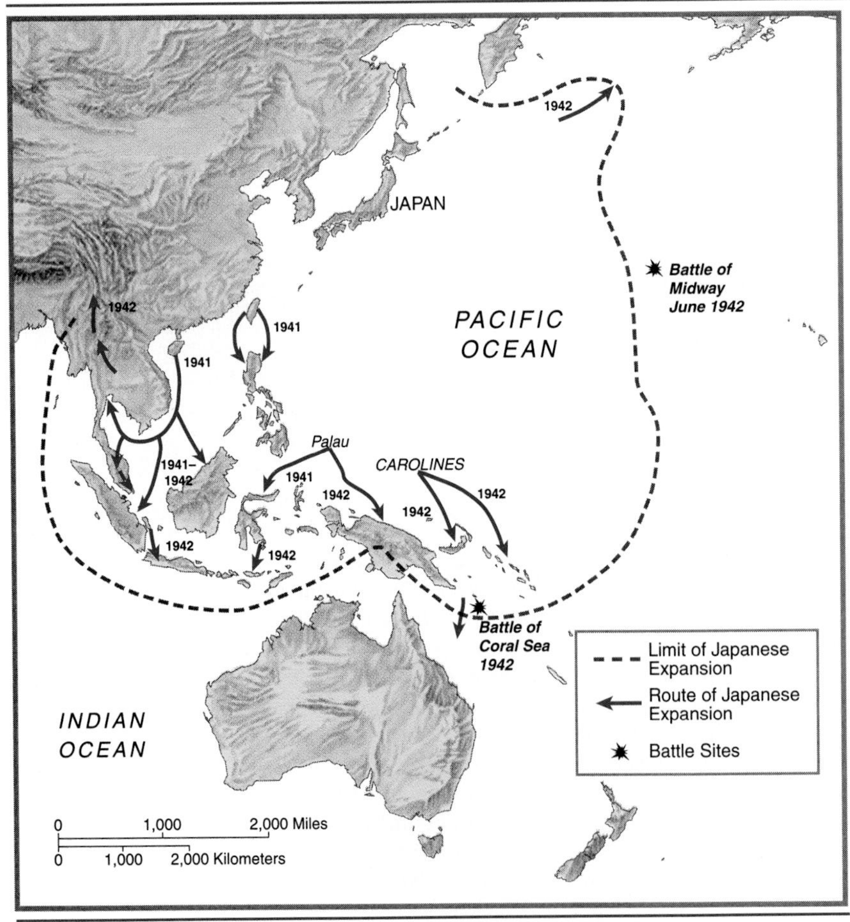

MAP 40.5 ***Japanese Expansion, 1941–1942.*** *Having lost their momentum in China by 1941, Japan looked to opportunities in Southeast Asia following the defeat of the French and Dutch in 1940. The Japanese desperately needed Indonesian oil after the American embargo in 1941. Japan attacked Southeast Asia and the Pacific, by land and sea, and overwhelmed most resistance until they were stopped by Allied forces at the Battle of the Coral Sea and at the Battle of Midway—thus sparing Australia and halting Japanese expansion to the central Pacific and Hawaii.*

By early 1942, the Japanese seemed invincible. They tried to sever Allied communications with Australia and contested the islands throughout the South Pacific. The Americans decided to fight a naval engagement in May 1942 in the Coral Sea. In the fierce fighting, each side lost an aircraft carrier, but the Japanese had fewer to lose. Yamamoto planned a major thrust in the east against U.S.-held Midway Island and Hawaii. Instead of concentrating his forces at Midway, Yamamoto divided them, and the Americans relied on reading the Japanese naval codes and some shrewd guesswork to win. The defeat of the Japanese at Midway saved Hawaii from invasion.

The rest of 1942 and part of 1943 were concerned with fighting in New Guinea and Guadalcanal in the South Pacific. Both engagements cost the Japanese heavily. Rather than take each Pacific island, the American strategy was to attack only strategic places, hopping over less important islands. This plan speeded up the American offensive and soon provided islands from which the Americans could bomb Japan.

Another result of the fierce fighting in the Pacific was the growing image of Japanese troops as suicidal warriors. During the battle for Tarawa, for example, the Japanese had 8 survivors from a force of 5,000. Savage fighting marked the Philippines, Iwo Jima, and Okinawa campaigns in 1944 and 1945. ***Kamikaze***, suicide bombers that sank and damaged some ships, took a heavy toll on the morale of navy personnel.

Because of the image of Japanese fighters as fanatical, U.S. planners grimly estimated that the invasion of the Japanese main islands would last for months, if not years, and that it would cost 1 million Allied casualties. As the Americans had recently tested an atomic bomb, they considered the option of using it rather than invading. U.S. leaders decided to warn the Japanese that the

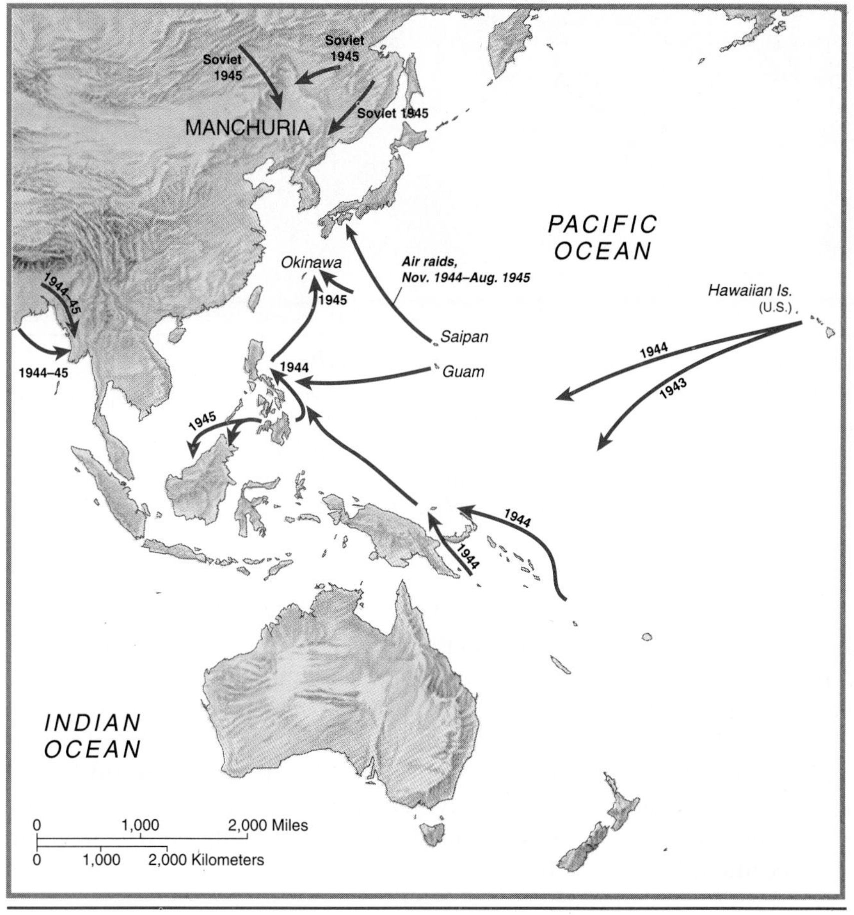

Map 40.6 ***Allied Attacks in the Pacific and Asia, 1944–1945.*** *The Americans and British carried out a series of attacks against Japanese forces in the Pacific and Southeast Asia in 1944 and 1945. Burma and the Philippines were two main targets of the Allied forces, along with certain strategic islands in the South Pacific region. Beginning in late 1944, U.S. airplanes began bombing Japanese cities on the home islands, especially on Honshu; other Allied land and sea forces attacked and took the island of Okinawa between April and June. In August, the U.S. dropped atomic bombs on the cities of Hiroshima and Nagasaki, leading to Japan's unconditional surrender.*

FIGURE 40.7 ***Destruction at Nagasaki.*** *Three days after the bombing of Hiroshima, the United States released a second atomic bomb over the city of Nagasaki, killing tens of thousands of Japanese. The surrounding hills absorbed some of the blast and prevented larger death tolls, although many later died of radiation poisoning. Before the bombing, the area shown in this photo was covered with residential and industrial buildings. The skeletal structure of the Mitsubishi Steel and Arms Works and the concrete walls of a school building can be seen at the foot of the hills.* Wide World Photos.

atomic bomb would be used on them if they refused to surrender unconditionally. Nothing came in reply, so the United States dropped the first bomb on Hiroshima on August 6, 1945. More than 50,000 people died within the first ten seconds. Then, receiving no unconditional surrender, on August 9 the United States dropped a second atomic bomb, on Nagasaki. For the survivors, women, men, and children, life became a horror with the added possibility of perishing painfully from radiation sickness. The combined effects of the bombs compelled Emperor Hirohito to opt for peace. On August 15, 1945, he announced Japan's surrender to the Japanese people, most of whom heard his voice for the first time. World War II ended with more than 60 million dead and atomic weapons looming over humanity like a threatening storm cloud.

WARTIME HOLOCAUSTS

Adolf Hitler had spoken for many years about a demographic revolution to "cleanse" Germany of the population that he considered inferior. In a deliberate and horrifying effort, the Nazis used the machinery of the nation-state to accomplish their goals. During World War II, **holocausts**, mass exterminations of peoples viewed as inferior, wiped out more than 11 million people, including around 6 million Jews.

A kind of trial run of the larger genocide of Jews and others took place between 1939 and 1941 during the Euro-African theater's first phase. Under cover of war, the Nazis organized systematic efforts to identify and remove to camps certain ethnic groups and disabled or otherwise incapacitated people. Hospitals and mental institutions were asked to surrender their old, senile, diseased, or mentally disturbed patients. In a few cases, children with malformed ears and those who were bedwetters were taken. Among the 170,000 to 200,000 people exterminated were disabled veterans from World War I. Around 30,000 severe alcoholics also were killed, with more being forcibly sterilized. By 1945, between 200,000 and 250,000 people had been sterilized for a variety of reasons.

Homosexuality became a crime in Nazi Germany, and around 220,000 homosexuals perished in the concentration camps. In the Weimar Republic, which preceded Hitler's state, laws relating to homosexuality had been increasingly eased, but when the Nazis took power these decrees were rescinded and a Department to Combat Homosexuality was created. Through informers, people engaging in homosexual acts were arrested. Interest in people of the same sex brought denunciation and placement in concentration camps. Lesbians in camps generally received somewhat better treatment than gay men. In the hierarchy of the camps, male homosexuals languished at the bottom. After the war, surviving homosexuals were placed in prison and forced to complete their jail sentences.

The Nazis scoured the German population in search of people whom they considered suited to the job of mass murder on a daily basis. Some candidates could not endure the slaughter, but others replaced them. A whole bureaucratic machinery gained experience with the initial massacre, and it ran smoothly in the later stages. Among officials who accomplished the deed were many who preferred this kind of activity to serving on the front lines, while others saw themselves as involved in an important demographic revolution. A few Germans risked their lives to shelter Jews or to smuggle them out of the country.

All sorts of horrors took place in the concentration camps. Medical experiments were performed, including injecting doses of poisons to ascertain what levels were fatal. Patients were placed in vacuum chambers to see how long they could survive with no air or reduced quantities of air. Dr. Joseph Mengele devoted his camp career to experiments on twins, whom he randomly killed and performed autopsies upon. Lamp shades made of human skin were prized by camp guards. Many inmates were used for labor, but in 1941 mass exterminations of Jews began. They were gassed in groups and incinerated in specially constructed ovens.

As the Germans conquered wider regions in Europe, they implemented their program against the Jews, Gypsies, Poles, and Russians. Jews suffered the largest numbers of fatalities in the death factories. Gypsies in Germany generally suffered extermination, while those in other countries died in smaller numbers. Perhaps as many as 250,000 Gypsies perished at the hands of the Germans.

Some countries refused to turn over their Jews to the Germans. Italian officials resisted what they felt to be barbaric demands from their German allies. Only after Mussolini fell and the Germans ruled Italy did large numbers of Italian Jews die. Bulgaria and Hungary refused to send their Jews. Romania opposed the Germans after the war turned in the Allies' favor, and Denmark evacuated most of its Jews to safety in Sweden. Japan also refused to cooperate with German demands to surrender its Jewish subjects. Croats, Slovaks, and Vichy French cooperated with the Nazis.

Germans grew uneasy with periodic revelations of the mass killings, but many pretended not to know and went about their lives. Others delighted in the fulfillment of the national socialist promises of the 1920s and 1930s. One German official in the occupied Ukraine, where 1.1 million Jews died, said that the Jews had been exterminated like cockroaches. By 1945, when all of the

FIGURE 40.8 *Nazi Death Camp.* *In death camps across Nazi Europe, millions of Jews were either worked to death or gassed to death and then cremated in ovens like this one at Majdanek, Poland. Poles, Russians, Gypsies, homosexuals, and others also perished in the camps.* Ria-Novosti/Sovfoto.

camps were liberated, the full magnitude of the genocide became apparent and horrified people around the world.

SOCIAL UPHEAVAL IN WORLD WAR II

Great changes were wrought around the globe in World War II. Women were called into factories and into other occupations normally assigned to men. Families were put under strain when one or both parents were absent for long periods. Ethnic groups also felt the pressures placed on them by the stresses of wartime and massive population movements.

Society under the Nazis

The German national socialists created a racial social hierarchy. Nazis defined Aryans as "pure" Germans, with blond-haired Nordic types often being considered the elite of the Aryan category. Most "defective" peoples like the disabled, the senile, or homosexuals had been taken away or exterminated by 1941. The Germans displayed a racial hierarchy of favor among forced laborers from other countries. French workers and blonds received preferential treatment, then came Czechs, then other Slavs, and finally the Jews and Gypsies. A similar hierarchy regulated the concentration camps.

Most Germans got used to the new social structure and savored its benefits. As the war progressed and it became increasingly clear that Germany might lose, the attitude of many became "Better enjoy the war, the peace will be terrible." Indeed, until Allied troops appeared on German soil, most Germans supported the Nazis, although some Germans did resist them. Hospitals under Roman Catholic jurisdiction resisted Nazi extermination plans by refusing to release their patients. Intellectuals like Dietrich Bonhoffer wrote and spoke against the Nazis, and many were sent to prison or to the concentration camps. Military conspiracies were hatched, and one nearly managed to assassinate Hitler in 1944.

Increasing losses of young German men began to alarm the Nazis, necessitating plans to offset the shrinking of the Aryan gene pool. Some considered enticing Germans from Latin America to become breeders for the state. Others urged that multiple wives be permitted for the remaining men. Certain factions within the Nazi government actively participated in the reclassification of some Poles and Czechs who "looked" Aryan, in order to maintain adequate supplies of "breeding stock." These pragmatic compromises with Nazi racial policies flourished.

A variety of social movements emerged from German youth. Hitler Youth groups were formed in the 1930s and became a major socializing force in Nazi Germany. Hitler Youth members received paramilitary training and the inculcation of Nazi values. Another group, the "swing youth," was attracted to the swing music that came from America. The swing youth appeared in large German cities in the 1940s and were largely from the middle class, with parents serving in the government. These young people frequented dance clubs where music by German swing bands imitating the one led by Benny Goodman performed. Because swing music had been associated in the Nazis' minds with American Jews and African Americans, it was considered racially impure and was strictly prohibited. Youth in working-class areas that had been dominated by socialist parties formed gangs that often clashed with Hitler Youth groups. The Edelweiss Pirates included hundreds of people aged sixteen to nineteen years old. They came from families of skilled or semiskilled workers and confined their anti-Nazi activities to minor acts of violence. A few collaborated with the German underground to help deserters, prisoners of war, and camp escapees.

The Nazis used repression to enforce social conformity. One measure involved the Morigen Youth Concentration Camp, which was established in 1940. Young people who displayed deviant behavior, emotional inadequacies, bad tempers, or incorrigible mischievousness were sent to the camp. A brutal regimentation program attempted to rehabilitate them, but the unreformed were shipped off to the regular concentration camps for extermination.

One popular program was the National Socialist Welfare Organization. It provided relief to war widows, orphans, and people whose homes had been destroyed by Allied bombings. As the war worsened, many Germans became totally dependent on this operation.

Another area of growth during World War II was urban planning. Hitler harbored schemes for radically redrawing the urban landscapes of most cities, and a network of architects and planners emerged before and during the war. Massive state buildings were proposed, some of which came under construction. The work went on partly because of bureaucratic inertia and largely because it kept the architects and others away from the front lines, as they had to direct the erection of state buildings.

Pressing against Social Barriers: The United States

Perhaps the most significant social developments in the United States were the wartime shifts that portended postwar change. During the war, more than 7 million women entered the workforce for the first time, and others joined the war effort in all branches of the military. Although more working-class women than middle-class women took jobs, middle-class women were more likely to climb the corporate ladder. Industrial managers offered financial inducements for women from the middle class, and this practice improved wages for all. Even middle-class women, however, did not do so well as men. In addition, managers quickly learned that middle-class women refused to tolerate the harsh disciplinary measures used against their lower-class counterparts.

When the war ended, many working women went back to home life. Women who headed households, however, could not afford to lose their jobs, and lower-class women resented being fired so that a man could be hired.

Women in the armed services numbered more than 200,000 and figured in the planning for peacetime as America's legislators debated a "G.I. [Government Issue or war draftee] Bill of Rights." Some women who served in the Women's Air Service Pilots and other groups were denied benefits. Other women who were veterans took advantage of the G.I. Bill and earned college degrees, which aided their social mobility.

African American soldiers fought in segregated armed forces units. After the war, most African American veterans resisted efforts to force them back into lifestyles shaped by traditional prejudice and discrimination. A limited number earned university degrees and entrance into new professions. Racial discrimination across the United States hampered their lives. In 1943, a threatened mass march on the nation's capital brought an executive decree banning discrimination at government-funded institutions. Federal government intervention was seen as an asset by many, although a few African American leaders favored segregation as a positive thing because they believed it eliminated racial bias.

A tragic episode in American history was the internment of Japanese Americans during World War II. Many United States citizens were inflamed by fear that American citizens of Japanese ancestry would commit acts of espionage and sabotage, though no evidence then or since has substantiated that fear. Nonetheless, the U.S. government ordered that anyone of Japanese ancestry residing in "sensitive zones" (areas along the Pacific coast of California, Oregon, and Washington) be confined in special camps. Within about a month, the roundup began, and ultimately tens of thousands of Japanese Americans were placed in a dozen "relocation camps" located mostly in inhospitable deserts and frigid remote mountain areas. Those interned found their dignity shattered and their constitutionally guaranteed rights shredded; they also lost property on which, having lost their sources of income, they could no longer pay taxes. Suicide and depression followed for some internees, but others persevered until their release in 1945. There was no comparable internment of citizens of German or Italian ancestry, and most scholars believe that racism was a powerful motivation for the internment of Japanese Americans.

Limited Social Change in Soviet Russia

The most significant social change in the Soviet Union was the immense loss of life. Most Soviet families suffered tragedy owing to the war. The deaths of 30 million people or more created a serious social and demographic crisis, especially on top of the great population losses of the 1930s.

Another wartime feature was the shift of large population groups from conquered territories. The conquest of the Baltic countries brought many Latvians, Lithuanians, and Estonians to places in the east, especially to Siberia. In addition, whole populations of Volga Germans and Tatars in the Crimea were moved away because the state doubted their loyalties.

THE WAR'S ECONOMIC COSTS AND CONSEQUENCES

Perhaps more than in any previous war, the importance of military supplies and logistics outweighed other strategic factors in World War II. By this time, refinements in weapons had reached the point at which technology played a more decisive role in victory than the sheer size of armies.

The German National Socialist Economic Plan

The national socialist economic vision was realized gradually. Trade in Europe was directed by Germany, and German currency became the standard European currency. Increasingly, the state took over industries and built a large economic empire with concentration camp labor. The last war year saw the power of the Nazi Party and the SS grow rapidly. Everything was to be controlled by the state.

Hitler feared that his wars might be undermined by unrest at home, so he concentrated on moderating the wartime suffering of the German people. Although rationing began on the eve of the war, the Nazis tried to minimize its hardships, and there was no total mobilization of materials and personnel until quite late. Nazi policy had long encouraged women to leave the industrial workforce and provided such generous economic benefits that many women left their jobs during the first twelve months of the war. Some women, however, continued to work in service jobs, for instance as maids in middle-class and upper-class households. The large-scale drafting of women into the industrial sector did not come until 1943 and even then did not reach levels comparable to those in Britain or Soviet Russia.

Systematic pillaging of conquered lands and peoples, as well as the use of forced labor, permitted Germans to enjoy a moderately good living standard for most of the war. The products and materials gained often went back to Germany for state needs. Within the first war year, substantial

UNDER THE LENS

World War II in South America

Accounts of World War II usually focus on Europe, Asia, North Africa, and the Pacific, considering South America peripheral to the conflict. Nonetheless, several South American countries were directly and significantly involved in the war. For the most part, their allegiances were determined by preexisting animosities, trade links, and the sentiments of powerful ethnic minorities.

At the outbreak of war, Brazil was one of the economic powers of South America, its prosperity riding on its rubber plantations. When the global rubber industry had opened plantations in Asia in the 1930s, Brazil initially had suffered. The war cut off Allied access to much of Asia, however, and Brazil again prospered following 1941. In recognition of its crucial economic link to the Allies, Brazil declared allegiance to their cause in 1942.

Uruguay, however, was a perennial enemy of Brazil, frequently clashing with Brazil over their common border. While Uruguay officially remained neutral, it was widely recognized that its sympathies (and probably aid) went to the Axis. Paraguay, however, was a perennial enemy of Brazil and Uruguay and declared itself one of the Allies. The Chaco War, a bitter border conflict between Paraguay and Bolivia between 1932 and 1935, had made these two countries enemies; Bolivia, not surprisingly, had no wish to be allied with Paraguay and declared itself neutral, while carrying out a pro-Axis policy. This stance pleased the politically powerful German-speaking minority in Bolivia.

Argentina was the most strongly pro-Axis of the South American countries. The considerable German segment of Argentina's population, coupled with Argentina's longstanding alliance with Uruguay, pushed the country toward the Axis. Postwar investigation strongly suggests that Argentina's "Colonels' Government," led by Colonel Juan Peron, collaborated extensively with Germany. Argentina's principal rival and enemy in South America, Chile, automatically united with the Allies.

In short, much of South America was involved in World War II, either overtly or through clandestine alliances. Countries arrayed on the same side did not necessarily share political views—they were united primarily by opposition to their traditional enemies. Countries with sizeable German populations often were pro-Axis, and countries with strong economic ties to the Allies usually became staunch Allies themselves.

Although no battles of World War II were fought in South America and only token South American forces were committed to action, the resources of these countries were significant in determining the war's outcome. In a period before the development of synthetic rubber and plastic, the rubber plantations of Brazil were critical to the Allied war effort, providing tires, gaskets, and other items. Chile's nitrate mining industry also was critical, because all major explosives were based on this naturally occurring substance. The denial of nitrates to the Axis powers, which had few sources within the territory they controlled, helped shorten the war and assure Allied victory. Pro-Axis nations of South America, in contrast, could offer the Axis powers only beef, tin, and wool, less critical war materials. After World War II, some South American countries gave shelter and support to many ex-Nazis.

numbers of Poles found themselves rounded up and shipped off to German factories. There they labored in poor conditions and lived under brutal treatment by Germans. If they became seriously ill or injured, they likely faced death as "useless mouths." French, Russians, and Italians (after 1943, part of the Allies) eventually were compelled to work with the Poles to make a forced-labor "army" of perhaps 8 million people.

The Revival and Domination of the U.S. Economy

World War II gave millions of American workers jobs and ended the Great Depression in the United States. State-directed policies created a vast military-industrial complex. Even before the formal war declaration in early December 1941, large sums had been devoted to rearming the United States. Around $13 billion was spent in 1939, and more than $30 billion was spent in 1941. The war years themselves saw growth of like magnitudes. Although the American government established certain strategic industries directly, it usually contracted with private producers for war materials.

War production was spread across the United States, reflecting congressional delegations' influence and preventing industrial concentration and vulnerability to attack. Many regions received substantial federal funds to supply the nation's war needs, and economic development spread all over the country. California in particular received an enormous amount of government funds to build weapons and provide supplies, and it became a major industrial state.

Between 1941 and 1945, the American economy grew by 50 percent, with steel output nearly doubling. Shipbuilding increased by a factor of ten and included around 51 million tons of merchant marine ships to haul war supplies. The industrialist Henry Kaiser used prefabrication methods in assembling merchant ships every few days. Aircraft production also increased tenfold during the war, for a total amount of 300,000 planes (out of a total of 750,000 worldwide). In 1944 alone, the United States turned out more than 100,000 planes. Other items included more than 500 million socks, 237 million cans of insect spray, and more than 3 million hot-water bottles. The United States rearmed the British and helped supply the Soviet Union. The Soviets received nearly 400,000 trucks and 2.7 million tons of gasoline; these facilitated the Soviet push into Germany.

One other American trend involved a change in what was regarded as "women's work." Before the onset of World War II, bank tellers, office clerks, and retail cashiers had been men. During and after the war, women more frequently worked in these jobs. The federal government also employed larger numbers of women during the war.

The Soviet Wartime Economy

Of the combatants, the Soviet Union mobilized its material resources and population most completely. This was possible because the Soviet economy had been restructured previously, between 1929 and 1941, and its various sectors already lay under state control. In addition, the Soviets realized that they faced the greatest fury of Nazi Germany. The government also eased its suppression of popular expressions of fervor and encouraged the rise of patriotism.

Stalin facilitated the dismantling and relocation of factories in the path of the German onslaught. By late 1941, more than 1,500 industrial plants were up and running in or beyond the Ural Mountains east of Moscow. Some were established in areas where winter already had arrived, and dynamite had to blast the foundations for the industrial works in the frozen soil.

Soviet control of production also facilitated the standardization of most weapons systems. This meant that large numbers could be produced quickly. In addition, tanks, planes, and guns produced in the Soviet Union during and after 1942 were often superior to their German counterparts.

The Soviet Union experienced one of the most disruptive assaults in its history; perhaps only the devastation by the Mongols in the thirteenth century could rival that of World War II. The peoples of the Soviet Empire endured great privation and personal loss, yet there was a growing pride in the ability of their armies to stop the Germans. Loss, mingled with hard-won self-respect, offered some hope for a future of peace and tranquility.

Japan's Wartime Economy

Direction of the Japanese economy for military purposes had commenced in the 1930s, before the onset of fighting in the Asian theater in 1937. In the

IN THEIR OWN WORDS

Soviet Views of the Early War

Nazi armies hit Soviet Russia with hammering body blows in 1941, nearly overwhelming all resistance. A range of reactions to the invasion has been recorded, and three from 1941 appear here. The first, arising from acceptance of Soviet propaganda that had promised total victory over the Nazis, is that the attack was insane:

> "Who do they think they are attacking? Have they gone out of their minds?" . . . "Of course, the German workers will support us, and all other peoples will rise up." . . . "Our men will hit them so hard, it will all be over in a week," said one worker. "Well, it won't necessarily be finished in one week," answered another. "They've got to get to Berlin. . . . It will take three or four weeks."

The opposite was occurring. Soviet armies were being overwhelmed, and the magnitude of the crisis did not dawn on the Soviet people until July 3, 1941, when Josef Stalin spoke candidly on national radio:

> . . . the enemy continues to push forward. . . . A grave danger hangs over our country. . . . It is essential that our people . . . should appreciate the full immensity of the danger that threatens our country. . . . The issue is one of life and death for the Soviet state, for the peoples of the USSR; the issue is whether the peoples of the Soviet Union shall remain free or fall into slavery. . . . All work must be immediately reconstructed on a war footing, everything must be subordinated to the interests of the front and the task of organizing the demolition of the enemy.

Increasingly, Stalin recalled the earlier victories of Russians over enemies like Napoleon. In fact, his speech was similar to one made by Tsar Alexander I in 1812 as French forces were approaching Moscow. During the war, perhaps for the first time, Stalin became a popular figure, one identified with Soviet Russia:

> All my life I will remember what Stalin's Order meant. . . . Not the letter, but the spirit and the content of this document made possible the moral and psychological breakthrough in the hearts and minds of all to whom it was read. . . . the chief thing was the courage to tell people the whole terrible and bitter truth about the abyss to whose edge we were then sliding.

Thus spoke a soldier about his reaction to Stalin's speech. Many soldiers gave the standard battle cry throughout the war—"for the motherland, for Stalin!"

---

next four years, further shifting and stockpiling of resources for war intensified economic tensions. But the outbreak of war in the Pacific theater pushed Japanese production and investment to a near-total effort.

Women and Korean nationals had been induced to enter industry in order to offset the drain of Japanese men from the labor market. Women had long been participants in the manufacturing sector, and their numbers grew after the late 1930s. Production and stockpiling had given the Japanese an edge in war equipment in the early months of the war in the Pacific theater, but the overall productive capacity of the United States eventually overcame that advantage. Also, the systematic destruction of Japan's merchant marine fleet by American submarines, surface ships, and airplanes began to have an effect in the latter part of the war. American ships and planes sowed mines in the coastal waters to hamper Japan's economy.

Despite the reduced importation of raw materials, Japanese workers achieved impressive production totals as late as 1944. In 1943, Japan had produced around 20,000 airplanes, and around 25,000 aircraft rolled off Japanese assembly lines in 1944. Massive bombing raids and Allied shelling of coastal areas beginning in early 1945 contributed to the destruction of Japan's military-industrial complex.

By the war's end, most Japanese were reduced to semistarvation. Some were forced to forage for wild vegetables and tubers in the countryside. Japan's once-powerful economy was in ruins.

Europe and Africa		Asia and the Pacific		Year	Events
			Asian theater of World War II, 1937–Aug. 1945	1937	Rape of Nanjing, Dec. 1937
				1938	
	Euro-African theater of World War II, 1939–May 1945			1939	Hitler announces plans to exterminate Jews in Europe, Jan. 1939 Germany attacks Poland, Sept. 1939
Holocaust, 1940–1945				1940	France falls to Germans, June 1940
		Pacific theater of World War II 1941–1945		1941	German invasion of Soviet Russia begins, June 1941 Systematic exterminations begin in Eastern Europe, Sept. 1941 Pearl Harbor bombed, Dec. 1941
				1942	German forces push toward Suez Canal, June 1942 Battle of Midway, June 1942
				1943	German army surrenders at Stalingrad, Jan. 1943 Russia stops German advance at Kursk-Orel, July 1943
				1944	Saipan falls to U.S., July 1944 Major air raids on Japanese cities begin, Nov. 1944
				1945	Atomic bomb levels Hiroshima, Aug. 1945

SUMMARY

1. World War II, consisting of three interlocking war theaters (Asian, Euro-African, and Pacific), began in 1937 and ended in 1945. At least 60 million people died, and terrible destruction convulsed many countries.

2. The Asian theater (1937–1945) followed a six-year expansion of Japanese imperialism into China. It wrought great loss of life and injury to 21 million people. During the war, Japanese atrocities sparked nationalism among the Chinese peasants.

3. The European theater (1939–1945) grew out of Adolf Hitler's grand plan to conquer and transform Europe in his racist vision. He took power in Germany, built the economy, and waged war on Czechoslovakia, Poland, and continental western Europe. He carried out his policy of eliminating "undesirables," a dress rehearsal for the Holocaust.

4. In North Africa, General Erwin Rommel defeated British units and threatened the Suez Canal. The British rallied and pushed back Rommel, and at the same time Americans landed to the west and destroyed the German and Italian forces in 1943. Africa became the launching pad for attacks on Italy.

5. Hitler attacked Soviet Russia, expecting a quick victory. He threatened Moscow, Leningrad, and the Caucasus oil fields but failed to win despite capturing 5 million Soviet soldiers. The Soviet counteroffensive carried through to Berlin by April 1945 and helped bring the defeat of Nazi Germany in May. Hitler committed suicide shortly before Germany's surrender.

6. The Pacific theater (1941–1945) began when the Japanese attacked Pearl Harbor and sank many battleships. The Japanese swept over more Pacific islands but were halted by United States naval forces in the Coral Sea and at Midway. Heavy fighting took place in the Philippines, Iwo Jima, and Okinawa. The United States dropped two atomic bombs, on Hiroshima and Nagasaki, to end the Pacific war.

7. The Holocaust brought the deliberate deaths of 11 million people, including Jews, Gypsies, Poles, Russians, and other groups. The machinery of destruction had been set up and run between 1939 and 1941, and the mass killings increased thereafter. Each intensification came during major military operations and reflected the national socialist goal of bringing about a racial demographic revolution.

8. Women gained new prominence in many countries. In the United States, women enjoyed improved wages and working conditions.

9. During World War II, African Americans entered the United States economy and the armed forces in large numbers. Japanese Americans, Tatars, and Volga Germans were oppressed by policies of their governments.

10. The economic dimension of the war left the United States and Soviet Russia dominant. The United States in particular benefited from a vast government investment program that produced a military-industrial complex and spread economic growth around the South and the West. Germans used massive importations of forced labor and the exploitation of conquered European lands to sustain their war machine. Japan mobilized its economic resources in the 1930s and built stockpiles of war materials that helped them in the first year of the Pacific war. Defeat left Japan in economic ruins, with many starving people by September 1945.

SUGGESTED READINGS

Barber, John, and Mark Harrison. *The Soviet Home Front, 1941–1945.* London: Longman, 1991. A study of a key area of Soviet Russia during World War II.

Glantz, David, and Jonathan House. *When Titans Clashed.* Lawrence: University Press of Kansas, 1995. A study of the war between Germany and Russia, 1941–1945.

Keegan, John. *A History of Warfare.* New York: Knopf, 1993. A standard examination of World War II and of war in general.

Pyle, Kenneth. *The Making of Modern Japan.* Lexington, Mass.: D. C. Heath, 1996. A survey of Japanese history and World War II.

Weinberg, Gerhard. *A World at Arms.* Cambridge, Eng.: Cambridge University Press, 1994. A thorough examination of World War II.

Last Spike Ceremony. *On May 10, 1869, at Promontory Point, Utah, east met west at the completion of the first railroad to span North America. Locomotives of the Central Pacific (left) and the Union Pacific (right) were brought nose-to-nose and christened with champagne. Similar celebrations attended the completion of railroad networks in Europe, Asia, and South America.* Union Pacific Railroad Museum Collection.

ISSUE 8

Technology Unites the World

On May 10, 1869, a group of executives, government officials, and workers gathered at Promontory Point, Utah, to celebrate the completion of the transcontinental railroad system that spanned the United States. They ceremoniously drove "the golden spike" that completed the last section of rail, then posed for photographs. Similar ceremonies marked the openings of the Chinese Eastern Railroad (1903), the Trans-Siberian Railroad of Russia (1905), the Transandine Railroad of South America (1910), and various other railway systems around the world. These events collectively formed a milestone in the march toward global interconnectedness.

Human beings are moderately puny creatures. Without technological assistance, they are limited to traveling only a few miles a day, carrying only a few things in their arms. Through technology, however, human beings have created ways of vastly increasing the loads that can be carried, greatly expanding the distances they can be moved, and speeding up the entire process. In addition, they have devised ways of carrying messages even farther and faster.

The movement of people or goods from one place to another is **transportation**, and the movement of messages is **communication**. For most of human history, the two were coupled closely. A person walking between communities to carry a message might as well carry physical objects also, because that person had to actually travel to the second community to transmit the message. Prior to the nineteenth century there were only a few modes of long-distance communication, such as the whistling codes of Madagascar and the drums used for long-range communication in parts of Africa. These techniques, however, were uncommon and restricted the communicators to relatively simple messages. Only in the nineteenth and twentieth centuries were technologies developed that permitted wide-ranging communication without movement of people or objects.

Improvements in transportation and communication technology had dramatic effects in uniting the world. A region that previously had little contact with other parts of the world might abruptly become connected with them. Sometimes this resulted in improved quality of life, as when the opening of new trade and markets permitted increased opportunity for entrepreneurs; sometimes it resulted in destruction and misery, as when a colonial power eradicated a local way of life.

NEW MODES OF TRANSPORTATION

There are two main measures of a transportation mode's utility. **Speed** is simply how fast goods are moved, and it is clearly an important measure, especially for perishable goods. Speed also is an issue with transportation through inhospitable zones, when food and water must be carried by the travelers. The other measure, **load**, is the weight of cargo that can be transported, and it, too, has obvious importance.

A fit human being can walk at about 4 miles per hour for about half a day, carrying about 50 pounds, resulting in a practical limit of transportation by simple human power: 50 pounds, 50 miles a day. A modern jetliner, in contrast, can travel at 600 miles per hour nearly all day (with stops for refueling and crew changes), giving a daily range of about 9,000 miles; its load can be up to 150,000 pounds. Surely, transportation technology has come a long way.

Early Transportation

The earliest innovations in transportation were designed primarily to increase the load, not the speed. When animal-drawn wagons were developed in southwestern Asia around 4000 B.C., they moved at about the same speed a person could walk, but they took advantage of the greater strength of draft animals and the fact that several animals could be harnessed to a single vehicle, greatly increasing the possible load.

Early boats, too, were quite slow as late as the eighteenth century. The *Mayflower*, the ship that carried the English to Plymouth Colony in Massachusetts in 1620, averaged only a little over 2 miles per hour for the 66-day trip. The load capacity of ships, however, has increased steadily since around 500 B.C.

Faced with a desire to increase the speed of transportation, as well as the load carried, engineers and designers could take two approaches: improve the vehicle or improve the route over which it passed. Water transportation, of course, was restricted largely to improving the vehicle, because the rivers and oceans could be modified only slightly and at great expense. Nonetheless, particularly in the nineteenth and twentieth centuries, some such improvements were made.

While some modifications in land vehicles were made from the earliest times through the eighteenth century, greater improvements were made in the routes over which those vehicles passed. Road systems at various times and places have stood out for their sophistication and effect on the speed of transportation. The Roman Empire in A.D. 100 had thousands of miles of paved roads stretching throughout its domain, as did the Maurya Empire of India in the fourth century B.C., the Qin Empire of China in the third century B.C., and the Inca Empire of A.D. 1400. In each case, the road system improved speed and transportation capacity dramatically, tying together the far-flung parts of an empire. The breakup of each empire, however, led to the degeneration of its road system, and transportation in subsequent times went into decline.

Reshaping the Route: Canals

While designs and styles of wagons and other vehicles changed over the ages, the first real attempt to change the face of land transportation came about with the development of transportation canals. Canals had been used for irrigation for thousands of years, but only around the seventh century B.C. did they begin to be used for transportation as

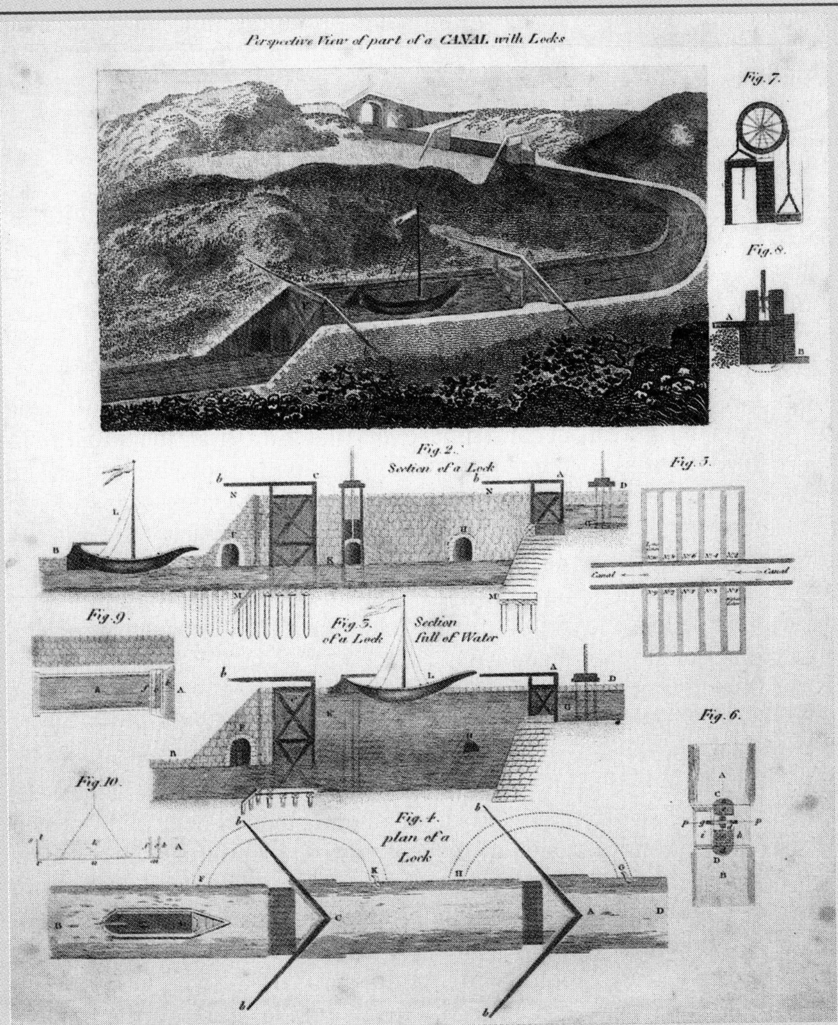

Figure I.8.1 ***Canal Locks.*** *A major problem of early canals was the regulation of water levels—a process needed to link distant points of the waterway at different elevations. The lock solved this problem, isolating a vessel in a closed dock and pumping water in or out as needed. This engineer's drawing of 1797 diagrams the apparatus.* Mansell/Time Inc.

well. At that time, Pharaoh Necho[1] of Egypt built a canal linking the Nile River and the Red Sea, major transportation routes of his era. Five centuries later, the Han Empire of China began building canals for both irrigation and transportation. Two centuries after that, the Romans built a canal connecting the Rhine River and the Zuyder Zee. Boats could carry far greater loads than wagons, and a canal permitted a boat to "sail" through land, although the construction of the canal was very costly in terms of labor.

These early canals were largely single links connecting two places, rather than a network of interconnected canals connecting many places, a **canal system**. The first major transportation canal system was the Grand Canal of China's Sui Empire, opened in the seventh century A.D. It was devoted solely to transportation, linking China's rich rice-producing centers with population and governmental centers so that grain tribute and taxes could be moved efficiently. The Grand Canal was refashioned by the Mongols in the fourteenth century and continued in use into the nineteenth century, by which time failure to maintain the canal plunged it into temporary disuse.

Canals in Europe apparently developed independently of those in Asia, and considerably later. Europeans had used canals from Roman times onward, but the utility of these canals was limited by the problem of connecting bodies of water at different elevations. Until the fourteenth-century invention of the **lock**, a mechanism for holding

[1] **Necho:** NEHCH oh

water in different parts of a canal at different elevations and moving a vessel from one elevation to the other, canal systems were impractical. Even after the invention of the lock, canal systems remained rare in Europe until the eighteenth century.

The reason lies with the huge investment required to build a canal. Private investors often were unwilling to risk such sums, even if they could afford them, and the building of major canals usually was left to governments. Canals came to be seen as sources of national pride, and they went hand-in-glove with the rise of nationalism in Europe. As land became more valuable and labor costs rose, however, planners turned increasingly toward other modes of transportation.

One special kind of canal has retained its importance through today: the canal connecting two seas. The most spectacular of these are the Suez Canal in Egypt, connecting the Red Sea and the Mediterranean Sea, and the Panama Canal in Panama, connecting the Atlantic Ocean and Pacific Ocean. The Suez Canal, completed in 1869, saved ships traveling between Asia and Europe the thousands of extra miles otherwise necessitated in rounding the southern tip of Africa. Its military significance was not lost on commanders in World War II and the Arab-Israeli War of 1967, and all sides sought to control it. The Panama Canal was completed in 1914, permitting ships to cross between the Atlantic and Pacific oceans without making the long and hazardous trip around the tip of South America.

Engine-Powered Vehicles on Sea and Land

The next great steps in transportation took place in Europe and North America, where inventors began using steam engines to power various types of vehicles. The steam engine, made practical by James Watt in 1782, could run on any fuel to boil water, using the resulting steam to power an engine. It was easy to adapt Watt's engine to turning a paddle wheel or a propeller screw, and the steamship was practical and in use by 1807.

The steam engine also was adapted to land vehicles. The first of these was the railway locomotive, in use by 1801 but truly practical only by 1829. The railroad was far faster than any contemporary form of land transportation and could carry far greater loads. The only liability was that it could travel only on specially constructed rails, which were quite expensive to lay. Its original use, therefore, was restricted largely to moving passengers relatively short distances between cities, limiting the amount of track laid. Later, especially in the United States, entrepreneurs would extend railroads into remote areas, with the expectation that development would be stimulated by easier access to industrial and population centers. Indeed, as noted in Chapter 32, the building of railroads itself was a significant industry in the second phase of the Industrial Revolution. In some countries, particularly those of Europe, the construction of a railroad system was viewed as a source of national pride and a part of the military defense system. On the railroads of most places around the world, more efficient diesel engines that burnt petroleum for fuel eventually replaced steam engines.

The final major innovation in land transportation, the automobile, was a European invention. The earliest automobiles had been powered with steam engines, but the first successful models, invented independently by Karl Benz and Gottlieb Daimler[2] in Germany in 1885, were based on internal combustion engines that ran on petroleum products. Between 1905 and 1915, the number of automobiles in use skyrocketed. In the United States, for example, 78,000 automobiles were in use in 1905, but 2.5 million were on the roads a decade later. Henry Ford and other American industrialists began building huge numbers of automobiles in America, starting a major American industry.

The rise of the automobile was linked to good roads, and in the era between 1890 and 1915, the responsibility for building and maintaining roads shifted increasingly from local communities to regional and national governments. These larger governmental units were more committed to the development of a good road system, and roads in many parts of the world improved substantially in this period. Automobiles or trucks could reach communities that were off the railroad lines, further uniting a nation. While these vehicles carried relatively small loads, they were rapid and were not restricted to railroad tracks.

[2] **Gottlieb Daimler:** GAHT leeb DYM lur

Transportation Takes to the Skies

The final major innovation in transportation was the development of the airplane. For many years after the Wright brothers' famous test flight of an engine-driven airplane in 1903, aviation was a sport of the well-to-do adventurer. Airplanes, though fast, could carry only modest loads and were generally dangerous and unreliable; they were fit for adventures but not for everyday use.

Technical improvements, however, led to greater trust. World War I showed that airplanes could be reliable, and public sympathy encouraged their increased use. The first international passenger service began in 1919, and regular use of airplanes for the carrying of mail began in many places in the 1920s. Famous flights, such as Charles Lindbergh's solo flight across the Atlantic in 1927, enhanced the reputation of airplanes, and their major role in World War II, in which 750,000 airplanes were involved, cemented their place in modern transportation.

The development of efficient jet engines in the 1950s and early 1960s meant that air travel was by far the fastest form of transportation. Some of the more troublesome side effects of jet travel, including the shrill screech that continued throughout the flight, were eliminated or reduced by technical refinements. While jet travel has remained limited to cities with sufficiently large airports, its speed and comfort have made it the transportation mode of choice for much travel; its decreasing cost has made it affordable to a larger segment of the world's people.

FIGURE I.8.2 *The First Zeppelin. Launched in Italy in 1907, this zeppelin marked the serious development of lighter-than-air ships. Consisting of a huge canvas bag filled with a very light gas and a gondola suspended beneath the bag, the zeppelin was a viable competitor to the airplane until the 1937 explosion of the* Hindenburg *in New Jersey—a catastrophe that was recorded on film and widely publicized.* Corbis-Bettmann.

NEW MODES OF COMMUNICATION

For most of human history, communication has been almost exclusively by the spoken word, with the speaker and hearer face to face. Two major revolutions, however, have permitted people to preserve their communications over time and to project them over space.

The First Communication Revolution: The Written Word

The first major revolution in communication came about when language was first written down. This occurred independently at various places in the world, earliest in Southwest Asia around 3000 B.C., and also in Mexico, China, and Egypt. The next step in the evolution of the written word was block printing, developed in seventh-century China, where entire plates were printed at once. A thirteenth-century Korean press utilized movable type, as did the fifteenth-century German printing press. The printing press permitted for the first time the mass production of inexpensive copies of writings. The written word no longer was unique, and readers in far-flung places could read copies of the same text. Later, magazines, newspapers, and handbills would convey messages to a mass readership. Education was the only limitation on the dissemination of information.

The significance of the printing press, coupled with widespread literacy, cannot be overstated. Printing permitted large numbers of copies of a text to be produced and transported inexpensively, spreading the author's message to a large and widespread audience. Scholars could communicate their ideas to one another, even if they never had met; in this way, each could build on the findings of colleagues, speeding the growth of their disciplines. Political, religious, and social reformers could encapsulate their ideas in inspirational words and spread them to potential supporters. Everyday people could learn of foreign lands and ways, sometimes encouraging them to immigrate or experiment with new concepts of government or society. Still, speaking, writing, and printing— important as they were— remained the only major means of communication into the nineteenth century.

The Second Communication Revolution: Electronic Communications

Many inventors had dreamed of means of long-distance communication, but the first practical scheme was not put into use until 1794. Claude Chappe[3] had invented an **optical telegraph**, with slats of wood mounted atop high buildings and moved via a system of ropes and pulleys. Different positions for the slats corresponded to codes for letters, and messages could be laboriously sent along lines of sight. By 1844, Chappe's optical telegraph consisted of more than 500 stations connecting 29 French cities and spanning more than 3,000 miles.

The defects of the optical telegraph, however, were obvious. It was useless at night or during cloudy weather. The ropes could foul in the pulleys or break; winds played havoc with the apparatus. Messages had to be retransmitted many times to carry them long distances, increasing the possibility of error. Finally, it was very slow.

Many scientists began experimenting with electrical signals to carry messages. A very cumbersome and ineffective electrical telegraph was put into operation in France in 1812, and practical systems were operating in England, continental Europe, and the United States by 1837. These electrical telegraphs transmitted short bursts of electricity over a wire according to a code, and a receiver at the other end decoded the signal. Each system initially was limited to a single landmass, because wires were needed. In 1866, however, a transatlantic telegraph cable was successfully laid, linking the Americas with the Old World. By 1900, there were few places in the world without telegraph links.

In the meantime, a new technology was developing: the telephone. Alexander Graham Bell, a Scottish-born American, transmitted the first sentence over telephone wires in 1876, and the advantages of this device were immediately apparent. Two-way conversations could be carried on between speakers with no code skills, the nuances of tone could be reproduced, and the communication could proceed at a normal speed. Thomas Edison and others refined the telephone to practicality in the next two decades. By 1915, a transatlantic telephone cable was laid, linking Europe and North America.

[3] **Claude Chappe:** KLOHD SHAHP

Figure I.8.3 ***Optical Telegraph.*** *This mechanical device was invented during the French Revolution and put to use in 1794 to provide communication between the cities of Paris and Lille. Although it was serviceable, with different positions of the arms denoting different letters, the optical telegraph was slow, and it was ineffective in darkness, fog, or heavy rain.* Deutsches Museum, Munich.

Both the telephone and telegraph required wires connecting the communicating parties, and inventors sought ways to increase the flexibility and decrease the cost of communication by eliminating the wires. In 1886, Heinrich Hertz,[4] a German scientist, produced "Hertzian waves," the electrical waves later used for radio transmission. By the late 1890s, Guglielmo Marconi,[5] an Italian scientist, was transmitting telegraph signals, and, in 1901, he successfully transmitted between North America and Europe.

Wireless telegraphy never had a major impact on communications, but radio transmission of voices and music certainly did. For the first time, communications could be electrically **broadcast** (sent out widely) to be received by anyone with the proper receiving device. This potential was realized first in the United States, when the Radio Corporation of America (RCA) began broadcasting music in 1920. Similar ventures proliferated in Europe shortly thereafter, though radio broadcasts in many other countries did not begin until after World War II.

Television was a logical outgrowth of radio, because most of its principles were the same. The difficulty of projecting a picture electronically was solved by 1923 by Vladimir Zworykin,[6] a Russian American scientist. The technology for television could have been implemented any time after this date, but it was not until 1939 that the first regular television broadcasts began, again initiated by the Radio Corporation of America. The popularity of radio and the general belief that the public would not be willing to pay more to receive pictures held up its introduction, and it was not until the economic boom following World War II that television took off.

The latest major communication advance can be seen as an extension of the telegraph. The **microprocessor**, the information-processing heart of a computer, converts messages into electronic impulses and can store or send these messages. Although they have many other uses, microprocessors are the innovation that has led to the "information superhighway" developed in the last years of the twentieth century: a vast network of interconnected microprocessors that can send messages from one station to another rapidly and inexpensively. Using microprocessors, a student in Houston can examine the library holdings of the University of Tokyo, a petroleum engineer in Iraq can consult professional literature otherwise unavailable in that country, and a freelance writer in India can send electronic mail to an editor in London inexpensively and rapidly.

The microprocessor, invented in 1958 by Jack Kilby and Robert Mason of the United States, consists of a chip of silicon on which are etched complex circuits that permit the microprocessor to

[4] **Heinrich Hertz:** HYN rihk HEHRTZ

[5] **Guglielmo Marconi:** goo YAY moh mahr KOH nee

[6] **Vladimir Zworykin:** VLAHD ih meer ZVOH ree kihn

carry out logical operations according to procedures encoded in the circuits. Every operation that a microprocessor can carry out could be accomplished—though in a more cumbersome manner—by conventional electronics. But the advantage of the microprocessor is that it can be mass produced inexpensively. The circuits are etched optically, meaning that the microprocessor is cheap enough to be widely purchased. The Univac computer, widely heralded in the 1950s, cost millions of dollars; it could be replaced in 1970 by a microprocessor that cost only $100,000; by the 1990s, a more sophisticated microprocessor cost less than a dollar. The microprocessor has been in use only for a few years, and it is not yet possible to assess the ultimate magnitude of its impact on communication.

THE IMPACT OF A SHRINKING WORLD

The march of technology has seen the inexorable improvement of the globe's transportation and communication potential. Today, a fifty-ton load can be carried across a continent in four hours by a jetliner; that same load would have taken three months for a team of more than 2,000 workers to transport in 5000 B.C.; using Southwest Asian technology of 3000 B.C., the task would have taken just as long but would have required only 100 workers; even as late as 1900, carrying the load by railroad would have taken about three days.

Prior to the nineteenth century, most transportation innovations were directed toward increasing the loads that could be carried. In the nineteenth and twentieth centuries, innovation has been directed more toward increases in speed, although loads have been increased as well. Communication advances associated with writing and printing have had major impacts on the world, but the modes of electronic communication developed since the nineteenth century have been qualitatively different. What are the impacts of these changes of the past two centuries on the world?

The economic change is obvious. As transportation has improved, the markets for goods have become broader, and items produced in one country may be found literally all over the world. This has provided some entrepreneurs with the opportunity for tremendous success, but it also has smothered others that might have been successful locally. The world trade in soft drinks is controlled largely by two American companies, and countless local beverage companies, particularly in the less industrialized countries, have been forced out of business by this competition.

These less industrialized countries, at a profound disadvantage in most economic transac-

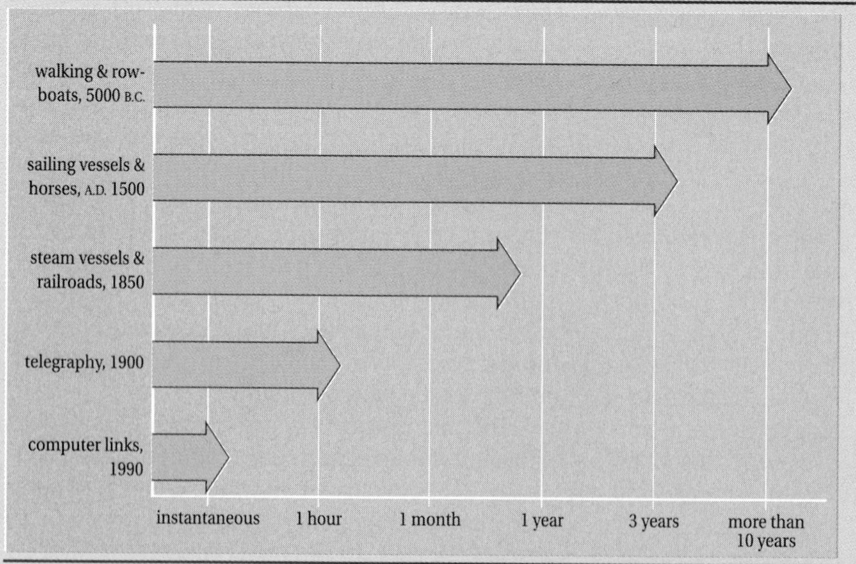

FIGURE I.8.4 ***State-of-the-Art Communication.*** *Changing technology has had a profound effect on humans' ability to interact with one another. As we discover faster and more efficient ways of sending messages around the world, we open up new avenues for trade and cultural exchange.*

tions, now sometimes find themselves with a competitive advantage over more industrialized countries, because their low labor costs may attract foreign industries searching to cut production costs. Many books are planned and laid out in New York or Boston, although often the actual printing takes place in Indonesia. Only inexpensive transportation could make such practices economically feasible.

Politically, the effects may be more complex. Improved transportation has enhanced the ability of powerful countries to use their military and economic might to coerce less powerful countries into dependent relationships as colonies, as allies dominated through military or political threat, or as countries whose economies actually are controlled by foreign corporations. On the other hand, the news media have become a powerful factor in international politics, graphically presenting conditions that, in an earlier era, would never have been recognized by the general populace. By drawing attention to abuses, the press can provide the focus for public pressure on governments.

At the social level, innovations in transportation and communication have broadened the horizons of nearly every person on the planet. There is a greater sense of shared background, interests, and skills in today's world than in any period that preceded it. Whether in Africa, Europe, or Latin America, newspapers carry many of the same stories and radios play much of the same music. This shared experience, an optimist might claim, has helped make people around the world relate to one another; a pessimist could point to intolerance and discrimination that argue otherwise. Certainly, however, this shared background, coupled with moderately inexpensive, fast, and reliable transportation, has increased the ease with which people can immigrate and successfully function in their new homes.

SUGGESTED READINGS

Clarke, Donald, ed. *The Encyclopedia of Transportation.* London: Marshall Cavendish Publications, 1974. A straightforward encyclopedia, emphasizing inventions and their operations. A good source for figuring out how a device really works.

Fabre, Maurice. *A History of Communications.* New York: Hawthorn Books, 1963. The New Illustrated Library of Science and Invention, vol. 9. A nice history emphasizing the development of writing, printing, and telegraphy, including some useful illustrations of devices.

Georgeano, G. N., ed. *Transportation through the Ages.* New York: McGraw-Hill, 1972. A series of essays on the development of roads, railroads, ships, canals, and aviation.

Smith, Anthony. *Goodbye, Gutenberg: The Newspaper Revolution of the 1980's.* Oxford, Eng., and New York: Oxford University Press, 1980. Primarily concerned with changes in newspapers brought by the electronic information revolution; also includes a brief history of newspapers.

Vance, James E. *Capturing the Horizon: The Historical Geography of Transportation since the Sixteenth Century.* Baltimore: Johns Hopkins University Press, 1986. A treatment of the geography of transportation, with considerable discussion of technological innovations and consequences.

HUMAN EXISTENCE ALWAYS HAS BEEN MARKED BY CHANGE, but the rate of change has increased over the millennia. In part, this has been caused by the inexorable growth of population. The cumulative development of technology also has been a factor, as greater technical capabilities have permitted actions with more wide-reaching consequences. Another key ingredient is the greater degree of connectedness between the parts of the world, opening the door to a wealth of transforming processes, including the fusion of ideologies from diverse cultural traditions, the expansion of economic markets, and military conflict. The twentieth century has seen the highest population levels, the most sophisticated technology, and the greatest degree of connectedness of all time, and the rate of change also has been greatest. This change has expressed itself in society, politics, economics, art, and virtually all other realms of human experience.

Baltic Demonstration. *In August 1989, citizens of Latvia and other Baltic states formed a human chain stretching across their countries to demonstrate their desire for independence*

PART NINE

ACCELERATING CHANGE

Part Nine explores aspects of this rapid change in the twentieth century, particularly after World War II. Chapter 41 discusses the Cold War era, the period of tensions between communist and capitalist countries that followed World War II. Chapter 42 examines the role of demography in the middle and late portions of the century, focusing on how and why populations have changed and what effects those changes have wrought. The part concludes with Issue 9, which considers the changing twentieth-century relationships between politics and ethnicity. These chapters and the issue provide windows on the swift and accelerating change that has characterized the twentieth century.

from the Soviet Union. This successful independence movement was one of many in the period since the end of World War II. Zoja Pictures / Gamma/Liaison International.

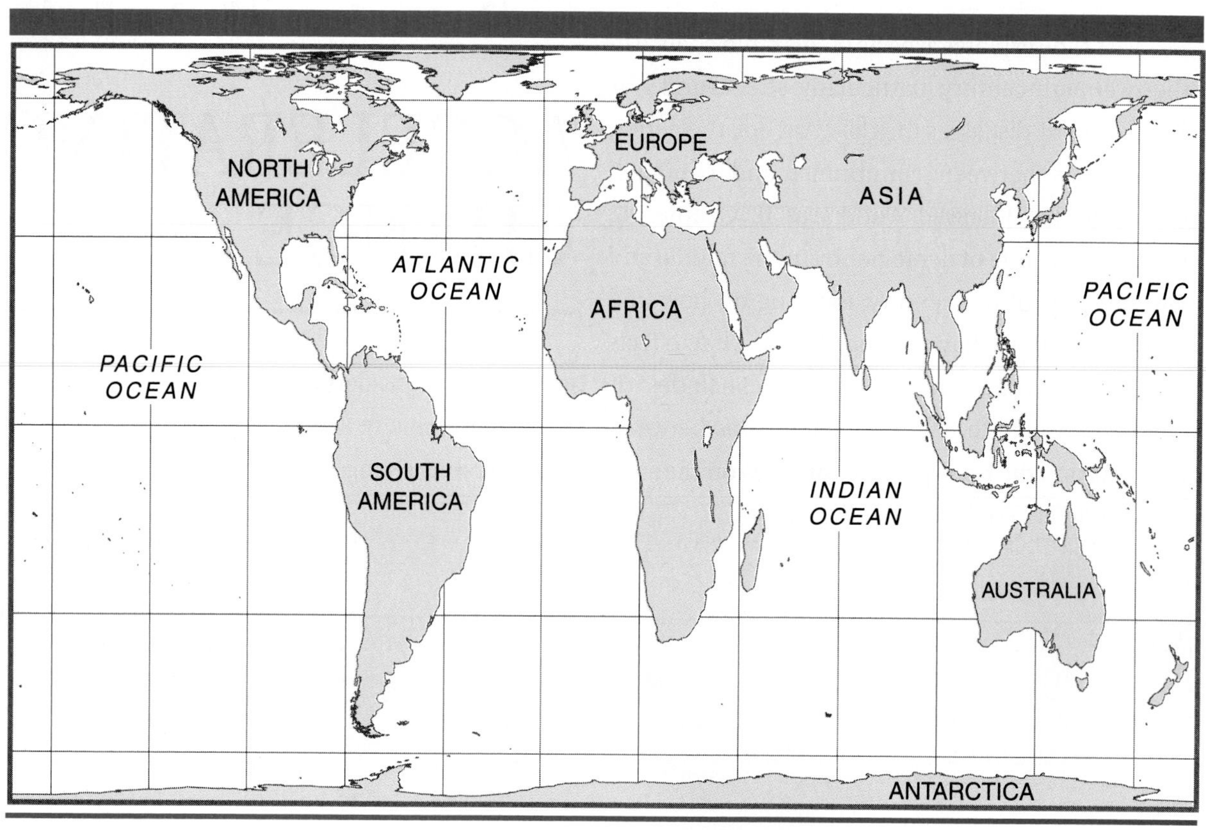
NORTH AMERICA
EUROPE
ASIA
ATLANTIC OCEAN
AFRICA
PACIFIC OCEAN
PACIFIC OCEAN
SOUTH AMERICA
INDIAN OCEAN
AUSTRALIA
ANTARCTICA

CHAPTER 41

The Cold War Era
1945–1991

From Stettin in the Baltic to Trieste in the Adriatic, an iron curtain has descended across the continent. . . . All are subject, in one form or another, not only to Soviet influence but to a very high and increasing measure of control from Moscow. . . . Far from the Russian frontiers and throughout the world, Communist fifth columns are established and work in complete unity and absolute obedience to the directions they receive from the Communist centre.

–WINSTON CHURCHILL

Sir Winston Churchill's "iron curtain" speech of March 5, 1946, set the tone for a global rivalry between two coalitions of countries, the U.S. alliance and the Soviet alliance. Scholars have called this rivalry the Cold War.

The Cold War era (1945–1991) was a time not only of political rivalries but also of accelerating change. Competition and conflict between the Soviets and Americans spread to Asia, Africa, and the Americas. The rivalry was economic as well as political. The United States and the Soviet Union developed economic blocs and struggled to dominate areas with important natural resources, such as petroleum. Unchecked economic growth, however, created serious environmental problems. Massive governmental funds were poured into universities and research centers, which became vital scientific research establishments.

Scholars often use the term **First World** to describe the U.S. alliance system and the **Second World** to refer to the Soviet alliance system. The

Third World is a commonly used term to refer to the nonindustrialized countries that did not initially support either of the alliances.

THE COLD WAR, 1945–1991

The **Cold War** is the name given to the intense and multifaceted rivalry that threatened to become a hot war between the Americans and Soviets. Key elements of the Cold War are:

—sharp ideological differences,

—an arms race,

—economic competition, and

—the formation of power blocs.

A rough balance of power existed between the American and Soviet power blocs, and major war involving them was avoided.

The Central Conflict

The seeds of the Cold War were sown in the last days of World War II. Only the United States and the Soviet Union had powerful military forces and the economic strength to impose their wills on others. American armies controlled much of Western Europe and Japan, while Soviet armies dominated Eastern Europe and parts of China. Britain had been powerful in the past, but its might had been undermined by the war.

Competition between the United States and the Soviet Union produced a massive arms race. Europe became the central Cold War stage, as the Americans helped rebuild the parts of Europe under their sphere of influence, and the Soviets turned their sphere of influence into a political and economic bloc. The competition became heated, especially with the onset of an expensive arms race. In 1945, only the United States possessed nuclear weapons capable of destroying cities. By 1965, although other countries also had these weapons, the Americans and Soviets had developed intercontinental missile delivery systems. They threatened the extinction of human beings on the planet.

Clear ideological differences shaped the Cold War. The Soviets touted socialism as the most modern economic and social system, the model that would win the Cold War. U.S. leaders promoted capitalism and democracy, claiming that they represented the "Free World." In fact, both Americans and Soviets backed unsavory dictatorships in order to expand and maintain their power.

Capitalism and Soviet-style socialism dominated global economics. Although economic integration had characterized the modern age, the Cold War stalled that process through the creation of two economic networks. Limited trade passed between the two blocs, but the overwhelming economic activity of each was internal rather than external. Although the United States had rebuilt the Japanese and Western European economies, American trade goods soon struggled to compete against materials from these capitalist rivals.

Anti-imperialist struggles often became intertwined with Cold War rivalries. In Vietnam, anti-French Vietnamese independence fighters received aid from China and the Soviet Union, while the United States gave its French allies generous aid to fight communist-backed guerrillas. In Angola, anti-Portuguese resistance fighters were aided by the Soviets, and, after winning power, the new Soviet-backed regime faced anticommunist rebels backed by the United States. These are but two of many examples.

The alliance systems developed their own power blocs with direct and indirect control of other countries. The Soviets refused to tolerate independent countries within their bloc. U.S. leaders helped overthrow governments in Guatemala, South Vietnam, and the Congo (Zaire). In addition, Cold War politics not only maintained the division of Germany but also perpetuated a division of Korea (North and South) and one of Vietnam (North and South).

Spies became an important element in the Cold War, and fear of foreign agents led to repression by suspicious governments. The Soviet Union had developed a network of spies upon the Bolshevik assumption of power in 1917. The Cheka and its successor organizations (including the KGB) trained foreign intelligence-gathering officials, often competing with agents of Soviet military intelligence in ferreting out secrets from the United States and allied powers. For its part, the United States relied on the Central Intelligence Agency (CIA) and the National Security Agency (NSA) to gather information.

Political oppression was common in the Soviet totalitarian system, and the United States went through an era when communists, their sympathizers, and those suspected of being either were regularly harassed or jailed. Witch hunts were promoted in many cities and towns across America, especially in the 1950s. Innocent people's careers were ruined by the anticommunist hysteria. A U.S. senator urged the banning of books about Robin Hood because he robbed from the rich and gave to the poor; he must have been a communist, in the senator's way of thinking. One famous example was the persecution of government officials by Senator Joseph McCarthy in the early 1950s. McCarthyism became the name given to political persecutions of this era.

The Cold War began in Europe and spread to Asia, complicating the Cold War alliance system. In 1949, the Chinese Communist Party gained control of the Chinese mainland and formed an alliance with the Soviet Union a year later. Within a decade, however, nationalist tensions and other factors shattered the Sino-Soviet agreement. Thereafter, China competed with both the United States and

FIGURE 41.1 ***Wartime Allies Meet at Potsdam.*** *From mid-July to early August 1945, leaders of three major Allied powers—Great Britain, the United States, and Soviet Russia—met in Potsdam, Germany, to iron out the details of peace agreements reached at the earlier Yalta conference. The resulting "Potsdam Agreement" provided, among other things, for the restructuring of the German economy and divided control of postwar Germany between the three Allies and France, another Allied country. Delegates to the conference also issued the "Potsdam Declaration," which demanded Japan's unconditional surrender. Pictured, from left to right, are Britain's newly elected prime minister, Clement Attlee, U.S. president Harry Truman, and Soviet premier Josef Stalin.* Corbis-Bettmann.

FIGURE 41.2 ***Hollywood Stars Protest Government Witch Hunt.*** *During the anticommunist probes of Congress, people accused of being communists were intimidated and maligned; the hunt for alleged communists in Hollywood was no exception and cost many their careers. The Hollywood stars in this October 1947 photo flew to Washington, D.C., to protest congressional tactics. Among those shown here are Richard Conte, Humphrey Bogart, Lauren Bacall, and Jane Wyatt. The hunt for communists continued despite the protest.* Corbis-Bettmann.

the Soviet Union for influence in the Third World. Vietnamese communists took control of Vietnam and eventually played off the Soviets and Chinese to become more independent from foreign domination or influence.

The Cold War in Europe

Europe was the central ideological battleground for the United States and the Soviet Union during the Cold War. As the establishment of a Soviet empire in Eastern Europe became clear, the United States announced the Marshall Plan, an aid program to Western European countries that had experienced difficulties reviving themselves after 1945. The U.S. financial effort worked exceptionally well, and, by the early 1950s, most states had achieved a measure of growth.

Germany had been divided by the Allies during the last stages of World War II. It remained divided for decades because Europeans, especially the Soviets, wished to keep it weak, fearing a German military revival that would lead to a national expansionist state. East Germany was supported

IN THEIR OWN WORDS

A Former Communist Speaks Out

In 1948, when the Cold War was in full swing, the House Committee on Un-American Activities called Whittaker Chambers to testify about his life as an agent for the Communist Party. In the course of the committee's investigation, Alger Hiss, head of the Carnegie Endowment for Peace and former member of the U.S. State Department, had been named as a communist agent by Chambers. Between 1948 and 1950, the Hiss case riveted Americans and publicized the fact that Soviet agents had penetrated the U.S. government. Representative Richard Nixon, a member of the committee, became famous as an anticommunist inquisitor, helping him win national political office.

In the book *Witness*, published in 1952, Chambers presents his side of the Hiss case and describes the reasons for his turning against the communist side:

> Almost exactly nine years ago—that is, two days after Hitler and Stalin signed their pact [Nazi-Soviet Non-Aggression Pact of August 1939]—I went to Washington and reported to the authorities what I knew about the infiltration of the United States Government by Communists. For years, international Communism, of which the United States Communist Party is an integral part, had been in a state of undeclared war with this Republic. With the Hitler-Stalin pact that war reached a new stage. I regarded my action in going to the Government as a simple act of war, like the shooting of an armed enemy in combat.
>
> At that moment in history, I was one of the few men on this side of the battle who could perform this service. I had joined the Communist Party in 1924. No one recruited me. I had become convinced that the society in which we live . . . had reached a crisis . . . and that it was doomed to collapse or revert to barbarism.
>
> In 1937, I repudiated Marx's doctrines and Lenin's tactics. Experience and the record had convinced me that Communism is a form of totalitarianism, that its triumph means slavery to men wherever they fall under its sway and spiritual night to the mind and soul. I resolved to break with the Communist Party at whatever risk to myself or my family. Yet, so strong is the hold which the insidious evil of Communism secures upon its disciples, that I could still say to someone at that time: "I know that I am leaving the winning side for the losing side, but it is better to die on the losing side than to live under Communism."

Chambers's words evoke his vision of a titanic struggle against evil, and his later testimony implicated members of a communist apparatus that had penetrated the government. Later, Senator Joseph McCarthy used the fear of communism to attack government officials, furthering his political career, until McCarthy was censured by the Senate for his unorthodox methods in hunting communists.

by the Soviets, and West Germany was bolstered by the Americans, British, and French.

Most other European states fell under the influence of a power bloc, and the forces of nationalism remained checked by the arrangement. In 1956, Hungary, a member of the Soviet bloc, tried to develop an independent defense and foreign policy, but massive force by the Soviets and their allies crushed the effort. Twelve years later, Czechs and Slovaks tried a moderate form of socialism, but, as the world tensely watched, Czechoslovakia also succumbed to invading Soviet forces. Except for a few incidents such as these, the division of Europe brought some measure of peace and stability during the Cold War era.

The military and political basis of the Cold War was in two pacts, NATO and the Warsaw Pact. NATO (North Atlantic Treaty Organization) united the United States, Canada, Britain, France, West Germany, Belgium, Norway, Italy, Greece, and Turkey in defense of Western and Central Europe. The Warsaw Pact bound the Soviet Union, Poland, Hungary, East Germany, Czechoslovakia, Bulgaria, and Romania to defend Eastern Europe. Although

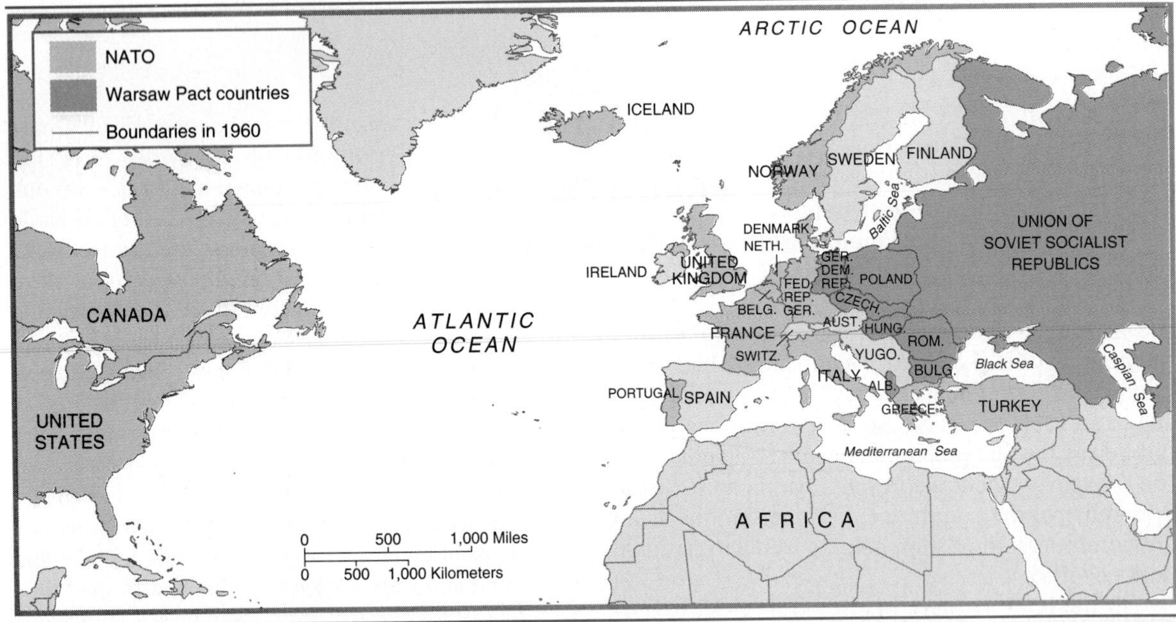

MAP 41.1 ***NATO and Warsaw Pact Countries in 1960.*** *By 1960, most of Europe as well as Turkey, Canada, and the United States were involved in NATO and the Warsaw Pact. Both the United States and the Soviet Union formed rival alliances that were characteristic of the Cold War. Although the two groups competed for significant parts of the whole world, much of their diplomatic and military planning centered on Europe.*

the two alliances concentrated enormously powerful armies in Central Europe, they never fought each other. The evolving balance of power had made warfare in Europe unwinnable.

The collapse of the Warsaw Pact came in 1989 and in a rapid manner that shocked many. After the Soviet leader Mikhail Gorbachev had been in power for a few years, some of the Eastern Europeans gambled that he would not use force to keep them in the empire. In 1989, the Berlin Wall, erected in 1961 to keep East Germans from fleeing to the West, was torn down by a popular movement. Communist governments fell in rapid succession, and newly installed national governments negotiated for the departure of Soviet troops stationed in Eastern Europe.

One of the most surprising and significant events, the reunification of Germany, came in 1990. This action not only destroyed the basis for a Soviet defense perimeter far from home, but it also resurrected a nation-state that had cost tens of millions of Soviet and Russian lives in two world wars. Although the absorption of East Germany into West Germany cost billions of dollars and caused social tensions, the united Germany has emerged as a major European power, especially economically. It threatens to rival the United States and other economic powers.

The final chapter of the Cold War came with the collapse of the Soviet Union in 1991. A failed takeover by elements of the Communist Party, the Soviet Army, and the KGB led to declarations of independence by Russia, the Ukraine, and other Soviet republics in December. Since then the fifteen countries of the former Soviet Union have bickered with one another, although some are beginning to seek some form of confederation. Russian communists and some nationalists have been calling for a reestablishment of the Soviet Union.

The Cold War in Asia

Asia became a major region of the Cold War tensions from the 1940s through the 1980s. Wars were fought in Korea, Vietnam, and Afghanistan. U.S. power suffered a serious defeat in Vietnam, and Soviet power suffered a significant defeat in Afghanistan.

FIGURE 41.3 ***The "Iron Curtain" Crumbles.*** *The Berlin Wall, erected in 1961, divided Germany, East and West, and was a visible reminder of the divisions between the American and Soviet blocs. In 1989, the wall was torn down, heralding the breakdown of Soviet power in Eastern Europe. Within a year, Germany was reunited and, soon after, Soviet Russia collapsed completely.* Alexandra Avakian/Woodfin Camp & Associates.

EAST ASIA. In 1945, Japan lay prostrate, having suffered tremendous losses in Allied bombing raids. The U.S. occupation, directed by General Douglas MacArthur, aimed to restructure Japan in order to render it incapable of fighting anew. The Americans wrote a new constitution and forced the Japanese to accept it. The constitution forbade the Japanese from having a military force, but as the Cold War developed, U.S. officials desired to rearm Japan as a major ally. The Japanese balked at acquiring an offensive military force but agreed to create a limited self-defense force.

Japan became a reliable ally with a stable political system. After political turmoil in the mid-1950s, two political parties merged, forming the Liberal-Democratic Party. It remained in power for thirty-seven years and dedicated itself to supporting the Japanese-American alliance. In addition, party leaders undertook measures to ensure economic growth, turning the Japanese economy into the world's second largest.

The Korean War (1950–1953) primarily concerned North Korea and South Korea, the United States, the Soviet Union, and China, although many other states also sent military units to fight there. Korea, a Japanese colony since 1910, had been partitioned in 1945, with the Soviets controlling the North and the United States administering the South. With Soviet backing, communist North Korea invaded the relatively democratic South on June 25, 1950. North Korea's aggression brought a military reprisal by the United Nations. The UN, planned by the Allies during World War II, had the power to wage war against aggressors. In June 1950, while the Soviet Union was boycotting the UN Security Council, the United States took advantage of the Soviet absence to push the UN to a declaration of hostilities against North Korea.

The invasion of South Korea had been a dream of Kim Il Sung (1912–1994), communist head of North Korea. Initially, Kim's battle plan unfolded with machinelike precision, but it eventually faltered. The initial thrust conquered most of South Korea, and U.S. troops and remnants of the South's army stubbornly held a small toehold along the coast. Then, General Douglas MacArthur staged an amphibious landing near Seoul, the capital of South Korea. U.S. soldiers moved out of their beachhead, threatening to cut off the retreating North Koreans. Soon, UN forces invaded North Korea, despite Chinese warnings of dire consequences.

In mid-October 1950, China's leader, Mao Zedong, felt that U.S. forces would invade Manchuria, China's newly conquered industrial base. After consultation with Josef Stalin and Kim Il Sung, as well as with China's leaders, Mao committed China to fight in Korea. Chinese forces dramatically turned the war's course. A few hundred thousand communist soldiers infiltrated the border and surprised the U.S. military leaders in November 1950. Although the Chinese pushed beyond the old border between North and South Korea, U.S. forces stabilized their lines and counterattacked. Soon, the conflict settled into a deadly war of attrition. In the summer of 1953, an armistice was signed, leading to an armed peace with both Koreas retaining about the same territory as before.

The Korean War produced several results. The Chinese had fought the Americans to a standstill and won international prestige, especially among Second and Third World countries. The Soviet Union benefited because its interests were advanced by the North Koreans and the Chinese. This kind of proxy war became attractive for both the Soviet Union and the United States.

The Korean people suffered massive casualties and immense destruction but rebuilt their country with outside assistance. With American aid, South Korea revitalized its economy and society. Military governments ruled from the early 1960s through much of the 1980s, and, although representative government suffered, the resulting political stabil-

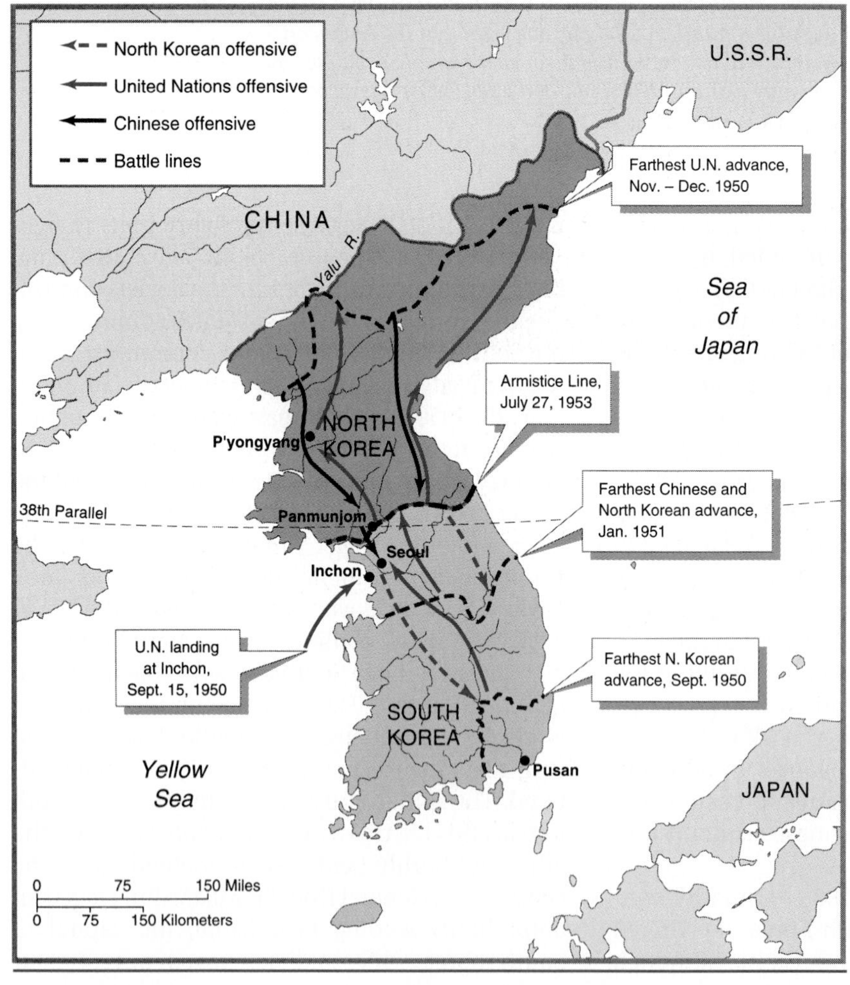

MAP 41.2 ***The Korean War, 1950–1953.*** *Korea, adjacent to Japan, China, and the USSR, became a focal point of Cold War activity during the Korean War. Although Soviet Russia did not fight in the war, its ally, China, did. The United States, a major participant in the war, used Japan as a staging area for actions in Korea. While most of the Korean Peninsula was fought over during the war, much of the conflict occurred along the 38th Parallel.*

ity helped engender general economic growth and prosperity. The North Koreans also rebuilt, but their economy did not prosper. They maintained an authoritarian government under the leadership of Kim Il Sung.

SOUTHEAST ASIA. The Cold War rivalry was complicated in Southeast Asia by the growing power of China. Another factor was the refusal of some countries, such as Burma (present-day Myanmar) to join any side. The U.S. created SEATO, the Southeast Asian Treaty Organization, a military alliance, to fight communism. SEATO countries joined the United States in the fighting in Vietnam during the 1960s.

The Vietnam War was two separate conflicts. The first war (1946–1954) was fought between the French and Vietminh. The **Vietminh** was an organization of Vietnamese communists and nationalists formed in 1941. Headed by Ho Chi Minh, a Vietnamese patriot and communist, the Vietminh took advantage of a power vacuum in Vietnam in 1945. Immediately, Vietminh agents organized independence groups, and, when World War II ended, the Vietminh launched a successful takeover from the Japanese. Vietnamese control remained until 1946, when the French returned, determined to maintain their empire.

War broke out in 1946 and lasted eight years. The Vietminh slowly took control of the countryside and gained a strategic advantage in 1949, when a Chinese communist victory in the Chinese civil war meant that Chinese material aid would be forthcoming. In 1954, the Vietminh won a major victory at Dien Bien Phu, compelling the French to admit defeat. European and Asian leaders agreed

FIGURE 41.4 ***Napalmed Children.*** *The Vietnam War of the 1960s and 1970s produced horrors on all sides that caused particular suffering for the people of Vietnam, especially in the South. This dramatic photograph captures the terror of Vietnamese children, some naked, fleeing from battle.* Wide World Photos.

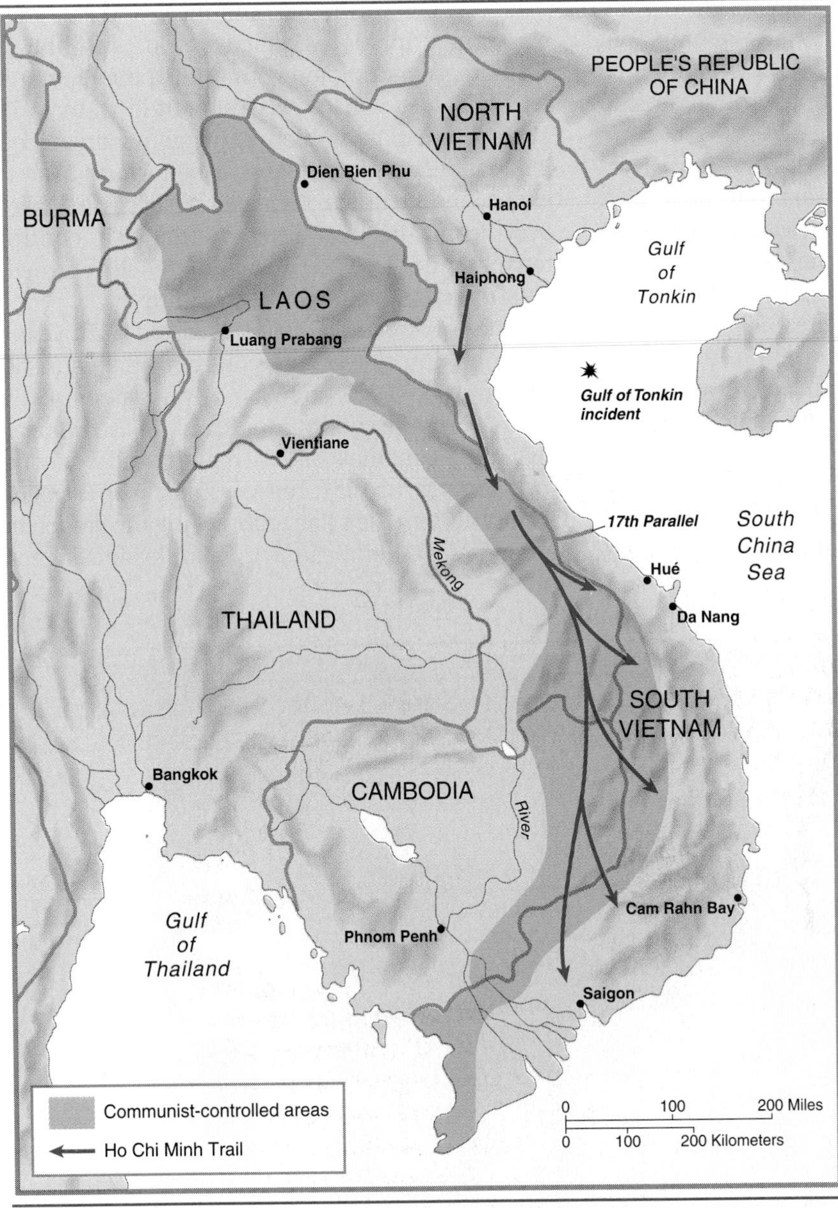

MAP 41.3 ***The Vietnam War, 1961–1975.*** *For the United States, the Vietnam War was fought in the 1960s and 1970s—for many Vietnamese, however, fighting for their country's independence began in the 1940s and continued with few respites until 1975. The war occasionally spilled over into Cambodia and Laos, and when South Vietnam fell to the communists in 1975, Cambodia and Laos soon came under complete communist control as well. During the course of the war, China gave significant aid to the North Vietnamese, as did Soviet Russia.*

at the Geneva Conference (1954) to divide Vietnam into southern (noncommunist) and northern (communist) areas and to hold national elections in two years to reunite Vietnam.

The United States refused to recognize the Geneva settlement and turned from aiding the French to entering the contest directly. The CIA, under the direction of U.S. President Dwight Eisenhower, organized a government in the South, renouncing elections. President Eisenhower later admitted that Ho Chi Minh would have won the vote. Soon, the communists organized a resistance movement in the South, the **Viet Cong**.

A second Vietnam War (1961–1975) pitted the United States and the allied South Vietnamese army against the Viet Cong and their North Vietnamese allies. A succession of U.S. presidents tried their hands at favorably settling the war in the South. Between 1963 and 1965, the collapse of the southern government and the introduction of

North Vietnamese army forces compelled U.S. leaders either to admit defeat or to use American troops to prevent the loss of the South.

The years from 1965 to 1975 saw the massive buildup of U.S. forces, a stalemate in the South, a growing antiwar movement in the United States, and the pullout of U.S. personnel. Although U.S. airplanes heavily bombed North Vietnam, American troops never invaded North Vietnam because they feared drawing the Chinese into the conflict, as had happened in the Korean War. U.S. President Richard Nixon tried a policy of turning over the conduct of the war to the South Vietnamese, but his invasion of Cambodia, which had been used as a military base by the Viet Cong, roused massive demonstrations in the United States that forced a more rapid withdrawal of American forces. A negotiated settlement between the North Vietnamese and Americans seemed to point the way to a resolution of the conflict. But a North Vietnamese attack in April 1975 triggered a rout of the South Vietnamese army a month later.

The Vietnamese communists took control of the South. They sent many Vietnamese to "reeducation camps," where some died and others toiled at hard labor. They also tried a variety of socialist economic measures to rebuild the country. Most failed, despite sizeable Soviet and Chinese aid.

In 1978, the Vietnamese invaded Cambodia. Although the Vietnamese toppled the Khmer Rouge (Cambodian communists), the Vietnamese found themselves stuck in an expensive occupation. After more than a decade of fighting and supporting puppet rulers, the Vietnamese withdrew at last.

Prior to the invasion by Vietnam, Cambodians suffered three years of tyrannical rule by the Khmer Rouge (1975–1978), who rivaled the Nazis in their ferocious assault on existing institutions and people. The Khmer Rouge emptied the cities and forced cityfolk into village centers. Millions perished, including Buddhist monks, intellectuals, and other members of elite groups. In percentages, the losses dwarfed those caused by virtually all other revolutionary governments. In the 1990s, the United Nations oversaw relatively free elections, but troubles have continued to plague the Cambodians to this day.

In 1965, the Indonesian Communist Party tried to take over the Indonesian armed forces, but failure led to mass reprisals by Indonesians who saw the botched coup as a Chinese communist plot. In the aftermath, several hundred thousand people died, including Indonesian communists and Chinese-Indonesians, many of whom were killed solely because they were Chinese. Since then, Indonesia has successfully followed a Western model of economic development, using oil to facilitate industrialization.

Britain granted Burma independence in 1948 and released control over its other Southeast Asian colonies somewhat later. Behind these actions was the realization that powerful national movements wanted self-rule and that armed resistance to them generally was futile. In Malaya, however, the British fought a communist insurgency by playing on the fact that some liberation fighters were of Chinese ancestry. Using ethnic rivalries and Cold War rhetoric to their advantage, the British defeated the insurgency. Nevertheless, the British abandoned the region by the mid-1960s, realizing that their global empire was lost.

SOUTH ASIA. Although the dominant force in South Asia was the antagonism between the Muslims and Hindus, Cold War rivalries surfaced there as well. India and Pakistan became rivals in the subcontinent, especially over the question of who should administer Kashmir, a strategic border territory mostly under Indian control. Indo-Pakistani Wars (1947–1948 and 1965) were fought with no decisive results. In 1971, internal upheaval in Pakistan exploded into a war in which East Pakistan (separated by 1,000 miles of Indian territory from West Pakistan) won independence, declaring itself the nation of Bangladesh. India fought on behalf of Bangladesh in order to split up and weaken its rival, Pakistan.

The Cold War came to South Asia when India allied itself with the Soviet Union and Pakistan allied itself with the United States. As the Chinese and Soviets became more estranged, the Indians and Soviets drew closer. In 1962, India and China fought a brief war in the Himalaya Mountains region, a war the Chinese won. Pakistan had already developed a military alliance with the United States and became closely tied with the Chinese. Pakistan also became a major base for anti-Soviet activities during the Afghanistan War (1979–1989).

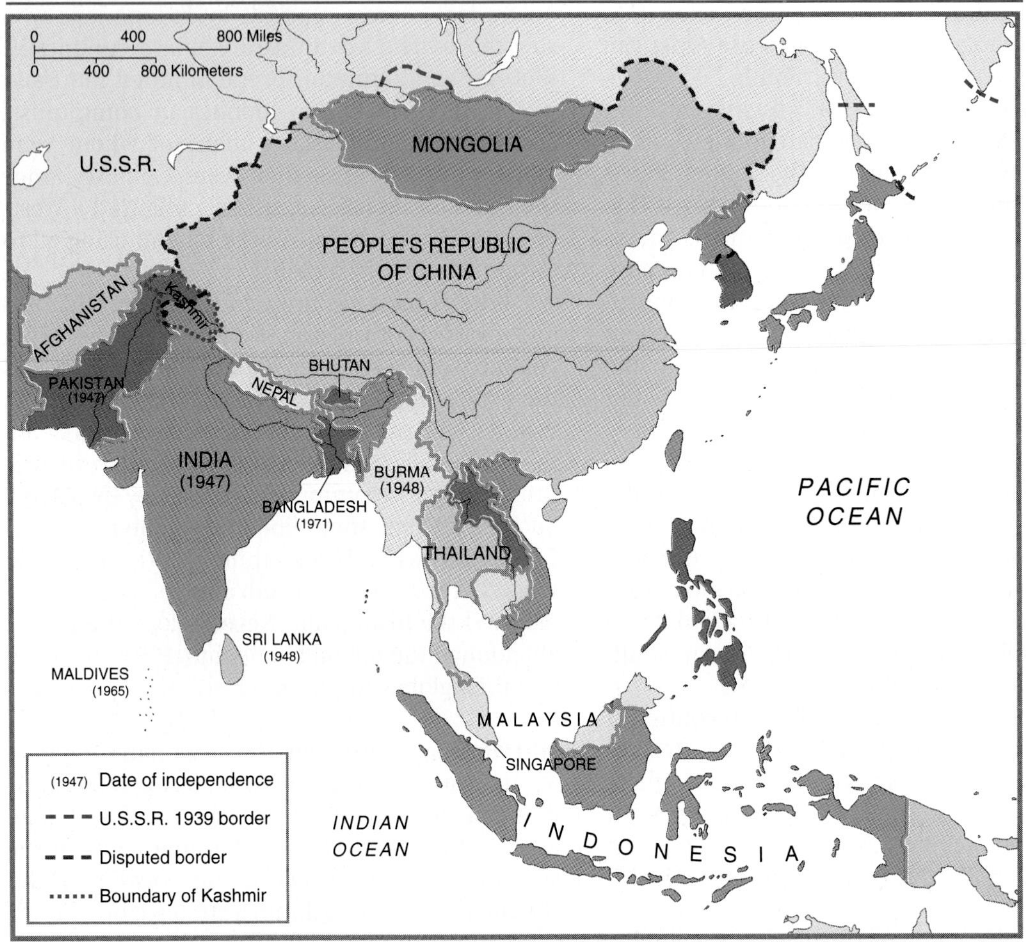

MAP 41.4 *South Asia in 1972. The British rule of South Asia and ultimate withdrawal in the late 1940s raised the problematic issue of the partition of India and Pakistan. These two South Asian powers fought several wars between 1947 and 1971. With the help of India, Bangladesh (formerly East Pakistan) broke away from West Pakistan in 1971. Since then, other countries have avoided foreign conflicts, although Sri Lanka has experienced a prolonged civil war.*

SOUTHWEST AND CENTRAL ASIA. The Cold War also intruded into Southwest and Central Asian politics. Many Islamic countries accepted Soviet aid in the 1950s and 1960s to offset U.S. aid to Israel. Egyptian President Gamal Abdul Nasser (1918–1970) threw out U.S. advisors and welcomed the Soviets. That meant abandoning the Western economic model and influence, as well as accepting Soviet aid and military advisors. Many countries chose Nasser's option, although Nasser's successor, Anwar Sadat, tossed out the Soviets in 1977, bringing Egypt back into the Western orbit. Syria and Iraq also developed close ties with the Soviets in the 1960s; they suffered when the Soviet Union declined and collapsed in the 1980s and 1990s.

A central concern for many Arab states was the state of Israel. As seen in Chapter 33, Zionists (Jewish nationalists) pursued the dream of a Jewish homeland in Palestine. After a time of immigration in the early decades of the twentieth century, Jewish leaders pressured the British government to have land assigned to them. Terrorism and guerrilla warfare forced the British to accede to the formation of Israel. Arab states, however, fought Israel in 1948, the first of several conflicts. Israel won in

FIGURE 41.5 ***Palestinian Refugees Awaiting Deportation.*** *The creation of the state of Israel in Palestine in 1948 led to war and the dislocation of large numbers of Palestinians. Over the following decades, most of them lived in makeshift refugee camps. During the 1960s, the Palestine Liberation Organization was formed to take back Palestine through the use of armed force.* Burt Glinn/Magnum Photos.

1948 and again in 1956, 1967, and 1973. The 1973 conflict brought Soviet threats of military intervention. In response, the United States went on a full nuclear alert, at a level just short of launching an attack on the Soviet Union. Since 1973, Israel has managed to negotiate a peace settlement with Egypt (1977) and to ease tensions with the Palestinians and Jordan. The United States has mediated in these agreements.

Iran strove to be a major power in Southwest Asia. It had substantial petroleum supplies and a thriving economy, but when an Iranian government nationalized British oil holdings in 1951, British and U.S. leaders began a policy of undermining Iran. Eventually, the government fell. In 1953, Shah Muhammad Reza Pahlavi, Iran's ruler, embarked on a program of modernizing Iran and arming it with Western weapons. Repression, especially against the religious hierarchy, fomented unrest that toppled the shah in 1979. The religious leadership that came into power abrogated the U.S. alliance and also destroyed communist influence. The Republic of Iran went its own diplomatic way in the 1980s and 1990s, and it became embroiled in a war with Iraq that lasted through the 1980s, resulting in millions of casualties.

Central Asia has been home to Muslims since at least the seventh century, and they number in the tens of millions of people of diverse ethnic backgrounds. In the nineteenth century, the Russian government conquered much of the region, leaving only Afghanistan under British control. During the collapse of the Russian Empire in 1917, many Central Asian states declared independence. However, the Soviets reconquered much of Central Asia. After the British left, the Soviets supported an unstable regime in Afghanistan.

The Soviet Union invaded Afghanistan in 1979 and soon found itself embroiled in a major conflict not unlike America's Vietnam War. Afghans have prided themselves on their independence and resistance to foreign rule. When the Soviets attacked, many Afghans fought back. After United States leaders provided surface-to-air missiles and

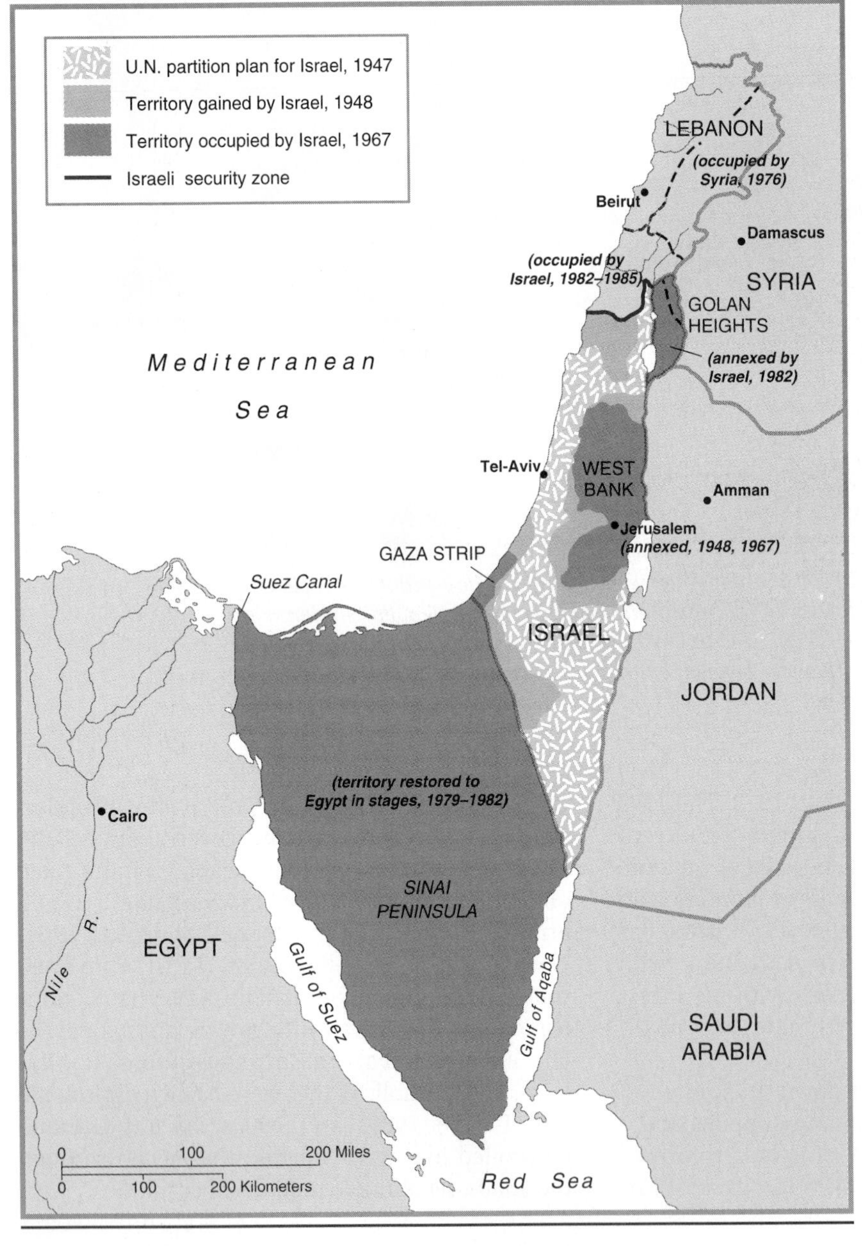

MAP 41.5 ***The Arab-Israeli Wars and Peace, 1948–1985.*** *Since its founding in 1948, Israel has fought a series of wars with its Arab neighbors. In the process, Israel has annexed significant territories and returned some conquered lands to Egypt in exchange for peace. During these conflicts, hundreds of thousands of Palestinians were rendered homeless and were forced to live in refugee camps.*

FIGURE 41.6 ***Afghans Celebrating on a Soviet Tank.*** *Although heavily outgunned by the Soviet army, the Afghans managed to defeat their northern neighbor, leading to eventual Soviet withdrawal. U.S. military aid improved the Afghans' chance of success. In this 1980 photo, a group of Afghan soldiers celebrate the capture of an enemy tank.* Alain Mingam / Gamma/ Liaison International.

other military assistance, the Afghan resistance fighters began to inflict heavy casualties on the Soviets, who began seeking a way to end the conflict. By 1989, the Soviets withdrew and their puppet government collapsed, and successor governments have proved unable to rule the country effectively.

The Cold War in Africa

Africans suffered from Cold War rivalries. The Soviets viewed Africa as an area for the penetration of its influence, and they hoped to appeal to the anti-imperialist African nationalists. As new states created one-party governments and adopted socialist economic policies, the Soviet Union gave military and economic aid to them. Angola, a former Portuguese colony, received Soviet aid, especially to fight off a rebel movement backed by the Americans. The United States had little interest in Africa until the Soviets began to appear there. Soon, however, the United States gave foreign aid, including military assistance, to African states. China gave help to a few African countries as well. When the Cold War ended, U.S. and Soviet aid vastly decreased, leaving many of the African states impoverished.

Kenya had been under British rule for many decades. In the 1940s and 1950s, the Kikuyu Uprising (the Mau Mau) fought against the British imperialists. The struggle lasted from 1952 to 1956 and then subsided until the British finally surrendered their control in the early 1960s.

One-party government characterized Kenyan politics, and the Kenya African National Union (KANU) represented a merging of the country's major parties. KANU's top leaders promoted their nationalist, pragmatic, and socialist goals. They created a mixed economy of state-run industries, along with those under private ownership. Similarly, when KANU developed its land policies, it preferred to have people purchase lands from the white settlers rather than undertake a nationalization and redistribution of land. The economy prospered until the late 1970s, when a recession hit most African countries. Social changes, like promoting universal education and improving the status of women, were introduced by KANU.

France controlled Algeria for more than a century, and more than 1 million French lived in that North African country, constituting Algeria's ruling class. In 1954, Arabs and Berber tribes revolted against French rule, and the fighting continued for seven years. Complicating matters was the fact that many French in Algeria detested the French government, fearing it would back the native Algerians. A brief uprising among the French in Algeria fizzled after the French president, Charles DeGaulle, took stern measures against it.

The Algerians overthrew the French, and the new Algerian government followed socialist policies to improve the well-being of its people in the 1960s and 1970s. Some prosperity came with the development of Algeria's oil reserves. In the 1990s, the rise of Islamic fundamentalist movements has complicated political life for the ruling elite, and repressive acts against the fundamentalist Islamic leaders have sent them underground. Elections that would likely have been won by the fundamentalists were canceled, leading to a bloody civil war.

The Cold War in Latin America

Latin Americans also became involved in Cold War rivalries. The United States had a long history of supporting dictators who adhered to its political and economic agendas. In Guatemala, a reforming government that threatened to overturn the existing sociopolitical status quo was toppled by the United States in the early 1950s. A precipitant to U.S. action was the nationalization of substantial property owned by the United Fruit Company, a U.S.-based business.

In 1959, revolutionaries overthrew the U.S.-backed Cuban regime and established a Marxist state headed by Fidel Castro. Two years later, a U.S.-supported invasion of Cuba failed. In October 1962, U.S. leaders had learned that the Soviets had built a missile base in Cuba; U.S. leaders viewed having Soviet missiles ninety miles from the U.S. mainland as intolerable. The Cuban Missile Crisis threatened to unleash nuclear war between the Cold War rivals. Although diplomats negotiated a

UNDER THE LENS

A Folk Hero of the Cuban Revolution

Ernesto "Che" Guevara (1927–1967) became a popular figure among revolutionaries and a cult hero among many young people in the 1960s and 1970s. Educated as a doctor in his Argentine homeland, Che roamed Latin America in search of a revolutionary struggle. He was in Guatemala when the United States helped overthrow the government, which had proved too anti-American. Later, Che Guevara joined with Fidel Castro to seize power in Cuba.

During the early 1960s, Che wrote extensively on revolution in Latin America. Following the lead of China's Mao Zedong, a man whom Che admired, he believed that the peasantry was the most important social force for revolution in Latin America. Thus, the countryside rather than the city should be the place where the revolutionaries should build their armies. Guerrilla warfare was to be the means of struggle to take power in the Third World. Once in control, the revolutionaries should use art and literature as vehicles to further the transformation of society, inspiring the people to change themselves. To promote that end, Che Guevara helped undertake a massive and successful campaign to spread literacy among the Cuban people.

Once in power, Che led an economic planning agency in Cuba. Very soon, he faced the task of motivating Cuban workers to help develop the economy. In the process, he hoped to transform people into socialists through the use of moral incentives. Through the popular education system, people were taught to help others for the good of society rather than for themselves. At the same time, Che Guevara did not rule out the use of material incentives to motivate people. But he believed that making material rewards the driving force in achieving economic aims corrupted people and led to class stratification, weakened communal solidarity, and distorted income equalization. This, of course, led away from socialist ideals.

By the mid-1960s, Che Guevara became disenchanted with the direction of the Cuban Revolution, leaving Cuba for new revolutionary pastures in Latin America. Fidel Castro, the Cuban leader, wanted to build communism in Cuba, relying heavily on the Soviet Union to accomplish that task. Che Guevara criticized the subordination of Cuba to a great power. He also believed that revolution within any one country had to take place in the context of revolutionary struggles and revolutions within the entire Third World. Thus, he was less interested in the Cold War as a struggle between the Soviet Union and the United States.

Che's romantic spirit brought him to South America. By the mid-1960s, he had been rumored to have been sighted in numerous places, and he had helped launch several unsuccessful revolutionary movements. Finally, in 1967, soldiers of a counterinsurgency campaign in Bolivia found and killed him. Che Guevara, who had inspired millions in life, became a martyr to revolutionary causes around the globe.

peaceful resolution of the crisis, the near-disaster sparked interest in tension-reducing measures. Soon, a series of arms-reduction treaties was signed by Soviet and U.S. leaders.

In the 1970s, the Sandinistas, a Marxist revolutionary movement in Nicaragua, overthrew a corrupt dictatorship backed by the U.S. government. The new state was recognized and aided by many Western European countries and the Soviet bloc. During the 1980s, however, elements of the U.S. government supported anti-Sandinista forces, despite specific congressional laws prohibiting intervention. U.S. President Ronald Reagan saw the illegal activity as part of the larger Cold War confrontation between the Soviet Union and the United States. The abandonment of covert U.S. aid and an election that ousted the Sandinistas reduced tensions there.

ECONOMIC TRANSFORMATION AND CRISIS

The Cold War severely taxed the U.S. and Soviet economies but provided growth for other countries. Third World countries, especially those in Africa, suffered from lack of outside investments; Cold War aid often provided critical funds though it stressed military rather than civilian projects.

The U.S. role in the Vietnam War (1961–1975) rent the United States' economic and social fabric. By the late 1960s, the United States could not fight a war and maintain an expensive welfare system implemented by President Lyndon Johnson. In 1971, President Richard Nixon responded to the deteriorating economic situation by freezing wages and prices, as well as taxing imports. In 1973 and 1979, two significant increases in petroleum prices rocked the U.S. economy. Anger with America's Cold War policies triggered massive antiwar demonstrations, galvanizing important segments of society. In addition, African Americans, Native Americans, women, and homosexuals challenged prevailing social practices, like racial and sexual discrimination.

In the 1980s, President Ronald Reagan accelerated a defense-spending program begun by his predecessor, President Jimmy Carter. This effort helped stimulate an economic boom that was enhanced by a mushrooming of export growth. By the mid-1980s, Reagan negotiated major arms-reduction programs with his Soviet counterpart, Mikhail Gorbachev, to reduce the formidable costs of the arms race.

U.S. Cold War activities benefited the Japanese economy. The Korean War, for example, turned Japan into a major military supplier for the U.S. army. The Toyota automobile company was nearly bankrupt when the United States placed orders for thousands of Toyota trucks, helping the company prosper. Japanese manufacturing output grew 50 percent from 1950 to 1951. The Vietnam War of the 1960s and 1970s also benefited the Japanese economy, which supplied some of the military needs of the U.S. army.

By the 1980s, Japan boasted the second-largest economy in the world and annual trade surpluses of around $100 billion. Large multinational corporations such as Mitsubishi and Sony produced Japanese goods that dominated many regional and national markets, leading to Japanese pride in their economic power. Many Japanese viewed the United States as a declining power, at least until the Japanese economy hit a prolonged slump in the early 1990s. American policy and investment had helped shape Japan into a major world power and ally.

Although some South Asian countries were among the poorest in the world, their economies gradually have developed, reducing poverty in the area by the 1990s. India initially concentrated on state-controlled industrial growth and received economic aid and technical assistance from the Soviet Union. It had achieved modest levels of economic growth by the 1990s. After 1991, major efforts were undertaken to open India to market forces, and economic growth has accelerated, especially in computer technology. Pakistan has been less successful in industrializing and has had to rely on financial assistance from abroad.

ENERGY AND THE ENVIRONMENT

The twentieth century became the era of petroleum because of the widespread use of the internal combustion engine. In addition, petroleum byproducts, such as plastics and various chemicals, have permeated modern societies, with the result that human beings have become dependent on oil.

FIGURE 41.7 ***OPEC's Growing Power.*** *The Organization of Petroleum Exporting Countries (OPEC) gained great influence in the 1970s and 1980s. Its members controlled a large proportion of the world's petroleum and began to set higher prices than ever before. Most industrializing and industrialized countries that relied on oil imports were hard hit; Japan was particularly vulnerable because it imported 99 percent of its petroleum needs. This 1980 American cartoon reflects the perspective that OPEC was ruining the new year with its policies.* © 1984, Pat Oliphant. Distributed by the Los Angeles Times Syndicate.

The industrial potential of petroleum had been discovered in the mid–nineteenth century, and its refinement made kerosene a popular fuel in the latter half of that century. The internal combustion engine created a demand for a new source of fuel. The British navy, for example, decided in favor of oil over coal for its ships' power in the years leading up to the outbreak of World War I. World War II soldiers and sailors relied even more heavily on oil, as evidenced by the Japanese drive to Indonesia's oil fields in 1942 and the Germans' fight for the oil fields in the Caucasus Mountains.

Western countries often enjoyed monopolistic control over many Third World nations' oil fields until the early 1970s. Then Arab nations banded with some other major oil-supplying countries to form a **cartel**, a group that produces a significant percentage of a material, that cooperates to fix production levels and prices, and that dominates international distribution of the material. This cartel, the Oil Producing and Exporting Countries (OPEC), controlled much of the global supply of oil and raised prices sharply on two occasions, in 1973 and in 1979. These steep increases caused severe budgetary problems for oil-consuming nations and sparked inflation. At the same time, many OPEC nations became wealthy, and they recycled these dollars back into Europe and the United States. Hard hit were Third World countries that also needed oil but had few funds to pay for their energy supplies.

The Persian Gulf War of 1991 showed the importance and dangers of petroleum production. Iraq had longstanding claims to Kuwait, which Iraq's Saddam Hussein seized in 1990. Because Iraq and Kuwait claimed a significant fraction of global oil reserves, this triggered a United Nations military response. After assembling a formidable armed force, including personnel from Saudi Arabia, Egypt, Britain, and others, U.S. leaders initiated a massive bombing campaign as a prelude to a ground offensive that lasted four days. Kuwait was freed, and much of the Iraqi army lay in ruins. Huge oil fires and spills gave the night landscape the look of a hellish inferno and horribly fouled the Persian Gulf. A deliberate act of ecocide had been committed by the departing Iraqi forces.

Although oil has remained supreme in the world, other energy sources, like coal, atomic energy, natural gas, wind power, and geothermal power, have become more widespread in usage. Coal has remained a common fuel in many parts of the world, although burning it causes air pollution. Atomic energy also became a major supplier of energy through power plants in the First and Second worlds.

Atomic energy couples great opportunities with serious liabilities. Power generation by this means often has proven expensive, but the needs of various industrial states, like those of Japan, encouraged the building and use of nuclear power plants. Japan lacked coal and oil resources and turned to nuclear power generation to supply some of its energy needs. One problem with nuclear facilities is their vulnerability to attack by terrorists. Another is the possibility that peaceful uses of atomic energy might produce enough fissionable material to construct atomic weapons. The Iraqis, for example, were in the process of building nuclear weapons but fooled inspectors about their intentions, and the North Koreans raised tensions in the Korean Peninsula by refusing to permit international inspectors to analyze materials produced by their nuclear power plants in 1995. Another problem with nuclear power plants has been the possibility of meltdowns of their reactors. In 1986, for example, a power plant at Chernobyl in the Ukraine exploded, spewing nuclear-contaminated materials across much of Europe. Nuclear waste disposal has been another serious problem.

A list of environmental issues began to dominate politics from the 1960s. People had become concerned about overpopulation, environmental degradation, and the waste of natural resources. Environmental sensitivity markedly increased in the 1960s and has brought change. Kenya, for example, has expended a significant amount of resources in enforcing its Wildlife Protection Act. Hunting safaris that seriously reduced the wild-animal population have been replaced by controlled tourist ventures with people wielding cameras rather than rifles. Local Kenyans have been lured into working in the tourist industry, lessening the attraction of poaching.

Industrialization has caused significant environmental degradation, especially since 1945. Industrial-waste sites in the United States have cost billions of dollars to clean up. In Japan, the Minamata disease caused by poisoning of rivers by industrial wastes was perhaps the first named

Figure 41.8 ***Victim of Environmental Poisoning in Japan.*** *A mother bathes her seventeen-year-old daughter who was born blind and physically disabled as a result of mercury poisoning. A local chemical plant dumped metal wastes into the water supply of Minamata Village; cases of environmental poisoning in the region became known as Minamata disease.* W. Eugene Smith/Black Star.

environmental affliction. Human beings who drank the untreated water began to display symptoms of severe nerve damage. Soviet-bloc countries had vast areas of industrial pollution from East Germany to the Ural Mountains.

Some environmentalists have warned people and their governments that the widespread use of fossil fuels has unleashed unprecedented amounts of carbon dioxide into the atmosphere. The layer of carbon dioxide permits the sun's energy through but traps it, as in a greenhouse. Thus, the earth's temperature will rise over time. If this process continues unchecked, they argue, an increase of the earth's temperature by a few degrees will cause disastrous weather and environmental changes. Other scientists have challenged these models, pointing to problems in accurately measuring the globe's temperature.

Air pollution has caused serious problems around the world since 1945. Industrial countries reported unusual levels of human respiratory problems and environmental degradation, and most cities felt some effects due to air pollution. Mexico City has had serious smog problems since the 1970s. Athens and Rome have watched the corrosive effects of smog on longstanding cultural treasures, like the Acropolis and the Colosseum.

SCIENTIFIC DISCOVERIES

World War II governments organized their scientists and technicians around a variety of war-related projects, and the onset of the Cold War fostered widespread state-funded scientific investigation. Although diverse countries were involved in massive scientific projects, the Cold War rivalry meant that the United States and the Soviet Union dominated.

World War II was a time when inventions like radar and airplanes were considerably improved. The U.S. government's most significant effort, the Manhattan Project, symbolized what a mobilized government might accomplish. The project's purpose was to develop an atomic bomb, and the United States spent around $2 billion to accomplish that task. It gathered and organized hundreds of scientists and technicians. They developed an atomic bomb that was exploded as a test in New Mexico in July 1945. For a few years, the United States monopolized this new weaponry, but the Soviets tested an atomic bomb in 1949. A few years later, both countries had detonated hydrogen bombs, much more destructive weapons.

A second war effort involved the development of rocketry, and the Germans invested much capital and human resources in that project. Late in the war, German rockets were launched against Britain, bringing limited death and destruction; more significant, they inspired great fear and anxiety among the British. U.S. and Soviet officials collared some of the top German missile scientists, and both powers' missile programs benefited from the knowledge derived from the Germans. When atomic bombs were attached to intercontinental missiles, they became strategic weapons systems of awesome destructive power.

Rockets facilitated the exploration of space. The Soviet Union surprised the world with the launching of *Sputnik*, the world's first human-made satellite, in October 1957. That event spurred the American educational system completely to revise its scientific and mathematics programs. Government funds flowed to these areas, and elementary and secondary schools developed a new emphasis on science and mathematics. Graduate schools reduced the amount of time necessary to earn a doctorate degree in order to train scientists more quickly. In addition, the U.S. government worked hard to overtake the Soviets in missile delivery systems. The arms race heightened fear of war and brought the creation of civil defense systems. American and Soviet schoolchildren underwent regular air raid drills during periods of the Cold War.

In the early 1960s, U.S. President John Kennedy challenged the American people and scientific community to land U.S. astronauts on the moon and return them safely before the end of the decade. A huge financial outlay and large-scale organization of scientists and engineers supported the moon race. Despite problems, American astronauts reached the moon on July 20, 1969, planting the U.S. flag there. The mood of America in the late 1960s, however, turned against such large-scale projects that seemingly did not benefit ordinary people. Although some additional programs of great size continued to receive money, only projects related to military needs were awarded consistent funding.

The federal government also spent considerable amounts of money on scientific research in universities across the United States. These funds helped provide the financial means for investigative projects, but they also helped foster a government-university complex that troubled many. Some feared the loss of the independence of university governance and academic freedom. Antigovernment feelings that surfaced in the 1960s and 1970s, fueled by concerns over the Vietnam War, caused soul-searching among academic scientists who lived off federal funds.

Other scientific and technological discoveries appeared outside government settings. Private industry spent large sums on research and development in the United States, and the Japanese and Germans began to outspend Americans in the 1980s. The International Rice Research Institute in the Philippines used U.S. and other funding to produce dwarf varieties of rice. These rice plants have higher yields of grain and sturdier stalks, preventing preharvest breakage under the weight of the grains. Now about one-fourth of the world's rice comes from these varieties. Yields increased about 100 percent per unit of area. These varieties, though, require chemical fertilizers and pesticides, putting them out of reach of many small farmers. These dwarf plants were primarily developed from 1967 to 1974.

SOCIAL CHANGE IN THE COLD WAR ERA

The pace of social change accelerated after 1945. Around the world, interest groups agitated for greater equality of opportunity in political, economic, and social arenas. In the ensuing decades, some of their goals were partly achieved, exemplifying the democratizing trend of modernity.

Expanded Suffrage and Office Holding

Voting rights and office-holding opportunities for women and ethnic minorities grew rapidly after World War II. Although women and some minorities had gained access to political systems in the nineteenth and early twentieth centuries in the West, most in other parts of the world had to wait until after 1945 to vote or to hold office.

In the West, women gained the franchise in the early twentieth century; office holding came somewhat later. Norway, for example, permitted women to vote in national elections by 1907, the same year they could vote in Wyoming, the first U.S. state to adopt female suffrage. Despite a lengthy struggle for the vote on the national level, the final, successful push for the vote came in World War I, when the extensive war-related service of women in the United States and Europe earned the respect of many men, who hastened the amendment process. U.S. women got the right to vote after the passage of the Nineteenth Amendment to the U.S. Constitution in 1920.

Since 1920, not only have women voted, but they have run for office. Although women have been elected as prime ministers in Norway, Iceland, Israel, and Britain, their numbers in office still represent far less than their percentage of the population. Margaret Thatcher of Britain held office through the 1980s, becoming one of the longest-ruling prime ministers in modern British history.

Asian women gained the right to vote after World War II. Japanese women, for example, got the vote only during the U.S. occupation (1945–1952). Women have run as candidates for

FIGURE 41.9 ***Prime Minister Indira Gandhi.*** *Indira Gandhi succeeded her father, Jawaharlal Nehru, as leader of India and governed from 1966 to 1977 and from 1980 to 1984. She and many other women emerged as national leaders during the Cold War era.* Wide World Photos.

Japan's House of Representatives, and a few have held office in the period since 1945. South Asians not only have given women the vote, but they have elected several women as heads of state. Indira Gandhi of India was elected as prime minister in 1966, remaining a powerful leader until her assassination in 1984. She promoted significant policies, including family planning to moderate India's rapid population growth. Benazir Bhutto won the prime ministership in Pakistan in 1988, becoming the first woman to head an Islamic state in the twentieth century. A military dictatorship ruled Bangladesh for most of its existence, but in free elections in 1989, Kaleda Zia was elected prime minister, and she held office for a brief time. Sirimavo Bandaranike assumed power in Sri Lanka after her husband's assassination in 1959, and she remained the dominant political figure in the 1960s and 1970s.

African women got the vote in the postindependence period, but because many states in Africa were dictatorial, the vote meant little. In addition, African women continued to hold limited economic and political power. When male-dominated nation-states passed economic laws or other measures, women's interests were generally ignored. Land reform in Ethiopia during the 1970s, for example, gave land to male family heads only; similar patterns were found in Cameroon, Mozambique, and elsewhere. North African states frequently have been guided by Islamic precedent, so women only gradually received the right to vote. They have not been able to gain much influence through elective office.

The matter of one's sexual preference in terms of office holding has been controversial in industrial states during the post-1945 period. Controversy arose as homosexuals openly espoused their sexual preferences when running for office. Election of homosexuals to high office in the United States has increased in the 1980s and 1990s. The U.S. Congressional Gay-Lesbian Caucus, for example, had more than twenty members in 1994. First World countries have been more tolerant of overt homosexual activity and office holding than those in the Third World.

Ethnic-minority participation in the electoral process has increased dramatically around the world, especially in the industrial world. African Americans were given the right to vote by an amendment to the U.S. Constitution in 1868. That constitutional guarantee, however, meant little in the South and other areas because restrictive measures often effectively kept African Americans from voting until well into the twentieth century. One strategy used to limit African American voting was the **poll tax**, a fee imposed on each voter. Many African Americans could not afford to pay the sum. Others failed to pass literacy tests that were given only to African Americans.

Voting restrictions continued until the American civil rights movement of the 1960s. Pressure put on Congress by large marches and rallies, including a massive march on Washington, D.C., led by the Rev. Martin Luther King, Jr., resulted in the passage of the Voting Rights Act of 1964, sweeping away state requirements that effectively kept many African Americans from voting. Other laws have been passed, and Supreme Court decisions have confirmed and extended these rights to all ethnic minorities. Out of one voting rights act in 1988 came the creation of electoral districts designed to facilitate majorities of certain ethnic minorities. Thus, members of these ethnic groups were more likely to win elections to the House of Representatives. The Supreme Court threw out some of the new districts in 1996. In addition, voter-registration drives have aimed at turning ethnic voting blocs into powerful political forces.

Between 1948 and 1991, South Africa followed ***apartheid***, a legal system of racial segregation and discrimination enforced by a minority white government. Black Africans were forced to submit to white rule while living under state-sponsored repression and poverty. In the early 1990s, Nelson Mandela, a major leader of the African National Congress (ANC), was released from years of imprisonment for his political beliefs. Mandela's release signaled the start of political reforms led by South Africa's prime minister, F. W. de Klerk. In the spring of 1994, South Africans of all races were permitted to vote freely for the first time: The ANC and Mandela were swept into power.

Toward Universal Education in the Third World

Universal education had generally been achieved in the First and Second worlds by 1945. After 1945, newly liberated countries in Asia and Africa adopted national goals of universal education. They saw education as the means to train people for the workforce, to improve people's chances of social advancement, and to implant ideas and val-

FIGURE 41.10 ***South Africa's Leaders Meet.*** *Nelson Mandela (center), F. W. de Klerk (right), and Mangosuthu Buthelezi (left) were frequently at odds in the negotiations that brought a representative government to South Africa in 1994. After freedom was achieved, these men sometimes posed for pictures to show their unity. While violence accompanied the fall of* apartheid, *peaceful actions and gatherings prevailed, giving hope for the future of South Africa.* Juhan Kuus/Sipa Press.

ues important to the nations' rulers. At the same time, families began demanding educational opportunities for their children because they realized that schooling could be a major road to advancement of the individual and thereby the family. Although universal education was often a government's stated goal, discrimination against women in societies in Africa and elsewhere meant that they seldom attained educational levels comparable to those of men.

The central government usually supplied the funds to create the educational infrastructure. In a few cases, like Kenya, a local system of education emerged. The Harambee Self-help Movement there permitted communities to build local schools with minimal governmental involvement.

One source of private education has come from religious schools. In parts of Africa and elsewhere, these schools were holdovers from imperialist times when Christian missionaries established schools. Many of these institutions carried over into independence. Muslim schools, often with religious leaders as teachers, flourished with little government support. Secular subjects have been taught in these schools, and, in countries like Pakistan, government decrees have insisted that basic Islamic principles and religious tenets be instilled in the students.

Public and private schools frequently followed Western education models and subject matter. The curriculum, usually Western, emphasized science and mathematics. In some extreme cases, such as in the Guyana educational system, students had to take London-based exams which had geographic detail about Britain that was alien and of little interest to Guyanans. Sometimes more latitude was permitted in literature and other humanities in using non-Western materials.

Expanding educational opportunity has been part of the process of democratization, one of the elements of modernity. Education has become the ladder to success for all people, but especially for women and minorities. People feel more ownership in governments that permit them to vote, hold office, and earn an education. That, in turn, helps officials govern more effectively.

ASIA		E. EUROPE	W. EUROPE / N. AMERICA		
				1940	
				–	
				–	
				–	
	Vietnam War, 1946–1955			–	Berlin airlift begins, 1947 Israel founded, 1948
			NATO, 1949–present	1950	
Korean War, 1950–1953				–	
				–	
		Warsaw Pact, 1955–1989		–	Hungarian Uprising, 1956 Suez crisis, 1956
				–	
				1960	
	Vietnam War, 1961–1975			–	Sino-Indian War, 1962
				–	Kenya becomes independent, 1963
				–	
				–	Six-Day War, 1967 Tet Offensive, 1968 Soviet troops invade Czechoslovakia, 1968
				1970	
				–	Indo-Pakistani War and Bangladesh independence, 1971
				–	
				–	
				–	Ayatolla Khomeini takes power, 1979 Soviet troops land in Afghanistan, 1979
	War in Afghanistan, 1979–1989			1980	
Iran-Iraq War, 1980–1988				–	
				–	
				–	
				–	Berlin Wall torn down, 1989 Reunification of Germany, 1990
				1990	

SUMMARY

1. The Cold War (1945–1991) lasted nearly fifty years and involved the great-power rivalry between the United States and the Soviet Union. The Soviet collapse in 1991 ended the Cold War.

2. Europe became the major place of Cold War rivalry. The Soviet Union suppressed uprisings in Hungary (1956) and Czechoslovakia (1968). A more relaxed Soviet policy in the late 1980s led to the independence of the Soviet bloc countries and Germany's reunification in 1990.

3. The Korean and Vietnam wars became battlefields of the Cold War and showed the limits of American power.

4. India and Pakistan, traditional rivals, became involved in Cold War politics, with India supporting the Soviet Union and Pakistan backing the United States.

5. A major conflict in Southwest Asia revolved around the formation of Israel in 1948. Arabs and Israelis fought many wars over who should control Palestine. In Central Asia, the Soviet Union failed in its effort to control Afghanistan during the 1980s.

6. African states threw off imperialist rule, gaining independence after 1945. Kenya and Algeria, for example, overthrew British and French colonial rule.

7. U.S.–Latin American relations were often tense, especially when United States leaders brought down a government in Guatemala and supported antigovernment Cuban and Nicaraguan forces.

8. The Cold War stretched the U.S. and Soviet economies to the breaking point, but it helped spur economic development in Japan and Western Europe. Many Third World economies heavily relied on foreign aid and suffered aid reductions when the Cold War ended.

9. Science benefited from government funding and organization, especially in projects like the atomic bomb program of the 1940s and the space exploration effort of the 1960s. Cold War rivalries, especially in military affairs, helped funds flow to scientific projects.

10. Petroleum became the dominant fuel of the twentieth century. Atomic energy offered another means to produce power but presented potential problems, including nuclear accidents and waste disposal.

11. Environmental degradation has become a major concern since the 1960s. Industrial pollution has fouled skies, and the careless disposal of industrial wastes has contaminated drinking water.

12. The growth of an environmental movement in the 1960s paved the way for a variety of government programs and policies.

13. Social change accelerated after 1945, bringing expanded voting rights and office holding to women. Ethnic minorities and homosexuals also benefited politically from more tolerant attitudes. Racial equality legislation passed in many countries, and universal education became a reality for millions.

SUGGESTED READINGS

Carson, Rachel. *Silent Spring.* Boston: Houghton Mifflin, 1962. A classic treatment of the overuse of pesticides, an environmental problem that kills many animals.

Goncharov, Sergei, John W. Lewis, and Xue Litai. *Uncertain Partners.* Stanford, Calif.: Stanford University Press, 1993. A revisionist interpretation of the Korean War in the light of Sino-Soviet relations.

Liss, Sheldon. *Marxist Thought in Latin America.* Berkeley: University of California Press, 1984. A standard treatment of Latin American socialist movements and leaders.

Nafziger, E. Wayne. *Inequality in Africa.* Cambridge, Eng.: Cambridge University Press, 1988. An examination of the economic policies of African governments in the Cold War era.

Walker, Martin. *The Cold War.* New York: Henry Holt, 1993. A survey of global history since 1945.

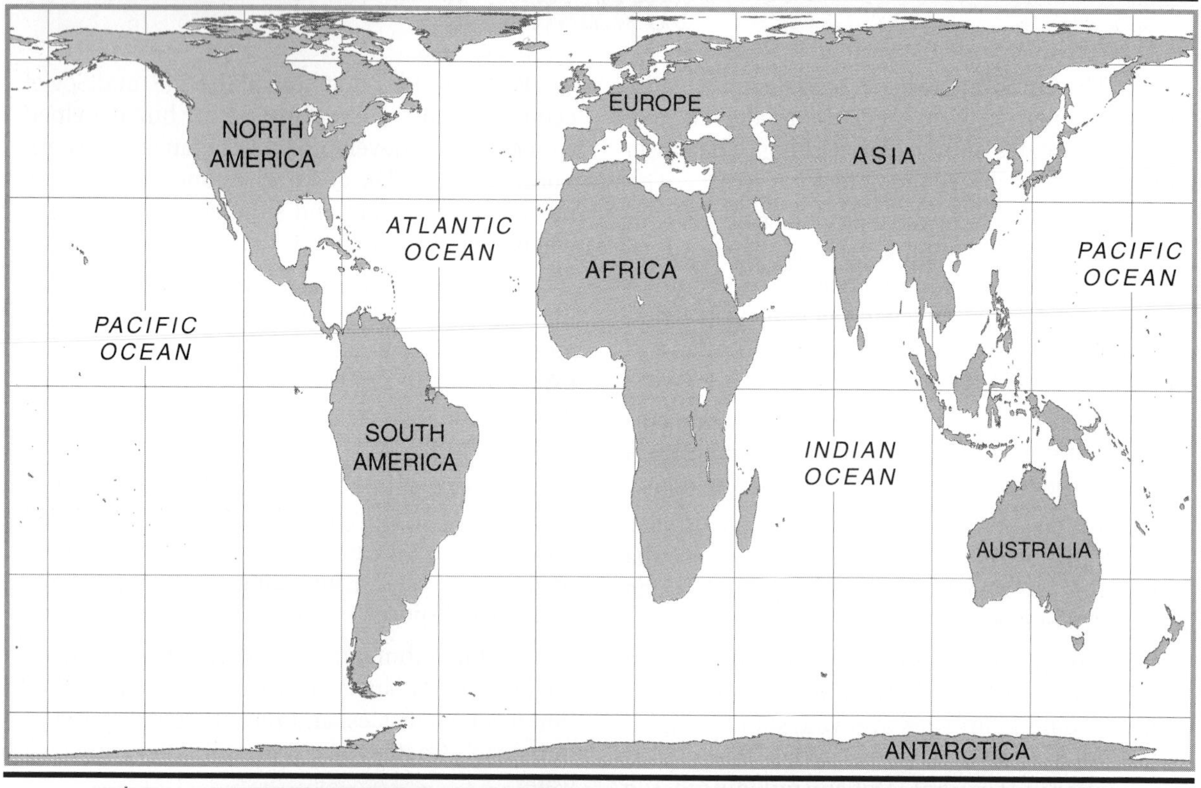

EUROPE
NORTH AMERICA
ASIA
ATLANTIC OCEAN
AFRICA
PACIFIC OCEAN
PACIFIC OCEAN
SOUTH AMERICA
INDIAN OCEAN
AUSTRALIA
ANTARCTICA

A Mother and Her Children at Ellis Island. *Ellis Island was the primary point of arrival for immigrants entering the United States in the first decades of the twentieth century.* Brown Brothers.

CHAPTER 42

Populations in Change

1945 Onward

In 1976, Pol Pot became the prime minister of Cambodia, a fertile Southeast Asian country of about 9 million people. In the following three years, Pol Pot's government oversaw the killing of at least 1 million and possibly as many as 3 million persons who were judged questionable in their loyalty to the state. Such "sins" as having a college education, speaking a foreign language, or wearing eyeglasses were considered signs of intellectualism (and potential disloyalty) and could lead to execution. One to 2 million persons died of widespread famines and the privations of forced labor; 1 million fled to Thailand. In all, about half of the population died or left Cambodia within three years.

The Cambodian case is unusual in its magnitude, but it is only one of many major population dislocations that have occurred around the world in the period since the end of World War II. The study of population, its changes in size and composition, and its movements is known as **demography**. The period beginning with the final years of World War II has been remarkable in the scale of demographic changes and the rapidity with which these changes have taken place.

One major factor in these changes is technology. Technological changes, particularly in food production and medicine, have helped extend human life; parallel changes in military technology have made possible the mass killing of huge numbers of people in a brief span of time. Improved, less expensive modes of transportation have made long-range migration more feasible.

A second factor is the sheer size of the human population by the twentieth century. The population in 1945 probably was about two billion people, far greater than at any previous time. With such a huge population, the number of adults of parenting age exceeded that of any earlier time, and the potential number of children born on any day was much higher than ever before. Population has continued to grow throughout the twentieth century, reaching a staggering 6 billion persons today.

These and other factors have combined to produce massive population changes in the latter part of the twentieth century, sending ripples through all aspects of life. Political policies, economic decisions, social policies, and wars around the world all have been shaped by changes in the size, composition, and location of population.

POPULATION SHIFTS IN THE WAKE OF WORLD WAR II

Some of the demographic effects of World War II have been documented in Chapter 40. The genocidal campaigns directed against Jews and other groups of people had major demographic effects, reducing their numbers by as much as half. In addition, battle and bombing casualties sometimes were high, producing significant decreases in population. Many other demographic effects of the war, however, related primarily to the movements of people over space.

The first major postwar population shift occurred in 1945, when millions of prisoners of war, political prisoners, and forced workers were liberated from Nazi German camps by allied military forces. Most returned to their home countries or regions, though some, particularly Jews, elected to move to places with less painful memories. Many Jews immigrated to Palestine shortly after World War II, and many others moved to the United States, Canada, and Great Britain.

A second major population shift was the expulsion of millions of ethnic and national Germans from Eastern European countries. Some came from families that had been living in these areas for generations, while others had moved there only in the 1930s, after German annexation of parts of Poland, Czechoslovakia, Austria, and Hungary; others were occupation forces in Romania and Croatia. The total number of Germans displaced by these actions was more than 12 million.

The expulsion of these Germans created a vacuum into which flowed millions of non-Germans, some of whom had been displaced during earlier German expansion. Nearly 2 million Czechs, forced eastward into Slovakia a decade before, surged back to their homeland; 3 million Poles who had sought refuge in eastern Poland and points farther east returned to western Poland. Millions of other Eastern Europeans moved westward into the lands these other Slavs had vacated.

A final major population shift occurred in the Baltic countries of Lithuania, Latvia, and Estonia. Traditional enemies of the Soviet Union, these countries were divided in their loyalties during World War II. Many who had fought against the Soviets migrated to Sweden, creating a flow of nearly a quarter of a million immigrants. Others stayed in these Baltic states, while another quarter of a million migrated to Poland or other parts of the Soviet Union.

In total, about 28 million Europeans migrated from one country to another in the aftermath of World War II. In Asia, Africa, and the other theaters of war, population movements were far less massive, although there were war-related migrations in China involving millions of civilians. Japanese occupations in Asia and the Pacific had included relatively little transfer of civilian Japanese populations to conquered regions, although the retreat of military forces at the end of the war involved about 3 million military personnel. Similarly, World War II in Africa had been focused on the northern parts of the continent, and the arid environment there had deterred major movements of people.

POPULATION MOVEMENTS TO BOLSTER POLITICAL CONTROL

Several major population movements in the postwar era were for political purposes. Some of these were voluntary, often in response to the creation of new countries and often with the blessing of one or more governments. Others were engineered by governments to consolidate their political control, transplanting huge numbers of people against their wills.

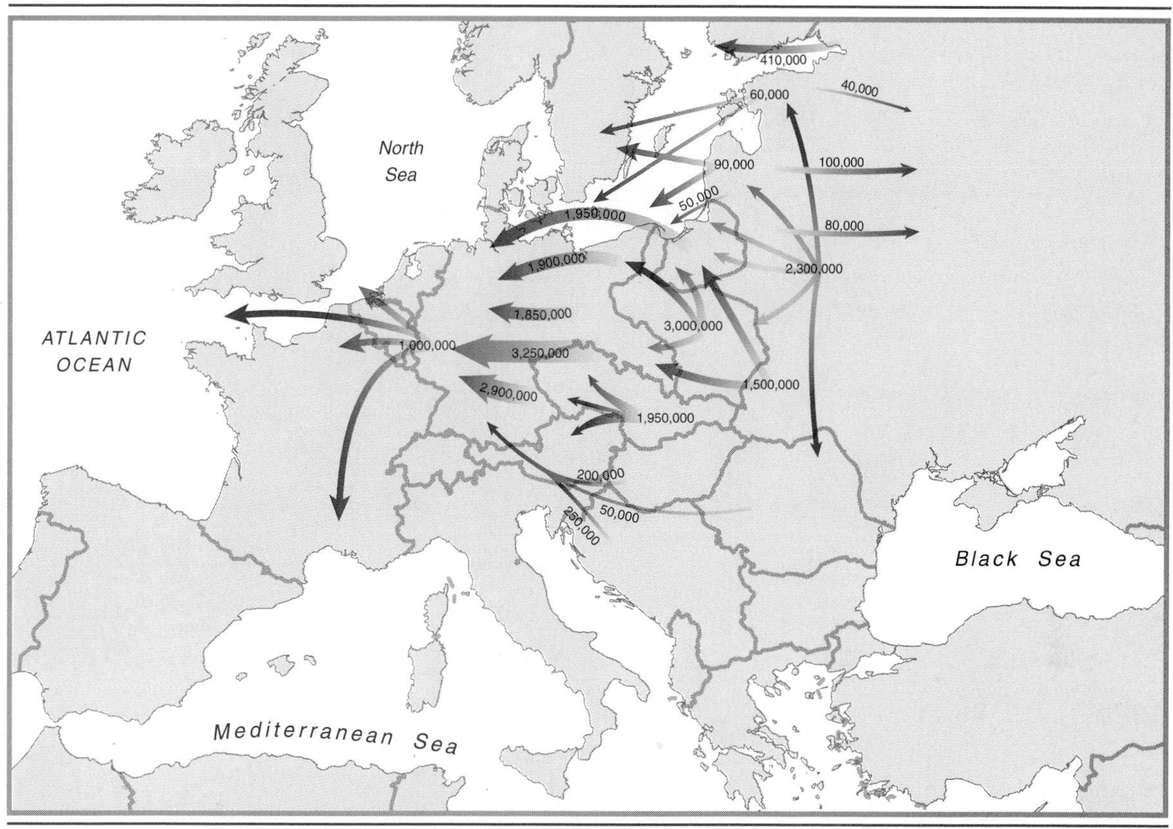

Map 42.1 ***Major Population Movements in Post–World War II Europe.*** *Following World War II, European countries underwent major population changes. Returning troops, refugees, and forcibly resettled peoples constituted most of these migrations.*

Voluntary Migration

Much of the voluntary migration following World War II consisted of members of one religious group moving to a state where they would dominate. Political and economic concerns have prompted most of the remainder.

INDIA AND PAKISTAN. Great Britain annexed the various Indian states into the British Empire following their conquest in 1757. Prior to this conquest, there had been no politically unified India, and separate states differed in government, religion, language, and social customs. The religious differences between Hindus and Muslims were strong, and these surfaced overtly in 1912. Indians had charged the British governor with arbitrary conduct against them, and the British were attempting to mollify the Indians by granting them elected seats to the British government's legislative council in India. In response to pressure from both Muslims and Hindus, the British agreed that some of the seats would be allocated to Muslims and some to Hindus.

The drive for Indian independence began among Hindu intellectuals, who established the Indian National Congress (INC) in 1885. In 1906, Muslim intellectuals founded the Moslem [Muslim] League, also dedicated to gaining independence from Britain. From the beginning, however, these groups were in conflict, because the INC envisioned an India dominated by the Hindu majority, while the Moslem League wanted to see India divided into separate Muslim and Hindu states.

These interests came to a head during World War II. In 1942, the INC and its leadership, Jawaharlal Nehru[1] and Mohandas Gandhi,[2] demanded immediate independence and threatened civil disobedience (and perhaps more violent

[1] **Jawaharlal Nehru:** jah WAH hahr lahl NAY roo
[2] **Mohandas Gandhi:** moh HAHN duhs GAHN dee

FIGURE 42.1 ***Mass Relocation during the Partition of India.*** *This photograph by Margaret Bourke-White shows Sikhs in bullock-drawn carts making their way to India from what had become Pakistan in 1947. Indian troops such as the soldier on horseback (middle, left) were given the task of protecting the Sikhs from possible violence during their migration.*

action) if it were not forthcoming. By this time, some renegade factions of the INC had raised the Indian National Army and actively were fighting alongside the Japanese against the British. Afraid that the INC would ally India with the Axis powers, the British outlawed the INC until the war ended. In the meantime, the Moslem League and its leader, Mohammad Ali Jinnah,[3] reiterated allegiance to the British and were permitted to continue operations throughout the war. During this period when the INC was illegal, the Moslem League prospered, gaining considerable political prestige and power.

In 1946, the British offered independence to India; and, recognizing the strength of the Moslem League, the INC reluctantly agreed to a division of the country in 1947. The predominantly Muslim provinces were in the far eastern and far western parts of the country, while the predominantly Hindu portions were in the vast central area. The central area became India and the eastern and western parts became the single state of Pakistan. (In 1971, eastern Pakistan became a separate country, Bangladesh.)

The major problem was that two rich states, Punjab and Sind, had totally mixed populations. Not only was there no clear majority there, but members of the Hindu, Muslim, and Sikh religions

[3] **Mohammad Ali Jinnah:** moh HAH mehd AH lee JIH nah

lived side by side throughout these states, with no simple spatial distributions by religion. Consequently, no simple partition was possible. Nonetheless, they were divided more or less arbitrarily into Indian and Pakistani portions, and civil violence was immediate and massive. An estimated 500,000 persons were killed during the partition of these states. A few million Muslims remained in areas controlled by Hindus, and smaller numbers of Hindus stayed in Muslim-controlled areas; both governments made special efforts to protect these minorities. Nonetheless, great numbers were unwilling or afraid to remain, and about 15 million people began the harrowing trek to the east or west.

A migration of this sort means more than merely leaving a familiar place. Migrants also leave behind lands owned personally or by their families, sacred shrines, jobs, and friends. The economic, religious, and social fabric of people's lives is torn irreparably.

ISRAEL AND PALESTINE. Other significant migrations of the same era were brought about by the creation of the new state of Israel. The British Empire included Palestine, the land around Jerusalem, sacred as the Holy Land for Jews, Christians, and Muslims. In the nineteenth century, Palestine had a predominantly Arab Muslim population with minorities of Christians and Jews.

In the late nineteenth century, intellectual European Jews conceived of Zionism, the nationalistic quest to establish a Jewish state in the Holy Land. From the last two decades of the nineteenth century onward, Jews from Eastern Europe began migrating to Palestine. Most merely sought to escape persecution in Europe, but some were Zionists intent on establishing a stronger Jewish claim for Palestine. The trickle of Jewish immigration grew to a flood by the 1920s and increased further in the 1930s, when Jews escaping Nazi Germany came to Palestine by the tens of thousands. In 1890, the percentage of Jews in Palestine

FIGURE 42.2 ***Jewish Settlers in Israel, 1949.*** *This family has migrated from Europe to Israel, where they will be farmers. Their future farm is marked at this stage by only a banner bearing a religious quotation in Hebrew.* Corbis-Bettmann.

was under 5 percent; by 1922, it had risen to 22 percent; by 1936, it was 29 percent. In 1946, on the eve of the establishment of the state of Israel, it had reached 32 percent. All of these figures reflect percentages in Palestine as a whole, though Jewish populations were concentrated in the parts of Palestine that eventually became Israel. (For comparison, Jews in 1997 constituted about 85 percent of the population of the area of former Palestine, that is, both Israel and areas of Palestine under Israeli control.)

In 1946, the British government announced its intention to withdraw from Palestine. The following year, the United Nations agreed to turn most of Palestine into the Jewish state of Israel; the remainder of Palestine would be merged with Transjordan to become the Arab state of Jordan. Although Arab Palestinian leaders rejected this agreement, David Ben-Gurion, a Zionist leader and first president of Israel, announced the creation of Israel on May 14, 1948, the day the British withdrew.

Fighting between the Jewish and Arab factions ensued immediately. Palestinian Jews received financial aid from Jewish communities around the world and from some Western governments; Palestinian Arabs received military aid from neighboring Arab states, including troops from Syria, Egypt, Jordan, Lebanon, and Iraq. The better-equipped Israeli forces were successful in resisting the more numerous Arab army, and Israel occupied much of the former Palestine. Israeli forces carried out systematic destruction of Arab villages, and Arabs continued guerrilla warfare; massacres of civilians occurred regularly on both sides. War broke out again in 1956, 1967, and 1973, and each time Israel expanded its occupied territories; these areas remain legally disputed today. Palestinian Arabs opposed the existence of Israel until their parliament reversed this opposition in 1996.

From the Arab viewpoint, Israel was seen as an intrusive state, claiming land that had belonged to Arabs for centuries. Because it was illegitimate, its violence against Arabs was unlawful; therefore, it was appropriate to return violence. From the Israeli viewpoint, God had given this land to the Jews, and Israel was a legitimate state. Consequently, it was legitimate to use force to defend it. These conflicting viewpoints persist largely into today.

As a result of the military conflict in Palestine, two-thirds of the Muslim and Christian Arabs in former Palestine left or were forced from their homes by the better-equipped Jewish forces. These displaced people sought and received refuge in neighboring Arab countries, and, as with any refugees, their suffering and loss was intense. The subsequent wars created even more Palestinian refugees, and major portions of the population lived as refugees for more than a generation.

From the 1960s onward, the Palestinian Liberation Organization (PLO) and its leader, Yasser Arafat, spearheaded Palestinian diplomatic missions, labor and consumer strikes, and terrorism to gain the creation of an independent Palestinian state. In 1994, a negotiated agreement between Israel and the PLO led to partial autonomy of a new Palestine, composed of some of the disputed lands occupied by Israel and comprising a portion of the pre-Israel Palestine.

Since the creation of Israel, Jewish immigration has continued to be a potent force. Immigration from Europe and North America was strong in the 1950s, then fell off in the 1960s and 1970s. A small surge came in the early 1980s with the coming of *felashas* (Ethiopian Jews) fleeing oppression in their home country. Immigration swelled massively in the late 1980s as the Soviet Union allowed Russian Jews to emigrate; the collapse of the Soviet Union further spurred Jewish immigration to Israel. Israeli leaders have used immigration as a political tool, settling Jewish immigrants in areas previously dominated by Arabs in order to secure a stronger claim to those lands.

Arab migration in Palestine and Israel has been of smaller scale and not always voluntary. Arab migration was strongest in the early years of Israel, when many left areas that had become Israel; about 1 million Arabs remained in Israel. Israeli policies of exiling Arab dissidents created a small but significant increase in the numbers of Arabs leaving Israel in the 1970s, 1980s, and early 1990s. Estimates of the numbers of Arabs displaced in Palestine range from just under 1 million to as many as 3 million persons.

VOLUNTARY MIGRATION ELSEWHERE. In the last decades of the twentieth century, civil wars wracked many countries, creating masses of refugees worldwide. In many cases, the successful faction committed atrocities against the losers or seized their property; in those and other cases, fears of such atrocities or seizures motivated thousands of refugees to flee their home countries. Many of these conflicts had an ethnic basis, and no one

IN THEIR OWN WORDS

Zionism and Arab Dislocation

Zionism arose from the insecurity of Jewish life in Europe. The dangers of discrimination, expulsion, and extermination led many Jews to seek a new homeland in Palestine. This was a nationalist quest, but many recent scholars have viewed it also as imperialism, taking a territory by force and subjugating the native inhabitants. Early Zionists supported this project with racist stereotyping of Arabs, as shown in this extract from a 1918 letter from Chaim Weizmann,[a] a prominent Zionist:

> The Arabs, who are superficially clever and quick witted, worship one thing, and one thing only— power and success. . . . The Arab, quick as he is to gauge a situation, tries to make the most of it. . . . The *fellah* [peasant] is at least four centuries behind the times, and the *effendi* [urbanite] . . . is dishonest, uneducated, greedy, and as unpatriotic as he is inefficient.

By implication, a Zionist claim to Palestinian lands would improve their management.

Those who implemented the Jewish seizure of Arab lands after the United Nations decree were well aware of the magnitude of population displacement that would be necessary to achieve their ends; however, they felt it was justified by the "rightness" of their goals. Moshe Dayan,[b] a high Israeli military official, reflected those attitudes in a statement in 1969:

> We came to this country which was already populated by Arabs, and we are establishing a Hebrew, that is, a Jewish state here. In considerable areas of the country [about 6 percent] we bought the lands from the Arabs. Jewish villages were built in the place of the Arab villages. . . . There is not one place built in this country that did not have a former Arab population.

Hundreds of Arab villages were systematically destroyed by Israelis, creating hundreds of thousands of Arab refugees.

An anonymous Arab woman provided the following statements about the events following the attack and destruction of her village in 1948:

> We slept in the village orchards that night. The next morning, Umm Hussein and I went to the village. The chickens were in the streets, and Umm Hussein suggested that I go and bring some water. I saw Umm Taha on my way to the village courtyard. She cried and said: "You had better go and see your dead husband." I found him. He was shot in the back of the head. . . . I stayed in Kabri [her village] six days without eating anything. I decided to leave and join my sister, who had fled earlier with her family to Syria. . . .

Not all Israelis supported these seizures of land. Hannah Arendt, an Israeli scholar, interpreted these events as follows:

> After the war [World War II] it turned out that the Jewish question . . . was indeed solved—namely by means of a colonized and then conquered territory—but this solved neither the problem of the [Arab] minority nor the stateless. On the contrary, the solution of the Jewish question merely produced a new category of refugees, the Arabs, thereby increasing the number of the stateless by another 700,000 to 800,000 people.

[a] **Chaim Weizmann:** HY eem VYZ mahn
[b] **Moshe Dayan:** MOH shuh DY ahn

could claim neutrality when political affiliation and ethnicity were viewed as essentially the same thing.

Refugees from Vietnam, Cambodia, El Salvador, Haiti, Ethiopia, and Rwanda, to name but a few, sought sanctuary in unprecedented numbers during these decades. Usually war or political oppression drove refugees to migrate, but sometimes persistent and systematic religious or ethnic discrimination was the cause. Christians in India, for example, have frequently complained that they are discriminated against in job hiring and other economic activities and that they sometimes are harassed and beaten.

Many of these came to the United States, France, and Great Britain, because those countries were allies in their cause or former colonial powers controlling the country before its independence.

FIGURE 42.3 *Vietnamese Boat People. Conditions in Vietnam deteriorated in the late 1970s, and many thousands of refugees fled by boat to neighboring countries. The refugees shown in this 1979 photograph are part of a group of 573 persons who spent forty-five days on a Malaysian beach until local authorities, considering them illegal aliens, ordered the refugees and their boats to be towed out to sea.* J. Pavlovsky/Sygma.

Others, often poorer people who could not afford the cost of fleeing to distant lands, sought shelter in neighboring countries, frequently at great risk to their personal safety.

For the most part, these refugees have become productive members of the country to which they migrated, but their presence sometimes has caused resentment among the long-time citizens. There are costs attendant to coping with a large flood of immigrants, including the providing of education and services. Sometimes these services must accommodate linguistic and cultural systems alien to the host country, and sometimes the long-time citizens fear that new immigrants will compete for scarce jobs or will form a criminal element. Racism also can create major barriers for those coming to foreign shores, and violent anti-immigrant groups have proliferated in Western Europe in the wake of increased immigration. Immigrants who may have endured the loss of everything in their native countries may find a different set of miseries in their adopted land.

A distinctive sort of voluntary migration, very different from that discussed here, took place in many parts of the world when former colonies and parts of empires were granted their independence. Some citizens of the former colonial power preferred to return to their home countries, often out of fear of violent freedom movements. In Kenya, for example, British colonists fled the Kikuyu (Mau Mau) Uprising in 1952, afraid that nativist orientation would lead to their deaths if Kenya gained independence. In other cases, racism or fears of economic instability led individuals to return to their home countries. In parts of East Africa, Indians and Pakistanis also fled newly independent countries for fear of violence or loss of their property. Although the numbers of such immigrants were relatively small, their departure often had significant effects on the newly independent countries, because they often controlled considerable capital that, if invested in the new country, could have smoothed the economic transition to independence.

Government-Mandated Migration in China and the Soviet Union

The examples just given have included cases where an individual deciding not to migrate might suffer considerable personal risk and economic hardship. Nonetheless, the individual had to make a choice, and some individuals elected to remain where they were. The cases that follow, however, are examples of migrations ordered and carried out by governments in order to consolidate their political power. In these cases, decisions were made by government officials, and the individuals destined to move had little or no say in the matter.

The People's Republic of China found itself in an awkward position in the 1950s: Its interior provinces were overpopulated, and some of its outer provinces had substantial majorities of ethnic non-Chinese. Tibet, for example, had been claimed by China since 1928 and had been seized by Chinese military forces in 1951. The majority of the citizens of Tibet were ethnically Tibetan, and the Chinese recognized the potential for an active freedom movement there. To avoid this, they mandated that millions of ethnic Chinese from the Chinese heartland move to Tibet. These numbers were great enough that ethnic Tibetans were swamped with ethnic Chinese, thereby reducing the likelihood of a successful independence movement. Comparable forced migrations of ethnic Chinese to the provinces of Xinjiang[4] and Inner Mongolia also took place.

[4]**Xinjiang:** SHIHN jee ahng

Similarly, the Soviet Union saw potential for independence movements in the eastern Prussia region (formerly part of Germany) and in the Baltic states of Lithuania, Latvia, and Estonia. To reduce the likelihood of independence movements, the Soviets forcibly moved several million ethnic Russians there and expelled many ethnic Germans, effectively diluting local political sentiments. Similar forced population movements were conducted by the Soviets in Central Asia and the Ukraine.

Such movements are relatively rare in history, largely because few governments have such complete political control that the populace will tolerate massive dislocations. These involuntary migrations are usually a sign that a powerful, totalitarian state is engendering considerable loyalty among the citizens of its core territories.

POPULATION GROWTH IN THE POSTWAR WORLD

Throughout the period of human existence, long-term population growth has been the rule, not the exception. In the latter half of the twentieth century, however, a new phenomenon has emerged. For the first time, large segments of the human population have reduced population growth drastically, sometimes creating stable or even decreasing population levels. At the same time, other population segments have grown at rates unprecedented in history.

The Demography of Population Growth

Whether or not a population grows is based on a simple equation: If the number of people surviving to maturity is the same as in the previous generation, the population is stable. Higher survivorship means population growth, and lower survivorship means population decline. Throughout most of history there has been a slow but steady increase in population, as each generation slightly outstripped its predecessor. The reason that population increase was not faster lay primarily in death, not birth.

In most of history, women typically have borne children more or less constantly throughout their childbearing years, many women bearing a dozen or more children. Incentives for parenting large numbers of children included having plenty

UNDER THE LENS

China's One-Child-per-Family Policy

Under the leadership of Mao Zedong, China had been tolerant of its rapid population growth. The rejection of traditional values during the Cultural Revolution, especially from 1966 to 1969, led to a new promiscuity, however, and China's rulers became concerned. It is unclear whether birth rates actually rose significantly as a result of this relaxation of traditional sexual restraints, but it drew attention to what Chinese leaders increasingly were seeing as a dangerous demographic problem.

By 1980, Deng Xiaoping, China's new leader, was convinced that a sharply increasing population would be disastrous for China. He believed that there would be insufficient jobs to employ everyone and that government funds needed for the economic transformation of China would have to be diverted to support the additional population. Accordingly, he decreed China's one-child-per-family policy.

This policy mandated that, except for thinly populated areas on the periphery of the country, every family should be restricted to one child. To encourage conformity to this mandate, the government conducted advertising campaigns to popularize the idea and provided birth control devices and abortions to put it into practice.

Enforcement of the policy was largely by persuasion. Block committees (civilian neighborhood leadership groups) were the source of the persuasion; they monitored mothers' menstrual cycles and encouraged their families to pressure them to have abortions if they became pregnant with a second child. The effect of this persuasion is difficult for most people outside Chinese society to appreciate, but the extreme value placed on conforming to the community's expectations made this a potent convincing force for Chinese women. Little formal punishment was prescribed, but children after the first were denied medical, educational, and other benefits normally provided by the state.

One stumbling block to the policy was the longstanding cultural value on male children. Parents whose first child had been a girl often were reluctant to accept that they would have no male descendant. Though illegal, female infanticide became more common, paving the way for a possible son. In attempts to overcome this bias toward male children, billboards and other advertising pictured happy parents with their single girl child.

The one-child-per-family policy has been quite successful at slowing population increase. By the 1980s and 1990s, however, problems related to its success were beginning to be evident. Services attuned to children, such as schools, were being underutilized, and it was recognized that caring for aged parents—traditionally shared by several children—would have to be assumed by a single offspring, providing that person survived long enough to do so. While the Chinese government has recognized the gravity of these problems, it has continued to implement the one-child-per-family policy and has done little to alleviate the problems it has spawned.

---

of offspring to assist with agricultural duties and having children to care for the parents in old age. In many societies, kinship has been reckoned through the male line, so male children took on great importance; having sufficient numbers of boys to ensure that one of them would live to maturity to carry on the family name and inherit property was incentive to enlarge families. Less frequently discussed by scholars but equally important was the general lack of reliable and safe means of birth control until recent years. The upshot is that most families had lots of children.

Having many children, however, did not guarantee that they all would survive to maturity. In fact, having a large family often strained the family finances to the point that food became scarce from time to time, the undernourished children became more susceptible to disease, and several children might die at once during an epidemic. Historical demographic studies around the world have shown that the average number of children surviving to adulthood rarely exceeded three per family. When taking other factors into consideration, such as premature deaths of mothers during childbirth

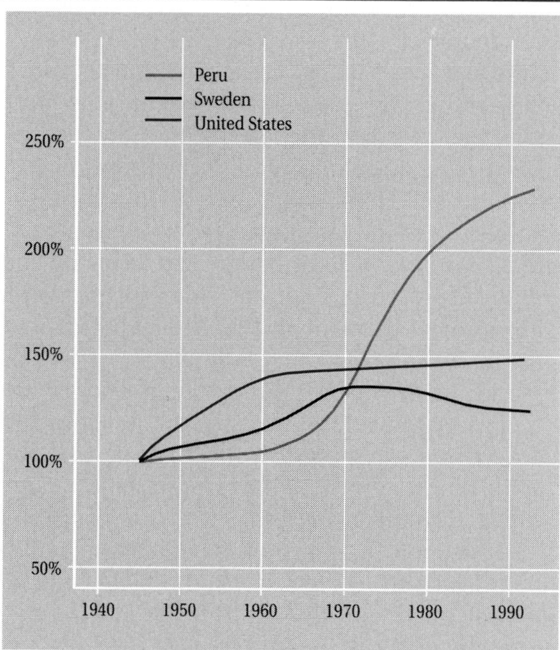

Figure 42.4 ***Population Growth Curves.*** *There are three basic patterns of human population growth in modern times. The most common pattern is that of Third World countries, where population growth tends to be continuous, as exemplified by the curve for Peru. A second common pattern, represented by population growth in the United States, is typical of most industrialized countries and shows a plateau as the population becomes more or less stabilized. A rare pattern, shown in the curve for Sweden, characterizes a few industrialized countries where population has actually decreased in recent years.*

and members of the society who never had children, the number of children per couple surviving to maturity averages 2.2, resulting in a modest rate of about 10 percent growth per generation.

Postwar Population Stability in the Industrialized World

World War II had brought many changes on the social front in the industrialized countries (the First and Second worlds), and these had profound impacts on practices affecting demography. The waging of World War II had revolved around industrial output, and the country with the greatest number of sophisticated tanks or airplanes and the fuel to power them was most likely to be successful. Because armies were predominantly composed of men, women were left to staff the effort on "the home front," and many factories were operated predominantly by women.

After the war, many of these women returned to domestic life, but some stayed on in the workforce. With the economic boom of the 1960s came expectations of luxuries that previously had been out of reach. In order to ensure the availability of a new car, a nice house, a swimming pool, or a vacation in Venice, many women entered the workforce, and families with both husband and wife working became increasingly common.

The demographic consequence of this was that it became inconvenient for a family to have children, because this might require that the wife leave her job, reducing the family income and placing those luxuries out of reach. At the same time, the cost of raising a child was increasing, especially because it was becoming more of an expectation that a child would attend college. In addition, the number of families engaged in agriculture had been steadily declining through the century, and the emphasis on industry during and following the war further decreased the number of farming families. While numerous children were an economic advantage on a farm, economically they were a liability to industrial and service workers.

The "baby boom" that lasted from the late 1940s to the late 1950s in many parts of the industrialized world tapered off, and birth rates fell off drastically. Until the postwar era, birth rates had remained more or less constant in the industrialized countries, and population growth had been high. In the postwar era, however, birth control had major impacts on birth rates for the first time. Various devices and techniques had been available for decades, but the development and popularization in the early 1960s of oral contraceptives, popularly known as "the pill," made birth control simple, unobtrusive, and inexpensive. Some religious leaders praised this new technology on moral grounds, believing it would diminish the population growth that they saw as threatening global welfare.

There were, however, dissenting voices criticizing birth control. The Roman Catholic Church, in particular, condemned all birth control technology as morally wrong and forbade its use by its adherents. Evangelical Christians and some Muslim fundamentalists joined their condemnation, as did some secular leaders, such as Mao Zedong. Surveys throughout the period in most industrial countries, however, showed that huge numbers of women (including Catholics and Muslims) used oral contraceptives. Various groups advocating the limitation of family size, such as Planned Parenthood and Zero Population Growth, became prominent and influential during this period.

With the reduced economic incentive for large families and the technology to keep birth rates low easily and inexpensively available, population in industrialized countries in the years following 1960 grew at much slower rates than before. Most industrialized countries reached a more or less stable population level by 1980, and some northern European countries actually were slightly decreasing in population. Previous economies, with their emphasis on small-scale agricultural production, would have been devastated by this demographic situation, but the industrial economies of the late twentieth century were able to thrive in this environment. The gradual shift during the last decades of the twentieth century to more information-based occupations was even more tolerant of a low rate of population growth, because even fewer numbers of workers were needed.

Population Growth in the Third World

While industrialized nations in the postwar era were trimming population growth, quite the opposite was occurring in the nonindustrialized countries of the Third World. There, population was growing faster than ever before, creating major economic, political, and social problems.

Countries of the Third World continued to be based primarily on small-scale agriculture. As a result, a family with many children continued to have advantage. Women seldom held jobs outside the domestic sphere, and there were few industrial jobs to entice them. Not only were there few incentives to limit the number of one's children, but birth control devices to do so were rare, unfamiliar, and often expensive. Under these circumstances, it is little wonder that birth rates remained high in most Third World countries.

Death rates for infants and children, however, began to drop rapidly in the postwar Third World. Improved communications technology, particularly television, had promoted wider knowledge of the Third World among the citizenry of industrialized countries, and that citizenry became more aware of the appalling health conditions in much of the rest of the world. With the economic prosperity that began in the late 1950s, industrialized countries set up an unprecedented number of programs to aid Third World people. Governments, churches, and private organizations began hundreds of programs to bring modern medicine and improved nutrition to remote corners of the world. The advances in medicine that had helped control disease among troops in World War II, as well as new advances churned out by public and private research organizations, were brought to cities and villages in Latin America, Africa, Asia, and the Pacific Islands. Probably the greatest impact came from preventative medicine, with immunization and education programs vastly decreasing childhood deaths from disease. The bringing of these medical treatments to the Third World is often called **the medical revolution**.

At the same time, scientific research was creating new strains of crops, new fertilizers, and new pesticides specially designed for Third World conditions. These technological advances, known collectively as **the green revolution**, sometimes doubled or even tripled the annual agricultural output of a community. The vastly increased food supplies made possible by the green revolution tremendously decreased hunger and the concomitant susceptibility to disease in the Third World.

The green and medical revolutions together substantially reduced infant and child death rates throughout the Third World. In countries like Guatemala and Nigeria, the likelihood that a child would survive to adulthood increased from around 30 percent to more than 80 percent. In effect, the next generation might be more than twice the size of the parents' generation, meaning at least a doubling of national populations every generation. Putting this in perspective, the rate of population increase became about twenty times that of the years preceding the green and medical revolutions. A plummeting death rate and an unchanged birth rate spelled rates of population increase unparalleled since the beginning of agriculture.

These rates of population growth produced both benefits and severe problems for the countries in which they occurred. On the positive side, families had to endure fewer deaths, and there

FIGURE 42.5 ***Medical Care in the Third World.*** *This American nurse of the organization* Médecins Sans Frontières *(Doctors Without Borders) provides medical assistance to Africans in Sierra Leone. Such volunteer programs from industrialized countries complement efforts by Third World countries to provide their citizens the benefits of medical advances.* Courtesy of Doctors Without Borders.

were plenty of children for agricultural tasks and carrying on the family name. The many problems, however, soon began to cause trouble.

As children grew to adulthood, they needed land to carry on their farming way of life. In earlier times, the numbers of surviving children eligible for inheritance was small, and a combination of clearing excess lands and dividing the ancestral lands could accommodate them. But with perhaps six or seven daughters (or sons, depending on the rules of inheritance) competing for the land, this strategy would leave inheritors with chunks too small for efficient farming. This meant the clearing of increasing amounts of land, often leading to deforestation, erosion, extinction of species, and general environmental degradation.

As agriculture became less attractive, more and more rural villagers found themselves drawn to the cities. Jobs often were perceived as abundant there, though the reality was quite different. The departing colonial powers that had ruled most Third World countries took much of the capital necessary for industrial development with them. Consequently, few Third World countries had significant increases in urban jobs, yet the population in the cities was growing faster than anywhere else. Shanty towns, wretched and unhealthful squatter districts inhabited by demoralized citizens with few options, grew up around many cities. Most who had gone to the city had given up any claim they might have held to agricultural lands and had no place to return to.

In the 1970s, there was great concern in the industrialized nations over unbridled population growth in the Third World. Books with provocative titles like *The Population Bomb* argued that this unchecked growth eventually would lead to various global problems, including inadequate food supplies, a degraded environment, and military conflict over land. One fear in some industrialized countries was that floods of immigrants would try to flee deteriorating conditions in their home countries, seeking a better life. Increasing numbers of applicants for immigration in many industrialized countries fueled this fear. Popular opinion in most industrialized countries was that people in the Third World should be educated to the problems of rapid population growth and assisted with the control of their birth rate.

In Third World countries, however, this sentiment usually was greeted with distrust. Many of these countries had only recently emerged from colonial control and believed that the population-control movement might be merely a trick on the part of the industrialized powers. If a country's strength is in its people, an attempt by outsiders to encourage a country to reduce its population growth could be seen as an attempt to keep the Third World weak, thereby avoiding possible threats to the dominance of the industrial powers.

In addition, religious objections to birth control continued, further reducing the effectiveness of the population-control movement. The opposition of the Catholic Church in predominantly Catholic Latin America and Islam in predominantly Muslim parts of Africa were especially significant. The Reagan and Bush administrations of the United States in the 1980s and early 1990s severely curtailed government foreign aid for birth control and forbade the use of aid for some measures to slow population growth, including voluntary abortion. These decisions had a major impact,

FIGURE 42.6 ***Shanty Town in Jakarta, Indonesia.*** *The growth of downtown Jakarta has engulfed many shanty towns around it. This 1979 photograph shows wealth and poverty juxtaposed within the urban landscape. In the shadow of a skyscraper, this single-family house will survive only a few more years before the family will be forced to relocate.*
Stuart Franklin/Magnum Photos.

PARALLELS AND DIVERGENCES

Foreign Migrant Workers

Migrant workers are laborers who travel from place to place to find work. Many leave their home country, either temporarily or permanently, because jobs are few. Migrant workers are most numerous when one country has surplus labor and limited jobs, while a neighboring country has a need for cheap labor. As a result, foreign migrant workers often are exploited, earning low wages for demanding or dangerous work. Still, they participate because they have few or no options to make equivalent wages in their own country.

A classic example of the long-term use of foreign migrant workers comes from the copper mines of South Africa. Until 1994, South Africa was ruled by a white minority that also controlled the economy of the country, including its mines. Work permits regularly were given to vast numbers of Zambians and other foreign nationals who were willing to work in the mines for lower pay than most South Africans would accept. The dust from copper mining is a low-grade poison, and miners suffered endemically from headaches and internal disorders; the risk of cave-ins and other disasters was moderately high, especially given that safety precautions historically were not strenuously enforced. The miners worked long hours with few holidays, and they were away from their homes and families for months or years at a time.

What made Zambians work in the copper mines? This employment was available to them, and it permitted them to earn more than any equivalent opportunity at home. Most of these miners were single young men in their late teens or twenties, and they intended to work only three or four years, enough to establish some savings so that they could start a business at home. Many were thwarted in this dream, however, because the costs of living in a copper camp could be high, and most workers sent a considerable portion of their paycheck to their families at home, leaving precious little for their savings. Sometimes ill health, brought on in part by the conditions in the mines, forced them to return to Zambia no richer than before.

The institution of the foreign migrant worker appears around the world when a relatively rich country is near a relatively poor one and there is access between them. Mexican farm workers in the United States, Algerian farm workers in France, Turkish laborers in Germany, and Ethiopian domestic servants in Kuwait—all are examples of the combined effects of overpopulation and unequal distribution of employment opportunity and wealth. And in all cases, there are dangers that migrant workers will be exploited by local employers who recognize their vulnerability and that they will be resented by local workers who see them as competitors. Cesar Chavez (1927–1994) organized the United Farm Workers Union in California in response to such problems in 1962 and after a multiyear strike was able to obtain better wages and working conditions for grape pickers. Similar unions have developed in many places around the world.

because the United States had been the primary world provider of such foreign aid. All in all, programs instituted by the industrialized countries had little effect in limiting population growth in the Third World through the 1970s and 1980s.

By the late 1980s, however, the negative effects of increased population were more evident in many Third World countries, inclining their leadership to become less hostile to attempts at population control. In 1994, at the historic Cairo Conference on Global Population, many Third World countries reversed their previous opposition and agreed that steps would have to be taken to reduce their birth rates in order to avert disaster.

FAMINE, CIVIL WAR, DEATH, AND DIVISION IN AFRICA

Along with rapid population growth in the continent as a whole, parts of Africa since World War II have experienced a series of demographic dislocations. These have included large numbers of deaths and vast movements of people, brought about largely by the combined factors of drought and ethnic factionalism.

The **Sahel**[5] is the semiarid region immediately to the south of the Sahara, cutting through Soma-

[5] **Sahel:** sah HEHL

FIGURE 42.7 ***Famine in the Wake of Drought.*** *The Sahelian drought and political upheavals that accompanied it led to mass starvation. This 1992 photograph from Somalia shows an emaciated corpse on a wheelbarrow, awaiting preparations for burial.* James Nachtwey/Magnum Photos.

lia, Ethiopia, the Sudan, Chad, Niger, Nigeria, Mali, Burkina Faso, and Senegal. It is there that the great African drought occurred. The Sahel is naturally quite dry, so it is marginal for agriculture and much of it is used for cattle pastoralism. Increasing populations in the Sahel have led to more intensive land use, which in turn has led to the killing off of natural vegetation, more rapid runoff of rainfall, and increased erosion.

A natural downturn in rainfall between 1968 and 1974 created a major drought, intensified by the environmental degradation induced by human overuse of the land. A second period of drought from 1983 to 1985 produced even more disastrous results. Since the beginning of these droughts, the desert has eaten up the Sahel at a rate ranging from 5 to 30 miles per year, making parts of these formerly productive lands essentially worthless for human uses. During the drought, agricultural and pastoral production throughout the Sahel was considerably diminished, and local food production was devastated. While this drought would have caused hardship under any circumstances, the political situation exacerbated the suffering and led to tremendous loss of life.

The drought and consequent food shortages caused unrest throughout the Sahel, and some political players were quick to take advantage of it. Aspirants to power sometimes fanned the fires of discontent, hoping to undermine the power of the ruling faction; leaders of the ruling faction sometimes diverted aid to members of their own tribe at the expense of other tribes. And various opportunists hijacked international aid shipments of food for sale and personal gain.

This situation led to widespread starvation in some regions, and when disease struck it had more devastating effects because of the undernourished

THIRD WORLD COUNTRIES

Trends	Year	Events
	1940	
Medical revolution, 1945–1980		Nazi concentration camps liberated, 1945
		India and Pakistan divided, 1947
		Israel and Palestine divided, 1948
Green revolution, 1950–1975	1950	
	1960	United Farm Workers Union founded, 1962
Sahel drought, 1968–1985	1970	More than 4 million Cambodians killed or displaced, 1976–1979
	1980	China's one-child-per-family policy implemented, 1980
	1990	Rwandan Civil War, 1994–1995
	present	

condition of its victims. The total number of deaths resulting from food shortages is unknown but clearly reaches more than a million. Further, civil wars in Somalia, Ethiopia, the Sudan, and Chad claimed hundreds of thousands more lives. These wars encouraged refugees to seek shelter with their fellow tribe members, who could be expected to be political allies. This often meant the crossing of borders, and there was considerable international flux of populations in the Sahel, often lasting well beyond the period of the drought.

Intertribal conflicts and demographic dislocations have not been restricted to the Sahel, however. In 1994, Rwanda, in Central Africa, was plunged into a violent civil war that was fought along ethnic lines. In the weeks that followed, at least 100,000 civilians were killed in a rampage of atrocities from both sides. Violence, disease in the wake of thousands of unburied corpses, and general deterioration of living conditions forced Rwandans of both factions to flee the country. In the most rapid refugee flight of its scale in history, more than three-quarters of a million Rwandans massed on and crossed over the borders with Tanzania and Congo-Zaire within days of the onset of violence. In a country of over 4 million people, nearly one-fourth had been killed or forced to flee in the first two weeks of the civil war, and the numbers rose in subsequent weeks and months.

Conditions in Rwandan refugee camps in Congo-Zaire were very difficult. Food and medical supplies were in short supply, doctors and nurses were few and overworked, sanitary conditions were compromised by the masses of people in restricted areas, and factional fighting was common. Although reliable estimates are not available as of early 1997, it is clear that large numbers of Rwandans died from disease and violence in these camps. In late 1996, political developments in Congo-Zaire led to the opening of a corridor through which Rwandan refugees could pass to Rwanda in safety. Over the course of only three days, nearly half a million refugees returned to Rwanda from Congo-Zaire in a massive but orderly population movement that was attended by remarkably little suffering and death. There was another wave of returning refugees from Congo-Zaire in early 1997, as Zairian rebel forces (who shared ethnicity with one of the Rwandan factions) threatened Rwandan refugees of the other ethnic faction. (In May 1997, the Zairian rebels overthrew the government and renamed the country as the Democratic Republic of Congo.)

The forces of factionalism, sometimes abetted by natural disasters, have kept portions of Africa in civil war and turmoil. The long-range demographic effects of such troubles are difficult to foresee, but it is clear that the fighting has claimed millions of victims, some of whom had the talents and skills to help guide these countries through their troubles. It also is clear that these conditions make many African countries unattractive to foreign investors whose capital is desperately needed to help stimulate economies and provide jobs for citizens.

SUMMARY

1. Demography is the study of population in all its aspects. The pace and scale of demographic change have increased dramatically since World War II.

2. Major population movements took place in Europe immediately following the end of World War II. Captives from Nazi Germany were released, Germans in eastern Europe were expelled, Slavs in eastern Europe moved into regions from which Germans had been expelled, and citizens of the Baltic states moved to Sweden and Poland. In total, about 28 million people moved from one country to another immediately following the war.

3. Voluntary migration, especially along religious lines, was important in establishing political control in states created after World War II. This was true in the case of India and Pakistan and in the case of Israel and Palestine. Many of these voluntary movements were of refugees fleeing violence. In the 1970s and later, large numbers of people seeking refuge from civil wars migrated to new countries.

4. Government-mandated population movements in China and the Soviet Union settled members of the majority ethnic group in outlying regions of their countries in order to forestall independence movements by ethnic minorities.

5. In postwar industrialized countries, birth control measures have reduced the birth rate to keep it in line with increased survivorship, the result of improved medicine and food supplies. These countries have had essentially steady population levels without growth.

6. In Third World countries, the medical and green revolutions have decreased child mortality, leading to rapid rates of population increase. The resulting overpopulation has led to environmental degradation and to various social and economic problems. Initially distrustful of efforts by industrialized countries to assist in limiting their birth rates, Third World countries in the 1990s recognized the problem and became more receptive to possible solutions.

7. Ethnic strife in Africa has resulted in widespread conflict, sometimes spurred by natural disasters. These conflicts often have resulted in great loss of life and major refugee flight.

SUGGESTED READINGS

Cornell University Workshop on Food, Population, and Employment. *Food, Population, and Employment: The Impact of the Green Revolution.* New York: Praeger, 1971. A detailed treatment focusing on the sociopolitical effects of the green revolution. Though fairly old, its information and conclusions remain current.

Fraser, T. G. *Partition in Ireland, India, and Palestine: Theory and Practice.* New York: St. Martin's Press, 1984. A treatment of these countries' national partition processes, applying a general model.

Koehn, Peter H. *Refugees from Revolution: U.S. Policy and Third-World Migration.* Boulder, Colo.: Westview Press, 1991. General treatment with an interpretation critical of U.S. policy in the 1980s.

Piore, Michael J. *Birds of Passage: Migrant Labor and Industrial Societies.* Cambridge, Eng.: Cambridge University Press, 1979. An elegant treatment of the general issues, drawing primarily on U.S. examples.

Signing of the Treaty of Waitangi. *Although the Maori were conquered by the British Empire, they maintained a significant presence and demanded the protection of their rights as the native peoples of New Zealand. Such protection was promised by the Treaty of Waitangi, signed in 1840 by Chief Tamati Waka Nene and Governor William Hobson; the treaty, however, was ultimately a failure.* Eileen Tweedy/ET Archive.

ISSUE 9

Ethnicity and Politics

When the legislative body that governs Papua New Guinea opened its 1996 session, it was composed of members representing more than a dozen parties, each with a core constituency defined by ethnicity. The ruling group consisted of a coalition of several of these parties that shared certain interests. No single ethnic group was able to dominate either society or government, a condition increasingly common in the modern world.

Ethnicity has been a factor in most politics throughout history. In the past century or so, however, the complexion of global politics has changed, placing ethnicity in a central position as never before.

THE MONOETHNIC STATE

The early civilizations, with the possible exception of that of ancient Egypt, were populated largely by citizens who viewed themselves as quite similar to one another. They spoke the same language, worshiped the same gods, followed the same customs, and—most important—considered themselves members of the same named group. Such a self-identified group that shares culture is called an **ethnic group**, and in some places ethnic groups are conventionally called "tribes." A state whose citizens are mostly from the same ethnic group or tribe is called a **monoethnic state**.

It was understandable that most early civilizations would be monoethnic states, because they were relatively small and isolated, developing in a more or less homogeneous region. As military technology and political organization evolved, however, states expanded their borders, overflowing into regions occupied by other ethnic groups. Sometimes these groups were absorbed into the dominant ethnic group, as when local tribes became part of the Inca following their conquest in fifteenth-century Peru. Other times, these groups retained their ethnicity but were denied full participation in society, as when the Normans who invaded England in 1066 denied Anglo-Saxons access to offices and various business enterprises, or when Anglo-Australians denied Aborigines the rights to vote or hold property. (Eventually the Normans and Anglo-Saxons in England merged to form a single composite English ethnicity; Aborigines have received the rights to vote and hold property but remain far less politically powerful than other Australians.) Minority ethnic groups can exist in a monoethnic state, but they must remain subordinate to the dominant ethnic group.

Nationalism, treated in detail in Chapter 33, fostered monoethnic states in Europe and lands under European control in the eighteenth and nineteenth centuries. The emphasis on a common past and culture, a great common purpose, and a national identity encouraged this development, but there was a serious problem. Many of these countries included substantial numbers of other ethnic groups. Efforts were made to bond some of them to the dominant ethnicity, as when Nazi German scholars went to great lengths to show the similarities in skull shapes between Germans and Czechs of the Sudetenland, arguing that these similarities indicated a previously unrecognized ethnic kinship. In other cases, ethnic groups were denied the vote, the right to own property, and other privileges accorded "regular" citizens; in this manner, South Africa's official *apartheid* policy of the 1960s through the 1980s set blacks apart from white citizens by law.

THE MULTIETHNIC STATE

The **multiethnic state** incorporates two or more ethnic groups into its citizenry and extends full privileges to them. Multiethnic states have developed in three main ways: as a result of the breakdown of empires, as the result of immigration from disparate places, and as a development out of colonial holdings.

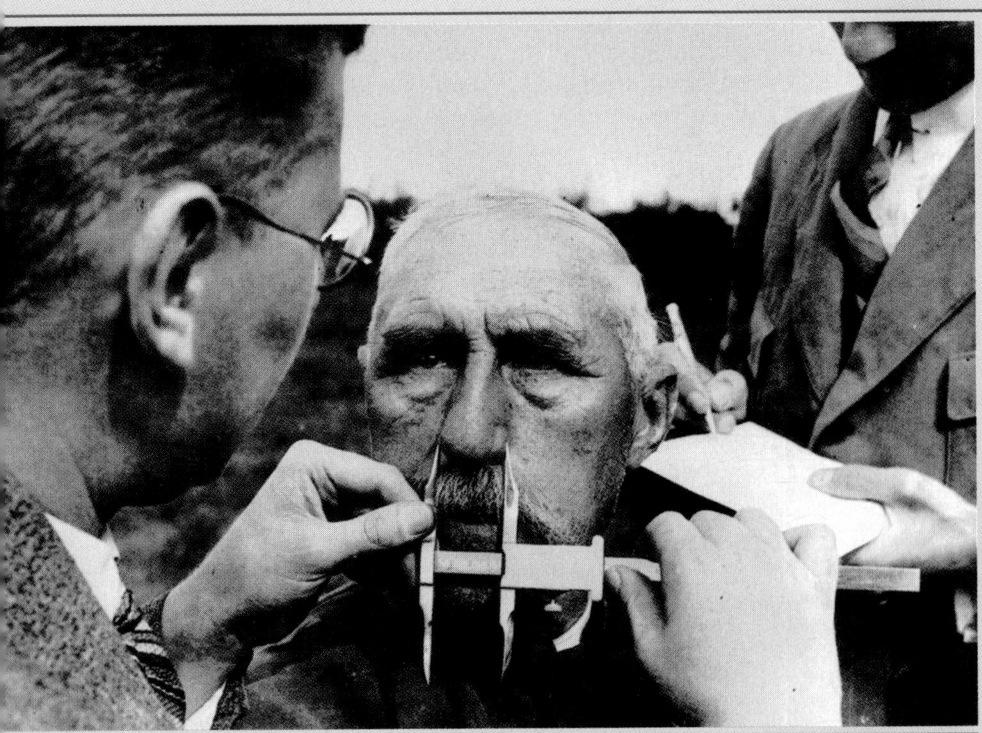

FIGURE I.9.1 ***Nazi Skull Measurement.*** *Anthropologists had measured skulls for decades, but under Nazi Germany the measurements took on a new purpose: the classification of individuals into ethnic groups to determine their fates. This photograph from 1936 shows two scientists from the League for Propagation of Racial Knowledge measuring a man to determine his "true" ethnicity. In later years, such measurements could lead to classification as a member of an "undesirable" group (Jew, Gypsy, or Slav) and to imprisonment or execution.* Ullstein Bilderdienst.

The Imperial Legacy

An empire, by definition, is a state that expands its political control over other peoples. Not every empire, however, is a multiethnic state, because some empires withhold political, economic, and social privileges from conquered peoples, reserving them only for the dominant ethnic group. The Roman Empire before the third century A.D., for example, had levels of citizenship for males and accorded some citizens rights withheld from others; only citizens of the highest level were granted the right to vote, various economic privileges, and the right to run for office. Consequently, the Roman Empire—despite its ethnic diversity—was not a multiethnic state.

Other empires, however, have been clearly multiethnic in their organization. The Aztec Empire of Mexico, for example, incorporated various ethnic groups into itself with full privileges. Some of these were allies and others were conquered peoples, but either way they maintained their distinctive ways of life and identification as Mixtec,[1] Tototepec,[2] or Mexica. This identification, of course, meant that loyalties sometimes were split, as when Tototepec rebelled against Aztec imperial rule, leaving its citizens to decide whether their personal loyalties lay more with Tototepec or with the Aztec Empire.

Lands of Opportunity

A second mechanism of multiethnic state formation is through large-scale immigration from diverse sources. This process began essentially with the European voyages of discovery of the fifteenth century and the subsequent colonial occupation of captured lands.

The European explorers of this era recognized little or no prior claim to land on the part of the American, African, Australian, or Pacific island peoples living on it. Indeed, a primary purpose of these explorations was to claim new lands for whatever European power was sponsoring the voyage. As a result, Europeans often viewed these new lands as "open," without inhabitants and, therefore, ready for immigration. In a more real sense, the demographic disasters that befell the native inhabitants shortly after the European arrival resulted in so much death that some places became truly open.

Some of these new lands were largely closed to immigration from individuals who were not citizens of the colonial power controlling them. In some cases, laws permitted immigration only by citizens of the home country. In other cases, opportunities were seen as sufficiently meager that immigrants from elsewhere were unlikely to choose to go there.

Other lands, however, were perceived as rich and attractive and drew immigration from many sources. Foremost among these was the United States, but Canada, Australia, Argentina, Brazil, and South Africa also drew heavy multiethnic immigration from Europe. Wave after wave of immigrants flocked to these countries, creating multiethnic populations of great diversity. Some ethnic groups, particularly non-Europeans, suffered official discrimination and were not accorded full privileges in the early years of these countries, but all now have official policies granting all citizens equal rights. With the granting of equal rights (in theory, at least), these countries became multiethnic states.

The Legacy of Colonialism and Imperialism

The final major route to a multiethnic state was along the rocky paths of colonialism and imperialism. Those lands unlucky enough to be conquered and controlled as colonies usually became multiethnic through one of two processes.

In the Americas, many colonies became multiethnic states by virtue of the distinction between Europeans and Native Americans. The names differ from country to country, but the general pattern remains the same: Those of pure or nearly pure European extraction are of one ethnic group, those of nearly pure American Indian extraction are considered another group, and those of mixed parentage are a third group. These three ethnic groups constitute the multiethnic aspect of American multiethnic states derived from colonies.

Why are there not several ethnicities for American Indians? Certainly there were many tribes at the time of European contact, and each viewed itself as a separate ethnic group. The demographic disasters of contact with Europe, however, reduced the numbers and power of American Indian

[1] **Mixtec:** MIHSH tehk
[2] **Tototepec:** toh toh TEH pehk

groups incredibly. As a result, American Indians in the twentieth century largely have banded together for mutual support. This merging of various tribes into a single interest group is known as **pan-tribalism**. While the economic, social, and political conditions of many American Indians are not good, pan-tribal political efforts have produced considerable gains in the past few decades, especially in North America and eastern South America. Successes have included return of lands, monetary settlements, and return of sacred items from museums. Another result of pan-tribalism has been the limitation of conflict among Native American ethnic groups over political power.

In Africa and Asia, the process of forming multiethnic states has followed a different course. In these continents, the division of the land into colonies was based on principles that made sense to the European conquerors, not to the local peoples. One tribe might be divided by a colonial boundary, and any colony was likely to have many tribes within it. When these colonial boundaries became national boundaries following independence, this meant that each country was a fragile coalition of tribes (many historically hostile to one another) and that tribal units sometimes were divided between countries. Because tribes largely equated with political parties, the political mix of any country was likely to be volatile.

Take Nigeria as an example. The boundaries of the British colony were established by the maneuverings of the British, French, and Germans, all of whom had colonies in West Africa in the latter half of the nineteenth century. Areas were thrown together into a single colony because the British could claim and hold them. This meant that tribal areas of the Hausa, Fulani, Yoruba, Kanuri, and Ibo were united into a single colony. Many of these groups were mutually antagonistic; portions of the tribal lands of most of them extended into adja-

FIGURE I.9.2 ***Meeting of the Amazonian Peoples.*** *This pan-tribal meeting held in Pará, Brazil, in 1995 was designed to build the solidarity of members of various Amazon Basin tribes, many of whom previously had been hostile to one another. Such meetings stress the common problems currently faced by all tribes, particularly the struggle to hold on to their territories in the face of encroachment by logging and mining interests.* Ricardo Azoury/Pulsar.

FIGURE I.9.3 *Zulu Rally in South Africa. These members of the Inkatha Freedom Party, an ethnic-based political party dominated by the Zulus, carry spears and shields. The function of these "cultural weapons," however, is primarily symbolic of the Zulu identity.* Oosterbroek Ken / Gamma/Liaison International.

cent colonies that were held by the French or Germans. The only glue holding the colony together was the colonial power.

Political movements between the end of World War II and the early 1970s left nearly all of Africa and Asia independent. What formerly had been colonies now were countries. Because the glue that once had held a colony together was missing, it was left to these new countries to try to form cohesive multiethnic states from the materials bequeathed them by colonialism and imperialism.

THE REASSERTION OF ETHNICITY IN INTERNATIONAL POLITICS

The years since World War II have seen ethnicity move to the fore as a factor in politics. Ethnically based political parties are active in every country that holds free elections. Civil wars are fought between rival ethnic groups, and multiethnic states are partitioned to produce monoethnic states. Some of the most dramatic of these developments have taken place as a result of the independence of former colonies and the breakup of the former Soviet Union.

Ethnic Politics in Former Colonies

In most of Africa and parts of Asia, political parties are highly identified with particular ethnic groups. In South Africa, for example, the first all-race election held in 1994 featured the African National Congress and the Inkatha[3] Freedom Party as major participants. Each party, however, drew its primary support from a single tribe or group of tribes; the Inkatha Freedom Party was supported by Zulus, and the African National Congress by a coalition of other tribes. The Moslem League and Indian National Congress, discussed in Chapter 42, were ethnically based parties instrumental in securing independence for Pakistan and India. Modern political parties in both countries draw much of their support from constituencies based on ethnicity and caste status.

These parties sometimes have formed the nuclei for hostile forces in civil wars. The 1994 civil war in Rwanda, for example, was a more violent and well-publicized version of conflict that had been ongoing in that country since 1962. The ruling party in 1994 was dominated by the Hutu tribe, but the leadership was inclining toward greater inclusion of the minority Tutsi tribe in its power structure. Upon the death of the Rwandan presi-

[3] **Inkatha:** ihn KAH tuh

dent, rumored to have been engineered by members of his own party antagonistic to his inclusion of Tutsi in the government, government (Hutu) and rebel (Tutsi) forces opened hostilities. The fighting in the weeks that followed was savage and marked by abundant atrocities committed by both sides. Refugee camps were shelled, pedestrians were hacked to pieces with machetes, and victims were dragged from their homes and shot in the street. What appeared on the surface to be random violence, however, actually was shaped mostly by longstanding tribal animosities.

The Rwandan example is by no means unique. The Congo (later known as Zaire) was wracked by a devastating civil war between 1962 and 1965. The Ibo tribe fought with government forces between 1967 and 1970 in an unsuccessful attempt to secede from Nigeria and establish Biafra as an independent state; in 1966 alone, seven military takeovers transferred power from one ethnically based party to another in Africa. The secession of Bangladesh from Pakistan (through a guerrilla war), the ongoing independence movement of Kashmir in India, and the ongoing insurgency in the Kachin region of northern Burma (Myanmar) attest that ethnically based political movements have been important in Asia as well.

The nature of the colonial experience in Latin America, as discussed earlier, has led to fewer ethnically based political movements of the sort common in Africa and Asia. In 1994 and 1995, however, a pan-tribal organization of Mayan Indians in the Chiapas region of Mexico took over several government buildings and carried on military operations for weeks before they settled into diplomatic negotiations with the federal authorities. This movement, however, was not aimed at autonomy or at the seizing of political control; instead, it was a highly visible means of publicizing government mistreatment of the Indians and forcing the Mexican government into political concessions.

The Ethnic Basis of the Breakup of the Soviet Union and Yugoslavia

In the late 1980s, regional sentiments in the republics comprising the Soviet Union were surfacing, and the Baltic republics of Lithuania, Latvia, and Estonia had declared their independence. In 1991, bowing to overwhelming sentiment, the government under Mikhail Gorbachev declared that the republics were free to decide whether they wished to continue in union with one another. Within a few months, the Soviet Union had been disassembled and transformed into over a dozen independent states. Many of those were monoethnic states with small minority populations, while others had sizeable minority ethnic populations and were taking steps in the 1990s to suppress or control those minorities in order to establish monoethnic states.

Figure I.9.4 ***Soviet Army Seizes Lithuanian Television Station.*** *In 1991, when Lithuania declared its independence from the Soviet Union, Soviet troops responded with massive force and on January 12–13 opened fire on unarmed protesters outside the national radio-television station in Vilnius; the army captured the building, killing thirteen persons and seriously wounding 100. The Lithuanian independence movement, however, persisted and eventually achieved its goal.*
Pascal Le Segretain/Sygma.

Throughout the former Soviet bloc, countries formerly welded together from smaller units have elected to split apart. Czechoslovakia voted to divide itself into the Czech Republic and Slovakia; the northern provinces of the Georgian Republic have continued military attempts to secede, as has Chechniya; and Armenia and Azerbaijan have continued to dispute their common boundary on the basis of ethnic distributions. These and many other splits and conflicts are rooted in ethnic issues long submerged under Soviet control.

Like the Soviet Union, Yugoslavia was a union of distinct ethnic groups held together by an authoritarian central government. In 1991, however, Yugoslavia dissolved as all its component states but Serbia and Montenegro seceded. Several years of bitter war ensued, particularly among Christian Serbs, Muslim Bosnians, and Christian Croats. Savage at times, the war has been marked by massacres of civilians and prisoners, the persistent blocking of food convoys destined for starving civilians, and widespread devastation. The United Nations and other international organizations made repeated diplomatic attempts to end the fighting and even resorted to military action to enforce cease-fires. By 1997, these efforts had achieved a tenuous peace and a fragile alliance between Croats and Bosnians, but it is unclear whether the region's peace will last.

ETHNICITY AND POLITICS IN THE TWENTY-FIRST CENTURY

It is ironic that, as twentieth-century transportation and communications are linking the world together in a way never before possible, the world is becoming politically more fragmented. The lesson to be learned is that mere contact is not enough to unite peoples politically. The might of major European powers was all that kept antagonistic ethnic groups together under colonial rule, just as Soviet power held together many multiethnic polities that now threaten to split apart. Now that these powers are diminished, how will people choose to organize themselves?

Max Weber, the early-twentieth-century sociologist, asserted that there were two conditions under which a group of people might voluntarily band together. First, they might see the mutual benefit in resisting some outside force; he called this the **associative bond**. Second, they might simply wish to be with others who shared beliefs, values, and customs; this was the **communal bond**. The associative bond favors multiethnic states, coalitions of equals founded on common need; the communal bond favors monoethnic states, states in which similarity is enforced by the absence or subordination of ethnic minorities. The absence of minorities can be brought about by careful placement of borders to encompass ethnic regions; alas, "ethnic cleansing" and other programs of extermination or relocation also have been used.

In the twenty-first century, countries will be straining between the conflicting benefits of these two kinds of bonds. On the one hand, larger, multiethnic states have greater resources and ability to cope with problems, including external aggression; they sacrifice the comfort of shared culture, however, forcing their citizens to adjust to one another's idiosyncrasies. On the other hand, smaller monoethnic states provide a strong body of shared beliefs and identity at the expense of the practical advantages of the larger, more diverse polity. At the end of the twentieth century, many people have opted for emphasizing the communal bond and the monoethnic state. The future may see a continuation of this decision or a return to the associative, multiethnic state.

SUGGESTED READINGS

Ingham, Kenneth. *Politics in Modern Africa: The Intertribal Dimension.* London: Routledge, 1990. A treatment of the tribal factor's significance in African politics, with abundant examples. Written before the demise of *apartheid* in South Africa and the massive (1994) intertribal conflict in Rwanda.

Kellas, James G. *The Politics of Nationalism and Ethnicity.* New York: St. Martin's Press, 1991. A general, theoretical treatment of the issue of ethnicity and politics, taken from the social science perspective.

Other information can be drawn from current newspapers and news magazines; it is almost certain that one or more similar conflicts will be active at any moment.

THIS VOLUME OF *THE GLOBAL PAST* HAS examined a great number of events, processes, ideas, and persons shaping world history in the past five centuries. When looking at these specifics, it may be difficult to see the long-term patterns of which they form a part. Part Ten points out some of these larger patterns, drawing attention to significant trends, cycles, and new directions.

Chapter 43 examines the arts and how they reflect their times. What do cartoons or murals say about changing political attitudes in the world? How did World War II affect French and Japanese films? How did blues singers fuse dissimilar artis-

tic traditions to create new art forms? Chapter 43 will explore these and other questions in its quest to show how art reveals insights into society.

Chapter 44 tackles the major theme of this text: how the world has become progressively more integrated over the past five centuries. It provides insights into the grand pattern of history for the modern era, helping us anticipate what the future may bring.

PART TEN

PERSPECTIVES

Technology in the Modern Era. *Fermenters like this one are used for the production of insulin, Interferon, and other medicinal drugs. Today's high-tech facilities mass-produce medicines through biochemical processes dependent on microorganisms existing in nature. One of the paradoxes of the modern era is that sophisticated procedures and technologies often rely on basic, natural processes.* Dan McCoy/Rainbow.

***Cartoon of* The Rite of Spring.** *When Igor Stravinsky's ballet* The Rite of Spring *opened in Paris in 1913, its radical innovations caused riots. This cartoon by Jean Cocteau, a writer, painter, and great supporter of experimental theater, shows a caricature of Stravinsky at the piano, flanked by puzzled-looking theatergoers.* V & A Picture Library.

Guerrilla Girls. *This New York–based coalition of artists uses art to express political protest; wearing gorilla masks, they hang posters to protest sexism and racism in the art world.* Deborah Outline.

CHAPTER 43

The Arts as Mirrors of the Modern World

"Art mirrors life." The name of the author of this quotation has been lost over the years, but the truth of the sentiment persists. Artists are the products of the forces that shape society at large. If this were not true, each artist would follow her or his own idiosyncratic creative urges, and there would be no styles distinctive to an age or nation.

Instead, we see the intimate linking of artists to their worlds. Successful artists choose themes relevant to their times, and they often select modes of expression that reflect the social, economic, and political realities of their environment. Even those artists who try to insulate themselves from the influences of the outside world are still shaped by them, because their ideas and concepts are molded by their culture.

As a result, the arts reveal society. They expose its strengths, its weaknesses, its sources of pride, and its fears. In effect, they are a mirror in which society, with all its beauty and blemishes, is reflected. Sometimes looking at society through the arts can reveal deep-seated concerns that are less obvious when viewed by different means.

FOLK ARTS, FINE ARTS, AND POPULAR ARTS

For convenience, the arts often are divided into three categories. **Folk arts** are those that have long traditions and are learned in informal settings, as when a parent teaches a child a folk song. Folk arts usually are viewed as received knowledge by the people who practice them, and innovation often is discouraged. As a result, they often are very conservative, changing only slowly. Folk art typically is perpetuated by amateur artists. The painting of hex signs on barns by Pennsylvania Germans is an example of folk art.

Popular arts are the forms of art that receive wide distribution and are appreciated by large numbers of people. The popular arts have exploded in the twentieth century, thanks to technology that permits huge numbers of people to experience art electronically. Radios, televisions, videocassette recorders, audio systems, film projectors, high-quality photoreproduction equipment, and a wealth of other devices permit billions of people daily to appreciate arts that otherwise would be available only to a few people in live performances or in art galleries. Popular artists usually are professionals, and the genre is very subject to crazes, fads, and brief periods of popularity of an artist or work. Doo-wop music of the 1950s, a form of a cappella rock-and-roll singing with lush melodies and close harmonies, is an example of popular art.

Fine arts are the elite wing of the arts, appealing mostly to a small group of enthusiasts, many of whom have academic training in the arts. Praised as intellectual and sophisticated by their proponents, the fine arts sometimes are disparaged as snobbish and pretentious by their detractors. The fine arts usually are produced by highly trained artists who simultaneously are part of an academic establishment and are rebelling against it. Many fine arts of the nineteenth and twentieth centuries reflect the attempts of the artists to break with traditional forms and create new, distinctive, modern forms. Fine artists usually are professionals, though their limited audience means that they rarely attain the financial rewards or fame of the popular artists. A Beethoven symphony is an example of the fine arts.

These distinctions are for convenience only, and the categories overlap somewhat. Count (William) Basie, the famous jazz musician, also wrote classical music, bridging the gulf between the popular and fine arts. Grandma Moses (Anna Mary Robertson Moses), the rustic painter of rural New York, achieved great fame and popularity, yet her art was essentially folk in character. Despite the vagueness of the boundaries of these categories, the terms frequently are useful in discussing the arts.

In their different ways, folk arts, popular arts, and fine arts all reflect the concerns, attitudes, and values of the time and place in which they were created. This chapter examines four themes that recur again and again in the arts of the modern period: nationalism, innovation, alienation, and fusion.

NATIONALISM

The rise of the modern nation-state created a demand for expressions of nationalism, and art became a major vehicle for these expressions. The modern nation-state demanded not just loyalty from its citizens; it demanded that they have greater loyalty to the nation-state than to any other ideology, polity, or entity. If the nation-state were to overcome the competing demands of a citizen's region, religion, family, and ethnic group, it required strong symbols that would remind citizens of their obligations to the nation-state. Art has proven particularly good at providing those symbols, particularly through expression in the popular and fine arts.

We saw in Chapter 33 how the nineteenth-century Romantic movement in the European fine arts fostered nationalist feelings. Drawing on stories, music, and themes prominent in folklore, it fostered distinctive national styles of music, dance, visual arts, painting, drama, and literature. While styles changed and Romanticism went out of vogue, national styles of musical composition continued. One of the best examples comes from the United States, where Aaron Copland (1900–1994) produced a body of overtly nationalist music during the middle decades of the twentieth century. His "Billy the Kid" drew on the story of the famous outlaw, using themes and rhythms from cowboy music; "Appalachian Spring" evoked the passing of winter in the mountains of the eastern United States, using themes from folk tunes; and "Rodeo" produced a rollicking image of steer ridin' and bronco bustin'. Copland's style had little of the emotion and exoticism of Romantic music, but he retained the emphasis on national style that had arisen with Romanticism.

National Anthems

A **national anthem** is a song that is adopted by a nation as a symbol, used at official occasions and often protected against desecration by law. While some countries and rulers were associated with particular songs prior to this date, the year 1795 marks the adoption of the first official national anthem. At that date, revolutionary France adopted "La Marseillaise"[1] as its national anthem. Originally titled "War Song for the Army of the Rhine," this song got its name from a band of revolutionaries from Marseilles in 1792. From there, it became a rallying chant of the revolutionaries, and—with new and less violent words—it was officially adopted as the national anthem of France.

Most other Western countries adopted national anthems during the nineteenth century, a period of nationalistic fervor, and these anthems became sources of great pride. Fine arts composers extracted musical quotations from them to represent countries, as when Peter Ilyich Tchaikovsky[2] included snatches of "La Marseillaise" in his "1812 Overture," indicating the Napoleonic army entering battle against the Russians. *Casablanca*, an American film set in a nightclub during World War II, includes a moving scene in which French and Germans sing their national anthems at the same time, each trying to drown the other out in obvious symbolism of their national antagonism.

During the Bolshevik Revolution, the Soviet Union adopted "Internationale" as its national anthem. This song previously had been a rally anthem of communists throughout Europe, calling for an international communist revolution, and it was logical to adopt it, given the Soviet Union's communist ideology. In 1943, however, the Soviet Union was in the midst of international conflict and feared defection of some of its member states during World War II; an anthem that emphasizes an ideology shared internationally is not the best symbol for a nation struggling to survive. Accordingly, the Soviet Union dropped "Internationale," replacing it with a new anthem called "Unbreakable Union of Free-born Republics," which remained in place until 1989. After the breakup of the Soviet Union in 1989, however, the "unbreakability" of the Soviet Union no longer was a credible theme, and individual states developed their own anthems, often resurrecting ones in use before 1917. Russians, however, were unable to agree on a replacement, as national competitions failed to provide an acceptable new anthem. Just before the 1996 Olympic Games, Russia hastily adopted a national anthem titled "Patriotic Song" so that gold medal winners would have an anthem to accompany their medal ceremony. As of early 1997, however, this anthem had no words, because there was

FIGURE 43.1 ***Anthem of Victory.*** *Evelyn Ashford, an American gold medalist in track at the 1984 Olympics, is emotionally overwhelmed during the playing of "The Star Spangled Banner" at the medal ceremony. National anthems are powerful artistic symbols often used to evoke nationalism.* David Madison/Duomo.

[1] **La Marseillaise:** lah MAHR say yehz
[2] **Tchaikovsky:** chy KOFF skee

no agreement on whether they should be militant or pacific, regionalist or international.

Japan also came to the end of the twentieth century with its national anthem in doubt. "Kimigayo,"[3] the Japanese national anthem, uses millennium-old words from an anonymous poem, coupled with a melody written in the 1870s. It was first performed for the Emperor Meiji's birthday in 1880, and it became the national anthem in 1893. "Kimigayo" was a potent rallying force during World War II, and it came to be associated with Japanese imperial expansion. During the 1980s and 1990s, Japanese political factions disputed the appropriateness of "Kimigayo" as a national anthem, ultranationalists favoring its retention and socialists wanting no anthem that reminded them of wartime imperialism.

Former colonies gaining their independence, especially since World War II, usually have adopted national anthems immediately. Most often these have been based on folk songs from the dominant ethnic group in the country. When the country has been based on a more or less equal coalition of ethnic groups, the song usually has been written on commission by a professional composer and has not used folk themes.

Revolutionary Posters

With the Bolshevik Revolution in Russia came a new form of art: the revolutionary poster. (See full-color illustration on p. A-32.) These posters were printed by revolutionary groups before and during the seizure of power, and the communist government printed them afterward. Between 1918 and 1921, more than 3,600 revolutionary posters were printed. They were posted at conspicuous places around cities and towns, inspiring support for the revolution, the revolutionary government, and its policies. In later years, the style of socialist realism created in the Bolshevik Revolution was adopted by communist revolutionary movements around the world.

This was not the first time that posted notices had been used in a revolution or other upheaval. Indeed, handbills with written messages had been posted during the French Revolution, the American Civil War, and at various occasions before then. The Russian posters, however, differed from their predecessors in the degree to which their art commanded attention. More than a century had elapsed between the French and Bolshevik revolutions, and printing had improved considerably. Even though printing in Russia was a bit less sophisticated than elsewhere in Europe, it was capable of mass producing fairly complex, multicolored posters. These posters featured art and bright hues and were far more arresting than the posters of previous eras. In addition, Russian revolutionaries pioneered the mass distribution of posters as a means of inspiring support.

The Russian poster drew on Russian folk art for some of its inspiration, but more direct input came from political cartoons that appeared in the satiric journals thriving between 1905 and 1907. These journals, mostly underground operations critical of the tsarist government, sprang up in large numbers following the 1905 massacre of citizens by tsarist troops on "Bloody Sunday" but were suppressed effectively by 1908. Their artists, however, were available when posters began being produced a decade later.

From these sources, the poster artists developed a distinctive series of styles. Most frequent were dramatic presentations of heroic or tragic figures in emotion-evoking poses. A woman and child might be seen cowering before blood-crazed tsarist troops; a heroic worker might be seen seizing a flag and carrying it forward in the storming of a position; a grandmother might be seen stolidly harvesting wheat to feed the soldiers at the front. These scenes were selected carefully to play upon the sentiments of the Soviet people and to encourage them to sacrifice for the cause.

Such posters were a departure from public art in the tsarist period. In that period, generals and royalty were the typical subjects of public art. With the revolution, the emphasis shifted to common people performing their parts in the successful operation of Soviet society. True to the communist ideal, workers were the most important group, and a great variety of occupations was portrayed. Women appeared prominently in many posters, providing role models for women who might otherwise have felt uncomfortable applying for work in a factory or as a miner.

The widespread use of posters extended well past the violent overthrow of the government and lasted throughout the process of revolution. During the establishment of the Soviet government, posters focused particularly on political and economic themes, using these to inspire support.

[3] **Kimigayo:** kee mee GY oh

FIGURE 43.2 ***Diego Rivera Mural.*** *In the early twentieth century, Diego Rivera and his fellow Mexican muralists decided that art should be rendered on public walls, where it would be available to both the poor and rich alike. This mural by Rivera presents a panorama of Mexican history from pre-Columbian to modern times.* Enrique Franco-Torrijos.

During periods of internal or external military challenges, posters tended to place greater emphasis on military and political issues. During calm times when the government was trying to promote social and economic development of the society, economic and cultural themes were dominant. The use of posters as a recognized arm of the state continued in the Soviet Union through the late 1970s, although they had lost much of their impact by the 1950s.

Mexican Mural Art

Mural art—the painting of pictures on walls—stretches back into Mexican prehistory, at least back to around A.D. 350. Modern Mexico shares this interest in wall painting, and many walls throughout Mexico bear marvelous murals. The tradition of mural painting is not unbroken from antiquity, however, and the twentieth-century boom in mural art traces back only to 1922.

The Mexican Revolution beginning in 1910 was a reaction to the elitist, antipeasant, anti-Indian policy of the Mexican government. By 1917, the revolutionaries had replaced the government, and there was a feeling that true social change would follow. In this atmosphere, a group of artists in 1922 decided that they should stop painting pictures on canvas to be sold to rich people; instead, they should paint scenes glorifying the common people of Mexico and the national past, and these should be painted on public walls, where all could appreciate them. Painters like Diego Rivera[4] (1886–1957) and José Orozco[5] led the way, and thousands of murals were the result.

[4] **Diego Rivera:** dee AY goh ree VAYR ah
[5] **José Orozco:** hoh SAY oh ROHS koh

UNDER THE LENS

Pre-Columbian Mexican Murals

Ancient Mexican Indians faced the walls of their temples and palaces with plaster and placed beautiful murals there. The best-preserved of these are at the ancient city of Teotihuacán, just north of Mexico City, and at the ancient Mayan site of Bonampak.

At Teotihuacán, the dry climate has preserved murals dating back to around A.D. 350. In these murals, physicians heal the sick, athletes play the ritual ball game that was both entertainment and worship, and fortunate souls cavort in the heaven of Tlaloc, the rain god. In the heaven scene, some people dance with linked hands, others play games with marbles, and swimmers frolic in abundant water. Trees, flowers, and butterflies are everywhere, and over it all rules the conventionalized representation of Tlaloc, with his blue feather headdress.

At Bonampak, different styles prevailed, and scenes were mostly of the rendering of homage. Subject peoples form lines to present tribute to a ruler, and rulers present offerings to the gods. Unlike the cavorting Teotihuacán figures, most of the Mayans stand rigidly upright with a standardized formal pose. This pose reveals a profile with a forehead that slants back, a curved nose, and a pendulous lip. These characteristics were used by the ancient Mayans to distinguish themselves from other ethnic groups in their paintings.

The Mexican muralists of the twentieth century created a new mural style, but they self-consciously incorporated elements from these ancient styles into their works. Diego Rivera's medical murals juxtapose ancient medical practices from Teotihuacán with modern medical clinics; the ancient gods from Tlaloc's heaven mingle and talk with Jesus and Christian saints, and their faces include both the slanted Mayan ones from Bonampak and the angular ones from Teotihuacán. His characters have ornamental curves emanating from their mouths, speech scrolls that were the conventional symbol representing vocalizations in ancient Mexican art. And personified Death, with a hollow skull and flowing robes, often stalked the inhabitants of murals, reflecting the prominence of death in both ancient Mexican and medieval Spanish folk culture. For Rivera and his contemporaries, the use of both Native American and Spanish imagery was critical to the creation of a national style of mural art.

The murals are in varying styles, but they have many common characteristics. All are more or less realistic, in recognition that highly abstract styles might be difficult for untrained citizens to appreciate. Themes emphasized a distinctive Mexican past and present, underscoring that the challenges of today are little different from those of the Mexican past.

These murals have inspired generations of Mexican muralists, and the tradition has flowed over the border into areas of the United States with large Mexican American populations. Diego Rivera and others painted murals in Chicago and San Francisco, and these inspired Mexican American artists to produce murals in the same style. The early murals are a blend of fine and popular art, but many of the later murals are truly folk art, with untrained amateurs producing beautiful and culturally meaningful works of art for passersby to appreciate. At both periods the murals have served to stimulate a sense of national and ethnic pride.

Fighting Ducks and Blazing Buzzards

The potential of films for fantasy was quickly appreciated by filmmakers, and the first animated cartoons appeared in the 1890s. They truly came into their own as popular formats in the 1930s, when depression-era melancholy in the Western countries could be chased away by an afternoon at a cinema, which necessarily included at least one cartoon. In the United States, Walt Disney, Warner Bros., and a few others produced the vast majority of cartoons, and they were widely distributed to theaters. Since then, they have been broadcast over television thousands of times, finding new generations of audiences.

One of the mainstays of American commercial cartoon films was unrestrained yet impotent violence. A pudgy fellow might be shot from a cannon and flattened against a brick wall, but after a suitably humorous sequence of reconstituting himself, he would be as good as ever. Cartoon characters were shot, stabbed, minced, blown up, and crushed on a regular basis, but their demises always were short-lived. In fact, it was critical to revive the characters to avoid distressing the younger members of the audience.

When the United States entered World War II, however, some cartoon films changed drastically. No longer mere entertainment, they became vehicles for promoting patriotism and national pride through the use of war plots. In some cartoons, characters made jokes about ration books, victory gardens, and other wartime emergency measures; these were interspersed throughout stories that otherwise were of the same nature as before the war. But other cartoons depicted the war itself, either directly or through a metaphor, and in these cartoons violence took on a more serious aspect.

FIGURE 43.3 ***Satire of Hitler.*** *This poster, titled "And Yet It Moves!," is a collage by John Heartfield, a German artist so disenchanted with Nazi Germany that he moved to England and adopted an English name. Its portrayal of Hitler as a sword-wielding ape on top of the world illustrates both Heartfield's contempt for Nazism and the power of art to make a political point.* Kunstsammlung, Stiftung Archiv der Akademie der Künste Berlin (Heartfield Archiv).

Cartoons depicted Germany's Adolf Hitler and Japan's General Tojo fairly regularly, and, after plot maneuverings, these cartoons invariably ended with a bomb falling on the villain. Other cartoons showed peaceful families of ducks swimming along or flying in V-shaped formations. Unprovoked, a squadron of buzzards would swoop down on them, sometimes firing machine guns or dropping bombs, and sometimes killing ducks. The buzzards typically would be shown with German-style helmets or with swastika armbands. After a suitable period of carnage, a hero would emerge, take to the air, and shoot down the villainous buzzards. They dropped, usually in flames.

These cartoons violated a basic convention of the genre: the invulnerability of the characters in the face of violence. Innocent victims sometimes died, and the villains almost always did. There were no resurrections in these cartoons, and viewers must have been moved by this. In the name of patriotism, cartoons were turned into propaganda vehicles to fuel support of the Allied cause in World War II.

Samurai Films in Japan

Historic dramas are a longstanding genre in Japanese drama, set in periods before the Meiji industrialization and Westernization of Japan. The film versions of these dramas, ***jidai-geki***[6] in Japanese, became popular in the 1950s and continue so through today. Most of these films are set in the shogunate period and portray proud *samurai*, down on their luck but retaining their honor. They are presented a virtuous task to complete, and the film depicts their attempts to do so.

One of the most famous of these films is *The Seven Samurai*, directed by Akira Kurosawa[7]

[6] ***jidai-geki:*** JEE dy GEHK ee

[7] **Akira Kurosawa:** ah KEE rah koo roh SAH wah

(b. 1929) and produced in 1952. In this film, a peasant village is terrorized by nearly 100 bandits who are trying to exact tribute, and the peasants try to hire *samurai* to protect them. The amount they can offer is too little to attract the *samurai*, who are, however, moved by the peasants' plight, and seven *samurai* set out to defend the village. As the plot advances, the *samurai* (assisted by the peasants, whom they have trained) fight skillfully and bravely, and the number of bandits is reduced; but so is the number of *samurai*. Finally, in a climactic scene, the *samurai* destroy the remaining bandits, but only two *samurai* survive. They muse that they may have won that day but that the fighters are always the losers.

Jidai-geki reflect many facets of postwar Japan. They underscore the tragedy of violence, but even more they present an image of a glorious and honorable past, desirable at the conclusion of an unsuccessful and brutal war. By stressing pre-Western themes, they are an act of passive rebellion against the Allied occupation of Japan from 1945 to 1952; the stress on violent military action contrasts markedly with the demilitarized government forced upon Japan by the terms of surrender in World War II.

Reggae's Message

Jamaica, the Caribbean country widely known for its resorts and foreign tourists, also is a country of abject poverty. Out of that poverty arose a form of popular music that was initially nationalistic but since has become an anti-imperialist symbol around the world.

In the 1950s, Jamaica had its home-grown African American music, calypso. It had a long tradition as a folk music, but it came to be associated with the sedate version played for tourists in expensive resorts. In the 1960s, influenced heavily by American rock-and-roll artists, many young Jamaicans developed a new form of music: reggae.[8] **Reggae** is a form of African Caribbean music, heavily influenced by American blues and rock and roll, with a distinctive rhythm that emphasizes the second beat of a measure.

The rhythm is catchy and good to dance to, but the appeal of reggae goes far beyond its musical virtues. The home of reggae is Trenchtown, a poor neighborhood of Kingston. There, such reggae artists as Bob Marley (1945–1981), Peter Tosh (1944–1987), and Bunny Wailer (b. 1945) adopted a political philosophy and lifestyle to accompany their music.

The sociopolitical wing of reggae was **Rastafarianism**, a movement dedicated to revitalizing pride in African heritage among Jamaicans and achieving racial equality. The first Rastafarians ("Rastas," for short) appeared in 1930, when Haile Selassie[9] was crowned emperor of Ethiopia, becoming the first native African national ruler since the conquest of Africa by European imperialists. Emperor Selassie was known as Ras Tafari ("Governor Tafari") before being crowned emperor, and it is from this title that Rastafarians derived their name. Rastafarians saw his ascension to the throne of Ethiopia as a symbol of the coming political and economic freedom for Africans in Africa and abroad.

The political climate of the 1960s transformed Rastafarianism. Drawing on freedom movements in Africa, the civil rights movement in the United States, and radical political movements (particularly in the United States), Rastafarians became more pressing in their demands. They believed the Jamaican government to be a relic of imperialism and Jamaica to still be in a neocolonial status, a place where ethnic minorities were systematically exploited and accorded little power in governance. Accordingly, they called for expanded political freedoms, economic development leading to financial independence, and recognition of Jamaica's African heritage.

These demands were championed by performers who had achieved superstar status in Jamaica (and sometimes abroad) through their reggae. Concerts might draw more than 100,000 fans, and the power of charismatic performers to move crowds is well known. The Jamaican government became very concerned that Rastafarianism might be a threat to security. At the same time, reggae lyrics began incorporating overt political messages, such as these phrases from "Get Up Stand Up" by Peter Tosh:

> Get up stand up, stand up for your rights.
> Get up stand up, don't give up the fight.
> . . . .
> And half the history has never been told.
> And now that children have seen the light
> They're gonna stand up for their rights.

[8] **reggae:** RAY gay

[9] **Haile Selassie:** HY lee sah LAHS ee

Such apparent calls to resistance and sometimes violence scared the government and police of Jamaica. Attempts to reconcile differences and mollify reggae activists were largely successful, although one performer, Peter Tosh, resisted these attempts. After several threats and one earlier attack, Tosh was murdered. While the police concluded that the murderer was an unidentified burglar, many people believe this was a political assassination.

In addition to their political views, Rastafarians advocated a form of life based partly on a return to nature. The supreme spirit, Jah, was said to inhabit all things, and reverence demanded that devout Rastafarians respect all living things. There were rules for the proper roles of men and women, advocacy of the use of marijuana (*ganja*) as a ritual drug, and expected standards of dress, including the signature male "dreadlocks," long hair crushed together into braidlike strands.

Reggae went through many changes in the late 1980s. Both Bob Marley and Peter Tosh, the greatest stars of the genre, had died, and a new generation of artists had arrived. The newer artists were less interested in political action and Rastafarianism, and the militant aspect of reggae abated.

FIGURE 43.4 ***Bob Marley in Concert.*** *Bob Marley (1945–1981), Jamaican singer, songwriter, and guitarist and the best known of all reggae artists, performs in front of a portrait of Haile Selassie. Selassie, also known as Ras Tafari, was the Ethiopian emperor who inspired Rastafarianism, a religious-cultural movement that originated in 1930s Jamaica. Marley's music expressed his commitment to Rastafarianism and the politics of nonviolence; the scale of his success brought his message to an international audience.* Peter Simon.

But the global influence of reggae remains. In a small village in Bolivia, on an Indian reservation in Arizona, along the street in any African city—a visitor can still hear the first wave of reggae with Marley, Tosh, and Wailer. While reggae no longer is the most popular style of pop music in Paris or Berlin, it is prominent throughout most of the Third World.

What is the attraction? First, this is Third World music. It was developed, written, and performed by individuals unaffiliated with the United States or any other industrialized power. While it arose out of nationalism, it has evolved into an agent of internationalism. Second, in many cases, it fuels African pride with its focus on Ras Tafari, its overt African orientation, and its African American performers. Even among non-African communities of the Third World, the focus on oppressed ethnic minorities is welcome. Third, it reflects values that resonate in many Third World societies: reverence for the land and living things, faith in a god, and a rejection of aspects of Western-style society. Fourth, the overt message of pride and the achievement of equality strikes a chord among many people around the world. Reggae is the international music of the oppressed.

INNOVATION

The pattern has recurred over and over again in nineteenth- and twentieth-century Europe, just as it had (to a lesser extent) in the seventeenth and eighteenth centuries. An artist in one of the fine arts has striven to develop a new style, a new message, or a new mode of expression. Finally succeeding in doing so, the artist presents this new kind of art to the world and is savaged by critics and public alike. The new art has succeeded too well in its goal: It is so different from its predecessors that consumers are unable to appreciate it.

Examples of this phenomenon abound in the fine arts of the Western tradition. One critic declared in 1854 that Franz Liszt, the great Romantic composer, was an ignoramus who clearly was unaware of what constituted the "correct" structure for a sonata, completely missing the point that Liszt was trying to reformulate the genre of sonatas to make it more flexible. When impressionist painting first appeared in France of the 1870s, it was ridiculed as "just a batch of daubs and paint blobs"; impressionists were forced to organize their own shows because established galleries would not handle their works. In 1913, a ballet called "The Rite of Spring" was produced in Paris; it was created by some of the greatest artists of the age, with music by Igor Stravinsky, choreography by Vaslav Nijinsky, and sets by Erté. Despite the all-star production team, the ballet was interrupted by laughter and catcalls from the audience, resulting ultimately in a riot between supporters and detractors. Critics maintained that the music was inharmonious and without discernible melody and that the dancing was merely awkward jumping around.

What these and many other cases have in common is that these artistic ideas, works, and movements were reviled when they were new but since then have been praised and declared great. The genius in these works led to their acceptance by critics and public alike, but only after some time had passed, allowing these people to become accustomed to their artistically radical new ideas.

What led artists to such drastic breaks with tradition, breaks that made their works initially unpalatable and unpopular? Three factors probably are most responsible:

- increased value placed on creativity, imagination, and intellectual stimulation;
- the progressive ideology; and
- artists' desires to distinguish themselves.

The increased importance of creativity, imagination, and intellectual stimulation often meant that some of the elements traditionally valued in art had to be sacrificed. Beauty, for example, had been a traditional yardstick of artistic success, but the innovators of the nineteenth and twentieth centuries increasingly were ready to jettison attractiveness if doing so meant a more creative, imaginative, or stimulating piece. In essence, the mental process of figuring out a work of art became increasingly dominant over the emotional process of enjoying it.

The progressive ideology of the nineteenth century contributed to this process as well. The basic tenet of progressivism is that improvement naturally arises out of change; consequently, any action that produces change is a step toward improvement. Innovation for innovation's sake was promoted by this ideology. In fact, innovation came to be perceived by many elite devotees of the arts as the litmus test for good art.

Finally, artists came to see themselves in a somewhat different light from their predecessors. In earlier centuries, artists were conceived first and foremost as skilled practitioners, persons whose manual and visual skills permitted them to produce well-crafted works of beauty; in the nineteenth century, artists began to be seen more as intellectual creators who devised new approaches to creating art. Being a mere practitioner of art was to risk being labeled as uncreative or derivative. The way to make one's name was to create a new style, not just to create works within a previously established style.

The fine arts in the past two centuries therefore have placed an ever-increasing value on innovation among artists, even at the risk of producing art that has little or no audience. Few in the public have the appropriate training to appreciate some cutting-edge works of art, and most have little interest in working hard to appreciate a work of art that may be neither attractive nor easily understandable. As a result, many modern musical compositions have never been played to an audience, galleries showing avant-garde paintings may have few visitors, and the circulation of modern poetry magazines remains small. In this sense, the fine arts have become attuned to a smaller intellectual elite than at any time in the previous five centuries.

The arts in the twentieth century became far more stylistically diverse than in any earlier time. Greatly divergent approaches were tolerated and encouraged. At the same time that Stravinsky was experimenting with dissonance and unusual rhythms, Edward Elgar was composing lyrical melodies and lush harmonies along more traditional lines; while Pablo Picasso was reducing people and objects to geometric forms, Georgia O'Keefe was painting realistic animal skulls in the desert setting of the American Southwest. This diversity makes it impossible to select a few examples that adequately represent the diversity of art in this period. Nonetheless, the examples that follow provide some idea of the range of innovation that has been tolerated and encouraged in the past century.

John Cage, the Prepared Piano, and the Organization of Sound

Prior to the twentieth century, classical music had seen its innovators, but the differences between their innovative music and that against which they were reacting, seen from the perspective of today, were quite small. In the twentieth century, however, the degree of difference between traditional forms of classical music and avant-garde forms became far greater. Some composers, such as Arnold Schoenberg, rejected the time-honored European system of harmony or even any system of harmony; others, like Lou Harrison, abandoned traditional modes of rhythm and its notation; still others, like Erik Satie, incorporated unusual sounds, like those of typewriters and shower hoses, into their music. One of the most innovative of these avant-garde composers was John Cage.

John Cage (1912–1992) was the son of an inventor, and he often considered himself an artistic inventor. After a brief stay in college, he dropped out to travel in Europe. He was largely self-taught in music and was acknowledged as extremely well read in a wide variety of fields, ranging from architecture to fungal botany. He first published musical compositions in 1932, and he remained productive through the rest of his life.

Cage was perfectly capable of writing beautiful music in more traditional styles, and some of his early works were of this sort. He preferred, however, to stretch the borders of music with new sounds, new ideas, and new forms. In fact, he redefined music as "the organization of sound," opening the door to all sorts of sounds not usually conceived of as musical.

Cage's first radically new piece was "Bacchanale," written in 1938 for what he called the **prepared piano**. The pianist was instructed to place various articles among the strings of the piano, resulting in buzzing, clunking, and whirring sounds during the performance. These sounds were largely unpredictable, varying from performance to performance, and most listeners found them unattractive. Cage's point, however, was not to make beautiful music but to make interesting music, and one way to make it interesting was to integrate new sounds into it.

In 1942, Cage published "Credo in Us," a percussion piece that incorporated either a radio or a record player, producing unpredictable sounds that interwove with the more programmed percussion rhythms. He carried this idea further in 1955 with "Speech," wherein several radios were tuned to different stations, and the resulting chance combination of sounds constituted the musical performance. Perhaps his most controversial work came in 1952 with "4'33"," a performance of 4 min-

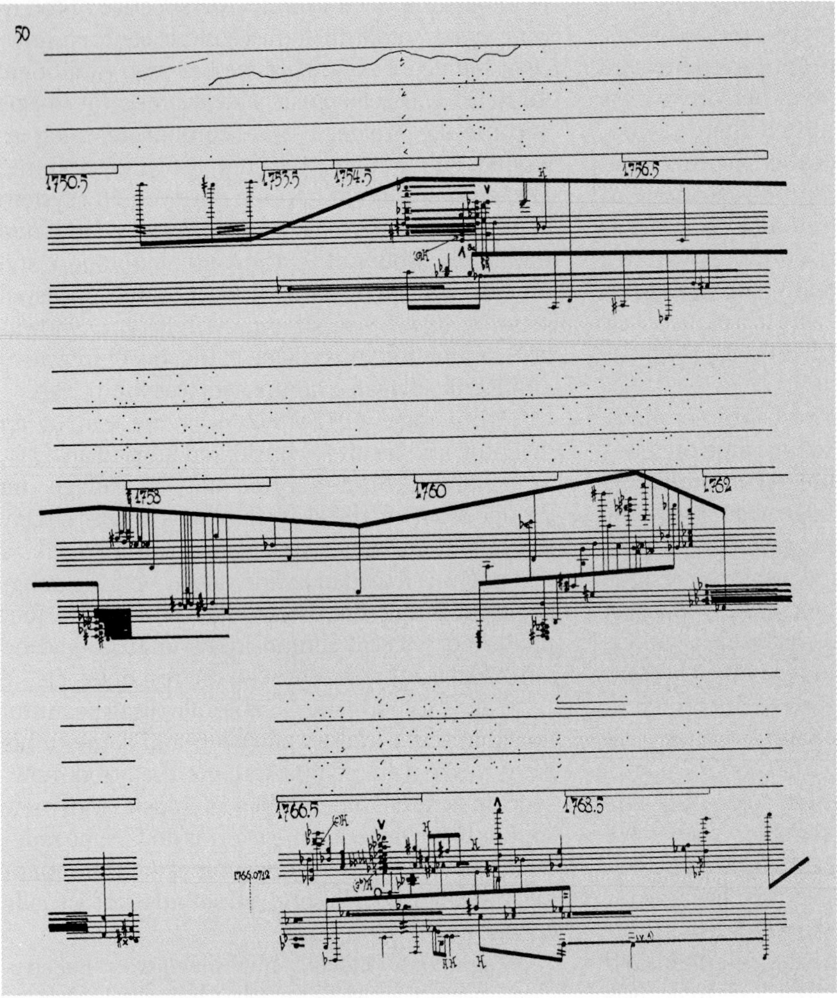

FIGURE 43.5 *John Cage Score.* *This page from Cage's* 34'46.776 *shows his disdain for convention. While the staffs and notes are reminiscent of those in standard musical usage, the score cannot be read traditionally, forcing the performer to interpret what is intended. Such purposeful confusion makes the piece radically different each time it is played.* ©1960 by Henmar Press Inc., 373 Park Avenue South, New York, N.Y. 10016.

utes and 33 seconds in which a performer sat on stage with any instrument, as silent as possible.

Needless to say, Cage received considerable negative reaction to many of his works. Some critics ridiculed him, and his concerts drew sparse audiences. Much of his music was damned because it required no skill to perform (and, some said, none to compose), and his detractors accused him of indulging in stunts in order to attract public attention. Yet he is considered a major figure in modern classical music. What makes John Cage worth examining?

Cage said, in effect, that there has been enough beautiful music composed. He was interested, rather, in expanding the world's vision of music beyond the attractive to include, potentially, every sound, no matter how ugly, dissonant, or grating. By having an audience listen to supposed silence, he felt that they would realize the wealth of sounds occurring during what is conventionally considered soundlessness. Because all sounds were equal to Cage, it mattered little that these sounds were ordinary or unattractive or outside the musician's control.

What mattered above all else to John Cage was to do something new. Attractiveness of the piece was to be sacrificed for raw originality; Cage's music was designed to appeal not to the spirit or to the senses but to the mind. As he wrote about his music, "Whenever I've found that what I'm doing has become pleasing, even to one person, I have redoubled my efforts to find the next step." To

Cage, music was a means of stretching the mind to experiment with new ideas, a set of progressive inventions, each farther from the starting point than the last. The result was a body of music intentionally placed as far from the historical continuum of fine arts music as the composer could put it, marking a major break in the Western musical tradition.

Abstract Expressionism

One of the more influential of twentieth-century fine art painting styles was **abstract expressionism**, a style characterized by an attempt to abandon previous artistic conventions and to emphasize the spontaneous, personal, free, unstudied, and intuitive aspects of art. Sometimes this meant abandoning planning and control and permitting chance to play a significant role in the production of the painting, much as chance played a role in some of Cage's music.

Abstract expressionist painters emphasized abstraction, the reduction of an image to simpler elements the artist considers most essential. The subjects of abstract expressionist paintings might be real objects or persons, but they are presented in a manner that makes them difficult to recognize. Alternatively, an abstract expressionist painting might be nonrepresentational, making no effort to depict anything more than a design.

There were two primary schools of painting within abstract expressionism. One, **action painting**, featured slashes of paint intersecting on a canvas; the other, **field painting**, used featureless and often overlapping masses of colors. Action painting was the earlier and led to field painting.

The pioneer of action painting was Jackson Pollock (1912–1956). Pollock was born in Idaho and raised in southern California, and some critics commented that his paintings had the grandeur and scale of the American West. He attended art school in New York and learned technique there,

FIGURE 43.6 ***Jackson Pollock in Action.*** *Jackson Pollock, an abstract expressionist known for his use of spontaneous techniques, would often hurl gobs of paint with his hands or sling paint from a brush whipped near the canvas. In this 1949 photo, Pollock experiments with different media.* Martha Holmes, *Life* Magazine, © 1949, Time Inc.

but his art remained relatively unaffected by contemporary artistic styles.

Pollock's early work in the 1930s depicted places and things, mostly people, in manners that were easily recognizable. By the 1940s, however, he increasingly was distorting his representations, and by the late 1940s he had abandoned all attempts to depict physical objects. Instead, he practiced action painting, hovering over large canvases and hurling dollops of paint at them from a swung brush. The resulting lines of paint intersected one another at various angles, partly determined by Pollock's planning but increasingly determined by chance. A sarcastic comment in the press dubbed Pollock "Jack the Dripper."

Pollock's devotion to action painting grew in part out of his absorption with violence. He was fond of barroom fisticuffs and idolized the semi-violent rebel-heroes of 1950s American films, such as Marlon Brando in *On the Waterfront*. By hurling paint, he felt that he was playing out his personal involvement with violence. Because art, in Pollock's conception, was a purely personal experience, the result had to be interesting to the artist.

And others found Pollock's art interesting. Many critics raved over it, some proclaiming him the greatest living artist. While most of the public was mystified by his art, wealthy clients bought it in quantities that permitted him a comfortable livelihood.

The second school of abstract expressionism, field painting, was pioneered by Willem de Kooning[10] (1904–1997). Born in the Netherlands but living most of his life in the United States, de Kooning discovered abstract expressionism and began working in it in the 1950s. His version was more cerebral and planned than Pollock's, prompting Pollock to say to de Kooning: "You know more, but I feel more."

Most of de Kooning's art depicts things, usually people, though they are reduced to masses of color. (See full-color illustration on p. A-32.) Sometimes a painting will be simply masses of flat color, emphasizing pure design and depicting nothing. His art usually is conceived of as more quiet and deliberate than that of Pollock.

Abstract expressionism was popular only from the late 1940s to the early 1960s, but it left a mark on modern painting. Just as Pablo Picasso's abstract art had taken a turn away from traditional painting styles of the 1920s, abstract expressionism signaled a radical departure from the evolution based on earlier forms, opening the door for all sorts of future innovations. Further, it marked the beginning of serious attention to American painters in international art.

[10] **Willem de Kooning:** WIHL ehm duh KOHN ihng

Free Verse

Of all the forms of Western literature, poetry in the sixteenth and seventeenth centuries clearly was the one most constrained by conventions of structure and form. Poems were of various named kinds, such as the English sonnet and the ballad, each of which was expected to meet certain requirements. An English sonnet, for example, was supposed to have fourteen lines, divided into three sets of four lines and a concluding pair; each of these sets of lines was expected to present a complete idea; each line was to have a meter, specifically to be made up of ten syllables, with every other syllable accented, starting with the second; the lines were supposed to rhyme with a pattern of *abab-cdcd-efef-gg*, wherein each letter represents a particular ending syllable of a line. These combined requirements placed sonnet writing under a daunting set of restrictions.

Poets from the seventeenth century onward tinkered with poetic forms, creating new ones, modifying old ones, and occasionally working outside the forms. It was only in the nineteenth century, however, that some poets stepped outside the forms altogether and created **free verse**: poetry that self-consciously avoided the traditional conventions of meter, rhyme, and structure. The first free verse was written by Walt Whitman (1819–1892), the American poet, in *Leaves of Grass*, published in 1855. Whitman introduced stanzas like:

> Has anyone supposed it lucky to be born?
> I hasten to inform him or her, it is just as lucky to
> die, and I know it.

Such verses flew in the face of traditional poetry: They had no rhyme, no discernible pattern of accented syllables, and irregular numbers of syllables per line. This freedom from predetermined structure is the essence of free verse.

IN THEIR OWN WORDS

"There Are Some Men"

Leonard Cohen is a contemporary Canadian poet who writes in free verse and other styles. The poem presented here, "There Are Some Men," is a tribute to a deceased friend written in free verse. It has five stanzas, each with a different number of lines; lines vary from two to ten syllables and have no regular pattern of accents; there is no rhyme. By rejecting these elements, Cohen frees himself to focus on creating a personal statement, individual in every particular, to memorialize his dead friend.

> There are some men
> who should have mountains
> to bear their names to time.
>
> Grave-markers are not high enough
> or green,
> and sons go far away
> to lose the fist
> their father's hand will always seem.
>
> I had a friend:
> he lived and died in mighty silence
> and with dignity,
> left no book, son, or lover to mourn.
>
> Nor is this a mourning-song
> but only a naming of this mountain
> on which I walk,
> fragrant, dark, and softly white
> under the pale of mist.
> I name this mountain after him.

As might be expected, Whitman's poetry was seen as radical and was greeted with considerable initial critical condemnation. The idea of free verse, however, was greeted with enthusiasm by some poets and critics, including Gustave Kahn, a French poet who in the 1880s coined the term and wrote a manifesto of how free verse would remove the fetters of poets. By 1900, free verse was well established and accepted among poets and poetry lovers, and it permitted new generations of poets to stretch the limits of the medium.

Generalizations are difficult with a medium as diverse and unconstrained as free verse, but it is fair to say that most free verse writers use the freedom from repetitive structure to create emphasis. A single word that stands out from the rest of the poem, for example, takes on special significance and begs the reader to pay special attention to it. This poem by E. E. Cummings, published in 1923, illustrates this well:

```
Buffalo Bill 's
defunct
          who used to
          ride a watersmooth-silver
                                        stallion
and break onetwothreefourfive pigeonsjustlikethat
                         Jesus
he was a handsome man . . .
```

Other poets have taken the idea of arranging words into visually interesting patterns even further, as when the words of a poem create the visual image of a bird's feather or a man smoking a cigar. Modern poets continue to develop new devices for presenting their art.

ALIENATION

Traditionally, the arts were expected to be uplifting, to provide a beautiful insight into reality. Consequently, the subjects and themes of art were primarily pleasant, attractive, and enjoyable. In the second half of the twentieth century, this changed dramatically. Literature and drama often focused on antiheroes, characters who had a certain charisma but were less than exemplary in their behavior or morals. Increasingly, stories ended unhappily and good characters remained unrewarded for their virtue. A cynic might contend that this view of life is more realistic than the one traditionally propounded, but it also represents a reorientation of the arts.

Many critics see this as a reflection of profound alienation in the twentieth century. Dissatisfaction with the wars, inequalities, and tragedies

FIGURE 43.7 ***Scene from* Une Si Jolie Petite Plage.** *This typical example of* film noir *features jaded cynics confronting one another and their collective depression. This genre developed out of the profound alienation of the era following World War II in Europe.* Museum of Modern Art, Film Stills Archive.

of the past has led many people to reject whatever they view as part of the historical baggage of the century. "Beatniks," "hippies," "punks," and others have been explicit about their alienation from and rejection of the societies they inherited, but other artists usually have encoded their rejection into their work.

Postwar Films

The medium of the film is ideally suited to popular arts. On the one hand, creating a film is a fairly expensive endeavor; on the other hand, the finished film can be easily reproduced for mass viewing. The two factors, coupled with the historic allure of the film to audiences, have made films in the twentieth century an ideal way to project ideas to a mass audience or to draw on that audience's sympathies and anxieties. While many of the filmmakers after World War II were trained in the fine arts, their films—largely for economic reasons—were typically directed toward mass audiences.

LE FILM NOIR. France had developed a successful film industry prior to World War II, an industry that had turned out a wide range of films, including historical dramas, comedies, sex farces, and the like. The devastation of war and enemy occupation, however, had throttled the French film industry, and, in the 1950s, France was trying to rebuild it. In this rebuilding period, many of its talented directors turned to a new genre.

This genre, known as ***le film noir***[11] ("the dark film"), focused on the dark, pessimistic, and gloomy side of life. One film of this genre is *Une Si Jolie Petite Plage* ("Such a Pretty Little Beach," 1948), directed by Yves Allégret.[12] The standard film blurb (used in movie descriptions in television guides) for this film describes it as follows:

> A murderer returns to the small seaside town where he spent his childhood, befriends the maid at the hotel, and after a few days kills himself.

[11] ***le film noir:*** luh feelm nwahr
[12] **Yves Allégret:** eev ahl ay GRAY

There is little that is cheerful in *film noir*. While many *films noirs* were critical and box-office successes in France, their gloomy nature was less popular with moviegoing audiences abroad.

Film noir is a logical outgrowth of **existentialism**, a philosophical movement linked to such thinkers as Jean-Paul Sartre[13] (1905–1980). Existentialism posits that the greatest problem facing anyone is existence itself, that reason and good intentions will not be enough to explain why things happen as they do, and that anguish at the failure to control the course of one's life is to be expected. Although its intellectual roots go back to prewar times, existentialism attained its greatest appeal in postwar France.

The appeal of existentialism to a war-ravaged France is obvious: It freed the victims from the obligation of trying to understand why they had suffered so greatly. According to existentialism, suffering is the natural state of humanity, and one's personal suffering—while perhaps intense and devastating—is only one share of the great misery of humanity as a whole. *Film noir* focused on and glorified suffering, making it the central theme. The pervasiveness of existentialism in the French film industry of the 1950s is evidenced by the fact that French critics of the period referred to *film noir* as "realism." *Film noir* gave audiences a means to acknowledge and accept their misfortune, providing an outlet for alienation.

GODZILLA AND MONSTER ISLAND. Just as in France, the film industry in Japan during the 1950s was trying to rebuild from the devastation of World War II. One of the successful genres of films developed in Japan during this period was the monster film. These films in almost every way are the opposite of the *samurai* dramas of *jidai-geki*. While *jidai-geki* are dramatic and very serious, monster films are light and usually provide abundant humorous moments. *Jidai-geki* typically attract the most acclaimed actors in Japan, while monster films usually attract less famous and less esteemed actors. While *jidai-geki* often are written with considerable literary skill, monster films are more likely to be written quickly and with little attention to symbolism or eloquence, lending them a "cartoonish" feel.

[13] **Jean-Paul Sartre:** zhahn pohl SAHR truh

But monster films still tell a great deal about postwar Japan. The most famous of them all, *Godzilla* (1956), features a dinosaurlike monster that is freed by an earthquake from a lava flow where it has been trapped for unknown eons. It then descends on Tokyo for no apparent reason, wreaking havoc as it goes. All attempts to destroy Godzilla fail, and it continues its rampage, making loud honking noises and tearing down buildings and power lines. Eventually, however, Godzilla simply goes away. Later films in the same series reveal other monsters, many of which live on Monster Island, and they take on varying positive and negative roles as they attempt to destroy Japan or protect it from other monsters. Many of these monsters were prompted to violence by American nuclear testing in the Pacific; in later years, some were aroused by air pollution, global warming, or increased ultraviolet radiation resulting from the humanly induced breakdown of the atmospheric ozone layer.

Japan is the only country to have felt the effects of nuclear weapons in war, and the Japanese have a unique appreciation of the magnitude of destruction that they produce. Monster films offer another version of utter destruction, sometimes unleashed by natural forces but more often released by unwise human use of the planet. Once set in motion, these processes cannot be controlled by human technology or effort. On the one hand, monster movies reflect a fatalism, recognizing that devastation may occur at any time; they reflect an alienation born of nuclear destruction, military defeat, and humiliation. On the other hand, they serve as a warning that human actions can easily result in unforeseen and destructive consequences.

Punk Rock, Grunge Rock, and Their Allies

From the 1960s onward, popular music has included some form of music that springs from the alienation and uncertainties of modern life. These have been variously known in different periods as "punk rock," "grunge rock," and other terms; the details of style have changed over the years, but the message has remained the same: The world is horrible, so all that is left is to have a good time.

These forms of music are not particularly distinctive musically, developing out of mainstream

FIGURE 43.8 ***Sid Vicious and Johnny Rotten of the Sex Pistols.*** *Alienation has been a significant theme since the middle of the twentieth century. The Sex Pistols, from their name to their musical style to their performance style, epitomized alienation in the mid-1970s and influenced the music of the 1980s. Their 1976 debut record, "Anarchy in the U.K.," brought punk rock into the mainstream, initiating the public to a genre known for its controversial expression of discontent.* Richard E. Aaron/Sygma.

rock and roll. They usually are characterized by heavy rhythms, simple melodies, and limited harmonies; singing styles are usually powerful, rasping, and coarse, with more interest in emotional effect than in raw beauty. As with so much modern art, the idea is not to produce a beautiful product but to produce an interesting product.

Dominant themes of the lyrics include sex, drugs, and violence, often reflecting a sense of despair. In essence, they say that we all will die soon, so we might as well experience as much sensory pleasure as possible, saving nothing for an uncertain future. Some lyrics focus explicitly on the probability of joblessness, nuclear war, or failed personal relationships. One minority form of this music advocates white supremacy and sometimes violence against other races. Probably no other form of art reflects the alienation of its creators so clearly as this one.

FUSION

As transportation and communication technology have improved over the last few centuries, the world's peoples have been in unprecedented contact with one another. Great distances separating places of residence no longer mean that people will have no knowledge of one another; immigrant communities around the world help make that contact face to face. The artistic result of this contact is **fusion**, the incorporation of ideas from various ethnic and national traditions into art. Fusion has been taking place for centuries, but the twentieth century has seen a quantum jump in the magnitude of fusion in the arts, including folk, popular, and fine arts.

"I Got to Sing the Blues"

No music has been more influential worldwide than that fusion of African and European music which developed in the American South in the centuries following the arrival of African slaves in the American colonies. We have no idea what name was given to this music by its originators in the seventeenth century, but it was ancestor to the blues, jazz, and rock and roll.

When African captives were brought to the Americas as slaves, they brought many elements of their culture with them. Because music was a prominent part of West African life, music was an important piece of culture carried in the minds of slaves. In the Americas, some African songs could be transferred directly, particularly rhythmic work songs that could be used to coordinate group activities in agricultural labor. Slaveholders forbade the practice of African religions by slaves, so African ritual songs had to be recast, but many doubtless resurfaced as Christian hymns and spirituals. New songs were invented using African principles, and some songs blended African and European elements.

There were common elements derived from Africa in most of these songs. Most had powerful rhythms, sometimes incorporating complex syncopations. Many employed call-and-response, an African principle whereby a soloist sings a line and a chorus sings a variant on it. Many melody lines generally ascended and then descended over a couplet or verse, again following a typical African pattern. Some of the harmonies of this music came straight from Africa, but others were borrowed from English or Scottish folk music. (The European population of the early colonial American South was largely of English or Scottish origin.)

Musically speaking, much stayed the same with the conclusion of the U.S. Civil War and the emancipation of the slaves in the United States. African American work parties still went to the fields and still sang the same types of songs; spirituals and hymns remained a prominent part of Christian devotion; and after-work entertainment continued to include music. There was, however, a significant change that had a profound effect on the development of African American music in the South: the barrelhouse.

A barrelhouse was no more than a bar, but in the segregated South of the late nineteenth and early twentieth centuries, a bar could serve only European American or African American customers. The barrelhouses run by and for African American patrons included music by semiprofessional entertainers, and barrelhouses became hotbeds of musical innovation. This setting saw the development of the **blues**, a form of African-inspired music characterized by distinctive rhythms, repetitive structure, and melody lines that generally descended from initial high notes.

Folk artists became popular artists as some found that they could eke a meager living off their music. Blues artists with such colorful names as Leadbelly, Blind Lemon Jefferson, Frankie Jaxon, Ma Rainey, and Cripple Clarence Lofton toured the African American barrelhouse circuit. The life was tough, working late hours in an establishment that focused on drinking and attracted many of the less savory elements of the community. Many a blues performer ended up murdered or in jail.

It was the blues of the barrelhouses that found its way to the cities and sparked the development of **jazz**, a more polished, innovative, and orchestrated outgrowth of blues. While blues focused on inexpensive instruments (guitars, spoons or other rigged-up percussion instruments, and voices), jazz used the whole range of instruments of the popular dance orchestras of the day, especially horns and woodwinds. Blues relied on repetition of moderately simple melodies and harmonies with complex rhythms, but jazz introduced greater complexity of melody, harmony, and especially structure. The greater complexity of jazz often meant that its performers had to be able to read music, while few blues artists had this skill. Both blues and jazz remained true to their African origins, retaining complex rhythms and call-and-response patterns.

Like blues, jazz originally was restricted essentially to African American performers. Jazz's rise in urban areas during the 1910s and 1920s, however, meant that the whole ethnic spectrum of America was exposed to it through clubs, records, and radio. By the 1930s, Americans of European and Asian extraction had joined the ranks of jazz performers. Europeans also listened to jazz, and all major European cities had their jazz clubs; many African American performers found the less racially charged atmosphere of Paris preferable to that of Macon or Memphis. Asia and Africa, particularly South Africa, also had some jazz clubs, although fans there were more likely to listen to jazz on records.

The birth of jazz did not mean the death of the blues. Rather, the blues persisted, largely in rural areas. After World War II, there was something of a revival of interest in blues that led to the development of **rhythm and blues**, an electrified and polished version of the blues, which developed into **rock and roll** in the 1950s. Early rock-and-roll music was mostly written and performed by African American entertainers, but versions (known as "covers") were performed by white musicians for white audiences. Cover versions typically had less prominent rhythms, less strident vocals, and a less emotional feel. Over the decade of the 1950s, however, covers became increasingly less common, and European American and African American versions of rock and roll gradually converged. This became especially so with the introduction of strongly blues-oriented British musicians like Eric Clapton and John Mayall in the 1960s. Rap music of the late twentieth century is a joint outgrowth of rock and roll and the African American oratorical tradition.

Born in the era of sophisticated transportation and communication systems, rock and roll spread

PATHS TO THE PAST

Leadbelly

Huddie Ledbetter was born in 1889 in Louisiana and became a folk blues artist who adopted the stage name of "Leadbelly" and eventually played the African American barrelhouse circuit. By the time of his death in 1949, he had accomplished something very unusual for an African American in that era: He had successfully crossed over into popularity in mainstream American music. While his music has been widely heralded for decades, his life is more controversial.

Some facts are clear. In 1918, he was convicted of manslaughter in a barroom brawl and sent to prison in Louisiana. Paroled in 1925, he was in a Louisiana prison again in 1930 and was paroled again in 1934. He went to New York City in that year and became a sensation as a performer and recorder of his own blues songs. He died a pauper in Bellevue Hospital in 1949.

Beyond these facts, however, it is difficult to find the real Leadbelly. His biography was written by John Lomax, the folk-song collector who managed him. In it, Leadbelly appears as an arrogant, hard-drinking, womanizing, violent man who was attracted to the life of a blues musician because it permitted him to indulge these vices. Lomax is portrayed as his would-be reformer, negotiating Leadbelly's release from prison in Louisiana and trying to assist him in adjusting to New York.

Leadbelly himself rejected this version of his life, saying, "Lomax did not write nothing like I told him." Subsequent historians have raised further doubts. Many of Leadbelly's songs were published under Lomax's name, and it appears that Leadbelly may have been exploited by Lomax and others appearing to befriend him. Certainly Lomax's involvement led to his financial success, while Leadbelly remained impoverished. Leadbelly's imprisonment clearly stemmed from a killing he committed, but it is equally clear that justice fell harder on African American men in the South in that era than on their white neighbors. As to the details of Leadbelly's character, different acquaintances have recorded different impressions.

Out of all this emerges a picture of the blues artist in a difficult world. Doubtless, some artists were attracted to the life because of the freedoms and license it provided, just as others rejected it for the same reasons. It would be difficult, however, to find a single blues artist who never had been cheated, exploited, or manipulated by management. And the life expectancy of the most prominent blues artists of this era was scarcely fifty years, suggestive of a hard life with dire consequences.

around the world. At the end of the twentieth century, virtually every country in the world has its own version of rock and roll. Some versions, like Puerto Rican *salsa*, Afro-Caribbean *zouk*, and Kenyan *benga*, have had influences on popular music internationally.

All of the forms of African American music have served a variety of purposes. Spirituals and gospel music engendered a feeling of community and have been a source of comfort for generations of the devout. The blues, sung as folk music on a back porch after work, provided a psychological release for individuals who were suffering from bad times. Many blues songs and some jazz had risqué lyrics that often carried a sexual meaning to the initiated. These must have provided entertainers with a chuckle, especially when white audiences failed to catch the hidden meanings of "smoking a cigarette" or "what it is that tastes like gravy (I'll betcha don't know)." And all of these forms of music gave professional musicians some level of economic mobility, providing them with a profession that permitted creative work and at least a hope of financial return.

Picasso and African Art

Pablo Picasso (1881–1973) was one of the most innovative and influential artists of the modern era. Predominantly a painter, he developed several styles, but his early work is of greatest interest to us here. Born in Spain, Picasso began his formal art training in Barcelona in 1896 but soon moved to Paris, where he became a sensation.

Figure 43.9 ***African Influence on Picasso's Art.*** *Modernist works by Pablo Picasso, such as his 1907* Bust of a Woman or a Sailor *(left), were profoundly affected by African masks that the painter first saw in the museums of Paris. On the right is a sickness mask from the Pende people of Congo-Zaire. The unmistakable relationship between such masks and his abstractions of human faces was acknowledged by Picasso himself.* *Left:* Art Resource Inc., N.Y. *Right:* ©1994 Africa Museum, Tervuren, Belgium. Photo by Roger Asselberghs.

In Paris, Picasso became entranced with West African masks. Made of wood and designed to be worn during ceremonies, these masks were well represented in Parisian museums, and Picasso studied them intently. He was particularly taken by the way a mask would effect a purposeful geometric distortion of a face. An almond-shaped mask, for example, elongated the face, then sharpened its features, especially at the forehead and chin. Picasso recognized that this kind of distortion of figures could produce interesting visual art, and many of his earlier works were devoted to this. These works were the first step toward the abstraction (simplification and distortion) that was to typify most of Picasso's work in his later years.

Picasso's use of African inspiration occurred in an era when Western artists still considered non-Western art to be "primitive" or simple. Part of Picasso's genius was his recognition that it was merely different. He tapped that difference to enrich his own artistic work, stimulating artists ever since to follow his lead.

Cuban Culinary Fusion

Cooking is not usually considered an art, though chefs regularly refer to the "culinary arts." Nonetheless, it is a creative expression that is as much shaped by its environment as any other art, and it profitably is considered a popular art form, one that frequently shows ethnic fusion.

As Cuban immigrants have streamed into southern Florida (mostly following the communist takeover there in 1959), Miami has become the capital for a new style of food, known variously as "Nuevo Cubano"[14] ("New Cuban") or "Cuban Fusion." Miami's population is equally divided between Latin American immigrants, mostly from Cuba, and native-born Americans of various ethnicities. Restaurateurs began developing Cuban Fusion cuisine in the 1980s, and it is widely eaten now by both Cuban and other Americans.

Cuban Fusion dishes draw on traditional Cuban cooking but are different in several ways. They are generally lighter and less filling than traditional Cuban foods, and they use a wider variety of ingredients. In addition to the black beans, spices, and fruits of Cuban cooking, Cuban Fusion uses luxury items of European cooking, such as caviar, lobster, and salmon; in addition, various Thai and other influences are clear, such as seasoning with fish sauce and garnishing with coriander leaf.

Cuban Fusion cooking can be a delight to the palate, but it has a strong symbolic meaning as well. To the hundreds of thousands of Cuban immigrants in Florida, it says that they are Americans now and have a joint heritage. To the rest of America, it says that Cubans have become a vibrant part of the ethnic mix of the modern United States.

SUMMARY

1. The arts are shaped by the time and setting of the artists who produce them. Consequently, they provide insight into history and society.

2. Folk art is produced by traditional, amateur artists; popular art is produced professionally for a mass audience; fine art is produced professionally for an elite audience.

3. Nationalism has been strongly reflected in the arts from the mid–nineteenth century onward, including in national anthems, revolutionary posters, Mexican mural art, animated cartoons, and Japanese *samurai* films. Romanticism and national styles in fine art music of the Western tradition also have reflected nationalist sentiments. Reggae has a more international message, appealing to oppressed peoples everywhere.

4. Innovation in the fine arts has become increasingly important since the late nineteenth century. Reasons for this have been an elevated evaluation of creativity, imagination, and intellectual stimulation; progressive ideology; and artists' desires to distinguish themselves. This sometimes has meant sacrificing traditionally valued elements such as beauty.

5. John Cage focused on interesting organization of sound, rather than traditional styles of music. Abstract expressionism, as practiced by Jackson Pollock and Willem de Kooning, created highly abstract paintings that contained random elements. Free verse, as pioneered by Walt Whit-

[14] **Nuevo Cubano:** NWAY voh koo BAHN oh

man, abandoned traditional structures of poetry. All of these are examples of artistic innovation.

6. *Film noir* in France, Japanese monster films, and punk (and related) music are examples of the effects of alienation after World War II.

7. Blues, jazz, rock and roll, and fusion cooking are examples of fusion in folk and popular art. Picasso's inspiration by African masks is an example of fusion in fine art.

SUGGESTED READINGS

Armes, Roy. *French Cinema.* New York: Oxford University Press, 1988. Chapter 8 deals with French realism and *film noir.*

Gaugh, Harry F. *Willem de Kooning.* New York: Abbeville Press, 1983. Good critical treatment of de Kooning's art, with good reproductions and some biography.

Govenar, Alan. *Living Texas Blues.* Dallas: Dallas Museum of Art, 1986. A short book tracing the history of blues in Texas, though it is generally applicable to the history of blues everywhere.

Kostelanetz, Richard, ed. *John Cage.* New York: Praeger, 1970. A collection of essays by and about John Cage.

Landau, Ellen G. *Jackson Pollock.* New York: Harry N. Abrams, 1989. There are many Pollock treatments, and this is one of the better combinations of biography, criticism, and good reproductions.

Manuel, Peter. *Popular Musics of the Non-Western World.* Oxford, Eng.: Oxford University Press, 1991. Compendious reference on local and international folk and (especially) popular music styles.

Nicholas, Tracy. *Rastafari: A Way of Life.* Garden City, N.Y.: Anchor Press, 1979. A simple account of Rastafarian beliefs and activities during the first wave of reggae.

Rodríguez, Antonio. *A History of Mexican Mural Painting.* New York: G. P. Putnam's Sons, 1969. Excellent treatment, focusing on Mexican murals in the twentieth century.

White, Stephen. *The Bolshevik Poster.* New Haven: Yale University Press, 1988. By far the most compendious collection and analysis of Bolshevik posters, containing far greater variety than any other treatment.

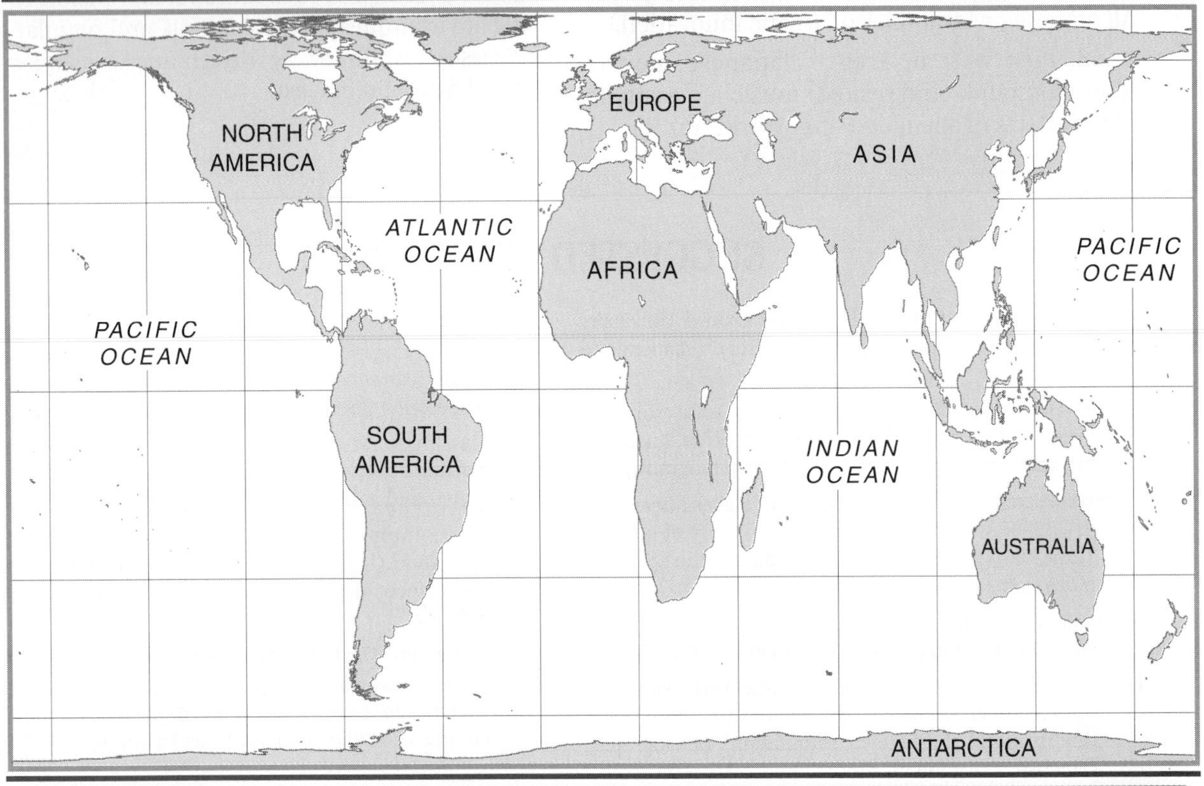

Kuwaiti Oil Fields Aflame. *Iraq invaded Kuwait in 1990, hoping to present the global community with a situation that could not be reversed. A military alliance of Europeans, Americans, and others ousted the Iraqis less than a year later. As the Iraqi Army pulled out, it set ablaze the oil refineries and fields. This act of ecocide, the deliberate destruction of an ecosystem, caused extensive, long-term damage to the surrounding environment. In this picture, an American soldier watches the inferno.* Jim Lukoski/Black Star.

CHAPTER 44

World Integration

In 1988, United Nations peacekeeping soldiers won the Nobel Peace Prize for their humanitarian operations around the world since 1945. This recognition reflected the importance of the United Nations as an international organization dedicated to global rather than national issues. In that sense, the United Nations represents the trend toward world integration in a time of resurgent nationalism.

A fundamental tension between integration and separateness has characterized the modern era. Throughout the modern era, transportation and communication technology have fostered greater connectedness and integration, including commercial links. At the same time, other factors have favored maintenance of local, ethnic, religious, or national identity.

ECONOMIC INTEGRATION AND CHALLENGES

Global economic integration has been a developing process, especially since the sixteenth century. By the early twentieth century, economic relationships had become interdependent, and unilateral actions by a country today often have international consequences. These consequences extend beyond the economic sphere to include political and environmental effects, sometimes global ones.

Economic Integration

Between 1500 and 1750, economic relationships increasingly spanned continents and oceans. The English, for example, established the Russia Company to develop better trade links with Russia, and the East India Company was formed by the English to conduct trade with India, China, and the Americas. The Dutch founded the East Indies Company to promote trade with peoples of the islands of Southeast Asia and Japan. The African slave trade was a significant example of trade between Africa, the Americas, Asia, and Europe. Underlying the growing economic connections were improvements in sailing technology that permitted goods to be more speedily transported.

Regional trade alliances, usually centered on empires, were also formed. Ottoman rulers developed impressive trade links within the area they controlled, as did the Mughals in India. And the Ottomans, Mughals, and Safavid Persians conducted significant interempire land trade. The same could be said about the Ming and Qing empires of China. These decisions by rulers of land empires increasingly left oceanic trade to Europeans, who also had better technology with which to navigate the oceans.

After 1750, the Industrial Revolution propelled the British and other industrializing nations to seek sources of raw materials and markets for finished products. Industrialization also brought increasing wealth and power to industrialists and their countries. Trade agreements were negotiated between Western countries and China, for example, extending trade links to new markets.

In the nineteenth and twentieth centuries, a developing international trade network sparked a standardization process. The metric system, for example, became increasingly accepted as the standard for weights and measures. Similarly, the British pound, which had become the major global currency in the nineteenth century, gave way to the U.S. dollar by the 1920s. French, which had been the accepted language for international diplomacy, has given way to English, which has also become the globally preferred language for scientific discourse, computer networking, and air-traffic control.

After 1500, economic growth and integration spurred the emergence of a prominent middle class in Europe. Merchants and bankers directed the economic transformation, while lawyers, clerks, and physicians benefited from the increasing opportunities to make a reasonable living. During the Industrial Revolution, the middle class became important not only economically but also socially and politically. Opportunities for members of the middle class to enrich themselves were greater in cities; chances for improvement were more limited in rural areas, where land use was often restricted to only a wealthy few.

Urbanization flourished as cities grew in numbers and in spatial area. Cities became more prominent as centers of economic activity, especially during the Industrial Revolution. Pittsburgh, Osaka, and Manchester, for example, developed into commercial and manufacturing centers. Railroad lines, highways, and airports increasingly integrated cities like these into a global trade network.

Beginning in the twentieth century, a series of political and economic crises rocked the international trade system, threatening economic integration. World War I weakened the economic power of the Europeans while strengthening the United States and Japan. Imperialist powers relied on their colonial domains as market areas free of international competition. World War II shattered the economic strength of most Western countries and Japan. Only the United States and the Soviet Union emerged with the economic power to establish trade blocs.

Since 1945, world trade has mushroomed, benefiting many countries, but national economic interests have unsettled the international economic order. Dominant economic countries in the aftermath of World War II concluded that economic prosperity depended on financial stability and cooperative planning. In 1945, U.S. and world leaders sponsored the Bretton Woods Conference, which set global currency exchange rates based on gold and the U.S. dollar. By 1967, a General Agreement on Tariffs and Trade had been negotiated and provided a fairly stable international trade network. With these mechanisms, a better-integrated trade system developed. In the 1980s and 1990s, a second General Agreement on Tariffs and Trade (GATT II) was negotiated, opening up national markets more than ever before.

On the other hand, regional economic blocs, such as the European Economic Community (EEC) and the North American Free Trade Agree-

Figure 44.1 ***NAFTA Cartoon.*** *The North American Free Trade Agreement caused controversy in American politics with many groups opposing the treaty. This cartoon captures the appeal of Ross Perot, a major NAFTA opponent who played on fears of losing jobs to promote protectionist trade policies. Perot's efforts failed as NAFTA passed in the U.S. Senate.* Rothco.

ment (NAFTA), have fostered more narrow economic interests. In 1951, a few Western European states began merging their economies, with the vision of eventually creating one economy. In 1958, the Treaty of Rome came into force, creating the European Economic Community. The EEC's economic output had exceeded that of the United States by 1980. Prime Minister Margaret Thatcher appreciated the financial benefits of British membership in the EEC. Although the British had stayed aloof from the EEC, the Thatcher government pushed hard to join the EEC and pushed for a single market with common manufacturing standards, trade regulations, and professional qualifications by 1992. Other European countries hoped to join the EEC but were excluded until the 1990s. NAFTA merged the markets of Canada, the United States, and Mexico. It was successfully negotiated in 1993, barely passing ratification by the U.S. Senate and offering modest economic gains since then. Thus, there has been tension between national and regional economic interests.

Challenges to Economic Integration

Although growing economic integration has characterized the era since 1500, special-interest groups have decried economic competition, asking for protection. **Protectionism** is the practice of sheltering local industries and businesses from international competition, and it has characterized national economic policies for much of the modern era.

Protectionist thought and economic practices developed in Europe during the seventeenth and eighteenth centuries. Mercantilist countries believed that they had to export more than they imported, and their leaders usually adopted high tariff rates, making cheap foreign goods more costly and protecting local products. As noted earlier, in the late seventeenth century, English textile manufacturers faced heavy competition from Indian cotton goods. After the manufacturers pled their case in mercantilist terms, high tariffs were slapped on the Indian imports, destroying the competition.

In the nineteenth century, many countries continued to practice protectionist policies. Russia, for example, used high tariffs to protect local industries, especially in the 1890s. The Chinese and Japanese lost control of their tariff policies because of the unequal treaties they were forced to sign with Western countries.

Protectionism reached a high point during the Great Depression. Country after country imposed high tariffs to shelter their national industries, motivated by the rise of nationalism. Although a few businesses were shielded, many others went bankrupt when their export markets dried up as high tariffs elsewhere ballooned the prices of manufactured goods. Their actions, taken to protect national self-interests, worsened the global situation. Indeed, the general trend was a shrinking global trade system, disrupting economic integration.

Since 1945, protectionist policies have been more subdued. Many countries concluded that the trade conflicts of the Great Depression hurt all countries and attempted to develop trade programs with more open markets. Although countries like Japan and South Korea have adopted mercantilist policies that protected certain industries, they have generally begun opening their markets to foreign trade competition. GATT II has further encouraged that opening trend.

The Soviet Union and China developed economic systems that lay largely outside the international economic order, hindering global economic integration. A significant part of the competition between the Soviet Union and the United States during the Cold War era was economic. In that sense, economic rivalry disrupted the general economic integrative trend. With the collapse of the Soviet Empire in 1991, however, prospects for greater economic unity on the global level have increased. In the late 1970s, China also opened its economy to international trade and investment, and Chinese leaders have eagerly sought membership in GATT and other global economic organizations. The Chinese economy has been the world's fastest-growing economy in the latter decades of the twentieth century.

In the 1980s and 1990s, a few U.S. leaders have worried about the loss of U.S. jobs and businesses from international competition, and they have fought the various trade agreements, such as GATT and NAFTA. U.S. trade unions have been very uncomfortable with policies promising low tariffs and easy access to the U.S. market. Although not a few jobs have been lost to economic competition from other countries such as Japan, the general trend has been toward significant job growth in the United States from a burgeoning export effort by U.S. businesses. For example, the U.S. and Japanese economies are so enmeshed that a trade war would have dire consequences for both.

The forces of economic integration and national interest have struggled with each other throughout the modern era. While most leaders recognize that national and global interests are linked, it is equally clear that they are not always identical. A policy may improve conditions within a country yet harm the global system; conversely, a policy may improve the world economy at the expense of national economic welfare. As a result, the tension between forces favoring and opposing economic integration produces periods when one or the other is dominant.

Environmental Consequences of Economic Integration

The increased pace of economic development and integration in the modern era has brought environmental problems with accelerating severity. Agriculture's spread and commercialization played a major role in the deforestation of continents and the erosion of soils. In addition, industrial pollutants have deeply affected people and ecosystems across political boundaries. Resource depletion has affected many countries, and the inadvertent modification of the earth's climate has threatened many people.

In the sixteenth, seventeenth, and eighteenth centuries, European colonists transformed the landscape of North America and Indonesia. Eastern North America was largely forest in 1500, but, by 1800, the massive stands of trees had largely been cleared for agricultural purposes. In Indonesia, many tropical rain forests were cleared for agricultural farmland.

Multiple factors have led to the clearing of forests around the globe, especially in the Third World, causing concern among environmentalists. Apart from agriculture, grazing by livestock has prevented reforestation in parts of the world. Demand for wood products, especially for the construction of houses, has led to heavy logging. Mining has also been a significant factor in reducing forests. The vast loss of forests troubles people who not only fear the destruction of unique ecosystems but who also lament the extinction of animals and medicinal plants. Once again, economic national interests conflict with international interests. Third World countries, for example, need to industrialize but are hindered by international commitments to preserve natural resources.

Air pollution has grown significantly with industrialization, and careless economic policies have caused problems that cross national borders. Fossil fuels, especially coal, have been notorious polluters of the air. In addition, they have caused acid rain, corrosive rainfall that kills trees and fouls lakes. Canada, for example, has suffered from acid rain coming from the United States, while Finland has endured acid rain problems coming from Poland. Massive fossil fuel burning in the nineteenth and twentieth centuries has also contributed to the **greenhouse effect**, the concentration of carbon dioxide in the upper atmosphere, which lets in and traps heat from the sun. This leads to global warming, which some scientists have shown to be a serious environmental problem.

The diminishing ozone layer in the upper atmosphere has also given great concern to environmentalists and citizens alike. Certain industrial gases, such as chlorofluorocarbons (CFCs), bind with ozone, reducing the amount of atmospheric ozone. Because ozone helps prevent harmful ultraviolet rays from entering the atmosphere, the reduction of the ozone layer can have serious health consequences, including increased incidence of skin cancer. In 1987, most countries finally agreed to reduce significantly their CFC emissions by the end of the twentieth century, showing international cooperation in attacking environmental problems.

Nuclear accidents, tests, and waste disposal have also caused problems that cross borders. In 1986, a Soviet nuclear plant exploded at Chernobyl, spewing nuclear radiation into the atmosphere and across Europe. Many Europeans suffered severe health problems because of this accident. U.S., Soviet, French, and Chinese nuclear

Figure 44.2 ***Deforestation in Brazil.*** *Destruction of the Amazon became a major environmental issue in the 1980s and 1990s. Evidenced here are the ravaging effects of strip mining, which has leveled a large section of the oxygen-producing rain forest. Such unchecked waste alarmed many in Brazil and around the world.* Antonio Ribeiro / Gamma/Liaison International.

FIGURE 44.3 ***Catastrophe at Chernobyl.*** *In 1986, a Soviet nuclear power plant in the Ukraine caught fire, releasing into the atmosphere massive amounts of radiation that caused death and disease. Although Soviet leaders initially denied any problems, they quickly reversed this policy and allowed critical reporting of the disaster.* Novosti, London.

tests have also caused serious air pollution by radiated particles that dropped over other countries. Environmentalists have become alarmed by the casual disposal of nuclear wastes, especially in the ocean. Toxic effects from nuclear materials can contaminate areas for thousands of years.

Other environmentalists have publicized the problem of overfishing in the oceans. Many countries have built and dispatched giant fishing fleets around the world, and they have developed major industries and created large numbers of jobs. Overfishing has already significantly reduced the numbers of edible fish. Fishing communities along the western U.S. coast have dwindled in size because of the absence of salmon in ocean waters. Thus, national interests can also disrupt people's livelihoods around the globe.

POLITICAL INTEGRATION

Since the end of the nineteenth century, internationalism has also begun to gather adherents who have reacted strongly against the conflicts brought by nationalism. Ideologies such as Marxism have developed partly in reaction to nationalist activities. Furthermore, cooperative unions, such as the League of Nations, the United Nations (UN), the Organization of American States (OAS), the Organization of African Unity (OAU), and the Arab League, have been formed to address issues beyond narrow national interests. At the same time, nationalists have decried international agencies and adherents, causing serious tensions.

Nationalism has been perhaps the most powerful political force in the nineteenth and twentieth centuries. It was a driving force, for example, behind the formation of Germany and Zululand. Nationalism also undermined the Russian Empire and helped oust imperialist powers ruling in Asia and Africa. In that sense, nationalism acted against integrationist trends and tendencies.

Some internationalist ideologies have developed in reaction to nationalism. Karl Marx saw nationalism as a by-product of the capitalist system and therefore doomed to disappear as the socialist system began to take hold internationally. His vision focused on class, especially the working class, and he argued that workers would eventually

FIGURE 44.4 ***Protests against Fishing Ban.*** *As some fishing grounds became severely depleted, various governments imposed bans on fishing. While many protesters at this 1996 demonstration in New England recognized the need to be more environmentally sensitive, their livelihood was dependent on fishing. Furthermore, they resented the fact that other governments ignored the bans and allowed their fleets to continue fishing.* © 1996 Josh Reynolds.

see that the ties binding them together cut across national boundaries. Marx encapsulated his vision in a memorable line from his *Communist Manifesto*: "Workers of the world unite."

Although world leaders had flirted with forming international organizations, the real impetus for international cooperative unions came only in the aftermath of the two world wars. The League of Nations was formed in 1919 to help implement the conditions of the Versailles Peace Treaties and to provide a body that would discuss problems affecting the international community. The League, however, failed to prevent World War II and disintegrated. The United Nations was formed in 1945 to deal with international crises and was more successful than the League. Neither body, however, could do much in the face of determined opposition by a major world power.

Regional bodies of cooperation have also come into existence in the twentieth century. The Organization of American States was formed in 1948 to deal with inter-American issues. In the 1950s and 1960s, it generally supported the United States' positions on diplomatic matters, prohibiting Cuba from participating in OAS activities. The Arab League came into existence in 1945 to discuss and mediate matters relating to Arab states. Its headquarters remained in Egypt until 1979, when Egypt signed a peace treaty with Israel. Then, Egypt's membership was suspended and the headquarters was transferred to Tunisia. The Organization of African Unity (OAU), a union that appeared

FIGURE 44.5 ***Meeting of the OAU.*** *The Organization of African Unity formed out of the need to discuss common issues in the aftermath of the collapse of imperialism in Africa. Many delegates to the OAU are dressed in Western clothing while others are wearing more traditional attire.* Laurent van der Stockt/Liaison International.

in 1963, has more than fifty African member states. All of these bodies are examples of political integration.

Thus, a kind of dynamic equilibrium has evolved in which international and national forces vie with each other. Sometimes one or the other has been temporarily ascendant, but, at least, a major world war has been averted, and some degree of political integration has been maintained.

RELIGIOUS INTEGRATION

Contrary to economic and political trends toward integration, religions have generally resisted integrating tendencies. Except for a few instances of ecumenism (bridging religious differences), the trend has been toward retaining and increasing differences.

Islam and Christianity became even more dynamic in converting peoples and encouraging migration of the faithful overseas in the Early Modern Era. Roman Catholic missionaries achieved considerable success in the Americas and the Philippines and more limited results in India, China, and Japan. Muslims were somewhat successful in spreading Islam in the Indian subcontinent, especially during the Mughal Empire. Their most successful proselytizing came in Indonesia and the southern Philippines and was directed by mystics and merchants. Thus, a major trend has been the development of religious communities through proselytizing and migration across widely disparate areas.

At the same time, Islam and Christianity were shaken by sectarian disputes. Shi'ites have persecuted Sunnis and Sunnis have persecuted Shi'ites in Southwest Asia. The Protestant Reformation and the Roman Catholic Reformation brought a

FIGURE 44.6 ***Mourning Khomeini's Death.*** *Millions of Iranians mourned the loss of the Ayatollah Khomeini, the religious leader who imposed a fundamentalist form of Shi'a Islam. Mass outpourings of grief were held in public places in the capital of Teheran and elsewhere.* E. Rad / Gamma/Liaison International.

split in Western Christianity. Religious wars convulsed parts of Europe in the sixteenth and seventeenth centuries.

Ecumenical trends have developed since 1945, but they have been limited in scope and have often been found at the grassroots level. Pope John XXIII (reign dates 1958–1963) promoted ecumenism during his papacy, though his successors have been less committed to it. Although some talks between Protestant and Catholic groups have been ongoing, little significant change has resulted.

More important has been the growth of religious fundamentalism, especially in Protestantism and Islam. **Fundamentalism** is the religious belief that posits strict adherence to practices supported by a literal interpretation of sacred texts. In a real sense, religious leaders have always claimed to be acting according to scripture. But religious fundamentalism in the twentieth century has evolved partly from the challenges of secularization. Religious fundamentalists have also frequently opposed ecumenical tendencies. Although fundamentalists have usually been a small percentage of a larger religious community, their skill at political organizing has given some of them significant influence.

WHITHER INTEGRATION?

One of the justifications of studying history is that we can learn from experience and thereby shape our futures more effectively. It is fitting, therefore, to conclude this book with an attempt to predict what the future will bring. With a mixed picture about current prospects for global integration, such a projection is challenging.

Despite protectionist tendencies in many if not most nations, the benefits of continued economic integration have become most compelling. With the signing of GATT II and NAFTA, powerful constituencies favoring opening trade have been encouraged. More international agreements will be negotiated and implemented. Perhaps some kind of agreement between the EEC and NAFTA will be proposed. Certainly, some form of NAFTA will bind the Americas early in the twenty-first century. At the same time, the close enmeshing of national markets will mean that serious trade disruptions would have a rippling effect through many countries' business and consumer sectors. Integration will make it more difficult for protectionists to implement trade-restricting policies. Global pressures to adopt environmentally friendly economic policies should increase tensions in the twenty-first century, as Third World countries continue to pursue national self-interest.

Just as the economic integration of Germany paved the way for its political integration, global economic integration will facilitate more political cooperation and decision making on an international level. Regional political associations might perhaps have a better chance of developing political unions. EEC countries, for example, have already used their close economic ties to begin developing common political institutions, a European Parliament. The United Nations will continue to be forceful when its interests coincide with those of powerful countries. At times, however, one or more strong countries will continue to thwart UN efforts in international disputes.

Religious tendencies will continue to run counter to integrative trends. Although limited attempts at religious ecumenism will continue, the pervasive direction will be toward maintaining sectarian differences. Religious bureaucracies will be very reluctant to share power with religious leaders from other sects. Furthermore, when religion becomes a part of the nationalist ideology, a powerful fundamentalist political force emerges, thwarting religious and political integration.

SUMMARY

1. Economic integration has been a general trend since 1500. The Industrial Revolution became the driving force behind global economic growth and closer economic ties. In the nineteenth and twentieth centuries, standardization became a major consequence of economic integration as first the British pound and then the U.S. dollar became the preferred international currencies. The metric system gradually became the accepted format for weights and measures, and English became the language of science, diplomacy, and air-traffic control.

2. The development of the noncapitalist Soviet bloc and China undermined global economic integration for most of the twentieth century, but the breakup of that autonomous system has meant better economic integration.

3. Economic integration has also meant that environmental problems can stretch beyond a country's borders. Massive deforestation of North America and Indonesia has occurred, while mining, agriculture, and housing construction have reduced forests around the world. Acid rain generated in the United States has harmed Canada's forests and lakes, and unrestricted use of chlorofluorocarbons has reduced the ozone layer's screening of ultraviolet radiation, increasing health problems such as skin cancer.

4. Tensions between internationalism and nationalism have developed in the modern era. International ideologies such as Marxism have focused on class rather than on the nation. International and regional cooperative unions, such as the United Nations, the Organization of American States, the Arab League, and the Organization of African Unity, have formed to promote discussion and solution of common problems.

5. Religious integration has been spotty at best. Although Christian and Islamic missionaries have actively spread their faiths, sectarian disputes sapped both religions. Religious fundamentalism has tended to highlight differences rather than commonalities among religions, and fundamentalists have become powerful by organizing political interest groups.

SUGGESTED READINGS

Franck, Thomas. *Nation against Nation.* Oxford, Eng.: Oxford University Press, 1985. A history of the United Nations, focusing on its relations with the United States.

Kaplan, Lawrence, ed. *Fundamentalism in Comparative Perspective.* Amherst: University of Massachusetts Press, 1992. Essays about Christian, Islamic, and Jewish fundamentalism.

Schama, Simon. *Landscape and Memory.* New York: Knopf, 1995. An analysis of nature in history, providing a historical context for environmental concerns in the late twentieth century.

Weston, Anthony. *Back to Earth.* Philadelphia: Temple University Press, 1994. A reassessment of the environmental movement and its future role in political movements.

Glossary of Terms

A

absolutism a system in which monarchs aim to achieve total control through a bureaucracy that is centralized along military lines
abstract expressionism one of the most influential of fine-art painting styles in the twentieth century, characterized by an attempt to abandon previous artistic conventions and to emphasize the spontaneous, personal, free, unstudied, and intuitive aspects of art
action painting a twentieth-century school of painting within abstract expressionism that was pioneered by Jackson Pollock; it emphasized the artistic process and featured intersecting slashes of paint across the canvas
African diaspora the enforced dispersal of Africans during the slave trade
agricultural-industrial slaves slaves who provide hard labor for commercial activities
Allies one of the two main blocs of united world powers that fought in World War II; it was composed of Britain, the Soviet Union, China, the United States, and Canada, as well as smaller countries
American exchange the process by which a variety of species, ideas, and technology that were previously isolated in one hemisphere passed between the Americas and the Old World
apartheid a legal system of racial segregation and discrimination enforced by a minority government; between 1948 and 1991 it was legal in South Africa, where it was enforced by a white minority government upon the black majority
asiento (ah see EHN toh) a subcontract that permitted a foreign trader to sell slaves in Spanish lands at fixed prices that were usually quite favorable to the trader
assembly line an American innovation, refined by Henry Ford in his automobile plant, that consisted of a conveyor system with workers standing along it, arranged in the order in which their tasks were to be performed
associative bond one of the two conditions asserted by the sociologist Max Weber under which a group of people might voluntarily band together, in this case for the mutual benefit of resisting some outside force. See also **communal bond**
Atlantic slave trade trade that carried slaves from Africa to Europe and the Americas via the Atlantic Ocean
Axis one of the two main blocs of united world powers that fought in World War II; it consisted mainly of Germany, Japan, and Italy

B

blitzkrieg literally translated as "lightning war," the term used for the German combination of air strikes and rapidly moving army ground vehicles during World War II
blues a form of African-inspired music that developed in the American South; it is characterized by distinctive rhythms, repetitive structure, and melody lines that generally descend from initial high notes
Bolsheviks Marxist supporters of Vladimir Lenin in early-twentieth-century Russia
bourgeoisie (boor zhwah ZEE) wealthy investors and their middle-class allies
broadcast to send out a message widely to be received by anyone with the proper receiving device, such as a radio
buccaneers pirates who raided Spanish treasure ships that were carrying gold and silver back to Spain from the Caribbean

C

cadres officials and activists under party direction in the People's Republic of China
call-and-response pattern a song pattern, common to West Africa and the American South, in which a leader calls a line and a chorus responds with the same or a similar line
canal system a network of interconnecting artificial waterways linking many places
capitalism an economic system wherein ownership is

private and individuals compete to increase their wealth, mostly unimpeded by government restriction

cartel a group, producing a significant percentage of a material, that cooperates to fix production levels and prices and dominates international distribution of the material

catastrophism a school of thought that sees the geological past as shaped primarily by major events such as earthquakes and floods

chattel slavery a system in which a slave is considered to have no more value than any other object and in which his or her humanity and personal rights are denied

Cheka a police force with hundreds of thousands of members that protected the Bolshevik state and, in 1918, undertook responsibilities that included guarding the *gulags* and frontiers and implementing a policy of state terror

cipher a method for making the meaning of a message unintelligible to an enemy or outsider by scrambling the letters so that only someone who knows the rules of manipulation can reconstruct the message

client governments local administrations that carried out the wishes of imperialistic governments

closed slavery a system of slavery that maintains a slave in that status for life

code a method for making the meaning of a message unintelligible to an enemy by substituting certain symbols for others

Cold War the intense and multifaceted rivalry that threatened to become an actual war between the United States and the Soviet Union from 1945 to 1991; key elements of the Cold War included sharp ideological differences, an arms race, economic competition, and the formation of power blocs

colonialism the process of establishing colonies, administering them, and extracting their wealth for the home country

communal bond a condition asserted by the sociologist Max Weber under which a group of people might voluntarily band together, in this case for the desire to be with others who share beliefs, values, and customs. See also **associative bond**

commune a model of economic organization in Mao Zedong's rural China that involved merging many cooperatives

communication the movement of messages from one place to another

communism a political system that aims to serve the people without supporting class domination

confederation a permanent union of equal states that cooperate for their common welfare

corporatism an element of national socialism involving the practice of combining owners, managers, and workers in a unitary whole within a business, factory, or industrial sector

cottage crafts the collective term for small-scale, home-based businesses run by independent artisans

Creoles the Spanish elite in nineteenth-century Central and South America

cultural relativism a concept developed by Franz Boas that all cultures should be viewed as equal in sophistication and value

D

daimyo (DY mee yoh) a Japanese territorial lord who was a retainer of a *shogun* in feudal Japan

deflation a steep drop in prices and wages

Deism a belief system that gained a following during the Scientific Revolution; it asserted that the universe functioned like a machine that ran by natural laws, and consequently its maker, God, had nothing left to do

demography the study of population and its changes in size, composition, and movements

depression an economic downturn involving long-term production drops, widespread unemployment, and deflation

detente the easing of international tensions through good-will gestures and negotiated arms-limitation treaties that was developed by the Soviet leader Leonid Brezhnev and the American leader Richard Nixon in the 1970s

diaspora (dy AS poh ruh) the forced migration and dispersion of a people

differentiation as applied to government, the idea that each governmental bureau must concern itself with a single function

Directory a group of five men who ran the executive branch of the French government and ruled the nation in conjunction with the legislature from 1795 to 1799

disease reservoir a population of animals that can contract a human disease and harbor the germs that cause the disease

domestic slaves slaves who perform household duties

E

economic revolution a transformation of a country's economic structure

elite revolution a revolution implemented by the ruling upper classes

empire a state that controls a large area that encompasses societies culturally different from itself; also, a group of states or territories that is ruled by a single power

enclosure the conversion of low-yield farming areas into pasturage for livestock in England

encomienda (ehn koh mee EHN duh) the institution that required American Indians to work for the Spanish colonists without compensation

Enigma machine a machine that automatically produced a complex cipher of any message that was typed into it; it was used by the Germans in World War II

Enlightenment an intellectual movement that championed the centrality of human reason and inspired eighteenth-century thinkers in Europe and North America

entrepôt (ahn truh POH) a colonial commercial center that served simultaneously as a collection center for goods to be shipped to the home country and as a distribution center for goods coming from the home country

estates groups of elite and other commoners who formed the assembly of the *riksdag*, which consulted with the king in seventeenth-century Sweden

ethnic group a self-identified group or "tribe" of people that has in common a culture and, sometimes, a language

ethnocentrism the belief that one's own ideas, values, culture, and cherished behavior patterns are socially, morally, or religiously correct and superior to others

evolution the concept that each species developed by modification from an earlier species

existentialism a philosophical movement linked to such thinkers as Jean-Paul Sartre that posits that the greatest problem facing anyone is existence itself; it attained its greatest appeal in post–World War II France

F

female infanticide the killing of female infants, a practice that usually increases during hard times

field painting a school of painting within abstract expressionism that was pioneered by Willem de Kooning and used featureless and often overlapping masses of color

le film noir (luh feelm nwahr) literally, "the dark film"; a film genre that was developed in France in the 1950s and focused on the dark, pessimistic, and gloomy side of life

fine arts the elite wing of the arts, produced by highly trained artists

First World the U.S. economic and political bloc of allied nations during the Cold War

folk arts those arts that are typically perpetuated by amateur artists; have long, unchanging traditions; and are transmitted in informal settings, such as from a parent to a child

Folk Islam the religious practices of ordinary Muslims, connected with the collapse of the Abbasid Caliphate in the thirteenth century

fossils the remains of ancient plants and animals

Free French an exiled government, founded by a group of French who were antagonistic to the Germans during World War II

free verse poetry that self-consciously avoids the traditional conventions of meter, rhyme, and structure; it was pioneered by the American poet Walt Whitman in the nineteenth century

full-rigged ship a ship with multiple sails set in various positions, allowing the vessel to take advantage of diverse wind conditions

fundamentalism the religious belief that posits strict adherence to practices supported by a literal interpretation of sacred texts

fusion the incorporation of ideas from various ethnic and national traditions into art

G

genocide the mass killing of individuals in a deliberate attempt to extinguish a racial, ethnic, or religious group

gentry a new elite social class formed in England during the Renaissance; it was not officially noble, yet was higher than the middle class and usually associated with rural property

geography the study of the ways in which people have used the planet's land and resources

ghetto originally, the Jewish section of an Italian city; any segregated enclave in cities around the world

glasnost policies of openness and discussion implemented in the Soviet Union by Mikhail Gorbachev in the 1980s

great art style an art style that occurs over a broad geographic area and is the dominant and often the only style within a culture, other than family-based folk art

green revolution technological advances in agriculture, such as drought-resistant crops, new fertilizers, and pesticides, that doubled or even tripled the agricultural output of a community and decreased hunger in the Third World during the post–World War II era

greenhouse effect the concentration of carbon dioxide in the upper atmosphere that traps heat from the sun, leading to global warming, which some scientists have warned is a serious environmental problem

guild system a hierarchical organization of merchants and artisans that regulated production of goods and worked for the common political, economic, and social interests of its members

gulags (GOO lahgs) labor camps in Siberia and northern Russia beginning in the Bolshevik Revolution

H

harem a place of confinement for elite Muslim women, where all adult males except for the head of the household are forbidden to enter

hereditary slavery a system of slavery under which children of slaves are also slaves

history the study of the human past, primarily through the interpretation of documents

holocaust mass extermination of a people viewed as inferior

Huguenots French Calvinists beginning in the sixteenth century

humanism a system of thought based on the study of human ideas and actions

I

ideology the complex of ideas and philosophy that directs one's goals, expectations, and actions

imperialism the process of forming, extending, or maintaining an empire; an economic and political colonial system of an industrial country needing raw materials and markets

import substitution the practice of relying on local businesses to fill the gaps left by the withdrawal of foreign imports

indenture a temporary position entered into voluntarily by impoverished individuals who transfer the rights to their labor to someone else for a specified term in exchange for transportation, lodging, monies, or other necessities

Indian Ocean slave trade the trade in slaves that passed through the coastal East African cities and northward, particularly to Southwest Asia

indulgences cancellation of punishments for committed sins; the sale of indulgences in Roman Catholicism was one of the abuses that led to the Protestant Reformation

Industrial Revolution the shift to the manufacture of most goods through mechanized factories and the changes that came in the wake of this shift; it originated in eighteenth-century England

inflation a pattern of sharply rising prices and wages

inquisition originally, an inquiry into what was being taught or preached by lay preachers in medieval Christianity; later, the inquiry by a designated church official into whether anyone held "correct" beliefs

intellectual class the social class that lives by the exchange of ideas

intellectual revolution a transformation of how human beings think about themselves and the universe around them

intendants royal representatives of Louis XIII of France who were appointed by Cardinal Richelieu to correct local abuses and extend state reach into distant regions

J

Jacobins a European political group during the Enlightenment who wanted the broadest male voting franchise, abolition of the monarchy, and price controls

Jacquard loom (ZHAHK ahr) a device, invented by Joseph Jacquard in eighteenth-century France, that could be fitted onto any existing loom, accelerating the process of weaving patterned cloth

Janissaries warriors of European extraction who composed the elite Ottoman military force

jazz a polished, innovative, and orchestrated outgrowth of blues that developed in American cities and used the whole range of instruments of the popular dance orchestras of the day, especially horns and winds

jidai-geki (JEE dy GEHK ee) the film versions of the historic Japanese dramas, set in periods before the Meiji industrialization and Westernization of Japan and often depicting *samurai* attempting to complete virtuous tasks

jihad (jee HAHD) an Islamic holy war; a holy struggle by the Islamic Ottoman Turks against their Christian or Muslim enemies

Junkers the landed nobility of East Prussia

K

kamikaze Japanese suicide bombers who sank and damaged some Allied ships by crashing into them during World War II

kimono (KEE moh noh) a robe-like Japanese outer garment

kulaks (KOO lahks) originally, wealthy Russian peasants; eventually, anyone opposing collectivization during Stalinist rule

L

laissez-faire (LEH say FAYR) minimal governmental interference in economic development

lateen sail a sail from the eastern Mediterranean that was adapted by the Portuguese; its slanted mast made it possible to sail almost against the wind

lifeways typical behaviors for a society

load a measure of a transportation mode's utility that measures the weight of the cargo that can be transported

lock a mechanism invented in the fourteenth century for holding water in different parts of a canal at different elevations and moving a vessel from one elevation to another

M

manifest destiny the nineteenth-century belief, popular among European Americans, that the United States should expand until it controlled the Pacific coast and beyond

manumission the freeing of a slave

means of production the way that people earn a livelihood
medical revolution the bringing of medical treatments such as immunization to the Third World in the post–World War II era
medreses (MEH dreh sehs) colleges built in cities of the Ottoman Empire
mercantile system a relationship in which a colony provides raw materials for the home country and the home country provides manufactured goods for the colony
microprocessor the information-processing heart of a computer, which converts messages into electronic impulses and can store or send these messages
middle class the intermediate socioeconomic class between the elite and commoners, composed of business and professional people in modern societies
Middle Passage the sea voyage in the Atlantic slave trade between Africa and the Americas
migrant workers laborers who travel from place to place to find work
mission a complex (designed for the religious conversion of native peoples) consisting of a church, dormitories, and farm or ranch facilities
model a picture of how or why a general process works
modernity a cluster of changes occurring after about 1500 in western Europe and Japan and by the nineteenth century across much of the world; it was characterized by a focus on progress, the application of science and technology, a secular understanding of the world, wide participation in government, determination of social status according to merit, and increasing economic domination by capitalism or socialism
Monists an influential group of German scientists in the late nineteenth century who expanded the idea of Social Darwinism, maintaining that ethnic groups were distinctive both biologically (racially) and socially and that not all peoples were equally fit
monoethnic state a state whose citizens are mostly from the same ethnic group or tribe
monoculture a practice whereby farmers focus on a single crop
monopolies the rights to exclusive legal control of an invention, a device, or trade
multiethnic state a state that incorporates two or more ethnic groups into its citizenry and extends full privileges to them
mural art the painting of pictures on walls
mutation a spontaneous development of a new trait as a result of an error in copying the biochemicals that carry the genetic code during reproduction

N

national anthem a song that is adopted by a nation as a symbol, used at official occasions, and often protected legally against desecration
national socialism a twentieth-century ideology that includes elements of nationalism, socialism, imperialism, and totalitarianism; national socialists, who believed that the nation is holy and harmonious and that all class conflict is evil, desired a powerful nation-state to control the nation's economy and an army in order to expand their ideology by conquest
nationalism an ideology that emphasizes one's social role as a member of a nation, often with a common language, shared historical experiences, and similar cultural traditions
natural selection a biological theory developed by Charles Darwin, which posits that, over time, a species' most adaptive traits are passed on and others are eliminated
New Economic Policy economic relaxation measures taken by the Bolsheviks during the peacetime period from 1921 to 1929 to permit economic recovery from the ravages of warfare
New World the area consisting of the Americas and the Pacific islands
Noh a Japanese dramatic form that originated in the Ashikaga Shogunate era; actors wearing masks rely upon gestures and voice rather than on facial expression to convey emotion

O

Old World the area consisting of Asia, Africa, and Europe
open slavery a system of slavery that provides realistic ways by which a slave can be freed
optical telegraph the first practical means of long-distance communication, involving slats of wood mounted atop high buildings and moved by a system of ropes and pulleys
Orgburo the organization bureau that handled administrative matters concerning the state apparatus during the Bolshevik Revolution

P

pan-Germanism an ideology favoring unity among German-speaking peoples of all nations
pan-tribalism the merging of various tribes into a single interest group
pantheism the belief that divinity is present in all creation
Party Secretariat the office that dealt with organizational issues relating to the Bolshevik Party
pellagra a deficiency disease resulting from a lack of niacin
perestroika the policy of restructuring implemented in the Soviet Union by Mikhail Gorbachev in the 1980s
period a span of time, defined by scholars for

convenience, during which conditions, events, and lifeways remained more or less similar and were distinctive from those of preceding and succeeding periods

periodic table Dmitri Mendeleyev's table of elements arranged in order of their relative weights and with groupings possessing similar characteristics

phrenology a now-discredited field of science adopted by the Monists that purported to relate physical characteristics to intellectual and moral worth

phylloxera (fih LOK seh ruh) an aphid from the Mississippi Valley of North America; it subsists by sucking plant juices from roots and devastated French wine grapes in the nineteenth century

Pietism a small Protestant sect that was sanctioned by the Prussian state and emphasized direct religious experience, personal conversion, and rebirth

pogrom an official riot in which bureaucrats led and incited mobs to persecute Jews in Europe

Politburo the political bureau that became the command center of the Bolshevik Party in Soviet Russia

political revolution a revolution that changes mainly the political structure of a country

poll tax a fee imposed on each voter and sometimes implemented as a strategy to prevent certain impoverished minority groups from voting

popular arts the forms of art that are typically perpetuated by professionals, are subject to fads, and receive wide distribution to large numbers of people

populist revolution a revolution implemented by the common people's seizure of power

praying towns in colonial New England, Calvinist communities where local Indians could come to learn the Calvinist religion as well as European skills and ways of life

predestination the idea that God preelects those who will receive salvation; a cornerstone of Calvinist theology

prepared piano a term coined by the composer John Cage to describe the process in which a pianist was instructed to place various articles among the strings of the piano, resulting in largely unpredictable buzzing, clunking, and whirring sounds during a performance

primary source a document that was written by a participant in or an eyewitness to the event, activity, or process being described or analyzed

progressivism the idea that things are getting better and better and that change is likely to bring improvement

proletariat factory workers

protectionism the practice of sheltering local industries and businesses from international competition; it has characterized national economic policies for much of the modern era

Protestant Reformation a period of religious protest that began in 1521 and resulted in the fragmentation of the Roman Catholic Church and the creation of Protestant sects

R

Rastafarianism the sociopolitical wing of reggae, and a movement dedicated to revitalizing pride in African heritage among Jamaicans and to achieving racial equality

rationalism the philosophy that maintains that reason is the only valid basis for determining actions or opinions

rebellion an uprising by people who seek to change the leaders rather than the political structure of a country

reggae (RAY gay) a form of Afro-Caribbean music developed by Jamaicans in the 1960s that is heavily influenced by American blues and rock and roll, with a distinctive rhythm that emphasizes the second beat of a measure

regimentation in Sweden, an emphasis on discipline and obedience in government and life

Renaissance an era of artistic, sociopolitical, and economic change that occurred in Europe from around 1350 to around 1600; it was characterized by an interest in Classical Greco-Roman forms

revolution a process of rapid and fundamental structural change

rhythm and blues an electrified and polished version of the blues (a musical form) that developed after World War II with a revival of interest in the blues

rock and roll a form of music that developed from rhythm and blues in the 1950s, when it was mostly written and performed by African American entertainers

Roman Catholic Reformation a reform movement within the Roman Catholic Church that began shortly after the Protestant Reformation

Romanticism an artistic movement originating in Europe and spreading to the Americas between 1780 and 1900; it emphasized feelings, imagination, and nature and was often employed as a vehicle with which to create a national identity

S

Sahel (sah HEHL) the semiarid region immediately to the south of the Sahara Desert, site of the great African drought, including parts of Somalia, Ethiopia, the Sudan, Chad, Niger, Nigeria, Mali, Burkina Faso, and Senegal

scientism the belief that science is the primary, if not sole, reality of human existence; the faith that the world is predictable and that it operates according to rules and principles that can be discovered

Second World the Soviet economic and political bloc of allied nations during the Cold War

secondary source a document in which information that has been gathered from primary sources is analyzed and digested, providing an interpretation of the event or process

secularism an ideology arguing that nonreligious ideas should be the organizational basis for society

segregation of tasks a major innovation of the Industrial Revolution whereby workers had only one small task to complete, and that task was repeated over and over again

serf a worker whose labor is owed to someone else, usually a feudal lord, and whose status is inherited by children, but who also retains certain personal rights and is not conceived of as "owned"

service gentry landlords who joined the army and served in the administration of Ivan the Great of fifteenth-century Russia

shah a ruler of Muslim Persia; the leader of the Persian Empire

shogun military dictator of Japan

Sikhism (SEEK ihz um) a monotheistic religion founded in sixteenth-century northern India; it began as an attempt to bridge the religious differences between Islam and Hinduism and was transformed into a religion of resistance to Mughal oppression

single-generation slavery a system of slavery under which the children of slaves are free

skraeling (SKRAY lihng) a Norse word meaning "impoverished one"; it was used to describe the Inuit, whom the Vikings encountered in Vinland

slavery the ownership and control of other people

Social Darwinism the idea that human society operates by a system of natural selection, whereby individuals and ways of life automatically gravitate to their proper station; the concept was developed by the nineteenth-century English philosopher Herbert Spencer

social history the study of everyday life in the past

social revolution a revolution that alters society

socialism a type of economy wherein property of all sorts is held by everyone as a whole

socialist realism a movement that stressed culture's ties to socialism, and a key element of Josef Stalin's cultural focus

source analysis a set of procedures developed by historians to determine whether a particular document is legitimate and accurate

soviets workers' administrative councils that led the anti-state effort during political unrest in Russia in the early twentieth century

Spanish Inquisition an inquisition that became a formal branch of the government in fifteenth-century Spain

speed a measure of a transportation mode's utility, based on how fast goods are moved

standardization of parts a principle of organization in the Industrial Revolution in which all examples of a particular mechanical part had to be the same so that any one of them could fit into its appropriate place

subordination a chain-of-command system

sultan an Islamic ruler, outside of Persia; the leader of the Ottoman Empire

T

terror the deliberate use of massive force to cow or eliminate opponents; it was used by revolutionists and antirevolutionists in late-eighteenth-century France, among other places

textual criticism the analysis and authentication of texts

Third World the nonindustrialized countries that did not initially support either of the Soviet or U.S. alliances during the Cold War (1945–1991)

totalitarianism a belief that an all-powerful nation-state should control all aspects of its citizens' lives

trans-Sahara slave trade the trade that brought slaves from sub-Saharan Africa to the Arab Berbers of North Africa

transportation the movement of people or goods from one place to another

triangular trade a trading system linking England, West Africa, and the Caribbean, involving sugar, rum, slaves, and manufactured goods

turbine a device consisting of an enclosed drum that was developed in the nineteenth century to harness water power; it replaced the waterwheel and increased the usable energy output of running water by as much as 30 percent

U

uniformitarianism the idea that the forces at work in nature today are similar to and at a scale comparable to those that operated in the past

V

Vichy France the puppet government that cooperated with the Germans following the fall of France during World War II

Viet Cong a communist-led resistance movement in the south of Vietnam formed in opposition to the noncommunist, U.S.-established government there

Vietminh an organization of Vietnamese communists and nationalists formed in 1941 and headed by Ho Chi Minh, a Vietnamese patriot and communist

voodoo a religion originating in precolonial West Africa and given over primarily to healing; also called *santería*

Z

la zarabanda (lah sah rah BAHN dah) a Cuban magical symbol (a right-angle cross in the middle of a circle)

Special Features

ENCOUNTERS

IN THEIR OWN WORDS

PARALLELS AND DIVERGENCES

PATHS TO THE PAST

UNDER THE LENS

Maps

Chapter 22
Excerpt from *The Nation and Its Fragments* by Partha Chatterjee. Copyright © 1984 by Princeton University Press. Reprinted with permission of Princeton University Press.

Chapter 23
Excerpt from *When China Ruled the Seas* by Louise Levathes. Copyright © 1997 by Louise Levathes. Used with permission of Oxford University Press, Inc.

Chapter 24
Excerpt from *Major Problems in American Indian History,* edited by Albert Hurtado and Peter Iverson (Lexington, MA: D. C. Heath, 1994), pp. 83, 84.

Chapter 25
Excerpt from *Voyages and Travels of an Indian Interpreter and Trader* (Toronto: Coles Publishing).

Chapter 26
Excerpt from *The Interesting Life of Olaudah Equiano,* edited by Robert Allison. Copyright © 1995 by Bedford Books.

Chapter 27
Excerpt from *Suleiman the Magnificent: Scourge of Heaven* by Antony Bridge (New York: Dorset Press, 1987).

Chapter 28
Excerpt from *Sources of Japanese Tradition* by William DeBary. Copyright © 1958 by Columbia University Press. Reprinted with permission of the publisher.

Chapter 29
Excerpt from *Readings in Her Story: Women in Christian Tradition,* edited by Barbara J. MacHaffie (Augsburg Fortress Publishers, 1992).

Chapter 30
Excerpt from *Women and Gender in Early Modern Europe* by Merry Wiesner-Hanks. Copyright © 1993 by Cambridge University Press. Reprinted with permission of the publisher.

Chapter 31
Excerpt from *The Enlightenment* by Ulrich Im Hof. Copyright © 1993 by Blackwell Publishing. Reprinted with permission of the publisher.

Chapter 32
Excerpt from "Human Documents in the Industrial Revolution in Britain" by Royston Pike in *Working in America: A Humanities Reader,* edited by Robert Sessions and Jack Wortman (Notre Dame, IN: University of Notre Dame Press, 1992).

Chapter 33
Excerpt from *The Emergence of Romanticism* by Nicholas Riasonovsky. Copyright © 1992 by Nicholas Riasonovsky. Used with permission of Oxford University Press, Inc.

Chapter 34
Excerpt from *The Nation and Its Fragments* by Partha Chatterjee. Copyright © 1984 by Princeton University Press. Reprinted with permission of Princeton University Press.

Chapter 35
Excerpt from *The Communist Manifesto* by Karl Marx and Friedrich Engels. English Translation in 1888 by Samuel Moore.

Chapter 36
Excerpt from A *History of Warfare* by John Keegan. Copyright © 1993 by Alfred Knopf. Reprinted with permission of Random House, Inc.

Excerpt from *The Collected Poems of Wilfred Owen,* edited by C. Day Lewis. Copyright © 1964 by New Directions Books, p. 5. Reprinted with permission of New Directions Books.

Chapter 37
Excerpt from *In a Shattered Mirror: The Later Poetry of Anna Akhmatova* by Susan Amert. Reprinted with the permission of the publishers, Stanford University Press. Copyright © 1992 by the Board of Trustees of the Leland Stanford Junior University.

Chapter 38
Excerpt from *The Penguin History of Canada* by Kenneth McNaught (London: Penguin Press, 1988).

Chapter 39
Excerpt from *The Search for a New Order* by W. M. Fletcher. Copyright © 1982 by the University of North Carolina Press. Used by permission of the publisher.

Chapter 40
Excerpt from *The Soviet Home-Front* by John Barber et al. (London: Longman, 1991).

Chapter 41
Excerpt from *Witness* by Whittaker Chambers. Copyright © 1952 by Random House. Reprinted by permission of Random House, Inc.

Chapter 42
Excerpt from *The Origins of Totalitarianism* by Hannah Arendt. Copyright © 1951 and renewed 1979 by Mary McCarthy West. Reprinted by permission of Harcourt Brace & Company.

Excerpt from "*Ha-Aretz,* April 4, 1969" in *The Question of Palestine* by Edward Said (New York: Vintage Press, 1979).

Excerpt from "The Zionist Occupation of Western Galilee, 1948" by Nafez Nazzal in *Journal of Palestinian Studies* 3 (3): 70, 1974.

Chapter 43

Excerpt from *The Spice Box of Earth* by Leonard Cohen. Copyright © 1961 by Leonard Cohen. Reprinted with the permission of the author, c/o Peter S. Shukat, Esq., Shukat and Hafer, New York.

APPENDIX 2

Global Change from 1500 to the Present

Full-Color Maps and Art

These color maps are here for your reference. We hope you will have reason to consult them over the course of your study of world history. You might use them to remind yourself of dates and locations in which certain civilizations thrived. They might cause you to notice which cultures flourished simultaneously and which bordered one another. At times, you might find yourself comparing these maps to the map of the world today and thinking about the historical influences on the world we now live in. We also hope you turn to this appendix whenever you need to find a good map quickly.

On each two-page spread you will find a collection of maps that illustrate the changes that came to one geographical area over the period of time covered in Chapters 22–44. The areas covered are Asia, Russia and the USSR, the Americas, Europe, and Africa. On the final page you will find two full-color examples of twentieth-century art.

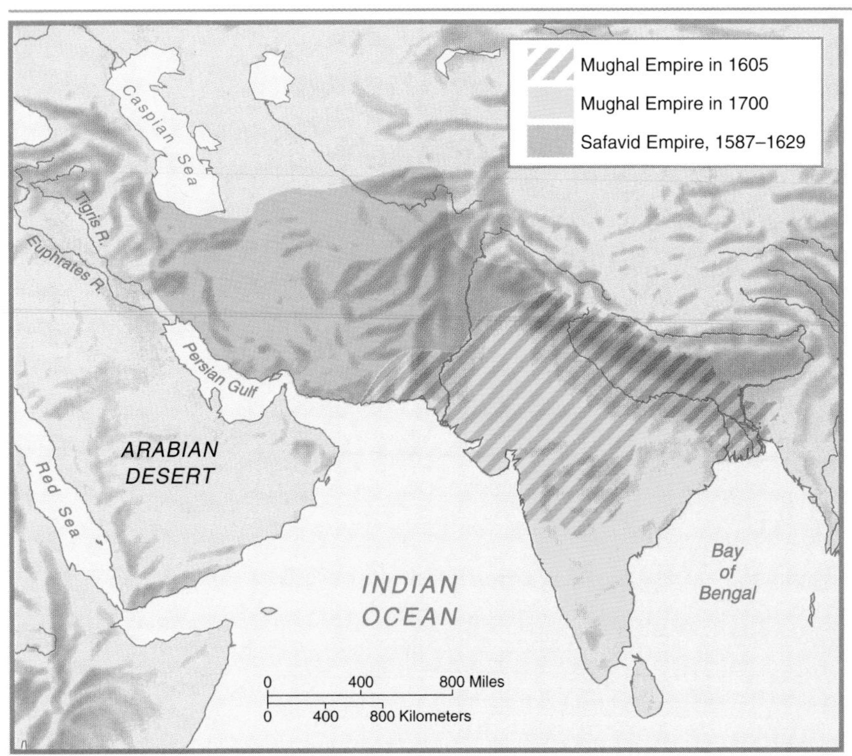

INDIA AND PERSIA, 1587–1700

THE QING (MANCHU) EMPIRE, 1644–1912

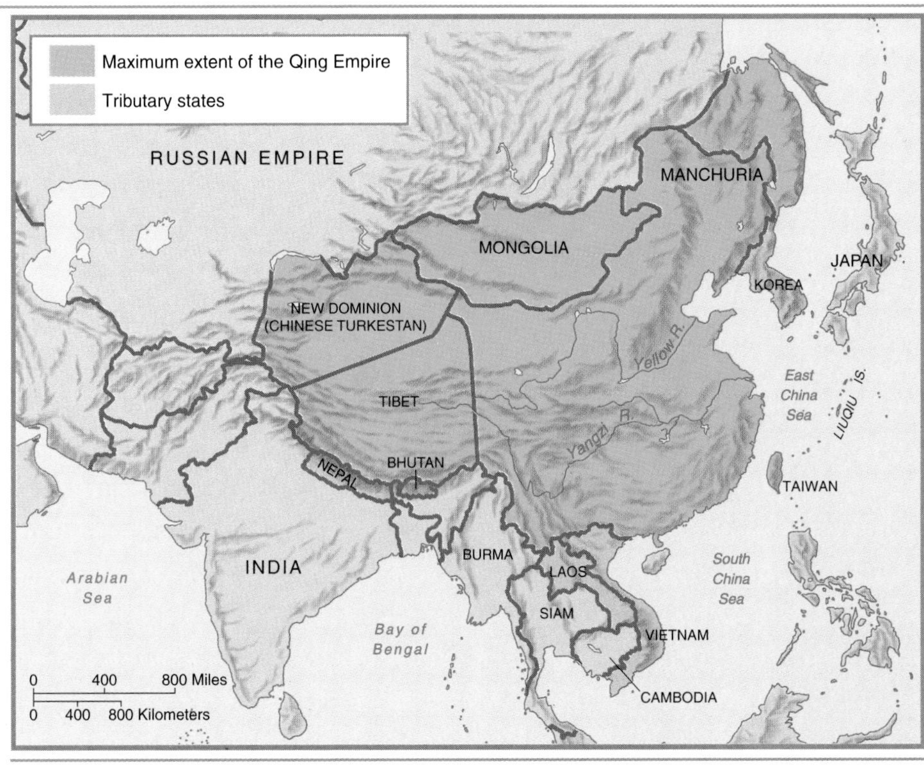

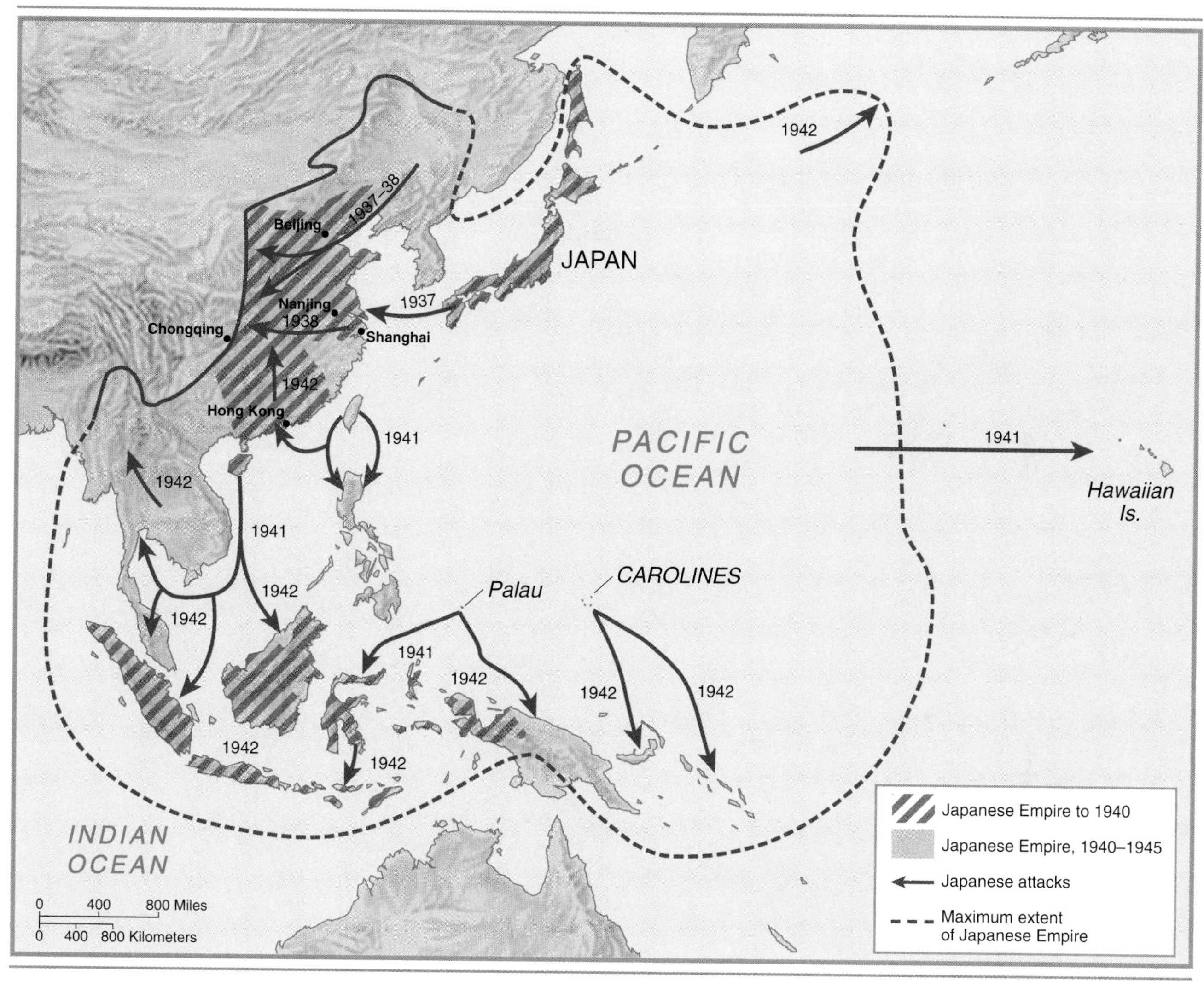

THE JAPANESE EMPIRE, 1931–1945

Asia, the largest continent, has seen a variety of empires in the last several centuries. In 1500, only the extreme western and eastern parts of Asia were under imperial rule (the Ottoman Empire and the Ming Empire in Ch. 28). Two hundred years later, the Ottoman (pp. A-20–A-21), Russian (p. A-22), Safavid, and Qing empires controlled most of the Asian landmass and its peoples (Chs. 27 and 28). From 1700 to 1900, imperial decline and European expansion through colonialism and imperialism overwhelmed the Safavid and Mughal empires. Most of Southeast Asia, too, fell under European imperialist rule. Japan became imperialistic in the 1890s and gradually took control of most of East and Southeast Asia, by the 1940s. Since 1945 (Ch. 40), these empires have dissolved, leaving in their wakes a complex array of independent states, many of which center on distinct ethnic groups. Nationalism has been a force for national unification and imperial dissolution.

BESSARABIA
(to Russia 1812)
MOLDAVIA
(1829)
Danube R.
HUNGARY
(to Austria 1699)
AUSTRIA
TRANSYLVANIA
(to Austria 1699)
KHANATE
OF CRIMEA
(to Russia 1783
BANAT
(to Austria 1718)
ROMANIA
(created 1858)
CROATIA
BOSNIA
(to Austria-
Hungary 1878)
ITALY
BULGARIA
(1878; 1908)
Black Sea
DALMATIA
(to Venice 1699–1797;
to Austria 1797 & 1816;
to Italy 1805–1809;
to France 1809–1816)
SERBIA
(to Austria 1718–1739)
MACEDONIA
(to Greece 1913)
ANATOLIA
ALBANIA
(1913)
GREECE
(1830)
TUNIS
(nominally subject
until 1881)
CRETE
(Turkey 1718;
to Greece 1908)
CYPRUS
(Br. Prot. 1878;
annexed by Britain 1914)
Mediterranean Sea
LEBANON
(Fr. Mandate 1920)
PALESTINE
(Br. Mandate 1920)
TRIPOLI
(Ottoman vassal until 1835;
Ottoman province 1835–
1912; to Italy 1912)
LIBYA
EGYPT
(1811; Br. Occupation
1882; Br. Protectorate
1914;1922)
Nile R.
0 150 300 Miles
0 150 300 Kilometers

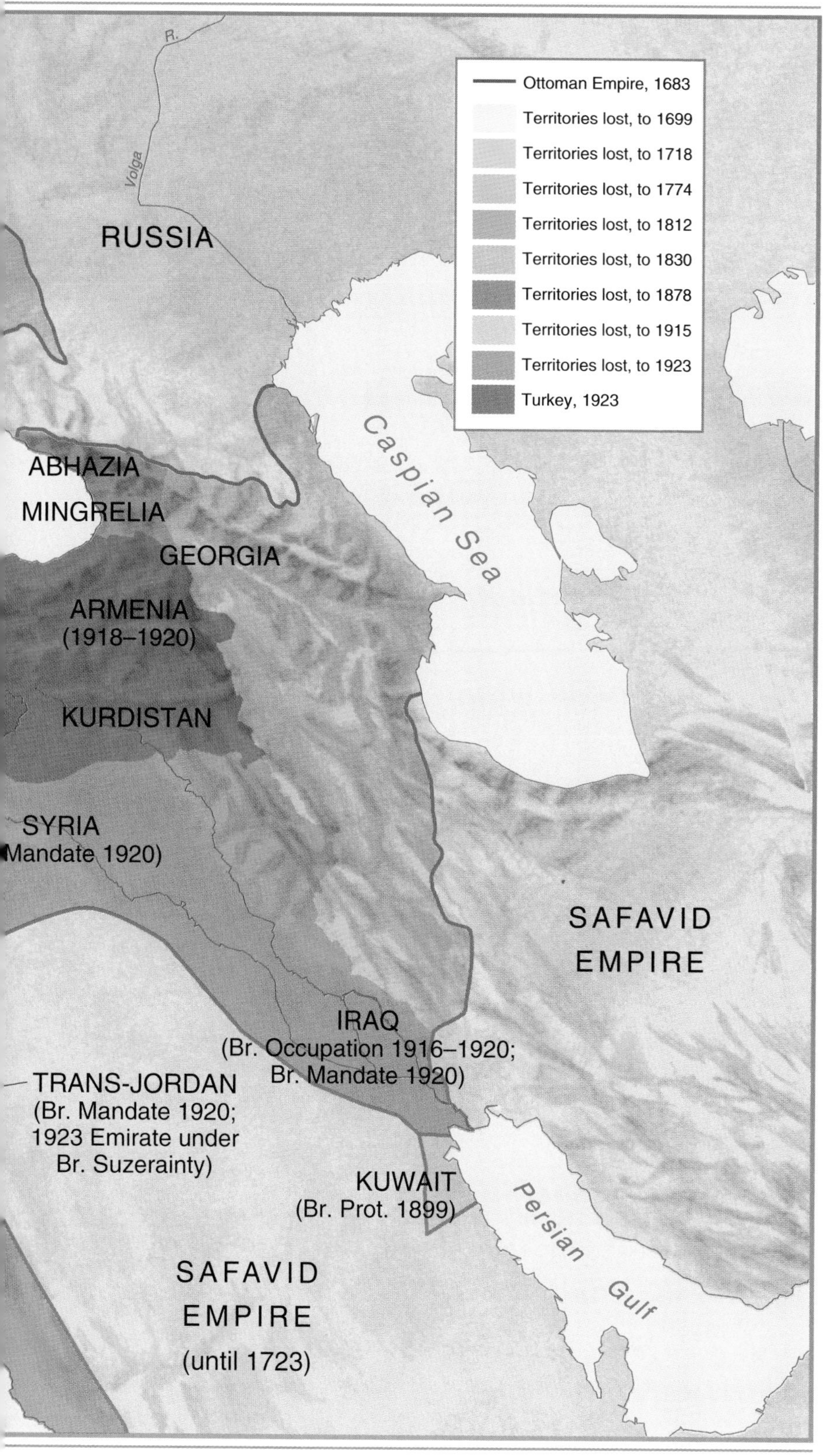

The Ottoman Empire, 1683–1923

At its height, the Ottoman Empire spanned three continents and ruled over 30 million people. One reason for the empire's longevity was its religious and ethnic toleration of its diverse citizenry, which included Asian Muslims, European Christians, and Jews. While the empire offered Muslims some advantages (like exclusion from a special tax), for the most part people of all backgrounds and faiths enjoyed shared freedoms.

By the early eighteenth century, however, stirrings of nationalism (Ch. 33) began to threaten the empire's foundations. Ethnic groups within the empire began to unite, often with support from Russia or European nations. During the nineteenth century, many independent nations emerged in the territories formerly under Ottoman control; by 1918, most of the original empire had been chipped away. The Ottoman Empire suffered additional losses as a result of its defeat in World War I; peace dictated by the Allies left little land and much resentment. This rage spurred Turkish nationalism and led, in 1923, to the establishment of the Turkish Republic and the end of an empire that had lasted almost five hundred years.

Russia and the Soviet Union, 1580–1989

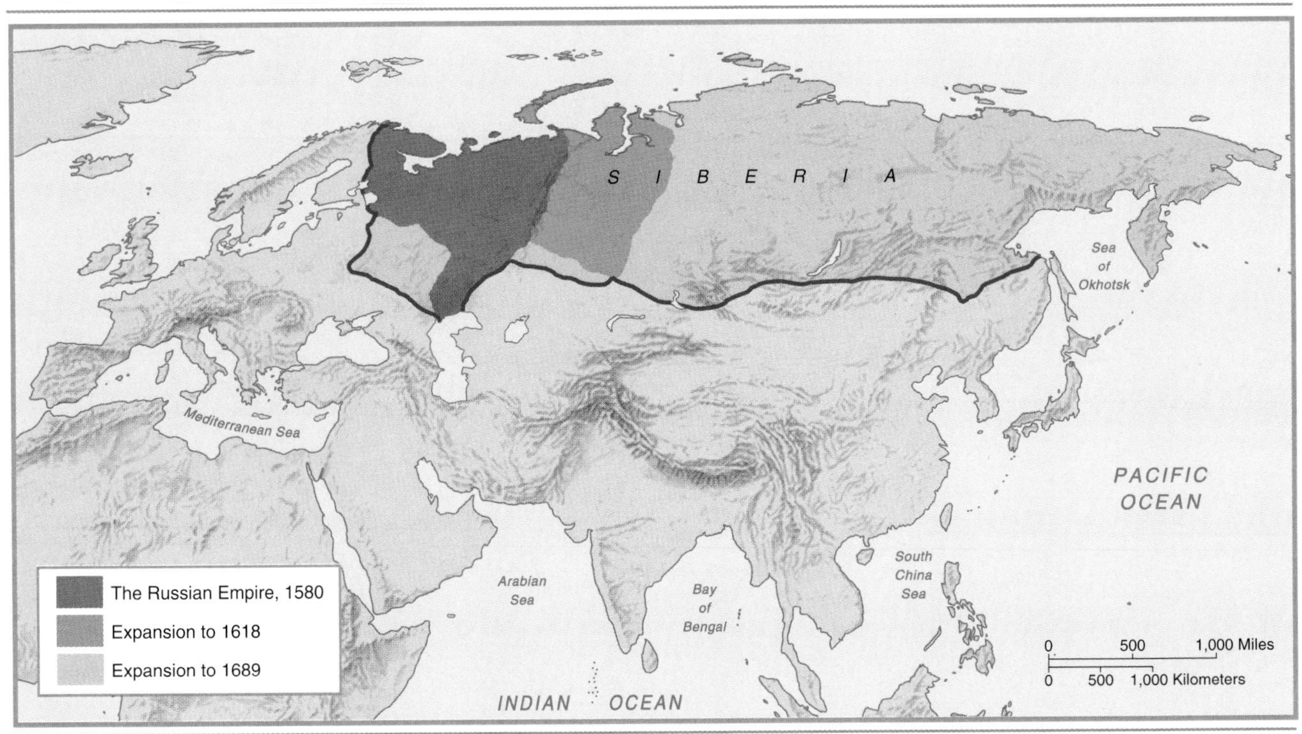

▶ **THE EXPANSION OF THE RUSSIAN EMPIRE, 1580–1689**

ORIGINALLY A EUROPEAN COUNTRY, RUSSIA BEGAN expanding into Asia in the mid–sixteenth century (Ch. 27). Siberia became the main avenue of expansion in the seventeenth century, with Russians reaching the Pacific Ocean during that era. Much of Central Asia was added in the nineteenth century. Although the Bolsheviks decried the previous colonial policies of the tsarist government, they reconquered most of the former imperial realm, adding Mongolia as a client state in 1919 (Ch. 37). The Soviet Empire held together until 1991 but by 1992 had dissolved into fifteen different states (Chs. 41 and 42), with Russia holding much of the territory it held in 1689.

▶ **THE SOVIET UNION, 1945–1989**

ARCTIC OCEAN
RUSSIA
FINLAND
SWEDEN
NORWAY
ESTONIA
LATVIA
DENMARK
LITHUANIA
GERMANY
POLAND
BELARUS
CZECH. REP.
UKRAINE
SLOVAKIA
AUST.
HUNG.
MOLDOVA
SLOVENIA
ROMANIA
CROATIA
BOSNIA & HERZ.
BULGARIA
SERBIA/ MONTENEGRO
MAC.
ALBANIA
GREECE
Black Sea
GEORGIA
AZERBAIJAN
ARMENIA
TURKEY
Caspian Sea
KAZAKHSTAN
Aral Sea
UZBEKISTAN
TURKMENISTAN
KRGYZSTAN
TAJIKISTAN
MONGOLIA
CYPRUS
SYRIA
LEBANON
ISRAEL
JORDAN
IRAQ
IRAN
AFGHANISTAN
PAKISTAN
NEPAL
BHUTAN
Mediterranean Sea
KUWAIT
BAHRAIN
QATAR
UNITED ARAB EMIRATES
SAUDI ARABIA
Red Sea
OMAN
YEMEN
BANGLADESH
MYANMAR (BURMA)
LAOS
INDIA
Arabian Sea
Bay of Bengal
THAILAND
SRI LANKA
MALDIVES
MALAYSIA
INDIAN OCEAN
0 500 1,000 Miles
0 500 1,000 Kilometers

Asia and Eastern Europe Today

BEFORE WORLD WAR II, many states in Asia and Eastern Europe were larger and more ethnically diverse. With war came displacement and death for millions of soldiers, civilians, and refugees. These conditions, and the social change they brought, have had tremendous short-term effects on the political map of the area (Issue 9 and Ch. 44). A stream of Jewish refugees settled in Southwest Asia, altering the region's ethnic balance. The establishment of Israel in 1948 did not resolve tensions between Arabs and Jews. Fighting in this region continues today.

India earned independence from British rule shortly after World War II to discover its own religious fragmentation. Two more countries, Pakistan and Bangladesh, have also emerged in South Asia. The ongoing Kashmir independence movement suggests that there may be more changes ahead.

As Russian power in Eastern Europe declined, ethnic ties flourished. Lithuania, Latvia, Estonia, Slovakia, Slovenia, Bosnia and Herzegovina, Serbia, and the Czech Republic are all less than fifty years old. These new states' borders were drawn to reflect the ethnic makeup of each region, though the continued fighting in the former state of Yugoslavia proves that social disputes cannot be settled by territorial divisions. With the breakup of the Soviet Union from 1989 to 1991, numerous countries (like Ukraine and Georgia) have emerged in Southwest and Central Asia.

The Americas, 1700 to the Present

THERE WERE major population movements from the Old World to the New World (Chs. 24–26) following its discovery by Europeans in the fifteenth century. The colonial peopling of the Americas brought millions of settlers, largely replacing the Native American population. The great surge in population movement, however, came in the nineteenth and twentieth centuries, when transportation became more available and less expensive. Reconstruction of migration statistics is notoriously unreliable, and these figures are only approximations.

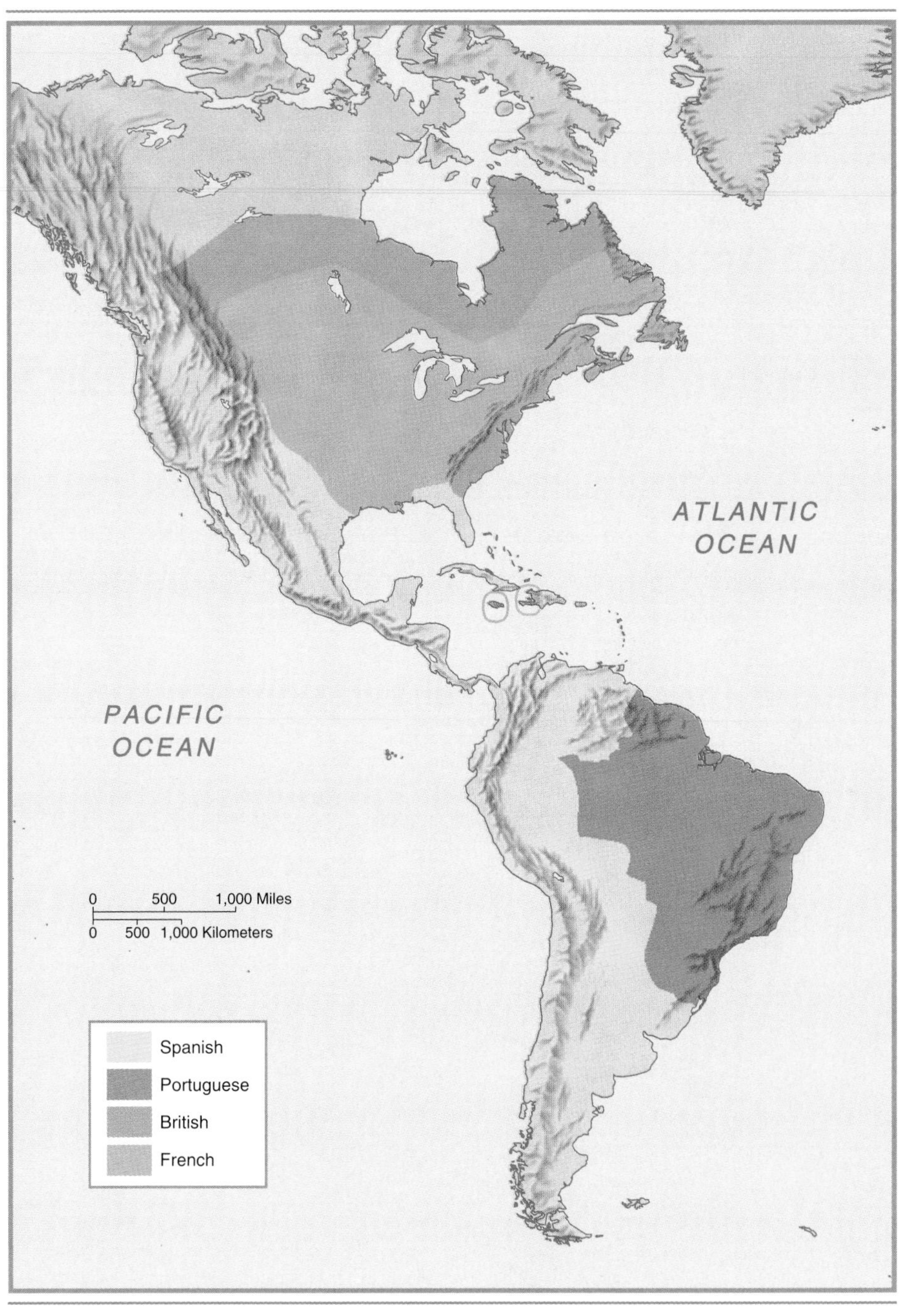

▶ **COLONIAL OWNERSHIP OF THE AMERICAS, 1700–1763**

From		To North America	To Mexico and Central America	To the Caribbean	To South America
		ESTIMATES (IN MILLIONS)			
Western Europe	Iberia	1	6		2.5
	Italy	11	1		1.5
	other countries	32	1		6
Eastern Europe		17	.2		.2
West Africa		6	2	5	12
East Asia	China	.2	.1		.2
Southeast Asia		3	.2		.1
Southwest Asia	Iran	.6			
	Arabia	.6	.1		
South Asia	India/Pakistan	.5		.1	

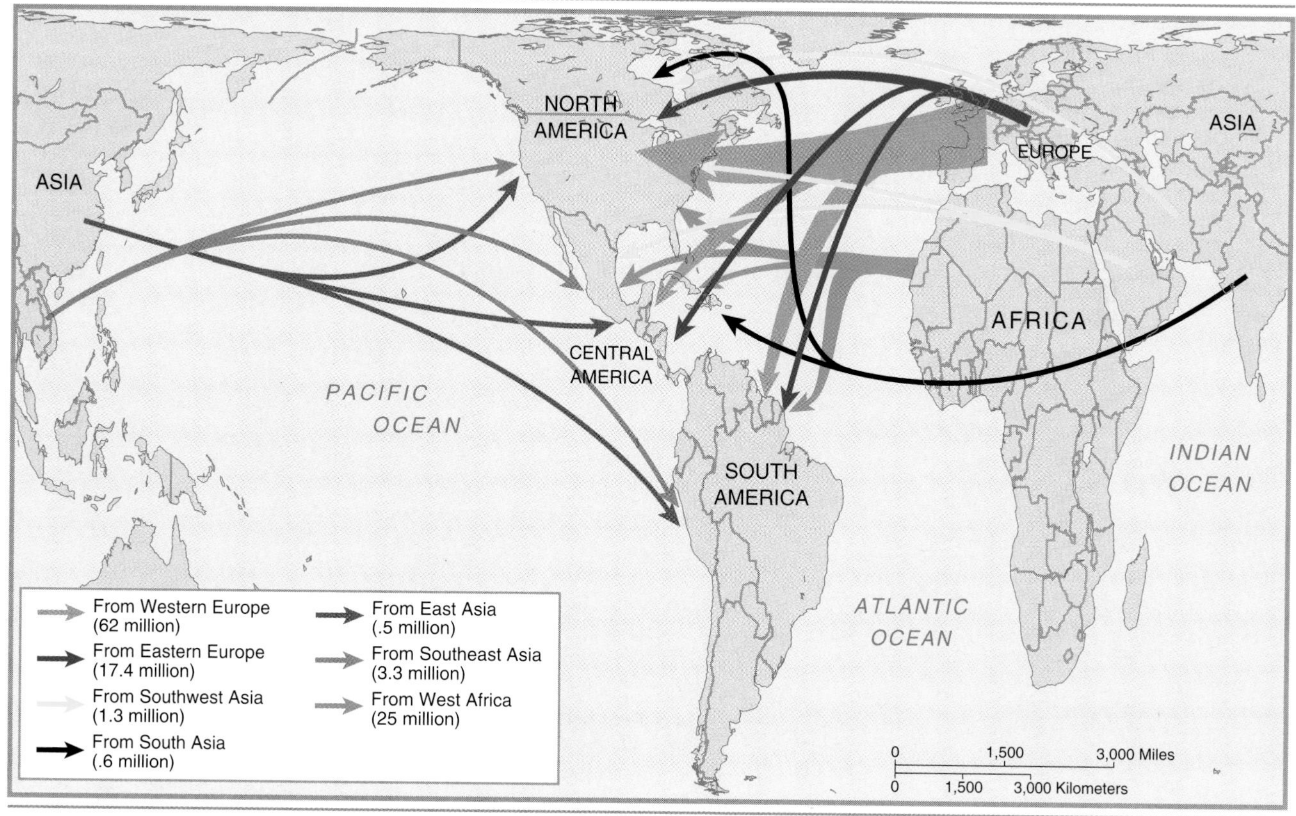

IMMIGRATION TO THE AMERICAS, SINCE 1500

Europe, 1560–1989

EUROPEANS HAVE ENDURED a variety of political systems in the centuries since 1500. By 1660, the Ottoman and Holy Roman empires could claim jurisdiction over large numbers of Europeans, and the hold of the Holy Roman Empire over its peoples was tenuous at best. The Swedes fashioned a Baltic empire that collapsed early in the eighteenth century (Ch. 30). The next major empire was created by Napoleon Bonaparte's conquests in the early nineteenth century (Ch. 31). It lasted until 1814 and was succeeded by the Austrian and Russian empires. Rising nationalist tensions in the Russian, Ottoman, and Austro-Hungarian empires helped precipitate World War I (Ch. 36), during which the Triple Entente (France, Russia, and Great Britain) fought Germany and Austria-Hungary. In World War II (Ch. 40), Britain and the Soviet Union allied (with the United States) to fight Germany and Italy. Central European states seemed to be allied and fighting against western and eastern European states in both wars. During the Cold War (Ch. 41), the Soviet Union and the United States formed alliance systems (the Warsaw Pact and NATO) that involved many European states. Since 1991, these military alliance systems have either collapsed or searched for a new purpose, but economic alliances and connections have continued to flourish and deepen.

▶ **EUROPE, 1560–1660**

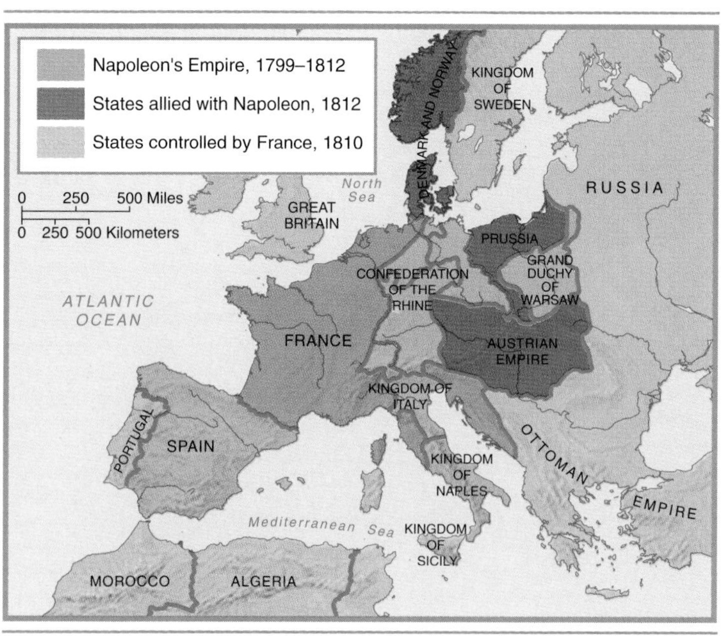

▶ **EUROPE UNDER NAPOLEON**

EUROPEAN ALLIANCES IN WORLD WARS I AND II

COLD WAR EUROPE, 1945–1989

AFRICA TO 1800

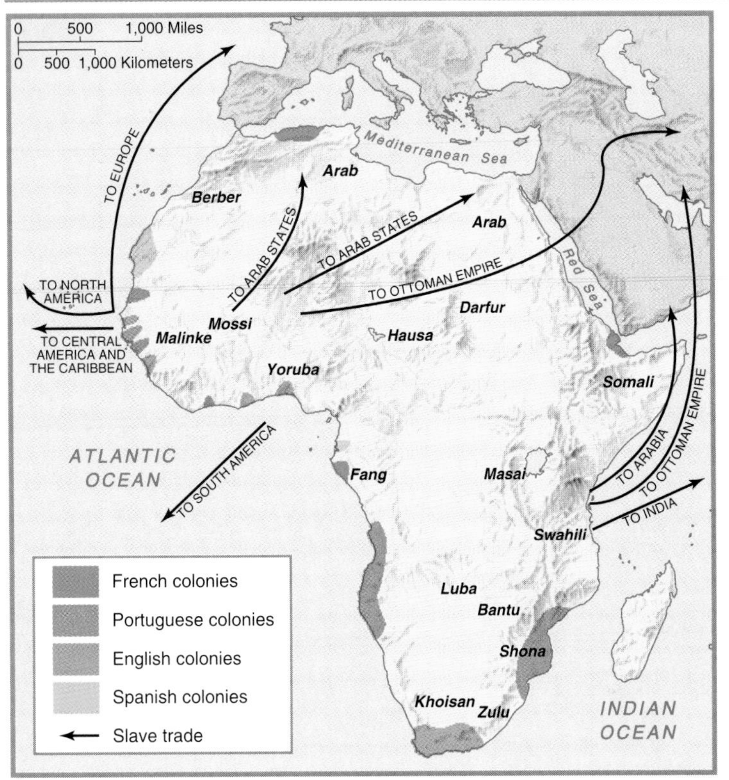

IMPERIALISM IN AFRICA, 1880–1914

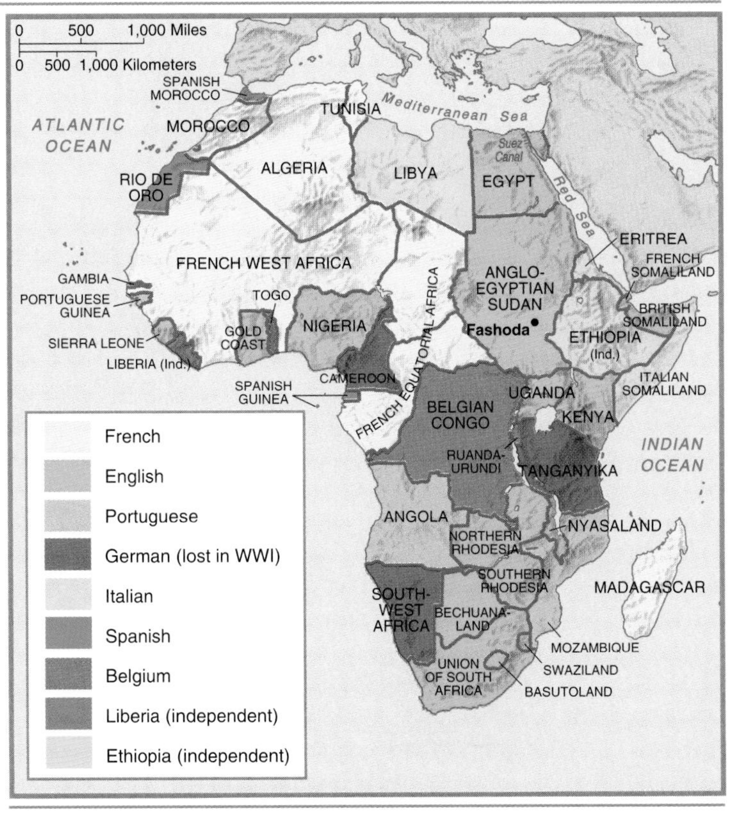

AT THE BEGINNING OF THE NINETEENTH CENTURY, European colonial powers were just establishing toeholds in most of Africa (Ch. 26 and Issue 6), though power rested primarily with native governments. By the end of that century, most of Africa had fallen to imperialist countries such as France, Britain, Belgium, and Germany (Ch. 34). Some territories passed from the possession of one European power to another, especially with the settlements following World War I. These territories remained under foreign domination until the late 1950s and after. By 1990, Africans had wrested control of their lands, gaining independence.

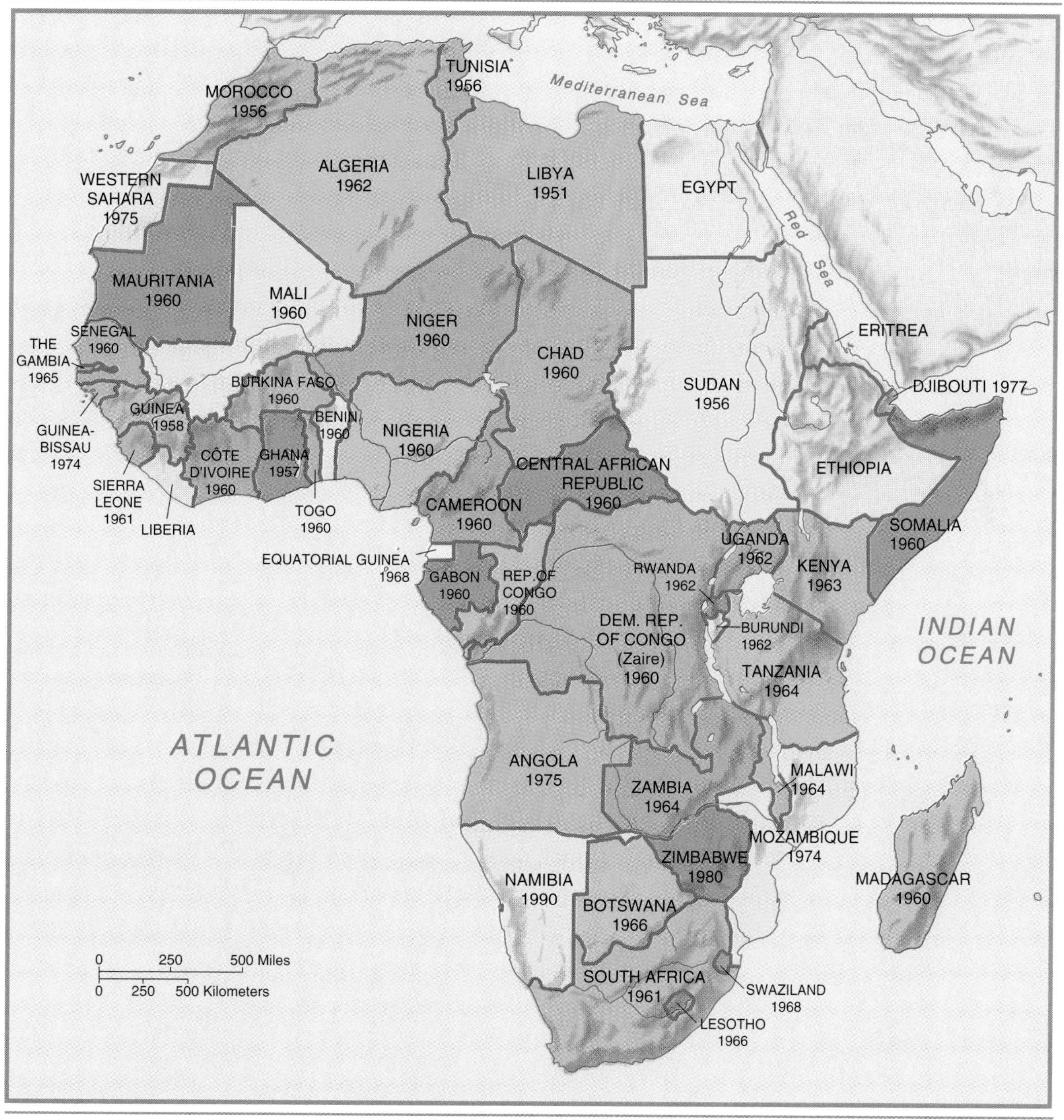

▶ **AFRICAN COUNTRIES EARN INDEPENDENCE, 1951–1997**

Two Examples of Modern Art

MODERN ART has grown out of the Western art tradition and reflects that heritage. At the same time, it has diverged significantly from traditional goals. These two works demonstrate elements of tradition (use of art for nationalistic or patriotic purposes) and divergence (use of abstraction for novel effects).

In 1920, Dmitri Moor's striking poster entitled "Have You Volunteered?" (right) challenged viewers to join the Russian revolutionary cause. The Bolshevik Party had seized power in Russia in 1917, and by 1920 the country was engaged in a major revolution. Red—used in the clothing of the Red Army soldier and the factory behind him—symbolizes the communist ideology and suggests the importance of the workers as the backbone of the Bolshevik movement. Many workers volunteered for the Red Army, bringing it to victory by 1921.

Unlike most abstract expressionist art, this 1964 work (below) by the Dutch-born painter Willem de Kooning depicts a particular subject, in this case a woman. Rather than record detail, however, de Kooning transforms the woman's image into layers of rich color that overlap one another.

Right: Courtesy of Stephen White, University of Glasgow. *Below*: Hirshhorn Museum and Sculpture Garden, Smithsonian Institution. Gift of Joseph H. Hirshhorn, 1966. Photo by Lee Stalsworth.

▶ **RED SHIRT POSTER**

▶ **WILLEM DE KOONING'S *WOMAN, SAG HARBOR***

Index

A note about the index:

Pages containing main coverage or description of a topic or person are set in **boldface** for easy reference. Entries include dates for important events and major figures as well as brief identifications, alternate names, and pronunciation guides when appropriate.

Parenthetical notations following pages refer to:

(illus.) for illustrations and graphs
(map) for maps
(table) for tables